The JOURNEY
of MODERN
THEOLOGY

FROM RECONSTRUCTION
TO DECONSTRUCTION

ROGER E. OLSON

An imprint of InterVarsity Press
Downers Grove, Illinois

InterVarsity Press
P.O. Box 1400, Downers Grove, IL 60515-1426
World Wide Web: www.ivpress.com
Email: email@ivpress.com

Revised portions of Twentieth-Century Theology, *©1992 by Stanley J. Grenz and Roger E. Olson, are incorporated into this book.*

InterVarsity Press® is the book-publishing division of InterVarsity Christian Fellowship/USA®, a movement of students and faculty active on campus at hundreds of universities, colleges and schools of nursing in the United States of America, and a member movement of the International Fellowship of Evangelical Students. For information about local and regional activities, write Public Relations Dept., InterVarsity Christian Fellowship/USA, 6400 Schroeder Rd., P.O. Box 7895, Madison, WI 53707-7895, or visit the IVCF website at www.intervarsity.org.

Cover design: Cindy Kiple
Interior design: Beth Hagenberg
Images: Karl Barth: ullstein bild / The Granger Collection, NYC—All rights reserved.
    Friedrich Schleiermacher: The Granger Collection, NYC—All rights reserved.

ISBN 978-0-8308-4021-2

Printed in the United States of America ∞

Library of Congress Cataloging-in-Publication Data
A catalog record for this book is available from the Library of Congress.

P	21	20	19	18	17	16	15	14	13	12	11	10	9	8	7	6	5	4	3	2	1
Y	31	30	29	28	27	26	25	24	23	22	21	20	19	18	17	16	15	14	13		

Dedicated to Rick

TABLE OF CONTENTS

PREFACE

This book is a revision of *20th-Century Theology: God and the World in a Transitional Age*, coauthored with Stanley J. Grenz and published by InterVarsity Press in 1992. It was intended to be a twentieth anniversary edition of that book with some added chapters. Plans changed and it became what you see—an almost entirely different book incorporating some material from the earlier one.

20th-Century Theology, which many people have come to call Grenz and Olson, has met with unexpected success as a textbook and reference book on modern theology. It has also been read by numerous individuals for their own information and (I hope) enjoyment. It won *Christianity Today*'s award for best book in theology for 1992. I have used it as my basic textbook in numerous sections of courses on modern and contemporary theology for the past two decades and have come to see certain flaws in it. So, when InterVarsity Press invited me to revise it for a twentieth anniversary edition, I was glad to do so. In spite of its strengths and positive reception, it needed updating and improvement.

Between that book's publication and this one's my coauthor Stan Grenz passed away tragically at age fifty-five in 2005. I will never forget the day in 1990 that he called me to inquire about my interest in writing a chapter or two in a book on contemporary theology InterVarsity Press wanted him to edit. Stan and I were relatively new friends. He left Munich, Germany, where he earned his doctorate in theology under Lutheran theologian Wolfhart Pannenberg, one year before I went there to study with the same theologian. A mutual friend put us in touch, and Stan was tremendously helpful in coaching me by telephone about life in Munich and about studying with Pannenberg. On my return, we met in Sioux Falls, where I had attended the seminary where he took up his first teaching position. My wife and daughter and I lived there for a few months as we transitioned back into life in the United States. Over the following years Stan and I developed a close friendship.

I jumped at the opportunity to write for Stan's book but dared to suggest that he and I write the whole book together. He agreed, and the rest is history. We worked hard to make *20th-Century Theology* read like a single-author book, which was not very difficult as we thought and wrote much alike. We enjoyed our partnership so much that we followed it with another co-authored book for InterVarsity Press entitled *Who Needs Theology? An Invitation to the Study of God* (1994). From 1990 on Stan and I roomed together at every annual national meeting of the American Academy of Religion and spent as much time together in between as possible given the great distances between us—especially when Stan and his family moved to Vancouver, Canada. His sudden death was a shock; it felt like the loss of a brother.

All that is to explain one reason writing this revision of *20th-Century Theology* was both painful and a joy. I felt almost disloyal at times as I rewrote all of Stan's chapters as well as mine. Part of the plan for this revision was to bring the story of modern theology up to date. I also intended to make it more user friendly, especially for students. As one critic of *20th-Century Theology* put it, the book read like we had something to prove. Indeed. To a certain extent we, wet-behind-the-ears young theologians that we were, had reviewers in mind too much as we wrote. And yet, I view this revision as an honor to Stan; I know he would be pleased with it and smile on it. His fingers are all over it—both in terms of its use of some of his material in *20th-Century Theology* and in terms of his influence on me.

Two major changes (besides the title) will be noted immediately by readers familiar with *20th-Century Theology*. First, the book begins with much new material on nineteenth-century theology. That was IVP's editors' idea. And I learned a lot as I conducted my research and wrote about important modern Christian theologians of a bygone era whose influence is still very much alive. I believe it is impossible to understand twentieth- and twenty-first-century theology without understanding nineteenth-century theology. That and the added chapters on postmodern theology make this a much bigger book. Second, the unifying motif is changed. The motif of *20th-Century Theology* was the transcendence and immanence of God. That was Stan's idea, and I liked it then. However, even then I felt we had to force some theologians into that motif; it did not feel natural in every case. The motif of this book seems more natural to me, especially given the expansion of material covered. The new motif is modernity and theological responses to it. Everyone talks about contextualizing the gospel, and they usually mean integrating it into a non-Western culture. This book is about how the most influential Western theologians (with Latin America here considered part of the West) integrated the gospel with modernity or did not. That is, some reacted against it. Yet, even those who reacted against modernity were influenced by it.

Of course, every book has its lacunae. The glaring one in this book is non-Western theologies. As everyone knows, Christianity is growing fastest in Africa and Asia, and those Christian communities are increasingly producing scholarly theologies. For the most part, however, they are not integrating with modernity, which may be a good thing, except where Western missionaries have influenced them or where their own theologians have studied in Europe or North America. Modern theology is not just theology done yesterday and today. Modern theology is theology done in the context of the cultural ethos called modernity. The theologians described, analyzed and evaluated in this book all have one thing in common besides being at least nominally Christian—they all wrestle with modernity, the cultural context stemming from the Enlightenment and scientific revolutions. There are other theologians of the same time period (nineteenth into twenty-first centuries). If they are not found here it is probably because they did or do not wrestle with modernity (or did not become influential and famous).

This book has taken years to research and write. The writing of the manuscript took place during January to July 2012 and that due to a sabbatical graciously granted by Baylor University. I want to thank Baylor's and Truett

Seminary's administrations for that gift and for my colleagues' and students' help and interest and support throughout the whole process of research going back at least two years. My special gratitude goes to my wife, Becky, who many times patiently waited as I finished a paragraph or page. And I thank my teaching assistants Brandon Morgan and Jared Patterson, who read my chapters, offered suggestions for improvement and tutored me in some areas where I was ignorant. Morgan's help is especially evident in the chapters on postmodern theology.

Finally, I dedicate this book to my brother Rick, who, like most older brothers, made much of my childhood miserable (smiley face goes here) but has become my father figure after our father slowly disappeared from our lives. Rick is a true genius, much smarter than I, and a reliable sounding board in all matters personal, spiritual and intellectual. If the world could only have greater access to his unparalleled common sense and native intellectual prowess, it would be a better place.

Roger E. Olson
Waco, Texas
Advent 2012

An Important Note for All Readers but Especially for Professors and Scholars

A reader will not get far in this book without realizing it is not a straightforward, objective, purely factual account of modern theology. Which is not to say it is not factual! If postmodernity has taught anything it is that there is no view from nowhere. Every historical survey is interpretive—a view from somewhere—even if it pretends to be about "just the facts." This is admittedly and unapologetically an interpretive survey of modern theology. It strives to be factual, but, inevitably, the author's and his sources' perspectives will intrude here and there.

The author and publisher hope that those who disagree with some of the book's interpretations and critical conclusions will still find the book useful—as a readable survey, gripping story, informative textbook and reference volume.

This book's primary intended audience is not scholars of modern theology but students, pastors and interested laypeople. Therefore, many esoteric scholarly debates about the movements and people discussed have been avoided or mentioned only in footnotes. It is, in other words, a kind of bird's-eye view of modern Christian theology. (Not every bird's, of course, but this bird's.) In other words, the intent is to portray for beginners, or readers needing a review, the basic contours of the subject. Think of it, then, as a satellite view of a city in which the major landmarks are visible (because the view has been enlarged) but not every detail is visible.

To be more specific, the accounts of the philosophers, theologians and movements given here avoid getting lost in the details of scholarly disputes over, for example, their changes. In the case of almost every person discussed, his or her thought evolved and changed somewhat over, say, forty years of writing. One of scholars' favorite pastimes is to debate such changes: When? Where? Why? How much? Because this is a survey for novices and not for scholars, such debates will largely be avoided. In some cases (e.g., Karl Barth) they will be mentioned in footnotes. This writer largely leaves it up to professors to add such dimensions into classroom lectures and discussions, using the chapters here as springboards. The goal here is to inform readers about the lives, careers, major ideas, legacies and possible problems of these thinkers. It is hoped that reading that much about a theologian, for example, will spark interest and further reading in primary sources.

Introduction

THE CULTURAL CONTEXT
OF MODERN THEOLOGY

M*odern theology is thinking* about God in the context of modernity—the cultural ethos stemming from the Enlightenment. The Enlightenment was the intellectual revolution, affecting all European and later North American societies, that began with the rise of a new rationalism in philosophy and science in the seventeenth century. Enlightenment thinkers "thought they had possession of a new knowledge and a new way of knowing which gave them a privileged position to judge the errors of the past and fashion the achievements of the future."[1] The Enlightenment, and its offspring modernity, will be the subject of some of the initial chapters of this book, so here only the briefest preview must suffice.

MODERNITY IS BORN IN A CULTURAL REVOLUTION
Many scholars date the beginning of the Enlightenment and modernity with French philosopher René Descartes (1596–1650), who launched a revolution in philosophy comparable to that of Copernicus in astronomy.[2] Ac-

---

[1]James M. Byrne, *Religion and the Enlightenment: From Descartes to Kant* (Lousiville, KY: Westminster John Knox, 1996), ix.

[2]Much of this initial material about Descartes's life and thought is drawn from A. C. Grayling, *Descartes: The Life and Times of a Genius* (New York: Walker & Company, 2005). The beginning of the Enlightenment is easier to identify than the birth of modernity. Here, modernity is not

cording to his own testimony, he wanted to discover knowledge that cannot be doubted. He lived during the Thirty Years' War (1618–1648) that devastated Europe; much of it was about conflicting religious beliefs and loyalties. Descartes wanted to know if there is any certain knowledge not based on revelation, faith or even sense evidence, as the five senses, he thought, can always deceive. In short, he was looking for rational certainty and thought he discovered it in the simple thought *cogito ergo sum*—an idea that launched an era—"I think; therefore I am." What he searched for and believed he found was indubitable knowledge, certainty, the ground of all certainty, a new foundation for knowledge including science and religion.

The result was, and has been up to the present, that Enlightenment-inspired thinkers tend to define knowledge as what one can be certain of, what cannot be reasonably doubted. Begin with a simple, clear and distinct idea that cannot be doubted, such as one's own existence (because to doubt one has to exist) and from it deduce an entire body of knowledge. Whatever is logically required by the foundational concept cannot be doubted and therefore is certain to be true. This is knowledge according to what modern philosophers call foundationalism. All else is opinion or superstition. Most early Enlightenment thinkers like Descartes saw this new approach to knowledge as an ally of orthodox Christianity; they thought it could be pressed into service for the defense of the faith. Something else happened over time as modernity developed out of the Enlightenment. Perhaps the Enlightenment poet and essayist Alexander Pope (1688–1744) expressed the unintended outcome of Descartes's and other early rationalists' Copernican revolution in thought best: "Know then thyself; presume not God to scan. The proper study of mankind is man."[3]

The other root of the Enlightenment, besides philosophical foundationalism, was the scientific revolution that took place at about the same time and also launched modernity. The exact beginning of the scientific revolution is much debated, but everyone agrees a major catalyst was Galileo Galilei (1564–1642), who proved, beyond any reasonable doubt, that the earth and other planets revolve around the sun—an idea proposed by Co-

equated with "the modern world" insofar as the latter is used politically of conquest and colonialism. Scholars who treat modernity that way tend to date its beginning with Columbus's "discovery" of the "new world" in 1492.

[3]Alexander Pope, "An Essay on Man," book 2, para. 1.

pernicus nearly a century before Galileo proved him right using mathematics and the new invention the telescope. What was so earthshaking about that? Simply that the Catholic church, of which he was a faithful member, had taught authoritatively for centuries that the sun revolves around the earth. Most Protestants agreed. (Luther condemned Copernicus as a heretic if not a lunatic.) Galileo's discovery called the authority of tradition into question; this was no dispute about different interpretations of the Bible but a major attack on religious authority itself.

Perhaps Galileo's main contribution to undermining religious authority was his "Letter to the Grand Duchess Christina" (1615) in which he declared science independent of theology and church authority. Galileo asserted that scientific fact must alter religious belief when they conflict. (He acknowledged theology's authority in matters of salvation.) The Catholic Church tried to suppress Galileo's discovery and new ideas about authority; it recognized the serious threat they posed to the stability of society and culture which was based on the church's authority (much of it confused with Aristotle's philosophy). But there was no holding back the flood of new scientific discoveries, many of which flatly contradicted what religious authorities, including theologians, had taught for hundreds of years.

Years after Galileo a devout Christian scientist and mathematician, Isaac Newton (1642–1727), added ammunition to the scientific revolution's assault on authoritative tradition. According to him, the entire universe is ruled like a vast machine by inexorable and mathematically describable laws such as gravity. Again, Pope expressed the popular Enlightenment sentiment: "Nature and nature's laws lay hid in night; God said 'Let Newton be!' and all was light."[4] Newton himself was more interested in discovering the date of the second coming of Jesus Christ than in science, but the effect of his discoveries and world picture added to the general impression of Europe's intellectual elite that tradition could not be trusted. Tradition, after all, said the universe operated by spiritual principles and beings. What could not be explained by observable and describable laws was explained by reference to a God of the gaps. Newton paved the way toward the closing of all the gaps, leaving no room for God or spiritual beings in the workings of nature.

---

[4]Alexander Pope's epitaph for Isaac Newton on his headstone in Westminster Abbey.

What was the effect of the scientific revolution's falsifications of some traditional religious beliefs and the churches' attempts to silence them? Andrew D. White (1832–1918), president of Cornell University and chronicler of the warfare between science and theology in Christendom, declared that the effect "wrought into the hearts of great numbers of thinking men the idea that there is a necessary antagonism between science and religion."[5]

This has been merely the simplest and most basic overview of the Enlightenment and its modern challenges to traditional Christianity; early chapters will lay them out in more detail. The point now is to say that something we call modernity arose out of these events of the seventeenth and early eighteenth centuries and gained momentum through later philosophers and scientists such as Immanuel Kant (1724–1804) and Charles Darwin (1809–1882) and that much of it introduced into the stream of Western culture impulses inimical to traditional Christianity.

MODERNITY CHALLENGES TRADITIONAL CHRISTIANITY

Before moving on to an introductory account of the ethos of modernity and its challenges to traditional Christianity it may be helpful to readers to know what is meant throughout this book by that phrase "traditional Christianity."[6]

Traditional Christianity is a much disputed concept. Here it designates what C. S. Lewis called "mere Christianity" in his famous book of that title—which is not to commit to every expression of Christian belief *Mere Christianity* contains. Although Christianity has always included much diversity, at least since the days of the apostles a rough doctrinal consensus prevailed to unite Orthodox, Catholic and Protestant Christians (even if not ecclesiastically). The fact that, at times, they have anathematized one another as heretics does not detract from the fact that they have traditionally agreed on certain basic beliefs. Spelling out that consensus would take another book, and many have done it. Here a few of the basic tenets of traditional Christianity will be pronounced.

The vast majority of Christians of all major branches believed in a personal God who transcends nature as its creator and who providentially rules over

---

[5]Andrew D. White, *A History of the Warfare of Science with Theology in Christendom*, 2 vols. (New York: Appleton, 1896), 1:167.
[6]I have spelled this out in much more detail in *The Mosaic of Christian Belief: Twenty Centuries of Unity and Diversity* (Downers Grove, IL: InterVarsity Press, 2002).

history. They also believed this God is supremely revealed in Jesus Christ, who is God incarnate and who performed miracles and was raised bodily from death (such that the tomb was empty). They believed that the Bible, however exactly defined and understood, constitutes a written revelation of God. They believed that the triune God, Father, Son and Holy Spirit, at least occasionally acts in special ways in human history to perform miracles that transcend anyone's ability to predict or explain rationally. They believed that faith is necessary for knowing God in the way that God wants to be known by humans and that religion is essential to fulfilled human life. They believed that Jesus Christ is both human and divine and the Son of God from heaven whose death on the cross provided salvation for fallen humanity and who will return to this world with judgment and redemption. This is, of course, only a minimal account of traditional Christianity. Many Christians will want to add to it, but the point here is that at least this is what all Christians of all churchly persuasions believed doctrinally for about a millennium and a half. And, at least, conservative Christians of all denominational persuasions still hold these beliefs.

There is more to this story of traditional Christianity, however, than doctrine. For a millennium and a half most, if not all, Christians also believed such things as that the sun revolves around the stationary earth. Here it will be assumed there is a qualitative difference, in terms of basic Christianity, between belief in a personal God and, say, belief that the sun revolves around the earth. To be sure, not everyone always recognized or held to that difference—as a difference of what is essential to Christianity as a religion. However, at least for our purposes here, "traditional Christianity" will generally refer to the broad doctrinal consensus. From time to time acknowledgment will be made that it also included some beliefs of a lesser nature that were falsified, not just challenged, by modern discoveries.

Evangelical theologian Millard Erickson (b. 1932) proposed recognition of a difference between "translating" the gospel and "transforming" it in attempts to contextualize the faith.[7] At the least, every culture has translated the gospel and Christian belief so that it can be understood by people of that culture. But does translation always involve transformation? Does the gospel itself, does

---

[7]Millard Erickson, *Christian Theology*, 3 vols. (Grand Rapids: Baker, 1983), 1:112–20. One critic said to me that these categories, "translating" and "transforming," are "static categories." My response was and remains, "Better static categories than no categories."

Christianity itself, change substantially from culture to culture? Must it? Are there, then, many Christianities and no "faith once for all delivered" and handed on from generation to generation and from culture to culture and shared by faithful Christians everywhere? That is a problem raised to intense pitch by modernity. Here it will be assumed throughout that there is such a thing as mere Christianity, traditional Christianity, that is always being negotiated, translated, with culture but that is not so tied to culture that every attempt at translation necessarily involves transformation of substance.

This will be an obstacle to some readers who believe there never has been even a basic Christian consensus that transcends its cultural expressions. Such people often reveal some apprehension, however, when they encounter extreme versions of Christianity. Hardly anyone believes that Christianity is compatible with anything and everything (which would make it meaningless). The assumption here will be, for better or worse, that basic Christianity has existed for two thousand years even if not everything that most Christians believed belongs to it. That the sun revolves around a stationary earth will be treated, for better or worse, as a secondary, common belief, not part of the core of Christian doctrine. It is not, for example, stated in the Apostles' Creed or any other Christian creed. That Jesus rose from the dead, however, is part of that doctrinal core. Modernity challenged both. But, it will be assumed here, the challenge to secondary beliefs such as the stationary earth is not a challenge to basic, essential Christianity in the same way as the challenge to miracles.

Another obstacle for some readers may be this book's assumption that traditional, classic, orthodox Christianity necessarily includes belief in the supernatural, by which here is meant the reality of unseen powers and agencies, especially God's, that are involved in special ways in history beyond the ken of science. The word *supernatural* conjures up all kinds of images and carries much baggage, especially in popular thought and language, but not all of that is meant here. A case of the supernatural in basic, traditional Christianity is the resurrection of Jesus. Traditional, orthodox Christianity has always included belief that Jesus was raised from the dead by the power of God in a manner that, in principle, transcends natural explanations. In other words, it was a miracle. What is not assumed here is that "supernatural" and "miracle" are necessarily contrary to science; belief in them does not necessarily conflict with science.[8] Nor does "the supernatural," as used here, assume a metaphysical dualism of realms such that reality is broken into two competing spheres—nature and supernature. As will be seen in several modern Christian thinkers (e.g., Thomas Reid and Horace Bushnell) "supernatural" and "miracles" do not necessarily imply such a dualism in which God must violate natural laws in order to act supernaturally.

MODERNITY BIRTHS A NEW CULTURAL ETHOS

Modernity is the cultural water Western people swim in. Do fish know they are in water? Neither do most people know about modern culture or modernity. To the average person "modern" simply means "what's happening now." That is better called "contemporary." "Modern" is the label for the cultural ethos, the *Zeitgeist*, the spirit of an age, that has dominated the intellectual life of Europe and North America for hundreds of years and has spread throughout the world. Modern theology is theology that seeks to contextualize Christian belief in the culture of modernity—sometimes by rejecting much of it. Theology that ignores modernity, however, pretending it is not real or to be taken seriously, is not modern theology.[9] All the theologians and theological movements described in this book are modern in the sense that they either consciously accommodate Christian belief to modernity or reject such accommodation while taking modernity seriously as a force with which theology must reckon—even if only by rejecting it. Many theologians, perhaps the majority discussed in this book, fall somewhere in between those extremes, acknowledging a need for theology to take modernity into account but accommodating to it cautiously or rejecting it only partially. Modern theological responses, even accommodations, to modernity fall along a spectrum and take on many different features, as will be seen.

So, what are the characteristics of modernity that make it such a challenge to traditional Christian belief? James Byrne rightly says,

---

[8]On this point and the entire subject of the supernatural, miracles and science, see chapters 3 and 4 of Alvin Plantinga, *Where the Conflict Really Lies: Science, Religion and Naturalism* (Oxford: Oxford University Press, 2011), 69–125.

[9]One might wonder if there are such theologians. Is it even possible for a twentieth- or twenty-first-century theologian to do theology without the influence of modernity? Perhaps not. However, some theologians seem more directly influenced by modern moves and consciously interact with them in their theologies. Those will be the main subjects here.

During the Enlightenment the dominant role which religion had played in European society, regulating everything from the appointment of kings and emperors to the rhythm of life which reflected the liturgical year, came under sustained pressure. . . . Quite simply the world gradually became, to use the later phrase of the sociologist Max Weber, a much less "bewitched" place.[10]

By "bewitched place" Weber (1864–1920) meant magical, supernatural, requiring divine or spiritual explanation for what happens. Weber was one of a host of largely secularized modern thinkers who sought to apply Enlightenment principles to spheres beyond the physical such as society; he was one of the fathers of modern, secular sociology. His view that the world, meaning both the physical and cultural realms, had been a "bewitched" place before the light the Enlightenment brought, has been commonplace among decidedly modern intellectuals and movers and shakers of society.[11] Byrne's point is that the culture the Enlightenment brought about, modernity, seriously undermined certain traditional ways of understanding the world. One of the ways it did that is what we call secularization—the demystifying and demythologizing of nature and the social order. Religious explanations had to take a back seat or get off the bus.

Byrne lists and describes several characteristic features of modernity stemming from the Enlightenment. The first one is "an emphasis on the power of 'reason' to discover the truth about humanity and the world."[12] That is not to say that nobody was reasonable before the rise of modernity during the Enlightenment. Great philosophers and theologians such as Thomas Aquinas (1225–1274) were reasonable in their own ways, but what the Enlightenment introduced was rationalism, foundationalism; it tended to reject all claims to revelation, faith or tradition as authoritative except perhaps within religious organizations and only about their doctrines. These, however, modernity has often reduced to mere opinion if not superstition. And this Enlightenment ideal of reason was meant to be objective— free of biases from tradition or revelation or religion. The ideal was the

---

[10]Byrne, *Religion and the Enlightenment*, 16–17.
[11]This is clearly the attitude of White, who explained that "in those periods [before the scientific revolution] when man [sic] sees everywhere miracles and nowhere law,—when he attributes all things which he can not understand to a will like our own,—he naturally ascribes his diseases to the wrath of a good being or to the malice of an evil being" (*History*, 2:1).
[12]Byrne, *Religion and the Enlightenment*, 5.

Sherlock Holmes–like view from nowhere—the purely rational thinker who followed the evidence and logic wherever it led without regard to vested interests or personal preferences.

Byrne's second general feature of the Enlightenment and modernity is skepticism with regard to "the venerable institutions and traditions of the past."[13] Skepticism about tradition comes in many shades and varieties, but overall and in general modernity encourages suspicion of tradition's truth claims. Sometimes that takes the form of extreme rejection of the past and its assumptions, and sometimes it takes the form of moderate, even healthy, questioning of traditions.

A third feature of the Enlightenment and modernity is the "emergence of a scientific way of thinking which offered intellectuals a viable alternative approach to knowledge from that which had dominated mediaeval thought."[14] Part and parcel of modernity is the belief that everything in the physical world is ruled by natural laws. Eventually that idea also crept into the realm of consciousness (with Freud) and society (with sociologists like Weber). The world, reality, was in process of disenchantment; the role of divine providence was gradually challenged and even pushed aside by extreme Enlightenment thinkers like Voltaire (1694–1778). The French *philosophe* wrote a biting, sarcastic poem after some Christians claimed that this is the best of all possible worlds, in spite of all evil and innocent suffering, because God rules over all and would have it no other way. God, if he exists, Voltaire responded, should explain his ways. No, the world is ruled by natural law and not by a capricious God. Not all Enlightenment thinkers went as far as Voltaire or the other *philosophes*, but the general impression sunk in among the educated elite that everything must be ruled by Newton's mechanical laws and not by God, despite Newton himself, who had claimed that physics is "thinking God's thoughts after him."

MODERNITY CREATES ACIDS THAT ATTACK TRADITIONAL RELIGION

Taken to their extremes, Byrne's three characteristic features of the Enlightenment and scientific revolution (and one might add, of modernity itself)

---

[13]Ibid., 7.
[14]Ibid., 10.

can be described as the omnicompetence of autonomous human reason, skepticism toward traditional beliefs not based on reason, including science, as virtuous, and scientism—a quasi-religion of the scientific method, extended to a worldview called naturalism—as the path toward progress. Not every Enlightenment thinker went to those extremes, but looking back over the centuries since Galileo and Descartes many people think their discoveries set Western culture's feet inexorably on those paths. There have been numerous attempts by philosophers, scientists and theologians to calm the troubled waters of culture by accommodating Christianity to modernity in various ways and to varying degrees. That is what much of this book is about—thinkers, especially theologians, who have attempted to reconcile the essence of Christianity with modernity, often by redefining that essence so that it is untouchable by the "acids of modernity."[15]

What are some other acids of modernity besides rationalism, skepticism and scientism/naturalism? One could add to these *secularism*—belief that life can be lived successfully without God or religion—which leads to the privatization of religion in which it has no voice in the public square. One could also add *historicism*—belief that everything in history is inextricably related causally to other historical events. And, finally, one could add *optimism*—belief that modernity, if lived out correctly in society, will lead to inevitable progress in overcoming misery of all kinds. Again, Voltaire stated it most bluntly and, admittedly, extremely, when he wrote that the demise of traditional religion and the rise of secular explanation would result in "less superstition, less fanaticism, . . . less misery."[16] But perhaps the single, overriding or underlying acid of modernity is *anthropocentrism*—placing the human at the center of knowledge. This process began in the Renaissance, but it became the *sine qua non* of the Enlightenment. Every other modern theme and acid of modernity arises from it and centers around it and assumes it. Again, Pope's saying about self-knowledge stands as the motto of the whole modern cultural revolution and its *Zeitgeist*: "Know then thyself; presume not God to scan. The proper study of mankind is man."

It would be a mistake to think that modernity, including these principles

---

[15]The phrase "acids of modernity" was coined by culture critic and essayist Walter Lippman in his 1929 essay by that title in *A Preface to Morals* (New York: Macmillan, 1929), 52–68.

[16]Quoted in Byrne, *Religion and the Enlightenment*, 19.

and impulses corrosive to traditional religion, led or necessarily leads to the demise of Christianity. As we will see throughout this book, despite predictions by some radical Enlightenment prophets such as Voltaire, Christianity has flourished throughout the era increasingly dominated by modernity. The result of modernity for Christianity, however, was nevertheless dramatic. As Byrne puts it,

> the nature of Christianity was up for grabs. Was Christianity primarily a personal faith in Jesus Christ, loyalty to the Pope, membership in a particular church, a commitment to the moral values of the gospel, an over-complicated version of a simple message, or just a very big mistake? All of these views and many others can be found in the Enlightenment.[17]

What the Enlightenment did, and modernity does, is not destroy religion in general or Christianity in particular but force them to reconsider themselves in several ways. Compared with the authority of the churches in society throughout the Middle Ages and well past the Reformation, churches increasingly had to take a back seat in the bus of knowledge. Knowledge has come to be defined as what can be proven by secular evidence and arguments. All else, including church doctrines, must be something other than knowledge, perhaps opinion or superstition. In response to this, many Christian thinkers went on a search for the essence of religion and Christianity that could not be undermined by Enlightenment knowledge. The resulting reconsideration of traditional Christianity led to its reconstruction—especially reconstructions of theology and doctrine. So radical did this project of reconstruction become that one wag commented that modern theologians became so afraid of being kicked in the ditch by modernity that they jumped there to avoid the pain of being kicked. That is an extreme analysis of modern theology; many modern theologians, as we will see, did nothing of the kind. Many valiantly attempted to defend traditional Christianity by criticizing modernity's tendency to overreach its own competence.

A caveat is in order at this point: Not everything introduced by the Enlightenment and modernity is automatically corrosive to religion in general or Christianity in particular. The point here is that, taken to extremes, certain tendencies of modern thought become corrosive to traditional Christian be-

---

[17]Byrne, *Religion and the Enlightenment,* 14.

liefs and that these major tendencies, even not taken to extremes, present challenges to traditional Christianity. Modern Christian theology has risen to those challenges in a variety of ways, and whether they are positive or negative is a judgment call made differently by observers and critics.

As this book will show, the theological responses to modernity have been wildly diverse—all the way from radical, secular theology of the 1960s to anti-modern fundamentalism. Still, one theme seems to run throughout most of them: a desire to reconstruct Christianity to make it immune from the acids of modernity and especially science. Even theologians who did not admit that as their project seem to have been driven by that motive. Might it be possible to redefine religion and Christianity so that the acids of modernity cannot harm them? Can they be made impervious to the ravages of the Enlightenment and scientific revolutions? It seemed to many movers and shakers of culture that White was right in his massive 1896 study *A History of the Warfare of Science with Theology in Christendom* that traditional Christianity always loses when it wages that war. But what if Christian theology could be redefined so that it has nothing to do with what the natural sciences study? One approach to peace between Christianity and science is to make science the sphere of facts and religion, Christianity included, the sphere of values. The German Enlightenment philosopher Kant hinted at such a separation and teased it out in *Religion Within the Limits of Reason Alone* (1793); many nineteenth-century theologians found in that proposal the charm that would end the war of science with religion.

One of the major themes of this study of modern theology is how various modern theologians have attempted to reconstruct or redefine Christianity in light of modernity and especially science. Some in this study have not engaged in that project; some have reacted to modernity's challenges by mainly rejecting modernity, especially its acids. Still, all of them, in one way or another, engaged modernity in conversation and were influenced by it. That is what makes them modern theologians. Near the end, we will look at some theologians who declare themselves, or are identified as, postmodern. That does not mean they ignored modernity and were unaffected by it. Even postmodern theologians belong under the umbrella rubric of modern theology insofar as they seek to conduct their theological work in relation to this cultural ethos called modernity. Paradoxically, one can be both modern and postmodern. One can be modern and at the same time anti-modern, as is the case with fundamentalisms of all kinds, including Christian fundamentalism.

So, in a general way, this volume is the story of Christian theology's attempts to relate Christianity to modernity. Modernity is not a time period but a mindset or cultural ethos, but it does seem to correlate with the era between 1650 and 1950 in Europe and the United States with its aftereffects lasting to the present.[18] Contemporary theology seems much less interested in correlating Christianity with modernity than was nineteenth-century theology or theology in the first half of the twentieth century. Still, if modernity is dead, its odor is still very much in the air.

There is no one overriding modern challenge to traditional Christianity to which every modern theologian responded. Miracles is one issue, and some modern Christian thinkers responded especially to that. Revelation that transcends reason's grasp is another issue, and some modern Christian theologians responded especially to that. Others, as will be seen, responded to other issues raised by modernity. So there is no single theme that ties all the theologians in this story of modern theology together except responding to modernity's apparent challenges to traditional Christianity. What ties them all together is their felt need to wrestle with the challenges of modernity to traditional Christianity—what was commonly believed, even taken for granted, by most, if not all, Christians for seventeen or eighteen hundred years before the Enlightenment and scientific revolutions.

MODERN THEOLOGIANS ACCOMMODATE TO MODERNITY

Throughout this book the phrase "accommodation to" (or some variant) will be used to refer to theologians' attempts to come to terms with modernity's ethos. In some cases accommodation implies only that—concern to take the new ethos into account in theology. In most cases it means more, something like subversion of the gospel, transformation of essential Christianity, by modernity. Every theologian in this book practices some level of accommodation, at least attempting to translate Christianity so that modern people can

---

[18]The "end of modernity" is a much debated concept. There is no absolute answer to when, or if, modernity as the dominant cultural ethos died. However, sometime shortly after World War II seems to be a reasonable estimate. After that what has come to be called postmodernity seems to have set in. No doubt there is much overlap.

understand it and so that its beliefs do not contradict material facts brought
to light by modern science, such as the sun-centered solar system. Not every
theologian accommodates by capitulating basic tenets of Christianity to the
acids of modernity, however. However, it is this writer's judgment that some
have. Rarely does this take the form of blatant denial of a core doctrine of
historic, orthodox Christianity. In almost every case it takes the form of reinterpretation that amounts to transformation. Again, these are not easy lines
to draw, but drawn they must be. This book will dare to suggest where and
when modern theologians have stepped over that line so that their modern
Christianity is no longer recognizable as authentically Christian.

One criterion for making that judgment is the category of the supernatural. All too frequently, in this writer's opinion, modern theologians
have capitulated to modern naturalism and skepticism about the very possibility of miracles.[19] This often results in radical reinterpretations of them
(e.g., Christ's resurrection) as events of faith rather than as events in time
and space. One of the flashpoints of controversy, perhaps even a watershed
issue, in modern theology is the concept of "act of God." What does it mean
in a culture shaped by modernity to speak of an act of God? Why this is a
problem will become clear in the first few chapters. The issue is not whether
God is creator and sustainer of the world, something virtually all modern
theologians affirm. The issue is whether God ever acts within the world, in
history, in ways that are beyond scientific comprehension and explanation.
That is, does God intervene in the course of nature to cause unique events
called miracles? Was Jesus' resurrection such an event? Traditional Christianity says it was. Modern theology is divided about it because of different
approaches to accommodating to modernity.

---

[19]An example is New Testament theologian Rudolf Bultmann (see chap. 5.b.), who interpreted
the New Testament and theology in general with the modern presupposition that "history is a
unity in the sense of a closed continuum of effects in which individual events are connected by
the succession of cause and effect. This continuum . . . cannot be rent by the interference of
supernatural, transcendent powers" (*Existence and Faith*, ed. Schubert Ogden [New York: Meridian Books, 1960], 291-92). Bultmann was not the first or last modern theologian to reconstruct Christian theology on the basis of that naturalistic principle. While "supernatural" may
not be a particularly helpful concept, because to some it implies a dualistic view of God and the
world, its denial by some modern theologians would seem to result in denial (often by radical
reinterpretation) of crucial events of salvation history such as the resurrection.

1

MODERNITY CHALLENGES TRADITIONAL THEOLOGY

The Context of Early Modern Theology

O*ne day in 1802* Napoleon Bonaparte, emperor of France, called as-tronomer Pierre-Simon Laplace (1749–1827), author of a controversial book about the universe based on Isaac Newton's discoveries of natural laws, to explain his cosmology. The emperor asked Laplace about the place of God in his account of the universe, its origin and workings. According to reports of the time, the astronomer replied, *"Je n'avais pas besoin de cette hypothèse-là"* ("Sir, I had no need of that hypothesis").[1]

To the average twenty-first-century European or American Laplace's statement may seem uncontroversial, but at the time it bordered on blas-phemy. Napoleon may not have been shaken by it, but church authorities and theologians throughout Europe and North America denounced such ideas as heresy. Laplace, however, was merely expressing what many edu-cated people in Europe were coming to believe—that the physical uni-verse could be explained without reference to a creator or anything super-natural. All the gaps in knowledge of the universe were being quickly

---

[1]Roger Hahn, *Pierre Simon Laplace 1749–1827: A Determined Scientist* (Cambridge, MA: Har-vard University Press, 2005), 172.

closed by the scientists of the Age of Reason. Before the Enlightenment
and scientific revolutions virtually everyone, Catholic and Protestant, believed God created and controls the universe and that supernatural
powers and forces keep it going. By the time of Laplace's publication of
Méchanique céleste (often translated "Cosmology") in several volumes
from 1799 to 1805, many devoutly religious men and women believed
science can explain much but could not by itself explain everything about
the world—especially its origin and design. Laplace's declaration that the
God hypothesis was nowhere needed in the physical sciences came as a
shock to them; some readily embraced it and some rejected it. It was now,
however, a claim to be reckoned with.

What if science could exhaustively explain the universe? Where, then,
would be God? What would be left to believe? Many contemporary
people will say religion has to do only with the inner world, the spiritual
salvation of the individual, but that is not what very many Christian
people believed in Laplace's time and before. Most Christians and other
religious people held to belief in what is called natural theology—the
absolute, rational necessity of God for any total explanation of the universe. Many Christians scoffed at Laplace and people like him as "in-
fidels"—unbelievers and skeptics. Over time, however, Laplace's point of
view gained traction and gradually began to replace natural theology
and challenge orthodox Christian claims about God as the creator, sustainer and providential governor of the universe. Christian thinkers
who cared about making the faith relevant to the growing modern
worldview began looking for ways to rescue Christianity from the
burden of increasingly incredible tradition and from the deepening impression that atheism was to be religion's inevitable replacement.

What brought about this crisis and the perceived need to accommodate
Christian theology to modernity? Laplace did not create the crisis; he
merely expressed it in a way nobody before had publicly stated it. To many
he was like the little boy in the fable of the emperor's new clothes who dared
to say the emperor was naked. What led up to his stark declaration and its
aftermath for theology was a long chain of events in both science and philosophy that define the revolution we call early modernity—the Enlightenment.

1.A. Science Revises the Heavens

It all started with the simplest of ideas, but one destined to revolutionize the Western world. In its December 31, 1999, issue, *Time* magazine announced its "man of the millennium" (which was ironic because the millennium did not officially end until a year later): Johann Gutenberg (1398–1468), inventor of the moveable type printing press. Perhaps it should have been a little-known Franciscan friar from England who was evading the Inquisition and hiding in Munich, Bavaria, under protection of the emperor in 1342. His name was William of Ockham (or Occam) (1285–c. 1349). Among other controversial ideas, Ockham expressed what came later to be known as Ockham's razor—that simple principle that when one cause sufficiently explains a phenomenon, more should not be posited. At the time, and long before and afterwards, people tended to appeal to two causes for most events—a natural one and a supernatural one. For example, if a person became ill, it could be both because of an imbalance in the body's humors and a demon. Also, celestial bodies such as planets were widely believed to be moved both by natural forces among them (such as some kind of magnetic field) and by angels. Ockham, much to the dismay of the church's magisterium, suggested that the simplest explanation was always the wisest and only one. Many scholars see in Ockham and his razor the subtle beginning of a cultural earthquake whose shocks were to be felt much later in the scientific revolution.

Ockham died of the plague in Munich, where there is no monument to his life or work[2] because he was excommunicated by the pope. However, his idea was later expressed in many different forms by luminaries of the scientific revolution such as Newton, who said, "We are to admit no more causes of natural things than such as are both true and sufficient to explain their appearances."[3] On the basis of Ockham's razor, modern science has gradually discovered the one, natural cause of most, if not all, physical objects and events in the universe and excluded supernatural explanations from the experimental sciences.

---

[2]This author lived and studied in Munich (1981–1982) and looked for such a monument. I was told there was one in the Franciscan church but could not find it. Perhaps it had been destroyed in the bombing of Munich during World War II.

[3]Quoted in Stephen Hawking, *On the Shoulders of Giants* (Philadelphia: Running Press, 2002), 731.

Copernicus proposes a revolution in science, and Galileo carries it out.
One of the most unfortunate events in modern Western history was the
Catholic Church's condemnation of Galileo Galilei for his defense of the
heliocentric model. Adding insult to injury (to the church's reputation) is
the fact that he was only semi-officially rehabilitated by Rome in 1992, when
Pope John Paul II expressed regret for how he was treated by the church.
The details of Galileo's condemnation are so complicated that no attention
will be given them here; what is important for our story is what Galileo
achieved and its effects on the scientific revolution that helped launch modernity and challenged Christian theology to search for ways to end conflicts with science. Suffice it to say that the church's treatment of Galileo
merely for publishing proofs of his discoveries did more to undermine
Christianity's credibility in the modern world than any other event.

Before Galileo, unchallenged tradition held that the sun and other celestial
bodies revolve around the earth. After all, Aristotle, an influential Greek philosopher almost baptized by the medieval church, said so. More importantly,
however, people believed the Bible said so. Psalm 104:5 (NIV) declares,

> He set the earth on its foundations;
>   it can never be moved.

To deny that the earth is unmoving and unmovable may seem like a trivial
matter to contemporary people, but that is only because they have become
used to it. To people in the sixteenth century, Nicholas Copernicus's suggestion that the earth revolves around the sun was shocking, so much so
that the Polish astronomer (1473–1543) had to publish his theory as a mere
model for making astronomical calculations and not as a statement of
literal fact.

Copernicus achieved a great leap of the imagination as he contemplated
the complicated model of the solar system universally held in his lifetime.
To account for the growing observations of the movements of the heavenly
bodies (planets, moons) around the earth it had to posit numerous strange
movings forward and backward. To Copernicus it was too complex; he was
looking for a simpler model of what we now call the solar system. His imaginative leap was to dare to think that perhaps all the planets, including the
earth, revolve around the sun. When he imagined that design, he found it

made for a much simpler, more elegant model that better matched what was being observed in planetariums. He gradually taught his theory to students who spread it around before Copernicus was prepared to publish it. He knew how controversial it would be. For years he worked on a book that would explain and defend this heliocentric model of the sun and planets, but it was published only as he lay dying. *On the Revolutions of the Celestial Spheres* was placed in his hands on his deathbed. As Copernicus feared, it created a firestorm of controversy and was widely condemned as heretical. Even Martin Luther declared that the Polish astronomer must be insane.[4]

Why is Copernicus's heliocentric model of the system of the "celestial spheres"—the solar system—called the Copernican revolution? Not because it posits the revolution of the earth around the sun! Rather, it placed observation and mathematical calculation at the center of natural science and began the overthrow of the authority of tradition.

Copernicus's memory has largely been eclipsed by that of Galileo, who first proved the heliocentric model of the universe factually true beyond doubt. Galileo was born in Italy and lived his entire life as a faithful son of the Catholic Church. He studied at the University of Pisa and taught mathematics and astronomy there and at the University of Padua, where he wrote some of his controversial scientific works. He came under suspicion by the Inquisition because he defended Copernicus's heliocentric model of the universe. The powerful Catholic Cardinal Robert Bellarmine (1542–1621) had declared publicly that Copernicus's system could not be held as true unless it could be proven by physical demonstration—something Bellarmine and other defenders of the traditional worldview thought impossible. Galileo thought he could prove it true by physical demonstration using new versions of the telescope that could see farther than those that existed in Copernicus's time. He also tried to prove it true by study of the tides, something that ultimately failed.

In 1616 Bellarmine and the Inquisition ordered Galileo to cease his attempts to prove Copernicus's theory true. For a while he obeyed, but in 1632

---

[4]Interestingly, a Lutheran theologian, Andreas Osiander, wrote the preface to Copernicus's book. However, he explained that its view of the universe was only a hypothesis meant for convenience of calculations and was not to be interpreted as a literal picture of the planetary system. Andrew D. White recounts Luther's vitriolic reaction to Copernicus in *A History of the Warfare of Science with Theology in Christendom*, 2 vols. (New York: Appleton, 1896), 1:126–27.

he published one of his greatest works, *Dialogue Concerning the Two Chief World Systems*, which laid the foundation for his proof. Ironically, given certain twists and turns of Vatican politics between 1616 and 1632, Galileo was permitted to publish the book. Soon, however, due to new vagaries of Vatican politics, the book and its author came under heavy criticism which led to a trial before the Inquisition. In 1633 Galileo was declared "vehemently suspect of heresy" and placed under house arrest. His books were banned, and he was forbidden to publish any more. However, during his house arrest, he continued to write books that would be published only in Protestant cities or only after his death.

Later, the world came to know of Galileo's mistreatment at the hands of the Catholic Church. It is widely believed that those who condemned him knew he was right, but they did not want his proof of Copernicus's heliocentric model disseminated publicly. Of course, it was too late. The credibility of the church sank to a new low in the eyes of educated men and women of Europe. The war between science and traditional religion in Christendom had begun, and science was destined to win virtually every battle from then on.

Galileo was dismayed by the controversy over his scientific discoveries and their publication. His main long-term contribution to the war between science and theology was inadvertent, which is to say he never intended it to be a declaration of war. That was his "Letter to the Grand Duchess Christina," written in 1615 and published in 1636 in Strasburg, a Protestant city. The letter had to do not so much with any specific scientific theory or discovery as with the roles of science and theology in the creation of knowledge.

The Grand Duchess Christina was the widow of Ferdinand de Medici, Duke of Tuscany, who had appointed Galileo to his professorship at the University of Pisa. The duchess was interested in potential conflicts between the new sciences and the Bible and asked for an explanation from a friend of Galileo, who conveyed the request to him. Galileo's response reveals a new attitude toward the relationships between science, the Bible and theology, one that caught on and became standard especially among devout scientists throughout the scientific revolution. (Not-so-devout scientists such as Laplace would adhere to it as well, but in a different way that did not afford respect to theology or perhaps even the Bible.)

It is impossible to grasp how revolutionary Galileo's explanation was without realizing that before it theology had been widely considered the queen of the sciences. (In that honorary title, given to theology during the Middle Ages, "science" means any and every orderly, disciplined way of studying and thinking. It was not limited to the physical sciences.) The revolutionary aspect of Galileo's new model for understanding the role of theology in relation to the physical sciences is his implicit declaration of independence for the latter from the former. In the long run, at least, it contributed to the dethroning of theology and its relegation to the status of a pseudo-science in the eyes of many Enlightenment thinkers. That was almost certainly not Galileo's intention, but true to the law of unintended consequences, it had that effect.

In the letter, Galileo confirmed to the duchess that he held the heliocentric model of the universe to be fact and not merely a device for making calculations about the future locations of planets and moons (which is how many of Copernicus's defenders managed to hold and promote it). That admission indirectly led to his much later trial and condemnation. More importantly, however, he declared that the physical sciences of observation such as astronomy rule in matters of knowledge about the physical universe even when they seem to contradict the Bible and do contradict theological tradition and doctrine. He argued that when such conflicts arise, it is theology that must adjust its thinking and teaching and not science. In effect, he was restricting theology to the spiritual sphere of salvation and living the Christian life (ethics) and enthroning the physical sciences of observation and deduction in its place in the physical sphere. Instead of one throne, there would now be two. Gradually, throughout the ensuing centuries, science's throne rose higher in the academic world.

Galileo went to great lengths to affirm the inspiration and authority of the Bible, but he appealed to the principle of accommodation to explain why it sometimes seems to state as fact things that cannot be true, such as God having eyes and hands and feet. Not everything in the Bible is meant to be interpreted as literal. Also, and more controversially, he stated that "the intention of the Holy Ghost is to teach us how one goes to heaven, not how heaven goes."[5] The real revolutionary statement in the letter, however,

---

[5]Galileo Galilei and Stillman Drake, *Discourses and Opinions of Galileo* (New York: Anchor Books, 1957), 173–216. Galileo knew that this epigram was not his originally; he was quoting another source. This saying had been around for some time before Galileo.

has to do with science's competence and theology's lack of competence in matters pertaining to physical reality so that theology's interpretations of the Bible in such matters *must be revised* when the material facts of science contradict them. Here is one statement to that effect:

> That in the books of the sages of this world there are contained some physical truths which are soundly demonstrated, and others that are merely stated; as to the former, it is the office of wise divines to show that they do not contradict the holy Scriptures. And as to the propositions which are stated but not rigorously demonstrated, anything contrary to the Bible involved by them must be held undoubtedly false and should be proved so by every possible means. Now if truly demonstrated physical conclusions need not be subordinated to biblical passages, but the latter must rather be shown not to interfere with the former, then before a physical proposition is condemned it must be shown to be not rigorously demonstrated—and this is to be done not by those who hold the proposition to be true, but by those who judge it to be false. This seems very reasonable and natural, for those who believe an argument to be false may much more easily find the fallacies in it than men who consider it to be true and conclusive. Indeed, in the latter case it will happen that the more the adherents of an opinion turn over their pages, examine the arguments, repeat the observations, and compare the experiences, the more they will be confirmed in that belief.[6]

Careful study of that declaration reveals what Galileo intended—that the burden of proof in matters of possible conflict between the Bible and science lies with theology if it insists on maintaining a traditional doctrine in conflict with science, and that it will fail if it resists the material facts of science. In the rest of the letter Galileo made clear his intention: that theology must bow to science in such cases and reinterpret Scripture so that it fits what science proves.

Once again, that may not grate on contemporary ears as it did on the ears of Galileo's contemporaries. Theologians were outraged when the letter was published in 1636. Some foresaw the consequence that Galileo himself may not have intended—the overthrow of theology as a science at all, especially in matters outside the realm of the spiritual (salvation, Christian life, church order).

---

[6]Ibid.

Newton pictures the world as a great machine. But we have not yet come to the biggest shock science had in store for theology. Science only began to revise the heavens with Copernicus and Galileo; it radically revised the heavens with Newton—again, against the scientist's own intentions. Newton's discoveries and others' interpretations of them seemed to relegate God to the spiritual realm, to the inner world of the human person, and out of the heavens—the physical universe and its workings.

Born in England and trained in theology, philosophy and mathematics, Newton was a precocious student who may even have been some kind of savant. He became a fellow, a teacher, of Trinity College, Cambridge University, in his early twenties. (His teaching location is ironic in that he did not believe in the Trinity, something he kept mostly to himself to avoid controversy.) Throughout his career as a professional mathematician who dabbled in many subjects, Newton was most interested in, and devoted most time to, biblical studies. He was obsessed with identifying the year of the second coming of Jesus Christ—a fact usually overlooked in college and university courses where he is studied. He was a devout but unorthodox Christian who harbored doubts about the deity of Christ and the Trinity. Still, in spite of his heretical beliefs, he thought of his scientific discoveries as supporting divine providence rather than undermining it. It disturbed him not at all that his discoveries seemed to make supernatural causes unnecessary; he interpreted his mechanical universe ruled by cause and effect as the sphere of God's providence. The study of natural laws, physics, was to him "thinking God's thoughts after him."

By many accounts, Newton was the greatest and most influential scientist who ever lived.[7] His *Philosophiæ Naturalis Principia Mathematica*, published in 1687, is considered one of the great classics of modern science. It laid the foundations for the mechanistic worldview that has been so beneficial to science and that challenged much traditional theology insofar as it ruled out miracles. Newton himself did not conceive that his worldview ruled out miracles; only his disciples and later interpreters drew that conclusion. Without doubt, however, it made belief in miracles more difficult and raised the question of how any supernatural events could be reconciled with the universe ruled by mathematically describable natural laws.

---

[7]Daniel Burt, *The Biography Book* (Westport, CT: Greenwood Publishing Group, 2001), 315.

Every high school student has heard the story of how Newton discovered the law of gravity. According to the legend, the scientist was sitting under an apple tree when an apple fell on his head and he instantly thought of the law of universal gravitational force—as if it suddenly popped into his head like the goddess Athena in full armor supposedly popped out of Zeus's head in Greek mythology. That is the stuff of legends and myths. However, it is probably based on something true; Newton may have told friends that he first thought of the law of gravity while reflecting on the fall of an apple from a tree. Like Copernicus's imaginative leap toward the heliocentric solar system, Newton's discovery of gravity may have been a great leap of the imagination sparked by a physical event observed.

$$F = G\frac{m_1 m_2}{r^2}$$

Fig. 1.1

What many people do not understand about Newton's law of gravity is that it, like all the rest of Newton's laws of nature, is mathematically describable (see fig. 1.1).

The purpose of providing the equation is not to lead into a detailed explanation but only to point out what many do not, but should, know about Newton's law of gravity and by extension all his laws of nature, including inertia. These are intended to be universal laws that can be described mathematically so that they can be used to predict future events in the natural world. Without them people would never have landed on the moon (or done much else in modern science). In other words, theoretically, if one knows the exact location and velocity of any body and all the bodies in relation to it, with Newton's laws he or she can predict precisely where it will be at any given time in the future. That means the universe of things, bodies, material entities, is closed to outside interference. Any supposition of possible outside interference throws a monkey wrench, so to speak, into the machine of nature, making it impossible to predict anything precisely.

This is why Laplace could claim that he had no need of the God hypothesis to explain the cosmos and how it functions. The world picture painted by Newton, intentionally or not, is that of a great machine that functions on its own in perpetual motion. The point is that only by imagining it as such can science predict the future—something essential to practical application of modern science. For example, soon after Newton's discovery of laws of nature, an astronomer named Edmond Halley predicted the precise year of the return of a comet later named after him. Using Newton's physics and mathematics, Halley predicted its return seventy-six years after its last appearance. It did indeed return in 1758—exactly seventy-six years after its appearance in 1682.

Feats like that demonstrated to everyone the competence of science based on natural laws understood as mathematically describable, which means unbreakable. If that is so, what does that mean for religion and especially for Christian belief in a supernatural God who acts providentially, with purpose and intention, in response to prayer? What about miracles? What about angels and demons? What about free will? So many questions for theology were raised by Newton's world picture that went beyond anything Newton himself asked or answered. Some Christian thinkers rushed to save the day by declaring Newton's physics proof of God; natural laws reflect a purposeful intellect who created them and uses them to work out his eternal purposes. Other Christian thinkers concluded it does not matter because religion has only to do with ethics—what ought to be—and not with physics, what is. Yet others suggested that if God is the author of the natural laws, as Newton himself believed, he can alter them and still keep the universe running in an orderly fashion so that science can do its business of calculating and predicting. All these and more answers will appear in our story of modern theology's attempts to respond to the acids of modernity.

The scientific revolution challenges traditional Christianity. The year was 1650—near the beginning of the modern era (which many date to 1648, the end of the Thirty Years' War). Bishop James Ussher of Ireland (1581–1656) published his landmark book *Annales Veteris Testamenti*, translated in 1658 as *Annals of the World* (not an exact translation of the Latin title), which revealed the date of the creation of the world as October 23, 4004 B.C. Ussher, a widely respected scholar, calculated the date of creation based on numerous factors turned up in his research, but his main source was the Bible itself. His methods need not detain us here. The point is that his chronology was widely accepted and worked its way into the footnotes and study notes of many English Bibles. For centuries conservative Christians depended on Ussher's research and conclusion; it was embraced by many as equal with Scripture itself. To deny that God created the entire universe in 4004 B.C. was tantamount to denying the authority of the Bible.

In 1925 American statesman and anti-evolution activist William Jennings Bryan (1860–1925) testified for the prosecution (and was, in fact, the lead prosecutor) at the famous Scopes "monkey trial" in Dayton, Tennessee. His combative counterpart, defense attorney and anti-fundamentalist crusader Clarence Darrow, asked Bryan about the age of a certain rock. Between 1650 and 1925, of course, much had happened in science. Using Galileo's methods and Newton's laws of physics and other discoveries of the scientific revolution, geologists had come to agreement that the earth was far older than Ussher claimed. By 1925 that the earth was millions of years old was settled fact for most educated people in Europe and North America. There were hold-outs like Bryan who, together with many other conservative Christians, saw modern science as the enemy of God. They often confused two issues—the age of the earth and evolution. Since evolution was in their view godless and reduced human beings to animals, they rejected the scientific claims about the great age of the universe as well.

Bryan looked at the rock held in Darrow's hand and paused. Bryan was a smart man and in many ways a modern man. He had served as Secretary of State under President Woodrow Wilson and had been his party's nominee for president in three elections. Then he said, "The Rock of Ages is more important than the age of rocks." Even some of Bryan's anti-evolution supporters laughed. Much of America laughed. (The Scopes trial was the first event broadcast live over radio nationwide.) Anti-evolution fundamentalists were humiliated and built their own colleges to protect their children from the godless atheism of modern science. There they continued to teach that the world was created about ten thousand years ago and that evolution is an atheist conspiracy to overthrow religion. Not all fundamentalists did this, but it became one way many fundamentalists fought back in the ongoing war between science and religion.

Progressive Christians, by contrast, often capitulated uncritically to the latest trends in science. They made peace with science by embracing whatever scientists said, even if it was merely a hypothesis yet unproven. The late nineteenth and early twentieth centuries saw many progressive, liberal Protestant theologians hastening to deny miracles because they thought to defend them would only extend the warfare between science and religion that religion seemed always to lose. One such progressive or liberal Protestant thinker was Andrew D. White, author of the influential two-volume *A History of the Warfare of Science with Theology in Christendom* mentioned earlier. In 1898 he concluded that the "dissolving away of traditional opinions regarding . . . sacred literature" was simply "the atmosphere of thought engendered by the development of all sciences during the last three centuries. Vast masses of myth, legend, marvel and dogmatic assertion, coming into this atmosphere, have been dissolved and are now dissolving quietly away like icebergs drifted into the Gulf Stream."[8] Many Christian theologians, as we shall see, agreed readily with him and sought to reconstruct Christian doctrines so that they would not be swept away by the tide of scientific discoveries.

What were and are some of Christian theologians' approaches to the war between modern science and traditional theology? What follows are generalizations; the approaches are probably as varied as the thinkers who proposed them. One was taken by Bryan and his fundamentalist cohorts: modern science, although valuable for some of its inventions, is to be resisted insofar as it conflicts with the literal, traditional interpretation of the Bible. Bryan and the fundamentalists followed a conflict model in relating to the scientific revolution and its results. Most of them, however, accepted that the earth revolves around the sun—a fact pointed out by their critics such as progressive Protestant pastor and theologian Harry Emerson Fosdick (1878–1969), who thundered from his pulpit in New York City's Riverside Church: "Shall the fundamentalists win?" His answer in that 1922 sermon was a resounding "No!"—meaning "unless we liberal Christians let them!"

Fosdick well represents another Christian approach to the war between modern science and theology: a dualist, accommodation model. Like most progressive, liberal Protestants of his time Fosdick was tired of the war between science and theology and opted to accommodate to whatever scientists said—including no miracles (because of the uniformity of nature most scientists then believed Newton's laws required). He urged modern Protestants to keep up to date with science and not fight against it. After all, he preached and wrote, Christianity is not about how the heavens go, or how old the earth is, but about the gradual dawning of the kingdom of God on

---

[8]White, *History*, 2:393.

earth through love and "Christian brotherhood." Fosdick provided a generation of twentieth-century American Christians with books explaining
the true essence of Christianity as ethical living, the social gospel, which
has nothing to do with the things science studies.[9] This approach is dualist
in separating science and theology into almost watertight compartments
where they cannot conflict because they are about entirely different subjects. It is radically accommodationist in bowing to every scientific discovery even if that discovery is only a hypothesis yet to be proven (e.g., the
naturalistic view of the universe as uniformly and universally ruled by
natural laws to the exclusion of miracles).[10]

Finally, some nineteenth- and twentieth-century Christians responded
to the war between science and religion growing out of the scientific revolution by cautiously correlating science's material facts with revelation's
venerable truths. This is the integrationist or correlationist approach to accommodation and is very similar to what Galileo intended in his letter to
the Grand Duchess Christina. Mediating theologian Bernard Ramm (1916–
1992), trained in science and theology, took this approach in *The Christian
View of Science and Scripture*,[11] in which he argued against both other approaches and called for Christian theology to adapt to the "material facts"
of science (such as the age of the earth) without capitulating to every scientific hypothesis, model or theory (e.g., naturalistic evolution).

Much modern theology is dominated by overt or covert attempts to respond
to the scientific revolution. To a very large extent, this book is that story.

1.B. PHILOSOPHERS LAY NEW FOUNDATIONS FOR KNOWLEDGE

The year was 1784; the so-called Enlightenment in European culture was at
its peak, and some philosophers were beginning to question its high-flying
claims about autonomous human reason and its potential to be objective,
know reality as it is in itself apart from revelation or faith and solve human-

---

[9]See Harry Emerson Fosdick, *A Guide to Understanding the Bible* (New York: Harper & Row,
1956).
[10]To be fair, not all fundamentalists rejected science entirely; the conflict model was practiced by
them in varying degrees. Similarly, not all progressive Protestants accommodated to every
whim of modern scientists, but they tended to rescue theology from defeat at the hands of science by separating them so that science explains the physical world while theology seeks to
explain the social world and way forward toward the kingdom of God on earth.
[11]Bernard Ramm, *The Christian View of Science and Scripture* (Grand Rapids: Eerdmans, 1954).

ity's problems. Immanuel Kant (1724–1804) published his essay "What Is Enlightenment?" to breathe new life into the movement. The way to do so, he thought, was to distill Enlightenment thought down to its basic principle—something all enlightened people could agree on.

People begin to think for themselves. What was Kant's answer that resonated with so many educated people first in Europe, then in America and later around the world? It is so simple that many twenty-first-century people, including many who think of the Enlightenment as something pernicious, live by it and take it for granted: *Sapere aude!*—"Think for yourself" or "Dare to know!" His first three sentences sound like a declaration of independence from authoritative tradition:

> Enlightenment is man's release from his self-incurred tutelage. Tutelage is man's inability to make use of his understanding without direction from another. Self-incurred is this tutelage when its cause lies not in lack of reason but in lack of resolution and courage to use it without direction from another. *Sapere aude!* "Have courage to use your own reason!"—that is the motto of enlightenment.[12]

Kant's essay goes on to reject knowledge imposed on people by religious and political authorities. For him, the essence of enlightenment is daring to question and use one's own reasoning ability to decide what to believe.

Many people take that approach to thinking and believing for granted, but that it is the right approach was new in the Enlightenment. Someone might point back to heroes of free thought such as Socrates and Luther, both of whom broke from the consensuses of belief in their own times and dared to think for themselves. However, they stand out as exceptions to the rule; before the Enlightenment it was generally thought wrong to think for oneself, and many who did died for it. For thousands of years the social expectation was to believe whatever authorities said whether they be traditional dogmas in religion or kings or customs. Kant was not calling for a new, revolutionary approach to knowing and believing; he was setting forth what he believed was the essence of the Enlightenment that had been going on for more than a century. He wanted its principle of free thought to be

---

[12]Immanuel Kant, "What Is Enlightenment?" in *The Enlightenment: A Sourcebook and Reader*, ed. Paul Hyland (London: Routledge, 2003), 54.

openly embraced by princes, kings and emperors. And he did much to bring about that embrace.

Sometimes the phrase "the Enlightenment" is used to cover both the scientific revolution (see 1.a.) and the revolution in philosophy that is the topic of this section. Sometimes it is used for only the philosophical revolution that corresponded to the scientific revolution. However, what matters is to grasp how revolutionary both together were in overturning ancient ways of thinking and knowing and replacing them with new mental habits. Most people can grasp that about the changes happening in science during the Enlightenment; they are more concrete and tangible in their results. For many, however, it is more difficult to understand why the corresponding changes in philosophy were just as earth-shaking and challenging to religion and especially Christianity. The acids of modernity brought about by modern philosophy were just as corrosive for traditional religion as were the ones created by the new sciences.

Philosophy has always been theology's main conversation partner, and for more than a thousand years, before the rise of modernity with the Enlightenment, philosophy was considered theology's handmaid. That is, philosophy was theology's servant. And throughout much of that millennium, philosophy was done by theologians or monks. During the high Middle Ages in Europe, if a person taught philosophy in a university he (it was always a he) was expected to either be ordained, that is, to be a priest, or live like one, that is, to be celibate. Even the Protestant Reformation did little at first to change that custom. Before the seventeenth century almost all philosophers in Europe were clergymen or lived the kind of life expected of clergy *and had to think within the boundaries of ecclesiastical tradition.* It was dangerous to think for oneself.

A case study in this is the twelfth-century philosopher Peter Abelard (1079–1142), who taught at the University of Paris. He was not ordained, but in true medieval fashion he was expected to live a celibate life. And he was expected to teach philosophy within the framework of authoritative tradition, which was Augustinian—the thought of the fifth-century church father Augustine (354–430). However, much had been added to and taken away from Augustine's thought by the twelfth century; it had been interpreted and reinterpreted. But those alterations had to be approved by popes.

(Most often, however, they happened gradually and were not even recognized as alterations.) The most influential philosopher of Abelard's time was a recently deceased French-English abbot named Anselm of Canterbury (1033–1109). Anselm used reason, logic, to prove traditional Christian beliefs, but he emphasized that he always approached that task with faith. His motto was "I believe in order to understand." In other words, faith seeks understanding. A good Christian, he and almost everyone else believed, accepts authoritative tradition and then puts reason in its service by adding proof to what is already believed by faith.

Abelard dared to question tradition and ecclesiastical authority. For one thing, he did not think celibacy should be a requirement for philosophers; he secretly married his patron's daughter. His patron sent thugs to break into Abelard's apartment and castrate him. More importantly, however, Abelard wrote a book whose title reflected his life's work: *Sic et Non* ("yes and no," circa 1121). There he demonstrated that authoritative tradition was flawed because one could find contradictory beliefs within it. Philosophy's task, for Abelard, was not merely to comment on traditional beliefs but to question them. For that Bernard of Clairvaux (1090–1153), preacher of the crusades, started a campaign to persecute Abelard, and Abelard almost certainly would have been burned at the stake had he not died of natural causes first.

So, Kant's principle of "think for yourself" was not entirely new with the Enlightenment. But there it took on a new, deeper dimension and was meant for all people. Within a short period of time during the seventeenth and eighteenth centuries it became acceptable to do philosophy outside the confines of the church and its tradition. It became acceptable and even required to question tradition and authorities in order to be considered a true philosopher. Because philosophy had always been theology's main conversation partner, the changes in philosophy challenged theologians. What were they to do with the new approach to thinking, believing and knowing? It took a long time for theologians to realize that they had to take Enlightenment thought seriously and not just react against it as something pernicious and evil. But even before they did that, they were being affected by it and, in small steps and to varying degrees, accommodating to it.

Descartes carries out a Copernican revolution in philosophy. Our story of the philosophical Enlightenment and the philosophical side of modernity begins in a small, stove-heated room in a house in Ulm, Germany, on November 10, 1619. Seldom is one date so little known and yet so momentous in terms of revolutionizing culture for centuries afterwards

René Descartes (1596–1650) is one of the most interesting philosophers in history. Many biographies of him have been published over the years, and new ones continue to appear 350 years after his death. He was a peripatetic intellectual and soldier, traveling all over Europe, fighting in battles, spying on influential political leaders for the Jesuits,[13] dabbling in occult "sciences" and teaching and writing. Most importantly for our story, however, is Descartes's determination to think for himself and to discover certain knowledge, that is, knowledge that could not be doubted, to shore up both the budding scientific revolution and religion whose doctrines were made increasingly doubtful in the aftermath of the Reformation and during the religious wars that ravaged Europe in the seventeenth century.

Descartes described what led up to his earth-shaking breakthrough in thought that helped launch the Enlightenment and modern world:

> Some years ago [referring to 1619] I was struck by the large number of falsehoods that I had accepted as true in my childhood, and by the highly doubtful nature of the whole edifice that I had subsequently based upon them. I realized that it was necessary, once in the course of my life, to demolish everything completely and start again right from the foundations if I wanted to establish anything at all in the sciences that was stable and likely to last.[14]

By "the sciences" Descartes did not mean just the physical sciences but all the disciplines taught in universities, including theology. Notice two things about this confession. First, long before Kant wrote "What Is Enlightenment?" Descartes was determined to think for himself. Second, he was seeking new foundations for truth and a method of discovering truth that would provide certainty. Before this, most people in Christian Europe assumed that faith plus reason, both working together within the context of tradition, provided certainty. Descartes was no longer convinced and dared to question everything.

---

[13]The fact that Descartes was a spy for the Society of Jesus, or Jesuits, who in turn worked for Catholic royal families such as the Hapsburgs, is well established by A. C. Grayling in *Descartes: The Life and Times of a Genius* (New York: Walker & Company, 2005).

[14]Quoted in ibid., 56–57.

On that November day in 1619 Descartes was traveling to the coronation of the new Holy Roman Emperor but was waylaid by intense winter weather. In that tiny room in that Ulm inn Descartes ruminated about the sorry state of so-called knowledge—not only his own but everyone's. That day and the night that followed seem to constitute one of the few known dates when the world changed. According to one biographer, that day and night "has gone down in anecdotal history as one of the fulcrums on which the Western world has turned."[15] Exactly what happened there and then is somewhat unclear because Descartes wrote about it much later and some of what he said was contained in diaries and notebooks now lost, but people who knew him well and wrote about him shortly after his death told the story based Descartes's own accounts. Apparently, if they are right, sometime during that day and night in Ulm Descartes broke through to a whole new way of seeking and finding knowledge. He laid it out eighteen years later in *Discourse on Method* (1637). According to many interpreters of philosophical history, this essay is "the dividing line in the history of thought. Everything that came before it is old; everything that came after it is new."[16]

Realizing that much, if not all, he had been taught was uncertain and some of it untrue, Descartes decided to start over and work toward certainty by doubting everything. He realized that his five senses could be deceiving him; they often do. Therefore knowledge based on sense experience is always uncertain. So he bore in and dug down into all that he knew, doubting everything, until he realized there is one thing he could not doubt—his own existence. "In this way, Descartes became one of those rare figures in history who have given the world a sentence that is a touchstone."[17] It is *cogito, ergo sum*—"I think, therefore I am." In other words, Descartes could not doubt his own existence as a thinking self because in order to doubt he had to think and in order to think he had to exist. This, then, was bedrock—the thinking self's own existence. From there Descartes deduced the logically necessary existence of God and the world and many other things dear to philosophy, religion and science. Insofar as ideas are clear and distinct and made nec-

---

[15]Russell Shorto, *Descartes' Bones: A Skeletal History of the Conflict Between Faith and Reason* (New York: Doubleday, 2008), 16.
[16]Ibid.
[17]Ibid., 20.

essary by logical connection with this bedrock, they must be believed. They constitute knowledge because of their rational certainty.

Descartes had much more to say in *Discourse on Method* and other writings such as *Meditations on First Philosophy* (1641), but the details of his epistemology need not detain us here. The relevant point is that, together with Galileo, Descartes launched the Enlightenment by daring to think for himself, apart from tradition, even to the point of doubting everything and then basing all knowledge on his own existence rather than God's. From Descartes on, then, modern thought has been obsessed with certainty, and knowledge has often been reduced to what can be proven with logical and/ or evidential proofs. Gradually, the realm of knowledge came to exclude things doubtable, and much that Descartes himself thought was true beyond a reasonable doubt later came to be doubted. What is important about Descartes is not what he believed but how he believed it.

Lest anyone think Descartes was anything else, we need to make clear that he thought of himself as a devout Christian. He did not intend to tear down or destroy Christian dogmas; he desired to give them a firmer foundation than ever they had. Is it his fault that later rationalists used his method to undermine traditional, orthodox Christianity? Or is there something inherently unchristian about Descartes's method—regardless of whether he used it to prove the existence of God and the soul and other Christian doctrines? The French Catholic mathematician, philosopher and mystic Blaise Pascal (1623–1662) thought so. Much later the Danish thinker Søren Kierkegaard (1813–1855) agreed with Pascal. Both, and many other Christians, believed that, in spite of his good intentions, Descartes's method served to undermine authentic Christian faith by replacing faith with reason. Before Descartes the watchword was "I believe in order to understand"; after him, for all kinds of Enlightenment rationalists influenced by his approach to knowledge, the watchword became "I believe only what I can understand." Faith was being replaced by autonomous human reason; knowledge was being redefined as that which can be known with certainty by autonomous human reason functioning apart from revelation, tradition or faith.

What became of Descartes, perhaps the first truly modern man? The end of his story is almost as interesting as the story of his great insight and new method of acquiring knowledge. Like Galileo, the French philosopher entered into correspondence with a royal acquaintance named Christina, only in his case she was the queen of Sweden (1626–1689), whose father, Gustavus Adolphus, led Sweden to victory in the Thirty Years' War. Christina was, by all accounts, not a particularly good monarch, but she was intellectually gifted and sought to bring the best of European culture, including philosophy, to her country. She invited Descartes to come to Stockholm to tutor her in philosophy. He went reluctantly, for he had an aversion to cold. Christina had him stand, bareheaded, at 5:00 a.m., tutoring her in an unheated library in her palace. Descartes hated it: "I think that in winter here, men's thoughts freeze like the water."[18]

In February 1650, less than a year after arriving in Sweden, Descartes fell ill, presumably from the frigid conditions, and died. But that was far from the end of Descartes. Soon after his death a near cult developed around his philosophy and his person so that in 1666 his body was disinterred, his bones put in a special copper box and transported to Paris where, in 1667, they were reburied in a church with great ceremony and even celebration (of his life) by his followers known as Cartesians. Between 1667 and contemporary times, the bones were lost—probably during the French Revolution.[19] However, Descartes's skull, which somehow had been left in Sweden, was recovered and now sits in the Museum of Man in Paris where it can be seen by the public. Ironically, the skull of the man who started an intellectual and cultural revolution that helped overthrow the dominance of traditional religion over people's thoughts is now a relic and the goal of philosophical pilgrims, much as saints' relics were worshiped by religious pilgrims in the Middle Ages.

Why so much focus on Descartes? Because he stood at the turning point between premodern and modern Western culture and profoundly challenged traditional ways of knowing and thinking about God and other matters dear to religion in general and Christianity in particular. He brought about a Copernican revolution in philosophy. Beginning with him, philosophy would no longer be the handmaid of theology and theology would no longer be the queen of the sciences. Beginning with him,

---

[18]Grayling, *Descartes*, 231.
[19]The story of Descartes's bones and skull is told in great detail by Shorto, *Descartes' Bones*.

knowledge began to be redefined as what people can prove (or justify) rationally apart from faith. In spite of his possibly good intentions, with Descartes, belief in doctrines founded on faith or tradition became opinion at best and superstition at worst. Autonomous human reason was inflated to become the criterion of all knowledge. The thinking self became the center of the world of thought, investigation and discovery. God was dethroned from the center and made a postulate of autonomous human reason. As much as theology tried to ignore Descartes or reject his rationalism and that of Enlightenment thinkers after him, it eventually had to deal with them. Descartes helped launch the modern world with its acids of modernity to which modern theology had to respond.

Locke argues for "reasonable Christianity." Descartes's rationalist method of grounding knowledge on self-evident foundations believed to be true a priori (i.e., without experimentation by sense experience) was not the only pillar of early Enlightenment thought. A somewhat different version of foundationalism arose in England in the later seventeenth century and flourished there and in North America throughout the following centuries. It is known as empiricism and rejects a priori truths of reason as the foundation for knowledge in favor of a posteriori (based on experimentation by sense experience) foundations for knowledge. The father, or at least main representative, of this Enlightenment approach to thinking and knowing was John Locke (1632–1704), like Descartes a Christian but one who revolutionized religious thought as well as politics and science. His best-known disciple was Thomas Jefferson, who worked Locke's ideas about politics and government into his Declaration of Independence (of the United States from Great Britain) in 1776. Jefferson was also influenced by Locke's ideas about religion and Christianity.

Perhaps Locke would not have approved, but in 1820 Jefferson, then in retirement from public life, took a razor to his Bible and created what he called "The Life and Morals of Jesus of Nazareth," which became the title of what later was called the Jefferson Bible. Jefferson's goal was to compile a New Testament (he did not care about the Old Testament except as literature) free of all irrational elements and composed exclusively of those teachings and actions of Jesus that Jefferson considered reasonable. Miracles were cut out, as were any sayings of Jesus offensive to enlightened minds. What was left was a relatively brief list of Jesus' sayings and deeds from the four Gospels; the Bible was reduced to a prop for Enlightenment morality. Locke may not have approved, but surely Jefferson was influenced by *The Reasonableness of Christianity* (1695). That manifesto of rational Christianity went through six printings in the following years and is still published and read by students of philosophy and religion in the early twenty-first century. It is a classic of Enlightenment religious thought.

Locke's life is not nearly as fascinating as that of Descartes, so his story will not detain us. He was a public intellectual in England who lived for a while in exile in Holland, a hotbed of Enlightenment philosophy and science because of its unique toleration of free thought. Locke worked as a tutor in various aristocratic families and became a civil servant in various agencies of the British government. So influential was he that, while in Holland, he helped select the new royal family for England after the so-called Glorious Revolution of 1688. While he was moving and working in different positions among the elite of English and Dutch society, Locke wrote several ground-breaking treatises that became classics of Enlightenment thought: *Essay Concerning Human Understanding* (1690), *A Discourse on Miracles* (1701), *A Letter on Toleration* (1689) and *The Reasonableness of Christianity*. These writings, especially *The Reasonableness of Christianity*, brought Locke into great controversy with church leaders in England over what they considered his rationalism, possible unitarianism (denial of the Trinity) and alleged implicit denial of the deity of Jesus Christ and his miracles.

Without question Locke's ideas were new and bold, but he "was always of the mind that his writings did full justice to the Christian faith."[20] According to Locke, quite in distinction from Descartes, the human mind is a *tabula rasa*—a blank slate with no innate ideas; knowledge does not begin with a priori truths such as one's own existence. Locke thought that approach to knowledge got a person nowhere outside the mind. He was interested in providing a philosophical basis for the scientific revolution as well as the political changes coming in Europe and America.

---

[20]I. T. Ramsey, "Editor's Introduction," in John Locke, *The Reasonableness of Christianity with a Discourse on Miracles and Part of A Third Letter Concerning Toleration*, ed. I. T. Ramsey (London: Adam & Charles Black, 1958), 8.

In his *Essay Concerning Human Understanding* Locke proposed an alternative rational approach to knowledge:

> *All ideas come from Sensation or Reflection.* Let us then suppose the mind to
> be, as we say, white paper [*tabula rasa*], void of all characters, without any
> ideas; how comes it to be furnished? Whence comes it by that vast store
> which the busy and boundless fancy of man has painted on it with an almost
> endless variety? Whence has it all the materials of reason and knowledge? To
> this I answer, in one word, from *experience*. In that all our knowledge is
> founded, and from that it ultimately derives itself. Our observation employed
> either about external sensible objects, or about the internal operations of our
> minds perceived and reflected on by ourselves, is that which supplies our
> understandings with all the materials of thinking. These two are the foun-
> tains of knowledge, from whence all the ideas we have, or can naturally have,
> do spring.[21]

Notice that phrase "can naturally have" in the final sentence. In other words, as a Christian, Locke was not denying (or at least wanted to appear not to be denying) supernatural knowledge through revelation and faith. However, that slight exception hardly makes a dent in his overwhelming emphasis on sense experience as the foundation of all true knowledge.

For Locke, then, normally speaking, all human knowledge derives from empirical foundations, from sense experience, another type of Enlightenment foundationalism. Much that we know is reasonable reflection on, that is, deduction from, sense experiences. We do not just have sense experiences; we interpret them using logic. Still, knowledge begins with simple ideas impressed on the mind by the five senses, and what follows in reflection and deduction must be based on and rooted in those. The implication is that anything we cannot experience through the five senses probably should not be considered knowledge.

Locke was the father of that branch of Enlightenment philosophy called empiricism. Descartes's approach to knowledge is usually distinguished from it as rationalism in the narrow sense of knowledge as rational, logical deduction from self-evident truths such as one's own existence. Locke's Enlightenment thought looks to the world outside the self as the source of

---

[21]John Locke, "An Essay Concerning Human Understanding," in *The Enlightenment: A Sourcebook and Reader*, ed. Paul Hyland (London and New York: Routledge, 2003), 41.

knowledge but nevertheless places the knowing self at the center of the universe of knowledge. It is the knowing self that has the sense experiences, reflects on them and creates complex ideas out of them.

Locke thought his new empirical philosophy was a great benefit to religion and even to Christianity. What it did was cut out all speculation about things beyond human experience and focus religion on what truly matters—ethical behavior. Locke's preface to *The Reasonableness of Christianity* is revealing about his biases and motives: "The little satisfaction and consistency that is to be found in most of the systems of divinity [systematic theologies] I have met with, made me betake myself to the sole reading of the Scripture (to which they all appeal) for the understanding of the Christian religion."[22] And what did he find in his "sole reading of the Scripture"? Primarily a "body of Ethics, proved to be the law of nature, from principles of reason, and reaching all the duties of life."[23]

Locke did not deny Jesus' miracles or his divinity, but he did downplay or neglect them. For him, Jesus was first and foremost "the Messiah," a great teacher of virtue who saves by his example. What Locke did not say is as instructive as what he did say. He never mentioned the Trinity, for example. He probably thought of that doctrine as extrabiblical speculation, unrelated to anything in human experience, and therefore unimportant. He would have gotten into trouble with the authorities for explicitly denying it or any other dogma of orthodoxy, so he left it aside. Locke's reasonable Christianity was a much scaled-down version of orthodox Christianity that focuses on ethics and morality. But what was most controversial about Locke's version of Christianity is the role he accorded autonomous human reason in it. Locke argued for belief in God's revelation in Scripture even though he drastically truncated the gospel. "Whatever God has revealed is true and must be the object of our faith," Locke insisted. However, and this is what was most radical about *The Reasonableness of Christianity*, "what actually counts as having been revealed by God, *that* must be judged by reason."[24] In his essay on miracles Locke declared that

---

[22]Locke, *Reasonableness of Christianity*, 24.
[23]Ibid., 62.
[24]James M. Byrne, *Religion and the Enlightenment: From Descartes to Kant* (Louisville, KY: Westminster John Knox, 1996), 107.

no mission can be looked on to be divine, that delivers any thing derogating from the honour of the one, only, true, invisible God, or inconsistent with natural religion and the rules of morality: because God having discovered to men the unity and majesty of his eternal Godhead, and the truths of natural religion and morality by the light of reason, he cannot be supposed to back the contrary by revelation; for that would be to destroy the evidence and the use of reason, without which men cannot be able to distinguish divine revelation from diabolical imposture.[25]

Later empiricist Enlightenment thinkers went further than Locke dared to go in redefining Christianity. Some of them are known in the annals of intellectual history as deists. Many consider Locke the true father of deism. It is impossible to know what he would have thought of the English deists' reconstructions of Christianity, but there is no doubt they thought they were his disciples (see 1.c.).

Enlightenment thinkers reconstruct philosophy and religion, and others push back. Throughout all this time from Descartes to Locke and beyond, the vast majority of European and American Christians were blissfully unaware of what was happening among the philosophers. There was little to no grasp of something momentous going on that would eventually shake the very foundations of culture including religion. Nevertheless, these new ideas in philosophy began to trickle down, first to the educated elite of society and then to the growing middle class who, by the 1700s, were finding the new ideas in philosophy, at least as they understood (or misunderstood) them, a welcome relief from the authoritarian dogmatism of the established churches and political authorities.

Throughout much of the nineteenth and twentieth centuries the Enlightenment, including both the scientific revolution and the revolutions in philosophy, was taught in European and American universities as a great liberation movement within culture, freeing people from the shackles of dead traditions and leading the way into the light of freedom to think and discover, to question and find new answers. "Modern" became a compliment; people embraced modernity with enthusiasm even when they did not understand its full implications. Religion and politics were the two fields of life most affected by the

---

[25]Locke, *Reasonableness of Christianity*, 84.

Enlightenment; it tore away at the traditional roots of both and sought to replace them with new plants. The French and American revolutions of the late eighteenth century were both stimulated by the Enlightenment, as were the ideas about government that replaced the overthrown ones. Divine right of kings was replaced by social contract; gradually hierarchical structures fell down and were replaced by individual rights. Traditional religion, especially theology and doctrine, were equally challenged and undermined. Several new ideas about religion and theology, inspired by the Enlightenment, came in to replace them. That will be the bulk of our story of modern theology.

Only conservative Christians and defenders of monarchy seemed uncomfortable with Enlightenment ideals until the beginning of what is called postmodernism in the late twentieth century. Postmodernism seeks to practice incredulity toward all metanarratives[26]—including the Enlightenment metanarrative. A metanarrative is a "big story" (usually a philosophy or ideology) that claims to explain everything. One loud protest against the Enlightenment and the modernity it spawned appeared in 1990 from secular philosopher Stephen Toulmin (1922–2009). *Cosmopolis: The Hidden Agenda of Modernity* raised questions about how liberating the Enlightenment was.

First, Toulmin lays out in stark form the "principal elements, or timbers, of the Modern Framework."[27] For example, "The 'human' thing about humanity is its capacity for rational thought or action" and "Emotion typically frustrates and distorts the work of Reason; so the human reason is to be trusted and encouraged, while the emotions are to be distrusted and restrained."[28] Toulmin argues that these and other principal elements of modernity, inspired by the Enlightenment, are ambiguous, and we should be ambivalent toward them. The Enlightenment and modernity have not been unmixed blessings. Toulmin concludes:

> At the outset, Modernity struck us as simple, straightforward, and beneficent. Here, at the far side of Modernity, its history proves more complex than we

---

[26]Jean-Francois Lyotard, *The Postmodern Condition: A Report on Knowledge* (Minneapolis: University of Minnesota Press, 1979).
[27]Stephen Toulmin, *Cosmopolis: The Hidden Agenda of Modernity* (Chicago: University of Chicago Press, 1990), 109.
[28]Ibid., 109–10.

thought. To begin with, we saw the story of Modernity as the onward march of human rationality, but this has turned out to hide ambiguities and confusions. Whether the seventeenth-century enthronement of "rationality" was a victory or a defeat for humanity depends on how we conceive of "rationality" itself: instead of the successes of the intellect having been unmixed blessings, they must be weighed against the losses that came from abandoning the sixteenth-century commitment to intellectual modesty, uncertainty, and toleration.[29]

Many postmodern people are less charitable than Toulmin about modernity. And not all of them are conservative Christians. Postmoderns in general are uneasy about modernity's claims about human reason and the ways in which the Enlightenment and modernity were hijacked and used to support and defend their vested interests by society's elites.

And yet, even many Christians eventually found value in at least some elements of modernity, and many felt compelled to go beyond reactionary rejection of the Enlightenment and modern science and begin to make peace with them. The story of how people who considered themselves both Christian and thoroughly modern sought to come to terms with the Enlightenment begins with a group of eighteenth-century thinkers who wrote about Christianity and sought to reconstruct it in the light of modernity. They are often lumped together as deists. A better term for them would be "natural religionists." The next section turns to their projects of combining early modern thought with Christianity in some kind of mutually transforming, integrative hybrid.

1.C. DEISTS CREATE A NEW NATURAL RELIGION

On a single day in 1697, in Dublin, the capital of Ireland, one book was publicly burned twice by the city's official hangman. One copy was burned in front of the Parliament House Gate. The book burning was ordered by the Irish Parliament, one of whose members publicly suggested that the author of the book should be burned with it.[30] The offending and offended book was one of the first treatises on the new religion later known as deism, better called natural religion. Its author was a noted Irish writer and sometime philosopher, John Toland (1670–1722). The book was *Christianity Not Mys-*

---

[29]Ibid., 174.
[30]Haig A. Boxmajian, *Burning Books* (Jefferson, NC: McFarland, 2006), 115.

terious with the subtitle *A treatise shewing, that there is nothing in the gospel contrary to reason, nor above it: and that no Christian doctrine can be properly called a mystery* and was published the year before its public burning. Fortunately for Toland he was not in Ireland when his book was burned; he was living and working in England. Toland was a disciple of Locke. He sought to apply Locke's rational philosophy to religion and Christianity in particular.

As explained in the previous sections of this chapter, the founders of the Enlightenment and scientific revolutions of the seventeenth and early eighteenth centuries were all Christians who at least pretended to be devout and orthodox. There is some reason to believe some of them may not have been devout or orthodox, but they did not attempt to oppose traditional Christianity. Some of their philosophical musings and scientific models conflicted with traditional, orthodox teachings of the churches, but that was not as obvious during their lifetimes as later. To a certain extent, Descartes and Locke, for example, became controversial for Christian thinkers and leaders because of their disciples, the deists or natural religionists. After *Christianity Not Mysterious* was published, many astute readers noticed how rooted its logic was in Locke's *The Reasonableness of Christianity*. Reading *Christianity Not Mysterious* indicated to many readers that it seemed to be almost a commentary on Locke's book, which had been published a year earlier. Was Toland simply bolder than Locke whom he greatly admired? Locke's book seemed less radical, but Toland's book raised questions about Locke's intentions.

Some years after Toland's book was published another deist manifesto appeared by another admirer of Locke—Matthew Tindal (1657–1733), who admitted inspiration from Toland. Tindal's 1730 book was titled *Christianity as Old as the Creation* with the subtitle *the gospel a republication of the religion of nature*. It became widely regarded as the "Bible of deism."[31] The author's thesis was that "the truths of Christianity have always been available to rational people from time immemorial. Hence, if the basic truths of religion can be known rationally, religion has no need of revelation at all."[32] Like Toland's book before it, *Christianity as Old as the Creation* created a furor;

---

[31]Byrne, *Religion and the Enlightenment*, 110.
[32]Ibid.

laws were passed in England forbidding any published attack on Christianity. A Tindal volume following up on *Christianity as Old as the Creation* was suppressed by officials and never published. Some openly deist writers were jailed. Some critics suggest that the only reason Tindal called his religion Christianity was to avoid prosecution. After all, he was not attacking Christianity! He was explaining and defending true Christianity.

Deism is a broad and ambiguous category, as is its better alternative, natural religion. Many students learn that deism is the belief that God created the world as a watchmaker creates a watch, with built-in laws, and then abandoned it or merely watched it operate without interference. The stereotype is of the deist God as an absentee landlord who is so transcendent as to be virtually useless for religion except as a moral governor of the universe who rewards good behavior and punishes (after death) bad behavior. Although there is some truth in that stereotype, it is not the whole story of deism. Natural religion is a better label because all the deists of the eighteenth century agreed on one thing—there is a religion of reason natural to all rational people that needs no special revelation from God or faith. Their views on God and God's relation with the world varied greatly. As a lot, they were trying to apply the new Enlightenment principles of Descartes and Locke and other early modern thinkers to Christianity to make it rational and truly modern.

Lord Herbert of Cherbury anticipates deism. A favorite argument among scholars of natural religion is when it began. Like most broad movements in thought, it is hard to pin down its exact starting point. Surprisingly, full-fledged natural religion seems to have begun early, before its time, that is to say, before there was a movement of deism. Lord Edward Herbert of Cherbury (1583–1648) was a British free thinker who wrote *De Veritate* (*On Truth*), first published in 1624. In it, the intellectual aristocrat, a baron and knight who served as a diplomat and general public intellectual, sought to solve the problem of Christian pluralism arising out of the Reformation. Thousands were being killed in the name of religion as Catholic and Protestant armies swirled around the Continent in a seemingly senseless orgy of violence known as the Thirty Years' War. France was the arena of another religious war—the Huguenot civil wars. (The Huguenots were French Protestants.) They included massacres on both sides in the name of God. Lord Herbert's own England was embroiled in a series of conflicts between Puritans and Anglicans that would soon break out into full-fledged revolution against the king.

In the midst of all that turmoil Lord Herbert put pen to paper and proposed a universal religion of pure reason composed of "Common Notions" agreed on by all reasonable people. He enumerated these ideas in five sentences:

1. There is a Sovereign Deity;

2. this Deity must be worshiped;

3. piety is closely linked to virtue, to good living;

4. wrongdoing must be expiated by repentance;

5. there is reward or punishment after this life.[33]

Lord Herbert expanded on these basic notions, borrowing from the tradition of scholastic theology but arguing that all of this can be found through reason alone without revelation. His intention was to provide a universal, rational religion to replace the many sects of Christianity so that the bloodshed could stop.

One interesting side light to *De Veritate* is that Lord Herbert was doubting whether to have it published. He knew how controversial it would be, not because his five principles would be rejected but because his claim that they can be based on reason alone would be considered heretical by many critics. (He was right about that.) By his own testimony recorded later, he was convinced to publish the book by a sudden loud noise in a cloudless sky.[34] Apparently Lord Herbert was still enough of a Christian to believe God gives signs to guide people (which is not to say it *was* a divine signal).

De Veritate did stir up controversy, but its author managed to weather it and go on to write on other subjects and die of natural causes the year the Peace of Westphalia was signed ending the Thirty Years' War. After his death his magnum opus was published—an exhaustive book on comparative religion seeking to support his claim that his five principles of natural religion are, indeed, universal in all world religions.

What was the significance of Lord Herbert's natural, universal religion of reason? One scholar suggests that "the importance of *De Veritate* is that it

---

[33]Ibid., 104.
[34]Ibid., 105.

made possible for subsequent thinkers to profess belief in God, yet to abjure revealed religion and established Christianity; the liberating effects of such a possibility for thinkers immersed in the daring discoveries of the new scientific age should not be underestimated."[35] Without doubt, then, Lord Herbert was at least a precursor of the deist movement of natural religion yet to come to full flower. He was also, along with Galileo and Descartes, one of the first modern men even if his fame is not as great as theirs. What made him modern? He dared to think freely about religion unbound by tradition and ecclesiastical authority. He had a greatly inflated view of autonomous human reason reaching out toward its omnicompetence. Finally, he omitted miracles or anything supernatural from his natural religion of reason. Later deists and natural religionists, especially religious free thinkers of the eighteenth century, would build on and extend his work.

Toland interprets Christianity rationally. When most people think of deism, names like Thomas Jefferson and Thomas Paine come to mind; they are often the examples of deism given in high school and college history textbooks. Better examples, because they influenced Jefferson, Paine and a host of later popularizers of deism, are Toland and Tindal. They and their controversial books have already been mentioned. Now it is time to take a closer look at real deism as exemplified by these two eighteenth-century writers who brought deism, or natural religion, to its scholarly apex.

First, however, it will be helpful to step back a moment and consider what conventional religion was like in the late seventeenth and early to mid-eighteenth centuries—a time of exploding new knowledge and budding free thought. For the most part conventional religion was static; nothing new was considered a sign of faithfulness by most people—the masses and the ruling elite alike. Theology was mired in scholastic debates over old controversies such as the order of the divine decrees of creation and predestination. Calvinism and Arminianism were still two main options dividing Protestant theology, and both assumed Scripture to be infallible and tradition to be authoritative.

A typical theologian of this time was Francis Turretin, who died in 1687, just a few years before the publication of Toland's *Christianity Not Myste-*

---

[35]Ibid.

rious. Turretin's influence was strong among Protestants through his massive system of Reformed theology, *Institutes of Elenctic Theology* (1679–1685), which was widely read and discussed among the faithful of Protestant orthodoxy. Typical of most Christian scholars of that time, Turretin was a determined defender of biblical inerrancy and authority. He went so far as to propose that the vowel points of the Hebrew Bible, the Old Testament to Christians, were inspired by God. He knew very well that they did not exist in the original manuscripts of the prophets, but he also knew that unless those vowel points added by the Masoretes, a group of eighth-century Jewish scholars, were inspired by God the exact meaning of portions of the Old Testament would be impossible to discern. This was the kind of Christian theology that seemed unreasonable to deists and free thinkers like Toland and Tindal.

One commentator on natural religion notes that

> in an intellectual climate in which critical biblical scholarship was virtually unknown and unconventional religious thinking of any sort looked on with suspicion, religious belief was generally presented as a unitary package in which the dubious and the simply unbelievable [e.g., Turretin's assertion of the divine inspiration of the Hebrew vowel points] were intermingled with the basic truths of faith. To an intelligentsia which had little freedom to voice criticisms of religion, treatises such as that of Tindal [and Toland] were a means by which they could continue to believe in God while justifying the futility of disputes between Christian sects.[36]

To many educated people, then, the deists' attempt to discover and expound a religion of reason, compatible with the new learning in philosophy and science, came as a breath of fresh air in the midst of an otherwise arid and sterile theological landscape.

Toland's *Christianity Not Mysterious* is a clever, and some would say coy, expression of natural religion. It is obviously indebted to Locke's ideas about religion and is firmly imbedded in the Enlightenment emphasis on reason. Nowhere does Toland openly deny any dogma of Protestantism (although he is not afraid openly to reject Catholic doctrines such as transubstantiation), but he subtly undermines the whole structure of traditional,

---

[36]Ibid., 109.

orthodox Christianity by insisting that nobody should, or even can, believe
that which is ultimately mysterious. He implies, at least, that much orthodox doctrine falls into that category. So it must be purged to arrive at
reasonable Christianity.

Toland's thesis is stated clearly: "Whoever reveals any thing, that is,
whoever tells us something we did not know before, *his words must be intelligible, and the matter possible.* This rule holds good, let *God* or *man* be the
revealer."[37] He was not rejecting revelation; he accepted that God has revealed truths the human mind cannot discover by itself. What he rejected
was the belief that any revealed truth could be beyond human reason, that
is, incapable of comprehension, unintelligible to the human mind when it
is functioning properly. He rejects the call "to adore what we cannot
comprehend"[38] and states, "The first thing I shall insist upon is, that if any
Doctrine of the *New Testament* be contrary to Reason, we have no manner
of Idea of it."[39] In other words, Toland was not just arguing that people
should not believe doctrines that are mysterious, in his particular sense of
that word, but that they cannot really believe them and requiring them to
do so leads to skepticism and rejection of the faith. The only specific, concrete example he offers is the Catholic doctrine of transubstantiation—that
in the Mass of the Catholic Church the bread and wine literally turn into
the body and blood of Christ. This he considered magic and beyond human
comprehension, unintelligible nonsense, a mystery nobody can really believe. But one has the sense that Toland believes there are many similar irrational beliefs in general Christian orthodoxy and Protestant theology as
well, though he does not mention them. He leaves to his readers to draw
analogies between transubstantiation, which it was not illegal to deny in
England, and doctrines of the Church of England (and other Protestant
churches) that it was illegal to deny.

What about original sin, total depravity, and the necessary illumination
of the Holy Spirit—doctrines dear to classical Protestantism? Don't these
help people to understand why they ought to and can believe in what is ul-

---

[37]John Toland, *Christianity Not Mysterious*, in *John Toland's Christianity Not Mysterious: Text,
Associated Works and Critical Essays*, ed. Philip McGuiness et al. (Dublin: The Lilliput Press,
1997), 41.
[38]Quoted in Peter Gay, ed., *Deism: An Anthology* (Princeton, NJ: D. Van Nostrand, 1968), 54.
[39]Ibid., 55.

timately mysterious to their minds? Toland rejects those beliefs as having anything to do with his argument. (He is careful not to deny them absolutely.) According to Toland, original sin does not result in any necessary defect of reason itself but only in "willful misuses of reason."[40] Appeal to "the illuminating and efficiacious Operation of the Holy Spirit" is unnecessary and unhelpful in trying to make inherently unreasonable doctrines believable.[41] What about revelation? Cannot God reveal truths that transcend reason's ability to comprehend them? Toland brushes aside any notion that divine revelation can violate reason. Truths once revealed, even if they could not have been reached by reason alone, must conform to natural reason, else they cannot be known. The deist rails against fideism— belief that some doctrines must be embraced by blind faith against reason. Reason is sovereign even over revelation.[42] For him, as for most if not all deists, there can be only one ultimate authority for religion, and that authority must be reason or else there will forever be the clash of competing claims about revelation and its truths that led to the wars of religion.

Toland's view of religion, its truth and knowledge of it, could not be made clearer than in this statement that begins much like Descartes long before with self-evident (a priori) truths:

> Were it not for those self-evident Notions, which are the Foundation of all our Reasonings, there could be no intellectual communication between God and Man; nor, as we are fram'd, can God ascertain us of any Truth, but by shewing its Agreement with those self-evident Notions, which are the Tests by which we are to judge of everything, even the Being of a God, and Natural Religion.[43]

What "self-evident Notions" was Toland referring to? At the least, one would be the law of noncontradiction, which rules out of all reasonable discourse, even out of knowledge itself, absolute logical contradictions such as (in a classical philosophical example): A = -A (A equals not A). Toland believed that traditional Christianity too often included such contradictory doctrines; one can only guess what they might be. The only one he openly

---

[40]Ibid., 68–69.
[41]Ibid., 62.
[42]Ibid., 118.
[43]Ibid., 116–17.

attacks is transubstantiation, but it is reasonable to assume he would have included, had it been legal to do so, the hypostatic union (two natures in one person of Jesus Christ) and the Trinity. Toland revered Jesus Christ but probably did not think him divine. He believed in the possibility of miracles but severely limited belief in them. He admitted that God, who created nature, may certainly alter its course. However, some claimed miracles are impossible even for God because they involve contradictions. Again, even miracles must be reasonable.

> No *Miracle* then is contrary to Reason, for the Action must be intelligible, and the Performance of it appear most easy to the Author of *Nature*, who may command all its Principles at his Pleasure. Therefore all those *Miracles* are fictitious, wherein there occur any Contradictions, as that *Christ* was born without opening any Passage out of the *Virgin's* Body; that a Head spoke some Days after it was sever'd from the Body, and the Tongue cut out; with Multitudes of this kind that may be met with among the *Papists* [Catholics], the *Jews*, the *Brahmins* [Hindus], the *Mahometans* [Muslims], and in all the Places where the Credulity of the People makes 'em a Merchandize to their Priests.[44]

What Toland is saying here is *not* that miracles are not contrary to reason but that the idea of a miracle is itself not necessarily irrational within theism—belief in God. However, the emphasis is placed squarely on a certain incredulity toward concrete miracles stories. One gets the distinct impression that he is unlikely to believe in any miracles, but he does not say so. The miracles he mentions as impossible because irrational are ones most people who might have read his book (i.e., educated people) would also reject because they are extrabiblical and border on superstition. But one has to wonder what Toland really believed about miracles and the supernatural. His inclination is most decidedly toward skepticism if not outright disbelief. Later deists, going further along Toland's trajectory, rejected miracles.

What was Toland's intent? He would say he was rescuing religion, specifically Christianity, from the dustbin of history where it would be relegated if it were not brought up to date with the Enlightenment and scientific revolutions. His critics and enemies said he was a cynical heretic, even

---

[44]Toland, *Christianity Not Mysterious*, 89.

an apostate, out to destroy religion. It may be impossible to know the truth of the matter. It is almost certain that he was out to undermine traditional Christianity. That he thought his project was a positive one, to rescue Christianity by reconstructing it for the sake of relevance, is probable.

What did Toland believe in and value in religion and Christianity? If we take him at face value, he believed in God. Unlike the popular caricature of deism, Toland, one of deism's main thinkers, did not think of God as an absentee landlord watching from a distance. In fact, Toland referred to himself as a pantheist—someone who believes God and nature are one and the same.[45] Furthermore, Toland believed every normal human being possesses a capacity called reason that enables him or her to distinguish truth from falsehood, and he believed that natural reason governs all knowledge, including religious belief. Finally, Toland believed that religion's primary function is to establish morality, to undergird and guide public and private ethical thinking and behavior. As Alexander Pope wrote, "For modes of faith let graceless zealots fight; His can't be wrong whose life is in the right."[46] What Toland did not believe is that traditional doctrines, forms of worship and ecclesiastical structures are sacrosanct. They are all open to criticism and radical revision as required by Enlightenment-based reason and science.

Tindal rejects special revelation. Tindal was Toland's successor as much as Toland was Locke's successor. He pushed deism and natural religion farther along the trajectory set by Descartes and Locke and the Enlightenment in general. He has been called "the most learned of all the Deists,"[47] and his *Christianity as Old as Creation* has been called "the deists' Bible."[48] Its overall thesis is that "if the basic truths of religion can be known rationally, religion has no need of revelation at all."[49] By revelation Tindal meant special revelation—truths revealed by God that cannot be known through rational reflection on nature alone. He did not mean to reject general revelation—truth about God knowable through reason working with nature

---

[45]Stephen H. Daniel, "Toland's Semantic Pantheism," in *John Toland's Christianity Not Mysterious: Text, Associated Works and Critical Essays*, ed. Philip McGuiness et al. (Dublin: The Lilliput Press, 1997), 306.

[46]Ernest Campbell Mossner, *Bishop Butler and the Age of Reason: A Study in the History of Thought* (New York: Macmillan, 1936), 57.

[47]Ibid., 75.

[48]Byrne, *Religion and the Enlightenment*, 110.

[49]Ibid.

alone. In fact, for Tindal, as for many deists after him, true Christianity and natural religion—universal truth about God knowable to all people always and everywhere—are the same:

> If God was always willing, that all men should come to the knowledge of his truth; and there never was a time when God intended men should have no religion, or such an imperfect religion which could not answer the end [purpose] of its being instituted by an infinitely wise legislator, this seems to my bewildered reason to imply that there was from the beginning but one true religion which all men might know was their duty to embrace. And if this is true, I can't well conceive how this character can conflict with Christianity without allowing it, at the same time, to be as old as the creation.[50]

For Tindal, as for most or all later deists, whatever is knowable about God has always been available to the senses and to reason. This includes, Tindal argued, God's existence, God's expectations of people and the fact of rewards and punishments in this life and in the next.[51] Whatever is important to Christianity is identical with the rational religion of nature; whatever is unknowable by reason and therefore not part of natural religion cannot be essential to Christianity. One commentator on Tindal's rational, natural religion explains that

> *Christianity as Old as the Creation* is what has been called "constructive Deism" at its best. Relatively moderate in tone and extremely shrewd in argumentation, it appropriated what was most persuasive in liberal Christianity, and left the supernatural component of that Christianity behind. Miracles and revelations, to the extent that they are authentic, merely confirm what God has revealed to the reason. The only true religion is Natural Religion, that is, a religion that acknowledges the fatherhood of God and the moral law of the universe.[52]

Another commentator on deism and especially Tindal noted:

> Natural Religion, which is about the only kind of religion that Tindal recognizes, is but an ethical system on a theistic background; it consists in ob-

---

[50]Matthew Tindal, *Christianity as Old as the Creation* (London: Routledge/Thames Press, 1995), 7. (I have made the text clear for readers of modern English; Tindal's text is in old English, which contains, for example, "f" in place of "s.")

[51]Gay, *Deism*, 102-9.

[52]Ibid., 102.

serving the rules that reason discovers. And anything added to this is a blemish. The whole of religion, according to the Deists, consists in performing all the duties of morality.[53]

What did people attracted to deism see in its much truncated, reconstructed account of Christianity? First, it offered a form of Christianity without dogmas to fight over; thus, insofar as it would be accepted, there would be no more wars of religion. Second, it offered a form of Christianity seemingly immune to the acids of modernity and especially to the onslaughts of the scientific revolution. Deism, natural religion, was wholly compatible with the new worldview of nature's uniformity—closed to miracles and supernatural divine interventions. Finally, deism preserved what many considered most important in religion and Christianity—morality. For Toland, Tindal and most other deists, God is the great architect and moral governor of the universe and Jesus is a prophet and example of human moral perfection.[54] This is the kind of Christianity many enlightened people of Europe wanted—one that is rational, moral, tolerant and immune to the passions of persecution and corrosive effects of modernity.

Deism's influence on America's founding fathers is well known and documented, in spite of some revisionist historians who wish to downplay it. Jefferson is a case study of deism's influence on them. Like Toland and Tindal, and under their direct influence, "Jefferson believed that reason, not revelation, was the path to true religion."[55] Therefore Jefferson famously included in "The Life and Morals of Jesus of Nazareth" (the Jefferson Bible) only what he considered consistent with natural reason, leaving out all the miracles and hard sayings of Jesus. The reason was that "Jefferson questioned many of Christianity's central beliefs and became a deist, and he differentiated between what he considered to be the moral teachings of Jesus and Christians' corruptions of those teachings"[56] that appear even in

---

[53]S. G. Hefelbower, *The Relation of John Locke to English Deism* (Chicago: University of Chicago Press, 1918), 138-39.

[54]Tindal struggled to include a high Christology in his rational Christianity, but the most he could say of Jesus Christ was that he was "a noble Example" and "the person sent from God who published" the "external revelation" (special revelation) that perfectly accords with universal "internal revelation" knowable through reason (*Christianity*, 8).

[55]Frank Lambert, *The Founding Fathers and the Place of Religion in America* (Princeton, NJ: Princeton University Press, 2003), 177.

[56]Ibid., 174.

the Gospels themselves. Jefferson believed that the divinity of Jesus was an invention of Jesus' "zealous disciples, not Jesus."[57]

Most deists remained adherents of traditional Christian churches, especially the increasingly tolerant Church of England (in America, after independence, the Episcopal Church). Those who belonged to the old Puritan churches (such as Presbyterian and Congregationalist) often found themselves invited to leave; many of them founded a new form of organized Christianity based on natural religion. The first Unitarian churches were founded by free thinkers and deists in England and North America in the 1770s. Early Unitarianism became a haven for Christians influenced by Enlightenment rationalism; it denied the Trinity as too mysterious for belief and rejected the prevailing, standard version of Protestant orthodoxy— Calvinism—as belief in an arbitrary and therefore irrational God.

Conservative Christian thinkers push back against deism. Not all religious rationalists rushed to embrace deism; many sought to use Enlightenment reason to defend orthodox Christianity including the deity of Jesus Christ and miracles. The most famous conservative rationalist (or rationalistic conservative) of the time was Joseph Butler (1692–1752), bishop of Durham, England, and author of *The Analogy of Religion: Natural and Revealed* (1736)—a rational response to Toland's and Tindal's natural religion. Butler agreed wholeheartedly with Locke and his ideological followers that reason is sovereign even in religion, but he disagreed with them that Christian orthodoxy contains much that is irrational. Butler's purpose in *The Analogy of Religion* was "to examine the facts of mankind [i.e., universal human experience] and of nature as they really are and to attempt to show from them the probabilities of things beyond human experience."[58] For example, according to the bishop, human experience indicates (not proves) the need of redemption such as Christ purchased in his atonement; for Butler, the doctrine of vicarious atonement is no irrational myth or superfluous addition to the simple religion of reason. It is, rather, the revealed confirmation of a "vague hope of reason."[59]

Butler did not even attempt to use reason to prove orthodox Christianity

---

[57]Ibid.

[58]Mossner, *Bishop Butler and the Age of Reason*, 81.

[59]Ibid., 96.

true. Instead he settled for using reason to demonstrate that natural religion's objections to Christian doctrines are not conclusive and that orthodox Christianity is not irrational but consistent with practical reason. He also sought to show that the deists' natural religion contains much that is itself beyond what natural reason can prove such as the immortality of the soul and rewards and punishments after death. What is notable about Butler, however, is how he adopted the standpoint and ethos of Enlightenment thought to defend orthodox Christianity. He was a thoroughgoing empiricist in the mold of Locke and used natural reason to point beyond nature itself. And, like Toland, he eschewed mysteries beyond any comprehension. His difference from Toland was that he believed all tenets of orthodox Protestantism reasonable even if not provable from reason alone. And that is what he, using Enlightenment methods, attempted to demonstrate in his *Analogy*.

Another eighteenth-century rational apologist for orthodoxy was William Paley (1743–1805), English clergyman and gentleman philosopher, who wrote *Natural Theology, or, Evidences of the Existence and Attributes of the Deity* (1802) in defense of belief in the God of traditional Christianity. Most of his arguments had been used before to fend off the skepticism of the deists, but Paley became famous for packaging them in a particularly lucid way. By the time Paley wrote *Natural Theology* many deists were becoming skeptical not only about doctrines such as the Trinity but also about any certain knowledge of God at all. Deism was gradually leading toward agnosticism or even atheism. Paley's most famous argument for the existence of a personal, intelligent, creator God was the watchmaker analogy. Paley argued that the human eye, for example, contains evidence of intelligent design and could not have come about by chance. He compared the eye with a watch found on a path. Would anyone think the watch came into existence by accident? Of course not. Similarly the human eye and the entire universe of nature must be the products of an infinite intelligence such as the God of orthodox Christian theism. Paley went on to defend many of the doctrines of Christianity from attacks by deists and Enlightenment free thinkers.

Many eighteenth-century Christians, including clergy and theologians, heaped scorn on deism as apostasy, believing it was a fad that could not take root and grow into anything truly threatening to traditional Christian

faith. Pietism and revivalism posed alternatives to deism and natural religion with emotional experiences of God that bypassed reason. In sum, the
eighteenth century became a cauldron of religious controversy and ferment
because of the Enlightenment and scientific revolutions, because of early
modernity and its acids.

Late in that century and early in the next several philosophers turned
against both orthodox Christianity and natural religion. They, too, are part
of the story of modernity's challenge to Christian theology. In truth it can
be said that these late eighteenth-century and early nineteenth-century
critical religious thinkers paved the way for the appearance of both atheism
and liberal theology in the nineteenth century.

1.D. CRITICAL PHILOSOPHERS LIMIT RELIGION TO REASON

The title of this section might indicate more of the same (i.e., deism, natural
religion). However, late in the eighteenth century and early in the nineteenth century the story of modernity and religious thinkers' responses to
it took a radical and unexpected turn that altered the course of Christian
theology for at least the next two centuries. Throughout the eighteenth
century, as religious thinkers grappled with the challenges of modernity to
traditional Christianity, proof of God's existence through reason was rarely
denied. Deists and defenders of orthodoxy agreed that there must be a First
Cause of all things and that it must be God. Causation was one principle
agreed on by free thinkers and traditionalists alike. It was also essential to
the scientific revolution. The whole scientific method depended on natural
causation. What we observe in nature must be caused by prior causes ruled
by natural laws. Rational religion, whether liberal or conservative, also assumed God as the causative explanation for nature itself. Gradually, steadily,
as a result of the Enlightenment and scientific revolutions, eighteenth-
century scientists and religious thinkers came to depend on the concept of
causation; using that concept opened up all possibilities for science and
modern, enlightened religion. The deists' natural religion depended on
causation, as did the traditionalists' defenses of orthodoxy using natural
theology and analogy.

Everything was thrown into crisis, however, when the empiricism of Locke
and his followers turned Enlightenment thinking against itself. If all

knowledge is based on sense experience and rational deduction from it, what becomes of this assumed reality of causation? Is it a rational concept? Can it be proven? Enter the radical skepticism of David Hume (1711–1776) that turned the reasonable science and philosophy of the eighteenth century on its head. However, it is not Hume so much as his German contemporary, Kant, who is important to the story of modern theology. Hume is important because reading him awakened Kant, as he confessed, from his "dogmatic slumbers"[60] and aroused him to rescue science and religion from radical skepticism. Kant's rescue, however, was purchased at great cost to traditional religion, including eighteenth-century natural religion/deism and traditional Christian theology insofar as it was based on natural theology (e.g., proofs of the existence of God). Finally, a third philosopher who engaged in thinking about Christianity, Georg W. F. Hegel (1770–1831), attempted to rescue (as he saw his project) rational religion, including true Christianity, from what he saw as Kant's radically reductive account of religion and Christianity.

Again, it is worthwhile to stop and consider why this story of modern theology engages so heavily, especially at its beginning, with philosophy. In order to answer that, I have to point ahead. Modern Christian theology, that is, theology that engages with modernity, begins with Friedrich Schleiermacher (1768–1834)—by far the most influential theologian of the nineteenth century who still casts a long and, some would say, dark shadow over twentieth-century theology. Liberal theologians tend to consider Schleiermacher a reformer and hero; conservative theologians tend to regard him as a villain. All agree, however, that Schleiermacher was to Christian theology what Copernicus was to astronomy (and by extension to science itself) and what Descartes was to philosophy. For better or worse, Schleiermacher revolutionized theology by carrying out a Copernican revolution in thinking about God. What makes him, rather than the philosophy we have been discussing, the starting point of modern theology is that he was an ordained minister and theologian, not a philosopher per se. True, Butler and Paley and many others who attempted to respond to deism and the acids of modernity in the eighteenth century were clergymen, but they did not deviate significantly from traditional paths of theology; they tried to

---

[60]Immanuel Kant, *Prolegomena to Any Future Metaphysic* (Indianapolis: Hackett, 2001), 5.

use Enlightenment modes of thinking to support traditional, orthodox theology. Schleiermacher, by contrast, as a pastor, preacher and professional theologian, allowed Enlightenment thinking, up to a point, to shape his reconstructions of Christian doctrines. Without capitulating to modernity, Schleiermacher attempted to accommodate it within his systematic theology *The Christian Faith*.

One cannot understand Schleiermacher's theology, or the theologies of later modern theologians, without first understanding the basic impulses of critical philosophers of the Age of Reason including Hume, Kant and Hegel, the subjects of this section. Once again, it is important to remember that, for better or worse, philosophy has always been theology's main conversation partner. In no era could theologians ignore philosophy and get away with it insofar as they intended their theological reflections to be public and relevant to culture. (Many theologians throughout the centuries and today try to ignore philosophy, but in most cases it is not difficult to show how they were and are influenced by philosophy even as they attempt to eschew it.)

Hume uses reason to undermine science and religion. By all accounts Hume was personally a congenial fellow. He was raised in a typical Scottish home and given a typical eighteenth-century Scottish education in both school and church. Very early, however, and probably as young as sixteen, he began to entertain serious doubts about the extremely strict teachings of the Scottish Presbyterian church that permeated all of Scottish society. It was heavily influenced by Puritanism with a harsh brand of Calvinism promulgated by means of three-hour church services every Sunday including a one-hour sermon and a one-hour lecture on doctrine.[61] According to one historian, the church of Hume's childhood and youth

> depicted God as an implacable despot, swift to wrath. . . . It held by the doctrines of election and reprobation in all their severity. . . . Both in church and in home the most relentless discipline was maintained. . . . The observance of the Sabbath was enforced with penalties. All other sacred times and seasons [e.g., Christmas] were deliberately ignored.[62]

---

[61]Norman Kemp Smith, "Introduction," in David Hume, *Dialogues Concerning Natural Religion*, ed. Norman Kemp Smith (New York: Macmillan, 1947), 4.

[62]A. J. Campbell, *Two Centuries of the Church of Scotland 1707–1929: The Hastie Lectures in the University of Glasgow* (Paisley: Alexander Gardner, 1930), 28.

Without doubt Hume's adult philosophy was, at least in part, a reaction against the religion of his youth. So was his adult personality, in contrast to his youth when he tried in vain to conform his mind and heart to his church's teachings and expectations. As a youth he was a shy loner absorbed in studies and obsessed with "confirming his moral character."[63] As an adult he was described as "extroverted, genial, somewhat pagan."[64] His favorite adult pastime, other than conducting research and writing, was playing cards with other gentlemen at The Poker Club of Edinburgh. Early he turned against Calvinism and religion in general—except for his own brand of religion, which was highly philosophical. It consisted mainly of belief in the existence of God (without proof) and the rational deconstruction of superstition. Hume scholar Norman Kemp Smith summarizes Hume's adult minimalist religion:

> Hume's attitude to true religion can . . . be summed up in the threefold thesis: (1) that it consists exclusively in *intellectual* assent to the "somewhat ambiguous, at least undefined" proposition, "God exists"; (2) that the "God" here affirmed is not God as ordinarily understood; and (3) as a corollary from (1) and (2), that religion ought not to have . . . any influence on human conduct—beyond . . . its intellectual effects, as rendering the mind immune to superstition and fanaticism.[65]

Hume studied to become a lawyer at the University of Edinburgh beginning at about age twelve, but he soon found his interests lay solely with philosophy and immersed himself in reading especially ancient Roman thinkers. There is no doubt, however, that he was fully acquainted with the Enlightenment and especially Locke's empirical philosophy, which he accepted and radicalized. Hume had no permanent career and was never given a professorship in spite of his noted intellectual achievements. He was widely considered an atheist. In his mature years he served in government positions in Paris and Edinburgh and tutored noble gentlemen in letters and arts. He was by all accounts an encyclopedist—a person of wide-ranging interest and knowledge who could write successfully on a variety of subjects. He spent fifteen years writing a multivolume *History of England* that won him fame if not fortune.

---

[63]Smith, "Introduction," 6.
[64]Ibid.
[65]Ibid., 24.

Throughout his adult life Hume was obsessed with two subjects—philosophical epistemology (theories of knowledge) and religion, bringing them into conversation in a way destructive to traditional religion both liberal (i.e., deist) and conservative (i.e., orthodox). Hume's most important books (for this study of modern theology) are *An Enquiry Concerning Human Understanding* (1748) and *Dialogues Concerning Natural Religion* (published posthumously in 1779). The latter was written in the form of a dialogue which makes it difficult to tell exactly what Hume's own views are supposed to be. However, most scholars believe his is the voice of Philo, the most skeptical of the three dialogue partners.

Hume was a follower of the empiricism of Locke. Locke disagreed with Descartes about innate ideas; he denied them. For Locke and all Enlightenment empiricists, all knowing begins with sense experience. That is, all knowledge of the external world is a posteriori—derived from perceptions and impressions. There is no knowledge a priori (immediate, self-evident, not dependent on experience) except in matters analytical, that is, matters of definition. Descartes, the strict rationalist, believed true knowledge comes from deduction; the mind discovers a self-evident truth lying within itself such as "I am." From there it deduces other truths such as "God is." Sense experience cannot yield certainty; pure logical deduction can. Locke agreed but argued that there are no synthetic truths a priori—that is, truths about the external world outside the dictionary that are self-evident and certain. All synthetic knowledge (all knowledge not having to do only with definitions of terms) is a posteriori, based on experience, and therefore at best probable. Absolute certainty is impossible in this realm. It is possible only in the realm of analytic truths (definitions). However, this did not bother Locke or those pushing forward the scientific revolution based on Locke's empiricism. Absolute certainty may not be possible in matters of science, but the kind of probability Locke envisioned based on sense experience and logical deduction from it was believed to be very high, so high as to amount to certainty.

Hume agreed completely with Locke about all knowledge of the world beginning with sense experience. In his *An Enquiry Concerning Human Understanding* the Scottish thinker declared that "all our ideas . . . are copies of our impressions."[66] By "impressions" Hume explained he meant "when we hear, or see, or feel."[67] Ideas are formed from reflection on impressions which are sensory perceptions. Hume went beyond Locke by radicalizing this empiricism and turning it against those Enlightenment thinkers like Locke, Newton and the deists who thought empiricism alone, without any admixture of a priori truths contributed by the mind, could arrive at the kind of knowing the Enlightenment was seeking—knowing with certainty (or even a very high degree of probability).

The problem Hume tackled, in a deconstructive way, was the gap between probability and certainty. The Enlightenment was all about discovering certain knowledge free from mere opinion, prejudice, bias or even faith. Such knowledge would be the key to unlocking the mysteries of the universe and, especially for the deists, to solving the problems of revealed religion that led inevitably to wars. One cornerstone in this Enlightenment foundation of knowing was causation. There Hume discovered a crack in the foundation. He wrote that "all reasoning concerning matter of fact seems to be founded on the relation of *Cause* to *Effect*."[68] Hardly anyone in eighteenth-century Europe would dispute that even if they considered God the chief cause of everything. Rational religion and science both depended on the idea of reasoning from cause to effect. The flaw Hume discovered is that causation (the relation between the supposed cause and its effect) is not itself an object of sense experience; it is at best a common assumption based on observation of regularities in the temporal connections between certain events. "From causes, which appear *similar*, we expect similar effects. This is the sum of all our experimental conclusions."[69] From this expectation we infer the reality of something called causation, but we never experience it. All we experience is that B always follows A. That A causes B is nothing more than an inference, a common belief. That B will always follow A we cannot say with certainty because we do not experience this force or thing called causation. In fact, Hume concluded, "we never can, by our utmost scrutiny, discover any thing but one event following another; without being

---

[66]David Hume, *An Enquiry Concerning Human Understanding*, ed. Eric Steinberg (Indianapolis: Hackett, 1977), 11.
[67]Ibid., 10.
[68]Ibid., 16.
[69]Ibid., 23.

able to comprehend any force or power, by which the cause operates, or any connexion between it and its supposed effect."[70]

Hume's discovery was a great blow to science and natural theology, both of which depend on the reality of causation. If causation is nothing but a common belief, how does it differ from superstition? Hume did not equate them. But he was raising a question about Enlightenment hubris; is certainty about the workings of the world, whether scientific or theological, possible? Or are we thrown back on belief?

In order to understand what Kant did, we need to remember and hold in mind this rather abstruse-sounding concept: Hume said that there can be no synthetic statements that are true a priori, and therefore certainty about the world outside the dictionary is always less than real certainty. But if certainty and knowledge are linked, as the Enlightenment wished and expected, then the whole modern project was in trouble. Hume went further. All knowing about the world outside the dictionary (i.e., synthetic truths) involves some element of belief. For science to do its business, it must believe in causation, which cannot be observed. But the Enlightenment, including the scientific revolution, was all about overcoming dependence on belief by establishing knowledge with certainty using reason.

What was Hume really up to? Did he enjoy being destructive with skeptical games? Not really. He thought it was a matter of principle to take things to their logical conclusions. For those, like him, committed to empiricism, facing its challenges had to be better than hiding from them. Hume was content to leave it that certainty is not possible in knowledge of the outer world, the world outside the dictionary. Science and religion would have to get along as best they could with probability and belief; it was for him a matter of muddling through. When asked how he handled these troubling matters personally Hume replied that he put them down and played cards with his friends.

What does all this have to do with religion? The answer should be obvious once one realizes how much eighteenth-century religion, both liberal and conservative, had come to depend on the reality of causation. Both natural religion (deism) and natural theology (conservative apologetics

---

[70]Ibid., 49.

using rational proofs of God's existence) assumed the reality of causation. The one thing they agreed on was that God is the ultimate cause of the world—its existence and design. Hume's *Dialogues Concerning Natural Religion* was like a bombshell falling on the search for a rational religion congenial with the spirit of the Enlightenment. And that meant on both liberals and conservatives because both depended heavily on proofs of the existence of God and the concept of God as cause of the world. Hume unleashed a calm, vicious attack on religion. In other words, in the *Dialogues* there is nothing of the anger and mean-spiritedness of, say, Voltaire. But neither is there a kind of ivory-tower raising of questions. Hume's assault was meant to devastate religion, except his own as it was summarized in three points above by Smith.

In *Dialogues* Hume (via the character Philo) uses his skepticism to attack and undermine the proofs of the existence of God involving causation. If there is no proof of any such thing, then any proof that depends entirely on it is invalid. At least that is what Hume attempts to demonstrate. Insufficient space here prevents a summary of all his arguments against natural theology, so here only one example will be given, and it should be adequate to show Hume's method of reasoning. The most popular argument for God's existence, and one almost everyone accepted as valid in the eighteenth century, was the argument from design (what is in the early twenty-first century called intelligent design theory). Paley's natural theology was a good example of it even though that was published after Hume's critique. The argument is, in brief, that the universe displays evidence of design in its intricacies and interconnections. Hume attempted to show that what design is observable falls short of proving an infinite, all-wise creator. Rather, he says, it could just as well point to a committee or a demented being given the disorder and decay in nature. Here is an example of Hume's criticism of the teleological argument:

> Look around this universe. What an immense profusion of beings, animated and organized, sensible and active! You admire this prodigious variety and fecundity. But inspect a little more narrowly these living existences, the only beings worth regarding. How hostile and destructive to each other! How insufficient all of them for their own happiness! How contemptible or odious to the spectator! The whole presents nothing but the idea of a blind nature,

impregnated by a great vivifying principle, and pouring forth from her lap, without discernment or parental care, her maimed and abortive children.[71]

Many educated people believed that Hume had devastated the teleological argument for God and thereby seriously weakened natural theology and natural religion. At the close of the *Dialogues* the skeptic acknowledges that a religious person can still take refuge in faith in a special revelation for belief in God,[72] but he is confident he has done away with rational religion as it was believed in by both deists and defenders of orthodoxy.

Hume also attacked belief in miracles—something that had little effect on deism but sought to undermine belief in Christianity based on the historicity of Jesus' miracles. In a little section of *An Enquiry* titled "Of Miracles" (Section X) Hume argued that for every claim of a supernatural intervention there is always a better explanation than miracle. But his overall presupposition of the uniformity of nature ruled out miracles from the beginning: "A miracle is a violation of the laws of nature; and as a firm and unalterable experience has established these laws, the proof against a miracle, from the very nature of the fact, is as entire as any argument from experience can possibly be imagined."[73]

Many enlightened people of Europe read Hume's *Enquiry* and *Dialogues* and concluded that both natural religion and natural theology were dead. Those who believed in God and Christian doctrine on the basis of faith alone were unfazed. But across Europe and in much of America Christianity had come to be linked so closely with Enlightenment reason, either in a free-thinking, liberal form or in a rationalistic, orthodox form, that Hume's skepticism, well argued and defended, came as a shock.

Kant rescues science from Hume's skepticism. Kant was by all accounts an odd person. In many ways he fit the stereotype of the eccentric philosopher. He was born and raised in the Prussian city of Königsberg (now part of Russia) and never traveled more than about ten miles from it. He lived his entire eighty years in a single city. To say the least, he was not the cosmopolitan man of the world many people admire. By contemporary psychological standards he was almost certainly afflicted with obsessive-compulsive disorder (OCD) and pos-

---

[71]Ibid., 211.
[72]Ibid., 227–28.
[73]Ibid., 76.

sibly agoraphobia (fear of leaving home, especially for crowded places). He rarely left home except to give lectures at the University of Königsberg and go for one daily walk. He was raised in a pietist home and church, but as an adult he rarely attended church. His neighbors set their clocks by his daily walk as his manservant carried his top hat, coat and umbrella in case it rained. He always walked at precisely 3:30 p.m. According to one story, Kant broke off lecturing one day because he was distracted by a student sitting in front of him missing a button on his tunic. Kant ordered the student to go back to his room, sew the button on his coat, and return so he, Kant, could resume the lecture. Kant may have been eccentric and reclusive, but he was extremely well read, including books by foreigners such as Hume. By his own admission, reading Hume awakened Kant from his "dogmatic slumbers" and set his feet on a new path of philosophy that many have called critical idealism. Much of Kant's philosophical project was devoted to rescuing science and religion from Hume's skepticism. His method and conclusions, however, were anything but comforting to advocates of eighteenth-century rational religion—deists and defenders of natural theology.

Kant has been hailed as *the* Protestant philosopher of the modern age. His influence cannot be overemphasized. It was Kant, according to historical theologian Claude Welch, "who more than any other single thinker cast his shadow over theology in the nineteenth century"[74] and, one might add, over much of twentieth-century theology. He was the Enlightenment thinker par excellence, but he criticized traditional rationalism and empiricism (the two main branches of Enlightenment foundationalism) and sought to combine their strengths and avoid both their weaknesses in his own massive, complicated and subtle critical philosophy. Here only the most cursory explanation of Kant's philosophy can be offered and only that which is necessary for understanding modern theology.

Kant wrote numerous massive volumes, and most of them are still in print in the twenty-first century. But by far his most influential works, especially for theology, were *The Critique of Pure Reason* (1781) and *Religion Within the Limits of Reason Alone* (1793). Though an Enlightenment thinker, Kant believed Enlightenment philosophy had reached an impasse and that

---

[74]Claude Welch, *Protestant Theology in the Nineteenth Century*, vol. 1: *1799–1870* (New Haven, CT: Yale University Press, 1972), 45.

Hume had simply pointed it out. He agreed with Hume's position that a consistent empiricism resulted in skepticism even about the reality of causation and many other things science needs to do its work. He also agreed with Hume that natural theology, especially the traditional arguments for God's existence, falls far short of providing certain proof of God. Still, unlike Hume, he was not comfortable leaving philosophy, science or religion mired in doubt. What was needed, Kant believed, was a new epistemology that would raise them above chronic skepticism. Such a new epistemology would have to alter both rationalism and empiricism, combining the best of both while omitting their worst features.

We have already seen that what Hume did (among other things) was point out that there can be no such thing as synthetic truth a priori. In other words, outside the dictionary, so to speak, there can be no certainty. A priori truth is always only analytical—about definitions. For example, no one can doubt that a bachelor is an unmarried man. But that is not because someone has gone around the world observing every bachelor and concluding that, yes, they are all unmarried men. It is true a priori that all bachelors are unmarried men because that is the definition of "bachelor." The same is true about circles; they are all round because being round is part of the definition of "circle." A priori truth is truth about which one can be absolutely certain because it requires no investigation or experimentation or even sense observation. A posteriori truth is truth derived from and dependent on investigation or experimentation or at least observation. For example, that the earth revolves around the sun is true a posteriori; there is nothing in the definition of "earth" or "sun" or even "solar system" that requires it to be true. It is true because careful observation, beginning with Copernicus and reaching its climax in Galileo, proves it true. But Hume's point was that strict, consistent empiricism can never yield certainty; no matter how sure we think a conclusion based on observation is, we know it could turn out to be wrong in some aspect. So, certainty exists only in the analytic realm; a priori truth is limited to that. In the synthetic realm, beyond the dictionary and perhaps the math textbook, all truth is a posteriori and therefore fallible.

Hume laid down the glove, and Kant dared to pick it up. He dared to seek for and claim to have found synthetic truths a priori, thereby placing science back on solid ground.[75] The cost to religion, at least natural, rational religion and theology, however, was great. Natural, rational religion and theology depended on metaphysics, that branch of philosophy that searches for the ultimate realities of things, powers, beings and forces behind appearances— things in themselves and not only in their appearances. God was believed to be the necessary ultimate cause of all other things, and God's existence, so natural theology and religion claimed, could be proven through observation of the world (e.g., its design). Kant agreed with Hume that this approach to religion had to die; it does not work. But why? Not precisely for the reasons Hume gave. Rather, Kant famously said, he had to sacrifice reason (in religion) in order to make room for faith. Whether that was sincere or not has been much debated; perhaps it was Kant's way of defending himself against charges of being a destroyer of religion. (People who think religion, true Christianity, *is* always ultimately a matter of faith and not reason regard Kant as an ally in spite of himself.) What did he mean?

Kant set out to discover a priori synthetic truth. In order to find it, he suggested a necessary Copernican revolution in philosophy. Rationalism, following Descartes, said that real knowledge, which it equated with a priori truth, exists independent of the five senses in the realm of thoughts. Logical deduction from one's own existence, for example, could bring a person to knowledge of God, the immortal soul and the unity of external reality (the "universe"). Therefore innate ideas, self-evident truths, are the starting point for knowledge. Empiricism, however, following Locke, said that real knowledge always begins with sense experience. The mind is a *tabula rasa*, a blank slate, onto which knowledge is impressed, like the impression a key makes pressed into wax, by sense experience. Kant believed that both rationalism and empiricism, taken alone, lead to dead ends of philosophy, science and religion. Somehow they needed to be combined. Kant assumed that empiricism is better overall than strict Cartesian rationalism. Logic alone cannot produce scientific discovery. Empiricism was

---

[75]What follows, the account of the basics of Kant's epistemology, is my summary of the main points of *The Critique of Pure Reason*, trans. Norman Kemp Smith (New York: St. Martin's Press, 1965), which is notoriously difficult to summarize. And quotations from it are usually not helpful in such a brief summary. I will leave it to critics to decide if I have done justice to it in this context—a very brief survey and explication for the purpose of understanding Kant's influence on modern theology.

the very foundation of science. But how to fix its flaws so expertly discovered by Hume?

Kant suggested that instead of thinking of the human mind as a block of
wax and knowledge as impressions formed on it by sensations, perceptions,
why not think of the human mind as an active, productive machine that has
gears and levers (metaphorically speaking) that take sense experiences and
shape them into knowledge? In other words, the mind should be thought of
not as an inert receiver but as something that receives *and* produces. It
shapes and forms raw data of the five senses into knowledge using innate,
cognitive functions that Kant called "forms of intuition" and "categories of
understanding." The forms of intuition are space and time. The categories of
understanding include causation—that all-important force Hume demonstrated cannot be observed and therefore cannot be known. To use a more
modern illustration, one Kant would enjoy were he alive today, the mind is
more like a computer program than a block of wax. It takes raw data and
organizes that data into knowledge, just as a computer program, for example,
takes a list of names entered randomly and puts them into alphabetical order.

What is the advantage of Kant's epistemology? It combines rationalism
and empiricism and provides a detour around their limitations. Kant agreed
with empiricists such as Locke and Hume that all knowing begins with sense
experience, but he agreed with rationalists such as Descartes and his followers that knowledge is not limited to sense experience. If Kant was correct,
and many people of the late eighteenth century and beyond thought he was,
then synthetic truth a priori has been discovered. If Kant was right, we can
always be certain that all knowledge will be organized in a certain way including causation. Every effect will have a cause *because* the human mind
contributes causation to the process of taking raw data contributed by the
sense and organizing it. It does not matter that causation is not observable;
what matters is that it is part of the mind's machinery, so to speak. Or, to use
a more modern metaphor, causation is part of the software of the mind. A
synthetic truth a priori is: All objects known through pure reason exist
within a network of causes and effects. This is synthetic because it is about
the world of experience and not just definitions. It is true a priori because no
experience is necessary to know it; it is self-evident because of the universal
operation of "mind." For Kant, then, once one stops thinking of the mind as

passive in knowing and realizes it as active in the knowing process, Hume's skepticism is overcome. Now science can get back to work because one of its key categories, causation, is placed once again on *terra firma*.

One main question usually arises when people first encounter Kant's critical idealist epistemology. (It is called that because philosophical idealism emphasizes the role of the mind in knowing and because, unlike absolute idealism, it does not say that mind is all there is.) Doesn't this mean that we can have no knowledge of things-in-themselves but only of things-as-they-appear-to-us? Kant's answer is emphatically yes:

> All our intuition [knowledge] is nothing but the representation of appearance; that the things which we intuit are not in themselves what we intuit them as being, nor their relations so constituted in themselves as they appear to us, and . . . if the subject, or even only the subjective constitution of the senses in general, be removed, the whole constitution and all the relations of objects in space and time, nay space and time themselves, would vanish. As appearances, they cannot exist in themselves, but only in us. What objects may be in themselves, and apart from all this receptivity of our sensibility, remains completely unknown to us.[76]

That is why metaphysics and natural theology must go; if Kant was right we can have absolutely no knowledge of things except as the mind shapes them, that is, if we are talking about pure reason—"scientific reason." Metaphysics was always thought to be in some sense scientific; natural theology was supposed to put religion, including Christianity, on a scientific footing alongside the natural sciences (if not above them). But if Kant was right, "scientific knowledge," knowledge of the world through sense experience and deduction from it, is limited to appearances. The *Ding-an-sich*, thing-in-itself, is beyond knowing. Kant thought science should not bother itself with this; science can get on with its business without worrying about whether what it studies exists in the noumenal realm (Kant's term for the realm of things-in-themselves) or the phenomenal realm (Kant's term for the realm of things-as-they-appear-to-us). Some scientists agree and some disagree, but Kant felt strongly that it should not matter. To think one is studying things-in-themselves is to engage in metaphysics and fall under Hume's skepticism.

---

[76]Kant, *Critique of Pure Reason*, 82.

The illustration about computer software might help explicate Kant's point here. Imagine a person whose only job is to observe and interpret data arriving on her computer through a network. The data always arrives organized alphabetically. (Perhaps it is, for example, a list of book titles and authors.) What is it to the person whether the data were entered into the computer network and its software in that form? Suppose the person asked her supervisor, "Is this data I'm receiving on my computer entered somewhere else, say on another computer on this network, in exactly this form?" The supervisor might say, "That's none of your business; it doesn't matter" (especially if he does not understand it himself). A person ignorant of computers and their capabilities would probably assume the data are being entered in that form somewhere by someone. But a person knowledgeable about computer software and its capabilities will suspect the data are not being entered in that form somewhere by someone and will assume some software in the network or on her computer is organizing it as it appears to her. But what difference does it make to her job? None. Think of Kant's "noumenal realm" as the person, computer and raw data on the other end of the network connecting to the employee receiving it in organized form. Think of Kant's "phenomenal realm" as what appears on the employee's computer screen. Think of Kant's "forms of intuition" and "categories of understanding" as the software that organizes the raw data between its entry (noumenal realm) and its reception (phenomenal realm). The point is that for the person receiving the data to be interpreted, it is true a priori that it will always be in (for example) alphabetical order. That is a synthetic truth a priori—something Hume thought impossible.

So, if Kant was right, science is rescued, but metaphysics, including natural theology and natural religion, is dead. That is because the person on the receiving end of the computer network cannot know anything about the raw data or its origin from where she sits. The data *as she receives and observes it* reveals nothing about its nature before she sees it. For all she knows, it might start as a meaningless jumble of bytes. Similarly, for Kant, there is no way to know anything about the raw data of our sense experiences, its origin, its nature before the mind receives and organizes it. But it would seem that by definition God belongs in the noumenal realm. What good is a God who is shaped by the mind? The same could be said of all the objects of metaphysics (e.g., the soul, the universe as a whole). Thus, in order to rescue science, Kant had to destroy metaphysics and with it rational, natural theology and religion.

If Kant was right, there can be no knowledge of God in the strictest sense of knowledge. As a leading Kantian scholar says, "If the only objects of knowledge are objects which have been determined as such in accordance with certain principles of knowability, there can of course be no knowledge of God."[77]

Kant limits religion to practical reason. That is not, however, the end of the story of Kant and religion. Kant was, in his own way, a very religious person. He wanted to rescue religion from his own epistemology as much as he wanted to rescue science from Hume's. How to do that Kant explained in *Religion Within the Limits of Reason Alone* (1793).[78] But what he wrote there depended much on another book—*Critique of Practical Reason* (1788). Kant divided reason into two realms: "pure reason," by which he meant reason as used by all the sciences, and "practical reason," by which he meant reason as it is used in the moral life. Kant used "transcendental reasoning" to demonstrate the necessity of the ideas of God, the soul and the universe as a whole (i.e., its unity). Here "transcendental" means imagining what must be the case from what is the case and positing its reality. According to Kant, religion arises from ethics, from humanity's experience of the "moral law within." He famously remarked, "Two things fill the mind with ever new and increasing admiration and reverence, the more often and persistently one's meditation deals with them: the starry sky above me and the moral law within me."[79] Kant believed there is a moral law within everyone and it is perfectly rational. It does not depend on revelation. He called it the "categorical imperative" and expressed it in two forms, the most famous of which is "Always treat other persons as ends in themselves and never as means to an end." For Kant this is the philosophical golden rule; every rational person

---

[77]F. E. England, *Kant's Conception of God* (New York: Humanities Press, 1968), 207. Although if Kant is right there can be no knowledge of God, there can be and *indeed must be* (Kant insisted on this also) the idea of God as a "transcendental concept." By that Kant meant a necessary idea. For Kant, however, the necessity of the idea of God says nothing about God's existence or nature.

[78]Again, as with Kant's account of critical idealism, what follows is a brief summary of the main points of *Religion Within the Limits of Reason Alone*, trans. Theodore M. Greene and Hoyt H. Hudson (New York: Harper & Row, 1960).

[79]Immanuel Kant, *Critique of Practical Reason*, trans. Werner S. Pluhar (Indianapolis: Hackett, 2002), 203.

intuitively realizes it is correct. However, he realized that abiding by it does not always bring happiness; in this life there is no automatic relationship between living morally and being happy. Therefore, there must be a place where moral living is rewarded with happiness. This everyone understands to be heaven, although Kant did not think of it in terms of traditional theology or even in biblical images. Based on the moral law within, Kant argued that practical reason requires that people believe in God and the immortality of the soul including rewards and punishments after death.

In *Religion Within the Limits of Reason Alone* the German philosopher contended that religion's proper function is to support ethics and morality. It is not about metaphysics as that is traditionally understood. Rather, "pure religious faith is concerned only with what constitutes the essence of reverence for God, namely, obedience, ensuing from the moral disposition, to all duties as His commands."[80] Even Christianity is limited to its ethical function, according to Kant; it is not at all about mysterious doctrines about God-in-himself such as Trinity or incarnation, although he never denied them. (Because he suspected Kant was implicitly denying these and other dogmas of the state church, the king of Prussia silenced Kant for a time, forbidding him to publish anything on religion. Eventually the imposed silence was lifted.)

Kant's view of Jesus Christ illustrates his view of Christianity as limited to practical reason—morality and ethics, especially duty to live according to the categorical imperative. For Kant, Jesus was simply "an example conforming to the archetype of a humanity pleasing to God."[81] Kant was clever at expressing his disbelief in things supernatural without explicitly denying them. For example, immediately after that definition of Christ, he wrote that "he [Jesus] is represented [in the Gospels] as returning to heaven, whence he came."[82] Notice that he did not say Jesus returned to heaven from whence he came; he only said Jesus is "represented as returning to heaven." On the basis of that alone he could not be accused of heresy, but anyone who understood the code imbedded in the phrase "represented as" realized Kant did not believe in the resurrection or ascension. Finally, the

---

[80]Kant, *Religion*, 96.
[81]Ibid., 119–20.
[82]Ibid., 120.

philosopher expressed Jesus' real significance: "He left behind him, by word of mouth, his last will (as in a testament); and, trusting in the power of the memory of his merit, teaching, and example, he was able to say that 'he (the ideal of humanity well-pleasing to God) would still be with his disciples, even to the end of the world.'"[83] In other words, Jesus' importance lies in his example and teachings, not in his incarnation or atoning death as in traditional, orthodox theology. Kant's Christology did not go much beyond that of the deists. And he saw religion's primary significance and purpose much as they saw it—as a support for ethics.

Enumerating and explaining all the tentacles of Kant's philosophy that extended out into modern theology, influencing it as no other philosophy, would consume hundreds of pages. Here a few must suffice.

First, Kant's dualisms between the noumenal and phenomenal and between pure reason and practical reason and his restriction of religion to the latter and especially to ethics provided the primary path of escape from conflict between science and religion for much of future theology. In other words, if religion, including Christianity, is not dependent on metaphysics or any belief about the outer world of nature and is limited to morality or duty, then it can hardly be affected by any new discovery of science. If Kant was right, science and religion are about entirely different matters. Later liberal theology picked up on this and often distinguished between "matters of fact" and "matters of value" (or "faith"), putting a wall between them so that theology, restricted to the latter, is about what ought to be rather than what is. Science is about the facts of the world, not about right and wrong or (as much later liberal theologians will insist theology is solely about) the kingdom of God. In a degraded way, the old saying that theology is about "how to go to heaven, not how the heavens go" was Kant's point entirely, although it is doubtful that he was interested in any plan of salvation other than doing one's moral duty. This dualism between facts and faith has become so prevalent in modern Christian thought that many people take it for granted, but it was Kant's invention even if some Christian mystics anticipated it.

Second, and closely related to the first point, many later theologians saw Kant as an ally in their inflation of revelation as the sole source of knowledge

---

[83]Ibid.

of God. Many conservative and neo-orthodox modern theologians thought Christianity is based entirely on special revelation and faith and not on reason or natural theology. That was hardly the consensus of most Enlightenment thinkers of the eighteenth century, but it arose as something of a Protestant consensus in the early twentieth century with Karl Barth (1886–1968) and his dialectical theology colleagues and followers. Bernard Reardon, a noted scholar of nineteenth-century religious thought, expressed Kant's significance for these more conservative theologians concisely: "Scientific reason might be absolute in its own realm, but its authority did not extend to revelation, which dealt only with the supersensible and addressed man at the 'higher' level of his moral personality."[84]

Kant gave modernity a new twist without abandoning its basic impulses. Barth expresses it well in his essay on Kant: "What is the significance of this man and of his work? . . . Our answer must simply be that it was in this man and in his work that the eighteenth century saw, understood and affirmed its own limitations."[85] In other words, Kant uncovered the limitations of rationalism without rejecting reason. No longer could the "heavenly philosophers of the eighteenth century"[86] blithely go on believing in the omnicompetence of pure reason. Reason could not reach to a world behind appearances, to things-in-themselves. Newton had defined science as "thinking God's thoughts after him." Kant drove a stake in the heart of that way of thinking about human reason. Yet, Kant did not turn against reason; he redefined it and delineated its limitations. As for religion, he took it out of the realm of the natural (or supernatural) and placed it firmly in the realm of the ethical. Because of reason's limitations religion cannot use reason to establish itself as fact in the same way science establishes, for example, the existence of a new planet in the solar system.

Hegel returns reason to religion. One hard lesson students of intellectual history, and perhaps especially philosophy and theology, quickly learn is

---

[84]Bernard M. G. Reardon, *Kant as Philosophical Theologian* (Totowa, NJ: Barnes & Noble, 1988), 179.
[85]Karl Barth, *Protestant Theology in the Nineteenth Century* (Grand Rapids: Eerdmans, 2002), 252.
[86]Intellectual historian Carl L. Becker argued that the eighteenth century was not a secular age and that its leading philosophers believed in and practiced a "heavenly philosophy" in which reason, as opposed to revelation and faith, could establish the truth of God and God's will for humanity: *The Heavenly City of the Eighteenth-Century Philosophers* (New Haven, CT: Yale University Press, 2003).

that an absolute is never absolute. Kant killed metaphysics and limited reason to the realm of appearances; Kant restricted religion to ethics. Yes, he did that for himself and those who followed his philosophy. No, he did not put an end to all attempts to use reason to reach absolute and ultimate reality. A notable dissenter to Kant's philosophy was born in the middle of Kant's lifetime and grew up to react strongly against Kant's limitation of reason to appearances and religion to ethics. Hegel was born into a middle-class family in Stuttgart, Germany. His father was an official in the Duke of Würrtemberg's government who wanted his son to become a minister. The son dutifully studied theology at the Protestant seminary of the University of Tübingen but switched to the study of philosophy. He associated with a group of philosophers that came to be called idealists in that they considered ultimate reality to be thought or consciousness rather than matter. For them, the material world is an extension of the mental world with God being the Mind (capitalized because it was generally equated with deity) from which everything else is derived. One of Hegel's closest friends and colleagues at the University of Jena, where he began his teaching career, was the philosopher Friedrich Schelling (1775–1854)—an advocate of absolute idealism, which saw Mind as the sole reality of which everything else, including matter, is an emanation.

Hegel did not accept absolute idealism; his philosophy would better be called something like dialectical idealism, with "dialectical" denoting the underlying unity of opposites. Hegel came to think that absolute idealism, such as Schelling's worldview, ended up portraying reality as "a dark night in which all cows are black"—in other words, an identity without real distinctions. Hegel knew well that reality is both unity and diversity, but he could not stomach Kant's dualisms. If dualism is final, Hegel thought, then all hope of knowing reality is dead. Hegel was not ready, as Kant was, to give up on metaphysics or rational religion. However, he knew well that Kant had killed traditional metaphysics that depended on ideas like causation to prove the existence of God. Just as Kant saw Hume as a problem to overcome, so Hegel saw Kant as a challenge to be met. And he attempted to meet Kant's challenge by turning traditional philosophy and religion around or on its head.

The Kantian problem Hegel confronted was the limitations of pure reason to the phenomenal realm and of religion to the realm of practical reason or ethics. To Hegel this was too great a sacrifice. He wanted to return philosophy to rational knowledge of ultimate reality and religion to rational knowledge of God. "Rational knowledge is an essential element in the Christian religion itself."[87] The only way to do this, however, was to overcome the dualisms of thought and being and of subject and object assumed or created by Kant. Hegel knew there was no going back to what was before Kant; he had no interest in deism or its form of natural religion. That, too, was bedeviled by dualisms that made real knowledge of ultimate reality impossible. In his magnum opus, *Phenomenology of Spirit* (1807), the speculative philosopher suggested that all things in philosophy could be made right again, that is, truly scientific, if it overcomes the dualisms of thought and being and of subject and object and instead thinks of consciousness itself as ultimate reality. In other words, the whole problem of Hume and Kant, according to Hegel, was their assumption that the order of knowing, or thought, and the order of being, or reality, are two different orders. So long as thought and being are divorced, Hegel believed, there will be no knowledge of ultimate reality or God. As Kant realized, the only "knowing," in that case, is "practical knowing," that is, positing the existence of God (and the soul) because God is a necessary idea to account for morality. But, Hegel the idealist asked, what if thought and being are not different orders, divorced from each other, but belong together so that thought itself reveals the nature of reality including God? Then consciousness is not finite and striving to grasp a reality other than itself (God or matter or whatever) that it ultimately cannot know. Instead, consciousness, mind, spirit, is infinite but dynamic—as is being, or God.

Consciousness itself, then, reveals ultimate reality just by its own structure because they are united, not separated. This great unity of all reality, consciousness and being united in a dynamic process, is not merely finite but is what Hegel called the "true infinite" that includes the finite in itself,[88] overcoming the difference between the finite and the infinite in a process of reflection through which "Absolute Spirit" (Hegel's concept of God as the Mind or Spirit) comes to self-awareness. There are, then, not two, separate

---

[87]G. W. F. Hegel, *Lectures on the Philosophy of Religion*, trans. E. B. Spiers and J. Burdon Sanderson, 3 vols. (New York: Humanities Press, 1962), 1:17.
[88]Ibid., 1:184–85.

realms of the noumenal and phenomenal, and human intelligence and consciousness is not limited because it is an aspect of Absolute Spirit. History, the upward march of cultures in time, is the process of Absolute Spirit coming to self-awareness through the evolving of human consciousness.[89]

Hegel posited the identity of the process of human thought, at its best and most logical, with the history of God or Absolute Spirit. "For Hegel . . . the structure of truly rational human thinking *does* bear witness to the structure of reality; not, however, because the structures of thought and of reality are similar but because they are, ultimately, one and the same."[90] Human thought and the cultures it creates evolve in a pattern of thesis, antithesis and synthesis.[91] An idea (or culture) is put forward which inevitably gives rise to its seeming opposite or antithesis. Thought, consciousness, strives to "sublate" thesis and antithesis by taking them up into a higher unity that leaves behind their contrary, conflicting elements. The higher unity is synthesis—the union of opposites that transcends them. The synthesis then becomes a new thesis confronted eventually by its antithesis, and the process continues. This is how consciousness works—not only human consciousness but also history itself, which is the career, as it were, of Absolute Spirit, Hegel's term for God. Through this dialectical process God comes to self-awareness in dependence on the world. This is called panentheism—an influential idea of God and the world in modern theology after Hegel. It emphasizes God's immanence more than God's transcendence. God and the world are always interdependent with God being the greater partner. Hegel expressed it best in his *Lectures on the Philosophy of Religion*: "Without a world God is not God,"[92] or, more precisely put, "the divine Spirit's knowledge of itself [happens] through the mediation of finite spirit."[93] Thus, humanity's coming to know God is God's coming to know himself.[94]

---

[89]Ibid., 1:206. The brief summary of Hegel's philosophy here is based on *Phenomenology of Spirit* and *Lectures on the Philosophy of Religion*. These are extremely complex philosophical treatises, and so any brief summary necessarily omits many points and steps of the argument.

[90]Quentin Lauer, *Hegel's Concept of God* (Albany: State University of New York Press, 1982), 79.

[91]No claim is made here that Hegel used the language or scheme of "thesis, antithesis, synthesis." This is a conventional way of describing Hegel's view of reality.

[92]Quoted in Lauer, *Hegel's Concept of God*, 272.

[93]Quoted in ibid., 134.

[94]Hegel, *Lectures*, 1:206.

How does humanity come to know God and God come to know himself? Through reflection on history as the activity of Spirit. Hegel believed strongly in a kind of upward progression of history and culture toward greater and greater degrees of unity, the whole process of which is revelation of God.[95] History itself cannot be understood without understanding it as the history of God or Absolute Spirit. For our purposes, to understand how Hegel's concept of God influenced modern theology after him, the key idea is panentheism—that God and the world, God and humanity are not foreigners or aliens to each other; they belong intrinsically and inseparably together in the process of mutual activity called the history of ideas. Thus, God is not "someone out there," "wholly other," the opposite of everything finite and limited, but the consciousness of the world coming to awareness of the unity of finite and infinite. One Hegel scholar says, "It does not seem adequate to interpret this [viz., Hegel's idea of God coming to self-realization through humanity's discovery of God in thought] as meaning no more than that God has 'created' the human spirit with a *capacity* to know the divine; it would seem more accurate to say that Hegel looks upon the human spirit as . . . an *offshoot* of the divine."[96]

What is the point of all this speculative thinking? Just this: only by supposing reality to be this way is knowledge of ultimate reality possible, and philosophy and religion, Hegel believed, are worthless without this pursuit. Hegel was saying, "Instead of looking at reality 'this way' (viz., through the lens of dualisms of subject and object, finite and infinite, noumenal and phenomenal) try looking at it 'this other way' (viz., through the lens of all reality as a dynamic process and activity of one great consciousness) and see if it doesn't afford a better approach to knowing the things both philosophy and religion really want to know." Suddenly, seeing reality "as this" instead of "as that" makes it possible once again to try to know ultimate reality, God, with hope of succeeding. According to Hegel, so long as finite and infinite, world and spirit, humanity and God are regarded as opposites over against each other they can never really know each other. Then religion, for example, has to be reduced to something less than itself such as morality (Kant).

---

[95]Ibid., 3:149.
[96]Lauer, *Hegel's Concept of God*, 134. Lauer later says that, for Hegel, finite spirit is a "moment" of absolute Spirit with "moment" meaning aspect or stage (not temporal moment) (147).

Hegel's philosophy is a great system into which there is no entry point. One has to begin inside it and look outward to see how it illumines reality and religion. It presupposes that the real is the rational and the rational is the real with both "real" and "rational" redefined. In other words, it starts from the presupposition that human reason, working at its best, is one with ultimate reality—God. Thinking about thought itself reveals God. God is the process of thought itself. But here "thought" does not mean "stream of consciousness," mind-wandering daydreaming. Here "thought" means philosophy's and culture's upward path through conflict between ideas and cultures toward unity.

According to one possibly apocryphal story, two philosophers went together to hear Hegel lecture on his view of reality as Absolute Spirit. As they left, one said to the other one, "That was magnificent! What a great mind! His philosophy is amazing in its complexity and rationality." The other philosopher responded, "But, you realize, of course, he thinks reality is actually like that." The first one replied, "Oh, well, then he must be crazy." Hegel's philosophy is truly one of the most subtle and complicated and difficult to grasp of all time. Here I have been able only to touch on some of its points relevant for modern theology. So, what are the consequences and results of Hegel's great vision of reality as Absolute Spirit/God dynamically moving toward self-awareness through human consciousness and culture?

First, Hegel did not take religion as literal description of reality. For him, religion, including Christianity, is but a set of symbols, representations of philosophical truths. Philosophy at its best (his) is religion conceptualized; religion at its best (Christianity for him) is philosophy symbolized. So, for example, for Hegel the Trinity is a symbolic representation of the dynamic process of Absolute Spirit coming to self-realization through its other, the world. There are three "moments" (stages, aspects) of the process that correspond to the symbols of Father, Son and Holy Spirit.[97] For Hegel, the incarnation is a symbolic representation of Absolute Spirit entering into the finite, of the ultimate unity of finite and infinite. For Hegel, the atoning death of Christ is a symbolic representation of the "suffering" of the infinite, of Absolute Spirit, as it experiences the agony of finitude. Hegel called this

---

[97]Hegel, *Lectures*, 3:12–13.

the "speculative Good Friday." For some, certainly not all, later modern theologians this opens up vast possibilities of reconciling religion, even Christianity, with modern thought. Religion is but symbolic representations of philosophical truths. This idea appears again, in altered form, in some twentieth-century existentialist theology in which the resurrection of Jesus, for example, is explained as a symbolic way of expressing the restitution of faith in the hearts of the disciples after Jesus' death.

Second, even for many who did not claim to understand all of Hegel's philosophy, his idea of God immanent within the world process seemed congenial to the nineteenth-century ways of thinking about evolution. And it seemed to overcome some of the traditional, objectionable images of God as so transcendent as to be untouched by human misery. God's immanence in history and in the world and even in humanity became a theme of much liberal theology in the nineteenth and twentieth centuries. Process theology, for example, though immediately dependent on another philosopher, Alfred North Whitehead (1861–1947), is greatly influenced by Hegel's panentheism in which the world and God belong inseparably together in interdependence. To many liberal Christian thinkers this helps solve the mystery of evil in God's world. God is not the transcendent, all-powerful controller of history; God is the immanent Spirit evolving upward together with humanity coming to self-awareness through suffering just like people.

Third, and finally, Hegel's philosophy of religion offered another way out of the conflicts between science and religion. Religion is not about the same subjects as science. Nor is it, as with Kant, merely about ethics. Religion is about honoring God by helping God come to self-realization by promoting the unity of humanity. The kingdom of God could be thought of as the unity of humanity which would also be the unity of God and the world. That has nothing to do with the physical world of laws of nature; it has everything to do with social reform and cultural creativity. The ideal society, without conflicts, would be the end of history and thus the kingdom of God in which opposites would coincide, synthesis would be achieved and the suffering of God would end in God's full self-realization in humanity. Perhaps to soothe the ruffled feathers of Prussia's king, who was sometimes dismayed by Hegel's philosophy, the philosopher speculated that Prussia was the end of history, the perfect social order, the culmination of the process of Absolute Spirit. Few agreed with him about that, but the idea of an end of history in the sense of human culture achieving its divine purpose and God coming to self-realization in that, caught on among many nineteenth-century theologians who dreamed of the kingdom of God as a perfect social order on earth. This fueled liberal optimism that only died away as a result of the twentieth century's world wars.

Hume, Kant and Hegel change and reenergize modernity. It would be wrong to think that Hume's skepticism, Kant's limitations of reason or Hegel's speculative philosophy reversed the tide of modernity sweeping through Europe and eventually over America. Hume challenged the exuberant optimism about reason and its potential to usher in a kind of utopia through science and natural religion that dominated elite European circles in the second half of the eighteenth century. But he was a thoroughly modern man in terms of skepticism toward magic, superstition and religion. He was one of the first completely secularized public intellectuals, and he was idolized by a large cadre of young modernists disillusioned with tradition and religion.

Kant challenged Hume's skepticism without in any way reversing his secularism. To be sure, Kant had his own faith, but it was largely a rational, philosophical faith drained of any hint of the pietism in which he was raised. And he was skeptical in his own way. No more than Hume did he want to support magic, superstition or traditional dogmas. Kant was also a thoroughly modern person whose essay "What Is Enlightenment?" came to be regarded as the manifesto par excellence of the Enlightenment ethos of independent, free thought. Also, Kant did more than anyone else to separate science and religion so that they could not conflict.

Hegel challenged Kant's limiting of reason, rejection of rational knowledge of God and reduction of religion to ethics. But no more than Kant did Hegel want a return to premodern religion or philosophy. He, too, was a thoroughly modern person in that he trusted in reason alone to deliver truth about God and the nature of reality. Unlike Hume and Kant, he was not an empiricist; he stood in the tradition of Descartes in terms of rationalism. He also believed in innate ideas and that the existence of God is built into the nature of logic itself. Nothing illustrates his modernity better than his motto that "the real is the rational and the rational is the real." For him, the human mind, unaided by supernatural, special revelation, is capable of grasping and understanding everything important about God and God's relationship with the world because it is a part of God's own consciousness and being.

All three of these thinkers affirmed the anthropocentrism of the Enlightenment. All believed that knowledge of God, insofar as it is possible at all, is dependent on knowledge of humanity. The human, not God, stands at the center of the proud edifice of knowledge. What could possibly be more modern?

However, something as proud as Enlightenment, modern faith in reason could not go long without itself being challenged. Of course there were loud condemnations of it as apostasy from the orthodox conservatives of Protestant theology. But they were not alone in criticizing Enlightenment rationalism, naturalism and anthropocentrism. Some extremely intellectual thinkers quickly pointed out its flaws. The next section will examine a disparate trinity of Christian thinkers who, without reverting to premodernity, launched their own individual assaults on modernity's triumphalism. Each in his own way attempted to reintroduce revelation and faith to philosophy. They are also crucial for understanding modern theology because much of modern theology consists of reactions against the pride, the optimism, the humanism and secularism of Enlightenment-inspired modernity.

1.E. REALISTS, ROMANTICISTS AND EXISTENTIALISTS RESPOND

Everyone has heard of the fictional "world's only consulting detective" Sherlock Holmes, the creation of Sir Arthur Conan Doyle, who has been immortalized in numerous short stories, novels, movies and television series. He has been played by more actors than any other character. Almost a century after Conan Doyle put down his pen for the last time, the character Holmes still appeals to readers. Numerous spin-offs have been written, striving to match the genius of the detective's creator in spinning a yarn about his exploits in defeating crime in late nineteenth-century and early twentieth-century England. Hollywood continues to produce movies based on the character. A series of novels is being published by various mystery writers all competing best to continue the saga of Sherlock Holmes and Dr. Watson.

Why mention Sherlock Holmes in a book about modern theology? There is precious little theology in any of the stories. The answer is, "Elementary!"

(Holmes frequently said that to the often nonplussed Watson.) Holmes represents the ideal modern man, the paradigm of an Enlightenment person. He was unemotional, objective, rational and committed to reaching conclusions only by evidence and logical deduction. He said nothing against religion but displayed no interest in it. He refused to take miracles or the supernatural seriously even when a crime seemed to have been perpetrated by a vampire or ghost. Above all, he had a steadfast and unwavering faith in observation and deduction. After finally discovering the truth about a crime, when he had seemed to be wrong about a piece of evidence, the detective declared to Watson, "I should have had more faith [in my methods]. . . . I ought to know by this time that when a fact appears to be opposed to a long train of deductions, it invariably proves to be capable of bearing some other interpretation."[98]

A person as detached, rational and dedicated to observation as Holmes may never have existed, but it would be surprising if Conan Doyle was not intentionally trying to portray the perfect model of an Enlightenment man of science and reason—the model modern man.[99] (Ironically, Conan Doyle himself was the opposite of Holmes. The author, though a medical doctor and therefore well acquainted with modern science, believed in communication with the dead and "garden fairies.") One can imagine Holmes sitting in his brother's Diogenes Club smoking a pipe and congenially conversing with Locke or Hume or even Kant. One way to understand the abstract concept of modernity is to think of a character like Holmes, who seemed to be the perfect embodiment of modernity's ideals for all people.

Pushing back against Enlightenment rationalism and skepticism. However, not everyone in Europe, Great Britain or America valued this ideal. Without rejecting the Enlightenment entirely or calling for a return to medieval times, many astute thinkers, both Christian and secular, pointed out weaknesses in this portrait of the perfect person of reason. Others responded critically to Hume's skepticism and Kant's and Hegel's idealisms. In brief, modernity, as it has been described here so far, did not

---

[98]Arthur Conan Doyle, "A Study in Scarlet," in *The Complete Sherlock Holmes* (Garden City, NY: Doubleday, 1930), 49.

[99]If all a person knows about the character Holmes comes from the movies about him starring Robert Downey Jr., he or she will know little about the original character to which Downey's bears little resemblance.

meet with unqualified or universal applause even among the educated elites
of Europe, Britain and America. Especially the movement called romanticism reacted against the ideal of pure, objective rationalism devoid of
emotion. A type of philosophy called Scottish common sense realism responded especially to Hume's skepticism. The Danish writer Søren Kierkegaard (1813–1855), the father of existentialism, harshly criticized Hegel's
rational religion of Absolute Spirit and advocated a return to faith as the
basis for authentic Christianity.[100]

Once again it will be helpful to point out what was at stake in all this
philosophical conversation and controversy. What was at stake was the very
concept of knowledge. What does it mean to know something? The Enlightenment, including the scientific revolution, redefined knowledge.
Before Descartes and Locke, at least for the most part, knowing included
believing, trusting in revelation and tradition. For people of a particularly
rational bent it also meant reasoning within the context of faith. Anselm's
motto, "I believe in order to understand," was the norm. Begin with faith in
revelation (e.g., the Bible) and tradition (e.g., the church's teachings) and
then use God-given reason, illuminated by the Holy Spirit, to interpret life
and the world in that light. The ancient philosophy of Aristotle had been
baptized by the Catholic Church during the Middle Ages, and its principles
of metaphysics were widely considered beyond doubt or question. The
knowing person was the person of faith—not necessarily blind faith but
faith working together with reason within the framework of tradition.

The Enlightenment challenged all that. Science was discovering that Aristotle had been wrong about many things. As a result of the Galileo affair,
many educated people, movers and shakers of culture and society and even
church, began to doubt tradition. Luther and the other Protestant Reformers had successfully challenged the authority of the Catholic Church
and even of the empire. Perhaps the foundations of the great medieval synthesis of church and society were cracked. Modernity began with this crisis
of trust in time-honored tradition. Gradually, as a result of the new science

---

[100]The extent to which Kierkegaard was reacting to Hegel himself is unclear and debated. Some
scholars argue he was reacting only to Danish Hegelians. However, Kierkegaard spent a good
deal of time in Berlin and was no doubt familiar with Hegel's own writings even if he does not
mention Hegel specifically.

and philosophy, knowledge came to be thought of differently. Now it began with doubting and questioning tradition. Now it depended on evidence and logic working outside and independently of the authorities of church and empire. Now it meant, as per Kant, thinking critically for oneself, using objective reason to establish facts and distinguish them from fancy. Gradually knowledge came to be limited to what reason can discover and prove. All else was increasingly being considered opinion if not superstition. The trophy knowledge was being taken away from metaphysics and theology and handed over to science and critical philosophy. Hume questioned whether even they could provide knowledge, and Kant argued that we can have no knowledge of the world outside the mind.

But not everyone was happy with this new arrangement. As this section will show, Thomas Reid (1710–1796) protested Hume's skepticism and appealed to common sense to reestablish knowledge. His philosophy of common sense realism caught on among conservative Protestant Christians who were shocked by Hume's skepticism and Kant's reduction of religion to ethics and morality. Samuel Taylor Coleridge (1772–1834), a British romanticist, appealed to intuitive knowledge especially in the sphere of spirituality and religion. He protested the Enlightenment's inflation of reason to the exclusion of feelings and especially Kant's limitation of religion to doing one's moral duty. Schleiermacher and Horace Bushnell (1802–1876) were influenced by romanticists like Coleridge. Kierkegaard scoffed at Hegel's rational system of reality as abstract and cold and completely foreign to Christianity, which he saw as requiring risk, obedience and sacrifice. Knowledge for the Danish thinker was linked to commitment, especially in religion. For him, the Enlightenment thinkers all favored the "spectator" posture toward knowledge; for him that is the antithesis of spiritual knowing. Kierkegaard's influence on theology would have to wait until the early twentieth century, when he was discovered by the so-called dialectical or neo-orthodox theologians such as Barth and Emil Brunner (1889–1966).[101]

Scottish common sense realism challenges Hume's skepticism. When scholars talk about the Scottish Enlightenment they may be referring to Hume or his contemporary philosophical nemesis Thomas Reid. They were

---

[101]The label "neo-orthodox" is controversial as applied to Barth, as will be explained in 5.a., Karl Barth Drops a Bombshell on the Theologians' Playground.

both philosophers profoundly interested in the new sciences, enamored with Newton and his laws of nature, and empiricists with regard to knowing. And they were both Scottish. There the similarities end. Whereas Hume is still celebrated as one of the greatest minds in the history of philosophy, Reid has become one of its most neglected figures.[102] During his lifetime and for about a century afterwards, however, Reid's philosophy was widely studied and discussed—especially in America, where his influence has been strongest.[103] Reid's reputation was built on contradicting Hume's skepticism about knowledge of the external world and its workings. Like Hume, Reid had a strong faith in reason, but he did not think skepticism was necessary or good.

Reid was born into a Scottish family of clergymen and scholars. His father was a minister of the Kirk—the Scottish state church (Presbyterian). His mother's maiden name was Gregory; her family was "the most important intellectual dynasty that Scotland had produced."[104] Several of his uncles and cousins were famous Scottish scholars. It was natural, then, for Thomas to study theology, become an ordained minister of the Kirk and teach philosophy and theology first at King's College, Aberdeen, and then at Glasgow University. According to one of his pupils who became his biographer, Reid was not the most flowery speaker, but

> such . . . was the simplicity and perspicuity of his style, such the gravity and authority of his character, and such the general interest of his young hearers in the doctrines which he taught, that . . . he was heard uniformly with the most silent and respectful attention [which was not always the case in university lecture halls then].[105]

Reid was a committed Christian who agreed with the doctrines of the Scottish church but sometimes criticized the fanaticism with which some clergymen promoted it from their pulpits. (The reader may remember this played a role in Hume's departure from the faith.) Nevertheless, "the Kirk's

---

[102]Colin Brown, *Christianity and Western Thought*, vol. 1: *From the Ancient World to the Age of Enlightenment* (Downers Grove, IL: InterVarsity Press, 1990), 259.

[103]Benjamin W. Redekop, "Reid's Influence in Britain, Germany, France and America," in *The Cambridge Companion to Thomas Reid*, ed. Terence Cuneo and René van Woudenberg (Cambridge: Cambridge University Press, 2004), 327–29.

[104]Alexander Broadie, "Reid in Context," in *The Cambridge Companion to Thomas Reid*, ed. Terence Cuneo and René van Woudenberg (Cambridge: Cambridge University Press, 2004), 37.

[105]Quoted in ibid., 35.

belief system and its institutions informed his soul, and therefore informed his philosophy also."[106]

Like Kant, Reid's thinking was stimulated by reading Hume, and he found his fellow Scotsman's skepticism wholly unnecessary and pernicious to both science and religion. Therefore he set out to demonstrate Hume's radical empiricism and skepticism wrong and wrong-headed. This he attempted in a trilogy of philosophical treatises: *An Inquiry into the Human Mind on the Principles of Common Sense* (1764), *Essays on the Intellectual Powers of Man* (1785) and *Essays on the Active Powers of Man* (1788). The label "common sense realism" can be misleading, for Reid's epistemology is not merely a restatement of common sense in the usual meaning. Today many people mean by it "what most people believe to be true most of the time" (or something like that). Reid's meaning is somewhat different and much more subtle. The underlying problem Reid was taking on was the meaning of knowledge. What do we mean when we say we know? What kinds of objects and ideas properly fall into the category "knowledge"? Reid believed much of the Enlightenment from Descartes to Hume had restricted that category too much so that, in the end, almost nothing could count as knowledge. That is ironic because the whole Enlightenment project was about determining true knowledge and separating it from mere belief.

Before delving into the basics of Reid's philosophy and its significance for this story of modern theology it will be helpful to define "realism." Reid's philosophy is usually labeled common sense realism, but that can be confusing because "realism" has different meanings in different contexts even in philosophy. Here, in Reid's philosophy, "realism" is opposed to "idealism," which he believed leads inevitably to skepticism. Idealism (see 1.d.) is the popular idea during the Enlightenment that mind and thought are more real than physical objects perceived by the mind. It also is the idea that what the mind knows is not objects themselves but ideas in the mind. Reid referred to idealism tied to empiricism as "the common theory of ideas" and sought to undermine it.[107] He saw the fundamental, underlying problem of modern

---

[106]Ibid., 32.

[107]John Greco, "Reid's Reply to the Skeptic," in *The Cambridge Companion to Thomas Reid*, ed. Terence Cuneo and René van Woudenberg (Cambridge: Cambridge University Press, 2004), 134–35.

foundationalism, beginning with Descartes, as the wholly unnecessary belief that knowledge is really only of one's own mind and its contents. Of course, the reason many Enlightenment thinkers adopted the common theory of ideas was for the sake of certainty. Presumably we can be certain of things in our own minds but never of external reality. Reid sought to demonstrate how this notion of knowledge led straight into Hume's skepticism, and he thought Kant's critical idealism was not much better.

According to Reid,

> Hume's position was destructive not only of Christian faith, but also of science and of common prudence. Underlying Hume's skepticism was the apparently reasonable and enlightened claim that we are "to admit [as knowledge] nothing but what can be proved by reasoning." Reid's immediate response was to retort, that if this be so, "then we must be sceptics [sic] indeed, and believe nothing at all." However, he wryly observed that Hume himself could not keep to this principle either in his daily life or in his philosophy. Nor, for that matter, can any skeptic. Over and over again, Reid pointed out that men could not live by skepticism alone. "If a man pretends to be a skeptic with regard to the information of the sense, and yet prudently keeps out of harm's way as other men do, he must excuse my suspicion."[108]

Again, Reid's underlying motive in contradicting Hume's skepticism was, like Kant's, to rescue science and religion, but he thought Kant's alternative to Hume's skepticism was almost as dangerous and destructive as it. Reid wanted knowledge to include much more than the radical empiricism or rationalism stemming from the Enlightenment would allow. His realism, then, refers to his belief that the human mind can know objects outside the mind *and* that it can know them at least relatively reliably—as they really are.

Reid calls philosophy back to common sense. Reid's first step was to call philosophy back to common sense. "Philosophy has no other root but the principles of Common Sense; it grows out of them and draws its nourishment from them: severed from this root, its honours wither, its sap is dried up, it dies and rots."[109] He thought too many Enlightenment thinkers were divorced from and

---

[108]Brown, *Christianity in Western Thought*, 1:263.
[109]Quoted in Terence Cuneo and René van Woudenberg, "Introduction," in *The Cambridge Companion to Thomas Reid*, ed. Terence Cuneo and René van Woudenberg (Cambridge: Cambridge University Press, 2004), 4.

even disdainful of things like ordinary language and how it functions. He also thought too many were driven by an almost irrational fear of being wrong which drove them to search for absolute certainty, limit knowledge to that and then despair when they discovered there is little about which anyone can be absolutely certain. Kant's search for synthetic truths a priori did not drive Reid; he assumed that synthetic knowledge (e.g., of the laws of nature and how they work) is always a posteriori and therefore at best true to a high degree of probability. And that is all science and natural religion need. Reid, therefore, argued that "the philosopher has no option but to join with the rest of humanity in conducting his thinking within the confines of common sense."[110]

But what did Reid mean by "common sense"? To repeat, he did not mean what many, perhaps most, people mean by it. He did not mean, for example, taking a poll and finding out what most people believe. Common sense in Reid's philosophy is not folk belief. Rather, by common sense the Scottish philosopher meant certain principles every sane human being shares with every other sane human being. The principles are necessary assumptions that lie at the foundation of all thought and practice. According to Reid, we are to trust these unless overwhelming evidence proves them unreliable. Most of the time, however, they are reliable, which is why sometimes scholars refer to Reid's philosophy as "reliabilism" instead of "common sense realism."[111] Reid believed and argued that "philosophical thought, like all thought and practice, rests at bottom not on grounding [i.e., undoubtable ideas] but on trust."[112] This flies in the face of Descartes's "methodological doubt" that launched the philosophical Enlightenment and in the face of Hume's obvious distrust of experience. This is another sense in which Reid's philosophy is realistic—he is willing to settle for something less than absolute certainty because he realizes such is normally not available outside the dictionary and perhaps mathematics.

Reid defined common sense, as he meant it in his philosophy, as "that degree of judgment which is common to men with whom we can converse and transact business."[113] Reid elaborates:

---

[110]Nicholas Wolterstorff, "Reid on Common Sense," in *The Cambridge Companion to Thomas Reid*, ed. Terence Cuneo and René van Woudenberg (Cambridge: Cambridge University Press, 2004), 77.
[111]Philip de Bary, *Thomas Reid and Scepticism: His Reliabilist Response* (London: Routledge, 2002).
[112]Wolterstorff, "Reid on Common Sense," 78.
[113]Quoted in ibid., 81.

> If there are certain principles, as I think there are, which the constitution of
> our nature leads us to believe, and which we are under a necessity to take for
> granted in the common concerns of life, without being able to give a reason
> for them; these are what we call the principles of common sense; and what is
> manifestly contrary to them, is what we call absurd.[114]

These are principles even the skeptic cannot escape. He may think he doubts
them and even say he doubts them, but his behavior indicates otherwise.[115]
Reid believed it is possible to extract these basic principles of common sense
from everyday language and practice of sane people. People who deny them
or live against them are always considered insane. We must trust that these
principles are right and true and that we can base knowledge on them.

What are these basic principles of common sense according to Reid?
One is that "there is life and intelligence in our fellow men with whom we
converse."[116] If that seems somewhat abstract, think of it this way: Suppose
someone asked you to prove other minds exist. You cannot, but everyone
acts as if minds other than their own exist. Belief in other minds than one's
own is basic. Since it cannot be proven, skeptics such as Hume should
doubt it. But they do not. People rightly operate on the assumption that
other minds exist. Anyone who seriously doubted it and lived as if other
minds do not exist would be put in some kind of treatment facility. Another
first principle of common sense is that "we have some degree of power over
our actions, and the determinations of our will."[117] In other words, according to Reid, free will is a "natural conviction necessary for moral
responsibility."[118] (Reid was not intending to take a side in the age-old
Christian theological dispute over predestination.) Reid argued that if
Hume were on a jury his skepticism about free will would disappear as he
held the defendant guilty.

Reid's first principles of common sense are too many to mention or
discuss here. Suffice it to say that he believed in and cogently argued for the
philosophical relevance of certain basic assumptions embedded in all
normal human behavior; these can and should serve as guidance mecha-

---

[114]Quoted in ibid., 85.
[115]Ibid., 87.
[116]Ibid., 79.
[117]Ibid.
[118]Cuneo and van Woudenberg, "Introduction," 13.

nisms for science and religion. For example, Reid believed bad Enlightenment epistemology that ignored common sense was a great threat to theism and that theism is important for individual life and the social order. Perhaps one reason Reid has lost favor in much modern philosophy is that he was a Christian philosopher; "he never wavered from his theism or Christian belief, and a temperate, sincere faith pervades his writings and his biography."[119] Much of Reid's philosophy was aimed at shoring up natural theology and the rationality of belief in God and in God's revelation. He believed that "once one gets one's theory of knowledge and evidence right, there is no remaining threat to religious belief or natural religion" and "there is as much reason to believe that there is a supreme being, as that there are minds besides our own."[120]

Reid's philosophy answered Hume's skepticism and Kant's restriction of knowledge to the realm of appearances by arguing that it is philosophically right to trust our sense—up to a point. One of his basic principles of common sense is that "those things do really exist which we distinctly perceive by our senses, and are what we perceive them to be."[121] Thus, causality, though not itself actually perceived, can rightly be deduced from sense experience. That it cannot be known with absolute certainty as Hume meant is irrelevant. Everyone, including Hume, behaves as if it is true. Trying to deny it leads to absurdity. This is important because Reid wanted to breathe new life into the traditional arguments for the existence of God. He believed in the logical validity of the cosmological argument (the argument from finite things to an infinite First Cause) and the teleological argument (from evidence of design in creation to an intelligent Creator). These arguments work only because we can and should trust our experience and because a high degree of probability is sufficient proof beyond a reasonable doubt. The demand for indubitable proof leads nowhere.

There is much more to Reid's philosophy than can be expounded here. He believed in and defended miracles philosophically. He used Newton's laws of nature to argue for "providential naturalism"—that nature itself is the work of

---

[119]Dale Tuggy, "Reid's Philosophy of Religion," in *The Cambridge Companion to Thomas Reid*, ed. Terence Cuneo and René van Woudenberg (Cambridge: Cambridge University Press, 2004), 289.
[120]Ibid., 290, 295.
[121]Wolterstorff, "Reid on Common Sense," 79.

God. Reid was what many would call a religious rationalist or a rationalist Christian. His epistemology is a version of foundationalism. He believed, with Locke, that the truth of revelation and its interpretation must be determined and guided by reason.[122] For many conservative Christians (and others) Reid's philosophy provided a sophisticated alternative to Enlightenment-driven rationalism that leads to skepticism. Some would draw a more or less straight line from Descartes to Hume and Kant. Reid had the courage, they believe, to use appeal to common sense to rescue both science and religion from the debilitating effects of Enlightenment rationalism's restriction of knowledge to what can be proven beyond any doubt—an impossibly high standard for ordinary human beings. Later we will see that Reid's common sense realism was taken up and used to defend orthodox Protestantism against the acids of modernity by the conservative theologians of the Princeton School of theology in the mid- to late-nineteenth century (e.g., Charles Hodge).

What about science and its perceived threat to traditional Christian doctrine? Reid did not feel that orthodox Christianity was threatened by the scientific revolution; it was threatened only by wrong interpretations of science. For example, he believed with Paley that many scientific discoveries were supportive of belief in God. The more science discovered, he thought, the more evidence of intelligent design was found. But what about Newton's laws of nature? Didn't Newton prove, perhaps in spite of himself, that there is no room for God to act in the natural realm? Reid offered an ingenious theory that, for many traditional Christian theists, solves this problem. For him, Newton's natural laws do not lock God out of nature. Rather, "the physical laws of nature are the rules according to which the Deity commonly acts in his natural government of the world. . . . God is the cause of them."[123] Because God is their author and they are his creations and tools, there is no reason why God cannot suspend them or use them differently when necessary for his providential purposes. In other words, according to Reid, a miracle is not a divine violation of the laws of nature; it is God's unusual activity within or around his own regularities of action.

Coleridge emphasizes experience in religion. Coleridge is one of those odd people of Christian history who is difficult to categorize, but many

---

[122]Brown, *Christianity in Western Thought*, 1:265.
[123]Quoted in Cuneo and van Woudenberg, "Introduction," 15–16.

place him with the movement in early nineteenth-century Europe called romanticism. Before expounding Coleridge's philosophy and theology it will be helpful to explain the romantic movement of which he was a part. In brief, romanticism was an Enlightenment-based reaction to the over-rationalizing tendencies of the Enlightenment. In other words, the romantics were poets (such as Johann Goethe) and musicians (such as Ludwig Beethoven) and philosophers (such as Johann Hamann) who were firmly planted in modernity but dissatisfied with certain aspects of modernism. Some were religious and even Christian, and some were more pagan in their worldview. But all agreed that the eighteenth century that had contributed so much to European and American civilization failed to take seriously enough the emotional, affective side of human persons and the spiritual, dynamic and spontaneous side of nature. They were reacting against the idea of nature as a machine and the ideal human person as an emotionless, thinking subject. One way to describe the movement is that "the Romantics inverted the Enlightenment hierarchy and put the creative above the rational."[124] That is to say, they would have been revolted by the Sherlock Holmes character insofar as he was treated as the model of a modern man. The romantics did not want to return to a premodern philosophy, religion or way of life; they wanted to balance the Enlightenment's emphasis on reason with an equal emphasis on the affective, the intuitive, the mystical and the artistic.[125] One thing they all agreed about was that knowledge must not be limited to what can be proven rationally.

There was a decidedly spiritual side to the romantic movement; romanticists may not have all been Christians, but they had a "feeling for and longing for the infinite."[126] They believed in a kind of universal sixth sense or faculty not known to the rationalists and empiricists of the eighteenth century. Rationalism and empiricism are fine when conducting scientific experiments in the laboratory, but they fail miserably when trying to understand oneself and one's place in the universe. True meaning cannot be discovered by mechanical reason alone. Furthermore, nature should not be

---

[124]Steve Wilkens and Alan G. Padgett, *Christianity and Western Thought*, vol. 2: *Faith and Reason in the Nineteenth Century* (Downers Grove, IL: InterVarsity Press, 2000), 26.
[125]Ibid., 24.
[126]Ibid.

viewed as a machine composed of inert matter. The whole drift of the Enlightenment and scientific revolution had been in that direction—materialism. The romantics believed "there is something mysterious about nature . . . that simply cannot be explained by recourse to materialism."[127] For religious romanticists, "the whole of creation throbs with the very life of God; provided one develops the capacity to perceive it."[128]

Coleridge was a full participant in the English romantic movement, which was composed mostly of poets like himself. Their poetry has sometimes been described as "metaphysical poetry" because of its themes of nature as alive and its emphasis on beauty as a pointer to something divine within all of nature. "Theirs was an attempt to build from the raw material of human experience and identify points of contact with the divine."[129] That raw material included the cosmic awe one feels when observing and contemplating a rainbow or sunset and the sense of right and wrong in conscience. Coleridge specifically mentions three such "mysteries" (which he also called "ultimate facts" of human experience) that point toward the infinite and divine above or within nature: conscience, responsible will and evil.[130] The English romantics such as Coleridge valued apprehension over comprehension. However, it would be wrong to think of them as irrationalists; they simply wanted an expanded and more dynamic idea of reason.

One Coleridge scholar says he "epitomized" English romanticism.[131] But the same scholar, echoing many others, says that he is "one of the most enigmatic and fascinating figures in the history of Christian thought."[132] A few facts about Coleridge's life and career will show why. Like so many other great Christian thinkers, he was born into a minister's home; his father was a priest of the Church of England, and Samuel's upbringing and education were not unusual for that station in life. However, his father, with whom he was particularly close, died when the boy was only eight, and he was then sent to what was essentially an orphanage. He graduated from Jesus College, Cambridge University, where he came under the influence of many of the

---

[127]Robin Stockitt, *Imagination and the Playfulness of God* (Eugene, OR: Pickwick, 2011), 12.
[128]Ibid., 19.
[129]Ibid., 8–9.
[130]Samuel Taylor Coleridge, *Aids to Reflection* (Port Washington, NY: Kennikat Press, 1971), 156.
[131]Stockitt, *Imagination and the Playfulness of God*, 8.
[132]Ibid., ix.

leading philosophers of his time including Kant, but he was especially attracted to the romantic writers such as poet William Wordsworth. By his
own account young Samuel was sickly and bookish. Throughout his life he
tended to be absorbed in the life of the mind with a somewhat mystical bent.
He grew up to be a poet supported by wealthy patrons and is best known for
romantic poems such as *The Rime of the Ancient Mariner* (1798)—an epic
poem still widely read and studied in English courses.

Coleridge struggled. As a young adult he became disillusioned with orthodox Christianity and became Unitarian for ten years. Then he returned
to the Church of England and trinitarian orthodoxy. For a time he planned
to create and lead a utopian community in America, but that plan fell
through and left Coleridge somewhat depressed. Some contemporary
scholars believe he suffered what is now called bipolar disorder. He was ill
much of the time and became addicted to opium, then used as a pain medicine. He went through long periods of inactivity when he lived with friends;
these were followed by periods of intense writing. His greatest work is his
classic *Aids to Reflection* (1825)—a collection of aphorisms about philosophy,
spirituality and Christian theology. He exercised profound influence on
many later theologians including especially Bushnell (see 4.b.).

Once Coleridge returned to orthodox Christianity he passionately defended it in writings such as *Aids to Reflection*, but he did not defend it in
the same way as conservative Enlightenment thinkers such as Butler and
Paley (see 1.c.). In fact, Coleridge's foil for much of his exposition of true
Christianity was Paley the natural theologian. He considered Paley's defense of theism not much different from deism in that both placed their
trust in sensory evidence and logic. For Coleridge that sucks the life out of
Christianity. He was speaking of Paley's conservative theism as much as
deism when he wrote that "the utter rejection of all present and living communion with the universal spirit impoverishes deism itself, and renders it
as cheerless as atheism."[133] For him, the truth of Christianity lies not in evidences or apologetics but in the need of it and its ability to satisfy that need.
In other words, Coleridge based spiritual truth on spiritual experience
which he called "the light within me."[134] By "the light within" he did not

---

[133]Ibid., 117.
[134]Ibid., 160.

mean some special sense that only Christians have; he meant a universal, intuitive sense of the divine. To those who denied having such a thing he wrote, "If any man assert that he cannot find it, I am bound to disbelieve him. I cannot do otherwise without unsettling the very foundations of my own moral nature."[135] For him, the ultimate proof of the truth of Christianity is that it takes up that sense and fulfills it. The analogy of a lock and its key points to what he meant. Christianity, the gospel, is the key that unlocks and opens up the intuitive sense of the divine in every person; it fits it better than any other system. Against all natural religion and natural theology and rational apologetics he wrote "the light within me, that is, my reason and conscience, does assure me, that the ancient and Apostolic faith . . . is solid and true."[136] (By "my reason" here Coleridge meant something like Kant's practical reason—the inner conviction of the moral law as a signal of God's transcendence and presence.)

Ultimately, for Coleridge, the whole Enlightenment, from Descartes to Hegel (who was mostly yet to come) was a huge mistake insofar as it limited truth and knowledge to what reason as defined by foundationalism can know. For him, this is especially true for Christianity, which is the absolute religion, the fulfillment of the human heart's desires. The Enlightenment treated Christianity as a theory, as speculation. That kills it. Coleridge insists that true Christianity is "not a philosophy of life, but a life and a living process."[137] In other words, knowing its truth comes in trying it on. Trying it on requires childlike humility. One of his aphorisms is, "There is small chance of truth at the goal where there is not child-like humility at the starting-point."[138] For him, as for much of Christian tradition before Descartes, spiritual understanding follows believing: "Belief is the seed, received into the will, of which the understanding or knowledge is the flower, and the thing believed is the fruit."[139]

Coleridge's defense of the truth of Christianity is that, according to him, no one has ever sincerely and earnestly tried it and failed to find true satisfaction and fulfillment in it. To the person who asks, "How is this [Christianity] to be proved?" he answers:

---

[135]Ibid., 154.
[136]Ibid., 160.
[137]Ibid., 201.
[138]Ibid., 193.
[139]Ibid., 195.

It has been eighteen hundred years in existence: and has one individual left a record, like the following? "I tried it; and it did not answer. I made the experiment faithfully according to the directions; and the result has been a conviction of my own credulity [gullibility]." . . . I fear that the unbelief . . . has its source elsewhere than in the uncorrupted judgment; that not the strong free mind, but the enslaved will, is the true original infidel in this instance.[140]

And

The proper and natural effect, and . . . the certain and sensible accompaniment of peace (or reconcilement) with God is our own inward peace, a calm and quiet temper of mind. And where there is a consciousness of earnestly desiring and of having sincerely striven after the former, the latter may be considered as a sense of its presence.[141]

Coleridge's romanticism appears in his willingness to appeal to intuition and experience for knowledge of truth. It also appears in his insistence that this appeal is not irrational or against reason. "Coleridge is adamant that Christianity is rational but that current definitions of rationality are so severely restrictive that they neglect the most important aspects of our life."[142] For him reason must include intuition and imagination—God-given faculties that people ignore or suppress to their own great loss.

How is Coleridge's romanticism a response to modernity? That should by now be quite obvious. Partly because of him and Christian romanticists like him, modernity had to make room for spiritual experience. Not everyone agrees; many philosophers have continued to affirm materialism and foundationalism with its attendant skepticism about spiritual knowledge. However, romanticism forced the door of the Enlightenment open so that at least spiritual experience could not be ignored or brushed aside as sheer fanaticism. Coleridge was no fanatic. One thing is interesting and possibly instructive about Coleridge's philosophy and theology. If it is true, science and religion cannot conflict. One great advantage of a romanticized Christianity would lie therein. Of course, there may be a cost to that. Coleridge argued that spiritual truth and knowledge do not conflict with scientific or speculative reason; they simply "do not run on the same line . . . neither do

---

[140]Ibid., 202.
[141]Ibid., 117.
[142]Wilkens and Padgett, *Christianity and Western Thought*, 2:49.

they cut or cross" each other. Put another way in *Aids to Reflection*: "the mysteries in question [Christian doctrines such as the Trinity] are not in the direction of the understanding or the (speculative) reason. They do not move on the same line or plane with them, and therefore cannot contradict them."[143] He means that they cannot contradict each other because they are about entirely different matters. Again, we are back to Christianity being not about how the heavens go but how to go to heaven. Or maybe not quite. Coleridge did not cordon off Christianity so that it has nothing to do with other knowledge; instead he saw spiritual truth as lying deeper than the matters of science and philosophy and transcending them. Perhaps a way of expressing Coleridge's view is to say that, in spiritual matters, science and philosophy raise questions that only revelation, apprehended by faith (including intuition and imagination), can answer satisfactorily. According to one scholar of nineteenth-century theology commenting on Coleridge's achievement: "What most distinguished his own account of the venture of faith . . . was his effort to explicate the rationality of it, to show that this venture is neither against nor beyond nor apart from reason, but is reason's own highest moment."[144]

Earlier, reference was made to a possible cost of Coleridge's division between scientific, speculative reason and spiritual reason including intuition. The cost might be what one twentieth-century theologian, Wolfhart Pannenberg (b. 1928), called the "ghettoizing of theology," a term he used frequently throughout his writings. By that is meant any special pleading for religious truth claims where they are not subjected to the same rigorous canons of reasonableness as other disciplines. Throughout the nineteenth and twentieth centuries repeated attempts have been made to expel theology from European universities because of this perceived ghettoizing of it. Perhaps Coleridge would argue that so long as universities include departments of the arts they should also include departments of theology. Theology and art are more alike than theology and, say, physics. But that is a far cry from the medieval ideal of theology as the queen of the sciences.

Kierkegaard challenges religious rationalism. He has been called "the melancholy Dane" and the founder of existentialism, but Kierkegaard was a

---

[143]Coleridge, *Aids to Reflection*, 203.
[144]Welch, *Protestant Thought in the Nineteenth Century*, 1:126.

Danish Christian prophet whose message was heard but not heeded during his lifetime. Only much later, in the twentieth century, would Kierkegaard's challenge to modernity and especially Christendom come into its own as it was taken up into the theologies of (among others) Barth, Brunner and Reinhold Niebuhr—three of the main figures of so-called neo-orthodoxy or dialectical theology. Barth, perhaps the most influential theologian of the twentieth century, famously confessed, "If I have any system, it consists in this, that always as far as possible I keep in mind what Kierkegaard spoke of as the infinite qualitative difference between time and eternity . . . God is in heaven, you are on earth."[145] Kierkegaard was hardly heard, let alone heeded, outside his native Denmark until then.

Kierkegaard called himself a "powerless poet,"[146] but he also clearly saw himself as a prophet and martyr. He was not a martyr in the sense of being physically killed for his beliefs, but he subjected himself to a kind of martyrdom in life by abandoning the civil norms of Danish society and launching increasingly bitter attacks on it and its state church. The main target of his biting sarcasm and incisive criticism was Hegel and all his followers. In the process, however, he launched a literary crusade against all of modernity insofar as it related to religion and especially Christianity. His martyrdom was ridicule heaped on him by polite society.

Kierkegaard's strange life might best be grasped by a few brief stories beginning with his death and ending with his childhood. He died a recluse in Copenhagen, where he lived most of his life, at the relatively young age of forty-two. His final years had been consumed by written attacks on the Lutheran state church and its leaders. He had alienated most of his family and friends over seemingly minor disagreements. However, such was his reputation as a literary giant and critic of the powerful elites of church and society that more than a thousand people attended his funeral, which was, to say the least, controversial. Writing from the point of view of the Danish bishop, a Hegelian whom Kierkegaard loved to skewer, his biographer reports that

---

[145]Karl Barth, *The Epistle to the Romans*, trans. Edwyn C. Hoskins, 6th ed. (London: Oxford University Press, 1933), 10.

[146]Louis Dupré, *Kierkegaard as Theologian: The Dialectic of Christian Existence* (New York: Sheed and Ward, 1963), 210.

inside the coffin—reportedly quite a small one—that was being driven out to the family burial plot [from the church in downtown Copenhagen] that November day lay the corpse of a person who over the years had become so impossible that now, after his death, it was really not possible to put him anywhere. For where in the world could one get rid of a dead man who had carried on a one-man theological revolution during the final years of his life, calling the pastors cannibals, monkeys, nincompoops, and other crazy epithets? What sense did it make to give such a person a Christian burial in consecrated ground? That this same person also left behind a body of writing whose breadth, originality, and significance was unparalleled in his times did not, of course, make the situation any less painful.[147]

Perhaps it would help make understandable the bishop's ambivalence about allowing Kierkegaard to be buried in the consecrated cemetery if one reads one of the melancholy Dane's last descriptions of the bishop and his church:

> In the magnificent cathedral the Honorable and Right Reverend Geheime-General-Ober-Hof-Prädikant, the elect favorite of the fashionable world, appears before the elect company and preaches *with emotion* upon the text he himself has elected: "God hath elected the base things of the world and the things that are despised"—and nobody laughs.[148]

Needless to say, the bishop did not attend Kierkegaard's funeral. At the graveside service, with still the thousand mourners attending, the deceased's brother tried to give a solemn eulogy but was pushed aside by his nephew, who ranted about Danish society's mistreatment of his uncle. This was considered the height of uncivil behavior at the time, and the nephew was fined for it. Kierkegaard's epitaph was not exactly what he had prescribed when he knew he was dying: "Here Lies That Individual."

Kierkegaard was indeed an individual; he refused to be put into any category and that was true of his personal as well as his literary life.[149] His preferred identity was as "a witness to the truth." He believed that he saw

---

[147]Joakim Garff, *Søren Kierkegaard: A Biography*, trans. Bruce H. Kirmmse (Princeton, NJ: Princeton University Press, 2005), xvii-xviii.

[148]Søren Kierkegaard, *Attack upon "Christendom,"* trans. Walter Lowrie (Princeton, NJ: Princeton University Press, 1968), 181. This is not, of course, the actual title of any church leader in Denmark; Kierkegaard was engaging in irony. An idiomatic translation might be "the Honorable Right Reverend High and Mighty Preacher."

[149]The biographical points here are taken from Garff, *Søren Kierkegaard*.

what others did not see, and he felt called to use his writing skills to point it out to them—sometimes under a pseudonym, sometimes under his own name. He was a prolific writer and spent most of his time as an adult producing books and essays. Many of them were critiques of modern, middle-class, European culture; others were careful examinations of the structures of human existence. Many dealt with theological themes. Kierkegaard is usually classified as a philosopher, but he was just as much a theologian. The one overriding concern of all his works was "the individual before God." He believed that "normal society," including the state church, had lost the truth of Christianity and of authentic existence which, he never tired of saying, meant standing out from the crowd and responsibly deciding what to become regardless of the customs and habits of that society.

Earlier, reference was made to Kierkegaard's martyr complex. Sometimes he seemed to provoke controversy, even inviting attacks on himself, his reputation and even his sanity. *The Corsair* was a leading Danish literary journal for which Kierkegaard sometimes wrote articles. He and its editors had a falling out in late 1845 and early 1846; the editors dared to criticize him, and he struck back angrily. The volley of editorials and essays became personal. At one point Kierkegaard wrote to the journal, "may I request that I be abused. It is just too terrible to experience the insult of being immortalized by *The Corsair*."[150] The editors took him up on his request and launched a vicious series of attacks on Kierkegaard including insulting caricatures of him on his daily strolls around Copenhagen. Soon bands of little boys began following him around town calling him names and imitating his somewhat awkward gait. People gawked at him and gossiped about him in the streets. Eventually Kierkegaard retired to his apartment and rarely went out.

Kierkegaard never married. As a young man he proposed to the love of his life, a young woman named Regine Olsen. There is no question that he loved her; his journals reveal it plainly. However, he broke off the engagement without explanation, which, in mid-nineteenth-century polite society, was considered a terrible breach of civility. Scholars have speculated a great deal about the reasons for it. Some have suggested that Kier-

---

[150]Quoted in ibid., 399.

kegaard believed there was a curse on his family because, as a youth, his father had cursed God. (His father grew up to become a very devout pietist Christian.) More likely the philosopher came to the conclusion that marriage to him would ruin Regine because he knew well his personality problems. Also, he probably thought she would not care to engage with him in conversations about philosophy and theology, the only two subjects that really interested him. His journals reveal that he loved her from a distance for the rest of his life. Later, she married and lived a long and happy life.

Like many creative geniuses, Kierkegaard had a troubled family life. His parents were not poor, but there was something wrong at home. "Sickness and death burdened the spirits of the household in which there were few diversions in any event. Toys were seen as superfluous, and Søren Aabye [his middle name] had to make do with his mother's yarn spindle as his only toy."[151] Some of his siblings died, including one brother who died before he was born and after whom he was named. His father was a dour merchant who suffered a guilt complex that drove him to the edge of religious fanaticism. Søren's journals never fully reveal the great disappointment that caused a falling out with his father during his adult years, but the father-son relationship was complicated, to say the least. The adult Søren remembered how, as a child, his father rarely let him out of the house but marched up and down and across the large living room with him pretending they were going for hikes in the country. Most scholars agree that Kierkegaard's childhood had much to do with his melancholy outlook and his religious and philosophical pessimism.

Kierkegaard's literary output was voluminous, so only a few of his major books will be mentioned here and only those that bear on philosophy and Christianity: *Either/Or* (1843), *Fear and Trembling* (1843), *Philosophical Fragments* (1844), *Concluding Unscientific Postscript* (1846), *Sickness Unto Death* (1849), *Stages on Life's Way* (1845) and *Training in Christianity* (1850). Some of his last essays have been collected and published as *Attack upon "Christendom."* The philosopher wrote on so many subjects it is impossible to expound all of them even briefly, so here the concentration will be on his ideas that bear on modernity and Christianity.

---

[151]Ibid., 9.

The prevailing winds of philosophy in Kierkegaard's time, especially on the European continent, were in favor of Hegel's rationalist philosophy and approach to Christianity. Kierkegaard set his face against it because he considered it a complete betrayal of true Christianity. But his criticism strikes at much more than just Hegel; it strikes at the heart of all rational approaches to Christianity. Hegel, but not only he, emphasized a continuity between God and humanity, between faith and reason. And he emphasized an objective, rational approach to knowing ultimate reality including God. Kierkegaard's first contradiction to Hegel and the whole Enlightenment is to claim that "truth is subjectivity." This is the main point iterated and reiterated throughout *Concluding Unscientific Postscript*, perhaps Kierkegaard's most systematic statement of his philosophy. That "truth is subjectivity" has been widely misunderstood. By it he did not mean relativism—that all truth is merely true in relation to the individual. When Kierkegaard declared that truth is subjectivity, he did not mean that truth is merely subjective. Rather, as anyone who reads the *Postscript* will see, he meant the most important truth of life, truth about one's own self and God, about ultimate reality, is always only known subjectively—by personal appropriation in decision, risk and commitment. It cannot be known rationally in the way one knows about a planet or a law of physics. There, in the realms of the physical sciences, objective rationality reigns, but in the most important matters of life subjective faith is necessary for knowledge.

Kierkegaard's point is best expressed whenever he talks about how one becomes a Christian. Against both orthodoxy and modernism he eschewed a rational approach to becoming a Christian. Instead,

> Subjectively, what it is to become a Christian is defined thus: The decision lies in the subject. The appropriation is the paradoxical inwardness which is specifically different from all other inwardness. The thing of being a Christian is not determined by the *what* of Christianity but by the *how* of the Christian. This *how* can only correspond with one thing, the absolute paradox. . . . Faith is the objective uncertainty along with the repulsion of the absurd held fast in the passion of inwardness.[152]

---

[152]Søren Kierkegaard, *Concluding Unscientific Postscript to the "Philosophical Fragments,"* in *A Kierkegaard Anthology*, ed. Robert Bretall (Princeton, NJ: Princeton University Press, 1946), 255.

In this one statement Kierkegaard flies in the face of the entire trend of the Enlightenment as it bears on religion. Spiritual truth, truth about ultimate reality, truth about God and oneself, can be known only as paradox, through inward appropriation by means of decision, in the heat of passion. There is no impersonal, objective, rational path to knowledge of God and the things of God including the purpose and meaning of one's own life.

Another famous (or infamous) quote of Kierkegaard often misunderstood is that becoming a Christian requires a "leap of faith." By that he meant (contrary to what many have thought) that

> without risk there is no faith. . . . If I am capable of grasping God objectively, I do not believe, but precisely because I cannot do this I must believe. If I wish to preserve myself in faith I must constantly be intent upon holding fast the objective uncertainty, so that in the objective uncertainty I am out "upon the seventy thousand fathoms of water," and yet believe.[153]

The leap of faith, then, is not an irrational, blind jump into something dark and unknowable. It is the risk one takes with one's life when one decides passionately to entrust oneself entirely and without reserve to God whom no one can possess as an object. Kierkegaard was by no means changing the *what* of Christian belief; he held basically orthodox Christian doctrines to be true. The issue for him is the *how* of belief and the *in what* one believes. Orthodoxy had made doctrines the objective of faith; a person is a Christian by believing certain doctrines. Enlightenment natural religion and Kant and Hegel had made the path to right belief, whatever exactly that was, rational objectivity: in other words, no risk or passionate inwardness but only cool detached rationality. Kierkegaard's main point is that in matters of the physical sciences knowledge may be indifferent to the object being studied, but in matters of spiritual life one can never be indifferent and grasp truth. Spiritual knowledge requires commitment and commitment requires risk and decision. The true God cannot be known at the end of a syllogism or by believing doctrines, however true they may be.

Why cannot the true God be known at the end of a syllogism? Kierkegaard posits two reasons. First, because people are always "actively in error," and, second, because God is "wholly other" than creatures and thus

---

[153]Ibid., 215.

can be known only as paradox. Much of Kierkegaard's literary output is consumed with scrutiny of human sinfulness as self-deception. He was obsessed with original sin but not with it as a doctrine about a prehistorical fall in a mythical garden. For him, original sin is the human condition of bondage to illusion, anxiety and despair. Sin, he declared, is a condition brought on ourselves; it is not inherited. But we all bring it on ourselves. There can be no explanation for it; it just is. "Man," he averred, "forges the chains of his bondage with the strength of his freedom."[154] In an incisive analysis of human existence Kierkegaard argued that original sin, fallenness, is the misuse of freedom to try to go beyond finitude. In other words, it is the attempt to become God for ourselves. Clearly he saw this at work in Hegel's philosophical system that confuses God with humanity. Fallen people cannot work their way out of the chains of bondage they have forged for themselves; only grace can do that, and only the leap of faith, the passionate decision to trust in God alone to overcome anxiety and despair, reaches it. This can happen only to "one individual at a time."[155] It is an individual, personal decision where the sinner is confronted by God and decides to trust him. It always involves a crisis and humiliation; it is never the reluctant conclusion of an argument.

The other reason God cannot be known at the end of a syllogism is because God is both wholly other than humans (except in the incarnation) and always subject, never object.[156] Kierkegaard was repulsed by Hegel's concept of God as Absolute Spirit, the "true infinite" that includes the finite. For him this turned God into an idol. As Pascal said before Kierkegaard, "The God of the philosophers is not the God of Abraham, Isaac and Jacob!" Kierkegaard agreed wholeheartedly, and that because philosophical theology, such as Hegel's or deism, makes God over in humanity's image rather than allowing God to be God over against sinful humanity. God is both more transcendent and personal than philosophical theology can ever know. Faith in God is a relationship, not mere knowledge, and it is an embrace of paradox, not the rational discovery of a system or synthesis of opposites.

---

[154]Søren Kierkegaard, *Philosophical Fragments*, in *A Kierkegaard Anthology*, ed. Robert Bretall (Princeton, NJ: Princeton University Press, 1946), 160–61.

[155]Kierkegaard, *Postscript*, 207.

[156]Ibid., 211.

For Kierkegaard, the ultimate truth of Christianity cuts across all rational knowledge; it is a paradox that cannot be resolved. Remember that Hegel believed reason can resolve all antitheses in the greater whole of a grand synthesis (ultimately his own system). This he called "the dialectic" (thesis-antithesis-synthesis). Against this Kierkegaard opposed his own dialectic in which opposites cannot be united in synthesis. "When the eternal truth is related to an existing individual, it becomes a paradox."[157] His favorite example is the incarnation. The truth and reality that faith grasps in its leap of faith is absurd to reason. It is that "the eternal truth has come into being in time, that God has come into being, has been born."[158] The paradox of the incarnation, however, is not just a fact to be learned and held in the mind. It is not just a doctrine to be believed. It is the ultimate fact that determines the believer's existence; it is the whole foundation of the believer's relationship with God.

Kierkegaard's life project was to understand Christianity—what it meant to be a Christian in Christendom.[159] He came to the conclusion that much that passes under the label "Christian" is not authentic. "When Christianity is made so attractive that pretty nearly everyone accepts it as a matter of course, then one can be sure it is not true Christianity that is being presented—not the Christianity of Him who made the taking up of one's cross the condition of discipleship."[160] He believed that the thrust of modernity had become to make Christianity tame and harmless, to bring it under people's possession and control. For him,

> Modern man has lost this notion [of true faith]. He sees everything historically and en masse. Christianity for him is an age-old philosophy of life which over the centuries has proved itself sufficiently that one need not commit himself personally to it. Thus Christianity loses its transcendent value; it does not shock any longer. . . . Everyone must rediscover himself as an individual alone before God. Christianity cannot be handed down in a tradition; every man who comes into this world must be shocked anew, and, in this shock, advance to faith or fall into despair.[161]

---

[157]Ibid., 219.
[158]Ibid., 220.
[159]Robert Bretall, "Introduction," in *A Kierkegaard Anthology*, ed. Robert Bretall (Princeton, NJ: Princeton University Press, 1946), xx.
[160]Ibid., xxiii.
[161]Dupré, *Kierkegaard as Theologian*, 36–37.

Clearly, from all that has been said (and it is so little compared with what Kierkegaard wrote on the subject), Kierkegaard's philosophy of life and view of Christianity conflicted with modernity's. And yet, he was not a premodern man. He did not advocate believing on authority, even the authority of the Bible (to say nothing of the authority of any church). Nor was he a mystic; he had no use for a universal "light within" or union with God through contemplation. His modernity showed in how he put the human individual, the human subject, at the center of his philosophy. For him, in "true Christianity [the individual] is first related to God and only secondarily to the community."[162] In the true church, the church militant, there are only individuals.[163] The true Christian is the "knight of faith," who, like Abraham, risks all to obey God's call even when doing so goes against everything tradition and the community believes and says. This kind if individualism is rarely found outside of modernity.

What was Kierkegaard's solution to the war between science and religion that developed during early modernity and goes on still in the twenty-first century? If Kierkegaard is right, the war is unnecessary. Science deals objectively with the objective world. It is about rational investigation of nature and its laws. True religion, Christianity, is about a relationship that is wholly subjective, inward, paradoxical and unknowable to science or philosophy *as* philosophy. The only problem for Kierkegaard (or any Kierkegaardian) is when science and philosophy overstep their boundaries and attempt to dabble in that relationship (e.g., saying it is an illusion because it cannot be proven). Kierkegaard picks up true religion, Christianity, and holds it above the fray of philosophy and science. They cannot touch it. And as for certainty, Kierkegaard has no use for it. True Christianity is about "objective uncertainty" which is faith, a miracle that happens only by decision, risk and passionate commitment. "The truth is precisely a venture which chooses an objective uncertainty with the passion of the infinite."[164]

Three Christian thinkers responded to modernity from within it. What has appeared in this section is that not all modern Christian thinkers bowed to modernity or accommodated to its acids. Reid and Scottish common

---

[162]Ibid., 198.
[163]Ibid., 197.
[164]Kierkegaard, *Postscript*, 214.

sense realism debated the Enlightenment's tendency to ignore or scoff at common sense experience. For Reid, knowledge includes much more than what can be proved by reason or sensory evidence, but Christianity is nevertheless closely related to, if not dependent on, rational arguments. It is still theoretically possible for objective reasoning, science in the broadest sense, to falsify Christianity; they do not exist in separate, watertight compartments. Nevertheless, once common sense, as Reid defined it, is allowed back into philosophy Christianity can be established as objectively true to a very high degree of probability.

Coleridge and romanticism reacted to modernity by rejecting rationalism in spiritual matters; reason must be expanded and made more flexible to account for all of human experience including the artistic and the spiritual. Theology is more like an art than a science in the modern sense. It begins with the inner light and uses broadened and deepened reasoning to understand what is already believed by faith. Science and theology cannot conflict any more than science and art can conflict.

Kierkegaard and existentialism responded to modernity by severing all ties between objective reason and faith so that, to the former, what the latter knows is absurd. What faith knows, however, is not at all like what science knows. The sciences study things; faith enters into a new world through a new relationship. When rational philosophy attempts to study God it only always creates an idol. True Christianity is from above and unknowable by things and methods from below. So, science and true religion, Christianity, cannot conflict; they exist in separate, watertight compartments.

Throughout modern theology, beginning with Schleiermacher, the subject of the next chapter, the crisis modernity brings to traditional Christianity and these broad philosophical responses, including deism, Kant and Hegel, will influence the ways in which Christian theologians respond to, react against or attempt to come to terms with and accommodate to modernity.

2

LIBERAL THEOLOGIES
RECONSTRUCT CHRISTIANITY
IN LIGHT OF MODERNITY

The story of modern theology begins with the rise of liberal Protestant theology. And liberal Protestant theology (henceforth, liberal theology) began with Friedrich Schleiermacher, who will be the subject of the first section of this chapter. There were liberalizing Christian thinkers before Schleiermacher, but they were not professional, church-related theologians. Schleiermacher was the first person in history to be both liberal and a professional theologian—someone paid to teach Christian theology. Previous subjects here have all been philosophers or writers or both. The ones we would call free thinkers (e.g., Toland and Tindal) were tolerated by the state and state church in part, at least, because they were not theologians.

What is liberal theology? It is a label much abused. Many people call any religious view they disagree with and think is somehow modern, as opposed to traditional, liberal theology. In that sense, even some conservative theologians have been labeled liberal by people more conservative than they. In other words, in much everyday usage "liberal theology" is what philosophers call an indexical term. It has no definite, established meaning; its meaning is tied inextricably to the user's own theology. For example, this

writer once taught at a Christian liberal arts college where the main Old
Testament professor espoused amillennialism—the belief that the thousand-
year reign of Christ during which Satan is bound (Rev 20) is the church age
and that there will be no literal thousand-year reign of Christ on the earth
after he returns (premillennialism). The majority of the college's constituents had, over the years, come to believe in premillennialism, so many of
them accused the Old Testament professor, whose view was the dominant
one for most of church history, of being liberal. He was not—he believed in
the inerrancy of the Bible! But because his interpretation of the Bible was an
unusual one to many constituents, they automatically labeled his view
liberal. That is not the meaning of "liberal theology" here. Here liberal theology will be treated as a historical movement and type of theology that
arose within Protestant churches and their teaching institutions in the
nineteenth century. It was and is a distinctly modern theology, which is
why its conservative critics often called it modernism.

Liberal theology is best defined as "maximal acknowledgement of the
claims of modern thought"[1] within Christian theology. It began as a
movement and type of theology within Protestantism in Europe, but later it
extended into some sectors of Catholic theology, where it has traditionally
been called modernism. In other words, it is not just any revision of traditional doctrine; it is revision and reconstruction of Christian doctrine in the
light of modernity, with "the best of modern thought" serving as both a
source and a norm for doctrinal critique and construction.[2] This was some-

---

[1]Claude Welch, *Protestant Thought in the Nineteenth Century*, vol. 1: *1799–1870*. (New Haven, CT:
Yale University Press, 1972), 142. There are other definitions of liberal theology, and one of the
leading ones is by liberal theologian Gary Dorrien of Union Theological Seminary in New York
City. In his three-volume history of American liberal theology entitled *The Making of American
Liberal Theology* (Louisville, KY: Westminster John Knox, 2001–2006) he defines liberal theology
as the idea that "Christian theology can be genuinely Christian without being based upon external authority" (*The Making of American Liberal Theology: Imagining Progressive Religion 1805–1900*
[2001], 1:1). However, Dorrien goes on to define it further in a way that seems in complete agreement with Welch: "Since the eighteenth century, liberal Christian thinkers have argued that religion should be modern and progressive and that the meaning of Christianity should be interpreted from the standpoint of modern knowledge and experience" (ibid.).
[2]By "source" here (and later) is meant that body of knowledge on which theology draws for carrying
out its critical and constructive tasks. Two traditional sources of theology are Scripture and tradition. By "norm" here (and later) is meant a criterion of truth, a touchstone of right belief. Scripture
and tradition have traditionally been treated as norms as well as sources of theology, but reason
has often also been used by traditional theologians as a norm if not a source of theological truth.
Liberal theology introduces modern thought as a source and norm of correct theology.

thing new. Never before in Christian history had any theologian openly admitted that his or her culture rightly functioned as a norm for theology's content. Nevertheless, looking back on the history of Christian theology, it is not difficult to see where culture, meaning especially some philosophy arising outside Christianity, functioned that way in spite of theologians' intentions. For example, some early church fathers such as Justin Martyr and Clement of Alexandria borrowed heavily from Hellenistic culture, especially Platonic philosophy, to express Christian beliefs in the largely pagan Roman Empire. Many would say they absorbed elements of Hellenism into their doctrines. The great church father Augustine was undeniably influenced by a philosophy called Neoplatonism, and the medieval Catholic theologian Thomas Aquinas drew heavily on the philosophy of Aristotle.

The difference between these historical uses of philosophy and liberal theology's is the latter consciously and reflectively accommodated to modernity. This theological method is best expressed by a late-twentieth-century self-identified liberal theologian who contrasts "conservative theology" with "liberal theology":

> As I understand it, conservative Christianity at its best will say "We ought to listen to the hypotheses of the present and take from them what we can, but ultimately the truth has been given to us in the past, particularly in Jesus, and the acceptance of that is our ultimate obligation. Everything the contemporary world might say must be judged by its conformity to biblical revelation."
>
> Liberalism at its best is more likely to say, "We certainly ought to honor the richness of the Christian past and appreciate the vast contribution it makes to our lives, but finally we must live by our best modern conclusions. The modern consensus should not be absolutized; it, too, is always subject to criticism and further revision. But our commitment, however tentative and self-critically maintained, must be to the careful judgments of the present age, even if they differ radically from the dictates of the past."[3]

For liberal theology, the "judgments of the present age" are driven by modernity. No liberal theologian would say that Christianity must bow to or accept uncritically whatever modernity says. However, liberal theology *is* the tendency to accommodate to modernity, in its present form at the

---

[3]Delwin Brown, in Clark Pinnock and Delwin Brown, *Theological Crossfire: An Evangelical/Liberal Dialogue* (Grand Rapids, MI: Zondervan, 1990), 23.

time, as far as possible without sacrificing the essence of Christianity. Critics argue that liberal theologians kept changing Christianity's essence to allow maximal accommodation to modernity.

Liberal theology's heyday, its age of development and optimism for dominance, was the nineteenth century (defined as 1799 to 1914—a cultural period more than a specific century).[4] Its leading theologians were strongly influenced by the Enlightenment including especially Descartes, Locke, Hume, Kant and Hegel but also romanticism. (They were not influenced by Kierkegaard, whose legacy for theology had to wait until after World War II.) That is not to say any of them agreed completely with the Enlightenment, but they all thought it was a permanent cultural revolution that could not be opposed without Christianity losing all credibility in the modern world.

Liberal theology is best understood by studying the leading liberal theologians (not always their popularizers): Schleiermacher, Albrecht Ritschl (1822–1889), Adolf Harnack (1851–1930), Walter Rauschenbusch (1861–1918) and others. However, a few commonalities can be distilled from their writings; these might help readers understand what the liberal movement in theology was and where that liberal theological ethos is still alive today.[5] First, a person, church or Christian organization is not historically, classically liberal without taking modernity seriously as an authoritative source and norm for contemporary theological reconstruction. Just because a theologian proposes something new does not make him or her liberal. Real liberal theology aims at reconstructing Christian doctrines to balance contemporary cultural relevance with faithfulness to Christian sources. Usually, and this is probably the *sine qua non* of liberal theology, relevance to contemporary culture is given equal if not greater weight than faithfulness to traditional Christian sources.

---

[4]Welch famously defined "nineteenth-century Protestant thought" as Christian theology from 1799 to 1914—from the publication of Schleiermacher's *On Religion: Speeches to Its Cultured Despisers* that launched a whole new era in Christian theology to the beginning of World War I, which brought a crisis in Christian theology that forced a change in the optimism of nineteenth-century theology. See Welch, *Protestant Thought in the Nineteenth Century*.

[5]For those who wonder from where I derive this portrayal of liberal theology I will mention some of my main sources, many of which are written by liberal theologians: Dorrien and Welch (already cited); Kenneth Cauthen, *The Impact of American Religious Liberalism*, 2nd ed. (Lanham, MD: University Press of America, 1983); William R. Hutchison, *The Modernist Impulse in American Protestantism* (Oxford: Oxford University Press, 1976); Peter Hodgson, *Liberal Theology: A Radical Vision* (Minneapolis: Augsburg Fortress, 2007); Donald E. Miller, *The Case for Liberal Christianity* (San Francisco: Harper, 1981).

Second, liberal theology was imbued with optimism about human potential; it tended be anthropocentric in its outlook and method. A favorite saying of the optimistic nineteenth-century *Zeitgeist* was, "Every day in every way things are getting better and better." Some people believed that the Enlightenment and scientific revolution would usher in a near utopia on earth—especially if Christians would get on board its progressive bandwagon. After World War I in Europe and World War II in the United States, scholars talk about "chastened liberalism" as this optimism dropped away.

Third, liberal theology does theology from below. There are two ways of doing theology: from above and from below. "From above" means accepting the authority of special revelation from God and interpreting it with the intention of constructing sound Christian doctrine. (This does not have to mean ignoring contemporary context; from above has to do with sources and norms for determining correct beliefs.) "From below" means beginning theological reflection with human experience and attempting to determine from that what can and should be believed. Traditional Christian natural theology was the attempt to do both—from below only as a rational support for what is believed from above. Liberal theology endeavors to discover knowledge about God from universal human experience. That does not mean rejecting revelation from above, but it does mean submitting that revelation to the criterion of human experience as its judge. Most often, it means believing that there is a revelation of God embedded in human experience.

Fourth, liberal theology tends to interpret the Bible critically, meaning that the Bible is recognized as the primary Christian classic but not as supernaturally inspired or infallible. Liberal theology appeared and grew up alongside the rise of higher criticism of the Bible—the effort to interpret the Bible historically like any other ancient book or collection of books. That does not mean that all liberal theologians reject any inspiration or authority of the Bible. Usually the Bible is said to be inspired "insofar as it is inspiring." Its authority is not absolute because there is no absolute authority except God, and nobody has direct access to God's mind.

To be sure, there are other common traits of classical liberal Protestant theology, but these are the programmatic ones that are necessary even to begin to understand the thoughts about Christianity of Schleiermacher and other liberal theologians. Other typical traits that are not necessarily universal but common among liberal theologians are a tendency to be skeptical about the supernatural and miracles (because of the scientific revolution); a general focus on Jesus' humanity and a tendency to reinterpret his deity as some aspect of his humanity; a preference for universalism—belief in the salvation of all people; and an assumption that truth can be found in all world religions even if Christianity is the absolute religion that fulfills the truth in all others.

2.A. FRIEDRICH SCHLEIERMACHER LAUNCHES A COPERNICAN REVOLUTION IN THEOLOGY

Scholars of modern Christian theology almost universally hail Schleiermacher as the father of modern theology. He has been called a "prince of the church" and one of the few giants of Christian thought,[6] the most influential theologian since John Calvin[7] and the founder of modern religious and theological thought.[8] He is to Christianity what Copernicus was to astronomy, Newton was to physics, Freud was to psychology and Darwin was to biology. That is to say, he was *the* trailblazer and trendsetter, the one thinker subsequent theologians cannot ignore. He is accorded such prominence not because he founded a particular school of theology or because all modern Christian theologians are his disciples. Rather, he deserves this place of honor because he initiated a new era in theology—an era that has lasted for nearly two hundred years and dominated by so-called liberal theology, including post–World War II chastened liberalism, and the various reactions to it.

Keith Clements was right to say that "over a whole range of issues Schleiermacher foreshadows approaches which we recognize as distinctively 'modern' or, as some may prefer, 'liberal.'"[9] No Christian theologian before him faced as squarely the problems posed for traditional Christianity by the scientific and philosophical revolutions of the Enlightenment. And

---

[6]Brian Gerrish, *A Prince of the Church: Schleiermacher and the Beginnings of Modern Theology* (Philadelphia: Fortress, 1984), 20.

[7]Richard R. Niebuhr, *Schleiermacher on Christ and Religion* (New York: Scribner, 1964), 6.

[8]Robert R. Williams, *Schleiermacher the Theologian: The Construction of the Doctrine of God* (Philadelphia: Fortress, 1978), 1.

[9]Keith W. Clements, *Friedrich Schleiermacher, Pioneer of Modern Theology* (London: Collins, 1987), 7.

none strove so valiantly to reconstruct Christian doctrines to make them compatible with the spirit of his age.

What is especially significant about Schleiermacher is not his particular reconstructions of Christian doctrines, as interesting as they may be, but the method and approach he took in trying to disentangle Christian beliefs from conflicts with modern thought and scientific discoveries. Whether or not he was conscious of it, he seems to have been driven by a desire to redefine both religion and Christianity so that they are immune from the acids of modernity. Some of his critics accuse him of using some of those acids to dissolve classical Christian orthodoxy, but he regarded his project not as rejection of anything but as reconstruction of almost everything in the light of classical Christian sources and human experience. Because his method and approach to doing theology were revolutionary and influential, that will be our focus here; some of his specific doctrinal revisions will be discussed to illustrate how he practiced his new method of theology.

Schleiermacher becomes the most influential theologian in Germany. Schleiermacher was not a theologian working out of sight of the public and without interaction with them. Quite the opposite, in fact. He was a cultural hero whose funeral in February 1834 was attended by tens, if not hundreds, of thousands of ordinary Berliners lining the streets in mourning as his funeral cortege passed by. He had served as a military chaplain and was regarded as a Prussian patriot and social and political reformer. He was widely known as one of the greatest preachers of his time, preaching eloquent sermons from the pulpit of Berlin's Trinity Church. He was a sought-after socialite who was invited to many of Berlin's salon gatherings to discuss the arts and culture. He helped found the University of Berlin and became dean of its theological faculty. He translated Plato's works into German and wrote numerous books on various subjects including a life of Jesus. His magnum opus was a systematic theology titled *The Christian Faith* (1821–1822, revised in 1830). Most scholars agree with Clements that "nothing on such a scale, and so systematic, had appeared in Protestantism since John Calvin's *Institutes of the Christian Religion* nearly three centuries earlier."[10] In this mammoth work Schleiermacher presented a system of Christian doctrine for modern people.

---

[10]Ibid., 33.

In order to understand Schleiermacher's project in theology it is important to visit his youth and education. His father was a minister of the Reformed Church who served as a chaplain in the Prussian army. When Friedrich was ten, the elder Schleiermacher had a deeply emotional religious experience through the ministry of a pietist sect known as the Moravians. They were a group of deeply devout Christians from Bohemia who settled in the eastern part of Germany in the seventeenth century and were instrumental in the evangelical renewal across Europe and in Great Britain. John Wesley was also influenced by them, as was Kierkegaard. Like all pietists, the Moravians believed in "heart Christianity" over "head Christianity." That is, they placed doctrinal knowledge second to experience of Christ in the "inner man" through conversion and a personal relationship with Jesus. They were forerunners of contemporary evangelicalism.

At age fourteen Schleiermacher was sent to a pietist boarding school and later to a pietist seminary. Somewhere in his early education he began to develop doubts about certain key doctrines of orthodoxy. In a letter to his father he expressed skepticism about the substitutionary atonement of Christ. His father reacted harshly, nearly disowning the son. Although they later reconciled, Friedrich never recovered his early acceptance of orthodox doctrines, much to his father's dismay. However, the pietist emphasis on experience and even feeling, "Christian affections," never left him. In a letter to his sister he affirmed that he was still a pietist only of a "higher order." His drift away from orthodox Protestant theology continued during his studies at the pietist university of Halle, where he came into contact with the philosophy of Kant and read widely in Enlightenment philosophies in general.

In addition to pietism and Enlightenment philosophy Schleiermacher was influenced by the relatively new movement called romanticism that swept through Berlin around the turn of the nineteenth century. As already discussed, romanticism was a reaction to the cold rationalism of the Enlightenment; it placed emphasis on human feeling, imagination and intuition. Consequently, it valued poetry and music as means of human self-realization and self-expression. Many of the young Schleiermacher's friends in the salon culture of Berlin were influenced by romanticism and thought they were not capable of being religious or Christian because they also accepted the Enlightenment's critiques of traditional dogmas. For many of them, romanticism served as a kind of quasi-religion. Schleiermacher's first book was addressed to these friends; its title was *On Religion: Speeches to Its Cultured Despisers* (1799). In it he tried to defend religion against the common misunderstandings that it is little more than dead orthodoxy or authoritarian moralism that stifles individual freedom and alienates people from their humanity. Early on, Schleiermacher was attempting to bring together in a kind of synthesis pietism, Enlightenment rationalism and romanticism.

In *On Religion* Schleiermacher tried to persuade religion's "cultured despisers" that true religion is a matter of universal human "feeling" (*Gefühl*) and has little to do with dogmas. True religion, he urged, is "an immediate relation to the living God, as distinct from submission to doctrinal or creedal propositions about God."[11] *On Religion* represents one of the first truly modern studies of religion and earned its author the reputation of a youthful genius.

Schleiermacher's two great books of theology are *On Religion* and *The Christian Faith.* To conservatives, orthodox traditionalists, these books represented a capitulation to the antisupernatural spirit of the Enlightenment age, a thinly disguised attempt to talk about humanity as if it were talk about God. To progressives they represented a liberation from outmoded authoritarian dogmas to a truly modern form of Christianity that would not conflict with science and would still be reasonable and relevant to contemporary culture. The books unleashed a hurricane of harsh criticism with charges of pantheism and the like. One critic composed a cruel play on words using the literal meaning of Schleiermacher's name ("maker of veils"):

> Der nackten Wahrheit Schleier machen,
> Ist kluger Theologen Amt,
> Und Schleiermacher sind bei so bewandten Sachen
> Die meister der Dogmatik insgesamt.
> (To make veils for the naked truth
> is the job of clever theologians;
> all masters of dogmatics are "Schleiermachers.")[12]

---

[11]Ibid., 24.
[12]Quoted in Karl Barth, *The Theology of Schleiermacher* (Grand Rapids, MI: Eerdmans, 1982), 186.

In spite of the criticism, Schleiermacher's books, especially *The Christian Faith*, also unleashed a flood of revisionist theologies seeking to follow Schleiermacher's steps in refashioning Christianity to speak meaningfully to modern, increasingly secularized audiences.

Schleiermacher died February 12, 1834, of pneumonia. His death came while he was taking communion with his family. As mentioned earlier, his death evoked a great response from the people of Berlin. His funeral eulogist, H. Steffens, described the scene:

> Never has a funeral similar to this taken place. It was not something arranged but a completely unconscious, natural outpouring of mourning love, an inner boundless feeling which gripped the entire city and gathered about his grave; these were hours of inward unity such as have never been seen in a metropolis of modern times.[13]

Schleiermacher responds to the Enlightenment and develops a new theological method. Schleiermacher's theology arose largely as a response to the cultural and intellectual context of his time. It was not a comfortable era for orthodox Christianity. The spirit of the age promoted a relative indifference, if not hostility, to religion.[14] The French writer Voltaire, for example, attacked the church so vehemently that he was driven out of Paris and spent much of his life in exile. In Germany certain philosophers raised serious questions about the right of theology to occupy places in the universities alongside other, more rational, disciplines. The French Revolution enthroned the "Goddess of Reason" in the Notre Dame cathedral in Paris.

In the midst of all this turmoil Schleiermacher discovered in romanticism a good-luck piece for making Christianity relevant to its "cultured despisers." In part, at least, the romanticists were children of the Enlightenment. They shared its fear of authority and dogmatic belief systems. But they wished to recover a sense of the livingness of nature and of the power of human feeling and imagination—all of which they thought had been lost in the rationalism and materialism of the Enlightenment. In this romantic emphasis on feeling Schleiermacher found his clue for reconstructing Christianity so that it would not conflict with the fundamental spirit of his increasingly modern culture.

---

[13]Martin Redecker, *Schleiermacher: Life and Thought*, trans. John Wallhausser (Philadelphia: Fortress, 1973), 213.

[14]Clements, *Friedrich Schleiermacher*, 11.

The English Enlightenment poet Alexander Pope succinctly expressed the spirit of modern culture: "Know then thyself; presume not God to scan. The proper study of mankind is man." The spirit of modernity is radically anthropocentric. But what if one could study God by studying humanity? What if one could truly know oneself only by knowing God and vice versa? What if it could be shown that religion in general and Christianity in particular are not inimical to humanity but essential to its true fulfillment?

Schleiermacher's ingenious and controversial project was to do just that—to base theology on human experience by showing that religion is rooted in and even identical with an experience essential to humanity.[15] And he attempted to reconstruct Christian doctrine so that it does not elevate God at humanity's expense but brings the two together in an intrinsic way. In contrast to Kant and Hegel, however, his endeavor was not to focus on practical reason (morality) or the history of culture (Hegel) but on intuition. He looked to a fundamental, universal human feeling that he called *Gefühl*—a German word with no exact English translation. By it he meant a fundamental, universal sense of being utterly dependent on the whole of reality, the infinite, God. For him this universal sense of God, this human intuition of God, functioned as a religious a priori—something that does not come at the end of an investigation but always already exists and cannot be denied without denying oneself.

Schleiermacher's theological method is called a Copernican revolution in theology because it put human experience, rather than authoritative revelation, at the center of the theological enterprise. He sought to avoid the pitfalls of traditional orthodoxy with its inflexible dogmatism and deism with its bland natural religion by treating theology as human reflection on human experience of God. Thus, religious experience, something he considered common to all people and nearly identical with being human, would become the true source of theological reflection instead of timeless truths of revelation, which he did not think existed.

The key to the success of his theological revolution lay in Schleiermacher's ability to establish religion as fundamental to human nature and existence and not reducible to anything else. In *On Religion* he attempted to

---

[15]Ibid., 15.

explicate the true nature of religion by mining both his own pietist heritage and the new phenomenon of romanticism. He tried to show that the essence of religion lies not in rational proofs of God's existence or in supernaturally revealed doctrines or in churchly rituals and formalities but in a "fundamental, distinct, and integrative element of human life and culture"[16]—the feeling of being utterly dependent on something infinite that manifests itself in and through finite beings. In other words, religion is not something some people have and others do not have, nor is it something that must be somehow acquired. Rather, religion is instinctive and intuitive within every human person.

This innate religious experience, *Gefühl*, does not connote a sensation; it is not "feeling" in the usual sense. Rather, for Schleiermacher, it is a deep, inner sense or awareness. It is "the immediate consciousness of the universal being of all finite things in and through the infinite, of all temporal things in and through the eternal."[17] Religion, then, is "to seek and to find this infinite and eternal factor in all that lives and moves, all growth and change, in all action and passion, and to have and to know life itself only in immediate feeling."[18] In other words, it is something like cosmic awe—the feeling of being very small and dependent and part of a greater whole that one sometimes has when looking at a beautiful sunset or a newborn baby. Remember that Schleiermacher was a romanticist! For him, this religious feeling (sometimes called piety and sometimes God-consciousness) is basic and universal in human experience; all people have it whether they reflect on it or not. And it cannot be reduced to some other aspect of experience such as reason or conscience.[19] Although it is totally distinct from these, Schleiermacher argued (in *On Religion*), it is just as essential to understanding humanity. Reason and conscience give rise to science and morality; piety gives rise to religion.

Consequently, and this is especially significant for our story of modern theology, Schleiermacher was willing to waive "all claims to anything belonging

---

[16]Terrence N. Tice, "Introduction," in Friedrich Schleiermacher, *On Religion: Addresses in Response to Its Cultured Critics*, trans. Terrence N. Tice (Richmond, VA: John Knox, 1969), 12.
[17]Schleiermacher, *On Religion*, 79.
[18]Ibid., 77.
[19]Ibid., 80.

to the two domains of science and morality."[20] But in return he wanted religion's cultured despisers to recognize religion as something *sui generis*—human in its own right and kind—and to refrain from trying to subsume it under science or ethics. Religion, he asserted, has a reality all its own: "Piety presents itself to you as the necessary and indispensable third to science and morality, as their natural counterpart, one no less endowed with that dignity and excellence which you attribute to them."[21] Schleiermacher was declaring theology's independence from science and ethics; the latter cannot conflict with the former because it is about something entirely different.

Not only did Schleiermacher want to distinguish piety and religion from science and morality, but also he wanted to distinguish them from dogmas and systems of theology. The latter are in themselves alien to true religion and are at best only human attempts to set forth piety in speech.[22] Religion can get along quite well without dogmas and concepts, he averred, but reflection on religious feeling needs and therefore creates them.[23] In other words, dogmas and concepts are inevitable products of religion, but religion is feeling and not them.

What about theology? If religion is feeling, what is theology? In the broadest and most general sense theology is human reflection on religion, that is, on piety or God-consciousness. However, Schleiermacher did not believe there is any such thing as generic religion, for piety always expresses itself in some concrete form of religious life and through some religious community. He adamantly opposed the Enlightenment search for "the" natural religion divorced from any concrete religious tradition or community and its form of worship ("positive religion").[24] Therefore, reflection on religion, which theology is, is always reflection on some particular form of religious life in light of God-consciousness.

In his systematic theology, *The Christian Faith*, Schleiermacher defined theology as the attempt to set forth the Christian religious affections in

---

[20]Ibid., 77.

[21]Ibid., 80.

[22]"Christian doctrines are accounts of the Christian religious affections set forth in speech." Friedrich Schleiermacher, *The Christian Faith*, ed. H. R. Mackintosh and J. S. Stewart, 2nd ed. (Philadelphia, Fortress, 1928), 76.

[23]Schleiermacher, *On Religion*, 140.

[24]Ibid., 300.

speech.[25] Christianity is a form of universal human piety, of being in dependent relation to God. He recognized a specific form of piety he called
the Christian God-consciousness. This is what he meant by "Christian religious affections"—the feeling of being totally dependent on the redemptive
work of Jesus Christ for the fulfillment of one's own relationship to God.
The Christian experience of God-consciousness formed and fulfilled in and
through Jesus Christ is the essence of Christianity: "the distinctive essence
of Christianity consists in the fact that in it all religious emotions are related
to the redemption wrought by Jesus of Nazareth."[26] Rather than being the
project of systematizing some supernaturally revealed set of propositions,
Christian theology attempts to set forth a coherent account of the Christian
religious experience. Because it is fundamentally an experience of God mediated in and through Jesus Christ, all doctrines must be centered around
and relate to him and his redemptive work.[27]

In other words, for Schleiermacher, theology is reflection on religious
feelings, on God-consciousness, attempting to put them into words. Everyone has God-consciousness to some degree of intensity. It exists in everyone,
if only subconsciously, as a potential for knowing God more personally and
relationally. That is religion. But religion always seeks to come to expression
in some specific and concrete form, in some relatively organized expression.
Christianity is the religion that has the ability to fulfill that potential of
God-consciousness for knowing God personally and relationally which is
redemption. Jesus Christ is the Redeemer because he had full and complete
God-consciousness. Christianity mediates his God-consciousness to his
followers. Theology is the attempt to bring these feelings and experiences to
expression in words and concepts, but the words and concepts are not
themselves part of God-consciousness or of the experience of being redeemed through Jesus Christ.

Schleiermacher's innovation in theology was his "turn to the believing
subject" and his or her religious experiences as the primary source and
norm for examining and reconstructing doctrines. Not some body of divinely revealed information but the experience of believers is the subject

---

[25]Schleiermacher, *Christian Faith*, 76. For the exact quote see n. 17 above.
[26]Ibid., 98.
[27]Ibid., 125.

matter and criterion for theology. For him this meant that theology must continually reexamine the doctrinal formulas to determine their adequacy to express Christian God-consciousness. All doctrines are human-made; none is sacrosanct. Everything about Christianity is open to revision except the experience itself. Theology's task is to hold the church's preaching and teaching to strict agreement with the best contemporary analysis of the Christian God-consciousness in order to determine how much of it is to be retained, how much is to be thrown out and how much must be revised in order to be kept.[28] In *The Christian Faith* Schleiermacher carried out this task with incisiveness and tenacity. He attempted to replace inadequate formulations of doctrine with ones he considered better for expressing Christian God-consciousness in the contemporary context. His basic working assumption in this task is that "every doctrinal form is bound to a particular time and no claim can be made for its permanent validity. It is the task of theology in every present age, by critical reflection, to express anew the implications of the living religious consciousness."[29]

Schleiermacher's theological method both incorporated the Enlightenment and sought to move beyond its limitations imposed on religion and theology. In keeping with the Age of Reason, his thinking centered around human experience, shunned authority and sought to build knowledge from below. He followed Kant in restricting knowledge of God to what can be experienced and in eschewing speculation about "God in himself" or any metaphysical subjects. However, whereas Kant wanted to restrict religion to the limits of reason alone, Schleiermacher restricted it to the limits of piety alone. His theological method appealed to romanticists in its emphasis on feeling and intuitive knowledge, while avoiding romanticism's subjectivism and irrationalism. Above all Schleiermacher broke decisively with the Enlightenment by insisting on the uniqueness of religion as an irreducible element of human experience and on the uniqueness of Jesus Christ as the highest expression of God-consciousness.

Schleiermacher redefines and reconstructs doctrines. Although Schleiermacher's specific reconstructions of Christian doctrines are not as important to modern theology as his method, several illustrate the effect his

---

[28]Ibid., 390.
[29]Welch, *Protestant Thought in the Nineteenth Century,* 1:72.

starting point could have on Christian beliefs. His reformulations also set the pace and tone for many future developments in liberal theology.

The Bible played an important, although not foundational, role in Schleiermacher's theology. Christian doctrine is not to be drawn primarily or exclusively from the Bible. Rather, all doctrines, he wrote, "must be extracted from the Christian religious self-consciousness [i.e., God-consciousness], i.e., the inward experience of Christian people."[30] The Bible is special in that it records the religious experiences of the earliest Christian communities. Further, the New Testament preserves for succeeding generations the perfect God-consciousness of Jesus and its impact on the first Christians. The authority of Scripture, however, is not absolute. Rather, it serves as a model for all attempts by later Christians to interpret the significance of Jesus for historical circumstances.[31]

Clearly Schleiermacher did not consider the Bible supernaturally inspired or infallible. Within it he found passages and even whole books that seemed to contradict true Christian piety.[32] The entire Old Testament seemed to him to lack the "normative dignity" of the New.[33] Furthermore, he did not believe that the Bible could or should be considered utterly unique. Whatever the influence of the Holy Spirit was in its writing should be seen as different only in degree and not in kind from the Spirit's influence elsewhere. For him, the Bible holds a relative authority for Christian theology insofar as and wherever it shows forth the pure model of Christ's own God-consciousness. However, it is the latter, reproduced in the consciousness and displayed in the lives of Christian people, and not the Bible itself, which is the ultimate criterion of truth for theology.

Schleiermacher reconceives God. Schleiermacher's reconstructions of the doctrine of God have been among his most controversial contributions to theology. They were driven and determined by his understanding of the pious God-consciousness of Christian people, their feeling of absolute dependence on God for their being and on Jesus Christ for their redemption. According to the German theologian, the attributes of God are not to be

---

[30]Schleiermacher, *Christian Faith*, 265.
[31]Ibid., 594.
[32]Ibid., 609.
[33]Ibid., 608.

taken as describing anything about God. To describe is to limit and divide, thereby taking away from God's infinity which is necessary because of everything finite's dependence on him. In place of the traditional understandings of God's attributes, he offered what has become a classic reformulation: "All attributes of which we ascribe to God are to be taken as denoting not something special in God, but only something special in the manner in which the feeling of absolute dependence is to be related to Him."[34] In other words, talk about God is always really talk about human experiences of God. Such statements describe not God-in-himself but a certain mode of experiencing God. Notice how this account of doctrines about God addresses Kant's concerns about the impossibility of knowledge of things-in-themselves. Schleiermacher did not agree with Kant about everything, especially Kant's reduction of religion to ethics, but he did agree that knowledge of metaphysics, realities behind experiences, is limited if not impossible.

Schleiermacher's account of God-talk makes all the more clear why for him the test or criterion for determining the proper attributes of God is the feeling of utter dependence.[35] In drawing out the implications of that experience he concluded that God, the one on whom we are absolutely dependent for everything, *must* be conceived as the all-determining reality, the ultimate cause of everything—both good and evil, the one who acts but cannot be acted on. Here is where Schleiermacher's Reformed theological heritage dovetails with his Enlightenment and romanticist sympathies. On the basis of God-consciousness, he posited that God must be conceived as even the cause of evil. In this he went beyond even most Calvinists. His argument was that if evil or anything else could be ascribed to any other agency than God, then God's omnipotence would be limited and to limit God in any way is to violate God-consciousness, which is the feeling of utter dependence on God for everything. Schleiermacher even required that sin be thought of as ordained by God as that which makes redemption necessary.[36]

Interestingly, Schleiermacher's idea of God's omnicausality fits nicely with the Enlightenment view of nature as ruled by cause and effect. If

---

[34]Ibid., 194.

[35]Ibid., 200.

[36]Ibid., 335. Schleiermacher rejected belief in the reality of Satan or demons. Both are personifications of evil thoughts that resist the good. See ibid., 156–70.

Newton was correct, and even if Kant's internalization of causality is true, the entire universe is ruled by unbreakable laws of nature. Free will would seem to be an exception, and many Enlightenment thinkers made it so. However, Schleiermacher's vision of God and nature is radical and comports well with Newton's view. Only, in contrast to Laplace, who said he had no need of the God hypothesis to explain the cosmos, Schleiermacher believed that human God-consciousness demonstrates the reality of God. Whether we admit it or not, we all intuit God. But the God we intuit and experience in our feeling of utter dependence *must be* the one who created and governs everything or else he, God, is dependent on something outside himself. That cannot be. The God of God-consciousness has to be omni-causal; he works through natural laws in the physical universe and through other secondary causes in humans' inner worlds. But the effect is the same; whatever is is from God, including sin and evil.

This means that for Schleiermacher miracles and prayer must be redefined. Miracles, in the sense of special events that abrogate the order of nature, would contradict the feeling of absolute dependence.[37] If I believe in a miracle, I am believing that God did not know what he was doing in the first place and learned something new that caused him to intervene in his creation. But that would make God dependent on something outside himself for that new knowledge and need to intervene. Schleiermacher did not absolutely deny miracles, but he said that *if* one occurred it must be believed to have been part of God's universal plan from the beginning and already built into the universe—determined to happen ahead of time. It cannot be a response to something new that happens. Therefore, it is not really supernatural. Whether Schleiermacher believed in any miracles, however, is doubtful. He did not believe in the resurrection of Jesus Christ.

This brings us to the problem of prayer. Schleiermacher did not absolutely deny the efficacy of petitionary prayer, but he demoted it to a status of spiritual immaturity. To ask God to change the course of events is to imply that it is somehow independent of God and that God is somehow dependent on the person praying to tell him what is best to do. The common saying that "Prayer does not change things; it changes me" expresses Schlei-

---

[37]Ibid., 178–79.

ermacher's view of prayer well. Petitionary prayer, he said, is not the most mature form of prayer. Mature prayer takes the form of praise and adoration and thanksgiving. However, *if* a person prays a petitionary prayer its effect may be to bring his or her consciousness into line with God's will. It will not change what was predestined to happen as if God in all his wisdom had not already foreordained everything wisely. Also, Schleiermacher suggested that occasionally God may answer a petitionary prayer, but if so, the prayer and the answer are "only part of the original divine plan, and consequently the idea that otherwise something else might have happened is wholly meaningless."[38]

It should be clear by now that Schleiermacher considered the whole category of the supernatural to be inimical to true faith. To him it conflicted with the proper God-consciousness of Christians. Schleiermacher believed that "supernatural" implies a God who stands over against the world, that God and creation relate to each other through relative independence. Christian piety, of course, apprehends God as the absolute, infinite power on which everything finite (including the whole of finite existence) is utterly dependent and which is itself absolutely independent of anything outside itself. Schleiermacher's elimination of the category of the supernatural provided a convenient solution to a pressing problem for Christianity in the age of science:

> On the whole, therefore, as regards the miraculous, the general interests of science, more particularly of natural science, and the interests of religion seem to meet at the same point, i.e., that we should abandon the idea of the absolutely supernatural because no single instance of it can be known by us, and we are nowhere required to recognize it.[39]

Thus, science and Christianity, properly understood, *in principle* cannot conflict. The former deals with proximate causes only, whereas the latter deals with the ultimate cause.

Finally, Schleiermacher found the doctrine of the Trinity problematic. He relegated it to a short conclusion at the end of *The Christian Faith*, stating coldly that it "is not an utterance concerning the religious consciousness."[40]

---

[38]Ibid., 180.
[39]Ibid., 183.
[40]Ibid., 739.

He did not flatly deny it, but he found its historical formulation so fraught with contradictions that it is virtually useless for Christian theology.

Schleiermacher's delineation of God's personhood and transcendence has formed a focus of much controversy. Some have mistakenly charged him with pantheism, a criticism unwarranted by his exposition of the doctrine of God in *The Christian Faith*. Although it is not pantheism, there is a general consensus that his doctrine of God is panentheistic and thus, together with Hegel's concept of God as Absolute Spirit, a prototype of much later liberal theology. Schleiermacher refused to separate God from the world or the world from God. God is personal, but not anthropomorphically so. That is, God is not to be thought of as a great humanlike being who rules the world from heaven afar. In that case the world would be "other" than God and form a limit to God's being. But even more importantly, God is not to be treated as an object of any kind because to do so would be to limit and finitize God. For Schleiermacher, God is the absolute, infinite, all-determining, suprapersonal power immanent in everything but beyond all distinctions creatureliness imposes on existence.

Schleiermacher reinterprets the divinity of Christ. What of Jesus Christ? How did Schleiermacher reconstruct the doctrine (Christology) in light of his source and norm of God-consciousness? He absolutely rejected the traditional, orthodox doctrine of the incarnation as hypostatic union (Chalcedon's "one person, two natures"), replacing it with a Christology based on experience of God-consciousness. He criticized the classical doctrine as illogical. According to him, two "natures" cannot coincide in a single individual.[41] In its place he substituted the concept of Jesus' *Urbildlichkeit* (ideality) and *Vorbildlichkeit* (power of reproducing it in others).[42] Jesus Christ is completely like the rest of humanity except that "from the outset he has an absolutely potent God-consciousness."[43] His perfect God-consciousness was not a product of humanity alone; it was not his own achievement. It was a product of God's activity in his life. However, it was a fully human God-consciousness. From birth on he lived in full awareness of his depen-

---

[41]Ibid., 393.
[42]Ibid., 379. For a good discussion of this see Niebuhr, *Schleiermacher on Christ and Religion*, 219–28.
[43]Schleiermacher, *Christian Faith*, 367.

dence on God. In Schleiermacher's description, "The Redeemer, then, is like all men in virtue of the identity of human nature, but distinguished from them all by the constant potency of His God-consciousness, which was a veritable existence of God in Him."[44]

According to Schleiermacher, this ideal God-consciousness that Jesus possessed is sufficient to express what the Christian calls Jesus' "divinity." It is his *Urbildlichkeit*—his being the ideal of human God-consciousness, the ultimate in perfect piety. Jesus' redemptive work lies in his communication of this God-consciousness to others. That is his *Vorbildlichkeit*: "The Redeemer assumes believers into the power of His God-consciousness, and this is his redemptive activity."[45] Schleiermacher left no doubt about his attitude toward traditional language about Jesus as God when he endorsed what he considered to be the consistent practice of the New Testament to ascribe to him only such attributes as express exalted humanity.[46] In other words, for Schleiermacher, Jesus differs from other human beings in degree only, not in kind. What was true of him could be possible for any person if God chose to give it to him or her. Clearly, for Schleiermacher, Jesus was *not* God incarnate in any traditional (i.e., Chalcedonian) sense.

Schleiermacher leaves a legacy of controversy. To anyone familiar with traditional, orthodox Christian doctrine, it should be clear by now why Schleiermacher has been so controversial. The focus of criticism has been his theological method and approach because his doctrinal reconstructions stem from that. One of Schleiermacher's most outspoken detractors was Karl Barth, perhaps the most influential theologian of the twentieth century. To a large extent his dialectical or neo-orthodox theology was a reaction to Schleiermacher and liberal theology. Barth accused Schleiermacher of trying to speak about God by speaking about humanity in a very loud voice. In other words, Barth accused him of making theology radically anthropocentric and setting the course at the end of which certain theologians of the mid-twentieth century proclaimed God dead.[47]

---

[44]Ibid., 385.

[45]Ibid., 425.

[46]Ibid., 424.

[47]Barth's criticisms of Schleiermacher are scattered throughout his writings. However, a volume of lectures Barth delivered on Schleiermacher contains some of his most trenchant criticisms. See Barth, *Theology of Schleiermacher*, 186.

That may sound extreme, and Barth was given to extreme criticisms of other theologians at times. However, non-liberal Christian theologians generally agree with Barth that, in spite of his genius and good motives, Schleiermacher's theology failed to do justice to the faithfulness side of the task of correlating Christianity with modern culture. It represents a severe accommodation to modernity. At bottom, Barth's and other more conservative theologians' complaint against Schleiermacher is that his attempt to set up the "feeling of utter dependence" as the primary source and norm for theology easily became a Procrustean bed for Christian doctrine. (Procrustes was the mythical Greek innkeeper who gave guests a bed to sleep in and then cut off body parts that did not fit on the bed or stretched parts that did not fill it. "Procrustean bed" has become a phrase in philosophy and theology for any concept that predetermines the outcome of research.) To critics of Schleiermacher's theology, his God-consciousness predetermined what portions of traditional, orthodox theology and even of the Bible could be kept and what portions had to be discarded or radically reinterpreted.

Most serious, perhaps, is the problem that Schleiermacher's theological method, like that of liberal theology in general, sets up something merely human as the well and touchstone of truth in theology. But how, then, does one avoid allowing anthropology to control the content of the message? How does one allow the Word of God to speak prophetically to culture? Schleiermacher began the trend within modern Christian thought toward loss of transcendence by refusing to acknowledge the possibility that God might wish to speak a word or commit an act that could not be anticipated within the horizon of human experience alone.

Besides his weak theological method, conservative critics point to Schleiermacher's Christology as evidence of his accommodation to modernity. All of the major Enlightenment thinkers from Locke to Kant had trouble affirming the deity of the man Jesus; they considered that doctrine irrational, and Kierkegaard affirmed that it is "absurd" but to be believed nevertheless. The reason they had trouble affirming the deity of Jesus Christ (and his bodily resurrection, miracles and second coming) is because they equated the rational with what is possible to understand within a naturalistic view of reality. Traditionally, the truly distinctive thing about Christianity is the doctrine of the incarnation—that God was born and walked among people and died. This is Christianity's "scandalous doctrine" that offends adherents of other religions and worldviews but makes Christianity good news. At least that is what conservative theologians, including Barth, have always believed. Schleiermacher's Jesus is a man and nothing more. True, he was a special man—the perfect human, but only human. Talk about God existing in him does not make him unique or unsurpassable by others. Schleiermacher's low Christology opened the door to pluralism—the idea that there are other saviors besides Jesus. No doubt he did not think so, but that is one unintended consequence of his accommodation to modernity.

Liberal theologians, who often prefer to be called progressive, do not see these criticisms as ultimate. To them the essence of Christianity is not a doctrine about Jesus Christ or anything else. (Note, however, that Barth did not say it is a doctrine but the event.) The essence is universal human religious experience represented by Christian symbols such as incarnation and atonement. And that essence must be reinterpreted in every age and culture. To hold inflexibly to ancient dogmas is to doom Christianity to irrelevance. To them, Schleiermacher was a great hero who opened the door to reconstructing Christianity so that it would not fall into cultural oblivion because of the acids of modernity. The acids of modernity cannot touch Schleiermacher's theology, which is not about metaphysics or nature but about the inner world of the individual in Christian community.

2.B. ALBRECHT RITSCHL AND HIS DISCIPLES ACCOMMODATE TO MODERNITY

Schleiermacher did not found a school of theology; almost no one is ever called a Schleiermachian. He set in motion a new trend in theology called liberal theology. A later German Protestant theologian, however, built on Schleiermacher's approach to doing theology from below and combined it with Kant's emphasis on ethics as the essence of religion, including Christianity. Ritschl did found a school of theology, and his followers were called Ritschlians, a term that came to be synonymous with classical Protestant liberalism throughout much of the late nineteenth century and early twentieth century. Its leading exponents were Harnack in Germany and Rauschenbusch in the United States. Both picked up their basic methods and insights about Christian theology from Ritschl and continued them in their own theological projects.

The opening portion of this chapter discussed the common features of liberal theology. Ritschl and the Ritschlians exhibited all of them. As a reminder and refresher, liberal theologians, in the words of one of its contemporary proponents, "agreed on the necessity of giving renewed strength and currency to Protestant Christianity by adapting it to the spiritual wants of modern man, even if much that the past had accepted without demur would have to be discarded."[48] Ritschl agreed and used the philosophy of Kant to translate (or transform) Christianity for the modern cultural context. His disciples used his basic theological approach as the basis for their individual theological projects. Around the turn of the century (1900/1901) Ritschlian theology was dominant in Germany and was being brought to the United States. When more traditional, conservative theologians talked about liberal theology at that time, they usually meant Ritschlianism.

Ritschl founds a new school of liberal theology. The key figure in late nineteenth-century liberal theology was Ritschl. While he cannot be compared with Schleiermacher in terms of originality, creativity or long-term influence (Schleiermacher came significantly before Ritschl and set the trend for him), he exercised such influence that from about 1875 until 1925 Ritschlianism was virtually synonymous with liberal Protestantism. Thus, whereas Schleiermacher founded an epoch in theology but not a school, Ritschl founded a school but not an epoch.

Ritschl was born in 1822 into a Prussian Protestant bishop's family. He was musically inclined as a child and early showed great intellectual ability. Young Ritschl began his theological studies at Bonn and continued at Tübingen and Halle, eventually returning to conclude his academic preparation at Bonn. (The German custom is for aspiring scholars to study at several universities.) During his university training he was influenced by Schleiermacher, Kant and the Hegelian New Testament scholar F. C. Bauer (1792–1860).

The aspiring young theologian received his first teaching position at Bonn in 1846 and moved to Göttingen in 1864 where he remained until his death in 1889. During his twenty-five-year tenure there he established a reputation as Germany's leading Protestant theologian. A generation of

---

[48]Bernard M. G. Reardon, *Liberal Protestantism* (Palo Alto, CA: Stanford University Press, 1968), 10.

Protestant pastors and theologians studied under him or were at least strongly influenced by his writings. Although he published many articles and books, Ritschl's most important work was his three-volume treatise titled *The Christian Doctrine of Justification and Reconciliation* published between 1870 and 1874. Its English translator, Scottish theologian H. R. Mackintosh, said about it, "Not since Schleiermacher published his *Christian Glaube* [*The Christian Faith*] in 1821 has any dogmatic treatise left its mark so deeply upon theological thought in Germany and throughout the world."[49]

Ritschl discovers Kant as his conversation partner. Much of Ritschl's importance for modern theology, like Schleiermacher's, lies in his approach to doing theology more than in his specific doctrinal reconstructions, as interesting as they may be. In the late nineteenth century Christianity seemed constantly to be losing ground to the secular sciences. Traditional Christian doctrine was under siege from forces of materialism and positivism—the philosophical idea that knowledge belongs only to areas of empirical provability.

Ritschl believed the conflicts between religion and the sciences were unnecessary and based on a misunderstanding: the failure properly to distinguish between two different types of knowledge—"scientific" (by which he meant not only the physical sciences but also the social sciences) and "religious." Scientific knowledge, he asserted, strives for pure theoretical, disinterested, objective cognition of things in themselves (or at least as they appear, as in Kant's philosophy). Science attempts to grasp the inner nature of reality from a position of neutrality. Religious knowledge, by contrast, consists of value judgments about reality. It interprets reality in terms of the value things have for the knower's ultimate fulfillment and moral well-being. Religious knowledge has to do with the value of things for achieving people's highest good. Another way of describing this distinction is to say that for Ritschl scientific knowledge can only be about the way things are, whereas religious knowledge is always about the way things ought to be. Such judgments can never be disinterested, objective or neutral. Nor should they be.[50]

---

[49]Albrecht Ritschl, *The Christian Doctrine of Justification and Reconciliation*, trans. H. R. Mackintosh and A. B. Macaulay (Edinburgh: T & T Clark, 1900), v.
[50]Ritschl's explanation of these two realms of knowledge may be found in ibid., 203-13. There

According to Ritschl and his followers, then, conflicts between the secular, academic, scientific disciplines and religion, including theology, arise only when people fail to observe this distinction between theoretical knowledge and religious knowledge. For him, "every cognition of a religious sort is a direct judgment of value." Consequently, we can know the nature of God and the divine in its essence only "by determining its value for our salvation."[51]

In contrast to Ritschl's viewpoint, traditional Christian theology normally incorporated some discussion of the elements of metaphysics. For example, theologians employed theoretical proofs of the existence of God to establish the rational basis for Christian belief, and they generally made some attempt to describe the nature of God in himself. Ritschl vehemently rejected any reliance of theology on metaphysics. For him such an approach was illegitimate mingling of scientific and religious modes of knowledge.[52] Philosophical proofs of the existence of God belong in the sphere of scientific knowledge, he argued, because they treat God as an object of theoretical interest whereas truly religious knowledge of God can never treat God as an object, that is, as merely part of the furniture of the universe. Theology is interested in God only insofar as he affects the lives of people morally by helping them achieve their highest good.

But what is humanity's highest good? For Ritschl, Christianity is the community of people who collectively make the value judgment that humanity's highest good is found in the kingdom of God revealed by Jesus Christ. No theoretical proof of this value judgment is possible or desirable, but neither is belief in it a mere subjective leap of faith. Rather, this assertion is rooted in the collective experience of Christians throughout the centuries. And its truth is supported by historical investigation into the unique calling and career of Jesus of Nazareth in whom Christians find their highest ideal for humanity perfectly displayed and achieved.

Ritschl admits that even science inevitably includes some value judgments because it is impossible for the scientist or philosopher to be purely objective. However, he makes a distinction between "concomitant" and "independent" value judgments. Religion, he avers, moves only in the realm of the latter, which are perceptions of moral ends or moral hindrances.

[51]Ibid., 398.

[52]Albrecht Ritschl, "Theology and Metaphysics: Towards Rapproachement and Defense," in *Three Essays*, trans. Philip Hefner (Philadelphia: Fortress, 1972), 164.

According to Ritschl, then, theology is the investigation of the collective religious and moral experience of the kingdom of God by Christians in the church. It is built on and centered entirely around the Christian community's valuation of the kingdom of God revealed in Jesus Christ as humanity's highest good. Theology seeks to construct a system of value judgments based solely on the effects of God on Christians' lives and the worth of those effects for their achievement of their highest good as human beings. To this end, it makes use of historical research into the self-consciousness of Jesus and the original effects his preaching of the kingdom of God had on the earliest Christians. Such historical research, Ritschl maintained, would preserve theology's value judgments from becoming mere flights of subjective fancy and give theology its own kind of scientific character. But this would be a unique kind of scientific character that is totally unlike other sciences because it cannot be objective or indifferent; it is tied inextricably to interest in the highest good—something the ordinary sciences do not seek or know anything about.

In short, for Ritschl and his followers, theology seeks to determine the true essence of Christianity distinct from its merely outward forms and expressions. Furthermore, it attempts to represent all doctrines in systematic relation to that essence as their controlling force.[53] What is that essence and controlling force? Simply put, it is the kingdom of God, which as we will see, did not mean for Ritschl some future millennial reign of Christ on earth or the institutional church. It is the "unity of humanity organized according to love."[54]

So, for Ritschl, what is theology's controlling source and norm? It is not the Bible as a whole but what he called the "apostolic circle of ideas" as determined by sound historical-critical research.[55] This research must not be carried out with total disinterest; that would be to violate the boundary between science and religion. Nevertheless, Ritschl was confident that

---

[53]David L. Mueller, *An Introduction to the Theology of Albrecht Ritschl* (Philadelphia: Westminster Press, 1969), 45–47.

[54]Ritschl's formal definition of the kingdom of God is rather lengthy and complicated: "the uninterrupted reciprocation of action springing from the motive of love—a kingdom in which all are knit together in union with everyone who can show the marks of a neighbor; further it is that union of men in which all goods are appropriated in their proper subordination to the highest good" (*Christian Doctrine*, 334–35).

[55]Mueller, *Introduction to the Theology of Albrecht Ritschl*, 33.

faithful, scholarly research would show that the kingdom of God is the essence of Christianity, its heart and soul, the kernel within the husk of accumulated church traditions, because it was the heart of the apostolic circles of ideas.

Ritschl's theological method bears striking affinities with Kant's philosophy. The latter was mediated to Ritschl through a philosopher at Göttingen named Hermann Lotze (1817–1881), who tried to ameliorate Kant's skepticism while holding to his basic epistemology. Although much controversy has revolved around the question of Kant's and Lotze's influences on Ritschl, this much can be said with confidence: Ritschl followed Kant in trying to expunge metaphysics from theology and in bringing religion into the closest possible connection with ethics. He eschewed all speculation into the nature of God-in-himself and sought to focus all theological reflection and reconstruction on God's effects on humanity (although he could also appeal to Luther for that focus because Luther had said we can know nothing about God in himself but only God in his redemptive work). Ritschl differed from Kant, however, in claiming that God really is known in his effects. And he disliked Kant's separation between the phenomenal and noumenal realms. In responding to Kant, Ritschl relied heavily on Lotze for the idea that the thing (in this case God) is really present and manifest in its effects (in this case revelation and salvation).[56]

Ritschl revisions God and God's kingdom. Ritschl's doctrine of God was profoundly affected by his theological methodology. The first and most striking evidence of that is that he had little to say about God in himself. He asserted that Christian theology is interested only in God's effects on people and in the value judgments appropriate to those effects. Ritschl said almost nothing about the Trinity, for example, because he viewed it as a doctrine about God's inner being above and apart from God's relation with the world, and therefore it could not be articulated as a value judgment. Similarly he saw no positive role for the traditional metaphysical attributes of God such as omnipotence, omniscience and omnipresence. Without explicitly denying them he seemed to dismiss them as lying in the realm of the theoretical rather than the ethical-practical and therefore irrelevant to true reli-

---

[56]For a good discussion of Lotze's influence on Ritschl see Philip Hefner, "Albrecht Ritschl: An Introduction," in *Three Essays*, trans. Philip Hefner (Philadelphia: Fortress, 1972), 27-28.

gious knowledge. For Ritschl, the primary Christian theological affirmation is "God is love."[57] To this he added that Christian faith requires that God be personal and transcendent or "supramundane."[58]

Ritschl was much more interested in the kingdom of God than in God himself. Jesus had proclaimed the kingdom of God, which, according to Ritschl, is the unity of humanity organized according to love. In other words, it is a social order within the world. Christian faith grasps this kingdom revealed in Christ as humanity's highest good. Faith, therefore, knows the God proclaimed by Jesus as love. Apart from this, it has no interest in any "being of God." But the German theologian went further. For him, the kingdom of God is not only humanity's highest goal and good but also God's own highest goal and good.[59] Perhaps the most striking thing about Ritschl's doctrine of God lies there. For him, God's own self-end, his reason for being, so to speak, is the same as humanity's—the kingdom of God. This echoes Hegel's idea of history as Absolute Spirit's (God's) process of self-realization. It at least verges on panentheism. And it seems, against Ritschl's own rules, a metaphysical statement about God.

In any case, Ritchl's identification of God's own end (telos or goal) as the kingdom of God in the world inclines his theology in the direction of immanence if not panentheism. Certainly many later liberal theologians drew this conclusion and openly embraced panentheism. Overall, partly because of Ritschl, liberal theology's emphasis in the doctrine of God fell on the divine immanence within history rather than God's transcendence over it.

Ritschl redefines sin and salvation. For Ritschl and his followers the kingdom of God is the inner meaning of the doctrines of sin and salvation. Because the kingdom of God is judged by Christian faith as the highest good, sin must be understood as the opposite of that kingdom.[60] Sin is not primarily a willful wrong act, for this understanding trivializes the concept. Nor is sin an inherited disposition, a view that robs it of the element of personal responsibility. In place of the traditional doctrine of original sin Ritschl posited the existence of a "kingdom of sin," a "whole web of sinful

---

[57]Ritschl, *Christian Doctrine*, 282.
[58]Ibid., 236, 281.
[59]Ibid., 282. Here Ritschl refers to the kingdom of God as God's own glory and personal end.
[60]Ibid., 329.

action and reaction, which presupposes and yet again increases the selfish bias in every man."[61] Sin is primarily selfishness. Its essential character lies in its contradiction of the ideal of human unity centered around love, which is the kingdom of God. However, sin is not inherited. It is universal, but no other reason can be given for its universality than that all individuals are born into a world of selfishness in which that disposition dominates everything until and unless Christians, because of their redemption through Christ, resist it and change it.[62]

Throughout Ritschl's theological writings the kingdom of God appears to have two foci—a religious one and an ethical one (although these are inseparable). The religious focus is justification, the moment of salvation in which the sinner is declared forgiven by God. The ethical focus lies in the assertion that God calls men and women to fulfill the ideal of love toward their neighbors. For Ritschl, salvation must include both foci.

In his doctrines of sin and salvation the revolutionary this-worldly aspect of Ritschl's theology is most clearly evident. He believed that salvation is not primarily a matter of achieving a state of blessedness in this life or afterwards in heaven, although he never denied it. Rather, salvation is primarily the full fruition of the kingdom of God on earth. Consequently, Christianity is not an otherworldly religion but a religion of world transformation through ethical action inspired by love.

Ritschl puts Jesus Christ in a new light. Perhaps the most controversial aspect of Ritschl's theology is his Christology. Once again, the kingdom of God is the controlling center of his doctrine, and Ritschl used it to replace those aspects of the traditional doctrine (hypostatic union) that he considered speculative and metaphysical and therefore foreign to true religion. For anyone wondering at this point what is so liberal about Ritschl, his Christology will reveal it.

Classical, orthodox Christology, following the Chalcedonian Definition of 451, affirms that Jesus Christ was and is one person possessing two distinct but not separate natures—one human and one divine. The person of this union

---

[61]Ibid., 350.

[62]Ritschl was in many ways the true father of the social gospel movement (to be discussed later in this chapter with Rauschenbusch), but he did not advocate radical social action to reform the political order. He was a defender of the social status quo, except he thought it could be improved through love.

of two natures is the eternal Son of God, the Word, the Logos, the second person of the Trinity. The two natures is the manner of his incarnation. He did not turn himself into a human being or merely put on human skin, so to speak, but took to himself a human nature and through it experienced human life and death. In this orthodox doctrine, Jesus' deity or divinity consisted in his having a divine nature alongside his human one. And it consisted in his *being* the eternal Son of God—that was and is his personhood. Ritschl firmly rejected this traditional formula on the ground that it is scientific rather than religious.[63] That is to say, for him, it confuses two different types of language and transgresses the boundary between science and religion.

According to Ritschl, this traditional doctrine is not a judgment of Jesus' value but a disinterested assertion of something Jesus is supposed to have possessed before and apart from any effect he had on people. The truly religious estimate of Jesus, he averred, is interested in his historical conduct and effects, his religious convictions and ethical motives, and not in his supposed inborn qualities or powers, "for not in the latter but in the former does He exert an influence upon us."[64] Therefore, the affirmation of Jesus' divinity, Ritschl argued, is a value judgment Christians make based on the worth of his life in effecting their salvation. Because he came as the unique bearer of the kingdom of God he is judged by Christians to have the value of God.

Ritschl was sensitive to the accusation that he reduced Jesus Christ to a "mere man." He spent many pages anticipating the criticism and defending against it. He interpreted Jesus' divinity as the unique "vocation" given to him by God his Father to be the perfect embodiment of the kingdom of God among humans—a vocation he fulfilled perfectly. Because he took this life task as his exclusive vocation and realized it perfectly, his very person became the historical influence that made possible the achievement of God's and humanity's highest good. Thus, Christians confess Jesus to be "God," for this is a value judgment based on his life's worth for God and humanity.[65]

Ritschl refused to discuss the origin of Jesus' unique "Kingly Prophethood." Such inquiry, he claimed, would lead into empty metaphysical speculation

---

[63]Ritschl, *Christian Doctrine*, 398.

[64]Ibid., 413.

[65]This is an interpretation of Ritschl's account of Jesus' divinity as it is presented at great length and complexity in "The Christian Doctrine of Christ's Person and Life-Work," chapter 6 of *Christian Doctrine*, 385–484.

and away from the sphere of value judgments into the sphere of scientific judgments of fact. However, he could not restrain himself from discussing the concept of Christ's preexistence. Here more clearly than anywhere else he fell into inconsistency by allowing an element of metaphysics to influence his thought. Apparently he could not settle for the conclusion that Jesus' accomplishment was a product of his own initiative and effort. Rather, it had an eternal source in the mind and will of God:

> As Founder and Lord of the Kingdom of God, Christ is as much the object of God's eternal knowledge and will as is the moral unification of mankind, which is made possible through Him, and whose prototype He is; or rather, that, not only in time but in the eternity of the Divine knowledge and will, Christ precedes His community.[66]

In other words, for Ritschl, Christ preexisted his human life on earth only in that he and his work are eternally known and willed by God. This affirmation of Christ's ideal preexistence seems blatantly to transgress Ritschl's self-imposed limits on theology. It introduces an element of metaphysics or ontology that cannot be supported or sustained solely by historical research into Christ's worth for human salvation. This affirmation goes beyond the sphere of value judgments and asserts the reality of a transcendent ground and origin of Christ, a sphere Ritschl marked off as speculative in his criticism of the classical doctrine of Christ's divinity. It also falls far short of classical, orthodox Christology which says Jesus Christ preexisted his birth on earth as the Logos, the Word, the Son of God and God the Son.

Central to Ritschl's theology is Christ's accomplishment of salvation for humanity. But how does that occur? Here Ritschl introduces the concept of Jesus' "vocational obedience" to the Father: Jesus perfectly fulfilled the way of life appropriate for the kingdom of God. His sinless life and voluntary death not only revealed the kingdom of God in history but also released it as a power for transforming the world. It appears, then, that Ritschl's main interest lay in Christ's historical life as a moral example and influence affecting history. Although he explicitly rejected any doctrine of the atonement that would make Christ the bearer of divine punishment for the sins of the world, Ritschl did not deny the special significance of Christ's

---

[66]Ibid., 469.

death.[67] The death of Jesus was part of his vocation of utter loyalty to the cause of God's kingdom.

Ritschl had little to say about Jesus' resurrection or exaltation (ascension). For all practical purposes he represented Jesus' continuing influence on the world as that of a powerful moral image that continually motivates, energizes and guides the community of God's kingdom, the church.[68]

Like Schleiermacher, Ritschl leaves a legacy of controversy. Ritschl's reputation as a modern theologian of lasting importance cannot be denied; he spawned a generation of liberal Christian theologians and pastors who used his "moralizing of dogma" to make Christianity relevant to an era influenced by Kant and Darwin and biblical criticism. Ritschl's fame was for his strong effort to extricate Christianity from unnecessary conflicts with Enlightenment-influenced science and philosophy. In an era in which Christian theology was increasingly accused of being irrelevant to ethical progress due to its concentration on another world, Ritschl brought his spiritual and intellectual powers to bear on drawing out the moralizing power of the central Christian truth of God's redemption of humanity in the kingdom of God here and now. As a result of his influence, a school of theology called the social gospel emerged especially in the United States. All that is to say that Ritschl's achievement seems to have been twofold: to disentangle religion, especially Christianity, from conflicts with science and to make Christian theology primarily practical.

But Ritschl has not been without his detractors and critics. Conservative evangelicals, and especially fundamentalists, castigated him as a heretic. A Scottish evangelical theologian, James Orr (1844–1913), wrote a book carefully exposing Ritschl's theology as non-Christian.[69] Barth criticized Ritschl and the whole school of liberal theology influenced by him for many of the same reasons he criticized Schleiermacher—that it is an attempt to do theology from below apart from the authority of God's revelation from above (God's Word). Here I will offer some of the criticisms found in Orr's and Barth's and other critics' writings about Ritschl.

---

[67]Ibid., 477–78.
[68]James Richmond, *Ritschl: A Reappraisal. A Study in Systematic Theology* (London: Collins, 1978), 203.
[69]James Orr, *Ritschlianism: Expository and Critical Essays* (London: Hodder & Stoughton, 1903).

First, if Ritschl is right, theology and science cannot conflict. That might seem to be an achievement. However, it is brought about in the same way Kant's philosophy of religion did in *Religion Within the Limits of Reason Alone*—by reducing Christianity to ethics. One critic says that "theologians are right to fear stirring up a science-religion conflict from which religion has nothing to gain and everything to lose, but they ought to prevent this fear from producing a form of intellectual paralysis."[70] In other words, the central problem with Ritschl's theological method lies in the extreme way he tried to rule out all discussion of God in himself *and* his failure to avoid that himself. Ritschl's attempt to limit theological God-talk to the realm of value judgments is problematic in several ways. First, it seems to remove theology from the realm of facts, handing that over to the sciences. That would seem to create the ghettoizing of theology that Wolfhart Pannenberg complained about (see 8.b.). Second, if theology cannot discuss the inner reality of God's being, it naturally will appear that God exists only in relation to humans. God will become dissolved in his effects until only his effects are considered important. To a certain extent this danger appears already in what some critics have seen as Ritschl's near identification of God with the kingdom of God.[71]

In addition to the problem of God's transcendence, Ritschl's limitation of theology to value judgments raises some serious problems for the public nature of theology. In spite of his good intentions, Ritschl's theology opened the door to the accusation of subjectivism. As critic James Richmond notes, "At points Ritschl's theology does *seem* to withdraw religion into a restricted area of its own, and abandon to 'irreligious' (i.e., profane) science or philosophy the wider realms of 'human knowledge.'"[72] While there is no doubt that Ritschl would react with horror to the common habit of modern Christians and others divorcing faith from facts, there is equally no doubt that he, like Kant before him, partly contributed to it.

Perhaps no dimension of Ritschl's thought has evoked more criticism than his Christology. Why did he discard the ancient Christian doctrine of the hypostatic union—that Jesus Christ was and is one person, the eternal

---

[70]Richmond, *Ritschl*, 105.
[71]Ibid., 114.
[72]Ibid., 120.

Son of God, with two distinct but never separate natures, divine and human? Part of the reason lies in what has been seen as his illegitimate and inconsistent rejection of metaphysics from religion. But another cause may be more ulterior. Richmond points it out: "Ritschl and his nineteenth-century contemporaries did not understand Christ's deity in terms of *substance*, nor of *consubstantiality* with God, simply because such terms had become in post-Enlightenment Germany [and one could add Great Britain and the United States] unintelligible, not to say meaningless."[73] In other words, Ritschl, like other liberal thinkers, tended to accept the consensus of modern, educated, Enlightenment-influenced society as a norm for theology. This led Barth and other critics to attach to Ritschl and other liberal theologians the label "culture Protestantism" (see 2.c.).

At least from an orthodox or even neo-orthodox Christian perspective, Ritschl's Christology suffers the same defect as Schleiermacher's. It is a purely functional Christology in which Jesus is great but differs only in degree and not in kind from other great people. Ritschl's formula that when Christians affirm the divinity of Christ they mean that he has the value of God for them says it all. In no realistic sense is Jesus "God with and for us." He was simply the person who, always foreknown in God's mind and will, opened up the possibility of God's kingdom in history among people and showed them what it looks like. Like Schleiermacher's Christology, this seemed to open the door to other saviors equal with Jesus Christ.

Ritschl anticipated this criticism of his Christology and attempted to forestall it by arguing that any religious prophet equal with Jesus Christ who might appear in history would stand in dependence on him and would therefore be subordinate to him.[74] The critic's natural response, however, is why? Ritschl's account of the person of Christ, like that of most liberals, falls far short of the high incarnational Christology of the churches dating back to the New Testament itself. In no sense is his Christ "God with us." Even a sympathetic critic like Richmond cannot help labeling Ritschl's Christology "impoverishingly restrictive."[75]

Having explained conservatives' criticisms, it is necessary to conclude

---

[73]Ibid., 172.
[74]Ritschl, *Christian Doctrine*, 465.
[75]Richmond, *Ritschl*, 205.

this analysis of Ritschl's controversial legacy by saying that hundreds of Protestant pastors and thousands of educated laypeople found in his theology the way to be both modern and Christian. For those who, because of the Enlightenment and modernity, felt it impossible to accept traditional, orthodox Christian doctrines, Ritschl showed that a person could still be a Christian without being premodern or antimodern. One influential Protestant theologian of the early twentieth century, however, dared to say publicly that this liberal type of theology is not Christianity; a leading secular social commentator publicly agreed and suggested that liberals like Ritschl and his followers should stop calling themselves Christians.[76]

Harnack popularizes Ritschlian liberal theology. Earlier it was noted that Ritschl's theology gave rise to a school of liberal theologians whose influence permeated the major Protestant churches of Europe and the United States around the turn of the twentieth century. Two members of that Ritschlian school stand out as especially important for our story of modern theology because of the creative ways in which they built on and extended Ritschl's theology: the German scholar Harnack and the American social reformer Rauschenbusch.

Harnack was perhaps the most brilliant and popular advocate of liberal Protestant theology at the turn of the twentieth century. He was professor of church history at the University of Berlin from 1888 until his retirement in 1922. His lectures drew hundreds of students, and his scholarly writings (approximately sixteen hundred titles) brought him great acclaim from the academic world. He was a confidant of Kaiser Wilhelm, who placed him in charge of several important cultural institutions including the Royal Library in Berlin. He was knighted by the kaiser in 1914 around the time he wrote Wilhelm's speech to the German people announcing his declaration of war against Russia and France—the beginning of World War I.[77] Like most other

---

[76]The book was *Christianity and Liberalism* (1923; Grand Rapids, MI: Eerdmans, 1946) by Presbyterian theologian J. Gresham Machen (1881–1937), a leading intellectual of the budding fundamentalist movement in the early decades of the twentieth century. The secular commentator who publicly agreed with him that liberalism is not Christianity was Walter Lippman (1889–1974).

[77]Martin Rumscheidt, "Introduction: Harnack's Liberalism in Theology: A Struggle for the Freedom of Theology," in *Adolf von Harnack, Liberal Theology at Its Height*, ed. Martin Rumscheidt (London: Collins, 1989), 24. It was then, in 1914, that "von" was added to Harnack's last name as a sign of his elevation to the hereditary German nobility. That is why here and elsewhere in

German theologians, including most liberal ones, Harnack enthusiastically supported the kaiser's war policies. This was one thing that helped turn his most famous student, Barth, against him. After the war Harnack was offered the post of ambassador to the United States by the new German government, an honor he respectfully declined. He died in 1930, but to this day a major government building in Berlin, the Adolf von Harnack Haus, stands as a monument to this towering figure in modern theology.

Harnack's widest influence came through the publication of a series of lectures he gave at the University of Berlin in 1899 and 1900 which were taken down verbatim by a student and presented to the professor. In 1901 the lectures were published in the United States under the title *What Is Christianity?* (The German title was *Das Wesen des Christentums*—"The Essence of Christianity.") The volume went through numerous editions and was widely read and quoted by liberal preachers and authors for the next thirty-five years (when liberal theology of the Ritschlian type began to fall out of favor).

In the book's sixteen lectures Harnack attempted to identify the central kernel of authentic Christianity, which he called the "Gospel," and to separate it from the "husk" of cultural forms in which it is communicated in the New Testament and in traditional, orthodox Christianity.[78] He set forth the thesis that Jesus proclaimed a message about God the Father, not about himself: "The Gospel, as Jesus proclaimed it has to do with the Father only and not with the Son."[79] According to Harnack, this gospel is simple and sublime, consisting of three interrelated truths: the kingdom of God and its coming, God the Father and the infinite value of the human soul, and the higher righteousness and the commandment of love.[80]

By the "kingdom of God and its coming" Harnack did not mean anything about a second coming of Jesus Christ or millennium on earth afterwards. By it he meant what Ritschl meant, a social order within history, inaugurated by Jesus, ruled by love. By "God the Father and the infinite

---

this book he is referred to as Adolf Harnack. That was his name for most of his life including his professional career as a theologian.

[78] Adolf Harnack, *What Is Christianity?* trans. Thomas Bailey Saunders (New York: G. P. Putnam's Sons, 1901), 13.

[79] Ibid., 154.

[80] Ibid., 55.

value of the human soul" he did not mean the immortality of the soul but human persons now. All are of infinite value because all have God as their father. By "the commandment of love" he did not mean anything supernatural, a gift of grace available only to those who believe and are saved; he meant a benevolence of all toward all of which all are capable because they have the same heavenly father.

Harnack found little of this gospel in the Old Testament. Even in the New Testament it is encrusted with fantastic stories of miracles, angels, devils and apocalyptic catastrophes. That is all mythology to be discarded. Furthermore, throughout its history, he argued, the church overlaid the simple gospel Jesus preached with husks of alien philosophical concepts such as the Greek identification of Christ with the Logos—a Greek idea foreign to the simple teaching of Jesus.[81] Harnack wrote a seven-volume *History of Dogma* (1886–1889) in which he developed what has come to be called the Hellenization thesis about early Christian doctrinal development. According to Harnack, the early Christians, especially under Constantine, Hellenized the simple gospel of Jesus by adding metaphysical concepts such as the Trinity and hypostatic union. These, he argued, are not part of the gospel but later accretions that need to be recognized for what they are—time-bound, culturally conditioned interpretations of the gospel that make no sense to modern people.

For Harnack, in spite of the sorry history of the Hellenization of Christianity, the simple gospel of Jesus has survived wherever Jesus' pure and simple message of the kingdom of God has been accepted as the highest and most glorious ideal known to humanity. This ideal is "the prospect of a union among men, which is held together not by any legal ordinance, but by the rule of love, and where a man conquers his enemy by gentleness."[82]

A leading twentieth-century theologian named H. Richard Niebuhr blasted Harnack's liberal theology by describing it as a theology in which "a God without wrath brought men without sin into a kingdom without judgment through the ministrations of a Christ without a cross."[83] While

---

[81]Ibid., 216–20.

[82]Ibid., 122.

[83]H. Richard Niebuhr, *The Kingdom of God in America* (1937; New York: Harper & Row, 1959), 193. For almost a quarter century Niebuhr was on the faculty of Yale Divinity School.

liberal Protestants hailed Harnack's stripped-down version of Christianity as congenial with modernity, conservatives and neo-orthodox regarded it as a pernicious denial of the gospel that sucks the life out of it. There is little doubt that Kant would have been proud of Harnack; his version of Christianity differed little from Kant's *Religion Within the Limits of Reason Alone.* And, like Kant's, Schleiermacher's and Ritschl's, it cannot conflict with science. No matter what science discovers, or even develops as theory, it cannot undermine or challenge or contradict Harnack's Christianity, which is primarily, if not only, about ethics.

Rauschenbusch gives voice to the social gospel. Harnack stopped short of applying the ideal of the kingdom of God to specific political agendas; he even harshly criticized those who would use it to fuel revolutionary reform movements. Rauschenbusch, however, spent most of his creative energies as a theologian doing just that.

Rauschenbusch was the son of a German Lutheran minister who emigrated to America and quickly became a Baptist. Walter had a profound conversion experience when he was only nine years old. Having sensed God's call to the ministry, he attended Rochester Theological Seminary in New York, where his father taught in the German-speaking department.[84] Unlike some liberal theologians, the younger Rauschenbusch always maintained a pietist spiritual ethos of devotion to Jesus Christ in a personal relationship. He was not given, as some liberals were, to denying orthodox doctrines. However, later in life he did engage in some fairly radical reinterpreting of certain doctrines and had little to say about ones he could not "moralize." He fits somewhat uncomfortably in the liberal category, but because of his Ritschlian influence and leanings he is usually put there.

Rauschenbusch's first position out of seminary was pastor of a Baptist church in Hell's Kitchen, a particularly impoverished section of New York City. There he became involved in the growing socialist movement and

---

[84]Many years later the German department of Rochester Theological Seminary, where both Rauschenbusches taught, split off, moved to Sioux Falls, South Dakota, and became North American Baptist Seminary, this writer's alma mater (MA, 1978). When I first arrived there Walter Rauschenbusch's portrait was hidden behind a door that always stayed open; it was purposely kept out of sight because the seminary had become quite conservative. Later, however, it was put back in the line-up of past professors' portraits where it belonged.

helped found a religious socialist newspaper.[85] In 1891 he spent several months studying New Testament in Germany, where he came under the influence of the Ritschlian emphasis on the ethical kingdom of God as the heart and soul of the gospel. When he returned to the United States he threw himself into the budding social gospel movement, becoming its most theologically able exponent and leading prophet.[86] In 1897 he became professor of church history at Rochester Seminary and through his writings and lectures promoted the political and economic transformation of the United States until his death in 1918. For much of his teaching career he was deaf, although he retained the ability to speak. He communicated with students by means of their written questions. By all accounts he was an extremely popular teacher and preacher whose books sold millions of copies and were influential in bringing about many of the social reforms associated with the progressive movement. He worked closely with other social progressives in Rochester, which was a hotbed of that movement. Among his acquaintances and colleagues in social reform were Elizabeth Cady Stanton, Susan B. Anthony and Frederick Douglass.

Rauschenbusch's books, written mostly for popular consumption, were not weighty theological tomes but practical applications of the ethical aims and ideals of the kingdom of God to concrete social life. Like Ritschl, he defined the kingdom of God as "humanity organized according to the will of God,"[87] and by "the will of God" he meant love. His most influential books were *Christianity and the Social Crisis* (1907), *Christianizing the Social Order* (1912) and *A Theology for the Social Gospel* (1917). He also wrote a volume of *Prayers for the Social Awakening* (1910).

The book that catapulted Rauschenbusch into fame was *Christianity and the Social Crisis*, in which he set forth in stark detail the extreme gap between

---

[85]It is shocking to some Christian ears to hear the phrase "Christian socialism," but many devout Christians were socialists in the later nineteenth and early twentieth centuries—before socialism came to be equated with Soviet Union-style communism. "Socialism" to Rauschenbusch did not mean collectivism or totalitarianism communism. For him, as for later Christian socialists such as Barth, Niebuhr and Paul Tillich, it meant democratic socialism. Many of its goals, such as abolition of child labor, social security and graduated income tax, became standard parts of democratic capitalism in the United States.

[86]Claude Welch, *Protestant Theology in the Nineteenth Century*, vol. 2: *1870-1914* (New Haven, CT: Yale University Press, 1985), 261.

[87]Walter Rauschenbusch, *A Theology for the Social Gospel* (Nashville: Abingdon, 1978), 142.

wealth and poverty in the United States and asserted that being a Christian in this social crisis meant working for the salvation of economic structures that perpetuate poverty. The essential Christian task, he wrote, is not so much to abolish drunkenness and adultery, as bad as those are, but "to transform human society into the Kingdom of God by regenerating all human relations and reconciling them in accordance with the will of God."[88] He specifically singled out laissez faire capitalism as part of the "Kingdom of Evil" in American life and called on churches to lead a new revival in which not only individual souls but also corporate entities and social structures would repent and be saved.

His second major book, *Christianizing the Social Order*, offered specific suggestions for the revival of justice and love he envisioned. He called for the socializing of major industries, support for labor unions and the abolition of an economy centered around greed, competition and the profit motive. All these changes he equated with the gradual Christianizing of the social order—a progressive approximation of the kingdom of God in human society.

Rauschenbusch's final book, *A Theology for the Social Gospel*, was published just one year before he died. It was his attempt at a systematic theology in which every doctrine would be "moralized"—brought into connection with the ethical kingdom of God that he, like Ritschl and Harnack, believed was the main mission of Jesus. There he attempted to redefine every doctrine in terms of the social and historical reality of the "Kingdom of Love." Nowhere in the book does Rauschenbusch openly deny any classical doctrine of Christian orthodoxy, but he reinterpreted many of them in light of the central unifying theme of the kingdom of God. For example, the main significance of Jesus lay in the new concept of God that he offered to humanity. Instead of portraying God as a monarch, Jesus "democratized the conception of God" by taking him by the hand and calling him "Father."[89] Rauschenbusch then defined salvation as "the voluntary socializing of the soul."[90] He did not deny personal salvation as forgiveness and being born again, but he added to these traditional dimensions the social dimension and argued that a person who claims to be saved but lives a competitive life of selfishness and greed, oppressing others, cannot claim to

---

[88]Ibid., 99.
[89]Ibid., 174-75.
[90]Ibid., 99.

be fully saved. For Rauschenbusch, salvation is a holistic concept that cannot be limited to individuals and their conversions to Christ. It must be understood as also applicable to social structures and social behavior.

The American social gospel movement represented the most practical and concrete expression of classical liberal theology. Most of its underlying theological methods and themes go back to Ritschl, but it combined them with an evangelical fervor for social reform absent in most European liberal theology. What made Rauschenbusch liberal was not that he denied the supernatural, miracles, the inspiration and authority of the Bible, the deity of Christ or any other great doctrine of orthodox Christianity. He did not. What made him liberal was that he tended to downplay doctrine as relatively unimportant compared with experience, and the experience he meant was human experience of needing the kingdom of God and seeing it dawn. He also looked for the "kernel" of gospel truth within the "husk" of tradition. Unlike some other liberals, he had no desire to discard the husk; he only wanted to get to the kernel, which he saw as the kingdom of God on earth coming through social reform. One theme he held in common with nineteenth-century liberal theologians was optimism; he seemed to believe the kingdom of God, a social order organized according to love and cooperation rather than selfishness and competition, is inevitable insofar as Christians put their minds to it and work toward it.

Classical liberal Protestant theology declines after the world wars. Although liberalism in theology remains a force to be reckoned with even in the twenty-first century, to a great extent World War I swept it away in Europe, which was devastated by that war whose meaninglessness killed optimism about history. Or perhaps it is better to say the Great War forced liberal theology to change. Existentialism, which rose to popularity between the world wars, modified and chastened it. The outcome was the neo-liberalisms of Paul Tillich and Rudolf Bultmann (see chaps. 5 and 6). Classical liberalism of the Ritschlian type thrived in the United States between the world wars because Americans interpreted the victory over Germany as "the war to end all wars" and the war to "make the world safe for democracy." In the United States, optimism survived the European devastation and extreme hardship. One of the greatest proponents of Ritschlian liberalism in America was influential between the wars: Harry Emerson

Fosdick Jr., pastor of Riverside Church in New York City, author of numerous books popularizing liberal theology, champion of liberal theology against the growing fundamentalist movement. His face graced the cover of *Time* magazine twice in the 1920s and 1930s. After World War II, however, a different mood set into American Christianity. The neo-orthodoxy of Barth and Emil Brunner become popular, and liberal theology went on the defensive. However, a chastened liberal theology reappeared with Tillich, who emigrated to the United States, and with the distinctively American form of neo-liberalism called process theology.

One more German classical liberal theologian deserves attention here before the story moves on to other subjects. Ernst Troeltsch (1865–1923) was, in his own way, just as influential as Ritschl and Harnack. But his influence was profoundly troubling even to liberal theologians because he dared to question everything, including the absoluteness of Christianity as the unsurpassable religion, something all theologians before him had taken for granted. Troeltsch introduced into the stream of Christian thought something called historicism. And for those who took him seriously and were influenced by that idea, nothing could ever be the same.

2.C. Ernst Troeltsch Relativizes Christianity

Up to this point we have been looking at the Enlightenment challenge to traditional Christianity primarily in terms of philosophy and science—how they brought about modernity with its acids such as rationalism, naturalism, skepticism and a secular outlook on life. While Christianity rose to the occasion of the challenge via liberal theology, traditional orthodoxy remained under a cloud for those who took modernity seriously.

Lessing digs an ugly ditch. One acid of modernity so far hardly mentioned is its critical-historical perspective on everything (except itself). The best way to understand this is through Enlightenment thinker Gotthold Ephraim Lessing (1729–1781), one of those individuals in the history of Western thought who left behind an aphorism that almost every student of modernity learns. It is that "accidental truths of history can never become the proof of necessary truths of reason."[91] (This aphorism even has a title:

---

[91]From Lessing's 1777 essay "On the Proof of the Spirit and Power," trans. Henry Chadwick (Palo Alto, CA: Stanford University Press, 1967), 51–57.

"Lessing's Big Ugly Ditch.") In other words, there is no bridge, as it were, from any historical event to absolute truth. That means two things. First, we can never have absolute knowledge of any historical event; at best we can know history only to a degree of probability because we are always finding out that what we knew about history was wrong. Remember that the Enlightenment had a penchant for finding certainty; Lessing is saying one cannot look for it in history. (Hegel would later argue one can find it by looking at universal history—history as a whole—but Lessing would have scoffed at that, too.) Second, even if one could have absolute knowledge about a historical event, there is no way to build a universal truth for everyone on it. Historical events are always open to differing interpretations.

In effect, what Lessing was saying is that if you base your Christianity on historical events such as Jesus' miracles or his resurrection, you have forever to wait for the next issue of *Archeological Review* to find out whether you can still be a Christian. But many orthodox Christians of Lessing's time did attempt to prove Christianity true by appealing to Jesus' miracles and his resurrection. Lessing saw that as a shaky foundation for the total commitment faith in Jesus Christ calls for. For him, then, only two things can possibly shore up religious faith in the modern age: either a priori reason (a lá Descartes) or "The Proof of the Spirit and Power," which was the title of one of his essays. Lessing did not find ground for certainty in either one; his own faith in Christ seemed to be based on a simple choice to believe because of the "fruits" of Christianity (its effects in history).

Kant's response to Lessing's ditch was to remove religion from reliance on history and reduce it to ethics, that is, to remove it from pure reason and place it in the realm of practical reason. Hegel's response, as already mentioned, was to base religion, indeed Christianity as he interpreted it, on a rational system of thought that included a necessary interpretation of universal history—history as a whole. Whether it is based on any specific event in history is left unclear by Hegel. For him, it probably was not. Kierkegaard ridiculed modern people's obsession with Lessing's big ugly ditch because for him authentic Christianity is not based on the Jesus of history or facts about him but on Christ contemporary with us in faith. (This is where the Danish thinker's pietist roots show.) Schleiermacher responded to Lessing by basing Christianity on God-consciousness. Ritschl and his followers based Christianity on the moral power of the gospel of the kingdom of God to transform individuals and society. All these responses still aimed at showing that Christianity is the absolute religion—the height, the fulfillment, the apex of religion compared with which all other religions are at best faint echoes and foreshadowings.

Troeltsch relativizes religion (but not absolutely). But none of these responses took Lessing's challenge as seriously as Troeltsch thought they should. Troeltsch insisted on taking it utterly seriously, which meant, for him and his followers, admitting Christianity's relativity as a historical religion. In other words, Christianity is not a religion of myths or timeless truths or supernatural revelations; it is a religion firmly rooted in history. It talks about God acting in historical events that are new; it looks forward to an end to history. It is not just a set of symbolic representations of universal human experience. Nor is it a set of dogmas dropped out of heaven. It is based on history and has a history: "The Christian religion is in every moment of its history a purely historical phenomenon, subject to all limitations to which any individual historical phenomenon is exposed, just like the other great religions."[92] That is Troeltsch's basic thesis about Christianity from a modern perspective.

What should modern Christians make of that in light of Lessing's ditch? Troeltsch declared something no one before him, including his liberal theological forebears, had admitted—that there can be no such thing as an absolute historical religion. A religion rooted in history, that is historical, is necessarily relative, nonabsolute. In other words, it is part of the network of historical causes and effects and changes along with them. It is one world religion among many. They are all, Christianity included, human creations. Christianity must be regarded by modern people as "a special instance of a self-understanding common to all religion."[93] To some this would seem to be a denial of Christianity, but to others it came as a great liberation—from having to think that all religious people in the world are wholly wrong except Christians. (Troeltsch lived and worked at a time when, through colonialism, trade and missions Europeans were coming to know world religions as they are and not as merely "heathenish" idolatries.)

---

[92]Ernst Troeltsch, *The Absoluteness of Christianity and the History of Religions*, trans. David Reid (Richmond, VA: John Knox, 1971), 71.
[93]Ibid., 131.

As we will see, Troeltsch did not think his historicized Christianity was false. What was false about it were claims that it is absolute. To him, Christians who think Christianity is absolute have to consider other religions false—whether wholly or partially. Christians who think Christianity is absolute also have to consider versions of Christianity other than their own false—whether wholly or partially. But it is impossible to deny that every actual, existing version of Christianity has a history. So, in order to believe that true Christianity (one's own version) is absolute, one has to believe in some nonhistorical Christianity that has not changed in history and will not change in the future. Where is that? This is why modern theologians, whether liberal or conservative, have sought for the essence of Christianity. That would be true Christianity that does not change—the kernel within the husk—which Troeltsch denied; for him the kernel and the husk are inseparable.[94] Troeltsch thought that the search for the unchanging essence of Christianity (or any religion) was a chimera, an illusion and an attempt to escape the reality of history. We are all caught in history and affected by it. All beliefs are historical and can be accounted for in terms of their historical contexts (historicism). In other words, if you could get in a time machine and travel back to any distant point in Christian history you would find that Christianity to be conditioned by its cultural context and in many ways foreign to your own.

Troeltsch's views were liberal, and he belongs in any thorough study of classical liberal theology. Remember the definition of liberal theology as "maximal accommodation to the claims of modernity." As one Troeltsch scholar put it:

> [Troeltsch] is . . . convinced that no modern man with a fully awakened historical consciousness can take seriously any religious point of view which is incompatible with modern historical thinking. Consequently . . . his concern is in large measure to accommodate the Christian faith to such thinking.[95]

However, he went beyond the typical liberal attempt to discover Christianity's essence, separate it from the accumulation of mythical accretions

---

[94]Ibid., 72.
[95]Thomas W. Ogletree, *Christian Faith and History: A Critical Comparison of Ernst Troeltsch and Karl Barth* (Nashville: Abingdon, 1965), 12.

and hold it as the absolute religion above all others. He also opposed conservative attempts to prove Christianity absolute by means of apologetics—whether conservative or liberal. He had little to say about Kierkegaard's inward leap of faith because he would have considered that another escape from the relativities of history and a sure way to make Christianity esoteric—that is, nonpublic. Troeltsch was the forerunner of what came to be called religious pluralism—the idea promoted by late twentieth-century Christian theologians that Jesus Christ is one savior but not the Savior. For pluralists there are many saviors even if Jesus is ours. Because of Troeltsch, almost all twentieth-century liberal and neo-liberal theologians gave up the idea of Christianity as the absolute religion and embraced its relativity.

Troeltsch becomes an influential but controversial liberal theologian. Troeltsch was born February 17, 1865, in a small town near Augsburg, Germany. His family was Lutheran, and his father was a medical doctor. Ernst had five siblings. His childhood was relatively uneventful, and he showed academic promise very early. He attended Erlangen University, where he studied philosophy and theology. The type of theology at Erlangen was dogmatic, and the inquisitive Troeltsch began to question how traditional Christianity fit with the modern world of science and philosophy he was beginning to embrace. By the time he left Erlangen for Berlin in 1885, he believed that Erlangen's approach to Christianity was "quite a different world, a world of marked theological demarcation from the reality of modern life and views opposed to Christian faith."[96]

At the University of Berlin Troeltsch immersed himself in modern philosophy and became acquainted with liberal Protestant theology. In 1886 he moved to the University of Göttingen to study with Ritschl, by far the most famous and influential of all the liberal theologians of Germany and perhaps the world. For a while he was an enthusiastic follower of Ritschl. Soon, however, he began to have doubts about some aspects of Ritschl's theology—especially its rejection of philosophy from theology and the idea of Christianity as the absolute religion. At the end of his studies at Göttingen, Troeltsch was awarded a prize for an essay he wrote on the philosopher Lotze's significance for Christian theology.

---

[96]Hans-Georg Drescher, *Ernst Troeltsch: His Life and Work*, trans. John Bowden (Minneapolis: Fortress, 1993), 15. Most of the biographical information here about Troeltsch is from Drescher.

After his studies at Göttingen Troetsch returned reluctantly to Erlangen to complete his seminary studies and become a licensed minister of the state church. During his oral exams his professors and others on the panel advised him to pursue an academic career instead of becoming a pastor. Nevertheless, he took a position as assistant pastor at a Lutheran church in Munich (a mostly Catholic city) that did not work out; he longed for more academic study. He returned to Göttingen, where he earned his doctorate. Gradually he began to retreat "from the idea of a self-sufficient dogmatics, isolated from the intellectual trends of [the] time."[97] He began to think more critically about traditional Christianity with the conviction that even liberal theology did not go far enough in updating and reconstructing it in light of modernity. One thesis of his public disputation (like a defense of a doctoral dissertation) was that "theology is as hard for the church to bear as to do without."[98] Troeltsch's biographer comments that "all his life he thought that it was hard for the church to do without theology, and the church itself to some extent validated the other half of his thesis, in that his theology was difficult for the church of the time to take."[99]

Troeltsch began his teaching career as a theologian at Göttingen, where, with friends, he began to develop what has come to be called the history of religions school of theology. This was a circle of like-minded young theologians who investigated Christianity from a purely historical point of view in order to make theology truly scientific. After Göttingen Troeltsch taught at the University of Bonn and then Heidelberg, where he met his wife and married at thirty-six. Finally, in 1908, he was awarded a prestigious position on the philosophy faculty of the University of Berlin. At that time, to move from theology to philosophy was almost scandalous. Many of his friends objected to it as a "flight from theology." (It is important to remember that there was a struggle over the status of theology in German universities because of the Enlightenment. For someone to move from a faculty of theology to a faculty of philosophy could be interpreted as taking a different side.) "For Troeltsch, however, the change to the philosophical faculty was not resignation nor a flight from theology. He remained committed to the-

---

[97]Ibid., 37.
[98]Ibid., 40.
[99]Ibid.

ology as he understood it, a theology with a foundation in the philosophy of religion and a marked historical orientation."[100]

Toward the end of his life Troeltsch became embroiled in German politics. At the end of World War I Germany was in political chaos. The kaiser abdicated and fled Germany, leaving German intellectuals like Troeltsch to pick up the pieces and build a new social and political order. During the last year of the war and the first few years afterwards, Troeltsch wrote opinion essays for a leading cultural newspaper. That brought his name to the attention of the founders of the Weimar Republic that replaced the German monarchy. He became a member of the Prussian parliament in 1919 and then served for a time as undersecretary of state in the Prussian Ministry of Culture. (Prussia was the most significant state of the unified Germany.) He continued to lecture at the university throughout his brief political career.

In January 1923 Troeltsch was preparing to travel to England to give guest lectures at several major universities when he became ill. He recovered, then relapsed and died suddenly on February 1. Harnack gave the funeral address in which he said, among more laudatory comments, that "he [Troeltsch] was not a comfortable person, and he made it very difficult for people to get to know him."[101] Anyone who has studied under a Prussian professor probably knows what that is like. Troeltsch's most recent biographer comments that

> what is striking . . . is the tremendous breadth of his interests, his activities and his publications. None of the subsequent great theologians could show anything like this, and the same was true of the very few before him. For the leading representatives of dialectical theology [e.g., Barth] Troeltsch (together with Harnack) was the last great representative of an epoch of theology which had come to an end, which was shaped by . . . an inappropriate assimilation to modern culture.[102]

During his lifetime Troeltsch published numerous books and hundreds of articles. He is best known, even outside of theology, for his massive work on *The Social Teachings of the Christian Churches* (1912). Among his most significant volumes of theology are *The Absoluteness of Christianity and the*

---

[100]Ibid., 127.
[101]Ibid., 316.
[102]Ibid., 317.

History of Religions (1902), *Der Historismus und seine Probleme* ("Historicism and Its Problems") and *The Christian Faith* (published posthumously in 1925). Troeltsch did not leave behind a school of theology, although he is closely associated historically with what is called the history of religions school (*Religionsgeschichteschule*), which was not a school as such but an interest and approach to studying religion and Christianity that emphasized their historical relativity. Already when Troeltsch died his star and those of other liberal theologians was waning as the sun of Barth and dialectical theology rose in the theological firmament. However, Troeltsch's influence has lasted especially among neo-liberals and those theologians who, like Van Harvey (b. 1926) and Gordon Kauffman (1925–2011), called themselves historicists.

Troeltsch's biographer Hans-Georg Drescher offers a fitting epitaph for Troeltsch:

> Troeltsch's life was devoted to a form of theology which addressed the basic questions of its time and tackled them constructively. This included the discovery of the non-Christian religions, the questions put to the Christian tradition by historicism, and the recognition in principle of the historical method, to mention only the most important factors.[103]

Troeltsch attempts to take modernity absolutely seriously. One cannot understand what Troeltsch was doing with Christianity without first understanding his context and concerns. No theologian or scholar of any discipline merely decides to write a book or article. He or she always has a concern and is always reacting to something in the intellectual environment and the cultural context. Pick up any scholarly book and study it carefully and you will discover the author's point of view as conditioned by some concern. In early Christianity, for example, Augustine was responding to heresies in the churches and to the fall of Rome. In the Middle Ages Thomas Aquinas was responding to the rising interest in the ancient Greek philosopher Aristotle in European universities. During the Reformation Luther was responding to corruption in the Catholic Church and to radical Reformers. As we have seen, Schleiermacher was responding to Kant (among others). Ritschl was responding to the threat of modern science to Christi-

---

[103]Ibid., xviii.

anity. There is no exception to this rule: Every theology is always being done in some context and out of some concern.

This is one way of getting at what Troeltsch noticed and took seriously. All historiography (historical research and writing about history) is biased, not necessarily in any negative sense, by the historian's context and concerns. There is no view from nowhere in history. No historian ever treats history, as an old saying goes, as "just one damned thing after another." The historian, like the theologian, always views history from a certain perspective brought about by his or her context and concern. This was also true of Troeltsch as a philosopher of history and theologian.

Troeltsch was determined to be as intellectually honest as possible. For him, that meant no special pleading in scholarship. Remember the struggle over the place of theology in the universities. It went on during Troeltsch's time. (The situation is different in the United States, where theology is normally taught and studied in seminaries. Even in the United States, however, many seminaries are attached to universities, and some scholars have questioned whether theology is a science or an art and thus whether it belongs in a university.) If there is one mark of modernity that underlies everything else about it, it is the demand for intellectual honesty and rejection of special pleading in scholarship. (Here "special pleading" means appealing to knowledge beyond criticism. And this "one mark of modernity" does not mean all modern thinkers lived up to it.)

Troeltsch worked and wrote about history and theology within the context of the state university. That is something foreign to most Americans unless they have lived in Europe. In Germany, for example, Christian theology is taught in the state universities by employees (professors) of the state. Troeltsch thought that at Erlangen, for example, theology was taught in a manner inappropriate to such a context. It was taught dogmatically. That was true not only there. Troeltsch, like many other, especially liberal, theologians, rejected that approach to theology as unscientific in the broadest sense—that is, engaged in special pleading, closing off its scholarship from criticism all other disciplines are normally subject to. He agreed with theology's scholarly critics that if theology is taught in the state university, it must not make truth claims uncritically. Theology must be a critical discipline and not a dogmatic one.[104] It is impossible to understand Troeltsch without taking seriously this context and concern. For him, "one either gives controlling place to the methods and conclusions of historical thinking or to the methods and conclusions of dogmatic thinking."[105] Only the former approach is compatible with being modern.

Troeltsch was convinced that even liberal theology had not yet taken modernity sufficiently seriously. For him, "to live in the modern world and to think as a modern man is to know 'the fundamental historicizing' of all one's thoughts concerning the shape and meaning of life."[106] He believed few philosophers, historians or theologians had yet fully grasped that reality. What did he mean by "historicism"? This is a key idea in Troeltsch's life work as a philosopher of history and theologian. He wrestled with it. He believed in it. He fought against its extreme versions. But it is the thread running throughout Troeltsch's work. It is not possible, however, to understand historicism without understanding what is meant by "absolute." It means unconditioned, unchanging and complete, not influenced by or dependent on environment, immutable, not partial. Historicism is the denial of anything absolute in history or even history as a whole. History, historicism says, and Troeltsch agreed, is composed of the individual, the conditioned and the partial. No piece of history or history as a whole is independent; history is a network of social forces and events that affect each other. One of Troeltsch's basic principles that he thought was fundamental to all modern historical research and understanding is "the historical and the relative are identical."[107] For him, "acknowledgment of this proposition can be evaded only by one who has deliberately or instinctively thrown up

---

[104]This situation still exists in the late twentieth and early twenty-first centuries, as this writer witnessed when studying theology in a German state university. For the most part, nontheologians have come to terms with theology being taught there, but it is looked down on insofar as it is not *wissenschaftlich*—"scientific." The classes I took were held in a building labeled "The Human Sciences." But the feel of the theology faculty area was like a seminary. The theologian I studied under, Wolfhart Pannenberg (b. 1928; see 8.b.), was still doing what Troeltsch was doing—trying to remove all special pleading from theology in order to prove that it, too, can be scientific. His major attempt at that is *Theology and the Philosophy of Science* (Philadelphia: Westminster Press, 1976).

[105]Ogletree, *Christian Faith and History*, 13.

[106]Benjamin A. Reist, *Toward a Theology of Involvement: The Thought of Ernst Troeltsch* (Philadelphia: Westminster Press, 1966), 61.

[107]Troeltsch, *Absoluteness of Christianity*, 85.

a bulwark to defend Christianity [or any religion or worldview] from the modern study of history."[108]

The reason this is important is that part and parcel of modernity is the belief that knowledge is based on reason and what reasoning with evidence can establish beyond a reasonable doubt. Reason, philosophy of history, shows that all of history is interconnected. Every event is explainable by forces and events before and around it, if not exhaustively at least in part. But that makes it not absolute; it makes it relative. The absolute in history would have to have dropped in from outside history and would then be not part of history. To be sure, some conservative theologians argued that there are two histories—ordinary world history and *Heilsgeschichte* (salvation history). The acts of God, including God's revelation, make up *Heilsgeschichte*. The ordinary historian, working with ordinary historical sources and studying ordinary historical events, does not have access to *Heilsgeschichte*, but the Christian theologian does. Troeltsch rejected this dualism as unscientific. History is history; if meaning is to be found and its discovery considered scientific, it must be found in history by historical research. For Troeltsch, "historical inquiry is not competent to deal with *Heilsgeschichte*, for the events of this history can only be known and apprehended as acts of God, which means they can only be known in faith."[109] But faith is not scientific; its truth claims involve special pleading. If theology is to be scientific and not esoteric, according to Troeltsch, it must take the relativity of history seriously and exclude from the beginning all appeals to the supernatural. In fact, "from the first Troeltsch insisted that Christianity must be treated like any other religion."[110]

So, back to historicism. What is it exactly? One definition is that "we [must] interpret and evaluate social and cultural phenomena, or for that matter all human thought and behavior, in light of the process of their development out of the past."[111] Thus, events in history are "always conditioned by their context,"[112] and this includes every point of the development of Christianity. This corresponds with the natural sciences that, in order to be truly

---

[108]Ibid.
[109]Ogletree, *Christian Faith and History*, 33.
[110]Welch, *Protestant Thought in the Nineteenth Century*, 2:280.
[111]Ogletree, *Christian Faith and History*, 21.
[112]Troeltsch, *Absoluteness of Christianity*, 66.

modern and scientific, assume that every effect has a natural cause. Supernatural causes play no role in natural science. By Troeltsch's time, around the
turn of the twentieth century, virtually all educated Europeans and Americans had come to accept that dictum about the natural sciences. What concerned him was that theology, which is inextricable from history, had not yet
fully come to terms with the parallel rule in historical research. Historicism is
that rule. To ignore or escape from it, Troeltsch believed, is to turn the clock
back to premodern Christianity, which means back to dogmatism and ultimately back to wars of religion. But to embrace the historical consciousness
of modernity, including historicism, has far-reaching consequences.

> The consequence of this historical method is the destruction of the dogmatic
> method in theology. No single historical happening can stand out from the
> rest of history as resulting from some exclusive divine causality. All is made
> relative. Yet historical method seeks universality; it does not allow any hap-
> pening to isolate itself from relationship to the entire development.[113]

In Troeltsch's own words, "the modern idea of history marks the end of
dogmatic conceptualization [of Christianity] which hypostatizes naïve
claims to validity with a few comparatively simple notions such as revelations or truths of natural reason,"[114] and "It dissolves all dogmas."[115]

Does this mean, then, that the educated, enlightened Christian has to
embrace relativism? Is there no meaning in history? What about Jesus? Was
Jesus nothing more than the product of historical forces in his past and
present, his cultural context? These are the inevitable questions that must
arise if historicism is taken with full seriousness as Troeltsch insisted we
must. Christianity cannot be the same once it has realized the truth of historicism. Historicist Christianity will be reconstructed Christianity, but the
only alternative is its demise as modernity becomes the norm for all of educated society. Or perhaps Christianity will sink into esotericism and become
a mystery religion cut off from any public role in society. That was hardly
thinkable to Troeltsch or his scholarly colleagues or to the state churches of
Europe. Many Americans in the early twenty-first century might not find it
that unthinkable. But Troeltsch was determined to rescue Christianity from

---

[113]Welch, *Protestant Thought in the Nineteenth Century*, 2:282.
[114]Troeltsch, *Absoluteness of Christianity*, 46.
[115]Ibid., 47.

becoming nothing more than a folk religion. He was also determined to rescue historicized (modern) Christianity from relativism; he firmly denied that relativity requires relativism.[116]

Troeltsch relativizes Christianity (but not absolutely). What historicism means is the denial of the absoluteness of Christianity. Even for Christians, insofar as they desire to be modern, Christianity cannot claim absolute validity. The reason is that "for Troeltsch there can no longer be any supernatural certainty. . . . Neither external nor internal miracle can serve as the court of appeal. Faith gives a certainty, but it must be understood and established in a different way."[117] What does that mean? Sometimes Troeltsch could be maddeningly ambiguous. Clearly he did not want to destroy Christianity or deny its truth. But he believed intellectual honesty required recognizing and admitting and coming to terms with its historical relativity. He was most definitely not a relativist in the ordinary sense of that word; he sought for values in history and believed in them. He also affirmed the validity of faith as a decision outside of historical research. For him,

> faith as it seeks to be certain that it has laid hold of the divine source and the divine goal, faith as it is connected to the historical person at the beginning of Christianity [Jesus], and faith as it is expressed in ethical decisions is in every case an act of responsible decision.[118]

However, as valid as faith is, for Troeltsch, because of historicism, the decision for it can never be an absolute one if it is going to be responsible:

> In those decisions, faith in God, faith in Jesus Christ, and acceptance of the moral claim can be held together, but always as a venture fraught with inner tension, uncertainty, and temporality. Every such decision will be a relative decision, an assertion of validity for us in our particular present, and will always have to be made anew as a creative act.[119]

In other words, the reflective Christian believer can choose for faith, but in light of the relativity of all reality, including history, in which Christianity arose and has always been embedded, such ventures of faith must remain

---

[116]Ibid., 89.
[117]Welch, *Protestant Thought in the Nineteenth Century*, 2:283.
[118]Ibid., 2:301.
[119]Ibid.

fluid and flexible and open to correction and should never be made dogmatically or to the exclusion of truth to be found elsewhere. The key word
is "ambiguity." Recognition of historicism and the relativity of Christianity
as a historical religion requires humility because it is always ambiguous. On
the one hand the believer ventures to have faith in Jesus Christ; on the other
hand the believer ought to acknowledge that historical research can never
prove this faith valid and that, in fact, the object of faith is itself, himself
(Jesus), historically relative and not absolute. Even the venture of faith
cannot avoid the fact that, for the modern person, "to wish to possess the
absolute in an absolute way at a particular point in history is a delusion."[120]

A key phrase in Troeltsch's affirmation of the validity of Christianity is
"for us." Troeltsch was willing to allow Christian believers to claim the truth
of Christianity and of Jesus Christ as the center of value, but only for us,
that is, for Westerners. This claim can be made with all its ambiguity and
openness to correction, all its relativity, but only for us, not for all people
everywhere. Intellectual honesty, historicism, requires that Christians realize and admit that their truth and values are tied inextricably to their
history—the development of Western culture. At one time in his career,
Troeltsch believed that historical research could demonstrate the "supremacy of the Christian religion."[121] Later, however, as he realized the full
logical consequences of historicism, he discarded that idea. There can be no
such thing as "the supreme" in history. The supreme would be the unsurpassable and unique. Historical consciousness makes all such talk obsolete.
So, in his mature thought, Troeltsch argued that all the great world religions
have their own validity; Christians should not try to evangelize them.[122]
Christians can and should believe that Christianity is "the highest religious
truth that has relevance *for us*."[123] However, "we cannot and must not regard
it as an absolute, perfect, immutable truth."[124]

As if that were not radical enough, Troeltsch also envisioned a future
time when Christianity, like everything else historical and tied to a civilization, will die out. The dissolution of the Christian religion will happen

---

[120]Troeltsch, *Absoluteness of Christianity*, 122.
[121]Ogletree, *Christian Faith and History*, 58.
[122]Ibid., 59.
[123]Troeltsch, *Absoluteness of Christianity*, 107, italics added.
[124]Ibid., 115.

with the breaking up of Western civilization.[125] So, what is of value in Christianity? Why embrace it?

Troeltsch envisions an absolute above the relative. Troeltsch's answer to why a person should be a Christian is difficult for many people in the postmodern world to grasp or understand. He was a child of his times, and one thing he did not take seriously enough was the relativity of his own historical consciousness and historical-theological formulations. Troeltsch's answer to the "Why?" of Christianity has to do with his belief that Christianity provides the only hope for a new "cultural synthesis." Europe and Western civilization that centers around it (he thought) needs such a new cultural synthesis for "the reconstruction of life and society in the years to come" and, for him, this is an "ethical task."[126] Since Christianity is inextricably linked with Western civilization, any progress in values in the future, any reconstruction of Western culture, will depend on drawing out the best values from its own heritage of which Christianity is a strong value-providing source. So, in a sense, Christianity has a relative absoluteness for Western civilization. Without it, Western, European-based culture has nowhere to turn for its values. Troeltsch very much wanted to preserve and strengthen Western Christianity's prominent role in Western culture and society for the sake of the unity and progress of that culture. However, for him, it is not dogmas that are most important about Christianity but "cult" and "community."[127] In other words, Christianity is primarily about the worship and life of the people of God in community and "the living encounter with Divinity in such community."[128]

Strangely, to some critics, Troeltsch did believe in an absolute, and he thought Christianity is the best route to it for us, although it can never finally or fully be reached. First, it is important to know that he believed in something called the religious a priori—a phrase he coined. It means that religion, the search for the divine, is necessary for humans. It is not that there is a God-shaped empty place in every human heart but that "religious life has an autonomous self-sufficient character deriving from its inner necessity. . . . In the idea of the religious a priori Troeltsch was seeking to show

---

[125]Ogletree, *Christian Faith and History*, 37.
[126]Ibid., 50.
[127]Ibid., 67.
[128]Ibid.

the rational character of the necessity of religion."[129] The religious a priori is "the feeling for the absolute in human experience."[130] That sounds like Schleiermacher and has close affinities with Schleiermacher's God-consciousness, but for Troeltsch it has no specific content. He believed the existence of this innate human religiousness could be demonstrated through historical research. It is a pointer toward something absolute, but it is not itself absolute. The religious a priori is an element of finite consciousness not dependent on history, but it has no form. It takes form in history in particular, concrete religious forms of life, that is, in world religions.[131]

The introduction of the concept of the religious a priori raises the question of something absolute that religion reflects or strives toward. Troeltsch believed in God and that "the religious dimension of human history is a revelation of the divine life."[132] But the absolute, God, never enters history; he cannot because that would make him relative. The absolute, God, stands beyond all historical appearances including specific religious traditions. Even though God does not enter history, so as to become part of it (Troeltsch clearly did not believe in the incarnation), God is present *to* history as the source and basis of all that has value.[133] "While the absolute as such cannot be a historical appearance or revelation, it continues to have bearing on the historical, giving it unity, direction, and power."[134] For Troeltsch, then, God is something like Plato's form of the good—the form of all the forms—that keeps the world of multiplicity from falling into chaos and moral relativism. But no religion can claim to possess this or express the religious a priori perfectly. Nevertheless, all the great world religions are attempts to connect with the divine and draw human values from that.

> He [Troeltsch] has argued that while the absolute as such always stands beyond history, still the relative values and achievements of history do have a relation to the absolute. They strive toward it, approach, indeed, even contain it within themselves though only in a relative way.[135]

---

[129]Welch, *Protestant Thought in the Nineteenth Century*, 2:273–74.
[130]Ogletree, *Christian Faith and History*, 41.
[131]Ibid., 72.
[132]Ibid., 39.
[133]Ibid.
[134]Ibid., 43.
[135]Ibid., 45.

The only way to make sense of this is to believe that for Troeltsch the transcendental absolute, the source and ground of all value, that toward which religion aims, is always only potential so far as humans are concerned. For him, "absolute truth belongs to the future."[136]

Back, then, to the question of why to be a Christian. While Christianity is not absolute and may even pass away, it is the best source of values for Western culture's future. To abandon it may be to lose all values. What else would serve as a source of values for the necessary reconstruction of Western civilization (e.g., after the world wars)? Troeltsch believed, however inconsistently, that somehow Christianity, at its best, is at least for us (i.e., for him and people of Europe and North America then) the best source to turn to and rely on for the "new and creative achievement" needed in the "reconstruction of life and society in the years to come."[137] He talked about "historical heirlooms" that need to be rediscovered and used for the construction of this new cultural synthesis. Empirical research into Western history and Christianity is the best hope of finding them and putting them to good use.

Strangely, because it seems inconsistent with other things he said about Christianity, Troeltsch also believed that Christianity, although not absolute, is "the normative religion, the religion that is normative not only for [contemporary Christians] but also for all history up to the present time."[138] The reader will not be blamed for gasping. Was Troeltsch contradicting himself? Not really. By "normative" he did not mean "absolute"; he meant that "among the great religions, Christianity is in actuality the strongest and most concentrated revelation of personalistic religious apprehension."[139] This was Troeltsch's way of avoiding relativism in all his talk about the relativity of Christianity. For him, compared with all other great world religions (he explicitly excludes the "primitive religions" from consideration), Christianity is superior in that it brings to expression better the common goal of all "higher" religious life. "The differences between religions . . . exist only in the depth, power, and clarity with which the higher life is revealed."[140]

---

[136]Troeltsch, *Absoluteness of Christianity*, 115.
[137]Ogletree, *Christian Faith and History*, 50.
[138]Troeltsch, *Absoluteness of Christianity*, 121.
[139]Ibid., 112.
[140]Ibid., 95.

Christianity is different in degree from other religions but not in kind. It displays greater depth, power and clarity in revealing the common aspirations of all of them. In that sense it is normative but not absolute.

So, for Troeltsch, all is *not* merely relative. Only history is relative. The absolute, God, the source of all meaning and value, is not part of history. No person or group within history can claim to possess this absolute absolutely. But it can be useful as a source and goal; plumbing the "richest and deepest values" of "our past" can put us indirectly and relatively in touch with it. But in that process we must never claim to have reached it to the exclusion of other traditions and communities. What flesh can be put on these bare bones of philosophy? Buried in his work is Troeltsch's presupposition about value. "He seeks those values which can unify human culture to the greatest extent."[141] For him, the "unity of humanity" is the highest value even if not an absolute one. Underlying that is the bedrock assumption, hardly justifiable from historical research alone, that "all of life is the expression of the divine Ground of life and the inner movement of this Ground towards a total meaning."[142] That sounds more like faith than the findings of historical research. But for Troeltsch it is only a "confidence," not something that can be proved.

Troeltsch finds hope and meaning in the historical Jesus. If Troeltsch was right, then, Christianity is only a relative good, only a Western religion, and destined eventually to die. One response to that has been to say that Christianity is not Jesus; Christianity is a religion while Jesus is the living person in whom Christians (whatever they are called) have faith. For most Christians throughout history, there is at least one absolute within history— Jesus as Lord and Savior. At the same time, some more radical philosophers of Troeltsch's time suggested that sheer historicism *ought* to do away with Jesus. What if he never lived? Isn't that possible if all historical knowledge is at best relative? Why is Jesus important if there is no direct access to the divine within history and every historical event, Jesus included, is conditioned by its context? Perhaps all that matters about Jesus is the image of a person who lived such a life.

Troeltsch would have none of that. He admitted that "our knowledge of Jesus is thoroughly relativized by historical criticism, and the 'inner ne-

---

[141]Ogletree, *Christian Faith and History*, 54.
[142]Ibid., 52.

cessity' of the connection with him is 'a very relative matter.'"[143] Yet, he could not dispense with Jesus as a real historical person. He strongly believed that "Christian faith would be undermined if the community of scholars should reach and sustain a negative result on the historicity of Jesus."[144] That is because "in Christianity, Christ is a significant symbol only because behind this symbol stands an actual religious prophet."[145] What is at stake in the historicity of Jesus and at least a bare knowledge of what he was like and said and did? Here is an example of Troeltsch's inconsistency about the absolute and the relative, noted above in the matters of the religious a priori and Christianity's normativity. On the one hand, Troeltsch answered that "nothing absolute and final is at stake in the historicity of Jesus."[146] Yet, strangely, he went on to say that "relatively speaking a great deal is at stake."[147] What does this mean? It should come as no surprise that he comes back to the importance of Christianity for the vitality of Western civilization and its values. "The most vital religious tradition available to us in our civilization is one which centers in the reality of this personal life."[148] What Troeltsch meant is best expressed by his interpreter Thomas Ogletree:

> While Troeltsch's understanding of history and faith's relation to history means that there is no ultimate or absolute necessity for the historicity of Jesus, still there is a relative necessity in that the richest and most vital religious tradition in our cultural circle looks to the person of Jesus Christ as the center of its cult and community. For this religious tradition to play a normative role in our present life, empirical historical research must be able to clarify his place and role as a historical person in that tradition.[149]

So, Troeltsch thought that the search for the historical Jesus being carried out by liberal New Testament scholars was a good thing so long as it was strictly empirical in its methods and did not smuggle into them philosophical or theological assumptions. He believed that such research does demonstrate the historicity of Jesus and the basic outlines of his life and

---

[143]Welch, *Protestant Thought in the Nineteenth Century*, 2:290.
[144]Ogletree, *Christian Faith and History*, 71.
[145]Ibid., 69.
[146]Ibid.
[147]Ibid.
[148]Ibid.
[149]Ibid., 71.

teachings. The point is the values Jesus communicated by his life and teachings. Troeltsch denied the church's historical dogmas about Christ as having any modern validity. For him, "no man awakened to the nature and force of modern historical thinking can intelligently claim that Jesus Christ is the unique son of God."[150] He rejected the bodily resurrection of Jesus as myth because it violates the "principle of analogy"[151] that all critical historical research must use in separating fact from fiction. The principle of analogy is that an event must not be absolutely unique, a bolt out of the blue, so to speak, unlike anything else in history, in order to be considered historical. All historical events are somewhat alike. An event like a bodily resurrection is so unlike other events that it cannot come under the historian's purview to study. Thus, it cannot be considered historical.

Troeltsch revisions dogma in light of modernity. What about the orthodox dogmas about Christ and the Trinity? What did Troeltsch say about them? Predictably, his conclusions about them in *The Christian Faith* (*Glaubenslehre*), lectures in systematic theology delivered by Troeltsch at Heidelberg, are governed by modern thought. Everything in Christian history must be submitted to the canons of modern philosophy and historiography for evaluation and possible reconstruction. In his lectures on "Jesus Christ as the Object of Faith" Troeltsch followed the trend of liberal theology by denying the classical doctrines of the incarnation and Trinity as inextricably tied to "ancient cosmology." He discussed the emergence of the idea of the "immanent Trinity" out of belief in the incarnation of the Logos in Greek Christianity. According to that, Jesus Christ was the incarnation of the Son of God, second person of the Trinity, equal with the Father and yet distinct from the Father. His judgment on all that is:

> Now that ancient cosmology has been eliminated from theology, and with the accompanying emergence of a human-historical view of Jesus, the Christian concept of God has grown independent of this basically Neoplatonic formula. The contemporary material exposition of the concept of God is developed purely out of Jesus' proclamation of God; but this makes it impossible to explain Jesus' religious significance in terms of the incarnation of the Logos. And this, in turn, spells the end for patristic, immanent doctrine of the Trinity. But

---

[150]Ibid., 75.
[151]Welch, *Protestant Thought in the Nineteenth Century*, 2:281.

the concept of the redemptive revelation of God, in Christ and through the Holy Spirit, still remains the most succinct summary of the Christian faith; and so this three-ness remains. But no longer can it be understood in terms of the immanent Trinity—only in terms of the so-called *economic* Trinity.[152]

In other words, according to Troeltsch, because of the change in world-views brought about by the Enlightenment, modern Christians cannot believe in a heavenly community of three persons who are somehow also one substance. Nor can they believe in a literal incarnation in which a human being is identified directly with God. The whole problem in these ancient beliefs is ontology or metaphysics; people no longer think in those ways.

What can modern people believe about God and Christ? Troeltsch wrote, "We no longer ground our faith on incarnation, but on revelation instead."[153] Our Christian confession now can be "we believe in the God the Father and in the Son and in the Holy Spirit; for we believe in the eternal Lord of the world, who was miraculously revealed in Jesus, and in his Spirit, which rules in history and leads us farther and farther into all truth."[154] Since he denied the immanent Trinity (God as three persons in himself), Troeltsch must mean that Christians can still embrace three "moments" or "aspects" of divine revelation. What they cannot do, and be modern, is believe in the ancient, creedal statements of orthodox Christianity including that Jesus Christ was God. He is only the (or a) revelation of God through the Spirit of God. Even this must be held lightly in view of the relativity of all history and knowledge.

Troeltsch leaves a troubled and troubling legacy. It almost goes without saying that Troeltsch has been very controversial. During his tenure at Heidelberg some church leaders tried to have him fired. He chose to leave there and move to the chair of philosophy at Berlin partly to escape them. Philosophers do not come under the same scrutiny as theologians. Troeltsch knew well that his whole program of historicized Christianity "calls for a fairly radical reinterpretation of the Christian faith."[155] Even many liberals were shocked by some of his conclusions and especially by his firm denial of the absoluteness of Christianity and of Jesus.

---

[152]Ernst Troeltsch, *The Christian Faith*, trans. Garrett E. Paul (Minneapolis: Augsburg Fortress, 1991), 105.

[153]Ibid., 107.

[154]Ibid.

[155]Ogletree, *Christian Faith and History*, 76.

However, many liberal Protestant Christians found in him a bracing honesty missing in dogmatic Christianity. Especially those known as pluralists, such as John Hick (1922–2012), appreciate Troeltsch and find him an ally in affirming the truth in non-Christian world religions and even in affirming other religions' founders as genuine saviors of those religions' followers.[156] The value in this, according to pluralists, is that it is necessary for world peace, as wars of religion are still happening. Only if the world religions affirm each other as true paths to God and ways of salvation can wars of religion be stopped.

Some of the harshest criticism of Troeltsch came from other liberal Protestant theologians. One of them, Wilhelm Herrmann (1846–1922), dismissed Troeltsch as lacking faith. According to Herrmann, following Schleiermacher and Ritschl, Christianity is not a matter of science or history but of faith. For him, "the truth and validity of religion is solely a matter of faith, residing in the immediacy of inner feeling alone."[157] Of course, Troeltsch would dismiss that as special pleading and unscientific thinking about religion. Herrmann's more famous student, Barth, however, launched an attack on Troeltsch, labeling his theology "culture Protestantism."[158] According to Barth, Troeltsch has identified Christianity with Western culture (especially German culture, which, for Barth, led in part to the phenomenon of the so-called German Christians [the name religious sympathizers of Nazism took]). Barth agreed with Troeltsch that ordinary history is relative, but he disagreed that there is no breaking into history of the absolute. For Barth, the whole point of Christianity is that God has broken into history in Jesus Christ. Again, Troeltsch would dismiss that as unscientific special pleading.

Many Troeltsch scholars, even those sympathetic with his overall project, have noticed a tension in his thinking and even an inconsistency. On the one hand, he eschewed any talk of the absolute in history, but on the other

---

[156]See John Hick, *The Myth of Christian Uniqueness: Toward a Pluralistic Theology of Religions*, ed. with Paul Knitter (1987; Eugene, OR: Wipf & Stock, 2004).

[157]Quoted in Ogletree, *Christian Faith and History*, 82. See Wilhelm Herrmann, *The Communion of the Christian with God* (New York: Putnam, 1906).

[158]For the history and meaning of "culture Protestantism," an epithet Barth used for liberal theology in general, see George Rupp, *Culture Protestantism: German Liberal Theology at the Turn of the Twentieth Century* (Atlanta: Scholars Press, 1977).

hand he affirmed a non-historical "Infinite Consciousness" in the religious a priori within history.[159] Also, Troeltsch never satisfactorily explained why the historical Jesus is essential for Christianity since Christianity, like all religions, has no essence. Troeltsch denied any "permanent core" of Christianity that does not change. Then why is Jesus Christ necessary as more than a myth or image? Why couldn't a Christless Christianity emerge and still be Christian? Troeltsch clearly did not want that, but some of his left-wing followers could not see why. They reduced Christ to an image without any necessary historical reality.

Conservatives, neo-orthodox and even moderate liberals have condemned Troeltsch as not even a Christian. Some of them have argued that he took liberal Protestant theology to its logical conclusion. Clearly he stands in the line of Kantian or neo-Kantian theology that reduces Christianity to ethics, even though he claimed to value "cult and community" above all else about Christianity. But the real value he saw in Christianity, and the reason to preserve it, is its "historical heirlooms"—values of use to Western civilization in constructing a new cultural synthesis. But, if somehow Christianity should disappear from the earth, what would be lost? Troeltsch would say nothing absolute but not absolutely nothing.

Perhaps the most neutral (if that is possible) challenge to Troeltsch is the postmodern one. A postmodern person would point out the irony that the German theologian relativized all historical reality except his own historicism. If he was right, then he too stood in a particular context with a particular concern and a particular response conditioned by the past and his cultural environment. He envisioned Christianity as a Western, mainly European religion. The century after him proved otherwise. In the early twenty-first century it is mainly a religion of the Global South.[160] Troeltsch envisioned the possible demise of Christianity but not its embrace by untold millions of non-Europeans. He was also a prisoner of late modernism, some would say the Enlightenment gone to seed. Rationalism and naturalism were his operating principles, even though he tried to resist extreme versions of both. But they, too, were and are historically conditioned

---

[159]Ogletree, *Christian Faith and History*, 53–55.
[160]See Philip Jenkins, *The Next Christendom: The Coming Global Christianity* (New York: Oxford University Press, 2002).

perspectives on knowledge and reality. Troeltsch wanted everyone else to be critical of their own standpoints, but he failed to be sufficiently critical of his own and tended to absolutize it in contradiction to his own historicism.

Perhaps the most damaging criticism of Troeltsch is the one already hinted at—that his near identification of Christianity with German culture and his project of developing a "new cultural synthesis" on the basis of European Christianity (he even called it Europaism) may have laid the groundwork for the emergence of German Christianity in the 1930s that hailed National Socialism (Nazism) as that new cultural synthesis. If there is nothing absolute in or about Christianity, and if Christianity has no permanent core, how is one to criticize the so-called German Christians as non-Christian? Troeltsch did not foresee this and would almost certainly have condemned it (his own political sympathies were left-leaning), but that says nothing about whether his theology inadvertently led to it.

2.D. CATHOLIC MODERNISTS ATTEMPT TO BRING ROME UP TO DATE

On September 8, 1907, Pope Pius X promulgated a papal encyclical titled *Pascendi Dominici Gregis* ("Feeding the Lord's Flock"). Papal letters to all the faithful are not rare, but this one fell like a bombshell on those Catholic theologians who considered themselves progressives. Their enemies, including the pope, called them modernists. These few liberal-minded Catholic thinkers were anything but a cohesive movement; some scholars say the movement was created by the Vatican.[161] These so-called modernists were a loose group of Catholic scholars "the aim of which was to bring traditional Catholic teaching into closer relations with current thought, especially in philosophy, history and social theory."[162] *Pascendi* accused them of being "insidiously hostile to the faith as officially understood and taught"[163]

---

[161]Gabriel Daly, "Theological and Philosophical Modernism," in *Catholicism Contending with Modernity: Roman Catholic Modernism and Anti-Modernism in Historical Perspective*, ed. Darrell Jadock (Cambridge: Cambridge University Press, 2000), 89. According to Daly, "Rome did much to create the monster it slew."

[162]Bernard M. G. Reardon, "Roman Catholic Modernism," in *Nineteenth-Century Religious Thought in the West*, ed. Ninian Smart et al., 3 vols. (Cambridge: Cambridge University Press, 1985), 2:141.

[163]Ibid.

and their movement of being "a synthesis of all heresies."[164] The pope then instituted a required oath against modernism by all bishops, priests and teachers of the church.

Pope Pius's repression of progressive Catholic theology was the capstone and culmination of a long process in which the Vatican reacted to modernity and to any and all alleged accommodations to it. The Vatican had never lifted the conviction of Galileo or expressed regret for the way it handled the Galileo affair. It still felt threatened by modern science and Enlightenment philosophy and especially Kant's philosophy, which it called agnosticism. But the intensity of the Catholic hierarchy's reaction against modernity was partly because of the French Revolution that many scholars blamed on extreme modernism—the Enlightenment taken to its logical conclusion. The leaders of the French Revolution of the 1790s placed a statue of the "Goddess of Reason" in the cathedral of Notre Dame in Paris and worshiped her there. They disestablished the Catholic Church and persecuted its leaders and priests. Throughout the nineteenth century the Vatican was deeply suspicious of anything that smacked of Enlightenment rationalism or secularism.

The Catholic hierarchy restrains progressive thinking in the church. In 1864 Pope Pius IX promulgated the Syllabus of Errors—a laundry list of mostly modern ideas and cultural trends deemed inimical to true faith. Among other things it condemned separation of church and state and "Bible societies." Most importantly, however, it condemned "modern liberalism" and deemed its proponents "enemies of the Church."[165] In it "faith was presented as intellectual assent to divine truths revealed by God and guaranteed by external signs, namely, miracles and fulfilled prophecies. Theology was scarcely more than a series of logical deductions from the premises extrinsically revealed by God."[166] The same pope who promulgated the syllabus declared Mary's immaculate conception (that she was conceived without original sin) a dogma. Many Catholics, especially progressives, saw this as an assertion of papal power. Vatican I, the twentieth

---

[164]Darrell Jadock, "Introduction I: The Modernist Crisis," in *Catholicism Contending with Modernity: Roman Catholic Modernism and Anti-Modernism in Historical Perspective*, ed. Darrell Jadock (Cambridge: Cambridge University Press, 2000), 1.

[165]Daly, "Theological and Philosophical Modernism," 95.

[166]Ibid., 96.

ecumenical council of the church, declared popes infallible when speaking as Pius IX did about Mary—that is, as the representative of Christ on earth. The council was a setback for liberalizing forces in the Catholic Church.

Pius X's *Pascendi* stood on the shoulders of the Syllabus of Errors and Vatican I but aimed specifically at a group of Catholic scholars deemed too progressive in terms of accommodating to modernity. They included especially, but not exclusively, French biblical scholar and theologian Alfred Loisy (1857–1940) and English Jesuit theologian George Tyrrell (1861–1909). These two modernists resisted *Pascendi*, which brought about their formal excommunications in 1907 and 1908 respectively. Among other errors, *Pascendi* condemned modernism for "vital immanence" (or immanentism), "agnosticism" and "neo-Kantianism."[167] By vital immanence the pope meant an inordinate emphasis on the presence of God in human experience; by agnosticism he meant the denial that God-in-himself can be known. "Neo-Kantianism" was a catch-all phrase for everything bad in philosophy throughout the nineteenth century. Most of all, however, *Pascendi* expressed strong criticism for a central tenet of modernism—"any notion that dogma may have evolved or that it may need to change again."[168]

Tyrrell accused *Pascendi* of "equating Catholic doctrine with scholastic theology and of having a completely naïve view of the idea of doctrinal development."[169] Loisy was hardly more receptive of the critical encyclical. The pair may not have been guilty of some of the charges listed in it, but there can be little doubt that they were guilty of belief in doctrinal development of a fairly radical nature—compared with traditional Catholic thought. They believed, contrary to the prevailing mood of the Catholic hierarchy, that Catholic theology needed to use the best of modern thought as a source for reconceptualizing and reconstructing church dogmas. They also believed that experience of God is more fundamental to Christianity than doctrine; doctrines are the secondary language of the church while prayer is its primary language. Thus, according to Tyrrell and Loisy, dogma needed to change better to express personal faith and modern culture. Their hope was that "from the inter-

---

[167]Oliver P. Rafferty, *George Tyrrell and Catholic Modernism* (Dublin: Four Courts Press, 2010), 10.
[168]Jadock, "Introduction I," 5.
[169]Rafferty, *George Tyrrell and Catholic Modernism*, 27.

action of the Christian life and modernity a new [Catholic] synthesis would arise."[170]

Many scholars, not just theologians, regarded *Pascendi* and the excommunications of the modernists as overkill. Lord Acton (1834–1902), an English Catholic nobleman and editor, commented on the Vatican's treatment of liberalizing tendencies in the Catholic Church by writing that the Catholic hierarchy had exercised a "zeal for the prevention of error which represses the intellectual freedom necessary to the progress of truth."[171] Indeed, modernism was the "final phase" of a trend of "liberalizing tendencies" in nineteenth- and early twentieth-century Catholicism.[172] *Pascendi* and the modernists' excommunications seemed to kill that progressive impulse by also condemning "practically all the identifiable modernist publications."[173] For the next half century Catholic theology would remain, for the most part, stuck in its scholastic and dogmatic past. However, modernism seemed to have lasting influence as it reemerged in a different form at the Second Vatican Council (Vatican II) in the early 1960s.

It might be helpful before continuing to define certain common terms used by modernists and their critics. Protestants are generally unfamiliar with these terms even though they have parallels in Protestant theology. First is "integralism," a term for conservative Catholic thought that is, in many ways, the opposite of modernism. "The basic Catholic integralist position held that all areas of human behavior are subject to judgment by church authority and therefore to papal authority."[174] Integralism was viewed by modernists as the reactionary impulse in Catholicism, whereas conservatives viewed it as the only protection of Catholic identity from erosion, if not extinction, at the hands of the acids of modernity. In the late twentieth and early twenty-first centuries integralism came to be used as a very broad term for conservative Catholics' reluctance to accept all the changes introduced by Vatican II. It might be equated with Catholic traditionalism.

---

[170]Ibid., 28.
[171]Reardon, "Roman Catholic Modernism," 146.
[172]Ibid., 147.
[173]Ibid., 149.
[174]Darrell Jadock, "Introduction II: The Modernists and the Anti-Modernists," in *Catholicism Contending with Modernity: Roman Catholic Modernism and Anti-Modernism in Historical Perspective*, ed. Darrell Jadock (Cambridge: Cambridge University Press, 2000), 82.

"Immanentism" or "vital immanentism" was one of the charges made by
the pope against modernism. In order to understand that term one has to
step back and look at a larger picture of Catholic integralist theology in the
nineteenth century. *Pascendi*, like other papal pronouncements, assumed
two realms—the natural and the supernatural. Protestants often use the
word *supernatural* for miracles, but in Catholic theology it has a broader
meaning. The supernatural is, for Catholic theology, the realm of grace.
Whatever is not part of nature is of grace, the supernatural. Thomas Aquinas
made much of this distinction. The Syllabus of Errors, Vatican I and other
nineteenth-century Catholic theological decisions baptized Thomism, the
basic theological framework of Aquinas, as official for all Catholic theologians. For Thomas, there are two distinct but related realms of reality—the
natural and the supernatural. The natural includes reason, what reason can
know without the aid of revelation or faith such as the existence of God.
The supernatural includes what can be known only by revelation, such as
that God is triune. Natural law, basic ethics, is part of the natural realm and
thus knowable by reason alone. Salvation is solely supernatural; it cannot
be achieved by reason or mere human morality.

"Immanentism" is the Catholic hierarchy's term for modernism's alleged
dissolving of the line between the natural and the supernatural so that
God's grace is embedded in the natural realm. Supposedly in modernism,
"the internal immanent apperception of God was to replace the objec-
tiveness of divine revelation."[175] In other words, immanentism would be the
idea that the human person, unaided by supernatural grace, can know God
personally and savingly.

"Intrinsicism" and "extrinsicism" are twin terms used much in modern
Catholic thought—especially by modernists and their sympathizers. Extrinsicism is modernism's term for traditional Catholic emphasis on the external
nature of revelation, truth and relationship with God. It is all extrinsic or
external to the human person. Everything of real value spiritually has to
come from without; God is above and beyond and outside of everything
human. Intrinsicism is the belief that God and grace are in some sense
always already present to the human person and especially that when the

---

[175]Rafferty, *George Tyrrell and Catholic Modernism*, 11.

persons are saved God's grace resides in them transformingly. "Modernist presuppositions stressed the interior antennae within human experience as the basis for the recognition of the divine at work in human history."[176] Thus, the emphasis is on inward spirituality. Extrinsicism emphasizes what is outside the person—objective truth, supernatural grace. The connection between immanentism and intrinsicism is obvious. The modernists preferred "intrinsicism," but their critics called their view immanentism.

Finally, "doctrinal development" has a technical meaning in Catholic theology not necessarily present in Protestant theology. It does not just mean that doctrines go through stages. Obviously the belief in Mary's immaculate conception was elevated to the status of dogma in 1854, but Catholic traditionalists who do not believe in doctrinal development argue it was always believed by the faithful. In other words, according to integralists, dogma does not come into being; a belief is elevated to the status of dogma. Catholics who affirm doctrinal development mean somewhat different things by it, but the modernists agreed that all doctrines are historical and should be treated as such. One scholar of the modernist movement identifies this as *the* theological core of modernism:

> The conflict between the concept of Christian doctrines as immutable and perennially valid, on the one hand, and, on the other, as culturally limited expressions of truths which are antecedent to their formulations constitutes the theological core of the Modernist crisis which occurred in the Roman Catholic Church between c. 1890 and 1914.[177]

Belief in doctrinal development is not unique to the time-limited modernist movement, however. Many Catholic thinkers have believed in some degree of doctrinal development, but the modernists made it a hallmark of progressive Catholicism.

Two Catholic theologians set the stage for modernism. Catholic modernism, like every other theological movement, had its antecedents and outside influences. The leading modernists were influenced to some degree by the whole Enlightenment and scientific revolution and especially by Kant, whose "critique of metaphysics is, from the standpoint of religion and

---

[176]Ibid., 10.
[177]Daly, "Theological and Philosophical Modernism," 88.

theology, perhaps the most powerful factor in bringing about the modern world."[178] However, two nineteenth-century Catholic theologians who were not condemned or excommunicated set the stage for modernism: Englishman John Henry Newman (1801–1890) and Frenchman Maurice Blondel (1861–1949). Both are heroes to various types of Catholics, and many of their devotees would not want them blamed in any way for modernism; they were not modernists themselves. However, Blondel has been called "the spiritual father of Modernism."[179] Newman's influence on modernism is beyond dispute, as both Loisy and Tyrrell gave him much credit for inspiring them. Again, however, neither Blondel nor Newman was ever disciplined, and Newman was always held in high regard by the Catholic hierarchy. Perhaps it did not grasp the radical nature of some of his ideas about theology.

Newman was an evangelical Anglican priest and professor of theology at Oxford who gradually came to believe in many of the doctrines and practices of the Catholic Church. He and a group of friends and colleagues began meeting to urge the Church of England to move closer to Rome. This group came to be known as the Oxford Group, and Newman has always been considered its leader. In 1845 Newman left the Church of England to become a member of the Catholic Church. Possibly for political reasons, Pope Leo XIII granted Newman the status of cardinal in 1879. The convert to Catholicism helped found the Catholic University of Ireland (today's University College, Dublin) and was a prolific writer on subjects related to theology, apologetics and church structure. Perhaps because he was a convert to Catholicism he was granted a great deal of leeway in departing from the strictest tenets of tradition. However, he was genuinely a passionate Catholic who loved the church and wanted it to be both faithful and contemporary without accommodating to modernity.

Newman's best-known writings include *Essay on the Development of Christian Doctrine* (1845), the book that most inspired the modernists; *The Grammar of Ascent* (1870), a volume of Christian apologetics; and his autobiography, *Apologia Pro Vita Sua* (1864). He is best known in Catholic circles as a great defender of the Catholic faith against Protestantism and

---

[178]Ibid., 92.
[179]Bernard M. G. Reardon, *Roman Catholic Modernism* (London: A & C Black, 1970), 55.

the acids of modernity. He was beatified (a step toward sainthood) by Pope Benedict XVI in 2010. Even many Protestants admire and revere Newman, often for *The Idea of a University* (1852), which laid out the model for a modern Christian university.

Newman's influence on modernism was through his understanding of the development of doctrine. In his *Essay on the Development of Christian Doctrine* the cardinal attempted to overcome the traditionalist idea of "an immobile church in possession of an immutable dogma"[180] and develop a model of "doctrinal development as a living process which presupposes a dynamic relationship between the gospel message and the church to which it was committed and within which it has to be newly understood and articulated in every age."[181] However, Newman was most definitely not touched by historicism, the idea of the relativity of all ideas including doctrines. He believed in the divine source of right doctrine and in its objectivity even though it needs to be understood and articulated in new ways in new cultural contexts and time periods. Still, this was a new idea for many Catholics, and the modernists picked up and elaborated on it.

Blondel was perhaps the greater influence on modernism; without his "philosophy of action" it would never have been born. According to one scholar of modernism "one can reasonably take Maurice Blondel's *L'Action* as the point of departure of Catholic philosophico-theological Modernism."[182] Some scholars even include Blondel in the list of Catholic modernists, but he would not be a good fit for that category because of his basic respect for and adherence to the pronouncements of the Catholic magisterium.

Blondel's life was not particularly eventful; he is known only as a Christian philosopher who taught at the University of Aiz-en-Provence in France. But he is widely regarded as the real founder of what is known as the *nouvelle théologie* ("new theology") that included twentieth-century Catholic reforming theologians such as Henri de Lubac, Hans Urs von Balthasar, Karl Rahner, and many others. His classic work of philosophy and theology that influenced modernism was *L'Action* (1893). It was "an attempt to construct a philosophical argument for revelation which was not vulnerable to the

---

[180]Daly, "Theological and Philosophical Modernism," 105.
[181]Ibid.
[182]Ibid., 102.

Kantian critique of metaphysics."[183] The central idea was anti-extrinsicism or, simply, intrinsicism—the idea that there resides within all human persons a spiritual presence that makes them open to God so that when revelation comes it is not alien or foreign but the answer to the question that humanity is. In other words, the book's thesis was that "openness to the truths of faith corresponds to a fundamental human aspiration."[184]

Blondel's philosophy of action was a response to the increasing secularism and agnosticism of Enlightenment-inspired modernity on the one hand and the extrinsicism of traditional Catholic thought on the other hand. Modernity, especially Kant's philosophy, tended to make God and God's revelation something alien to humanity, especially modern man. Traditional Catholic thought tended to do the same thing in a different way; it pitted the natural against the supernatural and vice versa so that everything of grace, including God's self-revelation, was foreign to natural humanity. Blondel tried to show that so-called natural man, the human person apart from supernatural grace, is always already open to revelation and salvation. By means of a careful, phenomenological examination of human thought and creativity, he attempted to show that these cannot be completed in the natural order alone.[185] "In terms more properly Christian, [the person] remains open to the 'outer' fact of revelation should it be offered."[186] This emphasis on a natural openness to revelation was regarded by Blondel's critics as an example of immanentism, but the Catholic hierarchy never disciplined him for it.

Nevertheless, Blondel's approach to transcendence and immanence, the supernatural and the natural, signaled a significant shift from common Catholic reactions to modernity which were almost uniformly negative.[187] Blondel found help for his argument in Enlightenment philosophy in spite of itself. Some regard his as a "mediating Christian philosophy and theology"—attempting to reconcile religion and modernity without doing vio-

---

[183]Ibid., 103.

[184]Phyllis H. Kaminski, "Seeking Transcendence in the Modern World," in *Catholicism Contending with Modernity: Roman Catholic Modernism and Anti-Modernism in Historical Perspective*, ed. Darrell Jadock (Cambridge: Cambridge University Press, 2000), 121.

[185]Ibid., 124.

[186]Ibid., 125.

[187]Ibid., 115.

lence to religion's integrity.[188] What he was attempting to do was show, using modern methods and emphasis on humanity, that there is an "immanence of transcendence" in human experience. To critics he was confusing the orders of nature and supernature and not keeping them distinct. He rightly rejected that criticism, but he was trying to overcome the stark dualism between them that antimodern Catholic thought had created. The other accusation was that his philosophy was an example of Enlightenment anthropocentrism—human-centeredness rather than God-centeredness. He rightly rejected that as well. All he was trying to do, sympathetic scholars say, was

> to decipher the traces of transcendence in human beings and society. . . . In his thesis Blondel . . . demonstrated that, in following the dialectical movement of our concrete choices and our deepest desires, we discover an incompleteness, a natural inachievability that cannot be filled without going beyond ourselves.[189]

In spite of Blondel's innocence in terms of not being a modernist, it is easy to see why the modernists were inspired by his philosophy. That will be clearer by the end of this chapter. Suffice it to say now that his way of thinking placed the emphasis on human experience rather than on extrinsic grace. Grace, the supernatural, revelation, are not extrinsic but intrinsic to human existence.

With Newman and Blondel the stage was set for the emergence of Catholic modernism. However, many of Newman's and Blondel's followers never joined with Loisy or Tyrrell in developing the perspective that came to be known as modernism. They seemed to be influenced as much by Kant and Schleiermacher as by Newman and Blondel. And for that the Catholic hierarchy could not forgive them.

Modernists find common cause against Catholic traditionalism. Scholars are generally agreed that three Catholic theologians form the nucleus of modernism: Austrian Friedrich Baron von Hügel (1852–1925), Loisy and Tyrrell. Von Hügel's role is more disputed than that of the latter two. Bernard Reardon, a scholar of nineteenth-century theology, dubs him "a decided pace-setter" on the periphery of the modernist movement.[190] His un-

---

[188]Ibid., 119.
[189]Ibid., 120.
[190]Reardon, "Roman Catholic Modernism," 158.

wavering loyalty to the Catholic church saved him from the persecution suffered by his two friends and colleagues. Von Hügel was definitely a progressive among Catholic thinkers, but he was also something of a mystic who dabbled in metaphysics and transcendentalist (like romanticist) thinking.[191] As a hereditary baron of the Holy Roman Empire he was independently wealthy, and as a natural intellectual he was self-taught in philosophy and theology. He never held office in the Catholic church or in any academic institution. And yet he was widely recognized throughout Europe and Great Britain as a man of great knowledge and spiritual wisdom. In 1920 he was granted an honorary doctorate by Oxford University, the first time a Catholic had received that honor since the Reformation. He lived in England much of his adult life and worked tirelessly there to bring German theology into English. It was he who invited Troeltsch to lecture at English universities. When he died he was buried in an English country cemetery, and by his own desire his tombstone says only "Whom Have I In Heaven But Thee?" Many late nineteenth- and early twentieth-century Christian spiritual writers and mystics consider him a modern saint of the contemplative life.

Von Hügel's modernism is not revealed in his writings except insofar as he elevated spiritual experience above dogma in judging the authenticity of religion including Christianity. Most of his theological writings were published after the modernist crisis ended with the excommunications that he survived. Most of them have to do with the spiritual life. His influence on modernism seems to be mainly in the area of encouragement of Loisy and Tyrrell and attempts to broker a satisfactory outcome of their conflicts with the Catholic hierarchy that ultimately failed. The main reason for mentioning him here is that in most treatments of Catholic modernism he is mentioned as one of them.

Reardon labels Loisy "the most impressive, because the most learned, subtle and eloquent, of the modernist leaders."[192] His 1902 book *L'Évangile et l'Église* ("The Gospel and the Church") was described by Tyrrell as the "classical exposition of Catholic Modernism."[193] His goal and aim throughout all his works was "adapting Catholic doctrine to the exigencies of contem-

---

[191]Ibid., 159.
[192]Reardon, *Roman Catholic Modernism*, 17.
[193]Ibid., 27.

porary thought."[194] In other words, he wanted to reform Catholicism without destroying it.[195] But his way of reforming it was to conform it, at least in part, to modernity. Loisy was a priest and professor of Hebrew at the *Institut Catholique* in Paris, but he published works in biblical studies and theology far beyond his narrow academic field. He was a champion of academic freedom and fought long and hard with the Catholic hierarchy to free Catholic biblical scholarship and theological reflection from its control. After his excommunication Loisy became professor of history at the *Collége de France* and described himself as "more pantheist-positivist-humanitarian than Christian,"[196] thus seemingly justifying the Catholic hierarchy's treatment of him.

Reardon describes Tyrrell as "Modernism's prophet, apostle and most conspicuous martyr" and "a truly religious thinker, with something . . . of the spirit of Luther in him."[197] His most important work was published after his death: *Christianity at the Crossroads* (1909). His most influential book reflecting his modernism published during his lifetime was *Medievalism* (1908), a harsh critique of Catholic traditionalism. He was a Jesuit, assigned by his order to teach theology at its Stonyhurst College in Lancashire, England, until he was expelled from the Society of Jesus in 1906. Most of his later life was consumed by controversy even though he defended the Catholic Church against its secular and Protestant critics. His problem was that he attacked the prominent theologians of the church and what he regarded as their reactionary views, which he labeled "medieval." Tyrrell was banned from the sacraments by his excommunication, but a sympathetic priest nevertheless performed the sacrament of last rites over him on his deathbed and made the sign of the cross at his burial in unconsecrated ground. For this the priest was disciplined by his bishop.

What did these modernists have in common? If they were not a cohesive movement, which most scholars agree they were not (in spite of the Vatican's description), why are they lumped together in that category? They were relatively united in two causes: to oppose the status quo in Catholic

---

[194]Ibid., 20.
[195]Ibid., 21.
[196]Ibid., 35.
[197]Ibid., 37.

theology and to integrate modernity into Catholic thought. One scholar of modernism says, "Their commonality came primarily from what they were seeking to avoid."[198] That was the idea that every theological proposal had to be judged by the "standards of neo-scholastic teachings and [by] unquestioning submission to papal authority."[199] Also, they opposed the idea of "the inerrancy of biblical and doctrinal statements"[200] including the pronouncements of the Catholic hierarchy (including the popes). They saw the Catholic Church and its theology as hopelessly outmoded by modernity and in danger of losing its educated members. They also regarded it as dictatorial and oppressive and wanted to free its scholars to think in new ways and explore new avenues of theology.

The modernists were also, however, opposed to Protestantism and especially liberal Protestant theology as represented by Harnack, whom both Loisy and Tyrrell criticized. "Though themselves influenced by liberal Protestantism, the Modernists did not find its views congenial."[201] They viewed liberal Protestantism as too individualistic and too eager to discard the visible and institutional church as the natural outcome of Jesus' teaching.[202] They also saw the liberal search for Christianity's unchanging essence as the search for a chimera. For them, the essence of Christianity is its power of self-adaptation to different cultural contexts. They rejected any "fixity in dogmatic forms," including Harnack's three timeless elements of the "gospel of Jesus."[203] Nevertheless, as Reardon rightly points out,

> Despite their objections to Protestant liberalism their viewpoint was in large measure determined by the criticism and religious philosophy of the Protestant *avant garde* of their day, especially its unquestioning assumption of secular "progressivist" values, its positivistic view of history, its restricted conception of the function of biblical criticism, and its sympathy with an immanentist metaphysic incompatible, when pressed to a conclusion, with the principles of Christian theism.[204]

---

[198]Jadock, "Introduction I," 3.
[199]Ibid., 8.
[200]Ibid.,10.
[201]Jadock, "Introduction 1," 17.
[202]Reardon, "Roman Catholic Modernism," 154–55.
[203]Ibid., 155.
[204]Ibid., 171.

Reardon also notes,

> In spite of certain points of diversity among them, the Modernists were united by a deep longing for and determination to promote such an intellectual renewal of Catholicism as would equip it for the task of confronting the twentieth-century world, not with suspicion or open hostility . . . but with a genuine understanding of its needs and problems.[205]

Also,

> Modernism could fairly be defined as the attempt to synthesize the basic truths of religion and the methods and assumptions of modern thought, using the latter as necessary and proper criteria. Hence a "modernist" interpretation of Christianity . . . will be one which seeks to reconcile the essentials of doctrine with the scientific outlook of the modern world.[206]

Catholic modernists find common ground. All that is to say that Catholic modernism, like classical liberal Protestantism, attempted to reconstruct Christianity in light of modernity, giving modernity maximal acknowledgment—the greatest possible influence without losing faithfulness in accommodation. Obviously, however, the pope and modernists' critics believed it, like liberal Protestant theology, stepped over that line. Exactly where that line lies is the problematic of modern theology.

More specifically, the modernists were united in their view of dogma or doctrine as developing through history. As Loisy stated the matter, "It has to be realized that the Church's conceptions are not truths fallen from heaven and maintained by theological tradition in precisely their original form. . . . They are the outcome of human need, and they register changes in the human outlook."[207] Loisy declared, "Truth alone is unchangeable, but not its image in our minds."[208] He used the analogy of a seed and the tree into which it grows. The seed is the divine mission of Jesus and Christianity is the institutional and doctrinal forms it took as it moved out into the non-Palestinian world.[209] There is no going back to that pure seed; it no longer exists. What exists now, and has existed ever since the seed was planted, are adaptations to culture and human need.

---

[205]Reardon, *Roman Catholic Modernism*, 12.
[206]Ibid., 9.
[207]Ibid., 31.
[208]Quoted in ibid., 85.
[209]Ibid., 73–74.

Another common, unifying theme of modernism is the priority of religious experience over theology and dogma. According to Tyrrell, "The function of religious doctrine is first of all to fix and embody the inward sentiment begotten of contact with the Divine; to describe it as accurately as it can be described in the language of another world."[210] To all modernists, experience is the essence of Christianity, if it has any essence at all, and that because "Christ did infinitely more than cast his truth into the shape of an absolute doctrine. Rather he disseminated it 'as a living thing in hearts that are alive, in order that it might grow there, and bear fruit, and propagate itself.'"[211] What this means is that the modernists recognized a "pre-linguistic form of truth" lying within Christian experience that gives rise to "symbolic and variable expressions" in "historically controlled formulas" which are doctrines.[212] Clearly, this is similar to, if not borrowed from, Schleiermacher. The modernists equated revelation with this inner experience of God. Revelation is not theology or dogma; it is God experienced in the soul: "man's consciousness of his relationship with God—a dynamic not a static thing."[213] Tyrrell elevated this experience of God to the status of "the test of the veracity of Catholicism."[214] For him, it is "not the political machinations [of] the Roman curia, but the mystical experience of the authentically lived Christian life. Indeed Christian living was [his] test of the authority of religious formula[s]."[215] So, for modernists, religious faith, including Christianity, is not at heart belief in orthodox dogmas but a living relationship with God. Revelation is not church pronouncements but the mystical experience of God within the faithful people of God. Theology is not timeless truths authoritatively promulgated by the magisterium of the church but human reflection on dogma's adequacy to religious need, experience and culture. Theology must above all be practical and shaped by prayer: "A religious belief is to be judged by its prayer value."[216]

---

[210]Quoted in ibid., 139.
[211]Quoted in Reardon, "Roman Catholic Modernism," 167.
[212]Daly, "Theological and Philosophical Modernism," 108.
[213]Reardon, *Roman Catholic Modernism*, 34.
[214]Rafferty, *George Tyrrell and Catholic Modernism*, 14.
[215]Ibid.
[216]Reardon, *Roman Catholic Modernism*, 41.

Finally, modernists were at one in their view of doctrines and dogmas as symbolic and not literal representations of spiritual truths. As Tyrrell put it, what is historically false may yet be poetically true.[217] For Loisy, dogmas are symbolic expressions of revealed truths that lie conceptually behind them; dogmas are secondary to those preconceptual truths of experience.[218] "All theological language is symbolic and its meaning in the end is elusive."[219] This is probably the modernist theme that troubled Vatican scholars the most because it seemed to devalue doctrinal formulas as mere symbols and thus relativize them. Could a professing Christian perhaps then confess, say, the doctrine of the Trinity and think of it as merely symbolic and not any kind of description of God? It is doubtful that the modernists meant that, but the Vatican theologians had reason to worry because this was common among liberal Protestants. But the modernists, together with most liberal Protestants, were protesting the conservative tendency to worship concepts by equating them with God himself.

Loisy challenges the authority of Catholic tradition. An interesting fact about Loisy's "duel with the Vatican" (his 1924 autobiography is titled *My Duel with the Vatican*) is that the very book that led to his excommunication, *L'Évangile et l'Église*, was a critique of Harnack's *What Is Christianity?* The French modernist theologian interpreted the German liberal theologian's book as a defense of individualist Christianity. Like any good Catholic, Loisy valued the unity of the visible and institutional church. He also believed dogma is necessary for the life of the church, something Harnack seemed to deny. Harnack was famous for his Hellenization thesis that the simple gospel of Jesus had been corrupted by later church tradition. Loisy was critical of the "immobility" of Catholic tradition in his time, but he defended the idea and reality of tradition and of cultural adaptation of theology. So, for him Hellenization was not necessarily a bad thing. Neither was change in the church's beliefs and institutional forms. For Loisy, in contrast to Harnack and liberal Protestantism generally, early Christianity was meant to grow and develop and not remain as it was in Palestine in the time of Jesus and the apostles.[220]

---

[217]Ibid., 141.
[218]Daly, "Theological and Philosophical Modernism," 107.
[219]Reardon, *Roman Catholic Modernism*, 34.
[220]Ibid., 108–9.

What Loisy objected to was not tradition or institutional forms of the church. In contrast to all Protestants and in loyalty to the Catholic Church he identified Christianity with the visible and institutional Church of Rome so much that when he was excommunicated he declared himself no longer a Christian because he believed there is no Christianity outside that church.[221] He wanted to reform the church, not destroy or abandon it.[222] In fact, Loisy's intention in all his advocacy of doctrinal criticism and change was "to stay as close as possible to traditional Catholicism so as to sacrifice only that which appeared to be irremediably condemned by reason and modernity."[223]

How did Loisy want to reform the Catholic Church? First, by "adapting Catholic doctrine to the exigencies of contemporary thought."[224] He believed the church in his own time was quickly becoming obsolete by trying to ignore modernity or merely denounce it without even attempting to understand it. Second, he wanted to reform Catholicism by freeing its faithful scholars, including especially theologians, from its dominating authority. He wanted to "leave reason free under the control of conscience" and not under the control of the Vatican.[225] He "argued against any attempt to have dogma determine the outcome of historical investigations."[226] What were some of the specific dogmas or doctrines Loisy wanted to investigate and possibly change without interference from or censorship by the Catholic authorities? One is the all-important doctrine of the person of Jesus Christ (Christology).

In contrast to liberal Protestants, Loisy did not consider the creedal definitions of Christology such as the hypostatic union expressed at the Council of Chalcedon in 451 wrong. To most liberal Protestants that particular doctrine, that Jesus Christ was the union of two natures in one person, is proof of how far the church under Constantine and his successors strayed from the simple and pure gospel of Jesus found in the New Testament. Harnack condemned it as evidence of the church's Hellenization. Loisy did not. He regarded it as the church's best attempt in that time and place to express its faith in Jesus and guard it against heretical teachings. What Loisy objected to was not doctrines

---

[221]Ibid., 21.
[222]Ibid.
[223]Ibid., 108.
[224]Ibid., 20.
[225]Ibid., 19.
[226]Jadock, "Introduction II," 21.

or dogmas such as the hypostatic union but their enshrinement as incorrigible for all times and cultures. He also objected to the church's view of such ancient dogmas as revealed truths. For him, the ancient christological formulas were human creations and symbols, not revealed truths. They are to be regarded as "no more than . . . inadequate . . . presentation[s] of the mysteries underlying the Christian life."[227] They are "protective coverings" over revealed truths which come in the form of experience, not propositions.

Loisy did not attempt to reconstruct Christology; he wanted to encourage and defend that project. One thing is clear, however, and it is that he did not consider the dogma of the hypostatic union valid for the twentieth century. His focus in Christology was on the relationship between the "historical Jesus" and the "Christ of faith." Many liberal Protestants pitted them against each other arguing that the church's image of Christ as worshipful God did not square with historical research into Jesus' self-consciousness as messiah. Loisy wanted theology to discover a new view of the Christ of faith consistent with the Jesus of historical research and keep them in close relationship.[228] In other words, the medieval church's image of Christ as the Pantokrator—ruler of heaven and all there is—seemed to Loisy incompatible with the Jesus of history who was a Palestinian peasant. But that does not mean there cannot be a better image of the Christ of faith for today that is compatible with the Jesus being discovered by historical research. For him it was a task of Christian theologians to come up with a new dogma of the person of Jesus Christ that will function in the same way as the hypostatic union but be consistent with modern sensibilities. Loisy did not reconstruct Christology that way himself, but a later Catholic modernist did.[229] His name is Hans Küng (b. 1928), and chapter 10 in this book will tell his story and that of his theology. For Küng, Jesus should be believed in today as God's "deputy and representative" among people.[230]

Tyrrell criticizes Catholic medievalism and theologism. One of Tyrrell's books was entitled *Medievalism* (1908) and was published around the time of his excommunication. By "medievalism" he meant the Catholic Church's

---

[227]Reardon, "Roman Catholic Modernism," 163.

[228]Reardon, *Roman Catholic Modernism*, 33.

[229]Küng is not part of the modernist movement. He is, nevertheless, of the same ethos as Loisy and Tyrrell.

[230]See Küng's Christology in *On Being a Christian* (New York: Doubleday, 1977), 391.

tendency to treat ecclesiastical pronouncements with the same authority as divine revelation itself.[231] "Theologism," a term he coined, means much the same. It is, he argued, the "pseudo-science" of theology that treats the enigmas and mysteries of Christian faith, Christian experience, as capable of exact determination.[232] It is the equation of faith with orthodoxy and making orthodoxy necessary for salvation. Tyrrell found it "all but impossible to imagine Christ . . . making salvation dependent on any point of mere intellectual exactitude."[233] More precisely, Tyrrell defined theologism as

> when theologians take the dogmas or articles of the creed and use them as principles or premises of argumentation, when they combine them with one another, or with truths outside the domain of faith, so as to deduce further conclusions to be imposed on the mind under pain of . . . heresy.[234]

For Tyrrell, as for Loisy, revelation is not propositional; it is rather "the self-manifestation of the Divine in our inward life."[235] And by "our" he meant all humans. He believed in a divine presence in all people. Theology is the attempt to put this divine presence into speech, and the dogmas it produces are always inadequate and relative. With Loisy, whom Tyrrell greatly admired, he considered doctrines and dogmas symbols of deeper, inexpressible experiential truth.

By medievalism, then, Tyrrell meant the hardening of categories that plagues conservative theology, especially Catholic theology in his time. Catholic medievalism tries to ignore culture and pretends to possess timeless propositional truths unaffected by culture. Modernism, according to Tyrrell, avoids blind worship of culture while acknowledging that God is at work there also and there can be no absolute finality because "the process of culture is unending."[236] The influence of Hegel is obvious in some of Tyrrell's descriptions of revelation such as "the gradual unfolding and self-embodiment of one and the same Spirit."[237] He contrasted the modernist with the medievalist:

---

[231]Rafferty, *George Tyrrell and Catholic Modernism*, 23.
[232]Reardon, *Roman Catholic Modernism*, 111.
[233]Ibid., 115–16.
[234]Ibid., 111.
[235]Ibid., 112.
[236]Ibid., 165.
[237]Ibid., 147.

Whereas the Medievalist, with his mechanical and static idea of ecclesiastical infallibility, canonizes the entire medieval synthesis [doctrinal system] indiscriminately, the Modernist, with his dynamical idea of a process that will infallibly work out right in the end; with his conception of our highest truth as ever alloyed with error . . . is one who discriminates and qualifies, who distrusts absolutism of every sort.[238]

As with Loisy, a good illustration of Tyrrell's modernist method of theology is the doctrine of the person of Jesus Christ, or Christology. His envisioned reconstruction of this doctrine would "recast the formulation of Christian belief in a manner that made sense to the modern world."[239] It had to avoid the errors of theologism and medievalism that baptize the ancient Chalcedonian Definition (hypostatic union) as true for all Christians in all times and places. For him the incarnation is a profound mystery; words and concepts cannot grasp it perfectly. However valid they were in their own time, the ancient words and concepts are incoherent to modern people who do not think in Greek philosophical terms such as *ousia* ("substance") and *hypostasis* ("person"). Therefore, the church needs new symbols to express the mystery today. And the criterion for reconstructing Christology is the "need of the soul," not metaphysical speculation.

For Tyrrell, "Christ is the most perfect translation of the Divine Nature and Character into terms of human nature and character."[240] Christ is the incarnation of "eternal [ideal] humanity," and "through Christ in whose manhood the ideal manhood is realized grace is spread abroad among men in order slowly to realize the ideal race, people, or Kingdom of God."[241] Thus, Christ, for Tyrrell, is the sacrament of all sacraments, the visible means of God's grace par excellence. His divinity did not need to be an exception to humanity, an invasion from outside. It was, rather, the intensification of the divine presence in all persons. Such a revisioned Christology could be ethically fruitful because it regards Jesus as the ideal toward which all persons should strive. This is very similar to liberal Protestantism's functional Christology.

---

[238]Ibid., 166.
[239]Rafferty, *George Tyrrell and Catholic Modernism*, 28.
[240]Reardon, *Roman Catholic Modernism*, 130.
[241]Ibid.

Another area of doctrine Tyrrell wanted to reconstruct in light of modernity was hell. He believed that much of the Catholic doctrine was sheer speculation and in place of it he urged "temperate agnosticism."[242] "By this he meant that Christians had to have a certain reserve about the more imaginative speculations of theologians concerning issues such as the justice of God."[243] Tyrrell came close to affirming universal salvation without actually asserting it.[244] For him, the idea of literal fire and eternal torment was offensive to modern sensibilities so that hell needed redefinition to be believed.

Modernism reaps a whirlwind of criticism but plants a seed of change. As a movement, if it ever was one, Catholic modernism died out with the excommunications of Loisy and Tyrrell. They had their disciples and defenders, but they hardly dared raise their heads. However, a whole series of twentieth-century Catholic theologians categorized as the *nouvelle théologie* harked back at least to Blondel if not to Loisy and Tyrrell. Some scholars believe modernism's ghost haunted the rooms and hallways of the Second Vatican Council in the early 1960s; others dismiss the idea as unwarranted by any of the council's pronouncements. But it is the spirit or ethos of modernism the first group of scholars is talking about. The ethos of openness to the modern world was cautiously embraced by Vatican II. Would it have been without modernism a half century earlier? It is hard to say, but it certainly would not have without the *nouvelle théologie* that was at least partially inspired by modernism.

A few late twentieth-century Catholic theologians seemed more directly influenced by Loisy and Tyrrell even though they rarely referred to them. One has already been mentioned: Küng, who has lobbied tirelessly for reformation of the church and for his efforts was declared "not a Catholic theologian" by the Vatican in 1978. Küng's writings echo many modernist concerns and conclusions. Other Catholic theologians who seem especially inspired by modernism are Edward Schillebeeckx (1914–2009), a Belgian, and David Tracy (b. 1939), an American.

Obviously modernism had its critics. The entire force of the Catholic

---

[242]Rafferty, *George Tyrrell and Catholic Modernism*, 25.
[243]Ibid.
[244]Ibid., 24–25.

magisterium was brought down on the modernists, although they were not guilty of all the heresies they were accused of. For example, they were not guilty of agnosticism, if that means denial of any knowledge of God including God's real existence. However, they did deny that God can be known "in himself and for himself." For them, God is known only in his relationship with us in history and in experience. They were opposed to metaphysics insofar as that means trying to use reason to peer behind the veil of appearances to grasp reality-in-itself. Without doubt they were too influenced by Kant for that. Perhaps their most basic departure from traditional, orthodox Christianity was their blurring of the line between the natural and the supernatural, between nature and grace. It is questionable whether the category "supernatural" meant anything to them. They believed in grace, but their emphasis fell on the graciousness of nature itself—God's inward presence in everything and especially in humanity. The problem with this is that grace, in order to *be* grace, has to be gratuitous—sheer gift. Grace that is always already immanent in everything is something less than free gift.

What about the modernists and modern science? By identifying revelation and its truth with an inward presence of God to the soul, they tended to follow the liberal Protestant path of separating science from religion and theology. They did not reduce the latter to ethics in Kantian fashion, however, but favored something like Schleiermacher's approach to defining religion in a way immune to the ravages of science and acids of modernity. And they argued strenuously for the Catholic Church to adjust its biblical interpretations of, for example, Genesis to the sure discoveries of science. Surely their emphasis on doctrinal development was motivated, even driven, by a desire to update Catholic beliefs to fit better with the Enlightenment and modernity including the ongoing scientific revolution.

3

CONSERVATIVE PROTESTANT THEOLOGY DEFENDS ORTHODOXY IN A MODERN WAY

The nineteenth century saw the rise of liberal Protestant theology—a new phenomenon in Christian thought that built on the Enlightenment and scientific revolutions and attempted to make Christian theology authentically modern while remaining faithful to the gospel of Jesus Christ. Not everyone agreed it was successful. Conservative, orthodox Protestants were shocked by some moves made by the liberals. Toward the end of the nineteenth century and into the early twentieth century several American denominations were rocked by heresy trials—primarily launched by conservatives to oust liberals from their seminaries. By the 1920s, however, things had turned around in the so-called mainline Protestant denominations and trials were going against conservatives. In 1925 the infamous Scopes "monkey trial" in Dayton, Tennessee, saw a showdown between liberal and conservative forces over evolution. The conservatives won a Pyrrhic victory; they lost in the court of public opinion. Princeton theologian J. Gresham Machen (1881–1937), the leading fundamentalist intellectual, was tried by his own Presbyterian denomination and suspended from its ministry in 1935 in part, at least, due to his continuing opposition to liberal theological influence in that denomination.

Fundamentalism Opposes Liberal Theology

The story of the liberal versus fundamentalist controversy within British and American Protestantism is a complicated and sordid one. On the American side, the conservative resurgence defiantly and sometimes militantly challenging liberal theology can be traced back to the disciples of the nineteenth century's leading conservative Protestant theologian, Charles Hodge (1797–1878), who has been called the nineteenth century's "pope of Presbyterianism."[1] Hodge taught for more than fifty years at American Protestantism's flagship seminary—Princeton Theological Seminary—and produced many books, including a three-volume systematic theology and numerous articles and lengthy critical reviews of other theologians' writings. He taught more than three thousand ministerial students of various denominations and stood throughout most of his century against liberal theology of all kinds and for traditional, Reformed orthodoxy. However, he did so with a decidedly modern flair.

Hodge was the second member of a dynasty of what is sometimes known as the Old Princeton School Theology (henceforth Princeton Theology)—the type of theology that reigned supreme at that seminary from its founding in 1812 until its moderate reorganization in 1929. (Conservatives like Machen considered the reorganization a tilt in favor of liberal theology. Soon after it he, together with other Princeton professors "in exile," founded the staunchly conservative Westminster Theological Seminary in Philadelphia.) The Princeton Theology dynasty began with Archibald Alexander (1772–1851) and continued through Charles Hodge to his son Archibald Alexander Hodge (1823–1886) and then Benjamin Breckenridge Warfield (1851–1921). The last member of the dynasty was Machen. Many others admired Hodge and the dynasty of which he was a part, but these five theologians are usually considered the core of the Princeton Theology, and it is usually considered the intellectual powerhouse behind fundamentalism. Hodge was, by all accounts, "its most characteristic and perhaps formidable representative."[2]

---

[1]Paul C. Gutjahr, *Charles Hodge: Guardian of American Orthodoxy* (Oxford: Oxford University Press), 3.

[2]David Wells, "The Stout and Persistent 'Theology' of Charles Hodge," *Christianity Today* (August 30, 1974), 11.

The term "fundamentalism" arouses many thoughts and feelings in people, but it was first used to name a movement of conservative Protestants in Britain and America to oppose liberal theology. If liberal theology was maximal acknowledgement of modernity, fundamentalism was maximal conservatism—intentionally and sometimes militantly preserving and defending the perceived heritage of Protestant orthodoxy that had reigned within Protestantism from the Reformers until the rise of liberal theology. In the early twentieth century fundamentalism was the defense of basic Christian doctrines from the acids of modernity and liberal thought. The origin of its name is much debated, but it may have had something to do with the publication in 1910 of a series of booklets called *The Fundamentals*. These contained articles by leading conservative Protestant theologians criticizing liberal theology and defending conservative Protestant doctrines. During the 1920s and afterwards fundamentalism took on a different flavor—one that was separatistic, even from fellow evangelical Christians, and often anti-intellectual. Beginning in the 1940s a group of fundamentalists became disillusioned with the direction the movement had taken and banded together to create a more moderate type of conservative Protestantism called neo-evangelicalism. The "neo-" was later dropped so that the movement became known as evangelicalism.[3]

From the 1980s through the 2010s especially American fundamentalists became politically active, began calling themselves evangelicals and were instrumental in creating the loosely organized phenomenon known in the media as the religious right. The one thing tying original fundamentalism and the religious right together over the course of a century is commitment to conservative Protestant values and doctrines and opposition to liberal theology. The original fundamentalists included left-leaning politicians such as William Jennings Bryan. The point is that original fundamentalism was not identifiably politically or economically conservative; most American fundamentalism since the 1980s has been.

The original fundamentalists revered Charles Hodge and the other Princeton theologians because he was a towering intellectual who held con-

---

[3]The story of the stages of fundamentalism and evangelicalism's emergence from it is told by, among others, George M. Marsden, *Understanding Fundamentalism and Evangelicalism* (Grand Rapids: Eerdmans, 1991).

servative beliefs and yet was respected by liberal theologians. Much of the belief system and approach to Christianity adopted by the older fundamentalists were drawn from Hodge and the Princeton Theology. A leading Hodge scholar says that "Hodge's worldview and particular biblical hermeneutic . . . provided the intellectual framework for twentieth-century Protestant fundamentalism."[4]

Why, then, include Hodge in this volume on modern theology? Many people wrongly equate "modern" with "liberal." In fact, the early fundamentalists contributed to this by labeling their opponents, the liberal theologians, modernists. However, "modern" is not necessarily limited to "liberal." As will be seen, Hodge used distinctly modern methods in his exposition and defense of conservative Protestant theology. Besides, a person can qualify as a modern theologian by being against modernity—as was the case with Kierkegaard. The Princeton theologians probably did not consider themselves modern, but especially Hodge stands squarely in the modern space and with a modern, if not modernist, posture. That is not to say he adopted everything of modernity; he did not. But, for example, he strove to demonstrate how authentic, orthodox Protestant theology could and must be scientific. Also, he borrowed heavily from and depended on the Scottish common sense philosophy of Reid (see 1.e.). Although Reid was responding to Hume, he was also standing on the shoulders of Locke and the empiricist branch of Enlightenment foundationalism. Hodge was also a foundationalist of sorts, a biblical foundationalist who went out of his way to argue that the divine revelation in the Bible is rational. It is safe to say that, in many ways, Hodge was modern without being modern*ist*. He was a fundamentalist before fundamentalism's descent into what one leading evangelical scholar called "orthodoxy gone cultic."[5]

Hodge Constructs a Modern Form of Protestant Orthodoxy

The day was April 24, 1872; the celebration was of Professor Charles Hodge's fiftieth anniversary of teaching at Princeton Theological Seminary. Hundreds of people came to the little town of Princeton, New Jersey, to praise the

---

[4]John W. Stewart, "Introducing Charles Hodge to Postmoderns," in *Charles Hodge Revisited: A Critical Appraisal of His Life and Work*, ed. John W. Stewart and James H. Moorehead (Grand Rapids, MI: Eerdmans, 2002), 2.

[5]Edward John Carnell, *The Case for Orthodox Theology* (Philadelphia: Westminster Press, 1959), 113.

seventy-four-year-old theologian. The town's shops and businesses closed their doors in his honor. Laudatory telegrams flooded in from around the country and Europe. After a series of encomiums by dignitaries, Hodge stood to speak and declared that he was proud to say that during his tenure as principal of the seminary "a new idea never originated in this seminary."[6]

People often snicker when they hear that line, but for Hodge and his colleagues and followers, it was a statement of achievement. The world was changing all around them; Christianity was being reconstructed in ways they considered extremely pernicious. Especially liberal theology, with its interest in making Christianity modern, was redefining the faith into unrecognizability. At least that was how Hodge and his cohort saw things. But it was not only liberal theology they abhorred. It was also revivalism—that uniquely American brand of evangelism and worship that stemmed from the two Great Awakenings. The two great revivalists of the nineteenth century were Charles Grandison Finney (1792–1875) and D. L. Moody (1837–1899); they introduced so-called new measures of evangelism that Hodge and his Reformed stalwarts considered manipulative and theologically unsound.[7] It is impossible to understand Hodge without grasping the seriousness of the situation as he and the rest of the Old School Presbyterians saw it. The winds of change were threatening to blow everything familiar away. Someone had to hold onto the traditions of Protestant orthodoxy and explain and defend them without accommodating to non-Christian philosophies and anti-Christian scientific theories (such as Darwinism). Hodge was the man for it.

Hodge Becomes a Success Story

Hodge was born into the family of a Philadelphia doctor, but his father died when he was a small child. Impoverished, his mother moved the family to wherever she could make a living—mostly by taking in boarders and washing and sewing. Hodge's biographer suggests these early difficult circumstances may have played a role in Hodge's adult proclivities:

---

[6]Gutjahr, *Charles Hodge*, 363.

[7]Among Finney's new measures for promoting revival were "letting women pray in public, praying for people by name, entering towns without the permission of the local pastors, and using something called the 'Anxious Bench' where people thought to be on the verge of conversion were seated and intensely preached at during revival meetings." Ibid., 162–63.

One cannot help but wonder whether Hodge's extreme aversion to change, which became one of his defining characteristics, had its roots in the instability that characterized his earliest years. His family's nomadic life coupled with the stresses brought on by poverty may well have helped form Hodge's strong attachment to rituals and ideologies that were based on time-honored traditions and provided various forms of stability.[8]

Charles spent much of his youth in Princeton, where his mother finally settled. He attended the College of New Jersey (now Princeton University) and the newly founded Princeton Theological Seminary (unrelated Presbyterian institutions). The seminary's theology professor, Archibald Alexander, became his mentor and friend for life. Hodge named his first son after him.

After graduating from seminary Hodge was ordained to the Presbyterian ministry and soon began teaching at the seminary. In 1822 he was appointed a professor and married Benjamin Franklin's great-granddaughter. In 1825 he founded a theological journal called *The Biblical Repertory and Princeton Review* (later shortened to *The Princeton Review*), which he edited for forty years; many of his theological writings were lengthy articles in its pages on many subjects. He became embroiled in Presbyterian politics and served for a time as the General Moderator of the denomination. In a division between Old School and New School Presbyterians over revivalism and the role of experience in Christianity he sided with the Old School, which tended to be more traditional. From 1826 to 1828 Hodge traveled in Europe, studied at German universities (Halle and Berlin) and listened to leading German theologians, including Schleiermacher, teach and preach. When he returned to the United States he was one of a very few American theologians thoroughly versed in German theology and biblical scholarship.

In 1841 Hodge published a best-selling devotional book that was also heavily theological entitled *The Way of Life*; it became one of a few standard books in nearly all Protestant church libraries and homes. It contained a staunch but pious explanation and defense of basic Protestant doctrine and morality heavily skewed toward Calvinism—Hodge's lifelong theological orientation. However, his magnum opus is his three-volume *Systematic Theology* published between 1872 and 1874; it became *the* textbook in the

---

[8]Ibid., 22.

title's subject in many seminaries throughout the next century and in some even into the twenty-first century. An astute Hodge scholar notes, "It would be difficult to overestimate the influence that this study has had and continues to have in forming evangelical beliefs."[9] Between those two books Hodge wrote many biblical commentaries. His last book was *What Is Darwinism?* (1874), in which he took a strong stand against Darwin's theory of natural selection without closing the door on some kind of evolution with intelligent design. He declared Darwinism, natural selection theory, "atheism."[10] Hodge interacted much with modern science but was critical and selective about what he would believe. He accepted the ancient earth as fact based on geology but rejected natural selection as only theory because of "the implications of Darwinism for the place of humans in nature."[11] In other words, he argued, if Darwin is right, human beings are nothing more than highly evolved animals. He could not see any way to integrate natural selection with biblical Christianity.[12]

A few thumbnail descriptions of Hodge from scholars who have studied him for many years will help illumine his theology in conversation, often debate, with other theologians and philosophers of his time. One says that "he had a deep quest for structure and a distinct intolerance for ambiguity."[13] The same scholar notes that, according to people who knew him well, including his grandson, the Princeton professor was a warm-hearted, gregarious and well-liked person with many friends and admirers.[14] He also notes that Hodge was "deeply at odds with the great intellectual drift of the

---

[9]Wells, "Stout and Persistent 'Theology' of Charles Hodge," 10.

[10]From an excerpt from *What Is Darwinism?* in Mark Noll, ed., *The Princeton Theology: 1812–1921* (Grand Rapids: Baker, 1983), 152.

[11]Ronald L. Numbers, "Charles Hodge and the Beauties and Deformities of Science," in *Charles Hodge Revisited: A Critical Appraisal of His Life and Work*, ed. John W. Stewart and James H. Moorehead (Grand Rapids: Eerdmans, 2002), 100.

[12]As will be seen later in this chapter, Hodge was not antiscience, but he insisted on distinguishing between proven facts of science and theories, and the latter he judged by the criteria of what he saw as scriptural teaching. Hodge's successor at Princeton, B. B. Warfield, did not have the same problem. He accepted theistic evolution. See David N. Livingstone, *Darwin's Forgotten Defenders: The Encounter Between Evangelical Theology and Evolutionary Thought* (Vancouver, BC: Regent College Publishing, 1984).

[13]Steward, "Introducing Charles Hodge," 10.

[14]Ibid.

nineteenth century"[15] and often seemed to "believe too much."[16] Another Hodge scholar refers to Hodge's proclivity for "pontification."[17] The same commentator describes Hodge's responses to theologians with whom he disagreed: "Even by the polemical precepts of his day, Hodge behaved extraordinarily like Zeus, pronouncing his high judgments and hurling his thunderbolts accordingly on the inferior mortals below."[18] One contemporary admirer of Hodge records that, when he was asked if he sinned as a youth, the theologian reported that he remembered cursing once at age thirteen or fourteen, but he immediately repented and never did it again.[19] Finally, Hodge's most famous and influential student, Warfield, reminisced about his teacher's manner in his lectures:

> After his always strikingly appropriate prayer had been offered, and we were settled back in our seats, he would open his well-thumbed Greek Testament— on which it was plain that there was not a single marginal note—look at the passage for a second, then, throwing his head back and closing his eyes, begin his exposition. He scarcely again glanced at the Testament during the hour: the text was evidently before his mind, verbally, and the matter of his exposition was at his command. In an unbroken stream it flowed from subject to subject, simple, clear, cogent, and unfailingly reverent. Now and then he would pause a moment, to insert an illustrative anecdote—now and then lean forward suddenly with tearful, wide-open eyes to press home a quick-risen inference of the love of God for lost sinners.[20]

Many questioned Hodge's grasp of his opponents' views, his style of refuting them or his seeming lack of awareness of his own presuppositions, but few, if any, ever questioned his sincerity or genuine piety. When asked to define Christianity, he wrote:

> Christianity objectively considered, is the testimony of God concerning his Son, it is the whole revelation of truth contained in the Scriptures, con-

---

[15]Ibid., 22.

[16]Ibid., 36.

[17]James Turner, "Charles Hodge in the Intellectual Weather of the Nineteenth Century," in *Charles Hodge Revisited: A Critical Appraisal of His Life and Work*, ed. John W. Stewart and James H. Moorehead (Grand Rapids: Eerdmans, 2002), 43.

[18]Ibid., 42.

[19]Wells, "Stout and Persistent 'Theology' of Charles Hodge," 11.

[20]Stewart, "Introducing Charles Hodge," 18.

cerning the redemption of man through Jesus Christ our Lord. Subjectively considered, it is the life of Christ in the soul, or, that form of spiritual life which has its origins in Christ, is determined by the revelation concerning his person and work, and which is due to the indwelling of his Spirit. In one [the first] sense we may affirm that Christianity is a doctrine, and in another [second] sense we may with equal truth affirm that Christianity is a life.[21]

By all accounts, Hodge was a deeply devout person who regarded real Christianity as both experience and doctrine.

Hodge Is Influenced by Reformed Scholasticism and Confessionalism

Hodge was not always as aware as he should have been of his own presuppositions. He seemed to think that everything he believed as a Christian had fallen from the pages of his Bible or the lines of the Westminster Confessions (the standard Presbyterian statements of faith including the Larger and Shorter Catechisms). Scholars studying him, however, have often noticed strains of previous theologies and philosophies at work in his theological reflections. Most notable among them are Reformed confessionalism, even Reformed scholasticism, and Scottish common sense realism (Reid).

Protestant scholasticism, of which Reformed scholasticism is one type, is an approach to theology that arose after the Reformation, which was, in many ways, a reaction against Catholic scholasticism and even scholasticism itself. "Scholasticism" originally meant "the theology of the schools" with the schools being the medieval universities. (Sometimes the term also includes the pre-university monastic educational centers out of which the universities arose.) However, later, "scholasticism" came to designate the approach to theology used there: a highly logical, rational method of theology that often used speculation to answer every conceivable question about Christian doctrine. An extreme example, which has become a caricature of that theology, is "How many angels can dance on the head of a pin?" The vast majority of the scholastics' energies, however, went into examining more important questions in great detail and using logic, working on revelation, to answer them.

The prime example of scholasticism is Thomas Aquinas, who taught at the University of Paris and wrote tomes of Christian philosophy and the-

---

[21]Ibid., 8.

ology. His classic work is *Summa Theologica*, a massive, multivolume set of questions and answers about God and salvation and every subject of interest to thinking Christians related to those. Thomas used the philosophy of the ancient Greek thinker Aristotle to answer questions not answered in Scripture or Christian tradition. Sometimes he relied on Aristotle to interpret Scripture (although Aristotle lived long before Christ). What made Thomas a model of scholasticism, however, was the architectonic structure of his theology. It is like a great medieval cathedral built up from a foundation with every part being necessary to every other part. In other words, it is extremely systematic. Every idea is logically dependent on every other idea. At least that was the ideal of scholastic thought. Whether anyone achieved that is questionable.

The Reformers Luther, Zwingli and Calvin left much to mystery. The first two never wrote a systematic theology even though their attitudes toward reason were different. Luther rejected reason and reveled in mystery; for him mystery was a sign of God's transcendence. Zwingli relied heavily on philosophy and logic but did not attempt to construct a medieval-like system of Christian thought. Calvin wrote *Institutes of the Christian Religion*, which is not scholastic in its presentation of Christian doctrines in that it leaves much about God in the realm of mystery. The *Institutes* is a great summary of biblical doctrine as interpreted by Calvin, but it is not systematic in a scholastic way. The Reformers scorned scholasticism and blamed it for much of the medieval Catholic Church's doctrinal errors (as they saw them).

After the Reformation, however, many Lutheran and Reformed theologians constructed scholastic-like systems of theology relying heavily on logic and attempting to answer questions the first Reformers left in the realm of mystery. One example is the debates among Reformed theologians over the order of the divine decrees: supralapsarianism versus infralapsarianism. The underlying question is: Which comes first in God's intention (not time)—God's decree to create the world and humans or God's decree to predestine the elect to salvation and the reprobate (non-elect) to damnation? Each school of Reformed theology (followers of Zwingli and Calvin) held to a different order of the divine decrees. A nonscholastic Protestant would probably label it a fruitless effort that leads away from the

Bible into speculation. Protestant scholastics, however, regarded it as an important question that needed to be settled for the sake of either God's absolute sovereignty (supralapsarianism) or God's goodness (infralapsarianism). A favorite question among Calvin scholars is which side he would have taken had he lived long enough to be involved in the debate. Many Calvin scholars believe he would have warned both sides against undue speculation and overuse of logic to peer into the mysteries of God.

Hodge was greatly influenced by Reformed scholasticism via the required systematic theology at Princeton when he was a student there. His own *Systematic Theology* is a restatement of Francis Turretin's highly scholastic *Institutio Theologiae Elencticae*.[22] Like most volumes of theology in that time, Turretin's was written in Latin. Students at Princeton were required to memorize portions of all three volumes. Turretin's scholasticism is illustrated by his desire to tie up every possible loose end of previous Reformed theology. He was a strong advocate of biblical infallibility, which he interpreted as meaning that because it is God's Word, and because God is its ultimate author, the Bible must not contain any mistakes, discrepancies or inconsistencies.[23]

But Turretin noticed a problem for his doctrine of biblical inerrancy: What about ambiguities? How can it be determined whether there are errors in Scripture if it is impossible to know exactly what a biblical text means? And the problem was that the most ancient texts of the Hebrew books of the Bible do not contain vowels; Hebrew did not originally use vowels. The best Hebrew texts in Turretin's time were the so-called Masoretic Texts dating from the seventh to tenth centuries. A group of Jewish scholars known as the Masoretes had added vowels to the Hebrew texts of what Christians call the Old Testament. The problem Turretin faced was: How can we trust that these Hebrew texts with their added vowel points reflect what the original, inspired prophets wrote? In order to secure the meaning of the texts, he argued that the vowel points added by the Masoretes were inspired, or that the Masoretes were inspired by God so that they

---

[22]Wells, "Stout and Persistent 'Theology' of Charles Hodge," 15.

[23]Hodge used "infallibility" for a concept of biblical accuracy his followers labeled "inerrancy." Some conservative theologians would distinguish between the two terms. It is doubtful that Hodge would.

inerrantly added the right vowel points. Otherwise, there are cases where it is impossible to be sure what the prophets meant when they wrote portions of the Old Testament or what the best existing texts of the Old Testament really mean. Apparently, in true scholastic style, Turretin was determined to nail things down, to remove as much ambiguity as possible. But to extend divine inspiration of the Bible to the Masoretes seemed even to many of Turretin's colleagues and admirers a stretch.

Hodge did not follow Turretin that far, but he greatly admired him and was strongly influenced by his theology. Commenting on Turretin and other, older Reformed scholastics Hodge wrote, "These antiquated writers have a thousand faults, it may be; they are stiff, they are prolix, they are technical, but they have one great merit—they always let us know what they mean. Their atmosphere, if wintry and biting, is clear."[24] He was contrasting Turretin's theology with the romanticist Protestant theology of his day, which he considered dreamy and vague, but he might have been describing his own theology.

Like Turretin, but perhaps more modestly, Hodge wanted his fellow English-speaking Protestant Christians to have a compendium of Christian doctrine in highly systematic form. His *Systematic Theology* reflects something of that scholastic mindset about truth. One Hodge scholar labels his approach to theology "rational orthodoxy" or "supernatural rationalism,"[25] meaning that

> truth was [for Hodge] a unity, and the truths of theology had the same logical status as the truths of science or philosophy, except that theology depended on authoritative revelation. The revelation was addressed to reason; it therefore presupposed reason, which had the task of judging the revelation's credibility by assessing evidences.[26]

Hodge himself wrote, "Revelation is the communication of truth to the mind. But the communication of truth supposes the capacity to receive it. . . . Truths, to be received as objects of faith, must be intellectually

---

[24]Quoted in Noll, *Princeton Theology*, 116.
[25]E. Brooks Holifield, "Hodge, the Seminary and the American Theological Context," in *Charles Hodge Revisited: A Critical Appraisal of His Life and Work*, ed. John W. Stewart and James H. Moorehead (Grand Rapids: Eerdmans, 2002), 123.
[26]Ibid.

apprehended."[27] He went on to explain what he meant by "intellectually apprehended" and the capacity to receive revelation. Not only must reason judge the credibility of revelation;[28] it is a criterion of what it is possible to believe. There are two principles of that criterion that apply to theology: "It is impossible that God should do, approve, or command what is morally wrong."[29] This appears to have the status of an axiom for Hodge. In other words, he treats it as true a priori. "We have a right to reject as untrue whatever it is impossible that God should require us to believe. He can no more require us to believe what is absurd than to do what is wrong."[30] Hodge then pronounces the second criterion of reason as applied to theology: the law of noncontradiction. "It is impossible . . . that God should reveal anything as true which contradicts any well authenticated truth, whether of intuition, experience, or previous revelation."[31]

This is not rationalism as Hodge understood that term and described that approach to knowledge. For him, Rationalism (he always capitalized it, perhaps to distinguish it from his own use of reason) is belief that a person should not believe, and indeed cannot know, what reason alone, unaided by revelation or faith, cannot discover. It refuses to believe anything on authority, even God's authority. He described Rationalism:

> Rationalism assumes that the human intelligence is the measure of all truth. This is an insane presumption on the part of such a creature as man. If a child believes with implicit confidence what it cannot understand, on the testimony of a parent, surely man may believe what he cannot understand, on the testimony of God.[32]

The problem should be immediately clear. As the scholar who labeled Hodge's theology "supernatural rationalism" notes, "He walked a narrow line."[33] Clearly he did not embrace rationalism in the most extreme sense, but by his own definition of basic rationalism, Hodge would have to be counted a rationalist of some kind in that his axioms for what it is possible

---

[27]Charles Hodge, *Systematic Theology*, 3 vols. (Grand Rapids: Eerdmans, 1973), 1:49.
[28]Ibid., 1:50
[29]Ibid., 1:51.
[30]Ibid., 1:52.
[31]Ibid., 1:51.
[32]Ibid., 1:41.
[33]Holifield, "Hodge, the Seminary and the American Theological Context," 123.

to believe set human intelligence as the criterion of what revelation can say. In this regard Hodge seemed to adopt a scholastic-like approach to theology. It is impossible to imagine Luther or even Calvin working with those axioms as criteria of what God can require people to believe. Kierkegaard would consider Hodge a scholastic *and* rationalist.

Another way in which Hodge was influenced by Turretin is their shared Reformed confessionalism. Turretin was Swiss; the doctrinal content of his theology was largely determined by the First and Second Helvetic Confessions—Reformed statements of faith written by leaders of the Reformed churches of Switzerland in the sixteenth century. The author of the *Institutio* helped write the Helvetic Consensus in 1675—a doctrinal statement reaffirming double predestination and limited atonement against a group of Reformed theologians in France who were allegedly watering down high Calvinist doctrine. Turretin's theology was intended only as an exposition of classical Calvinism. Similarly, Hodge's *Systematic Theology* was faithful to his own church's Reformed doctrinal confessions, the Westminster Confession and the Westminster Larger and Shorter Catechism, that famously begins with the question "What is the chief end of man?" The answer is, "The chief end of man is to glorify God and enjoy him forever." The doctrines of Hodge will not detain us here because there is nothing modern about them; they are his restatements and defenses of Presbyterian and Reformed confessions.

Hodge Is Influenced by Scottish Common Sense Realism

Almost every commentator on Hodge's theology notes the fact of its dependence on Reid's Scottish common sense realism (henceforth Scottish realism). Hodge probably did not think of it as philosophy and certainly not as part of the Enlightenment. One aspect of Scottish realism is to believe that all normal people have certain native capacities for knowing truth as it really is outside the mind. Advocates considered it a protest against philosophy insofar as that had been corrupted by skepticisms and speculations such as Hume's and Kant's. Hodge did not think his theology relied on philosophy, but neither was he against all philosophy. On the one hand he said, "The great majority of what passes for philosophy . . . is merely human speculation,"[34] and on the other hand, "Everything is conceded [in his system] to philosophy . . . which [it] can rightfully demand."[35] Careful examination of Hodge's method of doing theology and defending Christianity reveals the influence of Scottish realism, which Hodge would probably not deny, in spite of his apparent lack of interest in philosophical matters.[36] According to one of his contemporary admirers, he "imbibed" Scottish realism "without recognition."[37] (He was not alone in that, as Scottish realism was pervasive in nineteenth-century America.) Here it might be helpful to insert a thumbnail reminder of exactly what Scottish realism is: "Overall, the Scottish epistemology is static: the mind knows an external universe. The mind itself is substantive—it is a sort of thing that has certain features or characteristics. . . . To obtain scientific knowledge, the natural philosopher follows certain rules, more or less mechanistically."[38]

One evidence of the influence of Scottish realism is Hodge's repeated appeals to certain "laws of belief" implanted in human nature. These he held in high regard, elevating them to a critical position alongside revelation itself. "We are to try the spirits," he wrote, referring to the apostle Paul's admonition to the Corinthian Christians to be discerning about prophecies. "But how can we try them without a standard? and what other standard can there be except the laws of our nature and the authenticated revelations of God?"[39] Near the beginning of *Systematic Theology* Hodge reveals his reliance on Scottish realism by stating that his method in theology begins with certain assumptions which "are given in the constitution of our nature."[40] One law of human nature is that "we cannot believe without evidence."[41] "Faith," he wrote, "is not a blind, irrational assent, but an intelligent reception of the truth on adequate grounds."[42] His debt to Scottish

---

[34]Hodge, *Systematic Theology*, 1:58.

[35]Ibid., 1:59.

[36]Wells, "Stout and Persistent 'Theology' of Charles Hodge," 15.

[37]David Wells, "Charles Hodge," in *The Princeton Theology: Reformed Theology in America*, ed. David Wells (Grand Rapids: Baker, 1989), 58.

[38]Bruce Kuklick, "The Place of Charles Hodge in the History of Ideas in America," in *Charles Hodge Revisited: A Critical Appraisal of His Life and Work*, ed. John W. Stewart and James H. Moorehead (Grand Rapids: Eerdmans, 2002), 69.

[39]Hodge, *Systematic Theology*, 1:53.

[40]Ibid., 1:9.

[41]Ibid.

[42]Ibid.

realism is clear in statements such as "The Word of God is to be believed because of the authority or command of God manifesting itself therein in a manner analogous to the exhibition of his perfections in the works of nature."[43] In other words, just as there is a self-authenticating aspect to nature and our ability to grasp it as it really is, so there is a self-authenticating aspect to God's revelation in Scripture the meaning of which is open and clear to anyone who approaches it without bias. In both cases, the truth is outside the mind and capable of being grasped and understood as it really is because of certain laws of right mental activity.

Perhaps the clearest example of Hodge's dependence on Scottish realism is his frequent appeal to what all reasonable people know to be the case. For him, as for Reid and other common sense thinkers, "in reasonably uncomplicated matters, the collective judgment of ordinary people provided a test of truth."[44] Some truths are self-evident and intuitive and all normal people agree about them. The example given in chapter 1 of this book (see 1.e.) is that other minds exist. No sane person seriously questions that. Scottish realism goes further and argues that among our basic intuitions, what all normal people believe and rely on, is the objective, factual nature of external reality and the human mind's capacity to know it as it really is. This is direct contradiction to Kant's critical idealism in which space and time, among other things, are not features of external reality but functions of the mind that imposes them on the raw data of the senses. Scottish realism firmly rejects that. So did Hodge. For him, knowledge is the mind's grasp of reality; it exists when the contents of the mind correspond with external reality. In the 1950s American television program *Dragnet*, the main character, Sergeant Friday, repeatedly said to flustered witnesses to crimes, "Just the facts, ma'am"—as if there are ideas that are not infected by interpretation and that correspond perfectly with the world out there. That is Scottish realism at work.

Hodge Lays Out a Biblical Foundationalist Method for Theology
A cartoon published in a leading evangelical Christian magazine shows a diminutive pastor with huge glasses sitting dumbfounded behind his church

---

[43]Quoted in Noll, *Princeton Theology*, 134.
[44]Turner, "Charles Hodge in the Intellectual Weather of the Nineteenth Century," 50.

study desk. On the wall behind him is an attendance chart with a plunging arrow indicating dwindling attendance at his church. Sitting across the desk is one of his deacons, who says, "Well, pastor, maybe it would help if you didn't end every sermon with 'But, then, what do I know?'" One result of the Enlightenment, an aspect of modernity, is limitation of knowledge to what can be proven logically or scientifically. This was the crisis of modernity for theology. For many nineteenth-century movers and shakers of culture, strongly influenced by Enlightenment rationalism, religion does not include knowledge; it has the status of opinion at best. Some liberal Protestant theologians accepted that by driving a wedge between facts and values or between facts and feelings—relegating theology to the realm of values or feelings. They still considered theology a form of knowledge, but, in Hodge's view, by placing theology in a category other than fact, these liberal theologians conceded too much to modernity's secular spirit. The result is pastors who do not claim to know what they are preaching about. The preaching of the gospel becomes expression of feelings or opinion or mere moralizing. To a great extent Hodge must be understood as reacting to this nineteenth-century drift away from facts in religion. For him, it was crucial to restore theology's queenly status as a rational system of facts.

In the opening pages of *Systematic Theology* Hodge argued for the scientific status of theology as an orderly way of knowing truth. He did not mean it is exactly like one of the so-called physical or natural sciences, but it follows the same basic method of knowing. In stark contrast with Schleiermacher or Ritschl or any other subjective approach to theology Hodge boldly stated:

> The true method of theology is . . . the inductive, which assumes that the Bible contains all the facts or truths which form the contents of theology, just as the facts of nature are the contents of the natural sciences. It is also assumed that the relation of these Biblical facts to each other, the principles involved in them, the laws which determine them, are in the facts themselves, and are to be deduced from them, just as the laws of nature are deduced from the facts of nature. In neither case are the principles derived from the mind and imposed on the facts, but equally in both departments, the principles or laws are deduced from the facts and recognized by the mind.[45]

---

[45]Hodge, *Systematic Theology*, 1:17.

In another place near the beginning of *Systematic Theology* he reinforces and explains this method further:

> The Bible is to the theologian what nature is to the man of science. *It is his store-house of facts*; and his method of ascertaining what the Bible teaches, is the same as that which the natural philosopher adopts to ascertain what nature teaches. In the first place, he comes to his task with all the assumptions above mentioned. He must assume the validity of those laws of belief which God has impressed on our nature . . . [Hodge states the ones quoted earlier here] . . . which no objective revelation can possibly contradict. These first principles, however, are not to be arbitrarily assumed. No man has a right to lay down his own opinions, however firmly held, and call them "first truths of reason," and make them the source or test of Christian doctrines. Nothing can rightfully be included under the category of first truths, or laws of belief, which cannot stand the tests of universality and necessity, to which many add self-evidence. But self-evidence is included in universality and necessity, in so far, that nothing which is not self-evident can be universally believed, and what is self-evident forces itself on the mind of every intelligent creature.[46]

In other words, for Hodge, every science, including theology, has a "store-house of facts" with which it works. What makes something a science is mining its facts out of that fund objectively using intuitive, universal rules of reasoning (first principles). Such a rule for the natural sciences is that every effect has a cause. Such a rule for theology is that "nothing contrary to virtue can be enjoined by God."[47] Following this basically foundationalist approach to theology, using as foundations the Bible and first principles, the theologian can rightly claim to possess knowledge on a par with the natural sciences.

To be sure, Hodge was not aware of being under the influence of Enlightenment thinking, but even his most sympathetic contemporary interpreters recognize it. Surely Hodge would argue that his method of theology is not unique to the Enlightenment, but it is difficult, if not impossible, to find theological method stated this way before Hodge. Clearly he was responding to his own Enlightenment-based cultural context and attempting to defend theology on foundationalist grounds. Kierkegaard, for one, would

---

[46]Ibid., 1:10–11, italics added.
[47]Ibid., 1:10.

accuse him of stepping over onto modernist territory in all this emphasis on facts, reason, method and system. Theology does exactly what the natural sciences do? Theology is to the Bible what geology is to the crust of the earth? With some justification Hodge's proposed method of theology has been called the evangelical Enlightenment.

Mark Noll, a particularly astute and sympathetic interpreter of Hodge and the Princeton Theology generally, has been in the forefront of exposing this side of their theology. He comments that "their philosophical allegiances could at times leave them sounding like scientific positivists."[48] Noll is especially critical (though not condemning) of Hodge's tendency to treat theology as an objective science of objective facts. "Hodge's desire for disinterested theological method recurred frequently throughout his career."[49] In other words, Hodge seemed to want theology to imitate the Baconian scientific method which left little room for mystery. But, Noll points out, in one aspect Hodge departed from his own ideals of pure scientific objectivity. Again, Scottish realism enters the picture to muddy the waters. "On some critical issues, Hodge was in fact eager to use 'preconceived theories' to construct his theology."[50] At least according to Noll, when Hodge could not rely on the Bible alone he fell back on his idea of universal moral intuitions and first principles of reasoning and knowing supposedly built into the human constitution. Noll concludes, "Despite his well-published claims, a new theological idea had indeed arisen at Princeton. That idea was the selective, random, and unacknowledged functioning of Hodge's own moral intuitions as a guide for theological reasoning."[51] What Noll means is that even Hodge could not escape an element of subjectivity in theology.

Hodge Defends the Bible as the Foundation of the Science of Theology

Clearly one of Hodge's concerns was that contemporary theology, nineteenth-century Protestant theology, was mired in subjectivism. It seemed

---

[48]Mark Noll, "The Princeton Theology," in *The Princeton Theology: Reformed Theology in America*, ed. David Wells (Grand Rapids: Baker, 1989), 22.

[49]Mark Noll, "Charles Hodge as an Expositor of the Spiritual Life," in *Charles Hodge Revisited: A Critical Appraisal of His Life and Work*, ed. John W. Stewart and James H. Moorehead (Grand Rapids: Eerdmans, 2002), 198.

[50]Ibid., 202.

[51]Ibid., 205.

that Christian theologians were believing and teaching whatever seemed right in their own eyes, according to their own inner lights or feelings, or were succumbing to idealistic and rationalist philosophies just to be modern. No doubt he would have agreed with the quip made more than a century later that theologians were jumping in the ditch of irrelevance to avoid the pain of being kicked there by modernity. In response to one theological adversary he sharply criticized the nineteenth-century tendency to base religion on feelings regardless of objective facts:

> The theology of the feelings is declared to be the form of belief which is suggested by, and adapted to, the wants of the well-trained heart. It is embraced as involving the substance of truth, although when literally interpreted, it may or may not be false. . . . It insists not on dialectical [i.e., logical] argument, but receives whatever the healthy affections crave.[52]

What antidote would Hodge prescribe for this theological disease? His answer was to return to the objectively given revelation of God in the Bible and derive all doctrines solely from it. "We have . . . to restrict theology to its true sphere, as the science of the facts of divine revelation."[53] What, then, is theology's true sphere and task? "Theology . . . is the exhibition of the facts of Scripture in their proper order and relation, with the principles or general truths involved in the facts themselves, and which pervade and harmonize the whole."[54] In other words, theology's job, as it were, is to receive Scripture as God's objectively given, factual revelation of truth, discover from it the doctrines God wants us to believe and put them in an orderly system. This is the science of theology.

Hodge did not believe in leaving loose ends in explaining his idea of theology and its proper method. So, first, why believe Scripture to be God's factual revelation? Why is it not, as liberal Protestants tended to believe, the great Christian classic, inspired insofar as it is inspiring, insightful but not infallible? Hodge offers several reasons. First, he says of Christians, "We believe the Scriptures . . . because Christ declares them to be the Word of

---

[52]Quoted in Noll, *Princeton Theology*, 190.
[53]Hodge, *Systematic Theology*, 1:21.
[54]Ibid., 19.

God."[55] It must be received and believed "simply on his authority."[56] However, for Hodge that did not mean a leap of faith without reason. There is the inner testimony of the Holy Spirit. He wrote of a "spiritual apprehension and experience of the power of truth" in Scripture that makes it self-authenticating. In response to a theologian he thought was questioning the objectivity of revelation in the Bible Hodge wrote:

> When a man becomes a true Christian, when he is made a partaker of the precious faith of God's elect, what is it that he believes? The Scriptural answer to that question is, he believes the record which God has given of his Son. And where is that record? In every part of the Bible, directly or indirectly, from Genesis to Revelation.[57]

Was that all Hodge had to say for why a person should believe the Bible is God's revelation? No, but he thought it was the real reason why every true Christian so believes. In this he was no different from Calvin in whose heritage he stood. Calvin also rested the authority of the Bible on the inner testimony of the Holy Spirit. However, Hodge knew very well that without offering more objective reasons skeptics, including many liberal Protestants, would claim he was also appealing to subjectivity. In a long passage near the beginning of *Systematic Theology* Hodge offered what he considered objective supports for belief in the Bible as God's Word. These are what theologians usually call the "internal" and "external" evidences of the Bible as God's veridical revelation. Among the internal evidences Hodge cites are that the authors of the Bible claimed to be God's messengers, speaking by God's authority, and if they were not, then they were either fanatics or imposters.[58] Among the external evidences he cites is that "the Bible ever has been and still is, a power in the world. It has determined the course of history. . . . It is the parent of modern civilization. . . . Its effects cannot be rationally accounted for upon any other hypothesis than that it is what it claims to be, 'The Word of God.'"[59]

So, according to Hodge, the real Christian receives the Bible as God's Word rationally based on both subjective and objective reasons and evi-

---

[55]Ibid., 168.
[56]Ibid., 47.
[57]Quoted in Noll, *Princeton Theology*, 137.
[58]Hodge, *Systematic Theology*, 1:37.
[59]Ibid., 1:39.

dences. On the one hand he declared that "no amount of mere external evidence can produce genuine faith"[60] and on other hand that reason in theology, as in the natural sciences, "derives aid from the impulses of emotion [but] maintains an ascendency over them. In all investigations for truth, the intellect must be the authoritative power."[61] Noll points to this tension in Hodge's view of faith and reason as evidence that he never fully worked it out coherently. According to Noll, Hodge "never satisfactorily show[ed] how the pietistically defined faith that bulks large in his work related to the propositionally defined Christianity about which he also wrote a very great deal."[62] In other words, Hodge seemed to go back and forth between the subjective and objective poles in all his offerings of reasons for religious faith. That is clear in his separate explanations for the warrants for belief in the Bible as God's Word.

If the Bible is God's Word, God's revelation, what else must be true of it? First, for Hodge, "revelation" is "the supernatural, objective presentation or communication of truth to the mind, by the Spirit of God."[63] If the Bible is God's revelation, it is then the theologian's "store-house of facts."[64] Theology's task is to "take the facts of the Bible as they are, and construct [a] system so as to embrace them in all their integrity."[65] Hodge admits that the Bible is not a systematic theology, but, although "He [God] [does not] teach us systematic theology, . . . He gives us in the Bible the truths which, properly understood and arranged constitute the science of theology."[66] In other words, the Bible is God's given not-yet-systematized system of divine facts. Just as nature is not a system but yields one to the inquiring mind, so Scripture is not a system but yields one to the believing, inquiring mind. One might wonder why God would reveal a set of facts unsystematized if creating a system from them were his main reason for revealing it. Why did God not just reveal the system? Hodge does not attempt to answer that; he takes it for granted that this is what God did and creating the right system

---

[60]Quoted in Noll, *Princeton Theology*, 133.
[61]Ibid., 194.
[62]Noll, "Charles Hodge as an Expositor of the Spiritual Life," 191.
[63]Hodge, *Systematic Theology*, 1:8.
[64]Ibid., 1:10.
[65]Ibid., 1:13.
[66]Ibid., 1:3.

out of the Bible's facts is theology's task. And he assumes it is no esoteric task. Anyone whose mind is functioning properly could create the system even if only the person of faith can know it as true and properly understand it.

Hodge then turns to the classic ideas of Scripture's inspiration and infallibility, which he strongly affirms and defends—as they are rightly understood. The authority of the Bible, he argued, depends on its supernatural inspiration. "The infallibility and divine authority of the Scriptures are due to the fact that they are the Word of God; and they are the Word of God because they were given by the inspiration of the Holy Ghost."[67] He defined inspiration as "an influence of the Holy Spirit on the minds of certain select men, which rendered them the organs of God for the infallible communication of his mind and will. They were in such a sense the organs of God, that what they said God said."[68] Furthermore, this inspiration "extends to everything which any sacred writer asserts to be true"[69] including facts of history and cosmology. Hodge goes to great lengths to distinguish between "inspiration" and "mechanical dictation."[70] Inspiration left the authors conscious and aware and pressed into its service their personalities and cultural conditions. It did not make them automota—robots. Yet, Hodge warns, inspiration extended to the very words the human authors chose. Did that not override their free will and conscious personalities? No, Hodge argued. His Calvinism appears in his explanation (which many, no doubt, will not consider a real explanation):

> If God, without interfering with a man's free agency, can make it infallibly certain that he will repent and believe, He can render it certain that he will not err in teaching. It is in vain to profess to hold to common doctrine of Theism, and yet assert that God cannot control rational creatures without turning them into machines.[71]

Hodge did not explain exactly how this is possible; it remains his assertion.

According to Hodge, if God is the author of Scripture, inspiring the human authors and guiding them to the very words he wanted them to use, then the

---

[67]Ibid., 1:153.
[68]Ibid., 1:155.
[69]Ibid., 1:163.
[70]Ibid., 1:157.
[71]Ibid., 1:169.

Bible must be infallible. For Hodge it is an airtight, rational syllogism. However, he insisted that Scripture's infallibility is not just an assumption based on a syllogism; it fits the facts of Scripture. Nowhere does Scripture err. It is, he avers, "miraculously free from the soiling touch of human fingers."[72] But what about the alleged errors and discrepancies in the Bible? Hodge admits there are problems, things that have no quick or obvious solutions. For example, "one sacred writer says that on a given occasion twenty-four thousand, and another says that twenty-three thousand, men were slain." (He was referring to the discrepancy between 1 Corinthians 10:8 and Numbers 25:9.) Hodge's response: "Surely a Christian may be allowed to tread such objections under his feet."[73] He does not even attempt to solve the problem. According to him, "The errors in matters of fact which skeptics search out bear no proportion to the whole. No sane man would deny that the Parthenon was built of marble, even if here and there a speck of sandstone should be detected in its structure."[74] Also, these alleged discrepancies "can no more shake the faith of a Christian than the unsolved perturbations of the orbit of a comet shake the astronomer's confidence in the law of gravitation."[75]

Hodge Seeks to Reconcile Theology and Science

One interesting thing about Hodge's theology is his constant concern with comparing theology with science and even reconciling them. We have seen that the war between science and religion was a major factor in the development of modern theology. Hodge was also concerned to avoid that war, but he was not willing to place religion and science in separate compartments where they could not in principle conflict with each other. He rightly saw that as conceding to the natural sciences facts and therefore knowledge and relegating religion, including Christianity, to a subjective realm of faith or values. Noll notes "the continued Princeton desire to pursue theology with an ear to science and science within the bounds of theology."[76] What did this mean, then, for conflicts between science and Christian doctrine (which for Hodge means between science and the Bible)?

---

[72]Ibid., 1:170.
[73]Ibid.
[74]Ibid.
[75]Quoted in Noll, *Princeton Theology*, 141.
[76]Ibid., 46.

Hodge's view was that interpreters of the Bible must "bow to the facts of science, but the facts of Scripture may never give way to mere theories of science."[77] In other words, when a fact is established by science so that it is beyond doubt or question, if it seems to conflict with Scripture the latter must be reinterpreted to fit science. He admitted, "The Church has been forced more than once to alter her interpretation of the Bible to accommodate the discoveries of science."[78] He was thinking of the Galileo affair among others. So, according to the Princeton theologian, "the church . . . is willing that the Bible should be interpreted under the guidance of the facts of science."[79] He admitted that the traditional dating of creation in approximately 4004 B.C. is impossible given the facts of geology, so the word *day* in the first chapter of Genesis must mean "an indefinite period" rather than a twenty-four-hour day.[80] But Hodge strongly believed that "Darwinianism" is not a fact of science but a theory and theology need not accommodate to it. In fact, it must reject it. Overall, however, he was confident that, after all is said and done, there is no conflict between scientific fact and the Bible; conflicts are always only apparent and due to either misinterpretation of the Bible or science overstepping its bounds by attempting to promote theories as facts.

The details of Hodge's doctrinal statements in *Systematic Theology* are unremarkable; almost without exception he expounded and defended traditional Calvinist theology. Throughout his emphasis is on the greatness, majesty and absolute sovereignty of God, the total depravity of human beings, the atoning death of Jesus Christ as a penal substitution for sins to assuage the wrath of God and salvation of the elect by grace through faith alone. What Hodge set forth as the right system of biblical truth is classical high Calvinism. In the scholastic debate between the supralapsarians and the infralapsarians he takes the latter side. Much of *Systematic Theology* is consumed with contradicting heresies and wrong theologies. Everywhere he turned Hodge saw one great error running through Christian history that must be opposed—anthropocentrism or humanism:

---

[77]Ibid., 143.
[78]Quoted in ibid., 144.
[79]Quoted in ibid., 143.
[80]Ibid., 143–44.

He argued that from its inception Christianity had been plagued by the conflict between two competing doctrinal systems. The one, he said, "has for its object the vindication of the Divine supremacy and sovereignty in the salvation of men; the other has for its characteristic aim the assertion of the rights of human nature. It is specially [sic] solicitous that nothing should be held to be true, which cannot be philosophically reconciled with the liberty and ability of man."[81]

Hodge thought he saw the second doctrinal system shadowing the first, which he considered biblical and "Augustinian" (his code word for orthodox), in his own time and place as before. He placed special blame on Arminians, which he called "Remonstrants," for the gradual doctrinal declension leading to the crisis of liberal theology in his time. They represented among Protestants the second system and a slippery slope leading down into liberal heresy.

Hodge Leaves a Legacy That Leads to Fundamentalism

Worth quoting again is that "Hodge's worldview and particular biblical hermeneutic . . . provided the intellectual framework for twentieth-century Protestant fundamentalism."[82] Another critic says that Hodge could rightly be called a "biblicist and dogmatist."[83] Noll notes "Hodge's occasional willingness to treat the Bible as a simple reservoir of facts"[84] and says, "On such a trajectory [as Hodge's] the next step is fundamentalism."[85] These are strong words from scholarly admirers. What justifies them?

First there is Hodge's tendency to treat Scripture as a reservoir of facts—as a not-yet-systematized systematic theology. The emphasis clearly is on Christianity as a doctrinal system and Hodge left very little in his system in the realm of nonessentials. While he was personally generous, hoping for the salvation of the majority of people and believing that salvation does not depend on theological orthodoxy, his rhetoric was one of exclusion based on his vision of right belief. That is to say that he was the proverbial black-and-white thinker who left little in the realm of gray. Most doctrines were

---

[81]Wells, "Charles Hodge," 45.
[82]Stewart, "Introducing Charles Hodge," 2.
[83]Kuklick, "The Place of Charles Hodge," 76.
[84]Noll, "Charles Hodge as an Expositor of the Spiritual Life," 194.
[85]Ibid., 196.

either true or false; he had great difficulty seeing anything of value in Christian traditions other than his own.

Second, there is Hodge's almost total incomprehension of his own cultural influences. Theologian David Kelsey rightly notes, "Hodge was largely oblivious to his conditioning by cultural context."[86] He was unreflective about his Americanism and philosophical commitments and accommodations to distinctively American forms of Scottish realism. Noll gives Hodge a backhanded compliment: "The truly remarkable thing about the work of the Princetonians was that so much historic Calvinism remained even as they adjusted their thought to accommodate American intellectual conventions."[87]

Finally, Hodge seemed totally lacking in social and historical consciousness. He denied doctrinal development, preferring to think that all right doctrines fall directly out of the Bible and that his system of doctrines could be transported anywhere in the world at any time and be right for all Christians.[88] In many ways he was the extreme opposite of Troeltsch; Hodge rejected historicism to the point of being blind to how his own belief system was influenced by culture and history.

Hodge's critics rightly point out that all of that has to be understood against the background in which Hodge was working. Hodge saw all around him almost nothing but doctrinal declension and infidelity. "This context deeply affected the form and direction that Hodge's theology took."[89] In what they see as the cognitive and moral chaos of postmodernity, many twenty-first-century conservative Protestants are rediscovering Hodge, often in the form of more popular presentations of the same doctrinal system, and rushing to it as refuge.

---

[86]David H. Kelsey, "Charles Hodge as Interpreter of Scripture," in *Charles Hodge Revisited: A Critical Appraisal of His Life and Work*, ed. John W. Stewart and James H. Moorehead (Grand Rapids: Eerdmans, 2002), 227.
[87]Noll, "Princeton Theology," 28.
[88]Ibid., 58.
[89]Wells, "Charles Hodge," 44.

4

MEDIATING THEOLOGIES
BUILD BRIDGES BETWEEN
ORTHODOXY AND LIBERALISM

The nineteenth century seemed to be an era of special tensions in Christian theology. The full force of the Enlightenment was beginning to be felt in Christian theology itself. The acids of modernity were eating away at traditional Christian doctrines, and liberal theologies were attempting to rescue Christianity from oblivion by accommodating to modernity. Fear of conflict between science and religion became a near obsession among theologians. Atheism was rising for the first time in Western history with philosophers such as Ludwig Feuerbach (1804–1872) claiming that God is nothing more than a projection of humanity into the heavens. Secularity was setting into political life; revolutions were happening in many European countries. State churches were under threat after the French and American revolutions disestablished religion. There had not been a period of such upheaval for religion in Europe since the Reformation.

Most church historians and historical theologians looking back on the nineteenth century focus on a few relatively extreme defenders of orthodoxy such as Hodge or radical revisionists of Christian doctrine such as Schleiermacher and Ritschl. However, a third group of theologians attempted to present a via media, a third way, between Protestant orthodoxy and liberal revision. These do not receive as much attention because they are perceived by some scholars as not particularly interesting or as unsuccessful. It is always the bold, the innovative, the radical who are remembered. Middle ground is often equated with mediocrity. That is unfortunate, because some of these so-called mediating theologians were quite creative and paved the way for new developments in theology in the twentieth century. To those inclined toward liberal accommodation to modernity they look conservative; to those inclined toward preservation of orthodoxy they appear liberal. The fact is, however, that they were consistently neither. They display features of both. They are valuable partly because they demonstrate that overreaction does not have to be normative.

Mediating Theologians Moderately Reconstruct Christian Theology

"Mediating theology" is a technical term in historical theology. It is the English translation of *Vermittlungstheologie*, which is a category created by scholars of nineteenth-century theology for a few German theologians who consciously attempted to carve out a third way between Protestant orthodoxy and liberal Protestantism. They mediated between other extremes, too, as will be explained soon. The *Vermittlungstheologie* was a small movement. "Mediating theology" has come to be used for many more theologians than the original three or four always included in the original German movement. The German *Vermittlungstheologie* began with the founding of a theological journal in Heidelberg entitled *Theologische Studien und Kritiken* ("Theological Studies and Critical Reviews") in 1828. The founding editor defined mediating theology: "Mediation is the scientifically tracing back of relative oppositions to their original unity, through which an inner reconciliation and higher standpoint is gained by which they are transcended, the intellectual position arising out of this mediation being the true, healthy mean [middle]."[1] However, this Hegelian definition of mediating theology is fortunately not the only way of describing it.

Clearer, certainly easier to understand and less tied to Hegel's philosophy is Dutch theologian Hendrikus Berkhof's description of mediating theology:

---

[1]"Mediating Theology," in *The Dictionary of Historical Theology*, ed. Trevor Hart (Grand Rapids: Eerdmans, 2000), 360.

"Its representatives did everything within their power to guard against a hopeless estrangement between the Christian faith and modern, immanentistic, rational thought"[2] and "these theologians established a relationship between the gospel and the secularized culture of their day."[3] That was not the only relationship they tried to establish. They are remembered for attempting to bridge the gaps between: rationalism and supernaturalism, Hegel and Schleiermacher, theology and the life of the church.[4] If we broaden the category of mediating theology from the original *Vermittlungstheologie* to a whole movement of theologians like it we can see many nineteenth-century theologians in Europe and the United States attempting to forge a bridge between seemingly opposite forces impinging on Christian thought—most importantly perhaps between liberal Protestantism and Protestant orthodoxy and therefore between modernity and traditional Christianity.

The original *Vermittlungstheologie* group included several German theologians largely forgotten except by a few specialists in nineteenth-century theology: I. A. Dorner (1809–1884), Julius Müller (1801–1878) and Richard Rothe (1799–1867). Dorner is usually considered "the most influential of the mediating theologians."[5] His main concern was to mediate between faith as the subjective standard of Christianity and Scripture as Christianity's objective standard.[6] He also sought to combine aspects of Schleiermacher's "feelings" approach to the essence of Christianity with Hegel's highly rational, intellectual approach to religion without being trapped by either of them. Berkhof says of Dorner that he was "not the man of cultural breadth but of evangelical depth."[7] Of all the original mediating theologians he says the intellectual world of their day paid them little attention compared with Schleiermacher and Hegel, but "this theology, preaching, and teaching definitely enabled many younger theologians and members of the church intelligentsia at one and the same time to participate in their culture and to be Christians with a good conscience."[8]

---

[2]Hendrikus Berkhof, *Two Hundred Years of Theology*, trans. John Vriend (Grand Rapids: Eerdmans, 1989), 64.
[3]Ibid., 65.
[4]"Mediating Theology," 360.
[5]Ibid., 361.
[6]Ibid.
[7]Berkhof, *Two Hundred Years of Theology*, 67.
[8]Ibid., 65.

The term "mediating theology" also appears in the history of nineteenth-century American theology and is normally used of those American theologians who studied with German mediating theologians or whose theologies seemed to mirror theirs. American mediating theology is often called Mercersburg theology because its two best-known representatives, J. W. Nevin (1803–1886) and Philip Schaff (1819–1893), taught at the German Reformed seminary in Mercersburg, Pennsylvania. While there is no question that Nevin and Schaff were influenced by the German *Vermittlungstheologie*, their main interest seemed to lie in ecclesiology—the doctrine of the church. They were anti-individualists who emphasized the role of the church and tradition in theological reflection. They are not best known or remembered for the kind of cautious theological reconstruction for which Dorner, for example, is remembered. Rather, the American analog for German mediating theology in its broadest sense is Horace Bushnell (1802–1876), whose theology is best described as "progressive orthodoxy."[9] That label itself should indicate Bushnell's mediating interest in theology—mediating between liberal Protestantism and Protestant orthodoxy. One scholar of American theology says that Bushnell's "aim as a writer was to overcome the larger divisions in the culture."[10] Bushnell called his own approach to theology "Christian Comprehensiveness," which meant recognizing "the partial truth in opposed theological positions and mov[ing] beyond the opposition toward a higher harmony."[11] This is exactly what the German mediating theologians saw as their project.

Bushnell has usually been categorized as a liberal Protestant theologian. One scholar of American liberal theology calls him "the theological father of mainstream American liberal Protestantism."[12] Bushnell himself would consider that a dubious honor and probably reject it. The scholar admits, "Throughout his career Bushnell charged that higher critical scholarship [of the Bible] was presumptuous and spiritually destructive, especially in its re-

---

[9]E. Brooks Holifield, *Theology in America: Christian Thought from the Age of the Puritans to the Civil War* (New Haven, CT: Yale University Press, 2003), 452.

[10]Ibid., 453.

[11]Ibid., 454.

[12]Gary Dorrien, *The Making of American Liberal Theology: Imagining Progressive Religion 1805–1900* (Louisville, KY: Westminster John Knox, 2001), 111.

jection of the biblical miracles."[13] Bushnell was an ardent defender of supernaturalism even if he did engage in cautious reconstruction of classical Christian doctrines such as the person of Jesus Christ (Christology) and atonement in order to bring them up to date with modern consciousness. He had one foot firmly planted in orthodoxy and the other one firmly planted in post-Enlightenment, modern thought and was influenced by both Schleiermacher and Jonathan Edwards. He better fits the mediating category than any other, as the label "progressive orthodoxy" itself indicates.

Our two chosen representatives of mediating theology are, then, Dorner and Bushnell. The first is always included in that category; the inclusion of the second requires more defense. No doubt some scholars will object to it. The reader can judge its appropriateness after considering the section on Bushnell (4.b.).

Before plunging into Dorner's theological contribution it will be helpful to some readers to offer a few cautions to avoid confusion. Mediating theology is not the same as moderate theology. The label "moderate" is used by many American Christians in the late twentieth century and early twenty-first century to indicate avoidance of both fundamentalism and liberalism, which have largely become terms of opprobrium. However, it is widely used to cover so much that it is almost meaningless. For example, a moderate Baptist in the American South may be very different theologically from a moderate Lutheran in the Upper Midwest. Mediating theology is a specific approach to theology that attempts to bridge seeming opposites; it is not an attempt to land somewhere in a middle ground between extremes. Mediating theologians may, indeed, seem moderate to some readers, but that is not the best way of describing them.

Another caveat is that Dorner and Bushnell are very different theologians who warrant little comparison beyond the fact that both attempted to combine aspects of liberal Protestantism with Protestant orthodoxy. Dorner was a high-church minister of the Prussian Union (Evangelical Christian Church), a denomination that included Reformed and Lutheran members. (King Frederick Wilhelm III forced Reformed and Lutheran Protestants in Prussia together in 1817.) Dorner was an executive of that state church as

---

[13]Ibid., 123.

well as one of its leading theologians. His own orientation was more Lutheran than Reformed, but he drew on both traditions. Bushnell was a minister of the Congregational churches of Connecticut who pastored one Congregational church in Hartford for twenty-seven years. His theological orientation, then, was toward the American free-church tradition and the New Haven theology that was strongly influenced by the Second Great Awakening in New England. That is to say, a very moderate kind of revivalism influenced Bushnell even if he came to oppose revivalism. The emphasis was on religious feelings, much like Schleiermacher's but with a distinctly American flavor.

Two men could hardly be more different than Dorner and Bushnell. And yet, for that reason, they represent different types of mediating theology. What they had in common was influence by Schleiermacher (with whom neither agreed completely), attempts to bridge the perceived gap between the subjective and objective poles of Christian faith and thought, desire to combine aspects of liberal Protestantism with aspects of Protestant orthodoxy and the goal of bringing together as much as possible modern culture and church life. Both also engaged in reconstructing Christian doctrines with an eye toward modernity but without making modernity a source and norm of theology's content.

4.A. ISAAK AUGUST DORNER BRIDGES THE GAP BETWEEN LIBERAL AND ORTHODOX THEOLOGIES

The twentieth century's most influential theologian, Karl Barth (see 5.a.), wrote of Dorner in his book on nineteenth-century theology that "here we have for the first time a theologian who, while standing amidst the problems of the nineteenth century, points beyond them in his contribution to theological method and poses new questions to us by the new answers he gives."[14] That is high praise from Barth! He continued his discussion of Dorner by saying of nineteenth-century theology, "For the first time [in Dorner] something new presented itself."[15]

Dorner was born in the German state of Würrtemberg, a hotbed of pi-

---

[14]Karl Barth, *Protestant Theology in the Nineteenth Century*, new ed. (Grand Rapids: Eerdmans, 2002), 563.
[15]Ibid., 569.

etism, an influence we have seen before as a major factor in many nineteenth-century theologians' backgrounds. Pietism remained an influence in Dorner's Christianity even as he criticized it for its alleged tendencies to make the Christian faith purely inward. Dorner studied and taught at the universities of Tübingen, Kiel, Königsberg, Bonn and Göttingen. He ended his career with a chair at the most prestigious university—Berlin. "Not only was he a front-ranking theologian but also a keen churchman, keen to cement and extend the linkage between the Lutherans and Reformed in Germany."[16] Toward the end of his career he served as the lead executive minister of the Prussian Union Church. Throughout Germany he was widely regarded as a leading Christian theologian and church leader. He was also well known in Scandinavia through his friendship with Bishop Martensen (Kierkegaard's Hegelian nemesis) and in England, where, strangely, he was translated and studied by Nonconformists (Congregationalists).

In 1856 Dorner founded an influential journal entitled *Jahrbücher für deutsche Theologie* ("Annual Journal for German Theology"), which he edited until 1878. According to one Dorner scholar, "His career was . . . typical in its Teutonic industriousness."[17] Among his published books were a five-volume *History of the Development of the Doctrine of the Person of Christ* (1839–1840), the two-volume *History of Protestant Theology Particularly in Germany* (1867) and his four-volume *System of Christian Doctrine* (1879–1880). Dorner's most discussed theological work was a series of three lengthy articles on the attributes of God, especially God's immutability, published in 1856 through 1858 in *Jahrbücher für deutsche Theologie*. Ritschl burst on the theological scene soon after Dorner's *System* was published, and attention turned away from the latter to the former. Dorner's theology was eclipsed by the new school of liberal Protestant theology led by Ritschl and popularized by Harnack (see 2.b.).

Dorner believed the Protestant Reformation was left unfinished.[18] The nineteenth century gave special opportunity to do just that. The main problem left unresolved by the Protestant Reformers, according to Dorner,

---

[16]Stanley H. Russell, "I. A. Dorner: A Centenary Appreciation," *The Expository Times* 96 (December 1984): 77.
[17]Ibid.
[18]Ibid.

was the doctrine of God. Luther and Calvin and the other Reformers had concentrated so much on the doctrines of salvation that they left almost untouched the received medieval, scholastic idea of God as *actus purus*— pure actuality without potentiality. Dorner believed Protestant orthodoxy had unthinkingly baptized a doctrine of God heavily influenced by Greek philosophy and medieval theology. It was his job to discover a doctrine of God that would do justice both to God's livingness and immutability. The traditional doctrine came down heavily on the side of God's immutability and aseity—unchangeableness and self-sufficiency, so much so that God seemed unrelated to the world. Dorner wanted to achieve a doctrine of God that is truly relational without going so far as Hegel's panentheistic idea of God as Absolute Spirit evolving through history.[19] The mediating element in Dorner's reconstruction of the doctrine of God lies in his attempt to bridge between Schleiermacher's idea of God as unable to be affected by the world and Hegel's idea of God as wholly immanent in the world and undergoing change with history. It lies also in his dual commitment to modern *Wissenschaftlichkeit* (scientific rigor) and the Christian church and its tradition.

Dorner's reconstruction of the doctrine of God went virtually unnoticed for a long time because Protestant theology turned with Ritschl and his followers away from metaphysics and speculation about God-in-himself. The problem Dorner was trying to solve was considered irrelevant to the ethical nature of the gospel. However, Dorner sowed seeds that would sprout and grow in the second half of the twentieth century as theologians of various types became interested in relational theology—the idea that what happens in the world affects God.

Besides the doctrine of God's attributes and relation with the world, Dorner worked on the doctrine of the person of Jesus Christ—Christology. A new development in German theology (that spread to Britain and the United States) was so-called kenotic Christology. It is the idea that in order to become fully human the divine Logos, the Son of God, the second person of the Trinity, divested himself of divine attributes of glory for the sake of his incarnation and real humanity. Dorner was horrified by that idea, as it

---

[19]Claude Welch, "Isaak August Dorner: Introduction to the Texts," in *God and Incarnation in Mid-nineteenth Century German Theology: Thomasius, Dorner, Biedermann*, ed. Claude Welch (New York: Oxford University Press, 1965), 108–9.

seemed to him to rob God of his deity and make him too mutable. His new construction of the doctrine of God's immutability was aimed precisely at providing an alternative to kenotic Christology. So was his own idea of "progressive incarnation." These are the two most interesting and constructive areas of Dorner's theology, and both illustrate his method and approach as a mediating theologian. Dorner's Christology never caught on, and so the emphasis here will be on his doctrine of God and God's real relatedness with the world of time and change, concepts that were revolutionary in his day.

Dorner responds to philosophical and theological currents of his time. Dorner developed his theological proposals in response to Schleiermacher, Hegel and a then new German theology called kenotic Christology led primarily by Lutheran theologian Gottfried Thomasius (1802–1875). All three stimulated him to think in fresh ways about faith and God. During his theological career everyone was talking about Schleiermacher and Hegel as opposite religious impulses facing into the Enlightenment. Certainly the theologian and the philosopher did not like each other much. About Schleiermacher's emphasis on religion as the feeling of utter dependence Hegel quipped that if Schleiermacher was right Hegel's dog would be the most religious being of all. Schleiermacher held his fire in public, but everyone knew he did not favor Hegel's rationalistic approach to theology. He was probably thinking of Hegel's philosophy whenever he criticized treating religion as a system of thought.

For many mid-nineteenth-century theologians Schleiermacher represents an overemphasis on experience and feeling in religion; his theology was too influenced by pietism and romanticism and thus fell into the trap of subjectivism. Christian doctrine was treated as nothing more than the human attempt to bring religious feelings to verbal expression, but they are inadequate to the essence of Christianity. The result was a relativized theology open to individual interpretation and adjustment as well as to constant revision at all levels. Dorner was dissatisfied with Schleiermacher's subjectivizing of Christianity which seemed to remove it from the realm of knowledge. In contrast, Dorner's "constructive effort was throughout directed toward attaining an objective knowledge of religious and ethical truth as real (not merely ideal or ideational)."[20]

---

[20]Claude Welch, *Protestant Thought in the Nineteenth Century*, vol. 1: *1799-1870* (New Haven, CT: Yale University Press, 1972), 275.

Dorner was also dissatisfied with Schleiermacher's concept of God as unaffected by the world. According to him, Schleiermacher adopted the classical theistic view of God developed by the church fathers and medieval theologians and not altered by the Reformers. The great medieval theologian Anselm of Canterbury claimed that God does not feel anything, including compassion. For him the feeling of compassion is not in God but in us when we contemplate God's great mercy. The tradition handed down portrayed God as complete in himself such that what happens in the world could not affect him. Thus God is not relational with the world but only within his triune community. Dorner saw this strong idea of God's immutability in Schleiermacher's doctrine of God and criticized it. The problem he pointed at was the inconsistency between strong immutability and redemption through incarnation. Even Schleiermacher believed that God is the source and sole actor in redemption. Dorner's question was how that could be reconciled with the concept of God as an abstract, eternally self-sufficient being.[21] What Dorner was accusing Schleiermacher of was reducing God to something less than living; his God was static and thus unable to interact with the world. But interaction with the world is part and parcel of Christian redemption. A purely static God cannot be the redeemer even as Schleiermacher described redemption.

Dorner wrote, "According to Schleiermacher God is, to be sure, the living spiritual causality of the world, but he is related to the world eternally in the same manner; he wills and effects in the world eternally the same things that are already implicit in his willing of himself."[22] One Dorner scholar paraphrases the mediating theologian's critique of Schleiermacher's idea of God: "Schleiermacher may say that God is living and spiritual, but it would be more accurate to his conceptual scheme to say that his God resembles an eternal paralytic, incapable of historical action."[23] Traditional Christian theism, which Schleiermacher adopted and failed to reconcile with his reconstructed account of Christian faith, describes God as *actus purus*—pure actuality with no potentiality. In other words, God cannot

---

[21]Robert R. Williams, "I. A. Dorner: The Ethical Immutability of God," *Journal of the American Academy of Religion* 54:4 (winter 1986): 724.
[22]Quoted in ibid.
[23]Ibid.

"become" in any sense. Dorner doubted that this is compatible with many things Christianity traditionally says about God: God is love, God grieves, God repents, God responds to prayer. The biggest problem, for Dorner, is that the traditional view, including Schleiermacher's, portrays God in an unethical way. That does not mean it portrays God as acting unethically, but it constructs a view of God that has nothing to do with ethics. It empties the idea that God is love of any practical meaning if not of all meaning. For Dorner it was absolutely essential that theology be ethically fruitful. The abstract, unaffected deity of classical theism and of Schleiermacher's God who is the sole cause of everything but cannot be affected is not a God of love. So, according to Dorner, the doctrine of God needs reconstruction.

However much Dorner was opposed to classical theism and its use by Schleiermacher, he was just as much or even more opposed to its opposite—Hegel's evolving, ever-changing Absolute Spirit that is nearly identical with history itself. He saw this as playing with pantheism. That is not to say Dorner rejected everything of Hegel's philosophy of religion; he borrowed Hegel's idea of "the inner course of history": "He was convinced . . . not only that the inner course of history points the direction of further progress, but also that the final solution must emerge out of the moments that have appeared in history."[24] In other words, Dorner agreed with Hegel's idea of history as the unfolding of God's own life in time. However, he strongly disagreed with the extreme to which Hegel took this idea—to panentheism, where God and the world are interdependent. For Dorner, God's relation with the world, with time and history, is real. History affects God. That is why God is a living God and not the static God of classical theism. However, this entry of God into time must not be viewed with Hegel as necessary. If it is necessary for God's self-actualization, then it is not ethical. In order to be ethical it has to be free. Hegel's Absolute Spirit is not free in its relation with the world and has no independent existence apart from the world.

Before continuing, it will be helpful to stop and set forth two fundamental principles or axioms of Dorner's mediating theology as it pertains to God. First, God's essence is love, which means his power is ordered by love. Otherwise God is not ethical. Sheer power has nothing to do with

---

[24]Welch, "Isaak August Dorner," 111.

ethics. If God is truly good, the ground and source of ethics, of right and wrong, love must be not just one of his attributes but his essence. It follows from this that "if love—an ethical conception—is primary, then God's power is not unqualifiedly absolute, but is ethically ordered and directed by love. Further, to be loving God cannot be absolute in all respects, but must be able to enter into reciprocal relation with the world."[25] Dorner's second axiom balances the first one: "The whole historical life of God in the world takes place, not at the expense of the eternal perfection of God himself, but precisely by virtue of this permanent perfection."[26] In other words, because God is love, once there is a world, God must be in real relation with it such that the world affects God. However, this real relation with the world in which the world affects God cannot be a diminution of God's perfection but the expression of God's eternal perfection. In other words, God must be "the One who loves in freedom."[27]

Dorner faced a third theological current in his time that stimulated him to respond and develop an alternative, mediating view. That was the new kenotic Christology of Thomasius and other German and British theologians. Thomasius was the Lutheran professor of dogmatics at the University of Erlangen who is best known for his concept of God's self-limitation in the incarnation. The background problem was the real humanity of Jesus Christ. Thomasius and others believed that traditional theism made it impossible to think of Jesus' humanity as fully like ours. Luke 2:52 says he grew in stature, wisdom and favor with God and people. Orthodox Christology says he was truly God and truly human yet one person (hypostatic union). Classical theism portrays God as absolutely immutable, incapable of any change including suffering. (Remember Anselm, who argued that God cannot feel compassion.) So, the question Thomasius raised and attempted to answer is how the Son of God, God the Son, the second person of the Trinity, equal with the Father, truly God, could become incarnate. How could he be born, grow in wisdom, suffer and die?

---

[25]Robert R. Williams, "Introduction," in Isaak August Dorner, *Divine Immutability: A Critical Reconsideration*, trans. Robert R. Williams and Claude Welch (Minneapolis: Fortress, 1994), 4.
[26]Ibid., 23.
[27]This is Barth's famous formula for God in *Church Dogmatics* II/1. However, it is clear that this also applies to Dorner's concept of God's relationship with the world, and it is probably that Barth's doctrine of God was directly indebted to Dorner at crucial points such as this.

The traditional answer was that the divine Son of God did not undergo any change in the incarnation. He took on a human nature without in any way altering his own divine attributes of omnipotence, omniscience and omnipresence. But that inevitably requires Christians to think of the baby of Bethlehem being both ignorant (like any baby) and at the same time omniscient, all-knowing. It also requires Christians to believe that Jesus both did and did not suffer the pain of crucifixion. The classical formula was that in all these changes the Son of God was unaffected in his divine nature but experienced ignorance, growth and suffering through his assumed human nature. Thomasius believed this was an artificial explanation of the humanity of Jesus; it depicted it as an impersonal nature put on by the Son of God like a coat. He believed it was time to take the Reformation to the next level by reforming Christology away from classical theism, much of which was developed throughout the Middle Ages by Catholic theologians such as Anselm and Aquinas.

Thomasius, for all his dryness, was wrestling with modernity in two ways. First, he was responding to the modern revisionism of theologians such as Baur and D. F. Strauss (1808–1874), two luminaries of the Tübingen school of biblical studies and theology. Both seemed to deny the deity of Jesus Christ based on his true humanity which they believed was a given, something beyond serious question. They considered that incompatible with deity unless one took the Hegelian approach of identifying deity and humanity in a panenetheistic way. Thomasius was also responding to the overall tendency of modernity to emphasize becoming over being. This was a gradual, almost imperceptible change, but evidence of it was everywhere in nineteenth-century European culture with the rise of evolutionary ideas brought about by Hegel and later Darwin. The idea of God's absolute immutability needed reconsideration. Thomasius stepped up to perform that task.

According to Thomasius, humanity was created by God as a fit vehicle for incarnation: "it is evident that there is no hindrance in human nature to a real union with God" *because* God established the "possibility of . . . intimate union of God with humanity by the creation."[28] Some have seen

---

[28]Gottfried Thomasius, "Christ's Person and Work," in *God and Incarnation in Mid-nineteenth Century German Theology: Thomasius, Dorner, Biedermann*, ed. Claude Welch (New York: Oxford University Press, 1965), 40–41.

in this a hint of accommodation to Hegel's philosophy of religion. Thomasius's main contribution to modern theology, however, comes in his idea that, for the sake of Jesus' real humanity, the incarnation had to involve divine self-limitation:

> And thus we shall have to posit the incarnation itself precisely in the fact that he, the eternal Son of God, the second person of the deity, gave himself over into the form of human limitation, and thereby to the limits of a spatio-temporal existence, under the conditions of a human development, in the bounds of an historical concrete being, in order to live in and through our nature the life of our race in the fullest sense of the word, without on that account ceasing to be God.[29]

Thomasius was suggesting, arguing, that for the sake of Jesus' real humanity the eternal Son of God had to divest himself of the divine mode of being, by which he meant retracting his attributes of glory from activity to potentiality to be regained in full actuality through the ministry of the Holy Spirit during his life and through his resurrection and ascension. In practical terms, this means that Thomasius was saying Jesus Christ, although truly God, was not omniscient and omnipotent throughout his entire human life; he depended on the Father and the Holy Spirit for his supernatural powers of knowledge and action (e.g., miracles) rather than on his divine nature which became dormant when he became human.

So, Schleiermacher adopted classical theism and portrayed God as unaffected by the world. Hegel went to the opposite extreme, at least according to Dorner, and portrayed God as constantly evolving through history. Thomasius portrayed God as mutable through self-limitation, which he considered a via media between classical theism and Hegelian panentheism. Dorner disagreed that Thomasius had achieved the needed via media. According to Dorner, Thomasius had sacrificed too much of God's immutability with his kenotic Christology. How can God remain God and give up or divest himself of his divine attributes? Dorner did not like the idea of the incarnation as God's self-limitation; he preferred a different route to explaining God's relationship with time and change that preserved God's ethical immutability and real incarnation in Jesus Christ while portraying God as capable of *some*

---

[29]Ibid., 48.

change through self-actualization rather than self-limitation. "For Dorner, the incarnation meant divine fulfillment rather than temporary withdrawal into potentiality."[30] As mentioned earlier, Dorner's whole project in reconstructing the doctrine of God was to find a way to do justice to God's freedom and livingness equally. Schleiermacher and classical theism did not do justice to God's livingness, vitality, real relation with the world. Hegel did not do justice to God's freedom by tying God too closely with history so that God has no life of his own apart from the world. Thomasius did not find the right way to balance God's freedom and livingness.

Dorner reconstructs the doctrine of God's immutability. In his three essays on God's immutability Dorner attempted to formulate "an alternative to an abstract deity eternally actual apart from the world and a pantheistic deity immanent in and dependent on the world."[31] His overall thesis is that "the God which is a self-consciously accomplished synthesis of ethically necessary substance and ethical freedom is both immutable and mutable, and for this reason can enter into reciprocal relation with the world without loss or diminution of being."[32] In other words, Dorner sought a way, and thought he found it, of combining God's livingness and freedom in relation to the world. To protect God's freedom, so that God is not made a prisoner of history, God's immutable substance must be affirmed as eternal and independently actual without any creation. Otherwise, God becomes a prisoner of the world of time and change as with Hegel's Absolute Spirit. To take seriously God's real incarnation in Jesus Christ and other involvement in the world God's mutability, ability to change, must be affirmed as an ethically free choice. According to Dorner, "the received doctrine of dogmatics of the *immutability* of God will first and above all need numerous alterations, if God's *livingness* is to be able to be compatible with it."[33]

The first alteration Dorner suggests is to scrap the doctrine of God's simplicity which was part and parcel of classical theism. In the traditional doctrine of God, assumed by most Christian theologians before Dorner, God

---

[30]"Mediating Theology," 361.

[31]Williams, "I. A. Dorner: The Ethical Immutability of God," 735.

[32]Ibid.

[33]I. A. Dorner, "Dogmatic Discussion of the Doctrine of the Immutability of God," in *God and Incarnation in Mid-nineteenth Century German Theology: Thomasius, Dorner, Biedermann*, ed. Claude Welch (New York: Oxford University Press, 1965), 116.

must be ontologically simple, that is, noncomposite, in order to be God, the being greater than which none can be conceived. The reasoning was that if God were composed of parts, his being could possibly disintegrate. Perfection of being requires simplicity of being. Dorner disagreed. He accused the classical doctrine of God's absolute unity, simplicity, of borrowing too heavily from Greek philosophy and of being dangerous to the doctrine of the Trinity. While Father, Son and Spirit are not parts of God in a literal sense, they are aspects of God. Also, God's attributes are not all one; they are real aspects of God. Dorner says, "Now certainly God is not composite; but it does not follow that all those distinctions have no place in God."[34] Also, on the basis of strict simplicity of being "the divine being could not be living, but could only be rigid dead substance or equally lifeless law."[35] Dorner considered it absolutely necessary to posit a distinction within God between knowing and willing, a distinction classical theism denied. Without it, he argued, God's real relation with the world of free creatures active in time would be a charade. Necessary to God's loving, ethical relation with human persons in time is "a change in God's living self-activation" which requires a distinction between God's knowing and willing. That is, according to Dorner, for God to know something is not the same as to will it and vice versa. Otherwise, nothing creatures do can really affect God.

Dorner hangs his reconstruction of God's immutability very much on the incarnation: "It is undeniable that God, so far as he dwells in man [i.e., Jesus Christ], also leads an historical life in the world, enters into contact with time. . . . God changes the world . . . enters into temporality."[36] But the flip side of that is that the world also changes God. God could not fail to be affected by his own incarnation. There Dorner agrees with Thomasius, but he prefers to think of the change wrought in God as "self-actualizing of God" rather than "self-limitation of God."[37] But Dorner also hangs his reconstruction of God's immutability on the ethical relationship between God and free creatures. He argues if God created a world of "free powers" out of love, then not everything can be traced back to one absolute, timeless

---

[34]Ibid., 120.
[35]Ibid., 121.
[36]Ibid., 129.
[37]Ibid., 128–29.

decree, as in Reformed theology. Rather, "it can not suffice to trace everything from God's side to his bare omnipotent will. The relation of love, which is aimed at in the creation of free powers, resists the absolutism of bare power; the place of the latter is taken by a communion of love."[38] A communion of love must be a reciprocal relation and not a one-sided relation in which one party does all the effecting and the other party (or parties) receives all the affecting. Thus, Dorner courageously argued, "it cannot be said of the relation of God to the world that there is in God only pure act and nothing of bare potentiality."[39] In a radical declaration, at least compared with all previous Christian thinking about God, Dorner said that "consequently, it is to be taught that God *himself*, who on the side of generating power remains eternally the sole original principle, enters in the world of the ethical or of love into a reciprocal relation, yes, into the relation of reciprocal effect."[40] That is to say, God allows himself to be affected by his creatures, something Schleiermacher could not admit and classical Christian theism always has trouble affirming.

This revising of traditional theism raises many questions, and Dorner faces into them resolutely. Traditional theism, classical Christian theism as represented by all the Catholic and Protestant scholastic theologians, rested on an assumption that God's power and creatures' power are noncontrasting. That is, power to decide and act is not like a pie that has to be divided so that when a slice is taken there is less pie. Rather, most classical theists always assumed, and still do, that creaturely power is somehow also God's power. That is, it is on loan from God and therefore cannot resist God. If it seems to resist God, that must be an illusion. Human beings, creatures, have no autonomy over against God such that their power to decide and act takes anything away from God's. Dorner disagreed:

> Since God created what is free for the sake of the ethical, he has in a certain way set over against himself a being of the same kind, which can resist him. By the creation he has exposed himself to the creature's possible opposition and defiance, which for him is by no means simply a matter of indifference.[41]

---

[38]Ibid., 131.
[39]Ibid., 133.
[40]Ibid., 132.
[41]Ibid., 133.

One of the questions this raises is God's omniscience. If God is all-knowing in the strongest sense, then how can creaturely resistance be real resistance and how can creaturely freedom affect God? Here is where Dorner bit the bullet more than any Christian theologian before him.[42] Because there is real receptivity in God, some of God's knowledge is of possibilities actualized by the world of free beings.[43] Thus, in relation to the world of free powers, there is "a change even in the knowing activity of God himself."[44] Dorner explains:

> Thus if there is to be that which is free, there must be in God a double form of knowledge, one which is unconditioned and created immediately and eternally from himself, and one conditioning itself by free causalities. Through the latter, however, temporal history is again reflected into the divine knowledge itself.[45]

Dorner breaks, then, with the classical theistic notion of God's knowledge as timeless in which God always sees the past and future as now. For Dorner this destroys God's ethical relation with the world in which he must be free together with free creatures who have the power to resist his will: "Thus God's knowledge is a knowledge conditioned by contemporary history, interwoven and advancing with it."[46]

Does this mean, then, that for Dorner God is ignorant of the future for the sake of creatures and their freedom? First, Dorner would insist that the primary issue is not freedom but ethical relation. In other words, he was not interested in freedom for freedom's sake, as some humanists may be, but for the sake of God's real, loving relation with the world of free creatures. If everything is decided and rendered certain from God's side, then the relation is not ethical; it is merely a condition imposed by God. Love in a relationship requires freedom to resist that love. Second, Dorner did not like the idea of God's "ignorance." That is not how he envisioned the change

---

[42]Astute readers may know that something like Dorner's view was taught by the radical Reformer Faustus Socinus (1539–1604), who was declared a heretic by all the other Reformers because he denied the deity of Jesus Christ and the Trinity. What makes Dorner different is his orthodoxy on those subjects and his insistence that any limitation of God's knowledge is not a real limitation but a self-actualization.

[43]Dorner, "Dogmatic Discussion of the Doctrine of the Immutability of God," 134.

[44]Ibid., 136.

[45]Ibid., 135.

[46]Ibid., 136.

in the mode of God's knowledge brought about by creaturely decisions and actions. God never moves like creatures from ignorance to knowing. Rather, God knows all possibilities as possibilities and all actualities as actualities. That is, the future is not a blank slate; God sees, as it were, all that might happen. "The moments of actuality are woven [by God] into the world of his loving thoughts."[47] But this means that God actually, fully experiences the world historically with it in time.[48] He does not look on the world like an unblinking stare that sees everything as already actual. And as new things happen he experiences them as new.[49]

Traditional, classical theists like Schleiermacher and Anselm before him will inevitably regard Dorner's alteration in the doctrine of God as a full denial of God's immutability and categorize it with Hegel's doctrine of God and with process theology in twentieth-century theology. However, that is a mistake. Dorner said that "in all these respects there takes place also on [God's] side change, alteration, a permitting of himself to be determined— though to be sure *without there being called into question that immutability which matters.*"[50] The German mediating theologian emphasized God's immutability just as strongly as his mutability and perhaps even more strongly. However, true to his denial of divine simplicity, he affirms that God is both immutable and mutable in different respects. God's ethical essence is immutable, unchangeable, stable and reliable. Only his experience, including his knowledge, changes with the world and that only because he allows it. (In "experience" is included activity including God's responses to free creatures' decisions and actions such as prayer.)

So wherein lies God's immutability? Dorner is quick to affirm and press that God's eternal, unchanging essence is his goodness, his love. That never

---

[47]Ibid., 137.

[48]Ibid.

[49]Some readers may wonder if Dorner was an open theist. Open theism is a movement that arose among American evangelical theologians in the 1990s that denied God's absolute, exhaustive and infallible foreknowledge (see, e.g., Clark Pinnock et al., *The Openness of God* [Downers Grove, IL: InterVarsity Press, 1994]). There is some debate about whether Dorner should be considered a precursor of open theism. Welch seemed to think of him that way. Here is how Welch interprets Dorner on God's foreknowledge (and I agree): "though he knows by self-awareness all the possibilities for the activation of freedom, the knowledge of the actuality for which freedom decides can come to him only from the world" (Welch, *Protestant Theology in the Nineteenth Century*, 1:278). At the least this is what is called free will theism.

[50]Dorner, "Dogmatic Discussion of the Doctrine of the Immutability of God," 150, italics added.

changes nor can change. Dorner wrote that "God has to be called good simply because it is his nature to be good and because this his nature defines him directly."[51] Also, "Deity is to be conceived as the absolute actuality of the ethical [i.e., the good, love] . . . it must . . . possess an actuality in the being and essence of God."[52] For Dorner, this idea of God's immutable being as good, as love, provides the bridge between immutability and mutability in God because love always seeks freely to express itself both inwardly (the Trinity) and outwardly (in creation). This is how God is to be conceived successfully as both immutable and living:

> God in himself is to be conceived both as immutable, *viz.*, in respect of the ethical, and as living and free; but these two are not simply left existing alongside one another. Rather, the ethical immutability that is in God requires also for itself the livingness that is just as eternal; the ethically necessary points of itself to freedom as its means of actualization. The livingness of God, the principle of which lies in his freedom, is no less bound up with the ethically necessary through itself, through its inner essence; the free is for the ethically necessary. We must say, therefore, that there is in God not a fixed but a living immutability; but just as little is there in him a restless or unsteady livingness by which he could forsake himself; rather, God's livingness has also taken the ethical immutability up eternally into itself.[53]

To recap and clarify: Dorner is arguing that there is in God that which cannot change, his ethical nature as perfectly good and absolutely loving, while there is also in God that which changes *precisely because* his unchanging nature is love. That which changes is not God's essence but his free activation of love in creation and reciprocal relation with creatures. And God's free, reciprocal relation with free creatures is not one of self-limitation, as if God somehow became smaller because of it, but one of self-actualization. God unleashes potential in himself by freely entering into reciprocal relation with creation.

All this may be illuminated by pointing to two consequences that Dorner himself mentions. First, this vision of God requires a new hermeneutic of Scripture. Classical theism had to interpret much of the Old Testament as

---

[51]Ibid., 154.
[52]Ibid., 155.
[53]Ibid., 159.

anthropomorphic because it portrays God as being affected and changing. Dorner rejects that hermeneutic in light of his idea of God demanded by the incarnation:

> The preceding explication [of God's loving and free reciprocal relation with the world] forbids us to be so hasty in the recognition of so-called anthropomorphisms and anthropopathisms in holy scripture; rather it warrants allowing an important place to what has been called biblical realism. If only the ethical immutability of God is protected and strictly preserved, then we have enough to allow movement and alteration also to be reflected into God, into the world of his thoughts and his will, without any danger for the concept of God and for the divine eminence . . . ; yes, in the ethical concept of God we have the principle which requires this.[54]

Thus, Dorner can take utterly seriously, even literally, those Old Testament passages about God relenting in response to intercessory prayer whereas classical theism requires that they be dismissed as figures of speech.

The second consequence of Dorner's reconstructed doctrine of God is denial of the classical Reformed doctrine of predestination. Schleiermacher held to a strong view of God's foreordination and rendering certain of everything that happens. Dorner responds to him and to Calvinism generally:

> To be sure, God does not hand over the reins of government to the faithful; but neither does he want to make them automatons [robots], beings resigned to a determined will. From the very beginning, he has preferred to give his friends a joint knowledge of what he wills to do . . . , and to deal historicotemporally through them as his instruments, which as personalities may even co-determine his will and counsel.[55]

For Dorner, then, there is no always already decided divine decree that determines all that will happen. He considers that a nonethical understanding of God and God's relation with the world. His goal in this was not to emphasize free will but to underscore God's ethical relationship with the world of free creatures and free powers.

Dorner reconstructs the doctrine of the person of Christ. Dorner was ahead of Ritschl in the project of moralizing dogmas. His driving motive

---

[54]Ibid., 165.
[55]Ibid., 179.

was just that—to reconstruct traditional Christian doctrines so that they are not just speculative abstractions but ethically fruitful beliefs about God and Jesus Christ and humanity. Unlike Ritschl, however, he did not think it necessary to relegate doctrine to the realm of values divorced from facts. Instead, he wanted to reinterpret Christian beliefs as facts with value. The ethical, the good, reforms the facts and the facts inform the ethical. For Dorner, the realm of facts includes Christian beliefs, which are ethical.

After his reconstruction of the immutability of God, Dorner's best-known revision of doctrine is his idea of "progressive incarnation," a revised Christology. Again, in order to understand his proposal it is necessary to know something about the ideas to which he was reacting. We have already seen that he was reacting to Thomasius's kenotic Christology. But Dorner was dissatisfied with classical Christology, the hypostatic union, in general. He thought all Christologies before him tended to undermine either the deity of Christ (Schleiermacher), the humanity of Christ (much conservative theology) or the unity and integrity of Christ's person. For him, "the Christological task . . . is . . . one of so delineating the unity of the person, by virtue of a truer idea of the nature of God and of man, that in the total picture of the person both sides receive their full due, though apportioned according to the difference of the two states."[56] The key to his reconstruction is in that last phrase: "two states." For him, the incarnation was not a coming together of two persons (Nestorianism) or the blending together of two natures (Eutychianism) or two natures stuck together without affecting each other in one divine person (Chalcedon's hypostatic union). Rather, the incarnation was the progressive union of two states, or conditions, into one. The two are the loving, self-expressive activity of God, the "Logos," and the open, receptive, ethical humanity of Jesus Christ.

Dorner begins his reconstruction of Christology with the preexistence of Christ and the immanent Trinity (God-in-himself). According to him, the Trinity is a necessary feature of any sound, incarnational Christology because only if "God is distinguished within himself, [can] he maintain himself in self-impartation without self-loss, remaining in himself and also

---

[56]I. A. Dorner, "The Doctrine of Christ," in *God and Incarnation in Mid-nineteenth Century German Theology: Thomasius, Dorner, Biedermann*, ed. Claude Welch (New York: Oxford University Press, 1965), 181.

being active outside himself."[57] In other words, if God were a "simple monad," indistinguishable oneness, he could not become incarnate or enter into the world. However, Dorner feared that tritheism, belief in three gods, hovered around some traditional expositions of the doctrine of the Trinity, so he preferred "modes of being" to "persons" to express the distinctions within God. The Logos, the second of God's modes of being, is the only one of the three who can become incarnate because his function within the Trinity is to express God's love. Thus, the Logos, the Son of God, the second mode of being of God, is the preexistence of Jesus Christ.

Dorner continues his reconstruction of Christology by reinterpreting humanity as created for union with God and therefore not "foreign" to God. Although distinct, God and humanity are suitable partners; humanity is open to God and God is open to humanity. "Man's distinction from God . . . works out as need for God, receptivity to God. . . . Conversely, God's self-sufficiency . . . works out as efficacious willing of fellowship [with humanity]."[58] Thus, the incarnation is not the bonding together of two conflicting natures in one person but the indwelling and union of the Logos and the human Jesus through "impartation" and "participation together."[59] Dorner's brief summary of the incarnation is that "Christ is utterly the God-man in whom the eternal divine predisposition to incarnation achieves actuality, and humanity is elevated to unity with God."[60] Crucial to his idea of the incarnation is that both the Logos and the man must will the union and find self-actualization there.[61] "A self-knowing and willing of God takes place in this man."[62] In other words, the incarnation was not a self-limitation of God but a self-actualization of God. A potential in God became actual in the union of the Logos with the man Jesus.

People aware of the early christological heresies may think Dorner's idea of the incarnation sounds Nestorian. (Nestorius was a fifth-century Christian who taught that the incarnation was a union of wills between two distinct persons—the Logos and Jesus. His theory was condemned at the

---

[57]Ibid., 215.
[58]Ibid., 229.
[59]Ibid., 228.
[60]Ibid.
[61]Ibid., 236–37.
[62]Ibid., 237.

Council of Ephesus in 433.) However, Dorner denied that his Christology was Nestorian. There was, he argued, no double personality of Jesus. Rather,

> originally united with this man, the Logos determines his will. He is to be con-
> ceived as originally and from the beginning the living divine substratum of this
> person, but this substratum increasingly forms itself into Jesus' actual knowing
> and willing humanity, in order to bring the God-manhood to full actuality.[63]

Another way Dorner expressed it is that "in Christ God as Logos so united himself with Christ's humanity that this is the place of his absolute revelation."[64] But this union had to be progressive for it to be truly ethical. If Jesus did not freely receive the Logos and participate freely in this divine-human union it would not be an ethical event. So, "the human aspect is not merely passively assumed."[65]

All of that requires the incarnation to be progressive and not accomplished all at once. "The unity of the divine-human total personality was in the beginning still no perfect union."[66] Expressed succinctly but in somewhat more detail:

> The incarnation is not to be conceived as finished at one moment, but as
> continuing, even as growing, since God the Logos constantly grasps and ap-
> propriates each of the new facets that are formed out of the true human un-
> folding, just as conversely the growing actual receptivity of the humanity
> joins consciously and willingly with ever new facets of the Logos.[67]

Clearly, this is the strikingly different from Thomasius's kenotic Christology in which the Logos limits himself to be born and grow and die. There the union is complete from the beginning and the human aspect of Jesus has no say in the matter; it is passive. Dorner considered this an a-ethical Christology (besides one that makes God too mutable). It negates the love and freedom of the divine-human relationship. The man must freely receive God and God must freely initiate and respond to the man with the result that they come together in a perfect union of God-manhood. Far from being a self-limitation of God, this is God's self-actualization of love.

---

[63]Ibid., 39.
[64]Ibid., 241.
[65]Ibid., 253.
[66]Ibid., 250.
[67]Ibid., 247.

Dorner leaves a stimulating legacy with unanswered questions. Dorner is one of those figures in Christian history who is both extremely creative and ambiguous. He raised interesting questions, dared to forge new paths in attempting to answer them and left a set of ideas for later theologians to wrestle with. Above all he transcended some of the apparent either-or dilemmas of modern theology, uniting opposites even if, in the end, in an unsatisfying way.

Dorner's influence on later theology is clear in Barth and process theology (see 5.a.; 6.b.). Barth picked up on Dorner's idea of God's essence as love-in-freedom and defined God as "He who loves in freedom." With Dorner, Barth refused to be bound by classical theism and defined God's immutability, for example, as God's faithfulness and not as God's absolute changelessness. Dorner talked about a divine temporality in God, as did Barth later. Barth's debt to Dorner also appears in the idea of God's relationship with history as a realization of God's attributes rather than as a loss of his divinity. For Barth, as for Dorner, God's entrance into humanity, even his death on a cross, was the most perfect expression of God's deity, not something alien or foreign to it.

Dorner also set in motion a way of thinking about God's immutability that took a different direction (from Barth) in process theology and open theism. As different as they are, both of these twentieth-century schools of theology emphasize God's becoming as well as his being. Process theologians rarely, if ever, acknowledge Dorner as an influence, but the similarity is too striking to be accidental. Process theology talks about God's di-polarity—one pole being eternal and unchanging and the other changing with the world's changes. There is no doubt that Dorner would reject the extent to which process theology has taken this; its emphasis on God's immanence would be too extreme for Dorner. Nevertheless, Dorner opened up the possibility of process theology and open theism (with the latter being more consistent with Dorner's overall supernaturalism than the former) with his stringent critiques of classical theism and his proposal that God is both immutable and mutable.

One area of Dorner's thought barely touched on here is his response to modernity. Every theologian in this book is included because of his or her response to modernity. In what sense was Dorner a modern theologian? He was not particularly interested in responding to the scientific challenges to traditional Christianity. It seems that he did not think science needs to be a challenge to Christian faith. For him, Christian faith is embrace of the facts of revelation, but revelation is not identical with every proposition of Scripture. Revelation must be ethical; it is only that which shapes and forms ethical living. Human beings have "moral need"; revelation is that which meets our moral needs and faith is reception of that revelation with ethical decision and conduct. Thus, there is no question of conflict between science and religion, not because science and religion dwell in watertight compartments as with Ritschl but because religion is about salvation in its broadest sense. Science is about facts of the material world. Christianity is about "ethico-religious self-knowledge founded on experience" of revelation.[68] Such does not require belief in Scripture's infallibility or literal interpretation extended to cosmology.

Dorner was the mediating theologian par excellence. He sought to bring together in a higher unity many competing ideas: Protestant orthodoxy and modernity, classical theism and Hegelian divine becoming, Schleiermacher and Hegel on God's transcendence and immanence. His ultimate mediation was between conservative theology broadly defined (placing value on tradition and a general faithfulness to it) and liberal theology. He was neither but displayed features of both. With conservative theology he was concerned to conserve the best of Christian tradition. With liberal theology he was concerned to come to terms with modern philosophy, especially Hegel, without capitulating accommodation.

Perhaps Dorner's biggest failure was his Christology. Valiant as his attempt to reconstruct classical Christology was, ultimately it failed. The outcome is undeniably Nestorian in flavor. Dorner never could explain satisfactorily how the Logos and the man were one person in Jesus Christ. Kenotic Christology was revived by British theologians in the late nineteenth and early twentieth centuries and Dorner's progressive incarnation idea gradually died away, although it may have been revived somewhat by process theologians such as Norman Pittenger and John Cobb. Kenotic thinkers such as P. T. Forsyth (1848–1921) and H. R. Mackintosh (1870–1936) breathed new life into Thomasius's Christology while fixing some of its defects.

---

[68]Quoted in Welch, *Protestant Thought in the Nineteenth Century*, 1:277.

4.B. HORACE BUSHNELL SEARCHES FOR A PROGRESSIVE ORTHODOXY

Horace Bushnell was forty-six years old and had already pastored the North Congregational Church in Hartford, Connecticut, for fifteen years. Yet he was plagued by doubts and qualms about Christianity. As a student at Yale College he had made a decision for Christ during a revival and then studied to become a minister, but his Christian faith was primarily a matter of duty rather than experience. He had been reading devotional literature and praying for a spiritual breakthrough. One February morning in 1848 he emerged from his home study after a time of deep meditation and prayer. His wife instantly recognized something different about him and asked, "What have you seen?"[69] His simple answer was, "The gospel." Later, referring to this epiphany, the New England pastor-theologian wrote that he "was set on by the personal discovery of Christ, and of God as represented in him."[70] Apparently Bushnell's experience that day was life-transforming in a way similar to John Wesley's famous "heart-warming" experience at the Moravian meeting in Aldersgate Street. It was not when he became a Christian; it was when he experienced God in a direct, unmediated way, and it changed him forever.

As a result of his profound spiritual experience Bushnell preached a powerful sermon that was published and became an influential piece of nineteenth-century devotional literature. Its title was "Christ, the Form of the Soul." In it he proclaimed that

> Christian faith . . . is not the committing of one's thoughts in assent to any proposition, but the trusting of one's being to *a being*, there to be rested, kept, guided, molded, governed, and possessed forever. . . . It gives you God, fills you with God in immediate, experimental [experiential] knowledge, puts you in possession of all there is in him, and allows you to be invested with his character itself.[71]

From that day on, "Bushnell approached religion, Christianity, from an experiential viewpoint"[72] rather than from a primarily propositional, doc-

---

[69]The account is taken from William R. Adamson, *Bushnell Rediscovered* (Philadelphia: United Church Press, 1966), 19–20.

[70]Ibid., 20.

[71]Quoted in ibid.

[72]Ibid., 78.

trinal viewpoint. This is not to say he disdained doctrine. In fact, after 1848 he produced numerous books and articles about Christian doctrines but always related them to Christian experience. While before his epiphany Bushnell had "never lived a doubt-free day,"[73] after it he was certain of the truth of the gospel if not of traditional, orthodox doctrines. As a result of this mystical experience of God in Christ immediately present to his soul, he

> increasingly emphasized the transforming work of God's Spirit in rendering visible, to believers, the self-expression of God in creation. Thematically, he focused on the representation of God in Christ, the indwelling of Christ in the soul, and the Spirit-transforming mission of the Holy Spirit.[74]

Bushnell becomes America's most influential theologian. Almost every-one agrees that Bushnell was America's greatest nineteenth-century theologian. According to the author of a three-volume history of liberal theology in America, "Bushnell is the major theologian of nineteenth-century American Liberal Christianity and the key figure in its history as a whole."[75] Moreover, according to the same historian, Bushnell was "America's greatest nine-teenth-century theologian."[76] Another historical theologian labels Bushnell a genius and remarks, "He was a brilliant, transitional figure who intro-duced a new era in American religious thought."[77] Many scholars of American religious history put him in company with Jonathan Edwards and Reinhold Niebuhr, the greatest American theologians of the eighteenth century and twentieth century respectively. They are widely considered the trinity of great American Christian thinkers.

And yet, Bushnell never held an academic position other than tutor at Yale College. He was raised in a typical New England Congregational church by a Methodist father and Episcopal mother. The church was Cal-vinist in the Puritan tradition, something Bushnell would rebel against later in life. During college he flirted with skepticism and expressed serious doubts about the truth of Christianity, but as a result of his mental con-version he dedicated himself to becoming a minister and graduated from

---

[73]Dorrien, *The Making of American Liberal Theology*, 122.
[74]Ibid., 141.
[75]Ibid., xvii.
[76]Ibid., 111.
[77]Adamson, *Bushnell Rediscovered*, 13.

Yale Divinity School. His main professor there was an influential nineteenth-century theologian, Nathaniel Taylor (1786–1858), the leader of what came to be called the New Haven theology, a modified form of Calvinism. Bushnell was not impressed by Taylor and later turned away from what he considered his "essentially rationalistic" theology.

After some years tutoring Yale students, Bushnell was ordained and became minister of the North Congregational Church, where he remained until 1859, when he retired due to poor health. He died in 1876 after a prolific writing and publishing postretirement career. He was married and had three children, one of whom died in infancy. During his pastorate Bushnell was almost tried for heresy by his regional Congregational association of churches, but the case against him never came to trial because his congregation withdrew from the association in order to protect him. He was the center of a storm of theological controversy because he openly opposed what he considered the overemphasis on theology as rational and scientific by both liberals and conservatives. He entered into sustained dialogue and debate with the growing Unitarian movement that was sweeping up many Congregational churches. He thought that "the Unitarians and their opponents both shared the same rationalistic assumptions about theology, and he was evenhanded in his criticism of both groups."[78] "His whole life and work was a reaction against the formal, logical systematization of the New England theologians before him. . . . Bushnell approached theology from an experiential viewpoint."[79]

Bushnell was involved in public affairs, writing numerous articles about controversial social issues and events such as slavery, women's rights and the Civil War. He was a hawk about that war even though his own views on race and equality for women were typically backward by twenty-first-century standards. He was a community booster in his adopted city. After his death Hartford named after him the city park he worked tirelessly to create. It was his idea and became the first American city park funded entirely by taxes. While living briefly in California for his health, Bushnell helped found the College of California, which eventually became part of the University of California. He is best known, perhaps, as the "father of the

---

[78]Holifield, *Theology in America*, 453.
[79]Adamson, *Bushnell Rediscovered*, 78.

modern Christian education movement" because of *Christian Nurture* (1847), in which he rejected the revivalism model of Christian initiation in favor of one centered around Christian education in the home and church. He believed it was possible for children to grow up Christian without a born-again experience. One Bushnell biographer pays tribute to him:

> Horace Bushnell was a man of many interests and abilities as a naturalist, surveyor, road engineer, housebuilder, mechanic, park designer, traveler, fisherman, and preacher. His character and versatility distinguished him from other men of his day. It was this man of many talents who in the final analysis pushed open new frontiers.[80]

Bushnell's literary production was prodigious. He published eleven major books and many collections of sermons. He wrote numerous articles and editorials in journals and newspapers and carried on a lively correspondence with theologians in Europe and the United States. Some of his books became best sellers, read by thousands of nonexperts in theology. After his death his major works were collected and published in a seven-volume set. Some of his writings are still in publication in the early twenty-first century. Among his main works, besides *Christian Nurture*, were *God in Christ* (1849), *Nature and the Supernatural* (1858), *Christ and His Salvation* (1864) and *The Vicarious Sacrifice* (1866). He never wrote a systematic theology and did not consider theology properly systematic. He agreed with the pietist leader Zinzendorf that systems kill Christianity. However, certain common threads tied his diverse theological books together. The main one was Christ. As the editor of one collection of Bushnell's works says, "It cannot be too strongly emphasized that Christ was the magnetic center of [his] thought and ministry."[81]

Bushnell's books were written against the backdrop of theological controversies in New England Protestantism. He waded into most of those, attempting to overcome false dichotomies with higher perspectives that transcended either-or thinking. Some of his theological proposals met with consternation and even rejection; they were not always easy to understand even when written in fairly popular language. Furthermore, they laid out new proposals that pleased neither conservatives nor liberals. "His books

---

[80]Ibid., 22.

[81]H. Shelton Smith, "Introduction," in *Horace Bushnell*, ed. H. Shelton Smith (New York: Oxford University Press, 1965), 26.

were routinely condemned, he was shunned and isolated through most of his ministry, and pastors who embraced his views were forced to be discreet."[82] One constant theme throughout all his works was "all theological language necessarily falls short of complete objectivity" so that "there can be no absolutely objective or scientific theology."[83] He thought that many of the theological controversies tearing Christians apart from one another were based on tendencies to take divine revelation too literally and attempts to force revealed truths into absolute rational coherence. He reminded those prone to such misunderstandings that "we never come so near to a truly well-rounded view of any truth, as when it is offered paradoxically."[84] Needless to say, this did not sit well with most of the theologians of his time and place who were rushing to prove that theology is scientific.

Bushnell's theology was a series of attempts to reconstruct traditional Christian doctrines in such a way as to speak to the modern mind without capitulating to accommodation. Unlike liberal Protestants, he held firmly to the supernatural and defended it against increasing tendencies to reduce God's action to the mechanical forces of nature and states of consciousness. Unlike conservative Protestants, he wished to update doctrines to make them more adequate to Christian experience and modern thought, especially about law and ethics. He worked with one foot firmly planted in Christian tradition and the other one planted in the modern thought world. His theology has been labeled "progressive orthodoxy" for that reason, and it is why he is included here as a mediating theologian.[85]

Bushnell emphasizes imagination and metaphor over dogma. Behind every great theologian stands an influential philosopher, and behind Bushnell stood Samuel Taylor Coleridge. He was not Bushnell's only inspiration, but the New England theologian cannot be understood without knowing something about the English poet and philosopher (see 1.e.). Many people have tried to link Bushnell with Schleiermacher, but their common ground is romanticism, and it was mediated to Bushnell primarily by

---

[82]Dorrien, *The Making of American Liberal Theology*, 173.
[83]Smith, "Introduction," 37.
[84]Quoted in Welch, *Protestant Thought in the Nineteenth Century*, 1:260.
[85]For those who have trouble regarding Bushnell as a mediating theologian, that is how H. Richard Niebuhr described him in *The Kingdom of God in America* (Chicago: Willet, Clark and Co., 1937), 193.

Coleridge. This accounts for much of the difficulty people encounter in attempting to understand Bushnell; Coleridge was often obscure and so was Bushnell. They both thought of religion as primarily a matter of experience and theology as the inadequate attempt to express that experience in words that can never fully grasp it. By his own testimony Bushnell was restlessly preoccupied with finding a method for theology that would rise above the rationalism and dogmatism that was tearing apart New England theology. Coleridge's romanticism gave him the key to the method he was seeking.

One day, Bushnell reported, he read Coleridge's *Aids to Reflection* and found it "foggy and unintelligible."[86] Later, however, he returned to it, sensing he had missed something. This time, he later recounted, "all was lucid and instructive!"[87] What he found most helpful in Coleridge was the idea of the imagination as a "transcendently perceptive, creative, unifying power."[88] There is an old saying that "the imagination is the devil's playground." But "imagination" in that folk maxim and in Coleridge mean two different things. For Coleridge, and then Bushnell, imagination is a God-given creative faculty of the human personality capable of grasping truths unavailable to analytical reason. Imagination is synthetic; it sees unity where reason can see only contradiction. It works well with metaphors and images whereas reason insists on turning everything it can into propositions. Imagination can see patterns to which reason is blind. Bushnell was coming to think of theology as more an art than a science. This lies at the root of all his troubles with more rationally minded theological colleagues who insisted that theology mimic science. Bushnell was attempting to rise above Enlightenment foundationalism in theology without falling into irrationality.

The influence of Coleridge on Bushnell cannot be overemphasized; it was profound and pervasive. The pastor-theologian himself said that he owed more to Coleridge's *Aids to Reflection* than to any other book except the Bible.[89] Coleridge revolutionized Bushnell's mind, opening it to vistas of truth other, more systematic thinkers, could not see. For example, truth can be conveyed irreducibly in poetry and parables, as often is the case in

---

[86]Quoted in Dorrien, *The Making of American Liberal Theology*, 124.
[87]Ibid.
[88]Ibid.
[89]Ibid., 147.

Scripture. That truth cannot be translated without loss into rational propositions without killing it. For Bushnell, as for Coleridge, "it offends true piety and intelligence alike to claim that the meaning of God's self-expression in Christ can be defined by 'a few dull propositions.'"[90] Much of Scripture's meaning is "spiritual and poetic, not appealing to reason, rational proofs, or historical evidence, but self-authenticating."[91] With Coleridge Bushnell proclaimed that Christian truth is "spirit and life . . . not a datum of the natural understanding."[92]

For those beginning to struggle with Bushnell's appropriation of Coleridge, it may be helpful to pause and explain, first, that both regarded religion as primarily about transformation rather than information. Theologians might pay lip service to that truth, but Coleridge and Bushnell believed they denied it when they dogmatically insisted on creedal truth as the essence of Christianity. For Coleridge and Bushnell, the essence of religion is "a taste for the divine" and "intuitive knowledge of God"; the essence of Christianity is communion with God through Jesus Christ. Bushnell wrote that "there is more of the true light of Christ in one hour of highest communion with him, than the best scheme of theological opinions has ever been able to offer."[93] And, "it is not by opinion but by love that we most truly know God."[94] "True realizations of God are effected, not through opinion, but through faith, right feeling, spirit, and life."[95] Second, both Coleridge and Bushnell considered propositional doctrines, creedal formulas, secondary to Christian experience and at best feeble attempts to express what cannot be expressed adequately in words:

> Creeds and catechisms did not greatly impress Bushnell. Too often they had become formulas and rigid statements to be taken literally. Most theological disputes originated because the differing parties failed to separate truths from their forms, or to see that the same essential truth could be clothed under forms that are contradictory.[96]

---

[90] Ibid., 146.
[91] Ibid., 146–47.
[92] Ibid., 147.
[93] Horace Bushnell, "Dogma and Spirit" (from *God in Christ*), in *Horace Bushnell*, ed. H. Shelton Smith (New York: Oxford University Press, 1965), 65.
[94] Ibid., 59.
[95] Ibid., 61.
[96] Adamson, *Bushnell Rediscovered*, 106.

However, it would be wrong to conclude that Bushnell disdained doctrines or creeds; nothing could be further from the truth. He believed doctrines are necessary for the life of the church and the Christian so long as
they are not made into idols, so long as they are acknowledged to be
human attempts to express the inexpressible and kept open to revision.
Most of his writings were on doctrinal subjects and were aimed at deconstructing traditional dogmas treated as ideologies and reconstructing
them as models, complex metaphors. For example, Bushnell did not deny
the doctrine of the deity and humanity of Jesus Christ, but he found the
classical formula, the Chalcedonian Definition, the hypostatic union, seriously flawed and in need of revision. He agreed with many liberals and
other mediating theologians that it tended to fracture the person of
Christ.[97] He complained bitterly that the primitive church's simple faith in
Christ as God and man was replaced at Chalcedon (and before) by sterile,
arid speculation under the influence of Greek philosophy. In his account
of early Christian history, intellect won out over spirit; spirit became the
servant of dogma rather than vice versa.[98] Beginning in the second century,
Bushnell averred, "the truth of Jesus vanishes" from Christian theology
and is replaced by speculation.[99]

Nevertheless, Bushnell did not think all doctrines could be replaced
merely by quietistic contemplation and spiritual experience. The deeply
flawed Christology of Chalcedon had to and could be replaced by a more
vital concept based on God's revelation in Christ as divine self-expression.
"The reality of Christ," he declared, "is what he expresses of God."[100] He affirmed the preexistence of Christ, his virgin birth, his sinlessness, his resurrection and his essential humanity and divinity, but beyond that he advised
Christians to "suspend thy raw guesses at his nature, and take his message!"[101]
Ultimately, he argued, the incarnation of God in Christ is a mystery. All that
should be required of any Christian is his own confession: "I insist that he
[Christ] stands before us in simple unity, one person, the divine-human,

---

[97]Dorrien, *The Making of American Liberal Theology*, 152.
[98]Smith, "Introduction," 50.
[99]Ibid.
[100]Horace Bushnell, "The Divinity of Christ," in *Horace Bushnell*, ed. H. Shelton Smith (New
York: Oxford University Press, 1965), 180.
[101]Ibid., 182.

representing the qualities of his double parentage as the Son of God and the Son of Mary."[102] To those who accused him of denying Jesus' divinity because he rejected the classical doctrine of the hypostatic union (as something to be taken literally rather than symbolically) he declared:

> By the *divinity* of Christ, I do not understand simply that Christ differs from other men, in the sense that he is better, more inspired, and so a more complete vehicle of God to the world than others have been. [This was his understanding of the typical liberal Christology.] He differs from us, not in degree, but in kind.[103]

Bushnell was accused of heresy for allegedly denying the deity of Jesus Christ because he criticized the classical Chalcedonian Definition that Christ was one person with two natures. Bushnell responded by saying that he had no problem with that dogma so long as it is understood as symbolic and not as literal description of what Jesus was.[104]

Bushnell's view of the dogma of the Trinity was similar to his view of classical Christology's dogma of the hypostatic union of two natures in Christ. He rejected the traditional, orthodox dogma of God as three persons sharing one nature because it seemed speculative and metaphysical. "His view was that taking any position about the inner nature of God is wrong."[105] For him, the Trinity is primarily about worship, because "worship of God as triune holy mystery is the heart of vital Christian piety."[106] Again, as with the person of Jesus Christ, Bushnell based belief in God's triunity on God's self-expression in three forms: "The Trinity we seek will be a trinity that results of necessity from the *revelation* of God to man."[107] In other words, Bushnell was urging Christians strictly to avoid peering into God-in-himself, the inner life of God apart from the world, and to avoid creating and worshiping metaphysical dogmas such as the church's classical dogma of the Trinity. For him, God's threeness is not about a heavenly council of persons in heaven but about God's encounter with us in his self-expressive activity in Christian experience as that is reflected revelation and worship.

---

[102]Ibid., 185.
[103]Ibid., 160.
[104]Dorrien, *The Making of American Liberal Theology*, 152.
[105]Ibid., 153.
[106]Ibid., 157.
[107]Bushnell, "The Divinity of Christ," 169.

The classical dogma is fine, so long as it is understood symbolically and not literally as describing God-in-himself.

Bushnell's overall view of dogma is expressed in his statement that

> if it were possible to get religious truth into shapes and formulas having an absolute meaning, like the terms of algebra, as clear even to the wicked as to the pure, and requiring no conditions of character in the receivers, it would very nearly subvert . . . all that is most significant and sublime in the discipline of life.[108]

For Bushnell, "all that is most significant and sublime in the discipline of life" lies in the realm of the aesthetic rather than the metaphysical, the poetic and metaphorical rather than the literal and the experiential rather than the notional. The influence of Coleridge in all this is obvious. That did not mean, however, that Bushnell would not engage in vigorous theological debate. He did not think that all verbal expressions, all concepts, of God and Christ are equally valid. Some bring God's revelation and Christian experience to expression better than others. The purely intellectual, cut off from the doxological and ethical, kills whereas the experiential, the symbolic, the metaphorical gives life.

Bushnell introduces a new theory of language to theology. It is almost impossible to understand how revolutionary Bushnell's theology was without understanding his theory of language and especially the language of theology. Scholars largely agree that this was innovative and insightful while also being somewhat vague. It foreshadowed later twentieth-century and twenty-first-century theological ideas of religious language, but to his contemporaries it was almost beyond comprehension. It radically departed from the Scottish realism that so pervaded American theology both on the left and the right in the nineteenth century (see 1.c.). It would probably be welcomed by postmodern thinkers, but in Bushnell's time and place it was widely rejected as sheer skepticism about knowledge. To the Congregational theologian, however, it was a way to protect the mystery of God from being conquered and dispelled by overly intellectualized and metaphysical thought and speech about God. And it was the only way to clear the path forward from being blocked by timeless truths of doctrine that pretend to describe God once and for all.

---

[108]Quoted in Dorrien, *The Making of American Liberal Theology*, 151.

Most traditional theology assumed what is called the correspondence theory of truth, which is the belief that words and propositions can directly describe reality as it is. Kant threw a wrench into that by claiming that all we really know are things as they appear to us after the mind has organized them. We have no direct knowledge of things in themselves. However, Scottish realism was a response to Kant that heavily influenced both liberal-leaning and conservative theologians of Great Britain and the United States in the nineteenth century. So, most American theologians in Bushnell's time assumed that words about God can at least adequately, if not perfectly, describe God. For example, in the traditional view, to say that God is powerful is to say something meaningful, even literal, about God. God's power is at least proportionally analogous to human power. According to Bushnell, this assumption is false and the cause of much theological turmoil and controversy. People think they are disagreeing when that might not be the case. One theologian says that God predestines people to salvation; another theologian says God empowers people to exercise free will to be saved. Bushnell, as will be seen later, called for both sides of this long-standing debate between Calvinists and Arminians to realize they are talking in metaphors and images and therefore not necessarily disagreeing. God very well may be doing both things in some way beyond our comprehension. Words like "predestine" and "empower" are images, metaphors, not essences that perfectly match some divine reality. In fact, Bushnell agreed with Kierkegaard (probably without knowing it) that "we never come so near to a truly well-rounded view of any truth, as when it is offered paradoxically."[109] (Kierkegaard probably did not care about being well-rounded.) This offended many nineteenth-century theologians "who assumed that theology was the science of drawing and systematizing logical deductions from literal assertions of fact."[110] Bushnell offered an entirely different view of what theology is. It is based on his unusual theory of language.

Bushnell's theory of language is by far the most obscure aspect of his theology. Scholars have disagreed about it for more than a century. What can be said without fear of contradiction, however, is that he felt strongly that "all

---

[109]Bushnell, quoted in Welch, *Protestant Thought in the Nineteenth Century*, 1:260.
[110]Dorrien, *The Making of American Liberal Theology*, 143.

words are metaphorical."[111] According to Bushnell, the language of thought is always figurative, never literal.[112] The only exception he would allow to this rule about language was strictly analytical terms such as "circle." But unlike "circle," a word like "sin" bears a different meaning to every mind because it is, like all words that attempt to name realities outside the dictionary, a "faded metaphor." In other words, "At the moment that a conscious subject thinks discursively . . . the subject dresses its truths in forms that are not equivalents of its truths, but merely signs or analogies."[113] Much confusion and unnecessary controversy arise from people thinking their words are exact equivalents of the things they name. People wrongly confuse the symbols with truth itself. Rather, the words, the symbols, are like arrows that point at truth but never reach it. This is not the case in, say, algebra, but it is the case in everything pertaining to the physical or spiritual worlds.

For Bushnell, then, "language cannot convey any truth whole, or by a literal embodiment," which is why "a great many shadows, or figures, are necessary to represent every truth."[114] It is also why religion must involve a "cautious and salutary skepticism"[115] because "all theological language necessarily falls short of complete objectivity."[116] It also means that language is always striving to improve its ability to describe reality without ever achieving perfection. Language always needs "mending." What this means for theology, then, is that it "must produce . . . a decided mitigation of our dogmatic tendencies in religion."[117] Bushnell explained:

> The views of language and interpretation I have here offered suggest the very great difficulty, if not impossibility, of mental science and religious dogmatism. . . . Our apprehensions of truth are here only proximate and relative. I see not, therefore, how the subject matter of mental science and religion can ever be included under the fixed forms of dogma.[118]

---

[111]Ibid., 123.

[112]Ibid., 144.

[113]Ibid., 150.

[114]Horace Bushnell, "Christian Comprehensiveness," in *Horace Bushnell*, ed. H. Shelton Smith (New York: Oxford University Press, 1965), 111.

[115]Horace Bushnell, "Language and Theology," in *Horace Bushnell*, ed. H. Shelton Smith (New York: Oxford University Press, 1965), 104.

[116]Smith, "Introduction," 37.

[117]Bushnell, "Language and Theology," 102.

[118]Ibid., 97.

On the basis of this view of language, Bushnell argued that all creedal for-mulations and doctrines must be always open to revision in light of better expressions of Christian experience and revelation.

This raises the question of the nature of revelation and of Scripture for Bushnell. If all language is metaphorical, if all words are mere symbols, what does that mean for revelation and for Scripture? First, he did not identify revelation with Scripture in any straightforward way. "While ac-cepting the Bible as a revelatory vehicle, Bushnell declared that beyond the revelation of God contained in scripture 'the whole temple of being around us and above us is written over with spiritual hieroglyphs all radiant with light.'"[119] One must remember that Bushnell was heavily influenced by ro-manticism. He believed that in some mysterious way even human beings, the whole human race, is "embosomed in the eternal intelligence of God."[120] Thus, all people always already have a revelation of God within themselves by virtue of being created in God's image, "embosomed" within God's eternal intelligence and surrounded by God's self-expressive activity in nature. This is what traditional theology calls general revelation, and Bushnell believed in it.

However, Bushnell did not believe general revelation is adequate for a personal relationship with God. So, God has given a book, Scripture, more fully to reveal himself. Bushnell did not, however, view Scripture in any-thing like Hodge's way—as a not-yet-systematized systematic theology, a book of propositions waiting to be organized into a dogmatic system or a volume of timeless truths dropped from heaven. Rather, he viewed the Bible first and foremost as literature. As the literature it is, it is filled with diversity and even contradictions. "No book in the world contains so many repugnances, or antagonistic forms . . . as the Bible."[121] While that may sound critical, Bushnell did not mean it so. In fact, he was very critical of the budding discipline of higher criticism of the Bible. "Throughout his career Bushnell charged that higher critical scholarship was presump-tuous and spiritually destructive, especially in its rejection of the biblical

[119]Dorrien, *The Making of American Liberal Theology*, 125.
[120]Quoted in ibid.
[121]Bushnell, "Language and Theology," 96.

miracles."[122] Rather, his view of the Bible as revelation followed his theory of language closely. For him, "the kind of truth claimed by the scriptural witness is spiritual and poetic, not appealing to reason, rational proofs, or historical evidence, but self-authenticating."[123] It is supernaturally inspired by God, but it is nevertheless "a cryptic text loaded with truth-revealing paradoxes and outright contradictions."[124]

The key term in that last sentence is "truth-revealing." Bushnell had no trouble believing that truth can be revealed more adequately by imagery and even contradictions than by rational systems of propositions. That is because saving faith, the purpose of Scripture, is personal and not rational. Persons cannot be revealed in syllogisms or rational systems; persons are known in often seemingly contradictory ways. Bushnell fervently believed that Scripture is God's inspired literature in the form of a transforming grand narrative, a theodrama (to use a popular term of narrative theology), and not a disorganized system of timeless truths. He believed this view of the Bible will incline more toward personal experience of God through it and mitigate controversies about its proper interpretation. "The Scriptures will be more studied . . . not as a magazine of propositions and mere dialectic entities, but as inspirations and poetic forms of life; requiring, also, divine inbreathings and exaltations in us, that we may ascend into their meanings."[125] This view of Scripture, he argued, will result in "more union . . . and more of true piety enlightened by the Spirit of God—neither of which involves any harm or danger."[126]

Bushnell reaches toward Christian comprehensiveness. One of Bushnell's goals as a theologian was to break through the deadlocks of differing Christian confessions, especially Calvinism and Arminianism, unconditional election and irresistible grace versus free will. This controversy had been tearing Protestants apart for more than two centuries, and Bushnell could see no sense in it. Because Scripture is not a rational system of dogmas anyway, it is possible that both Calvinism and Arminianism have grasped different portions of the truth. "Christian comprehensiveness" is Bushnell's

---

[122]Dorrien, *The Making of American Liberal Theology*, 122–23.
[123]Ibid., 146–47.
[124]Ibid., 145.
[125]Bushnell, "Language and Theology," 103.
[126]Ibid., 105.

ecumenical project to unite seemingly opposite creedal traditions. "Unite the Arminian and the Calvinist, comprehend both doctrines, and we have the Christian truth."[127] After all, Scripture contains paradoxes. Surely affirmation of God's sovereignty and human free will, although seemingly incompatible, can both be embraced. Neither side has a corner on truth; both are picking up on certain images and symbols and poetic expressions of God's salvific will and power. There is no reason they cannot be held in tension with each other within the same church. Some critics thought Bushnell was overly idealistic and optimistic when he wrote, "When a man is able to comprehend the reality of all sects, casting away the unreality, he will be a full-grown proper Christian man."[128] So, "let Calvinism take in Arminianism, Arminianism Calvinism."[129]

Naturally, many theologians then and now find Bushnell's approach to ecumenism overly simplistic and even impossible. However, as one scholar reports, "those who mastered his distinctive method of theological inquiry usually experienced an exhilarating liberation from an increasingly scholastic orthodoxy."[130] Critics, however, accused him of relativism and carelessness about doctrine. Some said he would empty Christianity of all cognitive content and reduce it to warm, fuzzy experiences of God compatible with anything and everything. Nothing could have been further from Bushnell's intention. That is not to say his method might not have that result for some people. Bushnell's intention was to reunite Protestants and possibly even, in the long run, Catholics and Protestants. It is important to know that he was not advocating doing away with all creeds and confessions of faith. Quite the opposite. His attitude was the more creeds the better so long as none of them are taken as sufficient in and of themselves to capture the multifaceted nature of Scripture and of God. "Bushnell believed that almost every one of the historic creeds of the church, no matter how repugnant to one another, stood for an element of truth which should find its place in a more inclusive Christian confession."[131]

---

[127]Horace Bushnell, "Christian Comprehensiveness," in *Horace Bushnell*, ed. H. Shelton Smith (New York: Oxford University Press, 1965), 121.

[128]Ibid., 124.

[129]Quoted in Smith, "Introduction," 38.

[130]Ibid., 39.

[131]H. Shelton Smith, "Editor's Introduction" to Bushnell's "Christian Comprehensiveness," in *Horace Bushnell*, ed. H. Shelton Smith (New York: Oxford University Press, 1965), 108.

One example Bushnell loved to use to illustrate his view of Christian comprehensiveness is the multiple, sometimes seemingly contradictory, images of the atonement in Scripture. There Christ's saving death is described as sacrifice, example, transfer of guilt, battle against evil, substitution, and many other things. All are true. No single theory of the atonement can capture them all, and thus it is wrong to elevate a single doctrine of the atonement to exclusive status. All must be believed, confessed and preached. Problems arise when a person or church absolutizes one image to the exclusion of others.[132] So what, then, is the purpose of theology? Why even have doctrines? Bushnell attempted to answer the obvious question:

> Considering that Christian character is imperfect, liable to the instigation of passion, to be overheated in the flesh and think it the inspiration of God, Christian theology and speculative activity are needed as providing checks and balances for the life, to save it from visionary flights, erratic fancies, and wild hallucinations.[133]

Practically speaking, then, theology's role is to rule out of bounds certain claims about God as incompatible with God's revelation and with Christian experience. During Bushnell's lifetime waves of revivals spread over especially western New York state so that it became known as "the Burnt Over District." It was there that many sects and cults arose on the fringes of Christianity, and Bushnell was no friend of theirs. But his main concern was to provide a vision of theology that unifies Christians in the mainline of basic historic orthodoxy—especially Calvinists and Arminians.

To what extent was Bushnell's Christian comprehensiveness successful? During his own lifetime, not very. His proposal was greeted with animosity by most theologians of both the right and the left. However, after his death, something very much like it became the standard view of doctrinal differences in various ways. The ecumenical movement arose in the twentieth century, bringing about cooperation between rival Protestant denominations. Some formally united in spite of differing doctrines. Something like Bushnell's Christian comprehensiveness has become standard fare in pietist

---

[132]Bushnell, "Christian Comprehensiveness," 112.
[133]Quoted in Adamson, *Bushnell Rediscovered*, 107.

and postmodern Christian circles. In 1984 a leading Protestant theologian at Yale Divinity School published *The Nature of Doctrine*, which strongly parallels many of Bushnell's ideas, arguing that doctrines that seem to contradict each other do not necessarily divide Christianity. The reasons George Lindbeck (b. 1923) gave are not the same as Bushnell's, but the overall similarity of their proposals is so strong one has to suspect that the latter's influence trickled down to the former in some way. It is safe to say that twenty-first-century Protestantism has become Bushnellian in its view of doctrines. They are good in their right place, as signs and symbols, but dangerous if taken literally or elevated to exclusive truth status.

Bushnell defends the supernatural. All of the above might make Bushnell sound liberal, and that is how he is often categorized. However, there were also conservative aspects of his theology. One was his adamant insistence that Christianity includes belief in miracles. He was not willing to accommodate theology so far to modernity as giving up miracles like the virgin birth and bodily resurrection of Jesus. He did not think every biblical account of a miracle had to be taken literally, but he defended traditional belief in God's supernatural acts in salvation history. Again, he was seeking a via media, a third way, between orthodoxy and naturalistic materialism, which he thought Unitarians and many liberals came too close to embracing. He was "prepared to yield aspects of the Bible to scientific or historical correction if necessary, but conceded nothing to those who sullied the character or deity of Jesus. This was where progressive orthodoxy drew the line."[134]

It will be helpful to know the opposite poles of the theological debate Bushnell was trying to transcend with a mediating view. At least to his way of thinking, Protestant orthodoxy was too uncritical in its belief about every miracle story of the Bible. It insisted that if the Bible says an axe head floated, the Christian must believe it, even if it has nothing to do with Jesus or Christian experience of God. He did not believe it is necessary or right to take everything in the Bible literally. He took the Bible seriously without taking all of it literally. But he thought he took it more seriously than liberals were wont to. Unitarian and liberal theologians were dismissive toward miracles and the supernatural and sought to reduce Christianity to an ethical

---

[134]Dorrien, *The Making of American Liberal Theology*, 163.

way of life and Jesus as the ideal human being. His third way began with the assumption that "nature and supernatural are complementary poles of God's universal economy."[135] In other words, they should not be conceived as opposites or in some kind of conflict. He feared that modernity had pitted nature against supernature as if God were not author of both and as if nature were an autonomous realm over against God. In that case, the supernatural would be violations of the natural. This Bushnell set out to correct.

Bushnell attempted to reconceive both nature and the supernatural so that they do not fall into conflict with each other. This he did by comparing them with the body and the mind. Nature is the realm of things acted on. The supernatural is the realm of acting powers and not only God's.[136] The human will is supernatural in that it is not under nature's control. (Bushnell was not a believer in divine determinism; he believed in free will.) "Every act of will turns the laws of nature to ends that would not be affected [sic] by the unaided operation of nature."[137] (It is probable that in that sentence "affected" should be "effected.") In other words, in order to deny the supernatural entirely, one would have to adopt materialistic naturalism in which case there could be no free will. And if there is no free will, there is no evil. The whole category of evil depends on free will, Bushnell believed. "For him, only a supernaturalist Christianity can establish the reality of evil and only a supernatural God can save the world from it."[138] For Bushnell, if God exists, miracles and the supernatural cannot be thought impossible. Any truly theistic world view must include the possibility of divine acts that go beyond what nature does. Also, if free will exists, something transcending mere nature is automatically included. The difference between God's supernatural agency and human supernatural agency is merely a matter of degree.[139]

Bushnell was not content to rest there; he needed to redefine the whole category of "miracle" so that it does not fall into absolute conflict with the new view of nature stemming from the Enlightenment and scientific revolution. At the same time, however, he believed that much orthodox theology genuinely contributed to the increase in naturalism among educated

---

[135]Ibid., 158.
[136]Ibid., 159.
[137]Ibid.
[138]Ibid., 159.
[139]Ibid., 162.

Christians because of its conception of miracles. The problem, he believed, was with the idea of miracle as a suspension or violation of the laws of nature. People generally pictured a miracle as a divine incursion into nature from outside, interrupting nature's system of causes and effects. This was no longer tenable in light of the scientific discoveries of nature as a harmonious whole governed by laws. An interruption of the laws of nature would destroy nature. And a nature constantly being interrupted would not be predictable. Science depends on the predictability of nature. So, Bushnell insisted that a human person's act of free will is not an interruption of nature; it is a power acting on nature from within. But it is not part of nature. Similarly, God's acts in the world are not interruptions of nature; they are powers acting on nature from within. God is not only outside of nature; God is also immanent within nature. In fact, according to Bushnell, a proper concept of God must see nature as God's activity. The laws of nature are regularities of God's activity whereas miracles are unusual acts of God on nature. Science studies the regularities; theology also studies the special acts of God's providence.

Bushnell wrote a book on this subject titled *Nature and the Supernatural.* It shocked both conservative and liberals. To conservatives, the orthodox, it seemed to deny miracles. To liberals it seemed to deny nature as understood by modernity. Bushnell would say both were right, up to a point, because both misunderstood both nature and the supernatural. His whole purpose in the book was to defend Christianity against the increasing tendency to translate it into naturalistic categories.[140] Liberals made much of the category of the "personal," but Bushnell argued, "The very idea of personality is that of a being not under the law of cause and effect, a being supernatural."[141] Thus, as with free will, personality itself is "a properly supernatural power in man."[142] At this point Bushnell had also to break with his Calvinist heritage and especially with Jonathan Edwards, the great Calvinist revivalist and theologian of a century earlier. Edwards had taught that all human decisions and actions are under the control of the person's

---

[140]H. Shelton Smith, "Editor's Introduction" to Horace Bushnell, "Nature and the Supernatural," in *Horace Bushnell,* ed. H. Shelton Smith (New York: Oxford University Press, 1965), 131.

[141]Horace Bushnell, "Nature and the Supernatural," in *Horace Bushnell,* ed. H. Shelton Smith (New York: Oxford University Press, 1965), 132.

[142]Ibid., 135.

strongest motive which is ultimately controlled by God. Bushnell strenuously objected to that because it effectively did away with personality and
sin. Sin must be free choice even if it is influenced by hereditary sin and evil
in the social environment. Against Edwards Bushnell declared that man "is
under no law of cause and effect in his choices."[143]

So, for Bushnell, if the human person is a supernatural being, which he
is if he has free will, then God is also a supernatural being who acts, at least
some of the time, supernaturally. "If it be nothing incredible that we should
act on the chain of cause and effect in nature, is it more incredible that God
should thus act?"[144] But, again, our supernatural acts in and on nature and
God's are not "violations" or "disruptions" of the laws of nature because
nature is not an autonomous, iron-clad machine separate from God and us.
Rather, "nature . . . is only stage, field, medium, vehicle, for the universe;
that is, for God and his powers."[145] And, Bushnell might add, for us and our
powers under God. Once nature and the supernatural, nature and miracles,
are redefined in these ways, he believed, the whole problem of miracles
melts away. It is possible to be thoroughly modern in one's belief about
nature, without going to the extreme of naturalism, and thoroughly orthodox in one's belief about miracles, without going to the extreme of conceiving them as disruptions of nature.

This is a major reason why Bushnell must be categorized as a mediating
theologian rather than as a liberal theologian. (No one imagines him as a
conservative or wholly orthodox theologian.) Liberal theology in his time
had by and large sacrificed the category of the supernatural and of miracles
in accommodation to radical modernity. The popular liberal image of God
and nature then, as now, was of the hand in the glove with God represented
by the hand and nature by the glove. Nature is God's activity, but there can
be no violations of nature's laws. The scientist studies only the glove, not the
hand inside the glove. The theologian studies the hand. The two are wholly
compatible. The cost of that analogy was miracles. Bushnell found that to
be a line he could not cross. To do so, he believed, was to give up Christianity because it would mean denying the virgin birth, Jesus' miracles and

---

[143]Ibid., 138.
[144]Ibid., 139.
[145]Ibid., 151.

his resurrection. But he rejected the hand in the glove analogy for God and nature and replaced it with the analogy of the mind and the body. The body has its autonomic functions that do not depend on the conscious mind; the conscious mind can affect the body and does with every decision to move. Bodily movements are not all automatic, but acknowledging that the conscious mind can move the body in no way denies the body's autonomic systems. With tremendous effort and concentration thought can slow heart rate, but that does not mean heart function is being violated or interrupted. Its normal activity is being changed without destroying it. So God can affect the natural order without violating or destroying it. That is the supernatural. That is a miracle. That is a mediating theology of the supernatural.

Bushnell proposes a new view of the atonement. Bushnell wrote about many doctrines, but the one that caused the most controversy and that he is most remembered for is the atonement. Again, his project in reconstructing the doctrine of the saving significance of Christ's death was to provide a middle way between what he saw as two extremes. Protestant orthodoxy had baptized the penal substitution theory of the atonement as the essential doctrine of how Christ's death saves. This is often referred to as the objective view because it represents the atonement as a transaction between God the Father and Jesus. Atonement, then, is something that happens outside of the person being saved; it is done whether anyone experiences its saving effects or not. In this view, God the Father punished Jesus, the Son of God who is also human, for the sins of humanity or, as in classical Calvinism, the elect only. Jesus suffered the wrath of God against sin deserved by humans. He was humanity's substitute so that God could forgive those who repent and believe. This was considered the orthodox doctrine of the atonement by most conservative theologians and church leaders during Bushnell's lifetime.

The main alternative view was that Jesus' death on the cross was a great object lesson of God's love for humanity. This is often called the subjective view or the moral example theory of the atonement. It is subjective because it does not portray the atonement as having any effect on God; it is not a transaction between God and Jesus. Rather, its main effect, perhaps its only effect, is on humans—to demonstrate God's love to them in order to draw them to God in repentance and faith. Most liberal theologians of Bushnell's lifetime had come to embrace that doctrine of the atonement because it was considered more in keeping with the spirit of modernity, which had great trouble with traditional ideas of God's wrath poured out on an innocent man. The penal substitution theory appeared to many people of the nineteenth century medieval in its portrayal of God. Most importantly, however, to them it was an unethical view of the atonement. It had nothing to do with ethics or morality; it was saturated with Old Testament imagery of bloody sacrifices and could not be moralized.

Bushnell had been taught a third view of the atonement that was popular among New Haven's Yale theologians—the governmental theory. The idea was that Jesus did not suffer and die to appease God's wrath but to uphold God's moral government of the universe. In that view, God wants to forgive sinners but cannot without undermining his righteousness, so, in the person of Jesus Christ, God voluntarily suffers an equivalent punishment that every sinner deserves in order to uphold and display God's righteousness and love. This seemed to many of the New Haven theologians a compromise position between the traditional penal substitution theory and the moral example theory. It is objective and subjective at the same time. Most importantly, however, it is ethical. In this view God did not punish an innocent man, Jesus, with the punishment deserved by others. And the main motive of the atonement was not God's wrath; it was God's love. In the governmental theory, the atonement, although objective in that it made it possible for God to forgive sinners who repent, was subjective in its educative value. It portrays to sinners how seriously God takes sin while at the same time portraying how much God loves them.

Bushnell was dissatisfied with all the traditional theories of the atonement and wrote *The Vicarious Sacrifice* to offer an alternative view. Later, however, he became dissatisfied with the theory he developed there and wrote another book on the atonement titled *Forgiveness and Law* (1874). It was his last book, his swan song, and he was most satisfied with it. He believed he had finally broken through to the best metaphorical way of thinking about Christ's saving death. For him, all atonement theories are pictures; none do complete justice to the mystery of the cross. Some pictures are better than others insofar as they unite the truth in others while leaving behind their flaws. For Bushnell, in both *The Vicarious Sacrifice* and *Forgiveness and Law*, the main flaw in the traditional objective views, including the governmental theory, was the depiction of God as wrathful or somehow beholden to a law that requires him to punish sin before forgiving sinners. The main flaw in the traditional subjective view was its failure to explain why Jesus' death was necessary. Why couldn't God have shown his love in some other way than through a bloody sacrifice? Also, how does the moral example theory account for human guilt? It is inextricably tied to a Pelagian view of humans as basically good and sin as only ignorance; in it humans only need an object lesson of God's love.

In *The Vicarious Sacrifice* Bushnell argued that Christ's death was not a penal substitution but a vicarious sacrifice. What is the difference? To Bushnell, "vicarious" means "identification with," whereas "substitution" means "taking the place of." To him, punishing an innocent person for someone else's sins is unethical; a good God would not do that. Also, "a sin cannot rationally be transferred" from one person to another.[146] Furthermore, God did not need reconciliation with the world of sinners; sinners need reconciling with God. For these and other reasons, Bushnell could not embrace the penal substitution theory. However, neither could he embrace the moral example theory because it emptied the cross of power. So what did he mean by "vicarious sacrifice"? His clearest statement is that

> the true conception . . . is that Christ, in what is called his vicarious sacrifice, simply engages, at the expense of great suffering and even of death itself, to bring us out of our sins themselves and so out of their penalties; being himself profoundly identified with us in our fallen state, and burdened in feeling with our evils.[147]

In other words, Jesus was God, in a human person, identifying with our misery and thereby bringing us together with God's mercy. Bushnell stated that few moderns could believe that Jesus literally took humanity's sin and God's punishment on himself. However, it is necessary to believe, for the sake of the gospel, that Jesus "bore" our sins in his person on the cross. However, "the bearing of our sins . . . mean[s] that Christ bore them on his feeling, became inserted into their bad lot by his sympathy as a friend,

---

[146]Horace Bushnell, "The Work of Christ" (selections from *The Vicarious Sacrifice*), in *Horace Bushnell*, ed. H. Shelton Smith (New York: Oxford University Press, 1965), 281–82.
[147]Ibid., 280.

yielded up himself and his life . . . to an effort of restoring mercy."[148] The object of Christ's death was not to appease God's wrath or satisfy God's justice or to offer merely a moral example, although it was a moral example. The object, according to Bushnell, was "the healing of souls."[149]

In order to accomplish what the cross did accomplish, Bushnell argued, God must be capable of suffering and must have suffered the cross of Christ. Traditional, orthodox theology said that God cannot suffer because to suffer is to change. Suffering is evidence of imperfection. God is perfect and therefore cannot suffer. Bushnell threw that aside. He averred without apology that God suffers because he is love: "As certainly as God is love, the burdens of love must be upon him. He must bear the lot of his enemies, and even the wrongs of his enemies. . . . In his greatness there is no bar to this kind of suffering; He will suffer because He is great, and be great because he suffers."[150] This shocked many theological traditionalists because it seemed to pull God down from glory and power. Bushnell did not care. He saw one of the greatest effects of Christ's life and death as "humanizing God to men."[151] Many people mistakenly think that the motif of "God's suffering" began with Dietrich Bonhoeffer (1906–1945), who wrote in his *Letters and Papers from Prison* that "only the suffering God can help" (see chap. 7). This was picked up by Jürgen Moltmann (b. 1926) in *The Crucified God* (1974) and by many other avant-garde theologians of the twentieth century (see 8.a.). Bushnell, however, was one of the first Protestant theologians to argue that God himself, not only Jesus, suffers.

For good reasons, Bushnell was not satisfied with his account of the atonement in *The Vicarious Sacrifice*; it seemed to waffle between objective and subjective, never quite landing on a definite explanation of why Jesus had to suffer and die. So, near the end of his life, he published *Forgiveness and Law*, in which he laid out a similar, but more specific, explanation of why Jesus died and how atonement works. In a nutshell, he explained that all forgiveness involves suffering. God did not suffer in Jesus in order to forgive but because he was forgiving.

---

[148]Ibid., 282.
[149]Ibid., 293.
[150]Ibid., 309.
[151]Ibid., 307.

While preparing a sermon on "Christian Forgiveness," he suddenly saw that any real forgiveness of one's enemy demanded a personal sacrifice so great as to be actually self-propitiating in its effect. ["Propitiation" means appeasing.] Since that was true of man, he concluded that it must be true also of God. He revised his doctrine of Christ's work so as to include the element of divine self-propitiation. Thus his doctrine now acknowledged that God must be reconciled to man, as well as man to God.[152]

In other words, God literally could not forgive sinners without suffering, but he did not suffer their punishment. He suffered the pain of forgiveness.

Most scholars are agreed that Bushnell never did break through to a coherent doctrine of the atonement; his explanations were filled with images and metaphors but lacked any rational explanation. However, Bushnell would not consider that a devastating critique. Yes, he was interested in explaining the atonement to people, but he did not think there was any perfect explanation that would satisfy the rational mind. The atonement, like the incarnation and the Trinity, is a mystery to be adored and contemplated. Explanation is only for the sake of bringing Christ's death to bear on the healing of souls. His final account of the atonement in *Forgiveness and Law* did just that. Just as God suffers forgiveness, so we should undergo the suffering and pain of forgiving others.

Bushnell leaves a mixed legacy and uncertain reputation. During his lifetime Bushnell came under withering criticism from theologians to his right and left. Hodge dismissed him as confused and unworthy of the influence he had on the popular Christian mind. The leading American liberal theologian of that time, Theodore Parker (1810–1860), criticized Bushnell for not going far enough in his revisioning and reconstruction of Christian doctrines. Contemporary theology gives him mixed reviews. Gary Dorrien categorizes him as more of a "seer" than a theologian in the traditional sense.[153] One thing can be said with assurance: Bushnell became America's preeminent Protestant progressive theologian after his death. But his admirers and followers did not always hold to his mediating approach to theology. Many of them chose to emphasize his liberal side and ignore

---

[152]H. Shelton Smith, "Editor's Introduction" to Horace Bushnell, "Forgiveness and Law," in *Horace Bushnell*, ed. H. Shelton Smith (New York: Oxford University Press, 1965), 311.

[153]Dorrien, *The Making of American Liberal Theology*, 153.

his passion for the supernatural and the objective work of Christ on the cross. Gradually, disciples like Theodore Munger (1830–1910) and William Newton Clarke (1841–1912) turned Bushnell into an icon of liberal theology. That became his undeserved reputation: America's first great liberal theologian. Instead, he was intentionally a mediating theologian, which is why people have generally misunderstood him; his mediating approach made him seem ambiguous.

Why is Bushnell included in a book about modern theology? What was modern about his theology? First, he was influenced by romanticism and Hegel. His affinity with Coleridge has already been explained. The influence of Hegel appeared in his optimistic view of Christian comprehensiveness, which assumed that it would be possible to achieve something like a synthesis of all Christian truth by leaving behind the flawed perspectives and claims and combining the ethically useful elements in a higher unity. And the very mention of his concern for ethical usefulness of theology indicates his modernity. For him, as for many nineteenth-century theologians, Christianity's main value lay in its ability to heal souls and provide ethical guidance for life. He did not, however, reduce Christianity to ethics in Kantian style. Bushnell was always concerned to reconstruct Christian doctrines such as the atonement in such a way as to allow them to speak to the modern mind while at the same time remaining faithful to the gospel. His liberal tendencies appeared in the fact that if he detected that a doctrinal formulation was incapable of speaking to the modern mind, if modern people could not understand it, he was more than willing to reconstruct it. His conservative tendencies appeared in his constant concern to keep continuity between modern reconstructions of doctrines and traditional beliefs. Thus, progressive orthodoxy is the right label for Bushnell's approach to theology in the modern age.

We have seen how much nineteenth-century theology was attempting to reconcile science with Christianity so as to avoid conflicts between them. Bushnell shared that concern. In one sense, his entire view of language and especially theological language, and its resultant treatment of doctrines, is aimed at preventing absolute conflicts between science and theology. For him, doctrines are models, complex metaphors, that never accurately represent the realities they describe. Similarly, the Bible itself is literature filled with symbolism not to be taken literally. That is not to say it is divorced from history, but it is to say it contains obscurities whose interpretation must remain open to revision in light of new knowledge and understanding. For him it was not impossible in principle for theology and science to conflict, but any absolute conflict would be resolved by saying that the biblical and creedal material is just metaphorical and therefore does not really conflict with science. Finally, his concept of the supernatural was clearly intended to mitigate conflicts between the new scientific world view and theology. He would not give up on the supernatural, which reveals his conservative side, but he insisted on reinterpreting it in a way that minimizes any potential conflict with science. Science studies the regularities of God's activity in the world that we call laws of nature. Theology sees something more in them than science can see; it sees them as modes of God's continuing creation and providential work in the world. And theology, unlike science, can acknowledged irregularities in the midst of nature's regularities without describing them as violations or disruptions of the natural order.

The only one of Bushnell's books still in print in the early twenty-first century is *Christian Nurture*, and for that reason he is most remembered as the father of modern Christian education. Unlike some other of his books, that one is relatively easy to read. A twenty-first-century person delving into most of Bushnell's books, now dusty volumes on library shelves (often in some storage facility), will find his flowery language an obstacle to understanding. Also, there are no Bushnellians around to keep his memory alive. So, he has been largely relegated to the dustbin of American religious history and to books on nineteenth-century American theology. Similarity is not always evidence of influence, but it seems fairly obvious that Bushnell's influence, however indirect, is reappearing in twenty-first-century theology among the so-called emerging church Christians on the fringes of evangelicalism. They may call themselves postmodern, but their "generous orthodoxy" is not very different from Bushnell's mediating approach to theology—not in the details but in the general ethos.

5

NEO-ORTHODOX/DIALECTICAL/
KERYGMATIC THEOLOGIES REVIVE
THE REFORMATION IN THE
MODERN CONTEXT

The First World War began in 1914 and ended in 1918; it sounded the death knell of the nineteenth-century European intellectual ethos including classical liberal theology. The Second World War began in 1939 and ended in 1945 and included the Holocaust; it brought the same cultural crisis to the United States. The twentieth century has been called the genocidal century. Its horrors forced reexamination of the Enlightenment's optimism about inevitable progress through reason. It was reason, after all, that made the wars possible. Science turned out to be a mixed blessing as it contributed not only great advances in medicine but also killing machines and bombs. Germany was throughout the nineteenth century considered the cultural capital of modernity; from it flowed the ideas that shaped the later Enlightenment's philosophy and science as well as theology. Then came two world wars and the Holocaust. Disillusionment set in. The time was ripe for a new revolution in theology.

According to Karl Barth, the turning point was the day in 1914 he picked up a newspaper and read a statement by German intellectuals supporting

Kaiser Wilhelm's war policy. Among the names were most of his theological mentors, including Harnack, who wrote the kaiser's speech declaring war against France, Russia and Great Britain. Barth, a budding young pastor and theologian, was so dismayed that he began to reconsider the liberal Protestant theology of his education. Something was wrong, he concluded, with a theology that allowed its adherents to support such an evil and meaningless war. For that and other reasons, like many other European theologians, he began searching for a new theological paradigm. Eventually he found it in the dialectical philosophy and theology of Kierkegaard, the "melancholy Dane." Kierkegaard's governing motif was the wholly otherness of God. Liberal theology had identified humanity too closely with God. One American theologian described the God-human relationship as like an ocean (God) and a bay (humanity). Hegel's ghost had to be exorcised from theology once and for all, Barth thought. And Kierkegaard, who had so valiantly opposed Hegel and Hegelian-inspired theology, was to be the exorcist.[1]

Christian Theology Rediscovers Existentialism

"Neo-orthodoxy" was commonly used as a label for the Protestant theology that grew out of Barth's and other primarily European theologians' disillusionment with liberal optimism and overemphasis on God's immanence between the two world wars. It is an imperfect label, and hardly any theologians used it to identify themselves and their theological orientation.[2] It is even difficult to identify what all theologians commonly lumped together as neo-orthodox had in common. Perhaps the only thing is a reaction against liberal theology without embracing fundamentalism. However, most, if not all, also found inspiration in the philosophy begun by Kierkegaard called existentialism (to be explained later in this introduction). Some so-called neo-orthodox theologians preferred labels such as "dialectical theology," "new Reformation theology" and "kerygmatic theology." The first of the three

---

[1]The extent to which Kierkegaard's thought influenced the early Barth is much debated. Barth probably discovered Kierkegaard after already becoming disillusioned with liberal theology; Kierkegaard's existentialism then became an ally and tool in his development of dialectical theology.

[2]This author is aware of the controversy surrounding the label "neo-orthodoxy." Many scholars of twentieth-century theology reject it for a variety of reasons. One is that it was coined by dialectical theologians' critics and is therefore pejorative. Also, virtually no theologian has ever called himself or herself neo-orthodox. However, especially in Great Britain and the United States, the label came to be used for those theologians also often known as dialectical.

designates a Kierkegaardian defiance of Hegelian synthesis of opposites and especially of God and humanity. According to dialectical theologians, the relationship between God and humans, apart from the grace of Jesus Christ, always includes crisis and confrontation. Dialectical theology also indicates a preference for paradox over Hegel's "the real is the rational and the rational is the real." God's transcendence, wholly otherness, and human sinfulness mean that all our human thoughts about God ultimately end in confession of mystery and acceptance of paradox as sign of mystery.

The second alternative label, "new Reformation theology," points to neo-orthodox theologians' desire to breathe new life into the theologies of Luther and Calvin within a modern context. Barth and other new Reformation theologians believed liberal Protestant theology had succumbed to a religion of culture. The religious a priori had overtaken and replaced the Word of God and faith. The third label, "kerygmatic theology," suggests neo-orthodox theologians' emphasis on the Word of God, the gospel, over rational philosophical theology. For them, Christian theology ought to eschew accommodation to philosophies such as Kant's and Hegel's (which is not to say they always succeeded in exorcising those ghosts from their theological reflections). It ought instead to stick closely to God's Word in Jesus Christ and the gospel, what Barth called "the strange new world within the Bible," and avoid making theology the servant of any philosophy.

Throughout this section that encompasses several theologians associated with the Barthian revolt against liberal theology[3] the labels "neo-orthodox,"

---

[3]The terminology of revolt comes from the important book (for Barth studies) *The Barthian Revolt in Modern Theology: Theology Without Weapons* (Louisville, KY: Westminster John Knox, 2000) by Gary Dorrien, a professor at Union Theological Seminary in New York. Dorrien opens his book with a discussion of labels such as "neo-orthodoxy" and (to introduce a new one for this phenomenon here) "crisis theology." He rightly notes that Barth rejected all labels imposed on him including, especially, "Barthian." The Swiss theologian wanted only to be known as a "church theologian of God's free and sovereign Word" (1). A great deal of discussion, even debate, has taken place throughout the 1990s and the first decades of the twenty-first century about proper labels for Barth's theology and those associated with his theological revolution. That discussion has included several scholarly theories about how much of a revolution it was, what launched it and especially about stages in Barth's theological career. Dorrien provides a helpful summary of these discussions in his introduction, "Neoorthodoxy Reconsidered" (2–13). According to Dorrien, whose interpretation of Barth's theological pilgrimage comes from a liberal Protestant perspective, he always remained under the influence of his liberal theological mentor Wilhelm Herrmann (1846–1922) and that Barth's main theme throughout his theology remained the Herrmann-inspired idea of revelation as "self-revealing and self-authenticating" "Spirit-illuminated Word" (5). This contrasts with other interpretations of Barth's theological pilgrimage that emphasize decisive shifts from, for

"dialectical" and "kerygmatic" will be used interchangeably even though this author is well aware of the great debates happening in theology and especially Barth studies about them. And their use for several theologians traditionally (rightly or wrongly) labeled neo-orthodox should not be interpreted as implying complete agreement among them. What they shared are certain impulses vis-à-vis liberal theology and fundamentalism and especially a common tendency prophetically to correct what they saw as overaccommodation to modernity in theology. They also, at least at certain key points, shared an appreciation of existentialism as a tool for a new, nonliberal, nonfundamentalist approach to theology. Finally, they shared a common commitment to Christocentrism in theology, something they believed was lacking in much, if not all, liberal Protestant theology.

Perhaps the best overall description of neo-orthodox, dialectical, kerygmatic theology is that it is Christocentric. All those theologians usually labeled those ways were determined to avoid what they regarded as the anthropocentrism of liberal theology and the biblicism of Protestant orthodoxy. They rejected both liberal elevation of human experience to a source and norm of theology and fundamentalist treatment of the Bible as a paper pope. For them, the category "revelation" meant first and foremost God's self-communication in Jesus Christ, the Word of God in person. They tended to reject, in varying degrees of vehemence, natural theology and rational apologetics. These, they believed, always tend to take over theology and predetermine what it can and cannot say. They tend to become straightjackets that restrict theology to some rational framework of thought tied to a time-bound culture. Theology's sole job, dialectical theologians averred, is to express the truth of God's Word, the gospel of Jesus Christ, prophetically to fallen human people and to the church for its guidance. Above all, theology goes astray when it ties

---

example, early existentialism to mature Protestant orthodoxy. In contrast to another leading interpreter of Barth, theologian Bruce McCormack, Dorrien defends the concept of neo-orthodoxy with proper qualifications while arguing that Barth's followers, the "neo-orthodox movement," moved far from Barth in many ways. McCormack, author of the much discussed *Karl Barth's Critically Realistic Dialectical Theology: Its Genesis and Development 1909–1936* (Oxford: Clarendon Press, 1995), attempted to distinguish Barth from so-called neo-orthodoxy and to emphasize the continuity of Barth's theology as consistently (after his break from liberalism) critically realistic, dialectical and orthodox. All of this discussion and debate aside, Dorrien is surely right that Barth's great achievement and main theme is that "the appropriate test of Christian theology is not whether it conforms to or confirms any independent theory of reality, but whether it makes present the narrated Word of Christ in all of its sovereign freedom" (12).

itself to the culture of a particular time and place, including modernity.

However, kerygmatic theologians were not interested in expending time or energy fighting modernity; that, they believed, was the fundamentalist mistake. Fundamentalism became a slave to modernity by defining its form of Christianity over against it. Liberalism and fundamentalism were seen as odd twins insofar as both were obsessed with modernity—either accommodating to it to make Christianity believable to modern people or militantly opposing it to make Christianity distinctive in a separatist way. Dialectical theology was also different from mediating theology insofar as the latter was still interested in correlating Christianity with modernity and achieving a synthesis of or via media between liberalism and orthodoxy. That goal seemed too Hegelian to these twentieth-century theologians who saw the twentieth-century crisis posed to modernity and especially its myth of inevitable progress as a gift to the churches for recovery of the gospel. What is the gospel? For neo-orthodoxy it is that, in spite of God's wholly otherness and human finitude and fallenness, God's mercy and grace have been shown in Jesus Christ for salvation. The gospel also is that salvation is by God's grace through faith alone. But the other side of the gospel is that there is nothing human beings can do to bring God or his grace under human control, to domesticate and tame them. Humans are sinners through and through and without hope apart from God's Word and faith.

Earlier neo-orthodoxy was tied to existentialism. Doesn't that mean it was enslaved to a human philosophy? To be sure, some critics of dialectical theology have accused its theologians of inconsistency at that very point. All were to some extent influenced by Kierkegaard. Some also found support for their theological revolution in later existentialist thinkers such as Martin Heidegger (1889–1976). Their defense was that original existentialism was more a Christian protest against culture Protestantism than a philosophy per se. In a certain sense, existentialism was an antiphilosophy, especially if "philosophy" is defined as rational investigation into and speculation about ultimate reality (metaphysics) or secular accounting for knowledge based on reason alone (epistemology). For neo-orthodox theologians, anyway, the ultimate philosophies to be eschewed in theology were those of Kant and Hegel. Kant's *Religion Within the Limits of Reason Alone* was a special betrayal of Christianity, but so was Hegel's philosophy of religion. Both re-

stricted religion, including Christianity, to secular reasoning, predetermining what Christian truth can be.

Existentialism has had a checkered history since Kierkegaard. Some existentialist thinkers were and are explicitly Christian. An example is Gabriel
Marcel (1889–1973), a French Catholic philosopher who distinguished between "problem" and "mystery" and insisted that life's ultimate questions
are not merely problems to be solved, as in traditional philosophy, but mysteries to be embraced. Some existentialist thinkers, however, were atheists.
An example is Jean-Paul Sartre (1905–1980), another Frenchman, who
flirted with nihilism and rejected religion as a form of inauthentic existence.
What did all existentialists have in common? That is difficult to say. Existentialism is more a mood, an ethos, than a definite philosophy or system.
Many definitions have been attempted, but none capture existentialism perfectly. Its ethos is rebellion against all systems of thought, philosophies, theologies and ideologies that subject the individual to the system.

One popular definition of existentialism is "existence precedes essence,"
in which "precedes" means "takes precedence over." All existentialists seek
"authentic existence" where the individual is not determined by some grand
scheme. For existentialists, meaningful human life requires being "that individual," as Kierkegaard called himself, free of control by "the crowd." For
Kierkegaard and Christian existentialists, authentic existence comes only
through being in relation to God as an individual. For secular existentialists,
authentic existence comes only through self-determination, by creating
one's own life meaning in the face of possible meaninglessness of reality.
That takes courage to face and overcome despair. For the Christian existentialist, despair is the fruit of sin and its only cure is grace which is given to
each individual through his or her own faith.

Neo-orthodoxy's relationship to existentialism is not absolute or monolithic, but the rediscovery of Kierkegaard's thought helped shape neo-
orthodoxy, dialectical theology, at least in its beginnings in the period immediately following World War I. That was a time of tremendous pessimism,
especially in Europe, about the project of modernity. The time had come,
neo-orthodox theologians believed, to start over with modern theology
and this time disentangle it from the overreaching rationalism and anthropocentrism of the Enlightenment. The time had come, they believed, for

theology to regain its independence from philosophy and boldly follow the Word of God. The time had come to recover the gospel from its captivity to modernity without throwing the baby out with the bathwater as neo-orthodox theologians thought fundamentalism tended to do. For example, all dialectical theologians accepted higher biblical criticism so long as it did not domesticate the gospel within the Bible by predetermining what it can be using rationalism and naturalism as norms. Another way of saying the same is that for kerygmatic theologians, the gospel stands even over against the Bible although the Bible is its medium. But the Bible is not always already the Word of God; it becomes the Word of God in the moment when God uses it to call people into encounter with himself through repentance and faith. Without that encounter, the Bible is just a book.

So, who were the leading dialectical theologians? Three theologians most scholars put in that category are Barth, Emil Brunner (1889–1966) and Rudolf Bultmann (1884–1976). None accepted the label "neo-orthodox," but it has stuck to them anyway, especially in English-speaking countries. There were other, lesser-known theologians such as Friedrich Gogarten (1887–1967) and Eduard Thurneysen (1888–1974) who were originally with them in the formation of dialectical theology. This group eventually broke apart and wandered off in separate directions, but they all retained something of the original ethos of kerygmatic theology in spite of their serious disagreements over details. Neo-orthodoxy came to Great Britain and the United States mainly through Brunner, whose books were the first to be translated into English. British and American neo-orthodoxy had its champions (with decidedly British and American accents) in Thomas Torrance (1913–2007) and Reinhold Niebuhr (1892–1971). Eventually, especially in Great Britain and the United States, neo-orthodoxy came to be so closely associated with the theological method of Barth that many called it Barthian theology, much to that theologian's chagrin. To him, what others called neo-orthodoxy, dialectical theology and Barthianism was evangelical theology.

5.A. Karl Barth Drops a Bombshell on the Theologians' Playground

After seeing his liberal theological mentors' signatures attached to Kaiser Wilhelm's war policy, Barth became disillusioned with liberal theology itself. The liberal theologians' support for German imperialism led him to conclude that something must be terribly wrong with that theology, if it could be so quickly compromised in the face of the ideology of war. Looking back on that event, Barth recollected that he could no longer "accept their ethics or dogmatics, their Biblical exegesis, their interpretation of history."[4] He experienced another disillusionment with the liberal Protestantism of his education as he tried to preach it to his mostly working-class congregation in the little Swiss town of Safenwil. He found that liberal theology was useless in his weekly task of preaching. As a result, he undertook a careful and painstaking study of the Scriptures and discovered "The Strange New World within the Bible," to employ the title of one of his earliest articles. In them he found not human religion, not even the highest thoughts of pious people, but God's Word: "It is not the right human thoughts about God which form the content of the Bible, but the right divine thoughts about men."[5] Barth found a relevant message for his parishioners in the transcendent Word in Scripture and not in the philosophical theology of the liberal school of neo-Protestantism in which he had been trained.

During World War I Barth began work on a commentary on Paul's epistle to the Romans. Published in 1919, the commentary unexpectedly created a furor because of its harsh criticism of liberal Protestant theology. It was this book, *Der Römerbrief* (*The Epistle to the Romans*), that was said to have fallen like a bombshell on the playground of the theologians. In it Barth affirmed the validity of both the historical-critical method of studying Scripture and the doctrine of verbal inspiration, and he stated that if he were forced to choose between them he would choose the latter.[6] Barth criticized liberal theology for turning the gospel into a religious message that tells humans of their own divinity instead of recognizing it as the Word of God, a message that humans are incapable of anticipating or compre-

---

[4]Karl Barth, *God, Gospel and Grace*, trans. James S. McNab, *Scottish Journal of Theology Occasional Papers No. 8* (Edinburgh: Oliver and Boyd, 1959), 57. See also Karl Barth, *The Humanity of God*, trans. John Newton Thomas (Richmond, VA: John Knox, 1960), 40.

[5]Karl Barth, *The Word of God and the Word of Man*, trans. Douglas Horton (Boston: Pilgrim Press, 1928), 43. See also Karl Barth, *The Word of God and Theology*, trans. Amy Marga (London: T & T Clark, 2011), 25, for a slightly different translation.

[6]Karl Barth, *The Epistle to the Romans*, trans. Edwyn C. Hoskyns (London: Oxford University Press, 1933), 1.

hending because it comes from a God utterly distinct from them.[7] In essence, Barth was calling for a revolution in theological method, a theology from above to replace the old, human-centered theology from below inaugurated by Schleiermacher, whom Barth accused of trying to speak about God by speaking about man in a very loud voice. Throughout the commentary on Romans he emphasized the otherness of God, the gospel as a message humans cannot tell themselves, the difference between time and eternity and salvation as wholly a gift of God that cannot be in any sense a human achievement. These great truths, he argued, cannot be built up from universal human experience or reason; they must be received in humble obedience from God's revelation.

Barth becomes the world's foremost theologian without a doctoral degree. Barth was born in Basel, Switzerland, into a very religious family. His father was a lecturer at a college for preachers and identified with a fairly conservative group within the Swiss Reformed Church. When Barth was two years old his father accepted a much more prestigious position as assistant lecturer at the University of Bern. His family life was strict but generally happy, and he later remembered respecting his father greatly and being deeply attached to his mother.[8] On the eve of his confirmation in 1902 Barth resolved to become a theologian, not so much with preaching and pastoral care in mind, he later wrote, as with the hope of reaching a proper understanding of the creed, to replace the rather hazy ideas of it he had then.[9] He studied theology at the universities of Bern, Berlin, Tübingen and Marburg, eventually arriving at a theological position within the Ritschlian school of liberal thought. In Berlin he came under the influence of Harnack, and at Marburg he became a disciple of the Ritschlian theologian Wilhelm Herrmann. Later, he radically repudiated this theology, much to the dismay of his teachers.

Barth never earned a doctorate, although later in life he was showered with honorary degrees from many great universities. In 1908 he was ordained to the ministry of the Reformed Church and took a position as as-

---

[7]Ibid., 28.

[8]Eberhard Busch, *Karl Barth, His Life from Letters and Autobiographical Texts*, trans. John Bowden (Philadelphia: Fortress, 1976), 12.

[9]Ibid., 31.

sistant pastor in Geneva. There he occasionally preached in the same great hall where Calvin had lectured three and a half centuries earlier. Like most assistant pastors, he found the work unfulfilling and moved in 1911 to a small parish in Safenwil, a village on the border with Germany. There he met a fellow pastor named Eduard Thurneysen, and together they began rethinking liberal theology and exploring new avenues of Christian thought. For Barth the result was his *Epistle to the Romans* and the launching of a theological journal that became the mouthpiece of the new dialectical theology movement.

The label "dialectical theology" came from Barth's early emphasis on confrontation and crisis between God and humanity. "Dialectical" placed Barth in the sphere of Kierkegaard's philosophical method rather than Hegel's.[10] For Kierkegaard, because of human sinfulness and the wholly otherness of God, God's truth and human thought can never be smoothed out into a rational synthesis. Instead, the paradoxical truths of God's self-revelation must be embraced in a leap of faith. In his preface to the second edition of *The Epistle to the Romans* (1922) Barth expressed his debt to Kierkegaard:

> If I have a system, it is limited to a recognition of what Kierkegaard called the "infinite qualitative distinction" between time and eternity, and to my re-garding this as possessing negative as well as positive significance: "God is in heaven, and thou art on earth." The relation between such a God and such a man, and the relation between such a man and such a God, is for me the theme of the Bible and the essence of philosophy.[11]

Within a few months of its publication, *The Epistle to the Romans* became the focus of a heated debate. Some liberal biblical scholars and theologians dismissed it as the rantings of a religious fanatic, while others hailed it as a recovery of the true spirit of the Reformation. Some of Barth's teachers, including Harnack and Herrmann, were puzzled by its unhistorical and un-critical approach to the Bible. In spite of the furor, however, numerous

---

[10]This is not to suggest that Barth was uninfluenced by Hegel. Virtually no German-speaking late-nineteenth-century or twentieth-century theologian could be uninfluenced by Hegel. It is to say that his basic impulses were more consistent with Kierkegaard's emphasis on God's tran-scendence than Hegel's emphasis on God's immanence.

[11]Busch, *Karl Barth*, 10.

pastors, teachers and theologians found in it a badly needed corrective for Christian theology moving into the twentieth century. So influential was the commentary that many scholars date the end of nineteenth-century and beginning of twentieth-century theology with its first publication.

Largely because of the success of *The Epistle to the Romans* Barth was offered a position as professor of Reformed theology at the University of Göttingen in 1921. Shortly after arriving, he fell into serious conflict with the disciples of Ritschl, who had taught there in the previous century and who was still revered. Barth continued to write articles and books setting the Word of God over against human reason and accusing liberal theology of succumbing to the culture of Enlightenment rationalism. He argued that the greatest danger to the gospel was not that it might be rejected but that it might peacefully be accepted and made harmless by becoming just another possession of human reason and culture. In his eyes, for a century German theology had been subverting the gospel by making it respectable. Naturally, such polemics won Barth few friends among the reigning theological elite of Germany.

In 1925 Barth was offered a professorship at the University of Münster, where he stayed only five years before moving to Bonn in 1930. During this period a shift began to appear in his writing. Without forsaking his rejection of liberal theology, he began to emphasize God's "yes" to humanity in Jesus Christ more than the divine "no" that he had previously been pronouncing. He discarded his first attempt at a systematic theology titled *The Doctrine of the Word of God: Prolegomena to Christian Dogmatics* (1927) when he realized it was too influenced by existentialist philosophy. He wished to produce a truly theological theology independent of any philosophy and based solely on God's Word. Further, he wanted to emphasize the objectivity of God's revelation more than the subjectivity of human faith.[12]

---

[12]Barth's theological development from *The Epistle to the Romans* into his mature system of theology, *Church Dogmatics*, is the subject of much debate and controversy. Catholic Barth scholar Hans Urs von Balthasar argued for decisive shifts in Barth's theological journey in *The Theology of Karl Barth*, trans. John Drury (New York: Holt, Rinehart and Winston, 1971). However, McCormack challenged Balthasar's interpretation in *Karl Barth's Critically Realistic Dialectical Theology*. McCormack pointed out that Balthasar did not take into account Barth's 1924 *Göttingen Dogmatics* (a series of lectures Barth gave at the University of Göttingen he titled "Instruction in the Christian Religion"). McCormack emphasized continuity in Barth's theology from his break

In 1931 Barth wrote what many scholars consider his most important statement of his mature theological method: *Fides Quaerens Intellectum* ("Faith Seeking Understanding"), a study of the medieval scholastic theologian Anselm of Canterbury. Contrary to many interpretations of Anselm, Barth argued the great churchman was not a rationalist but a devout Christian scholar seeking to put reason into the service of faith. Anselm's ontological argument for the existence of God was not an attempt to prove God apart from faith, Barth claimed, but an attempt to understand with the mind what is already believed by faith. For Anselm, Barth reasoned, all theology is to be done in the context of prayer and obedience. This means that Christian theology cannot be an objective, dispassionate science; it must rather be the faithful understanding of God's objective self-revelation in Jesus Christ made possible by grace and faith alone. What is required for finding theological answers is "a pure heart, eyes that have been opened, child-like obedience, a life in the Spirit, rich nourishment from Holy Scripture."[13] In other words, Barth asserted, the presupposition of correct theology is a life of faith, and its mark is unwillingness ever to set itself in explicit contradiction to the Bible, "the textual basis of the revealed object of faith."[14]

Before his treatise on Anselm, Barth's theology tended to emphasize the negativity of the encounter between God and humanity. Beginning with it, his theology emphasized the positive knowledge of God found in God's self-

---

with liberalism through his *Church Dogmatics*. A third major study of Barth's theology that adds to the debate over Barth's theological development is Dorrien's *The Barthian Revolt in Modern Theology*. Dorrien argues for both continuity and discontinuity in Barth's theological development. One reason for what he calls the "contradictory profusion of readings of Barth" is that "Barth's thinking purposely defied categorization" (165). According to Dorrien, contrary to McCormack, Barth's theology does deserve the appellation "neo-orthodox" with proper qualifications (166–67). And while he admits that discontinuity and "shifts" in Barth's theology have been overrated by some Barth interpreters, he carefully traces out an "objectivizing turn" in Barth's theology (183–84). The debate about Barth's theological development will no doubt continue. The reason is, as Dorrien points out, that at least from 1924 on Barth "employed a considerable array of analogical models" (183). In other words, what Barth said, and at what time and in what way, often depended on the opponents he was countering. While his theology always emphasized certain themes, how those themes were played out changed somewhat throughout more than forty years of theological reflection and production.

[13]Karl Barth, *Anselm: Fides Quaerens Intellectum*, trans. Ian W. Robertson (London: SCM, 1960), 34.

[14]Ibid., 40.

revelation in Jesus Christ.[15] The negative element remained, in that Barth always opposed every form of natural theology—the attempt to gain knowledge of God from nature, culture or philosophy using reason alone. However, his emphasis shifted toward the possibility of true knowledge of God in Jesus Christ delivered by revelation grasped by faith. Shortly after completing his book about Anselm, Barth began work on his magnum opus, a systematic theology with the overarching title *Church Dogmatics* (which he never finished). When he died in 1968, he had written thirteen volumes. One distinctive, notable feature is the lack of any traditional prolegomena or philosophical introduction. Barth consciously omitted such because he was convinced that true theology must be the explication of God's Word and nothing else. Any attempt to ground the truth of God's Word in human reasoning, however devout and sincere, inevitably leads to theology's subversion by human, historical modes of thought and thus to "anthropocentric theology," the evil against which Barth fought so hard throughout his career.

---

[15]Again, as explained in note 12 above, this claim about a shift in Barth's theology is controversial. However, in his 1956 lecture "The Humanity of God" Barth admitted to making two changes of direction—a first and a "new" one. And he credited Balthasar, "the shrewd friend from another shore," for identifying them. Anyone familiar with Balthasar's book (cited in n. 12) knows his thesis of two shifts of direction in Barth's theology—one from liberal theology to an emphasis on what Barth himself called "diastasis" between God and humanity (negative) to an emphasis on analogy (positive), although Balthasar was not satisfied with Barth's analogy of faith and defended an analogy of being. This reference by Barth in "The Humanity of God" seems to support Balthasar's thesis of two shifts in Barth's theology, one around 1916 that led to *The Epistle to the Romans* and another around 1930 or 1931 that led to *Fides Quaerens Intellectum.* (See "The Humanity of God," in Karl Barth, *The Humanity of God,* trans. John Newton Thomas [Richmond, VA: John Knox Press, 1960], especially 44–45.) None of this is to deny continuity in Barth's theology; it is only to defend the idea that within the continuity there were changes in emphasis. Barth himself acknowledged this continuity within change and change within continuity in a 1938 essay titled "How I Changed My Mind," which was published first in *The Christian Century* and then in a book (*Karl Barth: How I Changed My Mind,* ed. John D. Godsey [Richmond, VA: John Knox, 1966]). There Barth spoke of continuity in his theology, at least since his break with liberal theology. He insisted that his change of mind was a "deepening" and "application" of "that knowledge which . . . I had gained before" (42). This "deepening" consisted, he averred, of ridding himself of the last remnants of a philosophical foundation and exposition of Christian doctrine. "The real document of this farewell," he claimed, was "the book about the evidence for God of Anselm" (43). "Among all my books," he said, "I regard this as the one written with the greatest satisfaction" (ibid.). In 1948 Barth again wrote for *The Christian Century* about how his mind had changed, this time about changes since 1938. He spoke warmly about how "to say 'yes' came to seem more important than to say 'no' (though that is important too)" (ibid., 51). Discontinuity within continuity seems to be the solution to the many debates about changes in Barth's theological development. At least that is how Barth himself regarded his theological development.

The presupposition of Barth's project in *Church Dogmatics* (henceforth *CD*) is that God establishes an analogy between himself and humanity in Jesus Christ. He contrasted this "analogy of faith" with the concept of the "analogy of being."[16] Knowledge of God is not an innate capacity within human nature or experience; it is possible only because God has graciously given Jesus Christ, who is both God and human. He establishes the analogy and one either sees Jesus as the Way, the Truth and the Life by faith, on the basis of revelation, or one does not. There is no proving it. In fact, every attempt to prove Christ borders on idolatry because it calls God and his revelation before the bar of human reason to give an account of itself.

Barth becomes anti-Nazi and more ecumenical. During the 1930s, while teaching theology at Bonn, Barth became deeply involved in the anti-Nazi Confessing Church movement in Germany. In 1934 he helped write the Barmen Declaration, which stated that Jesus Christ is the only Lord for Christians and the church. Like the early Christian declaration "Jesus is Lord," Barmen constituted an implicit criticism of the German Christians' elevation of Hitler to the status of new messiah. Barth saw the German Christians' acceptance of Nazi ideology as a form of culture Christianity, the normal outcome of natural theology, and he gave great encouragement to those dissidents within the German state church who opposed the Nazis. Because of his refusal to give the Hitler salute at the opening of his lectures or sign the required loyalty oath to Hitler, the German government summarily dismissed Barth from his teaching position. He was then offered the position of professor of theology at the University of Basel in Switzerland, where he taught until his retirement and lived until his death.

Throughout his twenty-seven years of teaching at Basel, Barth worked tirelessly on *CD* and numerous other books and articles and preached regularly at the city jail. He also attained a reputation as a Mozart scholar. Students from around the world flocked to hear his lectures in Basel. He held a monthly English seminar for British and American students. In 1962 he retired from full-time teaching and immediately embarked on his first trip to the United States, where he lectured at several universities and seminaries. His appearance at the University of Chicago was especially note-

---

[16]See Keith L. Johnson, *Karl Barth and the* Analogia Entis (London: T & T Clark, 2010).

worthy as he entered into public conversation with both liberal and conservative theologians. According to a popular story (which this writer confirmed with an acquaintance who was present), at the end of his lecture a student stood and asked Barth if he could summarize his life's work in a single sentence. Many in the Rockefeller Chapel were shocked by the student's audacity, but Barth immediately responded (paraphrasing) that he could in the words of a song he learned at his mother's knee: "Jesus loves me this I know, for the Bible tells me so."[17] *Time* magazine honored Barth with a cover story, and the University of Chicago bestowed on him an honorary doctoral degree.

The final years of Barth's life were difficult as his health failed and he found himself the object of harsh criticism from both the theological left and right. He was dismayed by the rise of secular theology and the theology of Christian atheism (see chap. 7). But he was greatly encouraged by the changes in the Catholic Church at the Second Vatican Council (1962–1965). Barth died at his home in Basel sometime during the night of December 9, 1968, with the strains of Mozart playing on his phonograph in the background. His death marked the passing of the twentieth century's most influential theologian; he was to that century what Schleiermacher had been to the previous one.

Barth develops a theological method based on God's Word and faith alone. As we have already seen, Barth's theological method had both a negative and a positive pole. Negatively, he eschewed any form of natural theology and never tired of analyzing and trumpeting the ways in which it subtly and inevitably leads to the cultural captivity of the gospel:

> Christian natural theology very respectfully and in all humility re-casts revelation into a new form of its own devising. But for all that its behavior is so respectful and forbearing, for all that it subordinates itself so consciously and consistently, natural theology has already conquered it at the very outset, making revelation into non-revelation. This will certainly show itself in what it does with the revelation that has been absorbed and domesticated by it.[18]

---

[17]This story has been given many variations over the years. Some have even claimed it must be apocryphal. Wondering that myself, I asked a theologian who was there, and he affirmed the basic accuracy of the story and of Barth's famous answer.

[18]Karl Barth, *CD* II/1, *The Doctrine of God*, part 1, trans. T. H. L. Parker et al. (Edinburgh: T & T Clark, 1957), 139–40.

Barth attempted to demonstrate how this subversion of the gospel had taken place in classical Roman Catholic theology, classical liberal Protestant theology and even in the German Christians' openness to the ideology of Nazism. From the history of theology and his own discernment of the sovereignty of God in the gospel message Barth concluded that

> the logic of the matter demands that, even if we only lend our little finger to natural theology, there necessarily follows the denial of the revelation of God in Jesus Christ. A natural theology which does not strive to be the only master is not a natural theology. And to give it place at all is to put oneself, even if unwittingly, on the way which leads to this sole sovereignty.[19]

Barth summarized his own position by declaring, "The possibility of knowledge of God's Word lies in God's Word and nowhere else."[20] That statement expresses the positive as well as the negative side of his theological method. In spite of the unreadiness of humanity for God and the impossibility of true knowledge of God through reason, nature and culture, in his sovereign freedom and grace God has revealed himself in human history and made possible the miracle of knowledge of himself. The single event in history in which God is revealed, according to Barth, is the event of Jesus Christ. And in Christ God reveals himself, not merely information or a way of life. For Barth, this means that "the eternal God is to be known in Jesus Christ and not elsewhere."[21]

But how can one know that this is true? Barth responded, "The proof of faith consists in the proclamation of faith. The proof of the knowledge of the Word [of God] consists in confessing it."[22] In other words, faith in Jesus Christ as the self-revealed truth of God is self-authenticating. For the Christian this is the fundamental fact on which everything else rests and which itself rests on nothing else. Faith is a gift of God.

Barth explains the relation of the Bible to God's Word. For Barth, the only source of Christian theology is God's Word. This Word, however, exists in three forms or modes. The primary form is Jesus Christ and the entire

---

[19]Ibid., 173.
[20]Karl Barth, *CD* I/1, *The Doctrine of the Word of God*, part 1, trans. G. W. Bromiley (Edinburgh: T & T Clark, 1975), 222.
[21]Karl Barth, *CD* II/2, *The Doctrine of God*, part 2, trans. G. W. Bromiley et al. (Edinburgh: T & T Clark, 1957), 191–92.
[22]Barth, *CD* I/1, 241.

history of God's acts leading up to and surrounding his life, death and resurrection. This is revelation proper, the gospel itself. The second form is Scripture, the privileged witness to divine revelation. Finally, the church's proclamation of the gospel forms the third mode. The latter two forms are God's Word only in an instrumental sense, for they become God's Word when God uses them to reveal Jesus Christ. The Bible, consequently, is not statically God's Word; God's Word always has the character of event. In a sense, God's Word is God himself repeating his being in action. The Bible becomes God's Word: "The Bible is God's Word to the extent that God causes it to be His Word, to the extent that He speaks through it."[23]

Barth's view of Scripture caused much controversy and criticism. Liberals accused him of elevating the Bible to a special position that nearly equaled the traditional doctrine of verbal inspiration, thus removing it from historical critical inquiry. Conservatives assailed Barth's subordination of Scripture to a nonpropositional event of revelation and his explicit denial of its inerrancy, some going so far as to label his theology a "new modernism." Both criticisms fall near the target, but ultimately they miss the mark. On the one hand, Barth did deny Scripture the status given it in classical orthodoxy. He distinguished between the Bible and the Word of God, affirming that "what we have in the Bible are in any case human attempts to repeat and reproduce this Word of God in human words and thoughts and in specific human situations."[24] On the other hand, he warned sternly against the danger of concluding that Scripture's divine inspiration— its special status as privileged witness to Jesus Christ—is merely a human value judgment. Its inspiration, Barth said, is not a matter of our own estimation or mood or feeling about the Bible:

> Certainly it is not our faith which makes the Bible the Word of God. But we cannot safeguard the objectivity of the truth that it is the Word of God better than by insisting that it does demand our faith, and underlie our faith, that it is the substance and life of our faith. For in so doing we maintain that it is the truth of the living God, beyond which there is none other, the power of which we are not allowed to doubt in face of the forces of human subjectivity, which we have therefore to know and recognize as such. But if this is true, then it stands that we

---

[23]Ibid., 109.
[24]Ibid., 113.

have to understand the inspiration of the Bible as divine decision continually made in the life of the Church and in the life of its members.[25]

That the Bible is the Word of God, then, in no way depends on the subjective experience of the individual or on scholarly conclusions based on internal or external evidences. For Barth, the Bible is the Word of God because again and again, apart from any human decision or initiative, God uses it to produce the miracle of faith in Jesus Christ. The church's proper attitude toward Scripture is one of obedience and submission because the only authority above it is Jesus Christ himself. The Bible mediates Christ's authority to the church. Furthermore, the Bible has authority over the church, because "it is a record, indeed historically it is the oldest extant record, of the origin and therefore the basis and nature of the Church. . . . Therefore Holy Scripture has always in the Church a unique and in its way singular authority."[26]

Clearly, Barth held the Bible in high regard, placing it over every human authority while subordinating it to Jesus Christ himself. Throughout *CD* he treated the Bible as if it were verbally inspired and doctrinally infallible. He never appealed to some other authority over against Scripture. On the contrary, he boldly asserted that under Jesus Christ and in complete agreement with him it is normative for Christian belief:

> What finally counts is whether a dogmatics is scriptural. If it is not, then it will definitely be futile, for we shall definitely have to say regarding it that in it the church is distracted, i.e., it is busy about other matters and is not doing justice to the scientific task set for it by the problematic nature of its proclamation.[27]

Barth places Christ at the center and recovers the doctrine of the Trinity. The structure of Barth's theology is thoroughly Christocentric. The beginning, center and end of every doctrine is the event of Jesus Christ—his life, death, resurrection, exaltation and eternal union with God the Father. At every juncture of theology Barth asked, What is the proper understanding of this in the light of God's act in Jesus Christ? This Christocentric structure provides the coherence and unity that makes

---

[25]Karl Barth, *CD* I/2, *The Doctrine of the Word of God*, part 2, trans. G. T. Thomson and Harold Knight (Edinburgh: T & T Clark, 1956), 534-35.

[26]Ibid., 540.

[27]Barth, *CD* I/1, 287.

Barth's massive theology systematic. For him, Jesus Christ is the singular and unique self-revelation of God, the Word of God in person. From this basic affirmation of faith Barth deduced the deity of Jesus Christ: "revelation is the self-interpretation of this God. If we are dealing with His revelation, we are dealing with God Himself and not . . . with an entity distinct from Him."[28] One of Barth's axioms is that behind the actuality must lie the corresponding possibility.[29] Thus, if Jesus Christ is who faith says he is— the unsurpassable *self*-revelation of God—then he must be in some way identical with God himself and not merely an agent or representative of God. Behind and within the actuality of the event of revelation, then, lies its possibility—the triune God.

The doctrine of the Trinity had become largely otiose throughout the nineteenth century. Liberals did not know how to moralize it, so it slowly fell away from their theologies. Conservatives paid lip service to it but did nothing with it. It remained a mere doctrine that functioned hardly at all in their theologies. During the last few decades of the nineteenth century and the first two decades of the twentieth century it appeared that the doctrine of the Trinity was a relic of the orthodox past. Barth revived it. He understood the doctrine of the Trinity as the only possible Christian answer to the question, Who is the self-revealing God? He averred, "Thus it is God Himself, it is the same God in unimpaired unity, who according to the biblical understanding of revelation is the revealing God and the event of revelation and its effect on man."[30] In direct contradiction to Schleiermacher's approach, Barth placed the doctrine of the Trinity at the beginning of his theology. He argued, "The doctrine of the Trinity is what basically distinguishes the Christian doctrine of God as Christian, and therefore what already distinguishes the Christian concept of revelation as Christian, in contrast to all other possible doctrines of God or concepts of revelation."[31]

According to Barth, then, God's revelation is God himself. God *is* who he reveals himself to be. He *is* his revelation. Consequently, Jesus Christ, as the unique and unsurpassable self-revelation of God, is identical with God and

---

[28]Ibid., 311.
[29]Barth, *CD* II/1, 5.
[30]Barth, *CD* I/1, 309.
[31]Ibid., 301.

therefore both truly human and truly divine: "Jesus Christ is not a demigod. He is not an angel. Nor is he the ideal man."[32] Rather, "the reality of Jesus Christ is that God Himself in person is actively present in the flesh. God Himself in person is the Subject of a real human being and acting."[33] Barth made absolutely clear that in talking about Jesus Christ he was talking about the incarnation of the second "mode of being" (*Seinsweise*) of God. Borrowing from Dorner, he preferred "mode" over "person," because to modern ears the word *person* inevitably implies "self"—a subjective center of thought, will and action. For Barth, God has only one "self" or personality.[34] If Jesus Christ were another self or personality different from the Father he could not be the Father's *self*-revelation. In Barth's estimation, Father, Son and Holy Spirit are the divine ways of being that eternally subsist within God in absolute unity. Yet their distinction forms the precondition for God's revelation in Jesus Christ and his spiritual presence within the life of the church. Thus, when Barth said that "God is Jesus Christ and Jesus Christ is God"[35] he meant this to be understood within the context of the Trinity: Jesus Christ is the second mode of being of God, the reiteration of the Father's own personality.

Barth defines God as "the one who loves in freedom." Although the doctrine of the Trinity is the center and heart of Barth's doctrine of God, he devoted most of an entire volume to the attributes or "perfections" of God's being (*CD* 2/1). He defined the being of God as "the One Who Loves in Freedom" and divided the divine perfections into two categories, the perfections of divine love and those of divine freedom. This rubric replaced the traditional duality of God's absolute and relative attributes in Protestant orthodoxy. Barth claimed that God's love and freedom must be equally emphasized and balanced in order to do justice to the God of Jesus Christ. God's love is his freely chosen creation of fellowship between human beings and himself in Jesus Christ.[36] God wills to be ours and wills us to be his.[37] This is revealed above all in God's gracious identification with sinful humanity in the cross of Jesus Christ: "The Way of the Son of God into the Far

---

[32]Barth, *CD* 1/2, 151.
[33]Ibid.
[34]Barth, *CD* I/1, 350–51.
[35]Barth, *CD* II/1, 318.
[36]Ibid., 273.
[37]Ibid., 274.

Country."[38] The perfections that express this great love of God are grace and holiness, mercy and righteousness, patience and wisdom.[39]

Without in any way qualifying God's being as love, Barth proceeded to emphasize the freedom of God in this love. While God's love for the world is real and eternal, it is not necessary. God would still be love even if he did not choose to love the world.[40] Barth was clearly thinking of liberal theology, especially that influenced by Hegel, when he warned, "If we are not careful at this point we shall inevitably rob God of his deity."[41] God has perfect love and fellowship within himself—in his triune life—before and apart from his love for and fellowship with the world.[42] Only in this way can pantheism be avoided and God's love for the world be truly gracious, Barth argued. If God needed the world as the object of his love, then his love would not be purely gracious love and the world would be necessary to God's being. God would, then, be robbed of his deity.

In contradiction to the entire drift of nineteenth-century liberal theology, influenced as it was by Schleiermacher and Hegel, Barth affirmed God's absolute transcendence over the world, which he conceived in terms of God's freedom: "The loftiness, the sovereign majesty, the holiness, the glory—even what is termed the transcendence of God—what is it but this self-determination, this freedom, of the divine living and loving, the divine person?"[43] In fact, God is God only because he is absolute in his relation with the world: "God confronts all that is in supreme and utter independence, i.e., He would be no less and no different even if they all did not exist or existed differently."[44] The perfections of God's freedom are unity and omnipresence, constancy and omnipotence, eternity and glory—all of which Barth creatively reinterpreted from Protestant orthodoxy while remaining faithful to the biblical witness and Reformation theology.[45]

In spite of his emphasis on God's freedom, Barth did not interpret God's

---

[38]Barth, *CD* IV/1, *The Doctrine of Reconciliation*, part 1, trans. G. W. Bromiley (Edinburgh: T & T Clark, 1956), 157–210.
[39]Barth, *CD* II/1, 351–439.
[40]Ibid., 280.
[41]Ibid., 281.
[42]Ibid., 275. For Barth, this "before" of God's inner-trinitarian love is not temporal but logical.
[43]Ibid., 302.
[44]Ibid., 311.
[45]Ibid., 440–677.

love for humanity as a mere whim, as something that adds nothing to the divine life and about which God has little concern. Rather, God's fullness of life within himself "leans toward" unity with creaturely life.[46] Furthermore, God does not remain a prisoner of his freedom but freely chooses to go out of himself into real fellowship with the world that reaches its deepest unity in Jesus Christ. In fact, this desire and decision for union with creatures in Jesus Christ was for Barth the ground and basis of the creation of the world itself. God created the world for no other reason than to enter into covenant fellowship with it in the incarnation, death and resurrection of Jesus.[47] Thus, Barth recognized no hidden God behind the God of love revealed in Jesus. Even though God could have reserved his life and love for himself alone and withheld it from the world, "He does not will to be God without us . . . and creates us rather to share with us and therefore with our being and life and act His own incomprehensible being and life and act."[48]

Barth envisions a universal election in Jesus Christ. Barth was a Reformed theologian; he stood within the Protestant tradition stemming from the sixteenth-century Reformer Calvin. However, he was not a typical Calvinist, even though he strongly affirmed God's sovereignty. Barth developed a doctrine of election, predestination, that is Reformed without fitting into the traditional TULIP scheme (total depravity, unconditional election, limited atonement, irresistible grace, perseverance of the saints). Often, more traditional Reformed people do not know how to handle him; with them and with Calvin he embraced unconditional election, but against them and Calvin he taught universal atonement and at least potential universal salvation.

According to Barth, the supreme event of God's entry into human history is the cross of Jesus Christ, in which the Son of God goes into the "far country" to take onto himself the divine wrath and rejection so richly deserved by sinful humanity. Thus, Jesus Christ is the one elect and reprobate (condemned) man, all other humans being included in and represented by him: "The rejection which all men incurred, the wrath of God under which all men lie, the death all men must die, God in his love for men transfers from all eternity to Him in whom He loves and elects them, and whom He elects

---

[46]Ibid., 274.
[47]Barth, *CD* IV/1, 50.
[48]Ibid., 7.

at their head and in their place."[49] Like his theology in general, Barth's doctrine of election is Christocentric if not Christomonistic. Jesus Christ is for him the only object of God's election and damnation. No "horrible decree" of double predestination divides humanity into the saved and the damned. Rather, all are included in Jesus Christ, who is both the electing God and the elected human, and the benefits of his saving work extend to all. Only he suffers the rejection of God, and he is God rejecting himself: "in the election of Jesus Christ which is the eternal will of God, God has ascribed to man . . . election, salvation and life; and to Himself He has ascribed . . . reprobation, perdition and death."[50] Thus, for Barth, predestination means that from eternity God decided to acquit sinful humanity at great cost to himself.[51]

But to whom does God's acquittal extend? Barth made clear that Jesus Christ is the *only* truly rejected person and that all humans are elect in him.[52] People may try to live godless lives in rejection of God, but "their desire and undertaking were nullified by God before the world began. . . . What is laid up for man is eternal life in fellowship with God."[53] Does this amount to the doctrine of *apokatastasis*, universal reconciliation? In his written responses to this question Barth refused to give an unequivocal answer: "I do not teach it, but I also do not not teach it."[54] Nevertheless, we can guess what the answer must be. As Hans Urs von Balthasar pointed out, "It is clear from Barth's presentation of the doctrine of election that universal salvation is not only possible but inevitable. The only definitive reality is grace, and any condemnatory judgment has to be merely provisional."[55]

Barth argues with Brunner about natural theology. One of the most unfortunate events in twentieth-century theology had to be the argument between Barth and his counterpart in Zurich, Emil Brunner. Brunner was professor of theology at the University of Zurich from 1924 until 1955. He was one of the original neo-orthodox, dialectical theologians whose voluminous theological output was nearly as influential as Barth's during the 1930s and

---

[49]Barth, *CD* II/2, 123.

[50]Ibid., 163.

[51]Ibid., 167.

[52]Ibid., 319–20.

[53]Ibid., 319.

[54]Quoted by Eberhard Jüngel in *Karl Barth*, 44–45. For Barth's direct statements about *apokatastasis* and universalism, see *CD* II/2, 417–18, and *The Humanity of God*, 61–62.

[55]Balthasar, *The Theology of Karl Barth*, 163.

1940s. During the 1950s, however, his star waned as Barth's waxed. Eventually Barth eclipsed Brunner in terms of fame and influence. Brunner published a three-volume systematic theology with the overarching title *Dogmatics* (1946–1960). It was used as the foundational text in seminary courses in systematic theology throughout Great Britain and the United States for many years and is still in print in the second decade of the twenty-first century.

Brunner had to emphasize his differences from Barth in order to distinguish himself from the Basel theologian. The two stressed their differences so emphatically that they fell out of friendship and reunited for a brief meeting only at the behest of American students near the ends of their lives. The cause of their alienation was Barth's caustic response to Brunner's 1934 essay "Nature and Grace." There Brunner took Barth to task for rejecting not only natural theology but also general revelation. Brunner wrote:

> The Word of God could not reach a man who had lost his consciousness of God entirely. A man without conscience cannot be struck by the call "Repent ye and believe the Gospel." What the natural man knows of God, of the law and of his own dependence upon God, may be very confused and distorted. But even so it is the necessary, indispensable point of contact for divine grace.[56]

Against Barth, Brunner presented a view of general revelation that he believed was fully consistent with the New Testament and the Protestant Reformers, especially Calvin and Luther. He eschewed any notion of a "natural knowledge of God" in the sense of proofs of the existence of God while maintaining that the image of God in humanity—the human person's capacity for receiving God's Word—remained in spite of the fall.[57] Recognition of such a bare, minimal awareness of God, Brunner believed, is indispensable to the missions of church and theology, because it calls them to articulate the faith in a way that can be understood. While human thoughts and questions cannot determine the content of the gospel, they must be taken into account in determining the manner of its proclamation.[58]

Barth responded to Brunner's essay with a thunderous "Nein!" ("no!"). That was, in fact, the title of his published response (*Nein!* 1934). He wrote,

---

[56]Emil Brunner, *Natural Theology, Comprising "Nature and Grace" and the Reply "No!" by Dr. Karl Barth*, trans. Peter Fraenkel (London: Geoffrey Bles, The Centenary Press, 1946), 32–33.
[57]Ibid., 58.
[58]Ibid., 59.

"I have to reply with a 'No!' to Brunner and the whole chorus of his friends and disciples and those who share his opinions."[59] The tone of Barth's essay was harsh, perhaps because he was at that time teaching in Germany and struggling with the Nazi temptation into which many German Christians were falling, as he saw it, because of their openness to natural theology. Barth accused Brunner of giving aid to that "theology of compromise," which was leading to the subversion of the German church to Nazi ideology.[60] Furthermore, he accused Brunner of implicitly denying salvation by grace through faith alone and falling back into the Catholic or (worse yet) the neo-Protestant (liberal) theology of salvation by advocating a cooperation between grace and human effort.[61] It is true that Brunner was much closer to the synergistic view of salvation espoused by Arminianism, although he would surely reject that label. In his *Dogmatics* he rejected unconditional election and affirmed a grace-enabled free response to the gospel on the part of the person who is saved.

Turning to an analogy, Barth asked about Brunner's view:

> If a man had just been saved from drowning by a competent swimmer, would it not be very unsuitable if he proclaimed the fact that he was a man and not a lump of lead as his "capacity for being saved"? Unless he could claim to have helped the man who saved him by a few strokes or the like! Can Brunner mean that?[62]

Barth rejected Brunner's minimal natural theology (which probably should not even be called that), which amounted to nothing more than acknowledgment of a point of contact for the gospel in every person, as a definite turn away from the gospel of grace and toward a compromise with the natural thinking of modern humans. The gospel, Barth asserted, stands in no need of any point of contact other than the one created by the Holy Spirit, which is always a miracle.[63] And the question concerning the how of proclamation and of theological and ecclesiastical activity should be rejected at the outset, he added, because "only the theology and church of the

---

[59]Ibid., 72.
[60]Ibid., 71–72.
[61]Ibid., 90.
[62]Ibid., 79.
[63]Ibid., 121.

antichrist can profit from it. The Evangelical Church and Evangelical theology would only sicken and die of it."[64]

Brunner was deeply and personally injured by Barth's harsh attack. Throughout his career he continually referred to it, attempting to clarify his own position and to criticize Barth's. In 1949 he wrote in the first volume of his *Dogmatics*:

> Barth, in the defense of his main concern—with which we are in entire and unhesitating agreement—in his great "Spring-cleaning" has cleared out and thrown away a great deal that had nothing to do with Natural Theology, but was an integral part of the truth of the Bible; owing to the one-sided way in which he has defended his cause, he has injured the legitimate claims of Biblical theology, and has thus created unnecessary hindrances for the promulgation of his ideas.[65]

Although the two giants of dialectical, neo-orthodox theology became reconciled, the rift they created (for which Barth surely bears most of the blame) will be remembered as one of the most unfortunate and ironic conflicts in twentieth-century theology. One result of it was Brunner's attempt to search out and expose every actual or potential heresy he could detect in Barth's theology.

A primary object of Brunner's criticism was Barth's doctrine of election, which he considered highly speculative and saw as leading inexorably into universalism. Perhaps he was attempting to return some of Barth's venom when he wrote that his doctrine of election "is in absolute opposition, not only to the whole of ecclesiastical tradition, but—and this alone is the final objection to it—to the clear teaching of the New Testament."[66] Brunner worked out his own doctrine of divine election in conscious opposition to both Barth and the classical Calvinist doctrine of double predestination. The problem with both, he averred, is that in speculating into the eternal background of God's gracious election they move beyond anything stated or directly implied in divine revelation.[67] Brunner rejected any "logically

---

[64]Ibid., 128.
[65]Emil Brunner, *Dogmatics: The Christian Doctrine of God*, trans. Olive Wyon, 3 vols. (London: Lutterworth, 1949), 1:236.
[66]Ibid., 1:349.
[67]Ibid., 1:312.

satisfying theory" of election[68] in favor of what he considered a thoroughly dialectical, and therefore biblical, understanding:

> To believe in Jesus Christ and to be of the elect is one and the same thing, just as not to believe in Jesus Christ and not to be of the elect is the same thing. There is no other selection than this, there is no other number than that which is constituted by the fact of believing and not believing.[69]

Barth sparks controversy and leaves a legacy of lively debate. For whatever reason, Barth's theology has been the subject of investigation, examination and even sharp controversy well into the twenty-first century. One of Barth's interpreters wrote that "anyone who risks an appraisal of Barth's theology is surrounded by dangers."[70] Barth's theological career began with controversy, and it comes therefore as no surprise that controversy and debate have surrounded his theological method and proposals. Heirs of liberal theology that he so vehemently rejected have often dismissed his approach as fideistic, as requiring modern people to sacrifice reason and return to the tutelage of religious authority.[71] Barth's admirers, however, have responded that those critics have not been very successful in answering Barth's accusations that their approach to theology leads to the cultural subversion of the gospel.

Barth argued that his theological method was truly scientific even if it was based on faith. According to him, every discipline is scientific in its own way depending on its object. Theology does not need to be scientific in the same way that, say, physics is scientific. Nor does psychology or political science. Theology is the study of God, and its source is God's Word. It is scientific when it is faithful to its source and object. Barth was all about recovering the autonomy of theology from having constantly to adjust to the latest whims and fancies of modern philosophy. He was himself modern, however, in rejecting a kind of literalistic approach to the Bible. For ex-

---

[68]Ibid., 1:353.

[69]Ibid., 1:320.

[70]G. C. Berkouwer, *The Triumph of Grace in the Theology of Karl Barth*, trans. Harry R. Boer (Grand Rapids: Eerdmans, 1956), 389.

[71]L. Harold DeWolf, *The Religious Revolt Against Reason* (New York: Harper & Row, 1949). Another, not liberal, critic of Barth's approach to theology is Wolfhart Pannenberg, who perceived it as "ghettoizing" theology by engaging in special pleading. See *Theology and the Philosophy of Science*, trans. Francis McDonagh (Philadelphia: Westminster Press, 1976), 265–76.

ample, he labeled the first few chapters of Genesis as "saga"—neither literal
history nor myth but narrative recounting of events in prehistory. But the
narrative is not like modern history-telling. It is filled with primitive symbolism and to us obscure references. This was one of his ways of avoiding
conflict with the natural sciences; he did not care about conflict with the
philosophies of the Enlightenment. To him they were, by and large, idolatrous. Barth could sound like a fundamentalist when doing combat with
liberalism and like a liberal when countering fundamentalism.

Overall, Barth's theological method succeeds in preserving theology's autonomy over against other disciplines that would dominate it. Theology, for
him, remains irreducibly the science of God's Word. However, his refusal of
every kind of rational justification of revelation leads theology beyond autonomy into isolation. If there are no intelligible bridges connecting theology
with other disciplines or with common human experience, how can Christian
belief appear to outsiders as anything but esoteric? It is one thing for Barth and
his followers to reject liberal theology's reduction of Christian belief to what
can be anticipated within the horizon of human experience; it is another thing
for him to eliminate any connection between belief and experience. South
African theologian Wentzel van Huyssteen summarized this problem well:

> Barth is justified in rejecting the reduction of the object of theology to man-
> kind's religious consciousness. . . . But the assumed axiomatic datum of God
> and His revelation offers no escape . . . because the positive quality thus given
> to revelation can offer no alternative to subjectivism in theology. A positiv-
> istic theology of revelation that adopts a highly esoteric method makes it
> extremely difficult to convince others that the basic tenets of theology—God,
> revelation, Holy Scripture, inspiration, etc.—are not the constructs of sub-
> jective whim, whether personal or directed by an influential tradition.[72]

Another criticism of Barth's theology is its alleged christological constriction. Even some of Barth's sympathetic critics used this term to describe
the extreme concentration on Jesus Christ present throughout his entire theology. Not only did Barth make Jesus Christ the center and heart of his theology, thereby being Christocentric, but he also restricted knowledge of and

---

[72]Wentzel van Huyssteen, *Theology and the Justification of Faith: Constructing Theories in Systematic Theology*, trans. H. F. Snijders (Grand Rapids: Eerdmans, 1989), 22.

about God to what is revealed in Christ. Balthasar described Barth's theology as an intellectual hourglass "where God and man meet in the center through Jesus Christ. There is no other point of encounter between the top and bottom portions of the glass."[73] The problem with such a move is that it leads to the denial of any general revelation, that form of revelation which seems to form the core of Paul's argument in Romans 1.

"Christological constriction" is perhaps too strong a term to serve as a fair description of Barth's theology. He preferred "Christological concentration." Certainly he did not deny the distinction between the Son, the Father and the Holy Spirit. And by no means did he blur the distinction between Christ and the world. Furthermore, the term is too polemical to do justice to Barth's contribution in bringing Christ back into the center of Christian thought, where he belongs. Nevertheless the Swiss theologian's extreme concentration on Christology gives his theology the appearance of being one-sided and of neglecting the roles of the Father, the Spirit and human beings in salvation history. American evangelical theologian Donald Bloesch (1928–2010) complained of Barth's "objectivism" of salvation. That is, from his perspective, Barth concentrated so heavily on Christ's objective work of salvation for all people that human decision and participation suffered neglect. Thus, according to Bloesch, Barth's christological concentration leads him to neglect the subjective side of salvation:

> It is our contention that Barth does not finally succeed in holding the objective and subjective dimensions of salvation in true dialectical relation. It seems that not only is the objective prior to the subjective but that the real decision has already been "resolved and actually accomplished in the eternal will of God."[74]

Other areas of possible weakness in Barth's theology that have been the focus of criticism are his treatment of Scripture and his doctrine of the Trinity. (Criticism of his doctrine of election has already been discussed.) Barth denied the inerrancy of Scripture. This is a problem for conservative theologians who wonder how he could spin out such a detailed system of theology as appears in *CD* without the Bible as his authority. And if it was

---

[73]Balthasar, *Theology of Karl Barth*, 170.
[74]Donald G. Bloesch, *Jesus Is Victor! Karl Barth's Doctrine of Salvation* (Nashville: Abingdon, 1976), 106.

his authority for faith and practice, how could it be filled with errors? Also, how does one move from a nonpropositional revelation and a Bible that "becomes the Word of God" to a holistic system of doctrine?[75] Simply stated, critics ask how his assertion of tension between God's Word and the doctrinal propositions of the Bible lends itself to such a highly developed biblical systematic theology. Apparently Barth practiced a higher doctrine of Scripture than he expressed.

One of Barth's greatest contributions to twentieth-century theology is his recovery of the doctrine of the Trinity, yet his handling of it has raised serious questions about its orthodoxy. Some critics argue that it reduces God to a single subject by identifying God's one essence with his person and by employing the term "modes of being" for the trinitarian distinctions.[76] In other words, it appears modalistic. This criticism has some validity in relation to the first volume of *CD*, in which Barth derived the triunity of God from the concept of revelation itself and emphatically identified God's personhood with his single essence or nature.[77] Yet even there he rejected modalism by affirming "the ultimate reality of the three modes of being in the essence of God above and behind which there is nothing higher."[78] In later volumes of *CD* Barth made clear his rejection of modalism and asserted the eternal and irreducible distinction between Father, Son and Holy Spirit by affirming an order of obedience within the eternal being of God while rejecting any subordinationism.[79]

Why is Barth included in a book about modern theology, besides the fact that his career happened in the time period and culture governed by the modern ethos? In truly dialectical fashion, Barth was both modern and antimodern. He certainly was not premodern. He was conversant with all the developments in science and philosophy associated with modernity. He could probe and expose the weaknesses in theologies that accommodated to modernity. In a way he was obsessed with modernity and especially with expunging its anthropocentrism from theology. He was not afraid of the acids of

[75]Klaas Runia, *Karl Barth's Doctrine of Holy Scripture* (Grand Rapids: Eerdmans, 1962), 174–88.
[76]Wolfhart Pannenberg, "Die Subjektivität Gottes und die Trinitätslehre," *Grundfragen systematischer Theologie, Band 2* (Göttingen: Vandenhoek & Ruprecht, 1977).
[77]Barth, *CD* I/1, 348–68, esp. 350.
[78]Ibid., 382.
[79]Barth, *CD* IV/1, 200–201.

modernity, but he developed a theology that was by and large immune to them. His theology has little to say about the workings of nature or cosmology or even epistemology in any philosophical sense. It is strictly a theology from above, a theology of the *kerygma*, the gospel, the Word of God, and not a theology of correlation that attempts to connect Christianity with the modern mind. And yet, his theology powerfully spoke into the profound disillusionment of modern people about the modern mind. It spoke to the hunger for transcendence and salvation left in the wake of the cultural crises of the twentieth century. It was and remains a powerfully antimodern modern theology.[80]

5.B. RUDOLF BULTMANN EXISTENTIALIZES AND DEMYTHOLOGIZES CHRISTIANITY

In 1941 world-renowned New Testament scholar Rudolf Bultmann published an essay that created a firestorm of controversy among theologians and church leaders throughout Europe and North America. And it drove a stake into the heart of his relationship with friends and colleagues, including Barth, who were dialectical theologians. Its title was "The New Testament and Mythology." In it the German scholar demonstrated his deep commitment to modernity, existentialism and the gospel of Jesus Christ, at least as he understood that gospel. According to Bultmann,

> It is impossible to use electric light and the wireless and to avail ourselves of modern medical and surgical discoveries, and at the same time to believe in the New Testament world of spirits and miracles. We may think we can manage it in our own lives, but to expect others to do so is to make the Christian faith unintelligible and unacceptable to the modern world.[81]

He continued by explaining that the modern *Weltanschauung* (worldview) makes it impossible to believe in much that one finds in the

---

[80]Such a paradoxical, counterintuitive claim does not sit well with everyone. I believe, however, that it well expresses the dialectical relationship with modernity one finds in Barth. Without doubt he was a modern theologian reconstructing theology in light of what he considered the best of modern thought without making modern science or philosophy a norm for doctrinal truth. Modernity formed the context of Barth's theology, and his attitude and handling of it was ambivalent. No doubt debates will rage for years about Barth's appropriations of modernity and modernity's influences on his theology. See, for example, Bruce McCormack, *Orthodox and Modern: Studies in the Theology of Karl Barth* (Grand Rapids: Baker Academic, 2008).

[81]Rudolf Bultmann, "The New Testament and Mythology," in *Kerygma and Myth*, ed. Hans Werner Bartsch (New York: Harper & Row, 1961), 5.

New Testament including everything supernatural. The only criticism of the New Testament, he argued, that is theologically relevant is "that which arises *necessarily* out of the situation of modern man."[82] And what arises out of the presupposition that must drive that relevant New Testament criticism? It is "the view of the world which has been moulded by modern science and the modern conception of human nature as a self-subsistent unity immune from the interference of supernatural powers."[83]

Bultmann demythologizes the New Testament. Bultmann labeled the supernatural worldview of the New Testament as "myth" and explained that myth does not mean fable or fantasy. For him, myth is a technical term for the attempt to express in nonliteral fashion "man's understanding of himself in the world in which he lives."[84] Ancient people, including the authors of the New Testament, expressed their self-understandings (their place in the universe, the meaning of life) in supernatural images. Modern people cannot believe those images literally. "The real purpose of myth," he argued, "is to speak of a transcendent power which controls the world and man, but that purpose is impeded and obscured [for modern people] by the terms in which it is expressed [in the New Testament]."[85] So, it is the job of the modern biblical scholar and theologian, Bultmann asserted, to demythologize the gospel message of the New Testament. This is what shocked his listeners and readers. He expressed this hermeneutical project succinctly:

> The importance of the New Testament mythology lies not in its imagery but in the understanding of existence which it enshrines. The real question is whether this understanding of existence is true. Faith claims that it is, and faith ought not to be tied down to the imagery of New Testament mythology.[86]

Instead, faith ought to uncover the underlying message about human existence hidden within the mythology but without discarding the mythology. Unlike some liberal theologians and biblical scholars, Bultmann did not want to strip away the husk (mythology, the supernatural) to discover the kernel (timeless essence) within it. His German word for his project is *Ent-*

---

[82]Ibid., 7.
[83]Ibid.
[84]Ibid., 10.
[85]Ibid., 11.
[86]Ibid.

mythologizierung; its only English translation, an unfortunate one, is "demythologizing." But the German does not imply a stripping away or discarding; it implies interpretation, as in getting inside the myths to discover their true meaning.

If Bultmann had been a nineteenth-century liberal theologian, perhaps the reaction to his essay would not have been so harsh. But he was widely perceived as being a key member of the relatively new dialectical theology, neo-orthodoxy movement, launched by Barth and Brunner. Neither of them had any problem with the supernatural, although they did not take every miracle story in the Bible literally. Bultmann's essay seemed to be a declaration of war on all literalism, and it was difficult for many of his critics to understand how he could claim to believe the Bible is in some special way God's Word while rejecting everything supernatural as myth. He did not reject it, but he did reject its literal interpretation. Bultmann, however, would ask if anyone in the modern world takes everything supernatural literally. For example, surely the disciples standing on the Mount of Olives watching Jesus ascend into heaven thought he went up. That is, to them, heaven was "up." That is why his ascension is expressed as ascent rather than disappearing. Now nobody thinks heaven is literally up. So everyone, consciously or unconsciously, demythologizes the ascension story, believing that Jesus must have disappeared out of their sight, or perhaps he did ascend into the clouds and then disappeared into that other dimension we call heaven.

Bultmann believed we must press on consistently with this to demythologize all supernatural events and beings in the Bible; none of them can be taken literally, not even the bodily resurrection and empty tomb of Jesus. That is what upset more conservative Christians, including Barth. But Bultmann's defense was that he was not denying the resurrection any more than others deny the ascension. He was interpreting it nonliterally so that modern people can understand it. Toward the end of his controversial essay, he explained:

> The resurrection itself is not an event of past history. All that historical criticism can establish is the fact that the first disciples came to believe in the resurrection. The historian can perhaps to some extent account for that faith from the personal intimacy which the disciples had with Jesus during his earthly life, and so reduce the resurrection appearances to a series of

subjective visions. But the historical problem is not of interest to Christian belief in the resurrection. For the historical event of the rise of the Easter faith means for us what it meant for the first disciples—namely, the self-attestation of the risen Lord, the act of God in which the redemptive event of the cross is completed.[87]

"But the historical problem is not of interest to Christian belief." What Bultmann was saying was that whether or not Jesus rose from the dead is irrelevant to faith. And he already made clear by his denial of the supernatural that he did not believe in the bodily resurrection or empty tomb; these stories are myths that evolved among early Christians to express the special nature of Jesus and his cross. But he was saying something even more. For him, outer history, events in the physical universe, other than the cross of Christ (there is where his conservatism shows) bear no spiritual meaning; only events in inner history, in the inner lives of people, their self-understanding, bear spiritual meaning.

In another place, *Jesus Christ and Mythology* (1958), Bultmann explained demythologizing even more concisely. It is not about destroying the myths of the New Testament, nor is it about denying anything. Rather, it is the recognition that

> it is the Word of God which calls man into genuine freedom, into free obedience, and the task of de-mythologizing has no other purpose but to make clear the call of the Word of God. It will interpret the Scripture, asking for the deeper meaning of mythological conceptions and freeing the Word of God from a by-gone world-view.[88]

Bultmann's critics, including Barth, can hardly be blamed, however, for thinking he was denying things essential to the gospel, most importantly the bodily resurrection of Jesus. But Bultmann was trying to dispel the suspicion on the parts of many mid-twentieth-century scholars, Christian and non-Christian alike, that neo-orthodoxy, dialectical theology, was just a new form of supernaturalism and therefore premodern and therefore untenable for modern people. Bultmann argued that he was trying to remove the "false stumbling block" (supernaturalism) so that the "true stumbling

---

[87]Ibid., 42.
[88]Rudolf Bultmann, *Jesus Christ and Mythology* (New York: Charles Scribner, 1958), 43.

block" could be heard by modern people. So, what did he believe is the core message within the mythology of the New Testament?

> This, then, is the deeper meaning of the mythological preaching of Jesus—to be open to God's future which is really imminent for every one of us; to be prepared for this future which can come as a thief in the night when we do not expect it; to be prepared, because this will be a judgment on all men who have bound themselves to this world and are not free, not open to God's future.[89]

The reason for this somewhat lengthy introduction to Bultmann is to explain immediately why he is important to this story of modern theology even though he was a New Testament scholar and not a theologian as such. His impact on theology was enormous; he seemed to many liberal-leaning Christians to make it possible again to be thoroughly modern and Christian at the same time. The old liberalism was virtually dead; this was a new kind of liberalism not tied to the old ideas of the essence of Christianity as God-consciousness or ethics. For Bultmann, the essence of Christianity, as will be seen, is the cross of Jesus Christ and the preaching of that cross that transforms people from inauthentic to authentic existence—concepts that spoke powerfully to many people steeped in existentialism between the two world wars. Why does Bultmann belong in a section on neo-orthodoxy or dialectical theology? Simply because he does not fit anywhere else and his sole concern in theology was with the Word of God and faith. Therefore, insofar as neo-orthodoxy or dialectical theology is also kerygmatic theology, as contrasted with the older liberal theology inspired by Kant and Hegel (in different ways), Bultmann fits here because his whole concern was with the kerygma as he understood it.

Bultmann becomes the twentieth century's leading New Testament scholar. Bultmann was born in 1884, the first son of a Lutheran pastor in a small town not far from Hamburg, Germany. One grandfather was a missionary in Africa; the other was a Lutheran pastor in Baden. He studied theology first at Tübingen, the crossroads of German theology where so many modern theologians studied at least for a while. Later he studied at Berlin and finally at Marburg, both great centers of academic theology. At Berlin he was influenced by Harnack and at Marburg by the other leading

---

[89]Ibid., 31–32.

liberal theologian Herrmann. His prowess in biblical studies was early recognized by his teachers and especially his main mentor, Johannes Weiss
(1863–1914), perhaps the leading liberal New Testament scholar of the late
nineteenth century.[90] He was ordained into the association of free Protestants, a group of German churches not formally part of the state church. He
began his teaching career at Marburg in 1912 but in 1916 moved to Breslau
in Prussia (now in Poland), where he stayed until 1920. His field of research
and instruction was New Testament.

Bultmann's first book, *The History of the Synoptic Tradition*, that launched
the discipline of form criticism, was published in 1921. Eventually he moved
back to Marburg, which he referred to as his "scientific home," there to
remain teaching New Testament until his retirement in 1951. He was active
in scholarship well into his retirement and lived a very long life, being the
last of the twentieth century's giants of theology to die (1976). His major
published works include the two-volume *Theology of the New Testament*
(1948–1953) and *History and Eschatology: The Presence of Eternity* (1954–
1955). The latter comprised his Gifford Lectures, the most prestigious
regular theological lecture series in the world. By his own confession, he
associated himself with the new dialectical theology of Barth, Brunner,
Gogarten and Thurneysen in the 1920s. What attracted him to it was that it

> rightly recognized, as over against the liberal theology out of which I had
> come, that the Christian faith is not a phenomenon of a history of religion,
> that it does not rest on a "religious *a priori*" (Troeltsch), and that therefore
> theology does not have to look upon it as a phenomenon of religious or cul-
> tural history. It seemed to me that, as over against such a view, the new the-
> ology had correctly seen that Christian faith is the answer to the word of the
> transcendent God that encounters man and that theology has to deal with
> this word and the man who has been encountered by it.[91]

This did not mean, however, that he rejected liberal theology entirely. He
remained with the liberal theologians in studying the New Testament
through the historical-critical method. That, and his increasing use of exis-

---

[90]These biographical details are taken from Bultmann's 1957 "Autobiographical Reflections," in
Existence and Faith: Shorter Writings of Rudolf Bultmann, ed. and trans. Schubert Ogden
(Cleveland: World, 1960), 283–88.
[91]Ibid., 288.

tentialism in hermeneutics, especially his demythologizing project, led eventually to his break from the neo-orthodox movement.

Perhaps most important for understanding Bultmann's theology is the influence of Martin Heidegger, his Marburg colleague and an existentialist philosopher. Bultmann admitted that Heidegger became "of decisive significance" for him. In Heidegger's philosophy he found "the conceptuality in which it is possible to speak adequately of human existence and therefore also of the existence of the believer."[92] Heidegger is best known for his extremely difficult *Being and Time* (1927), one of the most influential volumes of existentialist philosophy of the twentieth century. It represented a form of atheist existentialism and focused on the concept of authentic existence as contrasted with inauthentic existence. Kierkegaard stands in its background, but Heidegger's atheism distinguished him from the Danish philosopher-theologian. For Heidegger, there are two ways of being in the world for the individual (and the individual is what matters most): authentic existence and inauthentic existence. Authentic existence means freedom; inauthentic existence means being determined by others. Bultmann found there analogies to Christian concepts of sin and salvation and borrowed heavily from Heidegger's philosophy for his expression of the gospel for modern people.

Bultmann lived through the Nazi era and held onto his teaching position at Marburg while others, considered disloyal to Germany, were expelled from their posts by the Nazis. However, unlike Heidegger, Bultmann did not join the Nazi party or express any sympathy with its ideology or goals. He joined the Confessing Church movement when it began in 1934 and signed the Barmen Declaration. He referred to the German condition during the 1930s and early 1940s as "the Nazi terror." His brother died in a concentration camp. According to his autobiographical reflections, "when the Allies . . . finally marched in [to Marburg], I, along with many friends, greeted this end of the Nazi rule as a liberation."[93] Not all German theologians did. Unlike those who collaborated with the Nazis, Bultmann was allowed to continue teaching in the university. Heidegger was not.

Bultmann limits God's special activity to inner history. It is notoriously difficult to know where to begin describing Bultmann's theology, as he was

---

[92]Ibid.
[93]Ibid., 285.

not a systematic theologian. He was not even a doctrinal thinker per se; his field of study was New Testament and his main interest was hermeneutics. But for him hermeneutics meant discovering the meaning of the New Testament for modern Western people, people whose lives and thoughts are shaped by the Enlightenment and scientific revolutions. To borrow a concept from a hermeneutical philosopher, Hans Georg Gadamer, Bultmann was trying to "fuse the two horizons" of the New Testament and modern culture; he was trying to bring them together so that modern people could understand the true message of the New Testament. Demythologizing is a general term for his method of doing that.

One place to begin in trying to understand Bultmann's theology, or contribution to modern theology, is with his ideas about history. Nineteenth- and early twentieth-century liberal theologians had become obsessed with Christianity and history. Many of them were involved in the search for the historical Jesus, which meant distinguishing the real Jesus from the legends about him built up by his first-century followers who wrote the New Testament. This was widely thought by liberals to be a way to rescue Christianity from at least some of the acids of modernity. What can a rational investigation of the historical Jesus discover about him? Then, once that question is answered, Christianity is the religion of that Jesus based on his real teachings. Harnack was a perfect example of that approach; for him the essence of Christianity is believing and following the simple teachings of Jesus about the fatherhood of God, the infinite value of the human soul and the kingdom of God and its coming (without anything supernatural or apocalyptic).

In spite of his liberal tendencies, Bultmann regarded that project of basing faith on objective historical research a dead end. For one thing, the searchers came up with nothing reliable to be known about the Jesus of history divorced from the faith commitments of the New Testament writers. This was one of the crises facing liberal Protestant theology around the time of the First World War. Albert Schweitzer, missionary to Africa, expert on Bach and theologian (1875–1965), published his devastating critique of the search for the historical Jesus titled *The Quest for the Historical Jesus* in 1906. He argued that very little could be known about Jesus apart from faith in him and that what could be known had nothing to do with the liberal questers who wanted to turn Jesus into a first-century liberal theologian. Bultmann came to be convinced by Schweitzer's criticism and argued, based on his own historical-critical research into the Gospels, that virtually nothing can be known about the real Jesus from historical research alone, divorced from faith.

But Bultmann did not leave matters there, in skepticism. He was skeptical about history, but he believed very strongly in the Christ of faith. In order to understand that distinction in Bultmann (other scholars had their own versions of it), it is essential to understand his idea of God's action, history and faith and how they are related to each other. For him, following Heidegger, history is not merely the science of facts pursued in a nonpersonal, detached way. Rather, truly significant historical knowledge is always existential knowledge; it is personal and involves decision. Important to this idea of history is a distinction between two senses of history. The German language helps make this distinction. *Historie* is what happened in the past as it can be studied scientifically with detached, neutral research.[94] It is the realm of bare facts, with as little interpretation as possible. *Geschichte* is the past approached from the perspective of the question of human existence, that is, authentic and inauthentic existence. This makes past events no longer merely past but also, in a certain sense, present because they disclose one's personal being. Both *Historie* and *Geschichte* can be synonyms in ordinary German language, but Bultmann distinguished them this way. Another way of putting it is that *Historie* is outer history while *Geschichte* is inner history.

This distinction can be illustrated by means of a television series episode from the 1980s. In *Newhart*, the character played by comedian Bob Newhart ("Bob") owned a quaint New England inn. His handyman was played by comedian Tom Posten ("George"). Bob discovered that an old barn behind the inn once sheltered George Washington's horse, so he planned to

---

[94]This all-important distinction between *Historie* and *Geschichte* is discussed in several places in Bultmann's writings. One is Rudolf Bultmann, *The Presence of Eternity: History and Eschatology* (New York: Harper and Brothers, 1957), 117–22. It is explained in Norman Young, *History and Existential Theology* (Philadelphia: Westminster Press, 1969), 23–24. Bultmann's distinction was inspired by an earlier German theologian, Martin Kähler (1835–1912), whose small but influential book *The So-Called Historical Jesus and the Historic, Biblical Christ* (1892) first made use of it.

refurbish it and use it as an expensive annex to the inn with rooms for guests. On hearing of Bob's plan, George became agitated and refused to cooperate with the renovations. Finally, Bob found out from George that when he was a little boy and his father was the inn's handyman under a different owner, the barn was his favorite playground. He spent some of the best hours of his life frolicking in it. To Bob the barn was *Historie* only; to George it was also and more importantly *Geschichte*. This is a homely illustration of the difference between Bultmann's two kinds of history; for him it has to do with salvation. But the illustration helps understand that a single historical event or artifact can have very different meanings. One is objective and factual whereas the other is subjective and personal.

Bultmann believed that *Historie* has no meaning; meaning is found only in *Geschichte*. That is especially true if by "meaning" one intends significance for one's personal existence as either authentic or inauthentic. Such meaning cannot be found by observation of past events from some neutral vantage point. Rather, one must begin to find meaning with one's personal history. What is of greatest importance is personal, individual, inner history, that is, personal authentic existence. Furthermore, the present moment in *Geschichte* is the moment of decision between inauthentic existence, being a prisoner of the past, for example, and authentic existence, being open to the future. For Bultmann, authentic Christian existence is not focusing on past events in *Historie* but grasping the present in *Geschichte* as decision to trust God as one faces into the unknown future.

Another important point about the distinction between *Historie* and *Geschichte* is that for Bultmann, God does not "act" in *Historie* but only in *Geschichte*.[95] "Act of God" here refers to God's gracious gift of authentic existence; it is not tied to anything supernatural or any event in past history, *Historie*, except the cross of Jesus. But viewed from outside of faith, even the cross cannot be seen as *Geschichte* or as God's decisive act for the individ-

---

[95]The concept of "act of God" is an especially complex one in modern theology. As a good Lutheran, Bultmann believed, as did Luther, that, in some sense, everything real is an act of God because God is the all-determining reality. He was not a deist. However, the "acts of God" he was most interested in are those in which God grants authentic existence to people, saving acts. The particular issue was, for him, whether miracles such as the resurrection of Jesus Christ are special acts of God in the older sense, which he rejected, of supernatural divine interventions into nature and history. Such he rejected. But he believed that God acts—in the cross of Jesus Christ and in bringing persons to authentic existence through its proclamation, the kerygma.

ual's salvation. From that scientific, historical perspective even the cross is at best a martyrdom. Speaking of it from the perspective of *Geschichte*, however, the cross is God's great act of atonement. The resurrection happened and happens *only* in *Geschichte*. It happened in the disciples' inner histories as they received faith that the mission of Jesus did not end with his cross, and it happens in every believer's inner history when, through the preaching of the cross of Christ, faith happens. The resurrection is the rise of faith in Jesus Christ and nothing else.

Bultmann proclaims the cross and faith for authentic existence. In contrast to Heidegger, Bultmann believed that authentic existence, salvation, is solely the product of grace through the response of faith to the message of the cross. With Barth he regarded it as a miracle,[96] not in the traditional sense of a supernatural event but miracle as an act of God that cannot be experienced through human decision alone. It requires grace. Heidegger believed that authentic existence is a matter of decision; Bultmann disagreed and at that point became more conservative. For him there is no way of salvation, authentic existence, apart from the grace of God which happens on account of faith in the cross of Jesus. The cross was God's decisive act of acceptance; faith is the decision to throw oneself entirely and unreservedly on the God of the cross and trust in him alone for one's security in life and death.

This brings us to Bultmann's understanding of the Christian kerygma (gospel) and its relationship to faith. Following Paul, he maintained that the kerygma is the preaching of the cross and the resurrection as the salvation event, an event that forms an inseparable unity.[97] But by this he did not mean merely the objective facts of what happened with Jesus of Nazareth. For him, as we have already seen, meaningful history cannot be equated with uninterpreted, brute facts of the past. Already early in his career Bultmann had rejected all attempts to prove that Jesus' death and resurrection have atoning and forgiving power.[98] What is important is the meaning of the cross and resurrection, their continued significance as God's Word addressed to individuals today. As people hear the message of

---

[96] See Bultmann, "New Testament and Mythology," 22–33, and *Presence of Eternity*, 149–52.

[97] Bultmann, "New Testament and Mythology," 38–39.

[98] Rudolf Bultmann, *Jesus and the Word* (New York: Charles Scribner's Sons, 1958), 213.

the cross preached and respond with faith, the cross and resurrection become their contemporary experience and not past events.

Understood this way, the cross is God's liberating judgment on humanity.[99] The resurrection, which Bultmann refused to speak of as an event of past history because of its supernatural character,[100] refers neither to the return of a dead man to life in this world nor to the translation of Jesus to a life beyond.[101] Rather, it signifies the elevation of the crucified One to the status of Lord. As a result, "faith in the resurrection is really the same thing as faith in the saving efficacy of the cross," Bultmann averred.[102] The proclamation of this Christian message gives rise to faith, and faith is the willingness to understand oneself as crucified and risen with Christ. The kerygma, then, is the "place" where Jesus Christ confronts the person and becomes his or her "eschatological event." Through the kerygma, the living Lord brings the end of the old world of inauthentic existence for the believer and opens up the future as a realm of authentic existence. As noted already, for Bultmann, this event of the kerygma and faith and authentic existence is in no way dependent on historical knowledge of Jesus' earthly life. Thereby Christian faith is freed from dependency on the shifting sands of critical historical scholarship.

Bultmann's account of faith and its relationship with outer reality should sound familiar. It is a new version of nineteenth-century theology's various attempts to disentangle Christianity from science (broadly defined). For him, the bare facts of science, whether about the physical world or history, cannot falsify true Christianity. God does not act savingly there except in the cross event;[103] God acts savingly in the kergyma and the person who hears it with faith. Nothing science can discover or secular historiography can find can counter Christianity so conceived. Interestingly, though, even Bultmann could not sacrifice the cross event as essential for the event of faith and authentic existence. He was not worried that suddenly historians would find out that it did not happen; he felt sure that the crucifixion of

---

[99]Bultmann, "New Testament and Mythology," 37.

[100]Ibid., 39, 42.

[101]Walter Schmithals, An Introduction to the Theology of Rudolf Bultmann, trans. John Bowden (Minneapolis: Augsburg, 1968), 145.

[102]Bultmann, "New Testament and Mythology," 41.

[103]See previous note 95 for an important comment about "act of God" in Bultmann's theology.

Jesus did happen. But only the eyes of faith can see it as an act of God. Some of Bultmann's disciples challenged this seeming inconsistency. Two left-wing Bultmannians in particular, Fritz Buri (1907–1995) and Herbert Braun (1903–1992), objected to their mentor's insistence on keeping the cross as an act of God and argued that Bultmann should have demythologized the cross as well. For them, the whole idea of "act of God" is mythological, and authentic existence is possible through existentialist philosophy alone.[104] Bultmann rejected their criticism and held fast to the cross as the decisive act of God in history (both senses).

What did Bultmann mean by "authentic existence"? That is crucial as for him it is virtually synonymous with "salvation." The categories of authentic and inauthentic existence were borrowed from Heidegger. According to him, there are two modes of being in the world. People develop an authentic existence whenever they accept the challenge of being thrown into the world (no one asked to be here). By contrast, people develop an inauthentic existence whenever they lose the distinction between self and the world. In other words, authentic existence is taking responsibility for one's own life and facing into the future courageously without security based on things of the world. Inauthentic existence is allowing the social world to determine one's existence (e.g., blaming one's family for one's failings).

Bultmann employed this idea of two ways of being in the world to understand the distinction between the biblical terms "sin" and "faith." Inauthentic existence consists in the search for security and satisfaction in the world, that is, in the realm of the tangible, in one's achievements or in the past. That is sin—understanding oneself in terms of self apart from God. Authentic existence, in contrast, is the refusal to base one's life on the world but rather on intangible realities, coupled with a renunciation of self-centered security and an openness to the future. It is living in the world, but at the same time living over against the world, seeing the world "as if not," to employ Bultmann's phrase (employing a phrase of Paul [1 Cor 7]). This is faith—personal commitment to God in total trust and reliance on him for security and satisfaction. Through faith a new self-understanding emerges, for faith is an act of response to God in which the individual finds his or her

---

[104]For discussion of this debate see Helmut Gollwitzer, *The Existence of God as Confessed by Faith* (Philadelphia: Westminster Press, 1965), passim.

own true being. For Bultmann, this new self-understanding *is* salvation and comes only through the cross and it proclamation.

Bultmann points toward the future with a new concept of eschatology. Bultmann believed in the resurrection of Jesus; he also believed in the return of Jesus Christ, in the same way. That is, in neither case did he think these were or will be literal events in outer history; both are myths in the technical sense of attempts to express the inexpressible. As already seen, he believed in the resurrection of Jesus but not in the empty tomb. Why? Because, as he said on many occasions, we now know dead people do not come back to life, but also because an empty tomb has no existential significance. What is important is the rise of faith in Jesus as Lord in the experience of authentic existence now. The resurrection is an interpretation of the cross, that it was not the end of the mission of Jesus Christ. So Bultmann also believed in the return of Jesus Christ, not as a literal event in the future of *Historie* but as an event in the believer's inner history. It, too, is a myth in its outward expression, for example, in apocalyptic prophecies of Jesus coming on a white horse or on clouds. He did not expect that to happen. But what is important about the return of Christ, eschatology, is its meaning for the individual.

Bultmann's mentor, Weiss, taught, contrary to much nineteenth-century theology, that apocalyptic elements were not peripheral to Jesus' proclamation. They cannot be discarded as legendary additions by later writers. Instead, Jesus' message was thoroughly apocalyptic or eschatological in orientation. Weiss and Schweitzer, who agreed, concluded from this that a central concern of the New Testament, the imminent end of the world, had proven false. Even Jesus was wrong. Bultmann agreed and disagreed. He agreed that Jesus and the earliest Christian communities anticipated the soon arrival of the kingdom of God, a hope that was not fulfilled.[105] But rather than being forced thereby to a negative conclusion concerning the relevance of the New Testament message, he reinterpreted the eschatology of the New Testament. Bultmann moved behind the temporal sense in which that message had been given to what he perceived to be its true existential meaning. After all, he pointed out, even the New Testament writers themselves, Paul and John, had

---

[105]Bultmann, *Jesus Christ and Mythology*, 14.

spoken of eternal life as something received now by faith, a present, existential reality, and not a temporally future anticipation.[106]

Bultmann asked, "What is the importance of the preaching of Jesus and of the preaching of the New Testament as a whole for modern man?"[107] His answer was that the mythological framework in which the preaching of the coming kingdom of God appeared in the preaching of the New Testament is "over and done with."[108] That is, modern people not only cannot believe it; they cannot even understand it. So, according to Bultmann, we must discover the true, inner meaning of the eschatological myths. Here is how he describes that:

> Eschatological preaching [of the New Testament] views the present time in the light of the future and it says to men that this present world, the world of nature and history, the world in which we live our lives and make our plans is not the only world; that this world is temporal and transitory, yes, ultimately empty and unreal in the face of eternity.[109]

However, it is not only a negative message about life here and now. The deeper meaning of the mythological preaching of Jesus about the soon coming of the "Son of Man" and the breaking in of God's kingdom is

> to be open to God's future which is really imminent for every one of us; to be prepared for this future which can come as a thief in the night when we do not expect it; to be prepared, because this future will be a judgment on all men who have bound themselves to this world and are not free, not open to God's future.[110]

Bultmann continues his discussion of eschatology by arguing that even for John "the resurrection of Jesus, Pentecost and the *parousia* [return of Christ] of Jesus are one and the same event" experienced in that moment by the person who believes.[111] The resurrection of Christ and the return of Christ and the outpouring of the Holy Spirit—all are different mythological expressions of the reality of the new self-understanding in authentic exis-

---

[106]Ibid., 32–34.
[107]Ibid., 17.
[108]Ibid.
[109]Ibid., 23.
[110]Ibid., 31–32.
[111]Ibid., 33.

tence that happens at the moment of faith in response to the word of the cross preached. Eschatology, then, is not about the temporal future. Bultmann never questioned life after death; he believed in a heaven without attempting to picture it. What he was denying was the traditional Christian expectation of an end of the world, or return of Christ on clouds of glory with angels or final judgment on a great white throne. All these are images not to be taken literally. They are expressions of something that happens in an eschatological now with faith. The future, God's future, becomes open and emptied of fear and viewed as opportunity to live authentically for God.

Bultmann redefines God's transcendence. A final problem for which Bultmann sought an answer lies in the doctrine of God. The liberal theology of the nineteenth century placed strong emphasis on God's immanence. Barth launched a campaign against this emphasis based on Kierkegaard's concept of the "infinite qualitative distinction" between eternity and time, between God and creation. Bultmann joined Barth in this campaign. In fact, Bultmann sought to employ a radical application of the idea of God's transcendence to the entire spectrum of theology.

In one sense, Bultmann's concept of transcendence differed from that presented in the Bible.[112] According to his reconstruction, the ancient peoples held to a spatially divided, three-story universe, with God and heaven literally above and hell literally below. This cosmology, he argued, is unbelievable for modern people. The scientific worldview has abolished it. God's transcendence, therefore, can no longer be understood in spatial terms. In its stead, Bultmann offered a nonspatial understanding. Biblical transcendence refers to God's absolute authority.[113] So, transcendence, demythologized and existentialized, means that God stands before us in the moment of decision, addressing us with his Word and confronting us with the challenge of responding in faith, thereby receiving authentic existence.

This understanding of God's transcendence means that we can never speak of God objectively, that is, as an object. We can never speak of God "in himself." We can only speak of God in terms of what he does for us and in us.[114] God is literally unknowable apart from the individual faith re-

---

[112]Bultmann, "New Testament and Mythology," 3–8; *Jesus Christ and Mythology*, 11–32.
[113]Bultmann, *Presence of Eternity*, 95–96.
[114]Bultmann, *Jesus Christ and Mythology*, 71.

sponse to the divine self-disclosure in his Word. And his Word is the message of the cross. This self-disclosure is not the communication of facts about God or a body of knowledge. It is an occurrence that calls the individual to response. Thus, we cannot speak about God; we cannot speak in detached, impersonal, objective terms. We can only speak of God and to God. All theoretical talk about God, such as descriptions of his attributes, is precluded because it treats God as an object and has nothing to do with decision or authentic existence. But Bultmann went even further. For him, statements concerning God must also concern human existence. Theological statements about God are possible only when they are also about human existence. Critics have seen this as reducing theology to anthropology. More sympathetic interpreters have denied this.[115] However, there can be no question that for Bultmann, theology must always be translatable into statements about human existence.

What does all that mean for Bultmann's ideas about God? Since he was not a systematic theologian, he had little to say about traditional doctrines such as the Trinity. But he probably could not have been a systematic theologian; he did not think the gospel or God's transcendence allow it. God is so transcendent that he cannot be known or spoken of at all apart from the Word and its gracious effect in people's lives. Bultmann was dismissive of theological attempts to understand God's inner being. For him, Christianity is all and only about salvation. So, even Jesus Christ cannot be spoken of in terms of his deity, as if it were possible to have metaphysical knowledge of some divine substance in him. Even talk of his preexistence is out of bounds because it would be mythological. It could be spoken of only if it could be translated into language about authentic existence. It cannot be, so it is not relevant. For him, the only essential thing about Jesus was his death on the cross as God's supreme act of forgiveness and acceptance for those who believe. He rejected all attempts to develop a theory of the atonement. Another way of saying all that is that Bultmann was radically antimetaphysical; he tried to disentangle theology from metaphysics entirely. But, unlike the older liberals, he also rejected attempts to reduce Christianity to ethics. Theology has basically the function of clearing the field, so to speak,

---

[115]See Young, *History and Existential Theology*, 66–72; Bultmann, *Jesus Christ and Mythology*, 70.

of metaphysical obstacles and land mines so that the preacher and his or her listeners can cross over to the real obstacle, the cross. It is a real obstacle, Bultmann believed, because it demands repentance and faith.

Bultmann leaves a legacy of controversy and consternation. In spite of the subheading of this evaluative section, not everyone thought or thinks Bultmann was wrong. Many modern Christians have embraced his project as the way to rescue the gospel from the acids of modernity. One of its greatest virtues is that it makes conflict between science and Christianity impossible in principle. But at what cost? Critics have argued the cost is making Christianity irrelevant to anything in the physical world or history except the cross. To some it appears downright gnostic in its rejection of the outer world as irrelevant to Christian faith.

Before discussing criticisms, however, it will be helpful to point out areas of Bultmann's thought that draw, for the most part, agreement by Christian scholars of various theological orientations. At the heart of his project is a worthy emphasis on making the Christian message speak to questions raised by contemporary people. This is important because Christians often find themselves answering questions people are not asking. Likewise helpful is his assertion that truth is not merely objective, that is, facts, but to be fully received ultimate truth, truth about life and its meaning, must "grip the soul" of the believer.[116] Finally, Bultmann set forth a laudable attempt to reestablish the transcendence of God, supplying a needed polemic against overemphasis on God's immanence in liberal and neo-liberal theologies.

Both liberals and conservatives were unhappy with Bultmann's proposals. One of the harshest conservative critics (other than fundamentalists) is Reformed theologian Klaus Bockmuehl, who devoted two chapters of *The Unreal God of Modern Theology* (1988) to Bultmann. His conclusion about Bultmann's demythologizing program is that it "announces the rule of an alien ideology in the church."[117] That alien ideology is naturalism, the worldview that "human existence is closed to supernatural interventions."[118] He argues that this ideology is in need of demy-

---

[116]Bultmann, *Presence of Eternity*, 122.
[117]Klaus Bockmuehl, *The Unreal God of Modern Theology* (Colorado Springs, CO: Helmers & Howard, 1988), 22.
[118]Ibid., 19.

thologizing as it is a set of value judgments unprovable by science. Furthermore, Bultmann's embrace of it is inconsistent, as his radical disciples Buri and Braun saw. Bockmuehl says:

> The gospel regards the assertion that human existence is closed and unitary as a permanent, not just a contemporary, error. The gospel rejects this assertion just as Bultmann must reject is [sic] as soon and as long as he describes the truth and authenticity of human existence as a gift which can come to man only from without by an "act of God." That in itself characterizes any notion of man's independence and self-sufficiency as erroneous.[119]

Bockmuehl, like most conservative critics of Bultmann, is saying that the demythologizer took a leap of faith in embracing naturalism, an alien, unprovable worldview, and did so inconsistently. But his main criticism is that "we cannot agree that value judgments that . . . have no objective necessity can serve as criteria for criticism of the Christian message."[120] Bultmann, according to this analysis and critique, adopted a foreign perspective that is purely a value judgment, not based on facts, as the Procrustean bed for modern theology.

Liberal critics of Bultmann accuse him of abandoning reason and opting for sheer fideism. Indeed, his rejection of evidences or reasons for faith is about as radical as possible. In an article on faith in Kittel's *Theological Dictionary of the New Testament* (1933) Bultmann adamantly stated that true faith hangs suspended in midair without any support. It is sheer Kierkegaardian leap. It is incredible to the intelligence of the world.[121] Liberal theologian L. Harold DeWolf wrote *The Religious Revolt Against Reason* (1949) largely to refute Bultmann and other neo-orthodox theologians. According to DeWolf, Bultmann's approach to Christianity makes it esoteric and cuts it off from knowledge, relegating it to the realm of superstition.[122] DeWolf's critique of Bultmann's approach is quite different from Bockmuehl's in that it does not fault Bultmann for adopting naturalism as its basis. It accuses him of taking a flight from reason into the safe refuge of blind faith.

---

[119]Ibid., 21.
[120]Ibid.
[121]Rudolf Bultmann, "Faith," *Theological Dictionary of the New Testament* (Grand Rapids: Eerdmans, 1968), 174–228.
[122]DeWolf, *The Religious Revolt Against Reason*, passim.

Another avenue of criticism often taken against Bultmann is that his interpretation of Christianity leads to a privatized, individualized faith cut off from the social world and its problems. That is, Bultmann's existentialist emphasis runs the risk of excluding the corporate and social dimensions of Christian faith. Bockmuehl charges that "above all others in this [twentieth] century, he has made Christianity a private affair."[123] He placed little emphasis on the outworking of faith in the life of believer on the social plane or in community. His existentialist orientation fosters an inwardness that readily leads to ignoring the social and political implications of the gospel. Even more, his description of salvation as authentic existence had little to say about sanctification, the life of Christian discipleship in the world. It seems inappropriately focused on the individual's self-understanding.

Finally, questions have been raised and need to be raised about Bultmann's radically antimetaphysical view of God. Questions about God's being and attributes, even triunity, are deftly turned aside as irrelevant to faith. It is hard to resist the sense that he has drunk too deeply not only at the wells of existentialism but at Kant's trough as well. Bultmann's claim that we can speak of God only insofar as we are at the same time speaking about human existence places God's eternal nature beyond the boundary of human knowing and speaking. Thereby God is made literally unknowable. All we know are his effects on us. Bultmann claimed this as a virtue: "Not what God is in Himself, but how he acts with men, is the mystery in which faith is interested."[124] This restriction tends to reduce God's reality to human questions and spiritual needs. People who believe in God want to know who he is and what he is like. That curiosity can go too far, but some of it needs to be addressed. Bultmann blocked all attempts to say anything about God outside of human experience.

In some ways, Bultmann is the ultimate modern theologian. No one embraced modern naturalism and rationalism more fully, except that he cordoned off Christian faith from rationalism. Everything in the physical world and in history is subject to reason, and it limits religion severely. Bultmann made a virtue out of what he saw as a necessity. He made it impossible for Christianity and science to conflict. While that might seem

---

[123]Bockmuehl, *Unreal God*, 75.
[124]Bultmann, *Jesus Christ and Mythology*, 43.

good on the surface, it required a severe ghettoizing of theology away from other disciplines. At the same time, ironically, he connected theology so closely with existentialism that it could hardly speak on its own. It became the prisoner of naturalism on the one hand and existentialism on the other hand.

5.C. REINHOLD NIEBUHR REDISCOVERS ORIGINAL SIN AND DEVELOPS CHRISTIAN REALISM

If asked to name America's most influential twentieth-century Christian theologian virtually every historian and theologian would name Reinhold Niebuhr. He never regarded himself as a theologian[125] and never earned a doctoral degree in theology. And yet, during his lifetime he was recognized as one of the leading American public intellectuals. A decade after his death in 1971 a leading theologian declared, "It is difficult to find a theologian in the twentieth century who has exerted more influence on a nation's political life than has Reinhold Niebuhr."[126] That encomium is justified by the fact that several US presidents have named Niebuhr as a major influence on their political beliefs and public policies.[127] So influential was Niebuhr that his face graced the cover of *Time* magazine's twenty-fifth anniversary issue (March 8, 1948); the issue contained a lengthy article about the prophet of Christian realism. Ironically, however, Niebuhr's best-known contribution, at least to popular culture, may have been his 1934 "Serenity Prayer" well known to millions of people because of its use by various twelve-step groups such as Alcoholics Anonymous: "God, give us grace to accept with serenity the things that cannot be changed, courage to change the things that should be changed, and wisdom to distinguish the one from the other."[128]

---

[125]See Niebuhr's reflections in his "Intellectual Autobiography," in *Reinhold Niebuhr: His Religious, Social and Political Thought*, vol. 2 of *The Library of Living Theology*, ed. Charles W. Kegley and Robert W. Bretall (New York: Macmillan, 1961), 3.

[126]Paul Jersild, "Reinhold Niebuhr: Continuing the Assessment," *Dialog* 22:4 (fall 1983): 284.

[127]Frank A. Ruechel, "Politics and Morality Revisited: Jimmy Carter and Reinhold Niebuhr," *Atlanta History* 37:4 (1994): 19–31; John McCain, *Hard Call: Great Decisions and the Extraordinary People Who Made Them* (Boston: Twelve, 2007), 321–38; Benedicta Cipolla, "Reinhold Niebuhr Is Unseen Force in 2008 Elections," *Religion News Service* of the *Pew Forum on Religion and Public Life*, September 27, 2007.

[128]The prayer is found at the beginning of a published collection of Niebuhr's short writings titled *Justice and Mercy*, ed. Ursula M. Niebuhr (New York: Harper & Row, 1974), 1. See also June Bingham, *Courage to Change* (New York: Charles Scribner's Sons, 1961).

Without doubt Niebuhr was a theologian, in spite of his wife's identification of him as a preacher and pastor.[129] He began his career as a pastor and preacher at Bethel Evangelical Church in Detroit.[130] Later, however, he became America's leading social ethicist, journal editor, frequent commentator, State Department consultant, confidant of President Franklin Roosevelt, professor at Union Theological Seminary in New York and circuit-riding speaker at colleges and universities. Because his education was interrupted by family needs following his father's death he never earned the usual academic theological credentials. His highest degree was a master of arts degree from Yale Divinity School. Nevertheless, he became the dominant, shaping voice in the American religious community during the mid-twentieth century.

Scholars have frequently categorized Niebuhr as a neo-orthodox theologian.[131] Yet, he rejected that designation because he equated it with the theology of Barth, whom he repeatedly criticized.[132] Of the European neo-orthodox theologians and with reference to their anti-Nazism Niebuhr wrote in the 1950s, "Yesterday they discovered that the church may be an ark in which to survive a flood. Today they seem so enamored of this special function of the church that they have decided to turn the ark into a home on Mount Ararat and live in it perpetually."[133] His complaint was that Barth and the dialectical theology movement, while right in their opposition to the old liberal theology, had become irrelevant to social problems. Whether he was right is open to debate, but the point is that Niebuhr distanced himself from Barth and neo-orthodoxy because he was mainly interested in social ethics and politics. He thought they were too interested in systematic theology and in fighting against liberal theology.

In spite of his distancing himself from neo-orthodoxy there is good reason to include Niebuhr in this chapter. In spite of his dissatisfaction with neo-orthodox theology, or at least some of what he considered its flaws, he

---

[129]From Ursula Niebuhr's introduction to *Justice and Mercy*, 1.

[130]Most of the biographical facts about Niebuhr are taken from Richard Wightman Fox, *Reinhold Niebuhr: A Biography* (Ithaca, NY: Cornell University Press, 1996).

[131]See William Hordern, *A Layman's Guide to Protestant Theology*, rev. ed. (New York: Macmillan, 1968), 150.

[132]See Ronald H. Stone, *Reinhold Niebuhr: Prophet to Politicians* (Nashville: Abingdon, 1972), 122–25.

[133]Quoted in Fox, *Reinhold Niebuhr*, 235.

was also protesting against liberal theology under the influence of Kierkegaard. Although he did not mention the Danish philosopher-theologian very often, parallels between their approaches to Christianity are evident. Like Kierkegaard, Niebuhr was vehemently opposed to anything that smacked of Hegelianism such as optimism about history and belief that opposites can be synthesized. He emphasized the sinfulness of humanity and the transcendence of God. Some people would prefer to categorize him as a chastened liberal, but his differences from liberal, even neo-liberal, theology are so stark as to make that a poor fit. Perhaps it would be nearest the truth to say Niebuhr straddled the line between neo-orthodoxy and neo-liberalism (e.g., Paul Tillich). Let the reader decide.

Niebuhr rises to prominence as a Christian ethicist. Like Rauschenbusch, Niebuhr was the son of an immigrant German pastor, and his home and church were bathed in warm-hearted, pietistic Christianity. His father was a pastor in the Evangelical Synod, a Lutheran and Reformed denomination of mostly German immigrants that later became part of the United Church of Christ.[134] After finishing high school in Lincoln, Illinois, he attended Elmhurst College in suburban Chicago and then Eden Seminary in St. Louis before going to Yale, where he earned the bachelor of divinity and then the master of arts in 1915. His professional career began in Detroit, where he pastored a congregation of mostly assembly-line workers at the Ford Motor plant. There he gained firsthand exposure to the plight of those being exploited by the industrialists of the nation, an experience that had profound influence on his social orientation and theology. Gradually he began to favor a form of socialism as the only solution to the poverty and powerlessness of America's workers.

Early in his career, Niebuhr was enamored with the social gospel associated with Rauschenbusch and other liberal theologian and social ethicists, but he became disillusioned with their optimism about progress through persuasion and with their pacifism and hesitancy to exercise coercive measures to establish justice. Above all he became disillusioned with what he considered their weak views of human sinfulness and God's transcendence.

---

[134]Niebuhr's parents came to the United States from the same tiny principality (Lippe) in Germany that this writer's maternal ancestors came from around the same time. And both immigrated to the same Illinois town. They may well have known each other.

The social upheaval he saw during his years in the pastorate, such as attempts to put down strikes by force, caused him "to reconsider the liberal and highly moralistic creed which I had accepted as tantamount to the Christian faith."[135] The shortcomings of liberal theology extended beyond the social realm into the personal realm as well: "In my parish duties I found the simple idealism into which the classical faith had evaporated was as irrelevant to the crises of personal life as it was to the complex social issues of an industrial city."[136] In short, then, in Detroit the young pastor came to see that the liberal theology of his seminary training was insufficient to meet the challenges of twentieth-century pastoral ministry in all its dimensions.

Niebuhr's activities as a pastor in the thick of Detroit's labor disputes cata-pulted him to national prominence. In 1928 he was called to teach ethics at New York's Union Theological Seminary, which was then the most presti-gious Protestant seminary in America. There he taught until his retirement in 1960. He was instrumental in bringing Tillich and Dietrich Bonhoeffer from Germany to teach there; Tillich stayed for many years and escaped Nazi per-secution. Much to Niebuhr's chagrin Bonhoeffer returned to Germany, became involved in a plot to assassinate Hitler and was executed days before the end of the war. While teaching at Union Niebuhr became America's leading Christian public intellectual and was called to the White House on several occasions to advise President Roosevelt about Germany and just war. In 1939 he was invited to deliver the prestigious Gifford Lectures in Edin-burgh. His lectures were published in his two-volume magnum opus *The Nature and Destiny of Man* (1941), which in 2011 *Time* named one of the one hundred most influential nonfiction books of the twentieth century.

Besides *The Nature and Destiny of Man*, Niebuhr's best-known and most influential books include *Moral Man and Immoral Society* (1932), *An Interpre-tation of Christian Ethics* (1935), *The Children of Light and the Children of Darkness* (1944) and *The Self and the Dramas of History* (1955). Some of his most influential writings were articles and opinion columns in various publi-cations including *Christianity and Crisis*, which he edited from 1941 through

---

[135]Niebuhr, "Intellectual Autobiography," 5. For another statement by Niebuhr concerning his turn away from liberal theology see his "Ten Years That Shook the World," *The Christian Cen-tury* (April 26, 1939), 545.
[136]Niebuhr, "Intellectual Autobiography," 6.

1966. Many of his essays, columns and articles have been collected into anthologies, including *Love and Justice* (1957) and *Justice and Mercy* (1974). New books examining Niebuhr's life and theological contribution appear almost every year. That contribution has been hotly debated: some critics condemn Niebuhr as an apologist for and defender of power; others defend him as a man of peace and voice for the powerless. Fundamentalists tend to ignore him; liberal theologians were at first threatened by his tilt toward neo-orthodoxy and later came to appreciate him for his progressive social and political views. But it was against liberal idealism that this Christian ethicist first made his mark in theology. Throughout the 1930s Niebuhr was advocating for the United States to take a stand against National Socialism and fascism in Europe even if it meant going to war. Most liberal Protestant pastors of America condemned all wars as unjust, inclining toward pacifism by appeal to Jesus' Sermon on the Mount. For them, the kingdom of God was a possibility within history, something Niebuhr came to deny as an illusion. Niebuhr wrestled with his liberal heritage in terms of the tension between the ideal and the real, a tension he found central to the biblical message.[137] How do the realities of life in the present, tainted as they are by sin and evil, fit together with the ideal of the kingdom of God? Niebuhr found the liberal answer naïve, ill-advised and unworkable in the face of the threat of totalitarianism. In its place he sought to bring the biblical gospel to bear on the specific situations in which he found himself and thereby to discover how to apply that gospel to Western civilization as a whole.[138]

Niebuhr searches for a practical Christianity. Niebuhr's fundamental goal throughout his career was "to establish the relevance of the Christian faith to contemporary problems."[139] As a result, he refused to limit his endeavors to abstract theological discussions and eschewed all metaphysical speculations. He focused on being an activist, seeking to apply theological insights to politics, international affairs, human rights and economics. In

---

[137]Stone, *Reinhold Niebuhr*, 11. Also, *An Interpretation of Christian Ethics* constitutes Niebuhr's Rauschenbusch Lectures at Colgate-Rochester Theological Seminary and is a sustained critique of the social gospel's dissolution of the tension between the ideal and the real in history.

[138]D. R. Davies sees this as the connecting theme of Niebuhr's life's work in *Reinhold Niebuhr: Prophet from America* (New York: Macmillan, 1948), 95.

[139]Reinhold Niebuhr, *Christian Realism and Political Problems* (New York: Charles Scribner's Sons, 1953), 1.

every area he consistently sought to act as a prophet, encountering contemporary social life with the critique provided by the biblical message. He refused to tie himself to any ideology even though he favored socialism as an economic system. When socialists leaned too heavily toward communism and atheism, he abandoned them without sacrificing his belief in redistribution of wealth and the welfare state. As a prophet, he stood apart from parties and movements, whether theological or political, and strove to be an independent biblical thinker constantly pointing out the problems with all ideological approaches to solving social problems, whether right or left.

As a part of his social consciousness and prophetic criticism, Niebuhr engaged in a kind of Christian apologetics. He attempted to demonstrate the relevance of biblical Christianity to a society that had largely rejected the gospel, or, in his words, he was interested "in the defense and justification of the Christian faith in a secular society."[140] However, his apologetic employed a different approach from classical appeals to the reasonableness of Christianity. He had no interest in natural theology, proofs of the existence of God or demonstration of history as God's providential work. Rather, he attempted to set forth the Christian faith as providing meaning to life, but he maintained that "no ultimate sense of the meaning of life is rationally compelling."[141] In fact, the two central propositions of Christianity, that God is a person and that God has taken historical action to overcome alienation between people and God, "are absurd from a strictly ontological [i.e., philosophical] standpoint."[142] Whereas the reigning liberal theology of his day had sought to reduce the absurdity of the faith by reducing the biblical message to a set of timeless truths of ethics or metaphysics (following Kant or Hegel), Niebuhr advocated an apologetic that would make clear the ontologically ambiguous status of the concepts of personality and history.[143] In other words, these agreed-on realities cannot be understood coherently from philosophy or science alone. In the midst of such ambiguous but necessary realities, we must leave room for the nonrational, so that the challenging message of God's relationship to creation as

---

[140]Niebuhr, "Intellectual Autobiography," 3.
[141]Ibid., 17.
[142]Ibid., 19.
[143]Ibid., 20.

evidenced in the biblical symbols and myths can be heard without being watered down.[144] In all this, Niebuhr's debt to Kierkegaard is obvious.

So, if Niebuhr appealed to the nonrationality (or suprarationality) of Christianity's main concepts, wherein lay his apologetic? It can be found in his exposure of alternative philosophies of life as undermining or destroying essential facts of human existence. His special targets were what he saw as the two main philosophies of the modern world: naturalism and idealism. In *The Nature and Destiny of Man* he spent hundreds of pages deconstructing naturalism and idealism, showing how they distort and betray human values and how Christianity better accounts for those values and better explains the facts of human life. Naturalism is the belief that nature is all there is; it reduces humans to highly evolved animals. Idealism is the belief that humans have infinite potential because there is continuity between human mind or spirit and God or ultimate reality. It elevates humans to godlets.

Neither worldview, Niebuhr argued, does justice to obvious realities of human existence. Contrary to naturalism, humans are beings capable of transcending nature in acts of creativity and evil. Contrary to idealism, humans are limited and finite and even sinful, conditions they cannot overcome by themselves. Niebuhr believed, and argued, that only the Christian vision of humanity as finite and free, animals but created in God's image, mortal but possessing immortality as a gift of God can explain the facts of human life. He did not consider this a rational proof of Christianity; he considered it proof that Christianity is not irrational even if it is nonrational.

Niebuhr reserved his strongest criticism for idealism, which he saw as the main flaw in liberal theology and the cause of liberal pastors' and theologians' reluctance, if not refusal, to advocate war to protect civilization from the scourges of fascism and Nazism. Not until Japan attacked Pearl Harbor did many American liberal Protestants support the United States taking sides in the war that Hitler had started in 1939. Niebuhr looked behind their pacifism and isolationism to their underlying optimistic idealism about humanity. They thought that if enough Christians worked for

---

[144]For a development of the presence of this nonrational dimension of Niebuhr's thought see Hans Hofmann, *The Theology of Reinhold Niebuhr*, trans. Louise Pettibone Smith (New York: Charles Scribner's Sons, 1956), 73.

peace hard enough, peace would break out all over. With his contacts in
Germany and throughout Europe Niebuhr knew better and considered
America's Protestant pastors and theologians idealists who would play into
the hands of evil with their belief in inevitable progress through education
and persuasion. So, he tirelessly attacked the two basic tenets of the modern
faith of liberalism: the idea of progress and the idea of human perfect-
ibility.[145] So poignant was his critique that one contemporary declared, "No
single thinker has done more than Niebuhr to reveal the bankruptcy of
secular illusions and ideals in our time."[146]

Niebuhr believed Christians are called to effectiveness in society and not
only to obedience to ideals. He considered Jesus' Sermon on the Mount a
counsel of perfection, something impossible to live perfectly in this fallen,
sinful world. He also believed in radical evil in humanity, the reality of
original sin and depravity. He believed that liberal idealism would sacrifice
effectiveness out of fear of compromise. Niebuhr was confident of God's
forgiveness if and whenever God's people must participate in the lesser of
two evils, and he considered a war to stop Hitler and his Axis allies such a
necessary evil. Christian social ethics, then, must be practical. It cannot be
an idealistic confidence in human ability to achieve the perfect in this world.
Compromise, based on rational thought about realities, is a Christian virtue
insofar as it is necessary for justice. Niebuhr's disciples called this approach
to practical Christian social ethics "Christian realism." Liberals called it
pessimism. Niebuhr himself called it prophetic.

Niebuhr develops a Christian anthropology. A theme running
throughout Niebuhr's writings is the human situation. Why is it impossible
to create a perfectly just society or attain the ideal in any perfect form in the
realm of the real? His quest to understand this somewhat depressing reality
led him to classical Christian theology, specifically anthropology, the doctrine of human nature and existence. The constant presence of anthropology in Niebuhr's work led one commentator to conclude that

> Niebuhr's most significant contribution to the restatement of Christian the-
> ology in our generation is his exposition of the doctrine of man. Unlike sys-

---

[145]See Niebuhr, "Intellectual Autobiography," 15.
[146]Davies, *Reinhold Niebuhr*, 72.

tematicians like Aquinas or Barth who cover the whole corpus of Christian truth by the method of a *Summa*, Niebuhr makes one doctrine, brilliantly plumbed to its depths, the basis of his whole thought.[147]

Niebuhr was drawn to the doctrine of humanity because he discovered a profundity in the classical Christian doctrine lacking in secularism and liberalism. In his view, the rejection of classical biblical anthropological themes by liberal theologians was responsible for the central ethical problems of his time. Liberalism, he argued, had replaced "sin" with imperfections of ignorance, which an adequate education could overcome.[148] In contrast to this naïve, optimistic emphasis on human reason and faith in education, Niebuhr saw in biblical anthropology a realistic picture. As a result, his own anthropology, which undergirded his social ethic, reflected that of classical Christian orthodoxy, insofar as he sought to emphasize the two-sidedness of the human situation. He affirmed the high stature of humanity as created in God's image as well as the biblical theme of original sin as universal fallenness.

Niebuhr saw in both the reality of human behavior and the biblical message a paradox. Humanity is filled with potential for both good and evil. In *The Nature and Destiny of Man* he summarized Christian anthropology in three theses.[149] First, human persons are created and finite in both body and spirit. Second, humans are to be understood first and foremost from their standpoint in relation to God, that is, as created in God's image, rather than in terms of their rational faculties or in relation to nature. In other words, the meaning of human life is in God, not self or world. Third, humans are sinners and because of sin they are to be loved but never trusted. Niebuhr, then, was not interested in the human person as such. He rejected philosophies that spoke of humanity in abstract, ontological categories. Instead, similar to other neo-orthodox theologians, he was interested in the human person as a historical being, a being "before God" caught in the ambiguities of history. Thus, his writings focused on humans in terms of their double relation to God and to each other in society.[150]

---

[147]William John Wolf, "Reinhold Niebuhr's Doctrine of Man," in *Reinhold Niebuhr: His Religious, Social and Political Thought*, 230.

[148]Reinhold Niebuhr, *An Interpretation of Christian Ethics* (New York: Meridian, 1956), 23.

[149]Reinhold Niebuhr, *The Nature and Destiny of Man*, 2 vols. (New York: Scribner's Sons, 1964), 1:12–18.

[150]Hofmann, *Theology of Niebuhr*, 104.

According to Niebuhr, this Christian account of human nature and existence, rooted in the biblical prophetic tradition, is richer and thicker than the shallow views of naturalism and idealism. And liberal theology, he believed, had by and large succumbed to idealism, neglecting the finitude and fallenness of humanity. Niebuhr found the concept of sin most lacking in the modern mindset, including liberal theology. Liberal theology had discarded the doctrine of original sin; Niebuhr thought that was a great loss and the cause of much of liberalism's ineffectiveness in social ethics. He wanted to recover but reconstruct the classical doctrine of original sin. For him, the biblical story of the fall (Gen 3) is a myth in the sense of a narrative that expresses a universal truth.[151] Adam and Eve represent everyone; we are all fallen into sin. We do not inherit a sin gene or chromosome, nor does God impute sin to us because we are descended from Adam. All those ideas are dispensable. What is not dispensable is the truth the myth of the fall expresses—that we are all sinners unable to cure ourselves. The fundamental nature of original sin, the sin that underlies our individual transgressions, is refusal of creatureliness: in other words, idolatry of self.

According to Niebuhr, sin is a paradox. That is why the Bible expresses it in a story. It cannot be made rational. To make it rational is to explain it away so that it is no longer sin. The paradox is that sin is inevitable but not necessary.[152] There is no flaw in human nature that makes sin necessary; it is always responsible choice. But beneath the sinful choices we all make lies a sinful condition for which nobody is guilty. People are guilty only when they act out their sinful condition in transgressions. But how does it come about that original sin, the sinful condition, is universal if it is not a spiritual disease inherited from the first couple? Niebuhr turned to Kierkegaard to help understand this situation. The Danish philosopher used the concept of anxiety to explain the universal character of sin.[153] The paradox of freedom and finitude that characterizes the human situation leads to insecurity. We are limited by the natural processes of life (finitude), but we are able to stand outside them and foresee their perils (freedom). By nature we are bound and

---

[151]See Niebuhr's explanation of "myth" in "The Truth in Myths," in *Faith and Politics*, ed. Ronald Stone (New York: George Braziller, 1968), 24–25.

[152]Reinhold Niebuhr, *An Interpretation of Christian Ethics* (New York: Seabury, 1979), 52.

[153]Niebuhr, *Nature and Destiny of Man*, 1:182–83, 251–52.

limited; yet we are also free, endowed with the capacity to rise above nature (self-transcendence). This paradox creates insecurity and anxiety. Freedom tempts us to try to go beyond nature, but our feet are firmly planted in it. In this state of anxiety we turn to sinful self-assertion, the attempt to turn our finitude into infinity, weakness into strength, dependence into independence. The alternative is to trust God for our ultimate security. For whatever reason, all humans (except Jesus) attempt to become gods for ourselves rather than letting God be God the ground of our security.

For Niebuhr, then, sin ought to be understood in relationship to faith. Faith is acceptance of our dependence on God whereas sin is the denial of our creatureliness. This sin condition comes in two forms, two ways of seeking to escape insecurity and rise above anxiety. The first is sensuality, the attempt to deny human freedom by retreating into animal nature.[154] More basic and universal is the second form, the denial of our human limitations by asserting independence. This is the sin of pride, which can take several forms.[155] First is the pride of power by which we attempt to overcome insecurity by exercising power over others in godlike fashion. Second is the pride of knowledge by which we claim that our limited knowledge is absolute. Third is the pride of virtue by which we claim absolute status for our relative moral standards. Fourth is spiritual pride by which we endow our partial spiritual experiences with divine status. Not only is pride present in individuals, Niebuhr added, but it is even more pronounced in groups, for "the group is more arrogant, hypocritical, self-centered, and ruthless in the pursuit of its ends than the individual."[156]

Niebuhr defends Christian realism against liberal idealism. As a result of his experiences in the pastorate and his study of Christian sources and human existence, Niebuhr offered a profound and prophetic critique of the reigning liberal theology and social outlook of his time. He remained appreciative of much about his liberal heritage but found it necessary to criticize its idealism and overoptimism in order to push Protestantism toward effectiveness in transforming society even partially toward the kingdom of God. Liberal theology, he concluded, had identified the kingdom of God

[154]Ibid., 1:228–40.
[155]Ibid., 1:186–203.
[156]Ibid., 1:208.

with various human enterprises and social agendas such as Prussia (Hegel) and socialism (Rauschenbusch). Furthermore, liberal theologians had thought that the kingdom of God, which Rauschenbusch had identified as society organized according to love, could be brought about by peaceful persuasion without conflict or coercion. Against this liberal idealism Niebuhr advocated Christian realism, the idea that sinful human beings cannot bring about God's kingdom or even achieve anything perfect, but they can with God's help approximate God's kingdom in partial achievements of justice.

In *An Interpretation of Christian Ethics* Niebuhr set forth the thesis at the heart of Christian realism: "love may be the motive of social action [but] justice must be the instrument of love in a world in which self-interest is bound to defy the canons of love on every level."[157] He rejected what he termed the "moralistic utopianism"[158] and sentimental optimism of the liberal churches, finding there a mistaken conception that love is a simple possibility rather than "an impossible possibility."[159] The grace of God makes love a possibility; the sinful condition makes it an impossibility. What Niebuhr meant is impossible to grasp without realizing that he interpreted the love Jesus commanded as perfect selflessness, total lack of egoism, concern only for the person in need and not at all for oneself. While such love might be possible occasionally in one-on-one relationships (e.g., parent to child or between spouses), such love is impossible in large, corporate relationships (e.g., company management to workers or one nation-state to another). According to Niebuhr, normally, and especially in social behavior, there is no human act that is completely free of every taint of egoism. That is how deeply sunk sin is in human bones.

What, then? Shall we give in and abandon hope for righteousness in social settings? Not at all, according to Niebuhr. But neither should we expect too much. To expect one nation to love another with absolute self-abandoning benevolence is to sink into ineffectiveness. It is not possible

---

[157]Niebuhr, *Interpretation of Christian Ethics* (Meridian, 1956), 9. What follows here is this writer's attempt to put Niebuhr's "dialectic of love and justice" in *An Interpretation of Christian Ethics* and in various essays such as those in the anthology *Love and Justice* as simply as possible. Niebuhr's writing can be daunting; rather than quoting him I prefer to paraphrase him.
[158]Ibid., 155.
[159]Ibid., 110.

under the conditions of sin. And sin cannot be overcome by taking thought or by education or persuasion. Similarly, to ask workers exploited by their employers to love them and to expect employers to love their workers self-lessly is an idealistic illusion. (These were the things Niebuhr heard and read from liberal Protestant pulpits and in liberal Protestant publications.) Above all, Niebuhr thought it ridiculous and offensive for Christians to call on oppressed minorities to love their oppressors. But Jesus said, "Love your enemies" and "Do not resist evil." Again, Niebuhr interpreted those commands the same way he interpreted "If your right eye offend you, pluck it out": as counsels of perfection, impossible ideals to strive for without thinking they can be achieved perfectly. So, what is the relevance of an impossible ideal? Niebuhr devoted an entire chapter of *An Interpretation of Christian Ethics* to answering that question.

For Niebuhr, the impossible ideal set before us by Christ, and therefore by Christian ethics, is absolute, unadulterated love that never harms or even resists one's enemies. That is impossible in this sinful world of violence, exploitation and oppression. "The ethical demands made by Jesus are incapable of fulfillment in the present existence of man."[160] In fact, trying to live by that law of love leads to its opposite. Great harm can be done to a weaker neighbor under attack by a bully by "just loving" the bully. What Niebuhr was seeing was the coming war that would be launched by Hitler in 1939 against virtually all his weaker neighbors. What should the United States do? Love all the combatants equally? Most of the liberal Protestant pastors and theologians he was speaking to were pacifists, and that was their policy.[161] He heaped scorn on it while appealing respectfully to them to see the error of their ways. If they would have their way, the United States would sit on the sidelines of World War II "loving" both sides while millions of Jews and others died in the Holocaust. Niebuhr believed this would

---

[160]Niebuhr, *Interpretation of Christian Ethics* (Seabury, 1979), 35.

[161]It might be helpful to give an example of the kind of liberal Protestant pastor Niebuhr was talking to. Edwin Dahlberg (1892–1986) was an American Baptist pastor and social activist for peace. He was Rauschenbusch's teaching assistant at Rochester Theological Seminary and served as president of the Northern Baptist Convention and of the National Council of Churches. He helped establish the Fellowship of Reconciliation, a religious network of pacifists and peacemakers. Dahlberg worked tirelessly for peace throughout the 1930s into the 1960s. He was carrying on the legacy of his mentor Rauschenbusch. Niebuhr never names him, but clearly he was thinking of leaders like Dahlberg when he wrote *An Interpretation of Christian Ethics*.

be the most unloving thing possible. But he did not think war is loving, either. It is the lesser of two evils.

For Niebuhr, and this is the essence of Christian realism, love is necessary as the perfect standard toward which we must strive and by which we must measure the imperfections of all our acts. "Love is both the fulfillment and the negation of all achievements . . . in history."[162] It is the critical principle, given by Jesus himself, for prophetic criticism of all ethical behaviors. To think we can achieve it, outside of occasional acts of charity, is to lose it. Love stands over us in judgment, telling us that we have not yet arrived at perfection. The kingdom of God, the rule of perfect love, is an ideal that is always coming but never arriving, at least not by human social work. It is eschatological to the core—a future condition that pulls us toward itself and that qualifies all our partial accomplishments in social ethics. The moment someone thinks it has arrived, he or she has lost love's capacity, the kingdom of God's capacity, to reveal the imperfection of his or her achievement. To think one has arrived at it is to commit the sin of idolatry. We sinners *need* an impossible ideal to tell us we still have far to go. When we think we have achieved it we lose its value and identify ourselves and our social accomplishments with God.

Again, if love is impossible, what is possible? For Niebuhr, justice is the closest approximation to love under the conditions of sin.[163] Until the kingdom of God arrives, which will be God's doing and none of ours, we must settle for justice while keeping our eyes on love. This is called the dialectic of love and justice, and it is the soul of Christian realism. Love is unconditional and disinterested in questions of rights or deserts. Love is totally selfless. Love gives without asking any questions. Love never resists the other. Justice is the incarnation of love in concrete social relationships. Justice is freedom and equality and calculates rights and deserts. It uses reason to calculate the right thing to do. It uses coercion when necessary and resists evils like oppression and exploitation. Justice sometimes requires punishment; love always forgives unconditionally. Justice sometimes requires war; love never indulges in violence. But Niebuhr was not advo-

---

[162]Quoted in Larry Rasmussen, ed., *Reinhold Niebuhr: Theologian of Public Life* (Minneapolis: Fortress, 1991), 176.
[163]Niebuhr, *Interpretation of Christian Ethics* (Seabury, 1979), 80.

cating a dualism of love and justice because they are interdependent, especially for Christian ethics. That is the dialectical aspect of their relationship. They are very different principles that are nevertheless dependent on each other. Love is dependent on justice to work. Justice is dependent on love to be true justice and not revenge. Without love, justice does sink into a crass combat between groups asserting their rights and revenge against the wrong doers. Without justice love floats above the ground but never touches down to become effective in working out social problems caused by sin.

Returning to Niebuhr's critiques of naturalism and idealism, in his view naturalism empties justice of love because love is not a law of nature. It requires a transcendent source. Nature alone yields only self-interest as the highest value. But idealism empties love of justice and so never becomes effective in solving real problems. It prefers the heady spiritual mountain peaks impossible to reach to the rough-and-tumble plains where life happens and problems need solutions. According to Niebuhr, Christian liberalism, with its pacifism and idealism, abdicates responsibility for this world in favor of the dream of impossible perfection. Christians must learn to engage in the dirty job of doing justice while keeping one eye on the impossible ideal of love to purify justice by tempering it, for example, with mercy. For Niebuhr, the best apologetic for Christianity is its ability to offer an anthropology and social ethic that rises above the limitations of naturalism and idealism and that provides a prophetic principle that keeps always in play the difference-in-relationship of the ideal and the real, the perfect and the possible.

How did Niebuhr's dialectic of love and justice play out in specific social ethical issues? In politics it meant always striving for a balance of power in societies large and small.[164] Niebuhr firmly believed that power corrupts and that no person should be trusted absolutely. "Love everyone, trust no one" was one of his mottos. He thought that democracy was the right form of national politics, but it needed checks and balances and constant adjustments. In economics it meant constant redistribution of wealth without destroying incentives to produce. In international relations it meant the United States and other superpowers collaborating to keep peace and going

---

[164]Ibid., 69.

to war when necessary to protect weaker nations and ethnic groups.
Niebuhr was a strong believer in just war theory. In race relations it meant
contending with racist oppressors to bring about greater equality. Niebuhr's
comment about racism well illustrates his reasoning about love and justice:
"Only a religion full of romantic illusions could seek to persuade the Negro
to gain justice from the white man merely by forgiving him."[165] Martin
Luther King Jr. said that Niebuhr was even a greater influence on him than
Gandhi. People remember King as a pacifist, but his tactics, while not using
violence, often provoked violence. Niebuhr had strong opinions about a
wide range of social ethical issues and expressed them freely in *Christianity
and Crisis* and other publications. But his opinions about specific issues
were not as influential as his basic principles. People fleshed them out in
different ways.

*Niebuhr emphasizes God's transcendence and the realism of Christian
symbols.* Like Bultmann, Niebuhr was not a systematic theologian or doctrinal thinker. He was an ethicist but a theological ethicist. Also like
Bultmann, Niebuhr was strongly influenced by both Kant and Kierkegaard.
From Kant he took the view that humans can have no knowledge of things-
in-themselves without necessarily buying into all of Kant's epistemology.
He was an antimetaphysical thinker who viewed speculation about the reality behind appearances a waste of time. With Bultmann and many other
Kantian Christians he did not care about God-in-himself because we can
have no knowledge of that and it is irrelevant to practical life. That is to say,
he was not interested, in fact he was actively disinterested, in attempts to
understand the inner workings of the Trinity or the divine substance and
attributes or how the incarnation worked. It is difficult to know exactly
what he thought about doctrines like the virgin birth and bodily resurrection, as those were not his concerns. Whether and to what extent he
believed in the supernatural is up for debate.[166] From Kierkegaard, as al-

[165]Ibid., 141.
[166]One evidence of how widely varying interpretations of Niebuhr's Christian beliefs can be was
played out in a debate between theologians Stanley Hauerwas and Gabriel Fackre about
Niebuhr's Christianity. In his Gifford Lectures published as *With the Grain of the Universe*
(Grand Rapids: Brazos Press, 2001), Hauerwas argued that Niebuhr's theology was not Christian. Fackre responded with a lengthy and strongly worded refutation in *First Things* (October
2002): 25–27.

ready seen, Niebuhr took the idea that God's transcendence means mystery and all our thoughts about him will inevitably take the form of paradoxes based on biblical symbolism.

Two doctrines, or at least themes, of Christian theology were discussed by Niebuhr at some length because they were crucial to his ethics. Here Niebuhr's views of them will be expounded briefly with the caveat that he did not present them systematically or doctrinally in the usual sense, so his expositions were never intended to be complete accounts. They are the transcendence of God and the cross of Jesus Christ (atonement). For Niebuhr, both must be described using symbols. That corresponds to some extent with Bultmann's meaning of myth, although Niebuhr did not existentialize them to the same degree Bultmann did. Niebuhr was also not a literalist in biblical interpretation; he spoke about taking the Bible seriously without taking it literally. Exactly what he took literally and what he took nonliterally is not perfectly clear; he was not a biblical scholar like Bultmann. But he insisted that even though he tended to view revelation as symbolic, he took the biblical message with utmost seriousness and did not view it as a merely human account of religious experiences or the best religious thoughts of spiritual men and women. His view of the Bible and theology could be described as symbolic realism, the idea that symbols participate in the realities they symbolize and are not merely signs that can be exchanged for other signs without loss. The biblical symbols are irreducible because they are given by God to guide our thinking about mysteries that cannot be rationally comprehended. God's transcendence and the cross are two such symbols.

One thing that justifies categorizing Niebuhr as neo-orthodox is his emphasis on God's transcendence. In the face of modern denial, he sought to reaffirm the biblical idea of divine transcendence as a basis for both the judgment and the overcoming of the human predicament. For him, this dimension is set forth in the concept of the kingdom of God that has come in Christ and is to come as the culmination of history. On the one hand, only the idea of a transcendent God and the kingdom of God standing over against history could provide the needed point of judgment to check the human tendency toward pride.[167] These symbols stand as checks on all

---

[167]Reinhold Niebuhr, *Faith and History* (New York: Charles Scribner's Sons, 1949), 113.

human efforts. At every moment the kingdom of God remains a humanly unattainable divine ideal. On the other hand, the symbol of the transcendent establishes that the meaning of history is disclosed to the present, illuminating "the darkness of history's self-contradictions"[168] as it offers hope for a final completion of history in God.

Niebuhr saw hope expressed in three major eschatological symbols found in the Bible, none of which were to be interpreted literally but were nevertheless to be taken seriously.[169] The symbol of the return of Christ is an expression of faith in the sufficiency of God's sovereignty and in the final triumph of love. The last judgment affirms the seriousness of the distinction between good and evil. And the resurrection of all the dead implies "that eternity will fulfill and not annul" the variety found in the temporal process and that the dialectic of finiteness and freedom has no humanly devised solution.[170] Ultimately, the disclosure of the meaning of history, while perceived by faith, likewise serves the life of faith and the Christian witness in the world. Niebuhr concluded *The Nature and Destiny of Man* on this note. To live in faith means to find "ultimate security beyond all the securities and insecurities of history,"[171] that is, in the transcendent God of history. In 1939 Niebuhr expressed optimism that this type of faith could dissuade others "from the idolatrous pursuit of false securities and redemption in life and history."[172] He was referring to the temptations of ideologies such as fascism, Nazism and communism. The world was being thrown into the most devastating war in history because so many people sought meaning and security in idolatrous human projects that denied transcendence. But Niebuhr's point was that this is what always happens, sooner or later, when the symbol of transcendence, meaning and security found in a divine source beyond nature or humanity is denied and rejected. For him, this is the pathos of modernity. For all the great things it has produced, its deadly flaw is denial of transcendence, throwing humans back on themselves; anxiety feeds the search for security in themselves with the result that might becomes right.

---

[168]Niebuhr, *Nature and Destiny of Man*, 2:288.

[169]Ibid., 2:287–98.

[170]For Niebuhr's presentation of his understanding of the resurrection in terms of the human self, see *Self and the Dramas of History* (New York: Charles Scribner's Sons, 1955), 237–42.

[171]Niebuhr, *Nature and Destiny of Man*, 2:320.

[172]Ibid., 2:321.

The other important symbol for Niebuhr is the cross. Like transcendence it has a powerful effect on social ethics. For him, the focal point of Christian faith is the cross, for Christianity proclaims a gospel for which this event is central. In keeping with his rejection of the rationalist approach to reality, he cautioned that the meaning of the cross does not follow logically from observable facts of history[173] but is visible only to the eyes of faith. The cross is important because it is revelatory; it discloses the profound truth about humanity and about God. It speaks about the human situation. It shows the depth of the human predicament, our self-contradiction.[174] On the one hand, it is the declaration of divine judgment on sin; on the other hand it proclaims the divine love and forgiveness for sin. It is "a revelation of the love of God," yet only to those "who have first stood under its judgment."[175] The cross, then, provides the clue to the meaning of history, which lies in love, for it is "the myth [symbol] of the truth of the ideal of love."[176]

For Niebuhr, the cross has immediate significance for Christian social ethics. A person who knows he or she has been forgiven by God, something revealed in the cross, must forgive others. Justice must be tempered with mercy, and enemies, even when opposed and resisted, must not be hated. Niebuhr supported the Marshall Plan for rebuilding Germany after World War II precisely because it is never right to push down a conquered enemy who can be raised up with forgiveness and restoration. The cross stands for both judgment and mercy; the Christian must exercise both justice and mercy together.

Niebuhr leaves an ambiguous legacy filled with appreciation and criticism. Langdon Gilkey (1919–2004), himself one of the twentieth century's most influential theologians, taught theology at the University of Chicago Divinity School for many years. He oversaw the doctoral degrees of more than sixty students in theology, more than any other theology professor. He authored numerous books including *Naming the Whirlwind* (1970) and *Reaping the Whirlwind* (1976)—books that helped turn around the crisis in

---

[173]Niebuhr, *Faith and History*, 137.
[174]Gordon Harland, *The Thought of Reinhold Niebuhr* (New York: Oxford University Press, 1960), 20.
[175]Reinhold Niebuhr, *Christianity and Power Politics* (New York: Charles Scribner's Sons, 1940), 210.
[176]Niebuhr, "Truth in Myths," 31.

theology caused by the so-called death of God theology of certain 1960s radicals. Like Niebuhr, and partly because of him, Gilkey stood on the borderline between liberal theology and neo-orthodoxy. One of his last books was *On Niebuhr: A Theological Study* (2004). He spoke for a generation of American theologians when he testified, "I am vastly indebted to this [Niebuhr's] theology, and, as much as any person in another generation can agree with a thinker, I hold Niebuhr's theology to be amazingly profound and true to experience as I have known it—more so than any other viewpoint I have encountered."[177]

What did Gilkey find so valuable in Niebuhr's theology? He considered it the best synthesis of modernity and classical Christianity, especially as represented by Augustine and the Reformers. This is ironic, as Niebuhr, following Kierkegaard, did not believe in the Hegelian dialectic of synthesis of opposites. Nevertheless, Gilkey and others found in Niebuhr a way to combine the best of modernity with the best of the Christian tradition including biblical truth. According to Gilkey, Niebuhr's "synthesis reshapes and redefines them both."[178] Classical Christianity is interpreted in terms of modernity's emphasis on change and relativity of all forms, but modernity's commitment to progress is rejected. Modernity is interpreted in terms of classical Christianity's emphasis on the transcendent sources of meaning, but classical Christianity's literalism and authoritarianism are rejected. But, according to Gilkey, ultimately Niebuhr challenges modernity. "To Niebuhr . . . the modern religion of progress is not only partial, prejudiced toward Western and middle-class values; it is also empty of empirical validity, of spiritual validity, and, most important, of redemptive power in the face of the tragic character of life."[179]

It is worthwhile to quote Gilkey's final judgment on Niebuhr's theology because it represents a positive assessment that avoids the tendencies of theologians both right and left to condemn Niebuhr as either liberal (overaccommodation to modernity) or fundamentalist (rejection of modernity). Many, especially American mainline Christian theologians, agree with this

---

[177]Langdon Gilkey, *On Niebuhr: A Theological Study* (Chicago: University of Chicago Press, 2004), 223.
[178]Ibid., 248.
[179]Ibid.

generally positive evaluation of Niebuhr as a successful correlator of modernity and classical Christianity:

> Niebuhr's most fundamental argument was that human existence so viewed (i.e., in modern terms) must be viewed Biblically, in relation to the transcendent God who is continually related in judgment and in grace to our world; and that modern life must in turn be lived in faith, love and hope if it is to escape self-destruction and despair. Niebuhr's theology represents, therefore, a correlation, if ever there was one, between a modern ontology and Biblical symbols, a correlation in which each side reshapes the other— and makes possible a Christian existence within the precarious terms of modern life.[180]

"Correlation" is a better term for Niebuhr's achievement than "synthesis." His existentialism would forbid the latter without rejecting the former.

Stanley Hauerwas (b. 1940) strongly disagrees with Gilkey's evaluation of Niebuhr's achievement. Hauerwas is probably second only to Gilkey in terms of influence on a recent generation of young American theologians. He taught theology at Yale, Notre Dame and Duke University Divinity School and wrote many books on a wide variety of subjects, most of them dealing in some way with Christian social ethics. His Gifford Lectures were published in 2001 as *With the Grain of the Universe* and represented a sustained critique of Niebuhr's theology as not Christian. According to Hauerwas, Niebuhr did not successfully synthesize or correlate modernity and Christianity but capitulated to modernity ending up agreeing almost completely with American philosopher William James's (1842–1910) pragmatism and therefore secularism. Hauerwas was not impressed with Niebuhr's use of biblical symbols or his emphasis on transcendence; in the end he judged that Niebuhr had thrown a veneer of Christianity over modernity. He recognized that Niebuhr did not agree with everything of modernity, but his basic impulses were naturalistic and modern and not truly biblical or Christian. One area where Hauerwas especially scored Niebuhr is his defense of violence as sometimes a necessary evil. The Duke theologian accused the Union theologian of sacrificing too much of the biblical message about peace on the altar of modern nation-state militarism.

---

[180]Ibid.

Another pacifist theologian, a Quaker woman, criticized Niebuhr for allegedly omitting the Holy Spirit from theology. In *The Omission of the Holy Spirit from Reinhold Niebuhr's Theology* Rachel Hadley King accused Niebuhr of capitulating to modernity's naturalism in a manner similar to Bultmann. According to her, Niebuhr's entire theology is an attempt to rescue something of Christianity after traditional Christian supernaturalism has been discarded. The result is a devastating loss to Christianity because it makes any real God-creature relationship impossible:

> In Niebuhr's description of the converted sinner's relation to God at the Cross we see a great effort to describe some real intercourse between God and the human spirit. But Niebuhr is unconvincing here as he was unconvincing when he tried to describe revelation. And the reason is the same in both cases: any real Divine human intercourse would involve a breaking of the creation barrier and Niebuhr's thought will not admit this as a possibility.[181]

King was not merely criticizing Niebuhr for omitting the Holy Spirit from the Trinity; by "omission of the Holy Spirit" she was accusing Niebuhr of neglecting, if not outrightly denying, any real God-human relationship of interaction in which God supernaturally acts in the world to transform people. She knew Niebuhr emphasized God's forgiveness of sinners, but her problem with Niebuhr was what she saw as his overall naturalistic bent that seemed to rule out the Holy Spirit's inward work in forgiven people's lives.

Rushing in to defend Niebuhr from these attacks was Congregationalist narrative theologian Gabriel Fackre (b. 1926), who knew Niebuhr personally and found especially Hauerwas's criticisms unfair. Soon after *With the Grain of the Universe* was published Fackre wrote a lengthy article titled "Was Reinhold Niebuhr a Christian?" (*First Things*, October 2002). There, using quotations from Niebuhr's writings, he attempted to prove that Niebuhr did believe in the power of God in the world including the resurrection of Jesus Christ, something King had claimed Niebuhr denied. Fackre's answer to his own question was a resounding yes.

What is one to make of these radically different interpretations of Niebuhr's theology and social ethic? First, one has to remember that

---

[181]Rachel Hadley King, *The Omission of the Holy Spirit from Reinhold Niebuhr's Theology* (New York: Philosophical Library, 1964), 147.

Niebuhr was a dialectical thinker heavily influenced by existentialism and so he was not particularly concerned about certain questions including almost anything metaphysical. And, because of that mode of thinking and influence, he did not see any problem with paradoxes and apparent contradictions. In fact, they can be a sign of the mystery of transcendence. When reading the competing quotations from Niebuhr's enormous body of writings found in his critics and defenders the only conclusion must be that he was not completely consistent with himself. At times he seemed to deny the supernatural activity of God, including the bodily resurrection and empty tomb of Jesus, while at other times he seemed to affirm it. It is tempting to think that some of this depends on whom he was arguing against at a particular time. But these were not his central concerns. His central concern was always ethics and especially the relationship between love and justice. When it came to classical doctrines of Christianity he was often ambiguous or silent.

Niebuhr's critics almost always bring up his seeming pessimism about progress toward the kingdom of God. It seems to them that he undermined any motive to work for the kingdom, to strive to establish love in the social order. There is no doubt that he believed love can be the chief motive and, to a certain extent, achieved in small contexts of one-on-one charity and in the family. However, as critics are quick to point out, he laid down as an absolute principle that there is no human act free of egoism. So, perfect love is impossible for human beings under the conditions of sin, that is, within history before the kingdom of God arrives, in any context. Even more importantly, his ethic ruled out any idea of the kingdom of God being achieved by humans in history even temporarily. Critics claim that he broke the important biblical paradox of the "already, but not yet" nature of the kingdom of God. But they often forget or ignore that he did believe justice can be achieved even if not perfectly. And he was willing to settle for that rather than go with what he saw as the liberal tendency to identify the kingdom of God with democracy or socialism or any human social arrangement. His whole point was that once some human achievement or social order is identified with the kingdom of God there is no longer any reason to "mend its every flaw." Yes, Niebuhr was a pessimist, or realist, but he saw the twentieth century as vindication.

Finally, what of Niebuhr and science? Does the thesis that much of modern theology is constructed to avoid conflicts between science and Christianity hold in Niebuhr's case? According to Gilkey, it does hold. He devotes several pages of *On Niebuhr* to "The Influence of Science on Theology" with special reference to its influence on the Union theologian. Gilkey thinks that much of modern theology, including so-called biblical theology, by which he means neo-orthodoxy, constitutes a major capitulation to modern science and retreat from it. He thinks this was and is right, but he thinks especially in neo-orthodoxy, including Niebuhr, it was largely unacknowledged.

> If, therefore, one wishes to know why Niebuhr states that the original Biblical myths are no longer credible if understood as literal truth . . . clearly the major reasons lie in Niebuhr's acceptance of these developing scientific concepts of our human past. . . . Niebuhr was right (as was Kierkegaard) that there are excellent theological reasons for discarding a literal interpretation of the myths of creation and fall. But he seems (to me) sublimely unaware (or perhaps loathe to recognize) that the fundamental ground of this new "symbolic" rather than "literal" hermeneutic of the Scriptures was the influence of the new scientific understanding of nature and the new historical understanding of the ancient world.[182]

Indeed. If Niebuhr was right about the essence of Christianity as having to do with social ethics, and about the symbolic nature of revelation, then conflict between science and Christianity is literally impossible unless one views science as requiring naturalism, which Niebuhr rightly did not.

---

[182]Gilkey, *On Niebuhr*, 234.

6

CHASTENED LIBERAL THEOLOGIES
RENEW AND REVISE THE
DIALOGUE WITH MODERNITY

Liberal Protestant theology underwent a dramatic alteration during the period between the two world wars. Most obviously, it had to give up the myth of inevitable progress and accept a sense of the tragic. The category of sin was recovered even if fundamentally changed. The result of these and other amendments to classical liberal theology was the emergence of something that can be called neo-liberalism or chastened liberalism. Two of its most influential manifestations are the theology of Paul Tillich and a theological movement known as process theology. As different as they are, both sought to come to terms with modernity in light of the new situation of the twentieth century. Both sought to correlate Christianity with philosophy. Both attempted in their own ways to discover a settlement of the centuries-old war between science and religion.

Neo-liberalism displays continuity and discontinuity with the older, classical liberal theology of the nineteenth century. With the latter, neo-liberal theologians emphasize the immanence of God, usually embracing some form of panentheism.[1] God is viewed as radically present in the world and history if not dependent on them. Neo-liberal theologians also tend to do theology from below, from human experience, so that revelation is sought outside of Scripture in the structures of human existence and/or of nature. Also, neo-liberals usually view all doctrines as revisable in light of new discoveries in contemporary thought; "the best of contemporary thought" becomes a source and norm of theology. The supernatural is problematic for neo-liberals; most are theological naturalists who view God as the hand in the glove of nature or as a depth dimension in nature, and they tend to deny miracles. Earlier we defined liberal theology as maximal acknowledgment of the claims of modernity. Neo-liberal theology is a more nuanced, complex relationship with modernity but still regards the Enlightenment and scientific revolutions as crises that forced theology to abandon orthodoxy. Like the older liberals in theology, neo-liberals tend to have a functional Christology in which Jesus Christ is different from other humans in degree rather than in kind. He functioned as God rather than being God incarnate. Finally, neo-liberals, like their classical counterparts, are to a person universalists with regard to salvation (unless salvation is interpreted as a wholly this-worldly experience).

There are significant differences between the older liberal theology and neo-, or chastened, liberal theology. One is the change from optimism to realism. Almost all the older liberal theologians viewed humanity as infinitely perfectible and looked forward to the arrival of a kingdom of God on earth through reason and education. Enlightenment philosopher Lessing (referred to in 2.c.) wrote about the moral education of the human race. For him and for many nineteenth-century liberal theologians, that is Christianity's main task and, especially for late-nineteenth-century theologians, it

---

[1]"Panentheism" is a term whose meaning is undergoing some change in the first years of the twenty-first century. Originally, panentheism meant the idea that God and the world are interdependent realities existing eternally in a relationship of mutual reciprocity. That is, God has no existence totally separate from the world. This denies the traditional Christian idea of creation out of nothing (*creatio ex nihilo*). In the first decades of the twenty-first century some calling themselves panentheists seem to mean only something like "relational theism"—the idea that the world affects God. For detailed discussions of panentheism see Philip Clayton and Arthur Peacocke, eds., *In Whom We Live and Move and Have Our Being: Panentheistic Reflections on God's Presence in a Scientific World* (Grand Rapids: Eerdmans, 2004) and John W. Cooper, *Panentheism: The Other God of the Philosophers* (Grand Rapids: Baker Academic, 2006).

was expected to yield a kingdom of love among people through peaceful persuasion. Neo-liberals are chastened because of the horrors of the twentieth century. Also, neo-orthodoxy's renewed emphasis on sin affected many of them. Whatever the causes, chastened liberals are not as optimistic about humanity and progress as were the older liberal theologians.

Perhaps the most notable similarity between the older liberal theology and the newer one is the use of philosophy. Nineteenth-century liberal theologians were heavily invested in romanticism (Schleiermacher), Kant (Ritschl) and Hegel (nearly all were influenced by his emphasis on God's immanence in history). Neo-liberal theologians likewise view some particular philosophical movement as necessary for the needed reconstruction of doctrine in order to make it relevant to contemporary culture. Tillich, for example, as will be seen, relied heavily on twentieth-century existentialism in which he was deeply immersed. He even called it the "good luck" of Christian theology for modernity. Process theologians rely heavily on the process philosophy of Alfred North Whitehead (1861–1947) and one of his main American interpreters, Charles Hartshorne (1897–2000). They could very well have said that process philosophy is the good luck of modern theology. All neo-liberals find philosophy essential to contemporary theology.

The most notable dissimilarity between the older liberal theology and the newer one is, as already suggested, the problem of evil. Classical liberal theology tended to view evil, including sin, as selfishness out of which humanity is growing through the "socialization of the soul" (Rauschenbusch). It is the not-yet-ness of the kingdom of God, the drag of humanity's animal nature on its spiritual evolution. For example, for Schleiermacher it was lack of God-consciousness. For Ritschlians it was lack of ethical education and commitment. Neo-liberals tend to have a more profound view of evil as deeply rooted in human existence, not something that can be overcome by taking thought and putting forth great effort. Neo-liberals do not expect a kingdom of God, as a social utopia, on earth.

Someone approaching both classical liberal theology and neo-liberal theology must understand that both agree with Niebuhr that it is important, and possible, to take the Bible seriously without taking it literally. For both, and this includes Bultmann and Niebuhr as well, the Bible is *the* Christian classic but not absolutely authoritative or infallible. Its inspiration is its ability to inspire rather than having God as its author. People who expect Christian theologians to adhere to anything like the classical Protestant *sola scriptura* will be unable to understand neo-liberals.

Now, admittedly, this has been a quick and nontechnical portrait of liberal and neo-liberal theologies, their similarities and differences. Not all scholars of modern and contemporary theology will agree with all of it, and this writer knows of no comparative study of the two. Most who write about liberal theology tend to lump Tillich and process theology into the liberal category with Schleiermacher, Ritschl, Harnack, Rauschenbusch and Troeltsch while acknowledging some differences. Some separate them into two entirely different categories because of their different views of evil. In that case, then, there would be very few liberal theologians left. This writer sees great continuity between the older and the newer liberal theologies while acknowledging significant differences. But it must be acknowledged that Tillich distanced himself from liberal theology because of his tragic sense of existence and history that he shared with Niebuhr. And yet all the neo-orthodox theologians distanced themselves from Tillich because of his lack of emphasis on the kerygma. Process theologians usually gladly accept the label "liberal" while carefully distancing themselves from older liberal theology that tended to reduce Christianity to social morality. They are unapologetically interested in metaphysics, something both the older liberals and neo-orthodox disdained.

6.A. PAUL TILLICH DESCRIBES GOD AS THE GROUND OF BEING, A "GOD ABOVE GOD"

Tillich was, like Niebuhr, an American icon, a public intellectual whose portrait graced the cover of *Time* magazine (March 16, 1959). Throughout the 1950s and early 1960s he drew great crowds wherever he spoke. Langdon Gilkey recounts Tillich's arrival to speak in Nashville, where Gilkey was teaching theology at Vanderbilt University:

> Several faculty persons . . . worried that the audience to hear this "philosopher" would be miniscule and thus far outclassed by the overflowing congregations coming to hear a well-known evangelist from Florida. Why not put Tillich in our small Divinity School chapel and the evangelist in the University auditorium? . . . This anxious prophecy was far off the mark. Tillich

drew immense crowds each night, the auditorium being more crowded at the end than it was on the first night.[2]

While many listeners understood Tillich in spite of his heavy German accent and sometimes elusive, if not esoteric, ideas, others came because he was famous and came back because he had a personal charisma that made them feel he was addressing them personally. Gilkey reports overhearing one woman who heard Tillich in Nashville comment to a companion, "I did not understand a word of what that man said, but he was speaking directly to me every moment of the lecture."[3]

More than any other twentieth-century theologian Tillich deserves the title "apostle to the intellectuals."[4] In a manner reminiscent of second-century Christian apologists such as Justin Martyr he sought to communicate the essential truths of the Christian faith to the intellectuals among his contemporaries in their own thought forms. Toward the end of his life he acknowledged this overriding apologetic purpose and passion by confessing, "My whole theological work has been directed to the interpretation of religious symbols in such a way that the secular man—and we are all secular—can understand and be moved by them."[5]

Tillich's theological contribution is comparable to Barth's in terms of overall influence and effect although it is quite opposite in terms of approach. Like Barth, he produced a massive system of theology that influenced an entire generation of Christian thinkers and was granted the notice and acclaim of secular society as well. Unlike Barth, he strove for positive correlation, if not synthesis, between modern secular philosophy and Christian faith.

Although Tillich died in 1965, his legacy endures into the first decades of the twenty-first century. An international society of philosophers and theologians called the North American Paul Tillich Society continues scholarly discussion of his work. The centennial of his birth in 1986 saw a number of conferences devoted to his theology and its enduring signifi-

---

[2]Langdon Gilkey, *Gilkey on Tillich* (New York: Crossroads, 1990), 199.
[3]Ibid., 198.
[4]Robert W. Schrader, *The Nature of Theological Argument: A Study of Paul Tillich* (Missoula, MT: Scholars Press, 1975), 73–74.
[5]D. Mackenzie Brown, ed., *Ultimate Concern: Tillich in Dialogue* (New York: Harper & Row, 1956), 88–89.

cance. In 1977 a published study of North American theologians identified Tillich as the most important influence on American systematic theology.[6] During his lifetime he was recognized by secular culture as one of the greatest minds Christian theology had ever produced. Few theologians have received the honor and recognition accorded him by politicians, governments, universities and foundations. Even the media recognized his importance; several filmed interviews with him were produced for public television, and some are still available on the Internet in the second decade of the twenty-first century.

Tillich escapes Nazism and rises to worldwide fame in America. Like so many other German theologians, Tillich was born into the family of a Lutheran pastor.[7] He seems to have had a serious interest in theology and philosophy from an early age—possibly even as young as eight—and began moving toward a career in ministry at the age of eighteen. Like most university students in Germany at the time, he studied at several major German universities including Halle and Berlin, coming under the influence of critical philosophy, theology and biblical studies. During his education for ordination he determined to become a professor of theology and eventually received not only ordination in the Protestant state church but also appointment as *Privatdozent* (tutor) at the University of Halle.

Tillich's studies were interrupted temporarily by World War 1 in which he served as a chaplain. He spent time on the front lines of battle and not only officiated at the funerals of many soldiers—including some of his friends—but also helped bury them with his own hands. His encounters with mass death and destruction became a turning point in his personal life and faith. He suffered two nervous breakdowns and underwent a severe crisis of doubt that transformed his view of God. After the war, he accepted a teaching position at the prestigious University of Berlin and became in-

---

[6]Thor Hall, *Systematic Theology: State of the Art in North America* (Washington, DC: University Press of America, 1978), 94.

[7]Most of the biographical information here is taken from the authoritative biography of Tillich by his friends Wilhelm Pauck and Marion Pauck: *Paul Tillich, His Life and Thought,* vol. 1 (New York: Harper & Row, 1976). Wilhelm Pauck was one of Tillich's students and became one of his most intimate friends. There are several biographies of Tillich including one by his wife Hannah titled *From Time to Time* (New York: Stein and Day, 1973), which created a great deal of morbid fascination and controversy. Since this chapter is intended to be an introduction to Tillich's theology, the details of his private life, however fascinating, must be left aside.

volved with radical socialist politics. He was instrumental in the formation of a religious socialist movement and published a major book on the subject entitled *The Socialist Decision* (1933). During the 1920s he became a well-known figure in German academic circles. He left Berlin first for Marburg, then moved to Dresden and finally to Frankfurt, where he came into open conflict with the budding Nazi movement. When the Nazis came to power Tillich was labeled an "enemy of the state," and *The Socialist Decision* was burned publicly. In October 1933, the Gestapo began to follow him.

Had he stayed in Germany Tillich would almost certainly have ended up in a concentration camp. He was spared that fate by the invitations of Columbia University and Union Theological Seminary to move to New York to teach there. Tillich moved in 1933 and, with much help from Reinhold Niebuhr, eventually became acclimatized to American culture. He became a US citizen in 1940. Tillich taught at Union Theological Seminary until his retirement in 1955. During his twenty-three years there he gained great fame for his sermons, many of which were published, and for his theological reflections on many areas of contemporary culture including the arts. In 1940 he was given an honorary doctoral degree by Yale University and was cited as a "philosopher among theologians and a theologian among philosophers."[8]

During World War II Tillich secretly delivered radio addresses to the German people for the Voice of America and met with President Franklin Roosevelt at the White House in 1944. In the years immediately after the war he traveled widely, giving numerous lectures to enthusiastic audiences so that "only a few years before his retirement from the seminary, Tillich acquired a wide and enthusiastic public which clamored to hear him."[9] In his first volume of *Systematic Theology* (1951) he expounded his views on theological method, reason and revelation, and God. The second volume appeared in 1957 and dealt with the human predicament and Christ. Volume 3, published in 1963, focused on the theme of life and the Spirit as well as on history and the kingdom of God. His other publications such as *The Courage to Be* (1952) and *The Dynamics of Faith* (1957) appealed to a more popular audience, as did his sermons and public lectures.

---

[8]Pauk and Pauk, *Paul Tillich*, 1:198.
[9]Ibid., 1:219.

On retiring from the seminary, Tillich accepted the invitation of Harvard University's president to become university professor—perhaps the most prestigious academic position in the United States. It meant he was able to teach any course he wished and had great freedom to travel, research and write. His Harvard lectures were tremendously popular among students with hundreds filling the lecture hall an hour early to be assured of having a seat. A cult of personality formed around him, with students lining the sidewalk to the building in order to see him walk past. His lectures at other universities drew hundreds and even thousands of listeners in spite of the fact that some critics claimed his talks were nothing more than "unintelligible nonsense."[10]

Tillich received an invitation to John F. Kennedy's inauguration in 1961 and was seated on the platform with a small group of special guests. He received twelve honorary doctorates from major American universities and two from European ones. After retirement from Harvard in 1962 he became Nuveen Professor of Theology at the University of Chicago Divinity School and served as distinguished theologian in residence. His death on October 22, 1965, was noted in the *New York Times* with a brief editorial and front-page obituary.

Few theologians have ever received the public acclaim Tillich did. He was truly a legend in his own time. However, his life as a Christian theologian was marked by great ambiguity and controversy. He was beset by doubts about his own salvation and feared death greatly.[11] He promoted socialism while enjoying the benefits of an upper-middle-class lifestyle.[12] He was a renowned ecumenical Christian yet rarely attended church[13] and apparently lived a fairly promiscuous lifestyle.[14]

Such ambiguities well illustrate the destructive ambiguities and tensions that Tillich himself believed are inherent in finite existence. For him, doubt is a necessary element of faith, and alienation and estrangement lie at the very root of human life. The Power of Being—God—can help us gain courage to face the inevitable threat of nonbeing and to accept that we are

---

[10]Ibid., 1:250.
[11]Ibid., 1:275.
[12]Ibid., 1:274.
[13]Ibid., 1:251.
[14]For a balanced and generous account of Tillich's marriage and infidelities see ibid., 1:85–93.

accepted, but it cannot completely overcome these tensions and ambiguities of existence. In order to understand these themes, which are so central to Tillich's theology, we must make clear certain elements of his basic presuppositions and theological method.

Tillich presupposes philosophy as basic to theology. Understanding Tillich's theological method requires first knowing his presuppositions, the first of which is that theology should be apologetic. It must formulate and communicate its concepts in a way that truly speaks to the contemporary situation. By "situation" he meant the particular questions and concerns of people in culture, "the scientific and artistic, the economic, political, and ethical forms in which they express their interpretation of existence."[15] He was harshly critical of theologies, such as fundamentalism and kerygmatic theology, which neglected the role of this situation and tried, in his words, to throw the Christian message at people like a stone instead of attempting to answer the questions put to it by contemporary culture.[16] For him, in contrast, theology must be "answering theology"; it must adapt the Christian message to the modern mind while maintaining its essential truth and unique character.

Apologetic theology presupposes some common ground between the Christian message and the contemporary culture in which it is being expressed. The existence of such common ground is another basic presupposition of Tillich's theology. At the least, he believed, the questions implicit in contemporary existence can and must be answered by theology as it draws on divine revelation. If this were not possible, theology would be obsolete, because it cannot answer questions that are not being asked. Fortunately, Tillich believed, the fundamental questions raised by contemporary existence are indeed answered, specifically in the symbols of divine revelation.

A third basic presupposition of Tillich's theology is the crucial role played by philosophy in theology's apologetic task. In direct contrast to Barth, he believed that philosophy is indispensible to theology, because it formulates

---

[15]Paul Tillich, *Systematic Theology: Reason and Revelation, Being and God*, 3 vols. in 1 (New York: Harper & Row; Evanston, IL: University of Chicago Press, 1967), 1:3–4. Hereafter references to Tillich's systematic theology will read *Theology* plus volume number. The pagination for the volumes in the three-in-one edition is the same as for the separate volumes, which were originally published by the University of Chicago Press.

[16]Ibid., 1:7.

the questions that theology answers and because it provides much, if not all, of the form that those answers should take. Consequently, Tillich held philosophy in high regard: "No theologian should be taken seriously as a theologian, even if he is a great Christian and a great scholar, if his work shows that he does not take philosophy seriously."[17] Against the fideism of thinkers such as Pascal, he remarked, "The God of Abraham, Isaac and Jacob and the God of the philosophers is the same God."[18]

Closely related to the third presupposition is a fourth. The particular kind of philosophy most useful to theology is ontology, especially existentialist ontology. In fact, Tillich defined philosophy so as to make it virtually synonymous with ontology: Philosophy is "that cognitive approach to reality in which reality as such is the object,"[19] and ontology is the "analysis of those structures of being which we encounter in every meeting with reality."[20] Tillich would not settle for any definition or use of philosophy that stops short of ontology, because it is the true center of all philosophy[21] and its questions and concerns are implicit in every other approach to philosophy.[22] At its root, then, philosophy is ontology—the study of being. It raises ontological questions such as what it means to say that something *is*, what is ultimately real beyond all appearances, what is being itself beyond all particular things that have being and what structures are inherent in everything that has being. Hence, he declared, "philosophy asks the question of reality as a whole; it asks the question of the structure of being. And it answers in terms of categories, structural laws, and universal concepts. It must answer in ontological terms."[23]

For Tillich, ontology's usefulness to theology lay in questions it raises more than in the specific answers it offers. A helpful example is his delineation of the question of nonbeing, with which the ancient Greek philoso-

---

[17]Paul Tillich, *Biblical Religion and the Search for Ultimate Reality* (Chicago: University of Chicago Press, 1955), 7–8. This book, comprising only eighty-five pages, constitutes a major exposition and defense of theology's use of philosophy. It should be read carefully once before and once after reading his systematic theology.
[18]Ibid., 85.
[19]Tillich, *Theology*, 1:18.
[20]Ibid., 1:20.
[21]Tillich, *Biblical Religion*, 6.
[22]Tillich, *Theology*, 1:20.
[23]Ibid.

phers wrestled and which twentieth-century existentialist philosophers revived, although in a different way. For Tillich, this continued interest in
nonbeing was not surprising, because "anxiety about non-being is present in
everything finite."[24] It is natural for humans to wonder about their own status
in relation to being, because in their moments of deepest thought they realize
that they are finite, transitory, temporal. They might not be just as easily as be.
In fact, nonbeing belongs to their existence, for they are faced with the threat
of nonbeing at every moment. Nonbeing raises the question of a power of
being that overcomes the threat of nonbeing and upholds and sustains finite
beings. Such a power cannot be finite but must be "being itself" or the
"ground of being." Without it, finite existence would sink into nonbeing and
nothingness. In short, the ontological question of nonbeing and the power of
being raise the question of God, Tillich believed. In fact, without the ontological question, he argued, the answer theology sets forth—God—cannot be
understood. In his words, "only those who have experienced the shock of
transitoriness, the anxiety in which they are aware of their finitude, the threat
of non-being, can understand what the notion of God means."[25]

Ontology, then, is absolutely crucial to contemporary apologetic theology.
This is especially the case given the dominance of existentialist philosophy in
the twentieth century. In fact, existentialist ontology, Tillich said, is the
"good luck of Christian theology,"[26] because it raises questions that theology,
drawing on divine revelation, is particularly suited to answer. In this way,
questions and answers concerning ontology form the common ground of
philosophy and theology: "The structure of being and the categories and
concepts describing this structure are an implicit or explicit concern of every
philosopher and of every theologian. Neither of them can avoid the ontological question."[27] Of course, the approaches of philosophy and theology to
the question of being differ considerably. Philosophy takes the attitude of
detached objectivity while theology looks at ultimate being, the power that
overcomes the threat of nonbeing, with "passion, fear, and love."[28] Nevertheless, in order to deal adequately with ontological issues and concerns,

---

[24]Ibid., 2:67.
[25]Ibid., 1:62.
[26]Ibid., 2:27.
[27]Ibid., 1:21.
[28]Ibid., 1:22.

Tillich averred, one must take on both roles—that of philosopher and that of theologian. Every creative philosopher is some of the time a theologian,[29] and every theologian must also play the role of philosopher in order to analyze the existential situation of humanity and the questions implied therein. Philosophy and theology are two distinct but inseparable and interdependent "moments" or aspects of a fully orbed ontology.

A final presupposition of Tillich's theology is the special nature of human existence in ontology. This is best expressed in the assertion, made several times in *Systematic Theology*, that "man is microcosm."[30] By this, Tillich meant that the powers and structures of being appear in the human in a way not true of any other creature. Human beings themselves are open to and participate in the structures of being both below and above themselves, so that their being provides special clues to ultimate reality: "Man participates in the universe through the rational structures of mind and reality. . . . He participates in the universe because the universal structures, forms, and laws are open to him."[31] Therefore, ontological reflection must turn to humanity, not to nonhuman nature, if it is to formulate questions and answers about ultimate reality or being itself.

These presuppositions underlie and inform Tillich's entire thought. But they were also highly controversial and have been the source of much scholarly debate. Most philosophers, especially in the English-speaking world, have reacted negatively to his identification of philosophy with ontology and even more negatively to his assertion of the inseparability of philosophy and theology.[32] Many theologians have criticized him for making Christian theology the prisoner of "ontological speculation," thus jettisoning both the autonomy of theology and biblical personalism.[33] Perhaps the most damaging criticism is

---

[29]Ibid., 1:25. See also Tillich, *Biblical Religion*, 64–66.

[30]Tillich, *Theology*, 1:176, 260; 2:23, 120.

[31]Ibid., 1:176.

[32]For a good critique by a sympathetic philosopher, see John Herman Randall Jr., "The Ontology of Paul Tillich," in *The Theology of Paul Tillich*, ed. Charles W. Kegley and Robert W. Bretall (New York: Macmillan, 1964), 132–61.

[33]Reinhold Niebuhr gently criticizes Tillich for subverting biblical drama to ontological speculation in "Biblical Thought and Ontological Speculation in Tillich's Theology," in *The Theology of Paul Tillich*, ed. Charles W. Kegley and Robert W. Bretall (New York: Macmillan, 1964), 216–27. Kenneth Hamilton accuses Tillich of allowing a philosophical system of ontological speculation ("*logos* philosophy") to predetermine and control the content of the Christian message. See Kenneth Hamilton, *The System and the Gospel: A Critique of Paul Tillich* (New York: Macmillan, 1963), esp. 227–39.

that close inspection of Tillich's ontology reveals that it is eclectic. It attempts to combine totally incompatible strands of philosophy: traditional ontology rooted in Plato, Augustine and the German idealist philosophers and modern existentialist ontologies formulated by Heidegger and Sartre.[34]

Tillich develops the method of correlation for theology. Building on these presuppositions, Tillich proceeded to propose a method for theology that would be both faithful to the original Christian message and contemporary in expression—the method of correlation. This approach determined the entire structure and form of his systematic theology and is often considered one of his most enduring contributions to modern theology. He offered this method of correlation, which "explains the contents of the Christian faith through existential questions and theological answers in mutual interdependence,"[35] in conscious rejection of three inadequate alternatives. The first alternative, the "supernaturalistic," is followed by many Protestant theologians and is basically synonymous with theology from above. For Tillich it is inadequate because it ignores the questions and concerns (the "situation") of humans who are to receive the message and expects the Word of God to create the possibility for understanding and accepting its truth.[36] According to Tillich, in contrast, "man cannot receive answers to questions he never has asked."[37] No doubt Tillich was thinking of both fundamentalism and Barthian neo-orthodoxy here. The conservative might respond, "What if human beings, because of their fallenness, never ask the right questions?" Tillich believed that the right questions are present in human existence.[38]

The second inadequate traditional alternative, the "naturalistic" or "humanistic" method, is the opposite of the first, for it attempts to derive theological answers from the natural human state without recourse to revelation. In this method, typical of much liberal theology, "everything was said by man, nothing to man."[39] Tillich accused the humanistic method of overlooking the

---

[34]The analysis and criticism of this conflation is the subject of Adrian Thatcher, *The Ontology of Paul Tillich* (Oxford: Oxford University Press, 1978).
[35]Tillich, *Theology*, 1:60.
[36]Ibid., 1:64–65.
[37]Ibid., 1:65.
[38]Ibid.
[39]Ibid.

estrangement of human existence and the fact that revelation, which contains the answers, is something spoken to humans, not by them to themselves.[40]

Finally, Tillich rejected the "dualistic" method, which tries to combine the supernatural with the natural. Here he was referring to traditional natural theology, such as what has been common in traditional Catholicism since Thomas Aquinas. It posits two kinds of theological answers—those derivable from nature alone, such as the existence of God, and those which must be supernaturally revealed such as the Trinity. The problem with this method is that it tries to derive the answer (God) from the form of the question. In its place Tillich proposed the method of correlation which resolves natural theology into the analysis of human existence and supernatural theology into the answers given to the questions implied in existence.[41]

The method of correlation, then, is a form of fundamental theology (not fundamentalism) that substitutes for natural theology. Tillich's approach replaces the proofs of the existence of God that traditionally form a large part of natural theology with the question of God implied in human existence as analyzed by ontology. The method revolves around questions and answers. The questions are raised by philosophy through careful examination of human existence. The theologian must function as a philosopher in this first step of theology. The second step is uniquely theological, as the theologian draws on the symbols of divine revelation to formulate answers to the questions implied in human existence that philosophy discovers but cannot answer. The overall task of the theologian in both steps is to bring the questions and the answers together in critical correlation.[42] The content of the answers theology presents must be derived from revelation, but they must be expressed in a form that will speak to the existential concerns of human beings. So it, the form, must be derived from philosophy. The theologian's task is to interpret the answers of revelation so that they remain faithful to the original Christian message while becoming relevant to the questions asked by modern secular men and women.

According to Tillich, "God" stands as a preliminary example of how the method of correlation works:

---

[40]Ibid.
[41]Ibid., 1:65–66.
[42]Ibid., 1:64.

God is the answer to the question implied in human finitude. However, if the notion of God appears in systematic theology in correlation with the threat of non-being which is implied in existence, God must be called the infinite power of being which resists the threat of non-being. In classical theology this is being itself.[43]

The *Systematic Theology* follows this method. In the first part Tillich analyzed the nature of human reason under the conditions of existence, discovering that it contains the question concerning something that transcends reason while fulfilling it. Thus, reason itself, as analyzed by ontology, raises the "quest for revelation." Tillich then proceeded to interpret divine revelation as that which answers the questions raised by reason. A similar pattern is followed in the other four parts of the theology. In each case the answer takes its form from the question while its content is derived from revelation. At least that was Tillich's intention.

The method of correlation has received mixed reviews. Although some found it extremely helpful in presenting theology in a way that is both faithful and relevant, critics chided Tillich for giving philosophy too much independence from and authority over revelation. Tillich did restrict philosophy to the tasks of formulating the questions for theology and of determining the forms of the answers. But does not even this nevertheless accord to secular philosophy too large a role in theological construction and reconstruction? In defining the method of correlation Tillich did not require philosophy to be transformed or converted before launching into its task, thereby leaving philosophy "autonomous"—to use his categories—rather than truly "theonomous" or healed.[44] How can such a discipline, disrupted by the tensions inherent in finite reason, be trusted to formulate the questions rightly? Might not the substance and form of the questions serve as a confining prison or Procrustean bed onto which the answers of revelation must fit? As Christian philosopher George Thomas asked,

> Can a philosophical reason which has not been fully "converted" by the Christian faith correctly formulate the "structure" and "categories" of Being

---

[43]Ibid.

[44]The terms "autonomy," "heteronomy" and "theonomy" are crucial to Tillich's thought. The first refers to the rule of the self or individual over itself. The second refers to the rule of another over the self. The third refers to the self and other united in God, the ground of being.

and raise the deepest "questions" implied in existence? If not, will not the Christian "answers," whose form is determined by the nature of the "questions," be distorted or obscured?[45]

A common criticism is that Tillich's employment of the method of correlation did not match his ideal description of it. In spite of his intention to allow the content of the theological answers to be determined solely by divine revelation, in practice the content as well as the form became influenced, if not determined, by the philosophical questions. Thomas raised this with regard to Tillich's doctrine of God, in which he described God not as *a* being or *a* person but being itself and the ground of everything personal. In keeping with his own understanding of the Christian message as declaring that God *is* himself personal, Thomas asked whether "Tillich's statement of [the Christian view] has not been weakened at points by the intrusion into his thinking of an impersonal philosophy alien to the spirit of Christianity."[46] Theologian Kenneth Hamilton concluded that the method of correlation as practiced by Tillich takes nothing from the Christian message and everything from the ontological system of thought from which it begins. In practice, he argued, Tillich did not truly "correlate" questions and answers but interpreted the language of Christian faith so as to make it conform to his preconceived ontological system.[47]

Tillich correlates reason and revelation. The first part of Tillich's *Systematic Theology* attempts to establish a correlation between reason and revelation. In this section, he tried to uncover conflicts and questions inherent in reason that drive it beyond itself toward revelation. His goal was to show that "revelation is the answer to the questions implied in the existential conflicts of reason."[48] In contrast to those who see reason and revelation as opposed to each other, Tillich believed that "reason does not resist revelation. It asks for revelation, for revelation means the reintegration of reason."[49] In order to understand Tillich's concept of reason it is necessary to grasp something of his fundamental ontology of "essence and

---

[45]George F. Thomas, "The Method and Structure of Tillich's Theology," in *The Theology of Paul Tillich*, ed. Charles W. Kegley and Robert W. Bretall (New York: Macmillan, 1964), 104.
[46]Ibid.
[47]Hamilton, *System and the Gospel*, 124.
[48]Tillich, *Theology*, 1:147.
[49]Ibid., 1:94.

existence." This ontological distinction underlies much of his theology and makes its first significant appearance in his treatment of the nature of reason. According to him, reality as we know and experience it must be differentiated into two realms: essence and existence. Essence is the potential, unactualized perfection of a thing. It has ontological reality but not actual existence. Existence, by contrast, is actual and "fallen" from essence. Because it is cut off from its perfection while still being dependent on it, it is not truly itself.

The philosophical background of Tillich's distinction between essence and existence lies in Platonic thought.[50] Plato believed in an ideal world of forms or perfect patterns of things and a world of individual, existing things that are imperfect copies of the forms. Tillich adapted the Platonic distinction to fit his own purposes. Nevertheless, Plato's general ideas of essence and existence serve as the background to Tillich's use of these terms. For him, "existence" refers to what is both finite and fallen. It is limited as well as disrupted and distorted by the condition of being cut off from its true being. This is true of actual reason, or what Tillich called "the predicament of reason in existence"; it is fallen from the "essential nature of reason" and therefore suffers certain conflicts that it cannot itself solve.[51] Essential reason, or reason itself, is transcendent. It is the "structure of the mind which enables the mind to grasp and to transform reality."[52] It also includes the mind's capacity for logical reasoning, discovering means toward ends. Ultimately essential human reason depends on both a rational structure of the universe (the "logos of being") and on the fit between it and the mind's structure. Reason itself, then, is not merely finite.[53] It is that function of both the universe and humanity which makes discovery and knowledge possible. Therefore, it transcends everything merely finite.

Actual reason, or reason in the predicament of existence, is different. Like everything that exists, it is limited and estranged from its true essence, which gives rise to conflicts. This estrangement shows itself in reason's po-

---

[50]Thatcher, *Ontology of Paul Tillich*, 99–116. Here Thatcher discusses the various philosophical traditions that deal with concepts such as essence and existence and concludes that, although Tillich's use draws on several of them, the Platonic interpretation is dominant.

[51]Tillich, *Theology*, 1:80.

[52]Ibid., 1:72.

[53]Ibid., 1:82.

larities that belong together but under the conditions of existence fall into conflict and contradiction—polarities such as autonomy versus heteronomy, relativism versus absolutism and formalism versus emotionalism. Through a careful analysis of these polarities Tillich attempted to show that although reason itself cannot solve the conflicts, they nevertheless cry out for reconciliation. He concluded that the conflicts produced by these polarities lead inevitably to either a desperate resignation of truth itself or the quest for revelation, "for revelation claims to give a truth which is both certain and of ultimate concern—a truth which includes and accepts the risk and uncertainty of every significant cognitive act, yet transcends it in accepting it."[54] In other words, reason needs to be "saved" or "healed." It cannot heal itself, but it does reach out beyond itself for a power that will reunite it with its essential structure and thus fulfill it.

According to Tillich, the uniting of the polarities of reason is the task of revelation. It reestablishes the essential structure of reason under the conditions of existence "fragmentarily, yet really and with power."[55] Consequently, he defines revelation formally as "the manifestation of the ground of being for human knowledge."[56] Revelation is the manifestation of the power that reunites what is tragically and destructively separated, thereby saving, healing and bringing harmony out of conflict. It is the unveiling of the mystery of being, the "self-manifestation of the depth of being and meaning."[57]

Like many twentieth-century theologians, Tillich rejected the concept of revealed words or propositions. Revelation is never the communication of information. Rather, it is event and experience that can happen through many different media, including nature, history, groups and individuals, and speech. In fact, anything can become a bearer of revelation if it becomes transparent to the ground of being.[58] That is, whatever truly transforms existence, drawing it toward essence, reuniting them is revelation. Words and doctrines are not revealed, but whenever the depth of being manifests itself through language something sounds through, which is "the Word of God" or revelation. Belief in revelation as spoken or written words

---

[54]Ibid., 1:105.
[55]Ibid., 1:155.
[56]Ibid., 1:94.
[57]Ibid., 1:124.
[58]Ibid., 1:118.

from God is "*the* Protestant pitfall," Tillich claimed.[59] The Bible, then, is not the "Word of God" in any unique sense. For Tillich, "Probably nothing has contributed more to the misinterpretation of the biblical doctrine of the Word than the identification of the Word [of God] with the Bible."[60] The "Word" is God manifest. However, Tillich did find a role for the Bible in revelation. It "participates" in revelation as the document that records the event of final revelation in Jesus the Christ.[61]

Tillich differentiated between "actual revelation" and "final revelation." The former designates all events and experiences that manifest the power of being wherever and whenever they happen. The latter designates the ultimate, unsurpassable event of the healing power of the New Being (Christ) to which all other revelatory events and experiences point. What ultimately distinguishes Christianity from other religions is its claim "to be based on the revelation in Jesus as the Christ as the final revelation."[62] Of course it cannot prove this claim. However, Tillich attempted to show that this revelatory event—the appearance in a particular person in history of the universal healing power of the New Being—is final and unsurpassable because it heals or saves reason by overcoming its conflicts. It is the answer to the question of revelation implied in the structure of reason under the conditions of existence.[63] The existential conflicts of reason call for a power that is both universal and concrete, absolute and relative, a power that negates the finite while preserving it. Only such a reality can heal reason by reestablishing the essential harmony of its poles.

As the being who is determined in every moment by God and as the finite individual who sacrificed himself completely to the infinite while maintaining his individuality, Jesus the Christ passes the double test of finality of revelation.[64] By his life and death he revealed the power of self-negation, in that he presented a picture or symbol of something finite that does not claim to be final in its own right. Such a self-sacrificing finite being defeats the demonic conflict of existential estrangement and creates true

---

[59]Ibid., 1:157.
[60]Ibid., 1:159.
[61]Ibid., 1:158–59.
[62]Ibid., 1:132.
[63]Ibid., 1:147–55.
[64]Ibid., 1:135–36.

"theonomy," which cancels out autonomy (independence) and heteronomy (total dependence) while preserving the truth in both. This power of self-negation, the New Being, is "the Christ."

Jesus was the finite individual who Christians believe became the Christ by his self-sacrificing life and death. He did so because he refused the demonic temptation inherent in finite existence to claim finality for himself. This sacrificing of himself to the Christ made Jesus of Nazareth the medium of final revelation. For Tillich, this means that any Jesus-centered religion is a perversion of Christianity: "A Christianity which does not assert that Jesus of Nazareth is sacrificed to Jesus as the Christ is just one more religion among many others. It has no justifiable claim to finality."[65] We will discuss Tillich's Christology more fully later. However, the decidedly gnostic tone of this assertion cannot be passed over without comment. The Christology of the Gnostics was more dualistic than docetic.[66] Certain Gnostic sects required members to curse Jesus in order to demonstrate their knowledge of the Christ as someone separate from him. (This may be the background of Paul's condemnation of those who curse Jesus [1 Cor 12:3].) To be sure, Tillich did not encourage or condone cursing Jesus. However, his radical distinction between Jesus of Nazareth and "the Christ" echoes the Gnostic view.[67]

Tillich points to the "God above God." Tillich believed that he had successfully correlated reason and revelation by showing that revelation fulfills reason without destroying it and that reason raises the question of revelation, without which it would be a meaningless answer. Throughout his

---

[65]Ibid., 1:135.

[66]Gnosticism was a heretical movement within early Christianity that, among other aberrations, believed that Jesus Christ was not truly human. Docetism, held by some Gnostics, is the view that Jesus only appeared to be human and was not even a physical being at all but purely spiritual. The majority of Gnostics, however, held to a dualistic Christology. That is, they believed that the man Jesus of Nazareth was nothing more than the instrument of the heavenly redeemer "Christ" who came down from heaven to teach gnosis or wisdom to the spiritual ones. This Christ-spirit left Jesus before he died on the cross. The claim being made here is not that Tillich's Christology is full-blown Gnosticism in this sense but that it echoes the dualistic view of Jesus Christ that the early church condemned as heresy.

[67]In his excellent study of Tillich's Christology, *Paul Tillich and the Christian Message* (New York: Charles Scribner's Sons, 1962), George Tavard accuses it of being docetist (131–37). However, the heresy he seems to describe and attribute to Tillich is not so much Docetism as dualism. Nowhere does Tillich deny that Jesus of Nazareth was human. What he seems to do is deny the importance of Jesus' humanity except as it is negated and sacrificed to a purely spiritual power called the Christ.

discussion of reason and revelation, however, he referred to what is revealed as the power of being, the New Being, the ground of being, or God. What is revealed in final revelation, and to a lesser extent in universal revelation, is God, the religious word for the ground of being.[68] God is the power of love that heals reason by reunifying its polar elements, which in existence have fallen into conflict. Tillich's doctrine of God has created more controversy than any other area of his theology. Much of the discussion has arisen out of his well-known assertion that "God does not exist. He is being itself beyond essence and existence. Therefore to argue that God exists is to deny him."[69] Some of the furor arose from a simplistic misunderstanding of Tillich's technical use of the term "existence," which gives rise to the impression that he was an atheist. However, even some astute critics have argued that in spite of all his talk about God as being itself or the ground of being, Tillich *was* an atheist.[70]

It would be impossible to give here an adequate consideration of all the nuances of Tillich's doctrine of God or its various interpretations. Here we will only attempt to show that while he may not have been an atheist, his doctrine of God places such a strain on the immanence and transcendence of God that the follower of Tillich must choose between them. Further, opting for the nearly total immanence of Tillich's "God above God"[71] is consistent with his overall viewpoint. Mark Kline Taylor is correct that Tillich risked "tracing out God's transcendence so deep in the fabric of existence . . . that the meaning of 'transcendence' was stretched beyond recognition."[72]

If God is the answer, then what is the question? As we have seen, for Tillich the question must precede the answer and determine its form. Simply stated, God is the answer to the question implied in being: "What is

---

[68]Tillich, *Theology*, 1:156.

[69]Ibid., 1:205.

[70]One of the harshest attacks on Tillich is by Leonard F. Wheat, *Paul Tillich's Dialectical Humanism: Unmasking the God Above God* (Baltimore: Johns Hopkins University Press, 1970), the basic thesis of which is that "Tillich is an atheist, in the broadest sense of the word" (20).

[71]The "God above God" is a phrase Tillich used in *The Courage to Be* (New Haven, CT: Yale University Press, 1952), 186–90. It is meant to designate the God who transcends the supposedly finite God of theism because he is not *a* being but being itself.

[72]Mark Kline Taylor, *Paul Tillich, Theologian of the Boundaries* (San Francisco: Collins, 1987), 23.

being itself?"[73] According to Tillich, finitude is a mixture of being and non-being.[74] Therefore, he engaged in a complex and subtle ontological analysis of the structure of finitude in order to show that it raises the question of the power of being or being itself that can overcome the threat of nonbeing inherent in itself. The ontological question arises in human existence because of finite beings' awareness that they are not the ground of their own being, an awareness that comes to its most intense expression in the "metaphysical shock" that occurs when a person becomes existentially threatened by nonbeing (e.g., when it sinks in that one was nowhere before birth and will finally die).

If God is the answer to the question implied in human finitude, Tillich argued, he cannot be *a* being, even the highest being or most supreme being, but must be conceived as the power of being, power resisting nonbeing, infinite power of being or being itself.[75] Now this power of being (that answers the question of being and nonbeing) by definition cannot "exist"[76] because "existence" is a mode of finite being—the condition of fallenness or estrangement from essence. Every particular being participates in nonbeing, which is what makes it finite and in need of a power of being to uphold it in being. If God were *a* being he could not properly be the object of ultimate concern (faith) and the power that answers the question of finitude. Something else would then be God. This is what Tillich meant by "the God above God." The God who is being itself, or the ground and power of being, is superior to the supposedly finite God of traditional theism who is thought of as *a* being and *a* person.

Tillich struggled to express the transcendence of being itself while maintaining its immanence. He asserted that being itself is not the universal essence of everything, the underlying substance of the world, because being itself transcends the essence/existence split to which all things in the world are subject due to their element of nonbeing. Being itself does not participate in nonbeing and therefore infinitely transcends everything finite.[77] For Tillich this meant that because God is absolute and infinite, unconditioned and free,

---

[73]Tillich, *Theology*, 1:163.
[74]Ibid., 1:189.
[75]Ibid., 1:235.
[76]Ibid., 1:202–5.
[77]Ibid., 1:237.

nothing can be said about him that is not symbolic except that he is being it-self.[78] All other assertions about or descriptions of God are purely (not merely) symbolic. But, for Tillich, a true symbol, unlike a sign, participates in the reality it symbolizes ("symbolic realism"). So there is no such thing as a "mere symbol" in Tillich's vocabulary. And yet, there is always a gap between a symbol and that which it represents. Because God is beyond everything finite, all language about him must be symbolic *except* "being itself."

After affirming God's transcendence so strongly, Tillich turned to God's immanence. God and the world participate in one another. Everything finite participates in being itself, which is the structure of being in which every-thing is grounded.[79] Conversely, God participates absolutely and uncondi-tionally in everything that is, as its ground and aim.[80] God includes every-thing finite within himself in a dynamic, living process. In fact, it would seem that this "life" of God necessarily includes the world with all of its nonbeing.[81] For Tillich, then, God transcends the world and the world transcends God. God is immanent in the world and the world is immanent in God.[82] Para-doxically, God may be unconditioned, but so long as there is a world he cannot be outside of it or it outside of him, otherwise he would not be the truly infinite (shades of Hegel) and unconditioned but limited and condi-tioned by something outside himself. Therefore, the world exists "within" the life of God, and God is the being (but not the substance) of the world.

It should be clear why critics have not been completely pleased with Til-lich's position. Even as sympathetic an observer as Taylor concluded that "Tillich's understanding of transcendence was so thoroughly immanental that many remained perplexed about his meaning of God's 'otherness' or 'transcendence.'"[83] One of Tillich's most astute critics, Adrian Thatcher, went further, arguing that he failed to explicate the transcendence and im-

---

[78]Ibid., 1:238–39. Tillich's use of the term "infinite" is highly ambiguous if not contradictory. In some places he distinguishes God as being-itself from infinity and places him above the finite-infinite split (e.g., 191). In other places, however, he says that "that which is infinite is being itself" (239). In another place he says that God is infinite but includes the finite in himself and therefore is not strictly infinite (252). This is close to Hegel's concept of the "truly infinite" as opposed to "bad infinity."

[79]Ibid., 1:238.

[80]Ibid., 1:243–45.

[81]Ibid., 1:252.

[82]Ibid., 1:263.

[83]Taylor, *Paul Tillich*, 23.

manence of God coherently, so that he risked positing two separate ideas of God that cannot be integrated.[84] Overall, it would seem that the "God above God" is really beneath and within everything. These are metaphors borrowed from spatial reality to describe something nonspatial. Nevertheless, however different being itself, the power or ground of being, may be from particular finite things or even their totality (the world), it cannot be transcendent in any traditional sense. This is especially true in light of Tillich's emphasis on the mutual participation between God and the world. God is the being of the world. Transcendence means that he is not subject to the limitations and conflicts to which finite things are subject. He includes these limitations and conflicts in himself, and this contributes to his life. Concerning this Tillich wrote:

> In this view the world process means something to God. He is not a separated self-sufficient entity who, driven by a whim, creates what he wants and saves whom he wants. Rather, the eternal act of creation is driven by a love which finds fulfillment only through the other one who has the freedom to reject and to accept love. God, so to speak, drives toward the actualization and essentialization of everything that has being. For the eternal dimension of what happens in the universe is the Divine Life itself. It is the content of the divine blessedness.[85]

That this is a form of panentheism is beyond dispute. At the end of his system of theology, Tillich himself used the word to label his view.[86] God and the world are not identical, but they are ultimately and inextricably linked. One is reminded of Hegel's assertion that without the world God would not be God.[87]

Language such as that raises the problem of how a person relates to the being of the world, to the ground of being that is not *a* being or *a* person. On the one hand, Tillich stated, "The personal encounter with God and the reunion with him are the heart of all genuine religion."[88] But on the other hand, he asserted that the protest of atheism against a heavenly, completely

---

[84]Thatcher, *Ontology of Paul Tillich*, 87.

[85]Tillich, *Theology*, 3:422.

[86]Ibid., 3:421.

[87]G. W. F. Hegel, *Lectures on the Philosophy of Religion*, trans. E. B. Speirs and J. Burden Sanderson, ed. E. B. Speirs (New York: Humanities, 1962), 1:200.

[88]Tillich, *Theology*, 2:86.

perfect divine person is correct. Such a being would "exist" and therefore could not be being itself which God must be to be God. Still, Tillich did not want to say that God is impersonal. He explained that "'Personal God' does not mean that God is *a* person. It means that God is the ground of everything personal and that he carries within himself the ontological power of personality. He is not a person, but he is not less than personal."[89] Can one "encounter" and have any real relationship with the "ground of everything personal"? Tillich was well aware of this objection and the entire line of biblical personalism that underlies it. He strove to solve this dilemma by synthesizing ontology and biblical personalism. Ultimately, however, he failed. In the end he could only express his synthesis in a paradox: "Our encounter with the God who is a person includes the encounter with the God who is the ground of everything personal and as such is not *a* person."[90] Surely this satisfies neither reason nor religious experience.

Tillich believed that the God above God who does not exist but is being itself provides the final answer to the questions implied in human existence.[91] One cannot avoid the suspicion, however, that he allowed the form of the question to determine the content of the answer. It is difficult to understand how being itself can be the transcendent, righteous, holy and personal God of Abraham, Isaac and Jacob, the Father of Jesus Christ. Tillich himself seemed to affirm this when he said that he did not pray to being itself, the ground of being, but only meditated on it.

Tillich reconstructs Christology using existentialism. Tillich's Christology is similarly determined by the form of the question with which it is correlated. In "Existence and the Christ," the third part of volume 2 of *Systematic Theology,* he presented a powerful and controversial phenomenology of human existence. At its core is his interpretation of the fall of humanity, which he viewed as the universal transition from essence to existence that "is not an event in time and space but the transhistorical quality of all events in time and space."[92] The Genesis story of the sin of Adam and Eve is not to be taken literally, he argued, but is to be interpreted

---

[89]Ibid., 2:245.
[90]Tillich, *Biblical Religion*, 83.
[91]Tillich, *Theology*, 1:286.
[92]Ibid., 2:40.

as a symbolic expression of the predicament of humanity, our inevitable estrangement from essential humanity and therefore from God, the ground of being. Although he denied that this fall is ontologically necessary, Tillich averred that it is identical with "actualized creation."[93] In other words, the transition coincides with our exercise of free will. As soon as humans actualize their freedom, they fall from the state of dreaming innocence (a concept he borrowed from Kierkegaard), which marks their essential being in union with God, and enter into estranged existence. This gives rise to tensions, anxieties, conflicts, despair, guilt and all sorts of evils in human life.

According to Tillich, we ought not to understand the fall as an occurrence either in the history of the race or the individual but as a symbol for the universal human predicament.[94] At the same time, it is not a necessary structural feature of humanity. It cannot be derived from human essence but has the nature of an irrational leap for which humans are responsible.[95] This is Tillich's version of original sin. Critics have suggested that Tillich's view "ontologizes sin," or makes it necessary, because it represents it as identical with actualized creation. This interpretation is supported by Tillich's assertion that "man is caught between the desire to actualize his freedom and the demand to preserve his dreaming innocence. In the power of his finite freedom, he decides for actualization."[96] It appears, then, that the only alternative to falling would be to remain unactualized—to be only potentially human—in dreaming innocence. As soon as humanity actualizes itself it falls into estranged existence. Critics question whether this perhaps makes sin a necessary feature of humanity. In any case, Tillich made clear that the fall, the transition from essence to existence, is the "original fact" about humankind as we know it. Ontologically the fall into existence precedes everything that happens in time and space.[97]

Tillich believed that his analysis opened the door for a truly Christian Christology. Universally implied in human existence is the quest for a New Being that will break through estrangement and overcome anxiety and de-

---

[93]Ibid., 2:44.
[94]Ibid., 2:29.
[95]Ibid., 2:44.
[96]Ibid., 2:35.
[97]Ibid., 2:36.

spair by reuniting us with our essence. For Tillich, then, Christ is the answer. The Christian symbol of Christ is the symbol of the New Being appearing under the conditions of existence yet conquering the gap between essence and existence.[98] Christians believe that this New Being appeared in the life and death of Jesus of Nazareth. For Tillich, however, the name and details of his life are unimportant. He argued that if historical-critical research should ever happen to conclude that the man Jesus never lived, faith in the presence of the New Being within history would not be affected. "Participation, not historical argument," he explained, "guarantees the reality of the event upon which Christianity is based. It guarantees a personal life in which the New Being has conquered the old being. But it does not guarantee his name to be Jesus of Nazareth."[99]

In what sense, then, is Jesus special? Tillich flatly denied that Jesus was "God become man." The doctrine of the incarnation must be reinterpreted to mean that Jesus Christ was "essential man appearing in a personal life under the conditions of existential estrangement."[100] He also suggested that one could indicate the divine presence in Jesus by speaking of "essential Godmanhood" appearing in him.[101] In other words, for Tillich, Jesus was not "divine" and did not have a "divine nature." Rather, he manifested in and through his humanity an entirely new order of being—essential humanity under the conditions of existence participating in but conquering estrangement. In him humanity became "essentialized" within existence, which is, of course, a paradox. The original unity of God and humanity (that never was) was restored in Christ, although under the conditions of existence. No traces of estrangement between Jesus and God can be found in the biblical picture of Jesus the Christ.[102] In fact, this overcoming of estrangement *is* his Christhood. In this way Tillich replaced the traditional two natures Christology with his understanding of Jesus as the New Being, and thereby he substituted a dynamic relation for the older concept of a static essence.[103]

---

[98]Ibid., 2:120.
[99]Ibid., 2:114.
[100]Ibid., 2:95.
[101]Ibid., 2:94.
[102]Ibid., 2:126.
[103]Ibid., 2:148.

What made Jesus the Christ? Here Tillich's gnostic tendencies resurfaced. He said that Jesus "proves and confirms his character as the Christ in the sacrifice of himself as Jesus to himself as the Christ."[104] This clearly implies a dualistic Christology that separates Jesus and Christ from one another. Tillich claimed that he was trying to develop a constructive contemporary Christology that would preserve both the "Christ-character" and the "Jesus-character" of the event,[105] but he seemed to drive a wedge between them.

It should not come as any surprise that Tillich denied the bodily resurrection of Jesus. He preferred instead the "restitution theory": the effect of the New Being on the disciples led to the "restitution of Jesus to the dignity of the Christ in the minds of the disciples" after Jesus' death.[106] Similarly Tillich attempted to deliteralize the symbols of Jesus' preexistence as the Logos and his virgin birth, ascension and parousia.[107]

Again, in light of his Christology, it is necessary to ask whether Tillich allowed the form of the question to determine not only the form of the theological answer but also its content. His rather dubious analysis of human existence led to the need for a concrete yet universal power of essentialization, a "New Being," in history to reunite humans with their essential being. This power must be *from* God but cannot *be* God, because God, the ground of being, cannot appear under the conditions of existence. Yet Tillich admitted that even the appearance of the essential human being under the conditions of existence is a paradox.[108] Nevertheless, for Tillich, Jesus the Christ cannot be truly human and also God—and this because of the way he defined both and ruled out the two natures doctrine.[109] Therefore, Jesus must have been a human being who achieved a union with God that belongs essentially to every human being as potential.

Tillich leaves a legacy of nonliteral, nonsupernatural Christianity. Understandably, conservative theologians, including neo-orthodox, have ex-

---

[104]Ibid., 2:123.

[105]Ibid., 2:145–46.

[106]Ibid., 2:157.

[107]Ibid., 2:158–64.

[108]For Tillich's view of paradox in theology and especially the paradox of the New Being, see ibid., 2:90–92.

[109]Ibid., 2:147–48.

pressed dismay at Tillich's theology. Theologian George Tavard indicted Tillich's Christology:

> Paul Tillich has failed to account for the biblical picture of Jesus and for the Christological dogma as the Church has always believed it. He has paid lip-service to the dogmas. . . . But when he himself tried "to find new forms in which the Christological substance of the past can be expressed," the Christological substance vanished. The divinity of Christ has been rejected for fear of a Christological metamorphosis. And the humanity of Christ has been declared unknowable. Thus both the Christ-character and the Jesus-character of Jesus the Christ have been lost. Where the Council of Chalcedon, spearheading the Church, follows a ridge between two chasms, the Christology of Paul Tillich falls into two chasms one after the other.[110]

Tavard is referring to the two chasms of dividing the two natures of Christ (Nestorianism) and confusing them (Eutychianism). Insofar as Tillich emphasized the difference between the man Jesus and the Christ that appeared in him, Nestorianism appeared. Insofar as he emphasized the purely spiritual Christ, Eutychianism appeared.

Criticisms of Tillich's other failures have already been mentioned throughout this section. Among the ones most often raised against his theology are the prominence he gave to philosophy in theology, its underlying naturalism and its seeming depersonalizing of God. And yet, Tillich has his admirers well into the twenty-first century. Gilkey concluded his book on Tillich with this glowing endorsement:

> Tillich . . . marshaled almost all of life's negativities—the essential ones of finitude, the absolutely destructive ones of estrangement, and the frustrating ones of life's ambiguities—and has shown how the many names of the divine serve to answer these, our deepest needs. . . . In this sense, form and content, method and message, and, perhaps most important, his personal being and his reflections, were uniquely and powerfully united in Paul Tillich.[111]

What of Tillich's relation to modernity? First, and most obviously, he wholly adopted naturalism; there is no hint of the supernatural or miracles in his theology. Second, his theology is anthropocentric; it focuses on

---

[110]Tavard, *Tillich and the Christian Message*, 132.
[111]Gilkey, *Gilkey on Tillich*, 173.

human existence. Third, none of the acids of modernity except perhaps rationalism can touch this theology. But rationalism was not particularly popular in Tillich's day, especially among those under the spell of existentialism. And yet, the ghost of Hegel hovers over all in this theology. In fact, it is a strange hybrid of Kierkegaard and Hegel, something that should be impossible. Both would be turning over in their graves to think someone was attempting to synthesize them. Kierkegaard's influence appears in Tillich's embrace of paradox; Hegel's appears in his panentheism. In the end, looking back over Tillich's theology, there does not seem to be any area where science could threaten it. It is structured to be immune to science, including historical research. It is about depth dimensions of human existence and not about cosmology or the workings of nature or miracles or anything science investigates. It does not even seem to be about history. Whether that is a strength or a weakness is a value judgment.

6.B. PROCESS THEOLOGY BRINGS GOD DOWN TO EARTH

A critic of process theology declared that the only thing wrong with it is that it is such an attractive alternative to the Christian faith.[112] "Attractive" because if process theology is true, there is no problem of evil because God is not omnipotent. The God of process theology is not the God of classical Christian theism, which is why it has sometimes been called neo-classical theism. Why an "alternative to the Christian faith"? That is a matter of judgment, but for many critics it radically reconstructs many traditional, orthodox Christian doctrines and especially the doctrine of God. Its reconstruction project, for them, goes too far so that what remains afterwards bears only a vague resemblance to anything recognizably Christian.

Process theologians think that is a virtue because, to them, the traditional Christian God, being the omnipotent and all-determining reality, is a bad example. In a manner reminiscent of Tillich, a leading process theologian declared that "the holy, omnipotent Creator-Lord of history—Lawgiver-Judge—must be superseded."[113] The same process theologian then concluded, "Just as the people joined in the ancient cry on the death of a

---

[112]Robert Jenson, *God After God: The God of the Past and the God of the Future as Seen in the Work of Karl Barth* (Indianapolis: Bobbs-Merrill, 1969), 208.
[113]John B. Cobb Jr., *God and the World* (Philadelphia: Westminster Press, 1969), 40.

king, 'the king is dead; long live the king!' so I want to join the chorus that today is proclaiming, 'God is dead; long live God!'"[114] By that, John Cobb (b. 1925) did not mean that God is literally dead; he was referring to the concept of God in Christian orthodoxy. *That* God, he believed, is unbelievable in light of the Holocaust and other twentieth-century horrors. A basic presupposition of most, if not all, process theologians is that a good and omnipotent God would have stopped the Holocaust. If he had the power to prevent or stop it, and if he was absolutely and unconditionally good, he would have stopped it. Thus, God must not be omnipotent. One leading process thinker even wrote a book titled *Omnipotence and Other Theological Mistakes* (1984).

Process theology adds a new element to neo-liberal theology. Process theology is neo-liberal theology. Some process theologians such as Cobb proudly call themselves "liberal" without the "neo-." However, Cobb admits a difference between his kind of liberal theology and the older, classical Protestant liberalism of the nineteenth and early twentieth centuries:

> We liberals have come down the road from historic Christianity progressively using up the capital of our heritage and doing little to replenish it. We have come more and more to mirror our culture, or certain strands within it, rather than speak to it an effective word of judgment or healing. We do well to recognize that the liberal Christians of Germany became in the '30s the German Christians who could hail Hitler as a new savior.[115]

Cobb continues to explain the difference further and highlights the horrors and tragedies, humanity's inhumanity, of the same centuries that witnessed the Enlightenment and the rise of liberal optimism about humanity. His liberal theology is chastened liberalism. To fellow liberals he wrote, "We must face the endless perversity of our motives and the inevitable ambiguity of all our actions."[116] Cobb and other neo-liberals drank deeply at the wells of Niebuhr's Christian realism, and it altered their liberal theology with a note of pessimism about human achievement. The kingdom of God is not nearby awaiting the fuller moral education of the human race.

---

[114]Ibid., 41.
[115]John B. Cobb Jr., *Liberal Christianity at the Crossroads* (Philadelphia: Westminster Press, 1973), 12.
[116]Ibid., 24.

Nevertheless, in spite of the chastening element that makes process theology "neo-," it is a form of liberal theology. That appears in process theologian Delwin Brown's affirmation that "liberalism [his own self-identifier] holds that a view of God must in each age be reevaluated and reconceived in light of our best views about the world. The Christian concept of God must cohere with the rest of modern knowledge."[117] Then he speaks for all process theologians and many other "progressive Christians" when he explains:

> Liberalism at its best is . . . likely to say, "We certainly ought to honor the richness of the Christian past and appreciate the vast contribution it makes to our lives, but finally we must live by our best modern conclusions . . . our commitment, however tentative and self-critically maintained, must be to the careful judgments of the present age, even if they differ radically from the dictates of the past."[118]

In other words, maximal acknowledgment of the claims of modernity.

So, process theology is a form of liberal theology and displays continuity with that theological orientation going back to Schleiermacher, but it is chastened liberal theology and therefore deserves to be classified as neo-liberal theology along with Tillich and some other twentieth-century theological movements and individuals. But what new element does process theology add to neo-liberalism? What makes it distinctive and different from, say, Tillich's theology? The similarities and differences are both striking. On the similar side, process theology, like Tillich's theology, is heavily indebted to a particular philosophy. Tillich called existentialism the "good luck" of Christianity in the modern world. Process theologians could say the same about the process philosophies of Whitehead and Hartshorne. Both were philosophers who wrote much about religion and God. Whitehead, a highly respected mathematician and philosopher who taught at the universities of Cambridge and London and at Harvard University, wrote one of the twentieth century's masterpieces of religious philosophy entitled *Process and Reality* (1929). There he railed against "the doctrine of an aboriginal, eminently real, transcendent creator, at whose fiat the world

---

[117]Clark H. Pinnock and Delwin Brown, *Theological Crossfire: An Evangelical/Liberal Dialogue* (Grand Rapids: Zondervan, 1990), 82–83.
[118]Ibid., 23.

came into being, and whose imposed will it obeys."[119] In place of God as "ruthless moralist" or "unmoved mover," Whitehead advocated a view of God that

> dwells upon the tender elements in the world, which slowly and in quietness operate by love; and . . . finds purpose in the present immediacy of a kingdom not of this world. Love neither rules, nor is unmoved; also it is a little oblivious as to morals. It does not look to the future; for it finds its own reward in the immediate present.[120]

Process theologians find in Whitehead's cosmology and philosophy of religion more than just a conversation partner. They are to it what Plato's philosophy was to many early church fathers. Augustine confessed that it was reading the books of the Platonists that made it possible for him to embrace Christianity. Whitehead's philosophy is to process theology what Platonism was to Augustine and existentialism was to Tillich's theology. It is the framework for interpreting and reconstructing Christian doctrine for contemporary people. There is a sense in which process theologians seek to correlate Christianity with Whitehead's process metaphysics just as Tillich sought to correlate existentialist ontology with Christianity. But Whitehead's philosophy and existentialism have little in common beyond both being philosophies. They could not be more different. So one new thing process theology introduces into modern, neo-liberal theology is metaphysics and especially process metaphysics. Both Tillich and process theology elevate their favorite philosophies to the status of source and norm for modern theology, but they disagree about which philosophy is the right one for the task of reconstruction.

Another similarity between Tillich's neo-liberalism and process theology is a radical reconstruction of the doctrine of God and belief that a God beyond the God of traditional Christian theism must be found and made the cure for the maladies of traditional theism. Tillich thought the God of classical Christian theism is too finite because he is viewed as *a* being even if the supreme being. Process theology thinks the God of classical theism is too supreme, too other, too transcendent in superiority over the world.

---

[119]Quoted in Cobb, *God and the World*, 40.
[120]Alfred North Whitehead, *Process and Reality*, corrected ed. (New York: Free Press, 1978), 343.

And yet, both embrace panentheism. Whitehead said, "It is as true to say that God creates the World as that the World creates God."[121] The surprise is in the last phrase, "the World creates God." Whitehead also averred that the world is immanent in God which means that God's being and life include the world (like Hegel's "truly infinite"). Tillich's "God beyond God," the "ground of being" and "being itself," is impersonal or suprapersonal (whatever that means). One cannot have a personal relationship with the ground of being. Process theology's God, Whitehead's "fellow sufferer who understands,"[122] is *a* person and *a* being, admittedly finite even if supreme in relatedness and influence.

Why do process theologians choose Whitehead's philosophy as the basis for their reconstruction of Christian doctrine? First, existentialism began to wane in popularity and influence in the 1950s and 1960s, which is exactly when process theology began to develop. Process philosophy seemed like a better tool for theological reconstruction especially in the United States. (It never really caught on in Europe.) Second, certain radical theologians of the 1960s began to proclaim that "God is dead." Christian atheism was asserting itself in an increasingly secular period of American history (see chap. 7). Process thought seemed to provide a way to believe in God without those elements of theism that the death of God theologians said proved God cannot be believed in or worshiped in a century of horrors like the Holocaust.

Third, process philosophy seemed to many Christian theologians to provide a way to correlate rather than divide science and theology. Whitehead was a philosopher of science and believed his view of God was consistent with evolution and the new physics being discovered by Heisenberg and Einstein. Most of all, perhaps, process thought emphasized becoming over being in a time when change was being touted as more basic to reality than stability and immutability. Changes in philosophy and science filtered into the outlook of modern society imbuing it with a sense of contingency, transience and relativity.[123] The ultimate goal of process theology is to indicate the relevance of the Christian faith, especially its

---

[121]Ibid., 348.

[122]Ibid., 351.

[123]These dimensions of reality as the context for process theology are noted in Lonnie Kliever, *The Shattered Spectrum* (Atlanta: John Knox, 1981), 44–46.

conception of the relation of God with the world, in a culture increasingly permeated by a sense of becoming over being.[124] To this end process theologians employ a new dynamic outlook, borrowed from Whitehead (and to a lesser extent Hartshorne), that declares all of reality, including God, to be relational and in process.

Process theology speaks with many voices. Unlike some other modern theological movements, process theology has no single spokesperson. True, Whitehead is behind it all, but he was not a theologian; he was a philosopher without any particular Christian identity. Process theology proper began well after Whitehead's death. The leading process theologians stood on the shoulders of earlier liberals and were heavily influenced by a form of liberal theology called Boston personalism, which had a relatively brief lifespan. Nobody can pinpoint the birth of process theology, but it is relatively easy to identify its main representative thinkers. To a certain extent, they formed a school of theology even though they taught at different institutions. The Center for Process Studies was founded in 1973 at Claremont Graduate University and School of Theology in California to provide a think tank and networking center for all process theologians.

Several key process theologians are Hartshorne (who some would classify more as a philosopher of religion than a theologian), Cobb, Norman Pittenger (1905–1997), David Ray Griffin (b. 1939) and Marjorie Suchocki (b. 1933). Process theology is one of the first schools of Christian theology to attract women, and several women theologians have been influential in it. (Others besides Suchocki include Anna Case Winters [b. 1953] and Catherine Keller [b. 1953].) Hartshorne taught at various universities including Harvard, Chicago and the University of Texas in Austin, his final teaching post. He was active in philosophy into his late nineties, giving his last public lecture at age ninety-eight.[125] He authored many books in the philosophy of religion, several of which have to do with process theology. His two best-known contributions are *Omnipotence and Other Theological Mistakes* and *The Divine Relativity* (1948). In the latter book, he expounded a social view of God as not absolute or unconditioned but necessarily relational:

---

[124]See Eulalio R. Baltazar, *God Within Process* (Paramus, NJ: Newman, 1970), 1–23.
[125]Bruce G. Epperly, *Process Theology: A Guide for the Perplexed* (London: T & T Clark, 2011), 13–14.

What is a person if not a being qualified and conditioned by social relations, relations to other persons? And what is God if not the supreme case of personality? . . . Either God really does love all beings, that is, is related to them by a sympathetic union surpassing any human sympathy, or religion seems a vast fraud.[126]

Hartshorne exercised a tremendous influence over younger process theologians who may not have agreed with everything he wrote but agreed with his social concept of God as necessarily, not just contingently, related to the world.

Probably the most influential spokesperson for process theology has been Cobb, son of Methodist missionaries in Japan and a Methodist minister himself. He taught at Claremont School of Theology for most of his career and helped found the Center for Process Studies and the journal *Process Studies*. Among his best-known books are *A Christian Natural Theology* (1965) and *Christ in a Pluralistic Age* (1975). Cobb is perhaps the most articulate and passionate defender of process theology as a form of Christian theology, claiming it is Christocentric and not just a philosophy of religion. Pertinent to this book's theme of science and Christian theology in modernity is Cobb's statement in *A Christian Natural Theology*:

I have indicated [in this book] my conviction that a cosmology inspired by the natural sciences has played a dominant role in undermining Christian understanding of both God and humanity. I have developed at some length aspects of Whiteheadian cosmology, which, I believe, both does more justice to the natural sciences and creates a new possibility of Christian understanding of the created order including human beings, of God, and of religious experience.[127]

Another influential process theologian was Pittenger, a British Anglican priest and theologian who did more than anyone else to bring the process perspective to Great Britain. He taught for many years at General Theological Seminary in New York and then at Cambridge University. He wrote the first major study of Christology from a process viewpoint, *The Word Incarnate: A Study of the Doctrine of the Person of Christ* (1959). There Pit-

---

[126]Charles Hartshorne, *The Divine Relativity: A Social Conception of God* (New Haven, CT: Yale University Press, 1948), 25.
[127]John B. Cobb Jr., *A Christian Natural Theology* (Louisville, KY: Westminster John Knox, 2007), 178.

tenger offered a new, process-based Christology in which Christ was special in the degree to which he embodied

> that which God is everywhere purposing and in some fashion achieving in the affairs of men; . . . it is *he*, Jesus Christ, who decisively embodies this purpose and action and in the concrete results of his appearing has made a real, unmistakable and "unlosable" difference in the lives of men and in their understanding of God and of the world.[128]

In other words, and this is the general process approach to Christology, Jesus functioned as God by perfectly embodying, achieving and revealing God's purpose for humanity. In process terms, Jesus "prehended" (felt) God's initial aim for him supremely and achieved it perfectly, and therefore God was "in him" in a unique way different in degree, but not in kind, from his presence everywhere and to every person and actual occasion (entity).

Finally, Griffin is another leading process theologian who has worked closely with Cobb over the years. He was inspired to go into theology by hearing Tillich lecture. He then taught theology at the University of Dayton and, until retirement, at Claremont School of Theology, where he served as director of the Center for Process Studies. Griffin wrote several important books related to process theology including *A Process Christology* (1973), *Process and Reality* (1979) and *God, Power and Evil* (1991). His special area of concentration in theology has been the problem of evil to which he sees process thought as the solution. Cobb and Griffin co-wrote what is perhaps the most influential popular presentation of process theology: *Process Theology: An Introductory Exposition* (1976), in which they reject as inadequate traditional images of God as "Cosmic Moralist," "Unchanging and Passionless Absolute," "Controlling Power," "Sanctifier of the Status Quo" and "Male."[129] Instead, they propose thinking of God as "Creative-Responsive Love":

> Process thought, with its different understanding of perfection, sees the divine creative activity as based upon responsiveness to the world. Since the very meaning of actuality involves internal relatedness, God as an actuality is essentially related to the world. Since actuality as such is partially self-

---

[128]Norman Pittenger, *The Word Incarnate: A Study of the Doctrine of the Person of Christ* (Digswell Place, UK: James Nisbet, 1959), 164–65.

[129]John B. Cobb Jr. and David Ray Griffin, *Process Theology: An Introductory Exposition* (Philadelphia: Westminster Press, 1976), 8–10.

creative, future events are not yet determinate, so that even perfect knowledge cannot know the future, and God does not wholly control the world. Any divine creative influence must be persuasive, not coercive.[130]

Process theology, then, has no single spokesperson but has many representatives who have influenced thousands of seminary students, pastors, educated laypeople and theologians throughout the United States and Great Britain for about half a century. They agree on certain basic principles of theology, and it is those we will consider here. The areas of disagreement and debate among them will not detain us. And our case study in process theology will be Cobb, even though he is only one voice in the process choir.

Process thought envisions reality, including God, as an evolving organism. Process thought is basically synonymous with Whitehead's metaphysical philosophy, even though Hartshorne introduced what he saw as some corrections into it. It is not easy to grasp, but without understanding its basic concepts process theology will make little or no sense. Process theologians assume these basic ideas of Whitehead's about reality including God. One thing that must be understood is that for Whitehead and process theology God is not an exception to basic metaphysical principles but their chief exemplification. In other words, God is not the exception to everything else we know; God is the supreme example of what we can know about reality itself. So, in order to understand process thought, one has to cease thinking of God as somehow outside the world and as the exception to the basic principles of reality and how it works. One has to realize that God is subject to the basic principles of reality such as that *to be is to be related.*

Whitehead referred to his worldview as a "philosophy of organism"[131] because of its emphasis on "feeling," dynamic movement and "being present in another entity."[132] According to him, subjective experience is not unique to humans but is the clue to the fundamental nature of all reality.[133] Reality is composed of "actual occasions" or "actual entities" which are not physical but have the nature of energy events. These are the most basic building

---

[130]Ibid., 52–53.

[131]In *Science and the Modern World* (New York: Mentor, 1948) Whitehead offered a system of "organic mechanism" as a replacement for scientific materialism (76).

[132]Whitehead, *Process and Reality*, 80.

[133]Alfred North Whitehead, *Adventures of Ideas* (New York: Free Press, 1933), 177–78. This view is elaborated throughout *Process and Reality*, e.g., 246.

blocks of reality. All actual occasions prehend or "feel" those around them and are influenced by them. The moment one comes into existence it becomes part of a field of other actual occasions and is influenced by them. But, and this is the strangest thing to most people who first encounter this philosophy, every actual occasion has some degree of freedom and "decides" what to do about those influences. As it prehends the actual occasions around it, it decides whether to imitate them, cooperate with them or go against them. For Whitehead, "God is an actual entity [occasion], and so is the most trivial puff of existence in far-off empty space."[134] All of them exist in interdependency, influencing each other and freely deciding, at least to a certain extent, what to do with those influences.

For Whitehead, and process thought in general, reality is not static but dynamic process. Every actual occasion, entity, and the whole network of them that makes up the universe is constantly evolving. Nothing actual remains the same. Each entity is striving toward something and coming closer or falling farther away. They are all value-oriented, striving toward the realizing of some value.[135] Each actual occasion is an activity of becoming, a bringing together into a unity of "feeling" responses to the relevant past and the reachable future. Hence, each is dipolar, consisting of a "physical pole" (the past) and a "mental pole" (the achievable possibility). Each creates itself in the process of experiencing and responding.[136] Each occasion, entity, is embedded in a stream or field of occasions and is both dependent on it and able to transcend it.[137] Each is partially the product of past occasions that it prehends and partially self-creating.

An actual occasion comes into being through a process called "creativity" that is embedded in the process itself and then the actual occasion passes away. It prehends and is prehended. In other words, its achievement of value or not is "felt" by other actual occasions that come into existence after it. Each occasion is free to accept or reject the values it prehends from the past and those around it. Not only is an occasion influenced by other en-

---

[134]Whitehead, *Process and Reality*, 28.
[135]Alan Gragg, *Charles Hartshorne*, Makers of the Modern Theological Mind (Waco, TX: Word, 1973), 31.
[136]Whitehead, *Process and Reality*, 38. See also Victor Lowe, *Understanding Whitehead* (Baltimore: Johns Hopkins University Press, 1962), 38–41.
[137]Whitehead, *Process and Reality*, 309.

tities like itself; it is also influenced by what Whitehead called "eternal objects," which are potentials embedded in the process that an actual occasion can use or ignore in its own process of becoming. These are somewhat like Plato's forms, eternal patterns and qualities such as colors, emotions, pleasure, pain, justice and love. So, each actual occasion occurring is confronted with at least two types of realities it prehends and decides what to do with in its own process of becoming. Whitehead posited a third type of reality influencing actual occasions. Each occasion is confronted by an "initial aim,"[138] consisting of the best possible combination for the newforming occasion, which it is free to accept or reject. By means of this initial aim, the occasion seeks to create an enjoyable experience and be creative for the future by contributing to others' enjoyment. For Whitehead, this is God's main job—to provide every actual occasion with its ideal initial aim. To reverse an old saying, then, for Whitehead "God proposes but man [or every actual occasion] disposes."

Crucial to Whitehead's understanding of God is the presupposition that God is an entity, an actual occasion, among others in the world.[139] Like all actual occasions, God is dipolar, consisting of a primordial pole and a consequent pole.[140] His primordial pole refers to God as the principle of the process of the world.[141] God envisages the infinite variety of eternal objects, assigns the best ones to each actual occasion as their initial aim and lures them toward achieving their initial aims.[142] Therefore, God contains the entire range of possibilities and is therefore the fountain of value and novelty in the process. Yet, the primordial nature or pole of God is not actual but only potential. God also has a consequent pole, which is actual, in which God himself prehends the world he is attempting to influence. God's ultimate aim, based on his primordial pole, which is eternal and unchanging, is to create unity and harmony in the world. To the extent that

---

[138]Ibid., 130, 374.

[139]"God is not to be treated as an exception to all metaphysical principles, invoked to save their collapse. He is their chief exemplification." Ibid., 521.

[140]Whitehead delineates the dipolar nature of God in relation to the world in *Process and Reality*, 519-33. He also referred to God as displaying a threefold character: primordial, consequent and superject (134-35).

[141]In Whitehead's words, God is "the unlimited conceptual realization of the absolute wealth of potentiality. . . . Not *before* all creation, but *with* all creation." Ibid., 521.

[142]Ibid., 287.

God's aims are achieved by actual occasions and the world as a whole, his consequent pole, which is his actual life experience, is enriched. To the extent they are turned away, rejected, not achieved, his life experience is impoverished. Thus, God becomes, "the great companion—the fellow-sufferer who understands."[143]

These two dimensions, poles, of God produce an intrinsic relation between God and the world. Both need each other, and both are bound up together. As Whitehead concluded, "each temporal occasion embodies God, and is embodied in God."[144] In other words, to use a very homely and inadequate analogy, God is both like a coach and a sponge. Like a coach, God urges each actual occasion in the world to achieve his ideal aim for it. Like a sponge, God soaks up achieved or unfulfilled value in the process. God cannot force any actual occasion to achieve anything. All he can do is influence and persuade (the "divine lure"). The world's response to God's initial aims affects God, giving him his life experience for better or worse. This is the sense in which God is "in process"—constantly experiencing the world's achievements and failures. But that does not mean God is totally dependent on the world. God's primordial pole is eternal and unchanging. It is like his character and the reservoir of all values he draws on to give each actual occasion its initial aim. So, for Whitehead and process theologians, "reality" is a great network of actual occasions constantly coming into and passing away from being. Only God is eternal and unchanging (in his primordial pole) and only God is immediately present to every other actual occasion influencing it. Only God holds in memory every achievement and failure of other actual occasions.

Process theologians reconstruct God using Whitehead's philosophy. Three postulates about God summarize Whitehead's philosophical theism. First, God is not aloof from or unaffected by the world; rather, God and the world are interdependent. The emphasis here is clearly on God's immanence, for God is "an actual entity immanent in the actual world."[145] God is also transcendent in that he is eternal and intimately and immediately re-

---

[143]Ibid., 532.
[144]Ibid., 529. Whitehead adds, "The World's nature is a primordial datum for God; and God's nature is a primordial datum for the World."
[145]Ibid., 143.

lated to every actual occasion. God's transcendence refers to the divine inexhaustibility, enduring faithfulness of purpose and ability to utilize even evil for good ends.[146] However, lacking omnipotence, God cannot make good come from evil. He can only use evil in his plan for the world.

Second, God works in and through the world primarily through persuasion rather than coercion. God provides the lure, but each occasion has the prerogative to accept or reject it. Thus, when Whitehead offered images of God and the world, the two he chose were "tender care" and "infinite patience."[147] Process theologian Lewis Ford drew out the implications of this view: "Faith in this sense is reciprocal. Just as the world must trust God to provide the aim for its efforts, so God must trust the world for the achievement of that aim."[148]

Third, we ought not to view God in terms of omnipotence, but as the one who suffers with the world. Whitehead rejected the classical understanding of God as the divine despot, claiming that with that view "the Church gave unto God the attributes belonging exclusively to Caesar."[149] Nor is God omniscient in the classical sense of knowing the future. Like humans, God knows the future only as a realm of possibilities, never as actuality. Unlike humans, however, he knows all the possibilities.

Process theologians pick up with Whitehead's philosophical theism and Christianize it. One theologian who has been especially adept at that is Cobb. Whitehead's metaphysics exercised a profound influence on the Methodist theologian's rethinking of Christian doctrines for the modern world. The overriding motivation for Cobb's entire enterprise of neo-liberal, process theology was to resolve the problem of evil, which has been called the "rock of atheism" in the modern world. The first question and answer in Cobb's two-volume series *The Process Perspective: Frequently Asked Questions About Process Theology* (2003, 2011) is about evil and God's omnipotence. Similarly, an entire section of the second volume is taken up with Cobb's answer to the problem of evil. In both cases his answer is the same— that God is not omnipotent and therefore cannot stop evil. "The answer of

---

[146]Norman Pittenger, "Whitehead on God," *Encounter* 45:4 (1984): 328.
[147]Whitehead, *Process and Reality*, 525.
[148]Lewis S. Ford, "Divine Persuasion and the Triumph of Good," *The Christian Scholar* 50:3 (fall 1967): 235–50; reprinted in Delwin Brown, Ralph E. James Jr. and Gene Reeves, eds., *Process Philosophy and Christian Thought* (Indianapolis: Bobbs-Merrill, 1971).
[149]Whitehead, *Process and Reality*, 520.

process theology is, of course, that God's power is not the sort that prevents people from doing evil things. God calls and seeks to persuade. But this does not keep us from committing crimes."[150] Even a superficial reading of Cobb and most process theologians must result in concluding that this is the major attraction of the process idea of God. Cobb argues that even a self-limiting but omnipotent God is inconsistent with God's goodness:

> Even so [assuming God limits himself for the sake of free will], the question re-
> mains. Why, in extreme cases, when so much is at stake, does God not intervene
> forcefully to prevent extreme forms of evil? If God has the power to do so and
> refrains, just to be faithful to an unwise decision made long ago, we find it hard
> to admire such a foolishly stubborn God and even harder to love that God.[151]

Clearly, then, for Cobb and other process theologians, a main appeal of Whitehead's process idea of God is its solution to the problem of evil. However, as critics often point out, it solves it at a great cost. A God who is not omnipotent, a God possessing only the power of persuasion, cannot guarantee an ultimate victory of good over evil. Cobb agrees and is happy with that sacrifice.

Cobb, like other process theologians, found in Whitehead's process philosophy the best possible basis for the development of a natural theology that could assist him in the task of reconstructing the doctrine of God to make it intelligible to modern and postmodern people. He based this choice on what he perceived to be the intrinsic excellence of Whitehead's structure of thought (e.g., coherence and aesthetic appeal) and its congeniality to Christian faith.[152] On that foundation, he constructed an understanding of God that he thought is more compatible with biblical personalism and contemporary science than the various conceptions found in classical theology or in Tillich—the main alternative neo-liberal theology when process thought began to develop. The union of Whitehead and the Bible was facilitated by the convergence Cobb observed between the preaching of Jesus concerning the coming kingdom of God and the scientific picture of an

---

[150]John B. Cobb Jr., *The Process Perspective: Frequently Asked Questions About Process Theology*, ed. Jeanyne B. Slettom (St. Louis: Chalice Press, 2003), 1:5–6.

[151]John B. Cobb Jr., *The Process Perspective: Frequently Asked Questions About Process Theology*, ed. Jeanyne B. Slettom (St. Louis: Chalice Press, 2011), 2:128.

[152]Cobb, *Christian Natural Theology*, 203–14.

evolving universe. Human experience includes the sense that we are being called forward, but this experience cannot be explained solely by a mechanical universe. Rather, humans have a sense of being "lured" beyond what the past dictates, of being directed to something beyond.

This experience of being lured to the future, Cobb insisted, is not limited to humans. Rather, all nature is being called forward toward ever new possibilities of harmony and beauty. The source of this "teleological pull," he argued, must be conceived in terms of personality (that is, as will and love), in other words, as God. In short, Jesus' message and the scientific cosmology point to the same conception of God, namely, God as "the One Who Calls."[153] Therefore, Cobb employed Whitehead in his attempt to replace the classical view of God as the controlling power over the world. In its stead he introduced the idea of God as "Creative-Responsive Love,"[154] who relates to the world through persuasion, not coercion. According to process philosophy and theology, the initial aim God provides can be chosen or rejected. Rejection of it is sin. Cooperation with God in actualizing the divine initial aim is salvation. Cobb interpreted this to imply that the outcome of the process is unknown even to God so that he undergoes risk and adventure in the cosmic experiment while remaining the source of restless striving toward unity, beauty and harmony. That is God's creativity; creation is God's work of luring the world toward his vision of what it should be. Science answers questions about the beginnings of the physical world and how it works; theology provides answers about the source of value in it.

Clearly, Cobb's view of the God-world relation is panentheistic, and he acknowledges that:

> The doctrine that I am developing here is a form of "pan-en-theism." It is, in my understanding, a type of theism. But it differs from much traditional theism insofar as the latter stressed the mutual externality of God and the world, with God conceived as occupying another, supernatural, sphere. It differs from pantheism when pantheism is understood to be the identification of God and the world. Yet, in reality, panentheism is the synthesis of the central concerns of traditional theism and pantheism.[155]

---

[153]Cobb, *God and the World*, 42–66.
[154]Cobb and Griffin, *Process Theology*, 41–62.
[155]Cobb, *God and the World*, 80.

Thus, in Cobb's view, God and the world coexist in mutual interdependence. God is supreme in the sense that only he relates immediately to everything and only he has the power to give every new actual occasion its initial aim. However, in this view, God does not intervene supernaturally, there are no miracles, and the resurrection of Jesus is "a powerful symbol . . . of victory over loss and defeat" but not an emptied tomb.[156]

Cobb reconstructs Christology using process thought. Cobb utilized process philosophy to reformulate Christology as well as the doctrine of God.[157] Lying behind his reformulation is the allegedly "incarnational" relatedness of actual entities he found in Whitehead's cosmology. According to process thought, present occasions incorporate into themselves both past experiences and the initial aim offered to them by God. In a sense, then, the past is incarnate in the present.[158] Also, in process thought, there is no reason why two actual occasions cannot share the same "space." So, there is a sense in which God, the provider of every initial aim to every actual occasion, is incarnate everywhere without displacing anything. To the extent that an actual occasion accepts and embodies God's initial aim, it incarnates God.

According to Cobb, "Christ" is the primordial nature of God working in the world as "creative transformation."[159] It is the self-expressive activity of God. To the extent that an actual occasion such as a human being decides for God's initial aim, God's creative transformation, God's self-expressive activity, the Christ, is present in it.[160] So, what makes Jesus special? What justifies calling him "God incarnate" in any unique sense? Jesus is the Christ, Cobb explained, because he brought into history a distinctive structure of existence, in that the incarnation of Christ in him constituted his very selfhood. Jesus revealed the basic truth about reality, which, if we accept it, opens us to being creatively transformed as well.[161] In this way, Cobb offered what some have termed an "exemplification Christology."[162] He places greater emphasis on Jesus' role of exemplifying what is universally divine

---

[156]Cobb, *Process Perspective*, 2:118–22.
[157]Cobb summarizes his Christology in *Process Theology*, 95–110. For a fuller treatment, see John B. Cobb Jr., *Christ in a Pluralistic Age* (Philadelphia: Westminster Press, 1975).
[158]Cobb and Griffin, *Process Theology*, 22.
[159]Cobb develops this theme in *Christ in a Pluralistic Age*.
[160]Cobb and Griffin, *Process Theology*, 98–99.
[161]Ibid., 102.
[162]Ted Peters, "John Cobb, Theologian in Process" (2), *Dialogue* 29 (autumn 1990): 292.

than on the qualitative uniqueness of Jesus' work of salvation. Christians, in other words, put their faith in a Jesus who exemplifies a more universal principle, namely, that which characterizes the primordial nature (character) of God. Using the term "Logos" as another synonym for "Christ" and "power of creative transformation" and "self-expressive activity of God," Cobb explains in what sense Jesus was the Logos incarnate:

> [In Jesus, in contrast to all other people] the "I" in each moment is constituted as much in the subjective reception of the lure to self-actualization that is the call and presence of the Logos as it is in continuity with the personal past. This structure of existence would be the incarnation of the Logos in the fullest meaningful sense.[163]

If that is difficult to grasp (which it is), another, simpler statement of Cobb's may clear things up. For Cobb, "Jesus existed in full unity with God's present purposes for him."[164]

Thus, for Cobb, Jesus was not "God incarnate" in any traditional, substantialist sense. He certainly was not a second person of the Trinity taking on a human nature as in the classical doctrine of the hypostatic union spelled out at the Council of Chalcedon in 451. The structure of Cobb's Christology, like that of Pittenger and other process thinkers, is similar to that of Schleiermacher and Tillich. Jesus experienced God in a special way. His experience of God was so special that it is unique "so far as we know."[165] But the difference between Jesus and other humans is one of degree and not one of kind. Or perhaps a better expression is that the difference of degree was so great as to constitute a difference in kind. In any case, there is no reason in principle why another human being might not achieve the same structure of existence.[166] Furthermore, like Tillich, Cobb differentiates between "Jesus" and "Christ." "Christ" is what the man Jesus became through his acceptance of the divine initial aim for his life. "Christ" is a principle, not a person.

Process theology leads to some unorthodox but intriguing conclusions. If process theology is right about the structures of reality, including God's

---

[163]Cobb, *Christ in a Pluralist Age*, 140.
[164]Ibid., 141.
[165]Ibid., 142.
[166]Cobb admits this; ibid.

lack of omnipotence, even impotence except for the power of persuasion, then it naturally follows that there can be no guarantee of a final victory of good over evil. All process theologians who touch on eschatology agree about that. It would be entirely inconsistent with the fundamental worldview of process thought to believe that God or anyone or anything can assure final closure to history and the appearance of God's final kingdom of peace and justice. Cobb and Griffin take up the challenge of a process eschatology and hold out hope for future transformation, a new level of human existence, but ultimately there is no reason to expect it:

> There is no assurance [based on process premises] that the human species will move forward. It cannot stand still, but in the face of its massive dangers it may decay or even destroy itself. Even if this new level of human existence were attained, and other levels beyond it, there would be no End at which the process would come to rest.[167]

So far as we know, then, the future is more of the same. It depends on humans to determine whether there will be progress, but the idea of a final end is inconsistent with basic process principles.

What about personal survival of death? What about life after death? Some process thinkers have opted for "objective immortality" in which the deceased person is "remembered" by God and his or her influence for good or evil enters into the stream field of actual occasions being prehended by them. Other process theologians, especially Griffin and Cobb, opt for some version of subjective immortality in which something of the deceased person survives consciously in another sphere or dimension than the physical one. Cobb's caveat about this subject is revealing about process theology as a whole. He answers the question about life after death by warning that

> process theology is unapologetically speculative through and through. It seeks to find and tell the most likely tale. If the process thinker forgets the extreme limitations of the human mind in relation to the marvel of what is, valid and valuable speculation can turn into arrogant and destructive dogmatism. I do not know what happens at death, and am suspicious of all who think they do. But for me, as one deeply shaped by the Christ event, the most likely tale is one about a God who loves all creatures and calls us to love one

---

[167]Cobb and Griffin, *Process Theology*, 117–18.

another. My speculations about life and death and whatever may lie beyond death are grounded in that.[168]

In spite of that warning, however, Cobb does speculate about life after death. He envisions heaven as "the beatific vision—that is, God, whom we experience so vaguely and uncertainly in this life, is present to all immediately and without ambiguity."[169] Hell is the same thing, but for some, those who experience it as hell, "this is misery."[170] Insofar as they have developed a life of hate and not love, Cobb suggests, people will experience the beatific vision of God as hell because they do not love God. However, he holds out hope that even the worst people can be redeemed after death.[171]

Process theology raises questions for some and offers answers for others. By salvaging the positive features of the liberal tradition of the nineteenth century—especially the affirmation that the natural processes are the locus of God's redemptive work[172]—process theology attempted to reestablish the vitality of theology in the context of the twentieth-century scientifically oriented world. To this end it utilized the dynamic nature of reality set forth by the new scientific theories of physics and biology as the central plank in a new natural theology. In this way it sought to provide an alternative to the radical rejection of philosophy in theology found in neo-orthodoxy. For some twentieth- and twenty-first-century Christians, process theology rescued belief in God from atheism. That is, only process theology makes it possible for them to believe in God. Without any doubt it has appealed to numerous thoughtful Christians who have trouble believing in or worshiping a God who is the all-determining reality or even the omnipotent supreme being governing the world. One disciple of process theology testifies:

> Once persons begin to understand process theology's innovative ways of describing God's relationship with the world, the problem of evil, human creativity, and freedom, and the ethical and spiritual significance of non-human world, they recognize the unique contribution that process theology makes to understand religious life, social transformation, and ethical behavior.[173]

---

[168]Cobb, *Process Perspective*, 2:146.
[169]Ibid., 2:145–46.
[170]Ibid., 2:146.
[171]Ibid., 2:147–50.
[172]Daniel Day Williams, *God's Grace and Man's Hope* (New York: Harper and Brothers, 1949), 121.
[173]Epperly, *Process Theology*, 3.

Another adherent of process theology wrote about how it made it possible for him to understand God as friend. C. Robert Mesle said that he always thought of God as his friend but had trouble reconciling that with the traditional idea of God as providentially controlling everything in the world including evil and innocent suffering. Finally he discovered process theology, which gave him the intellectual framework for the loving friendship he experienced in God:

> Here is my Friend, freed of the insulting suggestion that divine love would willingly allow senseless suffering. Free, also, of supernatural hocus-pocus here is a genuine Friend who does everything divine power can do to defeat the world's pain and suffering. We know that in everything God works for good with those who love him (Rom. 8:28). This is a vision of God that liberal Christians should appreciate.[174]

Similarly appreciative testimonials can frequently be heard and read. Process theology has tremendous appeal especially in the face of genocide, child rape and murder and tsunamis that kill hundreds of thousands.

However, much of the response to process theology has been critical. Conservative Christians have condemned it as sheer heresy and anti-Christian. In 1987 a major volume of essays, critical of process theology in varying degrees, was published. The title was *Process Theology*, and among the authors were several philosophers who had written major articles or books examining and critiquing process theology. Most of the authors were self-identified conservative evangelicals. One was evangelical philosopher David Basinger. His approach is sympathetic to some of process theology's concerns, especially the problem of evil, but he argues that "the various process arguments [about God's power] I have concerned myself with in this book do not demonstrate the process theological system to be superior to that found in classical Christianity, especially its free will variant."[175] Basinger's critique is more philosophical than theological and aimed primarily at demonstrating that its claims to superiority over traditional Christian theism do not succeed.

---

[174]C. Robert Mesle, "A Friend's Love: Why Process Theology Matters," *The Christian Century* (July 15–22, 1987), 623.

[175]David Basinger, *Divine Power in Process Theism: A Philosophical Critique* (Albany: State University of New York Press, 1988), 115.

Not all critics of process theology have been as calm and moderate as
Basinger, however. Jürgen Moltmann has argued that process theology's
denial of God's creation of the world out of nothing leads to an unfortunate "divinization of the world."[176] In other words, it erases the line between God and the world, making them of the same species. It represents
a radical immanentism of God. Lutheran theologian Ted Peters (b. 1941)
holds that in process theology the concept of an "immanent creativity"
replaces the classical Christian transcendence.[177] In other words, for
Peters and many other critics, it seems that process theology has two
"gods"—one the personal God of the Bible (radically reinterpreted) and
"creativity"—an impersonal power that causes actual occasions to arise
within the world process. Peters goes on to score process theology's denial
of God's omnipotence: "The 'God the Father Almighty' confessed by the
creeds is either replaced or reinterpreted by a deity who is strong on persuasion but weak on potency."[178]

Questions abound in the critical literature about how worshipful the
God of process theology is. Is a nonabsolute God who did not create the
world and who cannot control it or ensure the victory of good over evil
worthy of worship? Is having good intentions and being the repository of
all values and coaxing the world toward harmony worshipful? Other questions arise about process theology's handling of revelation and Scripture.
Where exactly is divine revelation? Does natural theology, even Whitehead's metaphysic, control theology? How authoritative is the Bible? Not
very, so it seems to critics. Even more, questions arise about process theology's Christology. The person of Christ normally stands at the center of
Christianity; it is what defines something as Christian according to the ancient creeds. Is process theology's account of Jesus sufficient to form any
continuity with Scripture or tradition? Does it leave the door open to other
saviors? Many critics think the answers to these questions are obvious and
condemn process theology as non-Christian.

So, what has process theology to do with modernity? There is a lively
debate about that. Griffin has argued most vociferously that process the-

---

[176]Jürgen Moltmann, *God in Creation* (San Francisco: Harper & Row, 1985), 78.
[177]Peters, "John Cobb," 215.
[178]Ibid., 298.

ology is not a form of modern theology but a form of postmodern theology. However, his exposition of "postmodern" in his introduction to *God and Religion in the Postmodern World* (1989) seems tailored to fit process philosophy and theology. "Postmodern" is a popular label in much of the intellectual world, so it is not surprising that process theologians want to wear it. If something can be labeled postmodern, it gains a certain panache and is considered avant-garde and mysterious. In fact, it seems much more the case that process theology is a form of modern theology insofar as it claims to be rationally coherent, free of mysteries and paradoxes, naturalistic and anthropocentric. It is a form of liberal theology with real continuity with Schleiermacher and Hegel. Human experience is the real source and norm of its theology from below.[179]

What about science? How does process theology handle the issue of conflict between science and Christianity? It would seem that process theology is completely consistent with modern science and, in fact, is cheerfully willing to let contemporary scientific theories lead the way in theological reconstruction. However, not all contemporary science will agree with process theology that there is necessarily a depth dimension in reality called God or even creativity or "creative transformation." Whitehead argued, and all process thinkers agree, that the universe that science studies makes no sense without such a depth dimension. Without it there is no basis for novelty, let alone advance or values. However, critics of process theology point out that it cannot explain why there is something rather than nothing as there is no creator in any traditional sense. It is true that many scientifically minded philosophers and theologians have adopted the process perspective. Two of the best-known are Arthur Peacocke (1924–2006) and Ian Barbour (b. 1923). But what they seem to like about process theology is its limitless flexibility in adjusting to whatever science dictates. Other scientist-theologians such as John Polkinghorne (b. 1930), theoretical physicist and theologian at Cam-

---

[179]Some, perhaps many, supporters of process theology may tend to challenge this claim. I consider it valid based on process theologians' reliance on Whitehead's philosophy and their apparent obsession with the problem of evil and especially the Holocaust. I have had many conversations with process theologians, and they nearly always come around to their belief that if God is omnipotent, God should have and, indeed, would have stopped the Holocaust from happening. Therefore, God must not be omnipotent, whatever Scripture and tradition say.

bridge University, have not been as sanguine about the beneficial relationship between science and process theology. In an interview he revealed his estimation of process theology:

> My criticism of process theology is that its God is too weak. God has to be
> both the God alongside us, the "fellow Sufferer" in Whitehead's phrase, but
> also the one who is going to redeem suffering through some great fulfillment.
> To put it bluntly, the God of process theology isn't the God who raised our
> Lord Jesus Christ from the dead.[180]

---

[180]"An Interview with John Polkinghorne," *The Christian Century* (January 29, 2008), 30–32.

7

DIETRICH BONHOEFFER AND RADICAL THEOLOGIANS ENVISION A RELIGIONLESS CHRISTIANITY

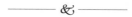

The April 8, 1966, cover of Time magazine displayed three words in large red letters on a black background: "Is God Dead?" The story lit a firestorm of controversy about a new movement in theology variously called radical theology, secular theology, death of God theology and Christian atheism. It reported on two little-known theologians, William Hamilton (1924–2012) and Thomas J. J. Altizer (b. 1927), who proposed a radical accommodation of Christianity to the secularity of the modern world. Altizer had just published *The Gospel of Christian Atheism*, in which he declared, "Now the time has come for theology openly and fully to confront the death of God, and whether or not a new form of theology will arise in response to this crisis, theology in our time can only refuse to speak of the death of God by ceasing to speak."[1] Together the two theologians published a book titled *Radical Theology and the Death of God*, in which Hamilton asked, "What does it mean to say that God is dead?" and answered his own question:

---

[1]Thomas J. J. Altizer, *The Gospel of Christian Atheism* (Philadelphia: Westminster Press, 1966), 15–16.

This is more than the old protest against natural theology or metaphysics; more than the usual assurance that before the holy God all our language gets broken and diffracted into paradox. It is really that we do not know, do not adore, do not possess, do not believe in God. It is not just that a capacity has dried up within us; we do not take all this as merely a statement about our frail psyches, we take it as a statement about the nature of the world and we try to convince others. God is dead. We are not talking about the absence of the experience of God, but about the experience of the absence of God.[2]

Soon after the *Time* cover story, numerous other publications and mass media hastened to popularize, examine and vulgarize this new theological movement. Conservative Christians wrote choruses with the refrain "God's not dead" and printed bumper stickers with the slogan "My God's Not Dead—Sorry About Yours!"

Theologians Radically Revision Christianity for a Secular World

The two catalysts of this uproar, Hamilton and Altizer, were taken aback by it.[3] They were concerned that more often than not, the popular press had distorted their message, and they, as well as others, sensed a compulsion to publish a number of books and articles interpreting it for educated laypersons because, Hamilton wrote, "it is important not to be satisfied with the news magazines, the weekly religious journals and *The New Yorker*."[4] However, the more they wrote and spoke on the subject, the clearer it became that the slogan "death of God" was highly ambiguous—even to them. Was it a historical event? A linguistic event? A cultural event? Or was it an affirmation of the divinity of humanity—the deepest expression of the immanence of God? All were possible interpretations.

One of the points Hamilton especially wanted to make was that death of God theology was not just "a complicated sort of atheism dressed in a new

---

[2]Thomas J. J. Altizer and William Hamilton, *Radical Theology and the Death of God* (Indianapolis: Bobbs-Merrill, 1966), 26–28.

[3]Hamilton and Altizer are generally considered the two main proponents of the death of God movement, although other theologians expressed their own versions of it. Two others who are often included as death of God theologians are Gabriel Vahanian and Paul van Buren. For a detailed analysis and critique of the phenomenon of death of God theology, see Jackson Lee Ice and John J. Carey, eds., *The Death of God Debate* (Philadelphia: Westminster Press, 1967).

[4]William Hamilton, "American Theology, Radicalism and the Death of God," in Thomas J. J. Altizer and William Hamilton, *Radical Theology and the Death of God* (Indianapolis: Bobbs-Merrill, 1966), 3.

spring bonnet" but a truly Christian form of theology. With this Altizer chimed in by asserting that only a Christian can truly affirm that God is dead.[5] For both of them, this is because Jesus Christ remains the best place to stand alongside suffering humanity against all dehumanizing and alienating powers, including the transcendent, sovereign God of Christian theism.

Dietrich Bonhoeffer was a well-known and beloved Lutheran theologian of the anti-Nazi Confessing Church movement in Germany during the 1930s and early 1940s. He is perhaps best known for his theological commentary on Jesus' Sermon on the Mount, *The Cost of Discipleship* (1937), and for his death at the hands of the Nazis for participating in a failed plot to assassinate Hitler. He was hanged at Flossenberg concentration camp in April 1945, just days before its liberation by the Allies. During his imprisonment he wrote occasional letters and essays that were later compiled by one of his students into the book *Letters and Papers from Prison* (published in several stages throughout the 1950s). Some of Bonhoeffer's statements were, to say the least, enigmatic and were open to various interpretations. Certain radical theologians of the 1960s focused on especially the phrase "world come of age" from a letter the prisoner wrote in which he mused about the path Christianity must take in the increasingly secular world. Bonhoeffer wondered if a new, "religionless Christianity" would emerge in response to a world that no longer felt any need of God or religion, in which Christians could no longer assume a God-shaped empty place in the human heart.

The labels "radical theology" and "secular theology" were coined to describe a mood in European and American theology that included, but was not limited to, Hamilton's and Altizer's death of God theology. Some of them affirmed God's reality but insisted on reinterpreting God as radically immanent in the world, including in its secularity. All agreed that the movement toward secularity begun by the Enlightenment could not be reversed and was reaching unforeseen depths for which traditional Christianity was unprepared. They took seriously what sociologists of religion called the secularization thesis—that modern, Western society focused on individualism and pluralism was on a trajectory toward total secularism that would not stop until religion was totally privatized if not obliterated.

---

[5] Altizer, *Gospel of Christian Atheism*, 102.

"Secularity" does not necessarily imply atheism; it does mean the belief that human life can be lived successfully without reference to God or anything transcending humanity. By "world come of age" Bonhoeffer may have meant a completely secular society; that is how most of the 1960s radical theologians interpreted his phrase. Whereas he only raised the question and hinted at some answers, such as "religionless Christianity," they attempted to describe and celebrate a Christianity completely accommodated to modern secularity.

The precise beginning of this radical 1960s theological movement is impossible to pin down. One possibility, however, is the publication of a little book that did not gain much attention by a relatively unknown theologian named Gabriel Vahanian (b. 1927). The book's title was *The Death of God: The Culture of Our Post-Christian Era* (1961). The book's thesis was that modernity had led to a post-Christian era in which God is not taken for granted and in which life is lived successfully without God. Existentialist philosopher Nietzsche had prophesied just such a cultural situation and even declared that it had begun when he wrote the parable of the madman who proclaimed "God is dead! We have killed him!" in the city square. Vahanian examined the meaning of that totally secularized culture for theology, but only some theologians noticed and paid attention. Just a few years later the world sat up and took notice when *Time* reported on Hamilton's and Altizer's follow-up on Vahanian's book.

Several other books played with the idea of God's death in culture and the meaning of secular Christianity in a world come of age without denying God's existence. In 1963 the Anglican bishop of Woolwich, biblical scholar John A. T. Robinson (1919–1983), published a paperback titled *Honest to God* that rocked Christianity in Great Britain and then in the United States. In it the bishop drew together strands of Bultmann's, Tillich's and Bonhoeffer's theologies to argue for a new view of God and Christianity accommodated to modernity in a radical way. In the book's preface Robinson stated his driving concern:

> I believe we are being called, over the years ahead, to far more than a restating of traditional orthodoxy in modern terms. Indeed, if our defense of the Faith is limited to this, we shall find in all likelihood that we have lost out to all but a tiny religious remnant. A much more radical recasting . . . is de-

manded, in the process of which the most fundamental categories of our theology—of God, of the supernatural, and of religion itself—must go into the melting. Indeed, though we shall not of course be able to do it, I can at least understand what those mean who urge that we should do well to give up using the word "God" for a generation, so impregnated has it become with a way of thinking we may have to discard if the Gospel is to signify anything.[6]

Throughout that book and some later ones, Robinson called for a radical deconstruction (not his term) of traditional theism including relocating God's transcendence completely in immanence within the world.

One theologian who had called for a moratorium on the word *God*, at least for a time, was an Episcopalian religion professor at Temple University, Paul van Buren (1924–1998). In *The Secular Meaning of the Gospel* (1963) he argued that in late modern, secular culture the word *God* has lost all meaning and so should be abandoned. Harvard University theologian and religion professor Harvey Cox (b. 1929) published *The Secular City* in 1965. It was a celebration of modern secularity, which he distinguished from secularism, as a fulfillment of certain motifs and trajectories in the Bible and Christianity. Cox, a Baptist theologian, called for Christian embrace of secularity and sacrifice of all vestiges of other-worldliness that take Christians' minds off the problems and needs of this world. In 1963 Colin Williams (b. 1921), executive director of the Department of Evangelism of the National Council of Churches, published *Where In the World? Changing Forms of the Church's Witness*. He expressed a theme running throughout all the radical, secular theologians' writings—that the church must redefine and reposition itself to be secular:

the Church must "let the world write the agendas" if it is to be truly the servant of God's mission in today's alienated and fragmented society—or, to put it another way, we must explore the thesis that the time has come to allow the Church to take shape around the needs of the world.[7]

For all of these radical, secular theologians, God, if we are to speak of God at all, must be recognized in the face of the neighbor in need and not in traditional religious ceremonies.

---

[6]John A. T. Robinson, *Honest to God* (Philadelphia: Westminster Press, 1963), 7–8.
[7]Colin Williams, *Where in the World?* (New York: National Council of Churches, 1963), 75.

The word *deconstruction* has been put to many uses in philosophy and theology. Most recently, in the 1990s and the early twenty-first century, it is associated above all with radical postmodernism, where it takes on a very technical, precise meaning in relation to unmasking the oppressive effects of belief systems and forms of life (see chap. 12). However, in a broader sense, the radical, secular theologians mentioned above, including the death of God theologians, were all engaged in a kind of theological deconstruction. There the term means what it sounds like—tearing down what has been built up. But it is not quite synonymous with "destruction." The latter may have no positive motive. Deconstruction is different from destruction in having a positive motive and purpose. For the radical, secular theologians it was to help Christianity survive in the coming secular world when people would no longer be religious. The older liberal and neo-liberal theologies assumed religion. They were all about reconstructing Christianity in the sense of re-modeling it. The radical theologians were not interesting in that project; they wanted to take traditional Christianity down and apart and replace it with a new, secular form of Christianity that would bear little to no continuity with traditional Christianity other than, as Hamilton expressed it, standing with Jesus in the midst of the world, seeking to meet its needs.

Another way of understanding radical, secular theologies is that, for all of them, God is no longer to be conceived as other than humanity. The "wholly otherness" that Kierkegaard and Barth spoke of must go. It is a relic of a time when culture was religious. In the late modern world, with all its secularity, God must be thought of as immersed in the world. The watch phrase would be "immanence of transcendence." God's transcendence *is* his immanence in humanity. That is not to say these radical theologians were pantheists. Those who continued to believe in God usually took their cue from Tillich, who described God as being itself or the ground of being. But for them, even Tillich was too God-centered, too focused on the in-finity of God, too allergic to anthropomorphism of God, trying with too much effort to distinguish God from everything creaturely and conditioned. For the 1960s radical theologians, God must be reconceived as present in the common struggles and needs and joys and triumphs of humanity without being identified with humanity in any simple way. They were much better at saying what they did not believe than what they did believe.

Bonhoeffer Becomes the Prophet of Religionless Christianity

Many books have been written and films produced about Bonhoeffer's riveting story. In the early twenty-first century, people are just as fascinated as they were ten and twenty years after his death. Every few years another biography or life story in film appears. In 2011 another massive, detailed biography of Bonhoeffer was published. This one, by bestselling author Eric Metaxas, was titled *Bonhoeffer: Pastory, Martyr, Prophet, Spy* and sold many thousands of copies. But what many people do not know is that he wrote shocking and, to some, heretical ideas in his Berlin prison cell between 1943 and 1945. Rightly or wrongly, the radical, secular theologians of the 1960s regarded him as their prophet.

Bonhoeffer was already a well-known theologian at the University of Berlin when Hitler came to power in 1933. Two of Bonhoeffer's early books had caught the attention of Barth, and the two formed a friendship with the Swiss theologian becoming, in many ways, the younger German theologian's mentor. Bonhoeffer was delivering a national radio address on "The Concept of the Leader (Führer)" soon after Hitler became Germany's chancellor (head of government). He was warning about the inherent dangers in the concept of "Führer" and was about to warn against the potential idolatry in it when he was cut off the air, possibly by agents of the new Nazi regime.[8] Soon he joined with Barth and other anti-Nazi pastors and theologians in founding the Confessing Church movement. Beginning in 1935 the young Lutheran dissident directed an illegal seminary for training ministers for the Confessing Church. This renowned school, eventually located at Finkewalde, followed an innovative format in theological education within the context of a close-knit community. The students and Bonhoeffer lived together, ate meals together, prayed and studied together. In addition to studying the academic disciplines associated with seminary education, the students learned to live the Christian life in genuine brotherhood and total dedication to the Lord. Before the seminary was closed by the Gestapo,

---

[8]Bonhoeffer's biographer, his former student Eberhard Bethge, strongly hints that it was "Goebbel's team" that "switched off" Bonhoeffer's microphone. He admits, however, that there is no way to know for sure. See Eberhard Bethge, *Dietrich Bonhoeffer: Man of Vision, Man of Courage*, trans. Eric Mosbacher et al. (New York: Harper & Row, 1977), 193–94. Many Bonhoeffer biographers have speculated about the event, but few, if any, were or are in a position to know about the event as well as Bethge.

Bonhoeffer wrote *The Cost of Discipleship* and *Life Together*—a theological account of Christian community (1939).

When war appeared inevitable, Bonhoeffer left Germany in 1939 to teach at Union Theological Seminary in New York. Soon, however, he returned to his homeland after telling his host, Reinhold Niebuhr, "I have no right to participate in the reconstruction of Christian life in Germany after the war if I do not share the trials of this time with my people."[9] On returning to Germany he was forbidden to speak publicly anywhere in the Reich. His brother and brother-in-law were both involved with Germany's Military Intelligence Service (the Abwehr), and they invited Dietrich to join them there. From that position he was able to work in the resistance movement together with them. Eventually they all became involved in the plot to assassinate Hitler that failed when the dictator survived the bomb planted by Claus von Stauffenberg. Bonhoeffer was arrested before the assassination attempt on suspicion of being involved in the anti-Nazi resistance movement. During his imprisonment for interrogation he wrote the documents now compiled by his student Eberhard Bethge in *Letters and Papers from Prison*. He was transported to a concentration camp and hanged after a brief trial on April 9, 1945. The camp doctor remarked afterwards, "In the almost fifty years I have worked as a doctor, I have hardly ever seen a man die so entirely submissive to the will of God."[10] Because of his courage and faith, even to death, Bonhoeffer has often been called a Christian martyr.

Bonhoeffer left a rich legacy of theological reflection. However, it is doubtful that he would be remembered as a great twentieth-century theologian were it not for the circumstances of his death and what led up to it and Bethge's tireless promotion of his mentor's memory. Among Bonhoeffer's theological writings are *Christ the Center* (originally titled *Christology* and first published as a volume from lecture notes in 1966) and *Ethics* (an unfinished volume reconstructed from Bonhoeffer's notes and published in 1955). However, Bonhoeffer is best known theologically for his enigmatic musings

[9]Cited in Edwin H. Robertson, "Introduction," in Dietrich Bonhoeffer, *No Rusty Swords: Lectures and Notes, 1928–1936*, trans. Edwin H. Robertson and John Bowden (New York: Harper & Row, 1965), 22. See also Bonhoeffer's *Gesamelte Schriften*, ed. Eberhard Bethge, 6 vols. (Munich: Christian Kaiser, 1965), 1:320.
[10]Wolf-Dieter Zimmerman and Ronald Gregor Smith, eds., *I Knew Dietrich Bonhoeffer*, trans. Kaethe Gregor Smith (New York: Harper & Row, 1966), 232.

in *Letters and Papers from Prison*. Some of those inspired the radical, secular theologians of the 1960s and have been widely discussed by theologians of many types since their original publication in 1953. Whether those 1960s theologians interpreted Bonhoeffer's ideas correctly has been hotly debated, including by Bethge. Nevertheless, some of them are striking enough to give a person pause to wonder whether Bonhoeffer may have been thinking along the lines in which some of those radical theologians later traced out.

In a letter dated April 30, 1944, Bonhoeffer revealed his driving theological concern: "The thing that keeps coming back to me is, what *is* Christianity, and indeed what *is* Christ for us to-day?"[11] This question was for him surrounded by a particular context that provoked it. That context was what he saw as the "world come of age" in which human persons operate autonomously, without sensing a need for divine grace or divine truth. In this world come of age, people no longer require God as a working hypothesis, whether in science, in human affairs in general or even, increasingly, in religion.[12] Bonhoeffer set about to deconstruct the religiousness that would no longer be needed or even thought about in the world come of age. It was a religiousness centered around the God of the gaps, the God who was called on to explain what could not be explained by any other means. God was used by religion and culture as a stop-gap for the incompleteness of human knowledge. This was an erroneous view of God all along, Bonhoeffer contended, and so its loss is no loss at all. This God of the gaps, a *deus ex machina*, was never the God of Jesus Christ or of authentic Christian faith. But theology had come to rely on the concept too heavily so that when the Enlightenment and science closed the gaps and God was no longer as necessary to explain things, Christianity seemed to suffer a credibility crisis. As this process reached its culmination and God was pushed out of increasingly larger dimensions of life, Bonhoeffer concluded, Christian theology turned to the inner life of the individual, attempting to retain at least that realm where God was still necessary.

Bonhoeffer saw a day coming when every gap would be closed and there would be no need to use God as an explanation for anything. What then?

---

[11]Dietrich Bonhoeffer, *Letters and Papers from Prison*, trans. Eberhard Bethge (London: Collins, 1953), 91.
[12]Ibid., 107.

"What is the significance of a Church . . . in a religionless world? How do we speak of God without religion, without the temporally-influenced presuppositions of metaphysics, inwardness, and so on?" he asked.[13] This concern was heightened, Bonhoeffer believed, by the failure of theologians to offer what he thought would be a helpful response to the adulthood of the world. In fact, in his estimation, the various attempts to accommodate the Christian message to the growing maturity of the world evidenced a common difficulty. They all built from the premise that individuals can be addressed as sinners only after their "weaknesses and meannesses have been spied out."[14] Such approaches demand that the apologist be able to point out to individuals that they are riddled with problems, needs and conflicts. For Bonhoeffer, however, this strategy is self-defeating, for it entails a denial of the maturity of the world (by which he meant modern society).

Bonhoeffer argued that Christianity must abandon all such approaches and adjust its witness. It can no longer attack "the adulthood of the world," for this attack is pointless, ignoble and unchristian.[15] Rather than polemics and apologetics, he called Christians to understand the world come of age better than it understands itself, namely, on the basis of the gospel and in the light of Christ,[16] and this because the autonomous world cannot truly understand itself unless it recognizes its relation to Christian faith. "We should not speak ill of man in his worldliness," he concluded, "but confront him with God at his strongest point."[17] Exactly what he meant is not clear; so many things Bonhoeffer wrote in *Letters and Papers* remain enigmatic. At the least, however, it is clear that he was calling Christians to take secular people seriously and not demand that they give up their independence, their strength, their knowledge and ability. Rather, so it seems, he was calling Christians to encounter modern, secular people on their own terms offering depth to their strength.

To this end, so that Christianity can still speak meaningfully to modern, secular people, Bonhoeffer advocated a "religionless Christianity." This phrase was intended to set forth his understanding of the true Christian

---

[13]Ibid., 92.
[14]Ibid., 117.
[15]Ibid., 108.
[16]Ibid., 110.
[17]Ibid., 118.

faith in the midst of the false religion he had already rejected earlier in his career. The concept of religion he criticized was religion built on an apologetic that begins with the assumption that all human beings are naturally religious, that they all have a God-shaped hole in their lives. Like Barth, he attacked as well the kind of religion that was based on a foundation of natural theology, man's search for God. He also dismissed a privatistic understanding of religion that limits it to the spiritual realm or is otherworldly in orientation. This approach makes religion magical, with God acting from the outside at the whim of humans. Finally, the kind of religion Bonhoeffer rejected was the attitude that introduces God as "the completion of a person's life, added at the boundaries of human need."[18]

According to the Bonhoeffer of the prison letters, the situation of the world come of age demands "a non-religious interpretation of biblical terminology."[19] He suggested that the erroneous theological conceptions widespread in the church ought to be replaced with an understanding that sees God as "the Beyond in the midst of our life."[20] We are to find God in what we know, he argued, not in what we do not know.[21] Further, in the contemporary world come of age we must view God as weak and powerless in the world, the one who "allows himself to be edged out of the world and on to the cross." Only in this way can God be with us and help us. "Only the suffering God can help" is one of Bonhoeffer's most often quoted sayings.[22] Thus the beginning point for a nonreligious interpretation of biblical terminology lies with a rejection of human religiosity, which in distress looks to the power of God in the world. We must abandon this imagery in favor of the God of the Bible "who conquers power and space in the world by his weakness."[23] All that Bonhoeffer meant with this picture of God is not clear, but one thing everyone agrees about is that the imprisoned theologian was focusing on the power of love over and in favor of the power of domination and control.

---

[18]For this interpretation of Bonhoeffer's understanding of religion, see Gerhard Ebeling, *Word and Faith*, trans. James W. Leitch (London: SCM, 1960), 148-55.
[19]Bonhoeffer, *Letters and Papers*, 120.
[20]Ibid., 93.
[21]Ibid., 104.
[22]Ibid., 122.
[23]Ibid.

Like Barth, but even more radically than him, Bonhoeffer emphasized the revelation of God in Jesus Christ so that all of God that we need is in him. That means the cross is not merely God's way of dealing with the guilt of sin; it is the revelation of God's very being as self-sacrificing love. Bonhoeffer did not want to say that God only *appears* weak on the cross. That demeans the cross as veiling God rather than revealing God. Perhaps more than anyone before him, the theologian in prison wanted to view the cross as the event of God. God *is* this event and this event *is* God. In true Lutheran fashion, Bonhoeffer did not believe in focusing on God in himself, and that was no Kantian rejection of knowledge of the noumenal realm. Luther had declared many times that we know nothing about God in himself but only God for us in Jesus. (The Reformer was not always completely consistent with that principle as when he speculated about a "hidden God" of wrath behind the merciful God revealed in Jesus Christ.) For Bonhoeffer, a key, if not the key, to understanding religionless Christianity is the realization that the cross of Jesus, his bloody and unjust death for us, is the most perfect revelation of God. Religion wants to go behind, if not around, the cross to find God in power, domination and control. Religionless Christianity looks on Jesus dying on the cross as God's way in the world. But that does not mean God is only humanity's victim; weakness and suffering is God's choice because of who he is, his character. It is God's way of saying yes to humanity:

> All that we may rightly expect from God, and ask him for, is to be found in Jesus Christ. The God of Jesus Christ has nothing to do with what God, as we imagine him could do and ought to do. If we are to learn what God promises, and what he fulfills, we must persevere in quiet meditation on the life, sayings, deeds, sufferings, and death of Jesus. . . . In Jesus God has said Yes and Amen to it all, and that Yes and Amen is the firm ground on which we stand.[24]

Bonhoeffer Advocates a "Holy Worldliness"

For Bonhoeffer, religionless Christianity, the theology of the cross taken ultimately seriously, must lead into what he called holy worldliness as the Christian's discipleship. He saw the chief temptation faced by Christians as with-

---

[24]Ibid., 130.

drawal from the world, especially from the modern, secular world, into pious enclaves cut off from the world or into private spirituality unrelated to the world. Another temptation is to view religion as one activity or dimension of existence alongside and in addition to others. But, according to him, the gospel is not a call to be religious in any of these senses. He rejected as unfaithful to the gospel any striving for detached, disengaged piety that viewed Christians as above or better than the rest of humanity. To be a Christian, he argued, does not entail any of the usual senses of being religious.

Rather, for Bonhoeffer, to be Christian means to participate in the life of the world as Jesus did. It is to serve God, not in some religious way or place, but in "the center of the village." Christian life is to be lived out in the midst of the world, not in retreat from it.[25] According to him, to be Christian in the world come of age means to "drink the earthly cup to the lees," for only in doing so is the crucified and risen Lord with us.[26] In other words, God is already there, where people are in all their ordinary, secular and especially suffering existences. If we want to be with God, we must go there where he is and not into some religious space sterilized of all that. Participation with God means sharing in the sufferings of God in the world. This conception, more than any other, constituted the culmination of Bonhoeffer's theology.[27] Sharing God's suffering means living a vulnerable life of responsibility for others. In *Christ the Center* Bonhoeffer defines Jesus Christ as "the man for others," so being for others is being with Christ. Speaking of the church, the imprisoned theologian declared that it is "her true self only when she exists for humanity."

Hence, the Christian is to aspire to be a human being, not a "saint" in the religious sense of someone who is otherworldly. In Bonhoeffer's poignant words,

> It is only by living completely in this world that one learns to believe. One must abandon every attempt to make something of oneself, whether it be a saint, a converted sinner, a churchman (the priestly type, so called!), a righteous man or an unrighteous one, a sick man or a healthy one. This is what I

---

[25]Ibid., 93.
[26]Ibid., 112.
[27]See Phillips's claim to this effect in John A. Phillips, *Christ for Us in the Theology of Dietrich Bonhoeffer* (New York: Harper & Row, 1967), 236.

mean by worldliness—taking life in one's stride. . . . It is in such a life that we
throw ourselves utterly into the arms of God and participate in his sufferings
in the world.[28]

Did Bonhoeffer have someone in mind as his model of holy worldliness?
He did not offer examples other than Jesus, so it is impossible to know. He
did not flesh it out, so to speak, in colorful word pictures that would lead us
to point at someone and say, "There! That's what Bonhoeffer was talking
about." It is clearer what he was against than what he was for, in terms of
specific behaviors. Withdrawal from the world, otherworldly piety, identification of spirituality with the trappings of religion—all those he was
against. Obviously he was also against Christians standing in the public
square and casting aspersions at passersby, calling them to repent and leave
behind their secular lives and join a religious community that is pure and
uninvolved in life's struggles. Many have suggested that, had he lived longer,
he would have held up Mother Teresa as the model of what he was advocating. Others have suggested Henri Nouwen, who left his academic life to
live, work and die in a community that sheltered and aided the mentally
handicapped. All that is for later generations to interpret and flesh out.
What is clear in Bonhoeffer is that Christianity must come to terms with
modern, secular life and that the way to that is the cross, meaning suffering
involvement, not escape or denunciation.

It is traditional at this point to turn away from Bonhoeffer's radical ideas
about religionless Christianity and holy worldliness to talk about another
side to his thought. Yes, the imprisoned theologian, together with his
radical musings, also wrote about the "secret discipline" Christians must
cultivate. Exactly what this meant, however, is as enigmatic and debated as
anything else in *Letter and Papers from Prison*. A clue to its meaning may lie
in the historical meaning. Surely Bonhoeffer did not make up a term or
borrow it without caring about its original sense. Early Christians in the
Roman Empire, before Constantine, used the phrase to describe the re-
straint baptized persons felt not to reveal certain deeper realities of the
Christian faith to outsiders who could not possibly understand and might
misinterpret them. Christians were often accused of eating babies, for ex-

---

[28]Bonhoeffer, *Letters and Papers*, 125.

ample, because of their talk about the Lord's Supper as the body and blood of the Son of God. There were certain things, in other words, best kept among Christians. Bonhoeffer seemed to have a different motive for maintaining a secret discipline among Christians. Devotion to God in prayer and praise continues in the discipleship of holy worldliness, but they have no place in public. In the midst of the secular world, "churchly language" has no place. Nor do any displays of religiousness.

That does not mean, however, that among themselves, and together with inquirers, Christians should not engage in prayer and the sacraments and worship. And it does not mean discarding personal devotions and prayer life. Rather, these traditionally religious practices ought not to be done in public, perhaps, for Bonhoeffer, because they inevitably seem otherworldly and self-righteous. In the contemporary cultural context in which talk about God has lost its meaning, traditional churchly language must remain silent, so that Christian speaking can be reborn out of praying for and working on behalf of others.[29] Based on his thoughts about Christian devotional life and community in *Life Together* it is fairly safe to say that Bonhoeffer valued traditional spiritual practices among Christians. However, based on everything he says in *Letters and Papers from Prison*, he believed the purpose of these is to enrich and support Christian involvement in the world on its behalf and to preserve the "*mysteries* of the Christian faith . . . from profanation."[30]

Bonhoeffer Redefines God's Transcendence in Light of Modernity

Bonhoeffer was profoundly impressed with the depth of modernity in twentieth-century Western culture. As he sat in his prison cell, ruminating on the state of contemporary society, what occurred to him was that the world had changed dramatically such that traditional Christianity could not be taken for granted. That is, people no longer assumed it as the glue holding them together; it no longer functioned that way as it did for many hundreds of years. Because of the Enlightenment and scientific revolutions, at least Europe and the United States were now irreversibly secular. But instead of bemoaning that fact and calling on Christians to resist and reverse

---

[29]Ibid., 160.
[30]Ibid., 95.

it, he saw it as an advantage. No longer could Christians believe in the God of the gaps or live according to cheap grace. ("Cheap grace" was a major theme of *The Cost of Discipleship* and was his term for taking the gospel and forgiveness for granted.) In this modern situation Christians would have to be serious about their faith, and that meant living cruciform lives.

One area of theology Bonhoeffer saw as especially affected by the world come of age is God's transcendence. Liberals had almost denied it. Dialectical theology seemed to have inflated it. Bonhoeffer wanted to redefine it. For him, the transcendent God is "the Beyond in the midst of the world," the reality of the ultimate that gives meaning to the temporal and nonultimate, the presence tapped by means of the secret discipline that gives sustenance to the believer and the church in their task of being in the world "for others." In a book he planned to write, the imprisoned theologian would say that

> transcendence consists not in tasks beyond our scope or power, but in the nearest Thou at hand. God in human form, not, as in other religions, in animal form . . . nor yet in abstract form—the absolute, metaphysical, infinite, etc.—nor yet in the Greek divine-human of autonomous man, but man existing for others, and hence the Crucified.[31]

He never lived to write that book or expand on that thought. Clearly, however, he found double duty for this new idea of transcendence. On the one hand, it does not conflict with modernity. It does not emphasize the supernatural, although it does not necessarily rule it out, either. On the other hand, it is truer to the gospel of God for us in Jesus Christ than traditional theistic notions of God in himself beyond the world ruling over it. Except for the lack of any idea of a "hidden God" or God as the all determining reality, it is very Lutheran. Luther loved to revel in the paradox of God's divinity in the suffering and dying of Jesus on the cross. Luther even talked about God dying on the cross because for him Jesus was "God deeply sunk in the flesh." For Bonhoeffer, that is true, but it is also true that God is deeply sunk in the face of the neighbor in need. In Bonhoeffer, God's tran-

---

[31]Ibid., 165. Note in this rendition of the text, "thou" has been substituted for "thing" in Bonhoeffer's definition of transcendence. For the basis of this change, see Eberhard Bethge, "The Challenge of Dietrich Bonhoeffer's Life and Theology," *The Chicago Theological Seminary Register* 51, vol. 2 (February 1961): 4.

scendence and immanence come together in a totally nonmetaphysical but gospel-centered way.

Including Bonhoeffer in a chapter with the radical, secular theologians of the 1960s is not meant to lump him together with them. Unlike Altizer and Hamilton, he was not a Christian atheist or even an advocate of secular Christianity in the same way as Cox. However, his musings in his letters from prison seemed to point in certain directions they traveled much farther than he did or perhaps would have. But we cannot know how far he would have gone with them.

Radical, Secular Theologians Pick Up Where Bonhoeffer Left Off

Cox represents that wing of 1960s radical theology that celebrated the secular without declaring God dead. In fact, thirty years after *The Secular City*, which introduced Cox and secular theology to American readers, he changed his mind about secularity and wrote glowingly about Pentecostalism in *Fire from Heaven: The Rise of Pentecostal Spirituality and the Reshaping of Religion in the Twenty-first Century* (1995). Between those two books Cox gained a reputation for being a theologian who tended to jump on whatever bandwagon popular culture was riding. Nevertheless, he has always been remembered as the American prophet of secular theology, a less radical form of radical theology than Hamilton's and Altizer's death of God movement.

Cox's concern in the 1960s was to answer the question he, and many others thought, was the pressing question facing the church then: "How . . . do we maintain an affirmation of transcendence in a culture whose mood is radical and relentlessly immanentist?"[32] Here, "immanentist" means God, however conceived, radically present in culture. According to 1960s sociologists, culture was inexorably becoming secular. According to Bonhoeffer, God is present in the world; God's transcendence is his immanence. Therefore, for Cox, God had to be thought of as present in secularity. Whereas traditional Christians were bemoaning the secularization of society, Cox and other secular theologians were determined to celebrate it as God's own work. Practically, this meant showing how the church ought to become

---

[32]Harvey Cox, "Afterword," in *The Secular City Debate*, ed. Daniel Callahan (New York, Macmillan, 1966), 197.

involved in building a new humanity, which is what Cox meant by "the secular city." This new humanity would be Bonhoeffer's "world come of age."

Basic to Cox's secular theology project was a specific understanding of the concept "secular." He used the term to refer to a specific point of view, a mood or outlook toward the world.[33] It designated a style of living marked by pragmatism and profanity; that is, the secular person's orientation is toward answering questions about what will work rather than metaphysical questions about ultimate reality behind appearances. Also, the secular person's concerns are wholly this-worldly and not with traditional religious questions.[34] Thus, the secular point of view emphasizes the temporal rather than the eternal and focuses on the needs and problems and joys of this world. The secular mood finds meaning in everyday activities and experiences rather than in pious, traditional religious disciplines. It highlights secular knowledge useful to ordinary living over the seemingly speculative ideas of theology and metaphysics. The secular outlook focuses on the autonomous, self-actualizing person as the source of whatever significance the human enterprise may have.[35]

In order to understand secular Christianity correctly, one must grasp Cox's distinction between "secularity" and "secularism." This is a major theme of Cox's 1960s theology. Other secular theologians worked with it as well. None celebrated secularism; all touted secularity as a work of God. "Secularity" refers to the outlook of modern science with its this-worldly concerns of finding solutions to human problems. The secular theologians hailed secularization as a liberating development. According to Cox, it delivered society and culture "from tutelage to religious control and closed metaphysical world-views."[36] "Secularism," in contrast, is the attitude that asserts that only through science is any trustworthy knowledge attainable and only the tangible and human affairs of this world are important. This attitude is dangerous, Cox argued, because it too readily becomes a new

---

[33]For a sketch of the secular point of view as set forth by the secular theologians, see John Macquarrie, *God and Secularity*, vol. 3 in New Directions in Theology Today, ed. William Horden, 6 vols. (Philadelphia: Westminster Press, 1967), 3:43–49. See also Charles C. West, "Community—Christian and Secular," in *The Church Amid Revolution*, ed. Harvey Cox (New York: Association, 1967), 228–56.

[34]Harvey Cox, *The Secular City* (New York: Macmillan, 1965), 60, 69.

[35]Ibid., 72.

[36]Ibid., 20.

closed worldview that can even function like a religion.[37] In other words, secularism is an ideology; secularity is a mood.

Secular theologians like Cox fought against secularism, claiming it to be an idolatrous pretension that ruled out anything spiritual. According to them and him, it is against the secularity promoted by the God of the Bible. In the words of one secular theologian:

> Secularism results from the inevitable tendency on the part of fallen man to make some aspects of his creaturely existence in the world an absolute which serves him in the place of God. Or man himself assumes the status of the absolute and becomes the object of devotion, hope and service "religious" in quality and extent.[38]

While opposing secularism, which is functionally atheistic, the secular theologians like Cox claimed that the secular outlook is legitimate and has its foundations in the Bible. The God of the Bible is immersed in the world and points his people toward concern for it and away from an otherworldly perspective. The secular theologians called Christians to a "believing secularity" and away from "idolatrous secularism."[39] One result of this would be a blurring, if not erasing, of the line between the church and the world on the basis of the reconciling work of Christ. Secular theologian William Fennell echoed Bonhoeffer:

> But since Jesus Christ is the one in whom *the world* is reconciled to God, the community seeks no separate existence for itself as a religious community in radical separation from the world. Rather, like its Lord, and in him, it exists for the sake of the world. It seeks in speech and action and attitude to interpret to the world the foundation in God of its true rather than false worldliness.[40]

Cox studied theology at Yale and Harvard and taught at Andover Newton Theological Seminary before joining the faculty of Harvard Divinity School in 1965. During the 1960s his secular theology found practical application

---

[37]Ibid., 21.
[38]William O. Fennell, "The Theology of True Secularity," *Theology Today* 21 (July 1964), 174–83, reprinted in Martin E. Marty and Dean G. Peerman, "Beyond the Secular Chastened Religion," in *The New Theology*, ed. Martin E. Marty and Dean G. Peerman, 10 vols. (New York: Macmillan, 1964), 2:33.
[39]Ibid.
[40]Ibid., 37.

in his activism in inner-city ministry and the civil rights movement. Later, during the 1990s, his religion course in the university became immensely popular as he focused much of his attention on correlating religion with popular culture. He appeared on numerous television programs to talk about religion and came to recant his view that culture's secularization is an inevitable process. Nevertheless, *The Secular City* remains one of the most read and discussed books of the 1960s and influenced many liberal-leaning Christians to focus their faith based activism on political transformation.

Cox's foundational thesis in *The Secular City* was that the process of secularization, rather than being inimical to Christian spirituality, is in profound agreement with Christian faith. This agreement arises from the fact that secularization is "the legitimate consequence of the impact of biblical faith on history."[41] In fact, secularity is dedicated to what is truly authentic and basic to the gospel, namely, liberty and responsibility. The call of the gospel to conversion, therefore, is an admonition to accept "adult responsibility" for the world.[42] In words reminiscent of Bonhoeffer in *Letters and Papers from Prison* Cox challenged Christians to find God in contemporary movements of secularization: "Rather than fighting and opposing secularization, we would do better to discern in it the action of the same One who called an earlier people out of endless toil, in a land where the taskmasters were cruel, and into a land flowing with milk and honey."[43] Cox's main concern was to draw out the implications of his thesis for the church. He asserted that the proper basis for a doctrine of the church lies in a theology of social change, even revolution,[44] symbolized by the image of the "secular city." (By "revolution" he did not mean violent overthrow of government. He was talking about radical cultural change.)

Because of its juxtaposing of two significant terms, "secular" and "city," this symbolic phrase represents positive goals of the gospel call: "The idea of the secular city exemplifies maturation and responsibility. Secularization denotes the removal of juvenile dependence from every level of a society; urbanization designates the fashioning of new patterns of human

---

[41]Cox, *Secular City*, 17.
[42]Ibid., 123; see also 121.
[43]Ibid., 191.
[44]Ibid., 114.

reciprocity."[45] As a result Cox found in the image of the secular city as the "commonwealth of maturity and interdependence" an apt symbol for the biblical idea of the kingdom of God.[46] In this sense, Cox became one of the founders of what later came to be called political theology—at least in the United States. For him, politics, in the broad sense of the right organization of humanity in community, was the source of unity and meaning for human life and thought. Politics was to replace metaphysics as theology's main conversation partner and field of investigation and expression. He declared, "What God is doing in the world is politics, which means making and keeping life human." Consequently, "theology today must be that reflection-in-action by which the church finds out what this politician-God is up to and moves in to work along with him."[47]

For Cox, this meant revising the Christian understanding of transcendence. God comes to us today, he asserted, in the events of everyday life and social change. In these events God is both the foundation of freedom and the basis of the experience that not everything is pliable and capable of being "transmuted into extensions of ourselves."[48] God lies behind the stubbornness of the realities that confront us.[49] But above all God comes as our partner who wants us to be interested in others, not in God. This idea led Cox to offer the climactic suggestion of his book, namely, that we might need to lay aside the word *God* in favor of another designation of the reality that confronts us in the secular city, a new name of God's own choosing that would emerge in God's own time.

Altizer Proclaims the Gospel of Christian Atheism

Altizer is generally considered the leading exponent of 1960s death of God theology or Christian atheism. During the height of the controversy launched by the 1966 *Time* cover article he was associate professor of Bible and religion at Methodist-related Emory University in Atlanta, Georgia. Although Emory's president defended Altizer's academic freedom, Altizer

---

[45]Ibid., 109.
[46]Ibid., 110, 116.
[47]Ibid., 255.
[48]Ibid., 262.
[49]For a similar interpretation of this enigmatic phrase, see Steven S. Schwarzschild, "A Little Bit of a Revolution?" in *The Secular City Debate*, ed. Daniel Callahan (New York: Macmillan, 1966), 151.

eventually left under tremendous pressure from the university's constituents. He then focused his attention on English studies and especially the postmodern style of literary criticism known as deconstructionism. Until his retirement he taught at the State University of New York in Stony Brook. In 2006 he published his autobiography, *Living the Death of God: A Theological Memoir*. Among his books after *The Gospel of Christian Atheism* were *The Self-Embodiment of God* (1977) and *Total Presence: The Language of Jesus and the Language of Today* (1980). As of 2012 he continues to make public appearances and speak on subjects related to the death of God. At one professional society meeting in 2005 he began his address to about five hundred professors of religion and theology with "Jesus was an atheist and we must all become atheists with Jesus!"

Altizer's writing style does not lend itself to easy interpretation. His friend Hamilton may have intended to praise him when he wrote that "Altizer is all *élan*, wildness, excessive generalization, brimming with colorful, flamboyant, and emotive language."[50] But that style is a major obstacle to understanding him. Another obstacle is his eclecticism. Altizer drew on a vast array of philosophers, poets and religious thinkers to concoct his unique recipe of thought. Among the most prominent influences are the philosophers Hegel and Nietzsche, but he also calls on the mystical poet William Blake (1757–1827). These three, he said, formed the primary sources for his theology. However, the indelible marks of Bonhoeffer and Tillich are also clearly visible in his thought. Hamilton and Altizer dedicated *Radical Theology and the Death of God* to Tillich, and in his preface to *The Gospel of Christian Atheism*[51] Altizer cited him as "the modern father of radical theology."

The overall theme of Altizer's Christian atheism is the absolute immanence of God in humanity "dissolving even the memory or the shadow of transcendence."[52] The passage through this death of God into radical immanence, he argued, is the "one clear portal to the twentieth century."[53] That is why it is necessary for theology—because theology must come to terms with the modern consciousness of humanity's full liberation and responsibility as

---

[50] Altizer and Hamilton, *Radical Theology and the Death of God*, 31–32.
[51] Altizer, *Gospel of Christian Atheism*, 10.
[52] Ibid., 22.
[53] Ibid.

articulated by its prophets who are the modern world's secular, profane minds: Freud, Marcuse, Sartre, Blake, Hegel and Nietzsche. These are the sources of Christian theology, according to Altizer, because they reveal the historical destiny of humanity in our time, "a time in which simply to share the universal condition of man is to take upon oneself a life without God."[54] Altizer viewed the death of God as an event in history and not just a symbolic expression of modern humanity's autonomy (as was more the case with Hamilton). He labeled this event the "self-annihilation of God" and interpreted it as the ultimate act of kenosis or self-emptying symbolized in the doctrines of the incarnation and the cross. This kenotic act of divine self-annihilation took place in Jesus Christ, so that God became identical with humanity by negating his own objective existence through finite life and death:

> The God who acts in the world and history is a God who negates himself, gradually but decisively annihilating his own original Totality. God is that Totality which "falls" or "descends," thereby moving ever more fully into the opposite of its original identity. God or the Godhead becomes the God who is manifest in Christ by passing through a reversal of His original form: thus transcendence becomes immanence just as Spirit becomes flesh.[55]

Thus, Altizer says, "the Christian proclaims the God who has totally negated or sacrificed himself in Christ."[56]

For Altizer, this self-sacrifice of God is an act of grace for the sake of the creature. By wholly and entirely identifying with creaturely existence, God affirms its being. Maintaining his independent existence in transcendence would destroy humanity's freedom and responsibility. Altizer saw this radical immanence of God as leading to an important and necessary practical conclusion: the one who affirms the death of God can overcome all forms of "No-saying" to life and say "Yes" to this world and life in it.[57]

Radical, Secular Theology Leaves a This-worldly Legacy

Without any doubt, 1960s radical, secular theology represents the deepest accommodation to modernity possible. In fact, some of it went beyond

---

[54]Ibid., 3.
[55]Ibid., 89–90.
[56]Ibid., 90.
[57]Ibid, 132–57.

anything envisioned by the founders of modernity, most of whom believed
in God. However, as already seen, modernity contained within itself a
strongly secularizing impulse. Bonhoeffer was no doubt right to see trouble
ahead for Christianity insofar as it held onto the God of the gaps idea and
attempted to base belief in God on phenomena that could not yet be explained by reason. As science closed those gaps and as philosophy increasingly went about its business without metaphysics or God, Christianity was
confronted with the task of rediscovering the place of God in life. For all of
the radical, secular theologians that place is politics in the broadest sense of
the word. For Altizer it replaced God. As will be seen, other theologians
picked up the challenge and went in different directions with it, but 1960s
radical, secular theology demonstrated how far theologians, unleashed
from traditional Christianity and the life of the church, can run with accommodation to modernity.

What effect did this seemingly ephemeral 1960s movement have on later
theology? One possible one is that culture began to turn away from theology, finding it difficult to take seriously as a discipline that can deny its
very object. Before the 1966 *Time* cover asking if God is dead and reporting
on the death of God theology, theologians frequently graced the magazine's
cover. Liberal theologian Harry Emerson Fosdick was on its cover twice in
the 1920s and 1930s. Other giants of modern theology who were on its cover
have been mentioned. After 1966, no theologian has been on *Time*'s cover.
A few have been featured in brief articles, but no *Time* cover story has been
about a particular theologian. Theology fell on hard times, perhaps partly
because of these radical theologians and their ideas, which were often distorted and misunderstood.

Another effect is that, although the radical, secular theology movement
died, the Pandora's box was opened and some later theologians dared to
continue with the motif of radical immanence of God in humanity. Among
certain postmodern philosophers and theologians especially the idea of
God's death or absolute absence, with no hope of return, has reappeared.
Slovenian philosopher Slavoj Žižek (b. 1949) has picked up the theme of
God's death and written much about it. He has appeared with Altizer, and
they have written together on the subject. Some have gone so far as to
identify him as Altizer's successor in radical theology. Among his main

works touching on God and religion are *On Belief* (2001) and *The Fragile Absolute: Or, Why Is the Christian Legacy Worth Fighting For?* (2000). Žižek could be considered a Christian atheist because, although he does not belong to any church, he promotes Jesus as the ideal iconoclast.

Another post-1960s thinker influenced by radical, secular theology is English theologian Don Cupitt (b. 1934), who taught Christian theology at Cambridge University from 1964 until his retirement in 1996. He is perhaps best known as the author and narrator of a British Broadcasting Corporation television series of documentaries titled *The Sea of Faith* (1984) which questioned many orthodox Christian doctrines in light of the plurality of world religions and discoveries of modern science. Cupitt's reputation as a radical theologian was sealed by *Taking Leave of God*, in which he wrote, "Modern people increasingly demand autonomy, the power of legislating for oneself. . . . A life lived in resigned acceptance of limitation and in passive obedience to God and tradition does not deserve to be called a moral life."[58] He continued by denying "theistic realism"—belief that God, an "immense cosmic or supracosmic Creator-Mind," exists.[59] And the main reason for taking leave of this belief and this God of Christian tradition is for the full humanity of people. So long as people believe in such a being, Cupitt, an Anglican priest, argued, they will not be fully mature and responsible for their own lives and for the world. However, he held onto and promoted "spirituality" without God. He allowed that the word *God* may not go away, but we have to invest it with new meaning:

> What then is God? God is a unifying symbol that eloquently personifies and represents to us everything that spirituality requires of us. The requirement is the will of God, the divine attributes represent to us various aspects of the spiritual life, and God's nature as spirit represents the goal we are to attain. Thus the whole of the spiritual life revolves around God and is summed up in God. God is the religious concern, reified.[60]

In other words, "God" is a cipher for human spiritual self-transcendence, but there is no being who corresponds with that word.

Not all those who find value in radical, secular theology, and certainly

---

[58]Don Cupitt, *Taking Leave of God* (New York: Crossroad, 1981), ix.
[59]Ibid., 8–9.
[60]Ibid., 9.

not all those who find value in Bonhoeffer's musings, are out-and-out atheists, however. Nor do they all celebrate secularity as a kind of savior of humanity from its minority. To what extent he is influenced by 1960s radical theology is unclear, but Irish postmodern Christian writer Peter Rollins (b. 1973) talks about the death of God and Christian atheism as antidotes to idolatrous religion that treats God as an object and especially as a support for ideological commitments. In *How (Not) to Speak of God*, he promoted "Christian a/theism" as deconstructive "as it always prevents our ideas from scaling the throne of God."[61] Authentic Christianity, Rollins avers, knows that we cannot grasp God, but "faith is born amidst the feeling that God grasps us."[62] In that book he was mainly concerned to use "a/theism" to guard against objectifying God (making God usable), but in *Insurrection: To Believe Is Human; to Doubt, Divine* (2011) he pushes it further such that one begins to wonder whether he believes in what Cupitt calls theistic realism. Like Tillich, Rollins denies that God exists, which may just be another way of expressing that God is not "thingy" or objectifiable. However, increasingly he seems inclined to push against any belief in God as at least potentially idolatrous, a dialectical move to be sure. At first Rollins seemed mainly concerned to protect God's infinity; in his later work he seems concerned more to ward off religious certainty and making God present. However, if a person emphasizes God's nonobjectiveness too strongly, it can easily lead to God's disappearance. Most of all, though, Rollins seems to be protesting the continuing tendency of Christians to view God as the God of the gaps, the *deus ex machina* who rushes in to solve problems which keeps believers from living real lives in the real world of suffering.

Secular, Radical Theologies Reap a Whirlwind of Controversy

One question that arises from examining 1960s radical, secular theology is whether it understood Bonhoeffer rightly. Many of Bonhoeffer's defenders, including his student Bethge, to whom many of the letters from prison were addressed, said they did not. In 1989 European theologian Georg Huntemann published a volume examining radical interpretations of Bonhoeffer titled *The Other Bonhoeffer: An Evangelical Reassessment of Dietrich Bon-*

---

[61]Peter Rollins, *How (Not) to Speak of God* (Brewster, MA: Paraclete Press, 2006), 25.
[62]Ibid., 30.

hoeffer. He argued cogently that even Bonhoeffer's most enigmatic suggestions in *Letters and Papers from Prison* have to be interpreted dialectically
and that the radical theologians failed to grasp this. According to him,

> Bonhoeffer's theology is a theology that can only be expressed in paradoxes,
> in the constant movement of a dialectic. The mysteries of Christian faith safe-
> guard the body of believers against secularization, but they also safeguard
> the world against religion. Church without world is ghetto, world without
> church is the well-lighted emptiness of a pedestrian mall.[63]

In other words, "religionless Christianity" did not mean for Bonhoeffer
abandonment of God or immersion in secularity. But it did mean Christian
immersion in the world and its needs. The truth seems to be that the Bonhoeffer of the prison writings was more radical than conservative Christian
interpreters acknowledge but less radical than the 1960s secular theologians thought.

Overall it seems safe to say that the 1960s radical, secular theologians
were unnecessarily caught up in a kind of romantic affair with secularity.
Not only did the secularity thesis turn out to be wrong, as at least American
society turned very strongly back to religion throughout the 1980s to 1990s,
but the theologians celebrating secularity were too willing to sacrifice anything recognizable as traditional Christianity to accommodate to what they
thought was the irreversible trend of modernity. Soon afterwards, in fact
even beginning during the 1960s, society was beginning to enter a new
stage called postmodernity. What exactly that means is still debated in the
second decade of the twenty-first century, but clearly the radical theologians of the 1960s were not yet aware of the door to religion and belief in
God the cultural turn away from secularism would open.

Even during the 1960s and in the immediate aftermath of radical theology's heyday, critics were challenging its celebration of secularity. Two of
the most constructive critical responses appeared in 1969 from sociologist
of religion Peter Berger (b. 1929) and theologian Langdon Gilkey. Berger
explored the "signals of transcendence" in ordinary human experience in *A
Rumor of Angels.* He suggested that modern society has the resources for a

---

[63]Georg Huntemann, *The Other Bonhoeffer: An Evangelical Reassessment of Dietrich Bonhoeffer,*
trans. Todd Huizinga (Grand Rapids: Baker, 1993), 74.

rediscovery of the supernatural. Years later he would repudiate the secularization thesis and acknowledge that religion has staying power even in a pluralistic, libertarian society such as the United States.

Gilkey raised the possibility of a renewal of God-language in a secular culture in *Naming the Whirlwind*. He criticized the death of God theologians for falling prey to a basic inconsistency. "Without god-language," he wrote, "this theology cannot consistently hold onto the category of the Lordship of Jesus Christ." It thereby relinquishes its sole touch with the Christian tradition and its claim to be a Christian theology.[64] Furthermore, Gilkey argued that Christian atheism's claim that contemporary human existence is entirely godless is "neither a true nor an illuminating picture of our secular life as it actually is."[65] To demonstrate this he explored in depth and detail the "dimensions of ultimacy" such as freedom and hope in human experience. Both Berger and Gilkey concluded that this theology fundamentally misinterpreted human experience by ignoring its openness to a transcendent beyond.

Devastating criticisms of radical theology brought the movement to an early demise, even though some of its themes continued or reappeared in later radical theologians as mentioned above. Most Christian thinkers, even those considered neo-liberal, rejected it as too extreme in its elimination of transcendence and emphasis on immanence. However, its most important legacy may lie in its challenge to late twentieth-century and early twenty-first-century Christian theologians to rediscover and reconstruct the transcendence of God in a way that would speak with power to the increasingly secular modern and then increasingly pluralistic postmodern mindsets. In one way or another most of the theological movements of the latter half of the twentieth century can be interpreted as responses to this challenge. Certainly the constructive theological work of Jürgen Moltmann must be understood in this way.

---

[64]Langdon Gilkey, *Naming the Whirlwind* (Indianapolis: Bobbs-Merrill, 1969), 148.
[65]Ibid.

8

THEOLOGIANS LOOK TO
THE FUTURE WITH HOPE

God does not yet exist. That is a startling statement, to be sure, but it lies at the heart of a theological movement that arose to counter 1960s radical, secular theologies that either denied any existence of God or immersed God in modern secularity. The movement has been variously called the theology of hope and eschatological theology. Its signal motif was the futurity of God, or God as the "power of the future." It attempted to recover a sense of Christian eschatology and link God's transcendence with futurity—a temporal metaphor for God's otherness as opposed to a spatial one. These theologians were responding to modernity in new ways that intrigued many Christians in the 1970s and beyond. They were also responding to the genocidal horrors of the twentieth century that many people were claiming to be the rock of atheism.

Jürgen Moltmann (b. 1926) and Wolfhart Pannenberg (b. 1928) were eschatological theology's main spokespersons. Both believed in the futurity of God and that God does not yet exist, short of the fullness of God's kingdom. Neither one believed, however, in process theology or any sense in which God is incomplete in himself. God's futurity, they averred, is true for humans but not for God. God has no future; he is already the power of the future that pulls history toward its final consummation in God's kingdom. But the point is that God is not the all-determining reality whose will and power are reflected in the events of history. God's will and power will be revealed when the kingdom of God arrives and is already being revealed proleptically in special events such as the resurrection of Jesus.

Moltmann's and Pannenberg's eschatological theologies responded to the cultural contexts of the mid-twentieth century. Protest atheism, with its arguments against belief in God based on the overwhelming evidence of gratuitous evils on a massive scale, gained strength during the 1960s. Atheists pointed to the Holocaust and Hiroshima to disprove the existence of the God of Christian theism, the all-determining and omnipotent God. They also argued that the God of traditional Christianity excluded human freedom and responsibility for this world. They based hope for the future on purely secular and humanistic principles. The 1960s theologians of accommodation responded by embracing the atheistic agenda, often reducing traditional Christian beliefs to symbols of human aspirations. Their God either dwindled away into almost complete immanence, as in process theology, or disappeared, as in Christian atheism. Theologians of reaction responded to the growing forces of secularization and atheism by retreating into fortresses of anti-intellectual emotion, mysticism or rigid confessionalism that satisfied itself with condemning the spirit of the age. Their God floated away from human problems into irrelevance, making appearances only in supernatural events of the distant past or the near future, as in apocalyptic dispensationalism, or in ecstatic events of the present, as in some manifestations of the charismatic movement.

Neither accommodation nor reaction, however, proved satisfying as a theological response to the revolutionary hopes and despairs of the times. In the middle of the confusion a book appeared from a virtually unknown young German theologian which seemed to many to provide the needed new approach for theology in the latter half of the century. Its title was *Theology of Hope* (1965). Its author, Moltmann, called for a shift to eschatology, to the traditional doctrine of the last things but reinterpreted and reconstructed, as the new foundation for theology in the late twentieth century. He declared,

> From first to last . . . Christianity is eschatology, is hope, forward looking and forward moving, and therefore also revolutionizing and transforming the present. The eschatological is not one element of Christianity, but it is the

medium of Christian faith as such, the key in which everything in it is set, the glow that suffuses everything here in the dawn of an expected new day. For Christian faith lives from the raising of the crucified Christ, and strains after the promises of the universal future of Christ.[1]

Many Christians in Europe and North America found Moltmann's theology of hope and promise a breath of fresh air in the aftermath of Bultmann's and Tillich's existentialized, nonsupernatural Christianity and in the middle of the radical, secular theologies that reduced Christianity to political activism. But Moltmann was not just repeating old eschatological formulas of escapism into God's other world; he was applying Christian hope to present political problems and arguing that belief in God's promised future energizes transforming action on behalf of humanity and the earth now.

Moltmann's efforts to renew eschatology as the basis for a new Christian theology were paralleled by several other theologians, most notably his colleague Pannenberg. They formulated their eschatological approaches to theology while teaching together at the Confessing Church's academy at Wuppertal, West Germany. Both were influenced by a philosopher named Ernst Bloch (1885–1977), whose three-volume work *Das Prinzip Hoffnung* (*The Principle of Hope*) (1938–1947) impressed both of them by its parallels with biblical faith in God's future. One of Pannenberg's earliest books was *Theology and the Kingdom of God* (1969), which, like Moltmann's *Theology of Hope*, emphasized God as the power of the future. For Pannenberg, as for Moltmann, the future kingdom of God, which is inseparable from God himself, is the central, unifying theme of Christian theology. Other theologians who joined with Moltmann and Pannenberg in emphasizing futurity as the "mode of God's being" were Carl Braaten (b. 1929), author of *The Future of God: The Revolutionary Dynamics of Hope* (1969), and Ted Peters (b. 1941), author of *God—The World's Future* (1992).

Moltmann and Pannenberg went their separate ways after their brief tenures as colleagues at Wuppertal, but throughout their theological careers, each in his own way continued to explore eschatology as the avenue to renewing Christian theology in the late modern world of increasing secularization and catastrophes. God seemed remote, even absent. The theologians

---

[1]Jürgen Moltmann, *Theology of Hope: On the Ground and Implications of a Christian Eschatology*, trans. James W. Leitch (New York: Harper & Row, 1967), 16.

of hope and eschatology did not want to return to the God of the gaps so eloquently rejected by Bonhoeffer and the radical, secular theologians. Neither could they see God as the providential ruler of history as traditional Christian theology portrayed him. Both wanted to recover a sense of God's transcendence but felt that modern theological attempts to do that were dead ends. As Tillich, and then John Robinson, had so emphasized, the idea of God up there is no longer meaningful. So Moltmann and Pannenberg, each in his own way, turned to "God ahead of us," "God of promise," "God as coming Lord" to describe God's transcendence. God is to the world as the future is to the present. Perhaps the most startling aspect of their common viewpoint is eschatological ontology—the idea that the future determines the present, an idea borrowed from Bloch that they believed is also biblical. The benefit would be that God is not the author of all the sin, evil and innocent suffering of history, nor is he powerless to do anything about them, as in process theology. God's seeming absence from this world is due to the "not yetness" of God's kingdom that will be and is already breaking in from the future.

8.A. JÜRGEN MOLTMANN RENEWS CONFIDENCE IN THE FINAL TRIUMPH OF GOD

In 1981 this writer moved with his family to Munich, Germany, to study theology with Pannenberg. He would rather have studied with Moltmann in Tübingen, but things worked out differently and Munich turned out to be a marvelous home for a year. The first time he turned on German television the broadcast featured Moltmann speaking passionately to a convention of disabled people. The speech was being broadcast nationally and in prime time. Moltmann's theme was a "Theology of Disability," and he spoke of God as "the disabled God," pointing his audience to the cross of Jesus Christ and speaking about the weakness of God in history. Moltmann was and is a national celebrity in Germany where, well into the twenty-first century, theologians are still considered public intellectuals. His books sell well and are read not only by other scholars or pastors but by thousands of educated laypeople as well. In the second decade of the twenty-first century, he is one of the last living world-class theologians.

Moltmann rises to prominence as a Protestant theologian. He was born in Hamburg in 1926 in a liberal Protestant home where he received more knowledge of Lessing, Goethe and Nietzsche than of the Bible. When he was a boy, Moltmann's parents moved the family to an intentional agricultural community outside Hamburg called Volksdorf ("People's Village"). It was an attempt at a utopia centered around gardening, healthy living and close community. But "there was no church in Volksdorf, nor would anyone have gone to it."[2] His parents and grandparents were free thinkers who had little time for religion but much time for the arts and philosophy. Toward the end of World War II the teenage Jürgen, like most German boys, was pressed into military service and spent nights manning anti-aircraft artillery in Hamburg. Many of his friends were killed during nighttime air raids and the ensuing firestorms that consumed Hamburg and other German cities. He was captured by Canadian troops in Belgium in 1945 and held as a prisoner of war for three years. War brought about a crisis of faith in Moltmann's life, as it had for Tillich, but the results were different:

> In the camps in Belgium and Scotland I experienced both the collapse of those things that had been certainties for me and a new hope to live by, provided by the Christian faith. I probably owe to this hope, not only my mental and moral but physical survival as well, for it was what saved me from despairing and giving up. I came back a Christian, with a new "personal goal" of studying theology, so that I might understand the power of hope to which I owed my life.[3]

Moltmann studied theology at Göttingen under teachers strongly influenced by Barth. Initially he became an ardent disciple of the master of dialectical theology. In fact, one of his earliest publications was a scholarly study of the beginnings of dialectical theology.[4] Although the influence of Barth remained, Moltmann later became more critical of the Swiss theologian's neglect of the historical nature of reality and the eschatological nature of theology.[5]

---

[2]Jürgen Moltmann, *A Broad Place: An Autobiography*, trans. Margaret Kohl (Minneapolis: Fortress, 2008), 5.

[3]Jürgen Moltmann, "An Autobiographical Note," in A. J. Conyers, *God, Hope and History; Jürgen Moltmann and the Christian Concept of History* (Macon, GA: Mercer University Press, 1988), 203–23.

[4]Jürgen Moltmann, *Anfänge der dialektischen Theologie*, 2 vols. (Munich: Christian Kaiser, 1962, 1963).

[5]For a definitive study of Moltmann's reception of and reaction to Barth, see M. Douglas Meeks, *Origins of the Theology of Hope* (Philadelphia: Fortress, 1974), 15–53.

Moltmann received his doctoral degree in theology in 1952 and served as pastor of a small Reformed church until 1957, when he joined the faculty of the academy at Wuppertal. There he collaborated with Pannenberg in the formulation of eschatological theology. After a brief stint at Bonn, Moltmann was offered the prestigious position of professor of systematic theology at the University of Tübingen and, except for brief stints teaching at American universities, remained there until his retirement in 1994. Throughout his career, even after retirement and into old age, he traveled all over the world lecturing on many subjects related to theology, politics, the arts and science, and he continued to write. Since the publication of *Theology of Hope* in 1965, he has continued exploring Christian theology with eschatology as his unifying theme. Among his major published works are *The Crucified God* (1973), *The Church in the Power of the Spirit* (1975), *The Trinity and the Kingdom* (1980), *God in Creation* (the Gifford Lectures; 1985), *The Way of Jesus Christ* (1990), *The Spirit of Life* (1992) and *The Coming of God: Christian Eschatology* (1996). The last book named comes closest to his magnum opus, the systematic statement of his life's work as a Christian theologian. Throughout it are sprinkled nuggets of Moltmann's theological wisdom that shed light on things he wrote earlier:

> the Bible is the book of God's promises, not of God's providence. It is the source for a historical theology in testimony, assailment, struggle and suffering, not for a speculative theology of universal history and a divine plan of salvation. The theology of hope is not a theory about universal history, nor is it an apocalyptic prediction. It is a theology of combatants, not onlookers.[6]

In *The Coming of God*, Moltmann argues that premillennial eschatology, belief in the coming kingdom of God on earth, does not, as often claimed, dampen activism for the transformation of the world now. In fact, he adamantly affirms that, if rightly understood, it energizes social and ecological activism. Of course, this is contrary to the usual theological consensus.[7]

In addition to writing, lecturing and teaching, Moltmann has been in-

---

[6]Jürgen Moltmann, *The Coming of God: Christian Eschatology*, trans. Margaret Kohl (Minneapolis: Fortress, 1996), 145–46.
[7]For an insightful examination and defense of Moltmann's unique premillennial eschatology see Brandon Morgan, "Eschatology for the Oppressed: Millennarianism and Liberation in the Eschatology of Jürgen Moltmann," *Perspectives in Religious Studies* 39:4 (winter 2012): 379–93.

volved in ecumenical dialogues with Catholics, Orthodox Christians, Jews, Muslims, Marxists and Pentecostals. There is almost no religious or ideological group he has not engaged with in conversation. His critical involvement with liberation theologies of all kinds has made him a major influence in revolutionary and political theologies of the latter half of the twentieth century and the beginning of the twenty-first century. His theology always inclines toward the practical and political. For example, *God in Creation* aims at encouraging and equipping Christian environmentalism. His many reflections on the Trinity, as in *The Trinity and the Kingdom*, bear on community formation and interdependence.

According to Moltmann, the real heart of Christianity, and therefore the true center of theology, is hope for the coming of God's "Kingdom of Glory," the divinely promised fulfillment of God's glory in the full freedom in community of humans as well as the liberation of creation itself from bondage to decay. Every part of his theology is permeated by this organizing motif. He maintains that eschatology has too often served as a useless appendage to theology, and even where it has been emphasized it has not been allowed full play. Instead of the traditional approach, he wishes to let the eschatological kingdom of glory in which God will be "all in all" determine the correct formulation of every Christian doctrine. He asserts that this reorientation toward the future is not only biblically sound but also points the way to solutions to the problems and impasses of contemporary theology.[8]

Moltmann reenvisions the future as the locus of being. One of Moltmann's primary concerns in theology has been to employ eschatological or "messianic" theology to overcome the conflict between God's transcendence and immanence through a creative reconstruction of the doctrine of God. He believes the concept of God as the "power of the future" will also help overcome the modern conflict between classical theism and atheism. He is also concerned to overcome the destructive separation between theological theory and Christian practice by providing a "critical theory of God" that will have direct social application. This eschatological reorientation of theology draws on several sources. Old and New Testament scholars Gerhard von Rad (1901–1971) and Ernst Käsemann (1906–1998) contributed to

---

[8]Jürgen Moltmann, "Theology as Eschatology," in *The Future of Hope: Theology as Eschatology*, ed. Frederick Herzog (New York: Herder and Herder, 1970), 9.

Moltmann's theology through their rediscoveries of the centrality of history and apocalyptic for Hebrew and Christian Scriptures. On the theological side, Moltmann was strongly influenced by Barth and lesser-known thinker Hans Joachim Iwand (1899–1960), who emphasized the eschatological and social dimensions of God's reconciling act in Christ's cross and resurrection.[9] By his own admission the theologian of hope was also influenced by pietist revivalist and socialist Christoph Blumhardt (1842–1919), who made the coming kingdom of God on earth vital to everything in his ministry and theology. In an article Moltmann declared, "My 'Theology of Hope' has two roots: Christoph Blumhardt and Ernst Bloch."[10]

Bloch was an atheist and a revisionist Marxist philosopher at Tübingen who blended biblical themes of eschatology into his scientific social analysis. For him, hope for a perfect "homeland" where the individual overcomes all alienation and is at one with oneself is a fundamental human instinct and one that drives history through revolutionary change towards utopia. The philosopher developed an ontology of "not-yet-being" in which the as-yet-unrealized social utopia exerts power over the present and past, giving rise to human "transcending without transcendence."[11] Moltmann borrowed much from Bloch's ontology of the future but added a powerful critique of transcending without transcendence. He regarded Bloch's belief that humanity can face the future in hope and transcend its circumstances toward utopia without God as an illusion: "A historical future without heaven cannot be a forecourt of hope and the motivation for any historical movement. A 'transcending without transcendence' such as Bloch proposed turns infinity into indefinite endlessness and makes the striving for fulfillment merely an 'on and on.'"[12]

It is possible to interpret much of Moltmann's thought as an attempt to provide an answer to Bloch without negating the latter's valuable contri-

---

[9]Meeks claims that "Iwand's theology must be considered the most crucial generating force in the theology of hope." *Origins of the Theology of Hope*, 34.

[10]Jürgen Moltmann, "The Hope for the Kingdom of God and Signs of Hope in the World: The Relevance of Blumhardt's Theology Today," *Pneuma: The Journal of the Society for Pentecostal Studies* 26:1 (spring 2004): 4.

[11]Marcel Nuesch, *The Sources of Modern Atheism: One Hundred Years of Debate over God*, trans. Matthew J. O'Connell (New York: Paulist Press, 1982), 189.

[12]Jürgen Moltmann, *God in Creation: A New Theology of Creation and the Spirit of God*, trans. Margaret Kohl (San Francisco: Harper & Row, 1985), 180.

bution to Christian theology. On the one hand, he finds Bloch's "atheism of hope" a challenge to Christian theology to make eschatology the medium of its thought.[13] On the other hand, he warns that Christian hope, while utilizing insights from Bloch, must resist the religious reductions inherent in the atheism of hope.[14] Bloch appreciated Christianity's apocalyptic vision of a future kingdom of God on earth while harshly criticizing its dependence on "heavenly transcendence" as unrealistic and abstract. Throughout his writings, Moltmann attempts to show that Christian hope is anything but unrealistic and abstract and that, in fact, hope without God is groundless and shallow. As Marcel Neusch reports, against Bloch

> Moltmann maintains that Christian hope is in fact not an abstract utopia but a passion for the future that has become "really possible" thanks to the resurrection of Christ. By entering into history the resurrection of Christ introduces a *novum* which gives substance to hope and opens up to it a definitive horizon (an *ultimum*) that does not signal the end of history but is rather a real possibility for human life and for history itself.[15]

Moltmann is not an accommodationist theologian; he does not allow a secular philosophy such as Bloch's atheism of hope to predetermine or control his reconstructions of doctrines. Yet, together, Barth and Bloch form the odd couple of Moltmann's theologial background (with Blumhardt). Barth's dialectical theology provides the theological raw material, whereas Bloch provides the stimulation and philosophical conceptuality for Moltmann's new interpretation of Christian hope.[16]

What Moltmann borrowed from Bloch is the ontology of the future or eschatological ontology. It is the idea that being, or the power of being, the source of being, lies not in some timeless realm above or in the past but in our future. Moltmann believed this is wholly compatible with biblical revelation because, as will be seen next, for him, revelation has the nature of promise rather than epiphany or "unveiling." In eschatological ontology, which Pannenberg also appropriated from Bloch, the future, rather than

[13]Jürgen Moltmann, "Hope Without Faith: An Eschatological Humanism Without God," trans. John Cummings, in *Is God Dead? Concilium*, ed. Johannes Metz, 16 vols. (New York: Paulist Press, 1966), 16:37–40.
[14]Ibid., 16:36.
[15]Neusch, *Sources of Modern Atheism*, 211.
[16]Meeks, *Origins of the Theology of Hope*, 18.

the past, determines the present. It is admittedly counterintuitive or para-doxical. The only way to make sense of it is to remember that for many German intellectuals "thought" and "being" are inseparable. So, if the future defines (*bestimmt*) the present, it also determines (*bestimmt*) it. (The German verb for "to define" is also the word for "to determine"—*bestimmen*. *Bestimmt* is its present tense.) That the future defines the present is beyond doubt; what a historical event means will be determined only by its outcome. For the German mind, that means both cognitively and ontologically. Thus, insofar as the present depends on the future for its ultimate definition or meaning, it also depends on the future for its being. For Moltmann and Pannenberg, then, the coming kingdom of God both reveals the true meaning of and ontologically determines the present. This was Bloch's point, only he did not believe in a real coming kingdom of God. For him future utopia was only an image.

Moltmann redefines revelation as promise. By his own confession, Moltmann intends his theology to be "biblically founded, eschatologically ori-ented, and politically responsible."[17] However, his methodology is somewhat more complex. In fact, there is reason to doubt whether he has a coherent theological method in any traditional sense. This lack of systematic approach arises partly from his own lack of interest in orthodoxy. "I am not so con-cerned," he wrote, "with correct but more with concrete doctrine; and thus not concerned with pure theory but with practical theory."[18] He sees the task of theology not so much as to provide an interpretation of the world as to transform it in light of hope for its ultimate transformation by God.[19] Another reason for his lack of systematic or scientific methodology lies in his belief in the provisionality of all human knowledge in light of the incompleteness of reality short of its eschatological fulfillment. Only when the kingdom of glory promised by God arrives will we "know as we are known" and "see as we are seen." Until then all thought about God must be full of tension.[20] Contra-diction lies at the heart of reality as history because the future, if it really is future and not just more of the same, contradicts the present and the past.

---

[17]Moltmann, "Autobiographical Note," 222.
[18]Ibid., 204.
[19]Moltmann, *Theology of Hope*, 84.
[20]Moltmann, *The Experiment Hope*, trans. M. Douglas Meeks (Philadelphia: Fortress, 1975), 50.

If anything is axiomatic for Moltmann it is that the future is new and not merely an extension of the past. This is another dimension of eschatological ontology and runs like a thread throughout his entire body of writing tying it all together. For him, reality is not a predetermined or self-contained system of causes and effects but is historical in nature, and "hope has a chance of a meaningful existence only when reality itself is in a state of historic flux and when historic reality has room for open possibilities ahead."[21] This means, then, that the future is not completely inherent in the present.[22] Rather, the future (and God as the power of the future) is the ground and origin of reality's new possibilities, working them into the present and in this way having mastery over it.[23] In this ontology, then, the future is "ontologically prior" to the present and the past. It is not becoming from the present, but coming to it, drawing the present forward into totally new forms of reality. This means that theological categories and concepts must be open-ended, always ready to be superseded and revised in light of the future as it occurs.

Because he holds to such an eschatological epistemology, it is no wonder that Moltmann does not elevate rigid rational consistency and systematic coherence as theological virtues. He is not particularly concerned that theology be scientific in the modern sense. Dialectical thinking about the future's contradictions of the present cannot help but give rise to paradoxes, and it often ends in doxology rather than logical conclusions. For Moltmann, then, "theological concepts become not judgments which nail reality down to what it is, but anticipations which show reality its prospects and its future possibilities."[24] This is not to say that he is an irrationalist who rejects any sort of methodology and revels in irrationality. He does not merely throw out ideas with no basis or interconnections. Although he does not specifically mention Tillich's method of correlation, his theology seems to aim at some sort of answering function. But its concepts are not derived from nature, human existence or anything of the world as it already is. Rather, like Barth, he explicitly rejects natural theology (including anthropological

---

[21]Moltmann, *Theology of Hope*, 92.
[22]Moltmann, *God in Creation*, 202.
[23]Moltmann, "Theology as Eschatology," 11.
[24]Moltmann, *Theology of Hope*, 35–36.

theology) because it presupposes that God is already manifest in the existing order of the world. For Moltmann, the present world is "out of order," so to speak; only in the future kingdom of glory will God be manifest, because he will then be "all in all."[25] Yet even though God's being cannot be proved by reason or evidence, anticipatory knowledge of God from "traces of God" in nature is possible for those who know and love God.[26]

Moltmann's rejection of natural theology as any sort of preamble to Christian theology is almost as complete as Barth's. However, unlike Barth, he holds out real hope for theology's ability to speak relevantly to secular people by drawing on revelation's answers to meet their needs and questions. He describes theology's task in a way similar to Tillich: "If it is correct to say that the Bible is essentially a witness to the promissory history of God, then the role of Christian theology is to bring these remembrances of the future to bear on the hopes and anxieties of the present."[27] The basis for a true natural theology, then, lies not in proofs of God from the world as it is, but in the sighs and groans of creation for redemption. Ultimately, only Christian hope, based on God's revealed promises for the future, can make happiness in the present possible because "hope makes us ready to bear the 'cross of the present.' It can hold to what is dead, and hope for the unexpected."[28] Therefore, concern for meeting the questions of the present with answers drawn from God's revelation of the future lies at the center of Moltmann's theological method.

But what is "revelation" for Moltmann? Again, he disappoints those expecting a tidy definition. His descriptions of revelation developed over time. However, the most important category for understanding revelation is "promise." Through a meticulous examination of Scripture, he discovered that both Israel and the early church regarded the primary form of God's presence and appearance among them as promise for the future.[29] But Moltmann carefully distinguishes the religion of promise from "epiphany religions" that view God's presence and appearance as unveilings of what exists eternally, timelessly, in some heavenly realm above history. Such an interpretation, Moltmann avers, serves to provide comfort in the midst of troubling change

---

[25]Ibid., 282.
[26]Moltmann, God in Creation, 64.
[27]Moltmann, Experiment Hope, 8.
[28]Moltmann, Theology of Hope, 32.
[29]Ibid., 95-229.

by annihilating history and to provide sanction to the political and cultural status quo by linking it with the eternal.[30] For him, the epitome of epiphany religion is the Greek philosophical theology with its obsession with timelessness (Parmenides) and with an eternal realm of forms behind reality (Plato). But this theology is not merely a relic of the dead past, for Moltmann traces its effects in philosophy and religion throughout two millennia of thought up to and including Barth's concept of revelation.[31]

In contrast to revelation as epiphany, Moltmann argues that Israel experienced God's word and presence as a history of promise and faithfulness to his promises. This experience of revelation fundamentally altered conceptions of history and the status quo: "Under the guiding star of promise this reality is not experienced as a divinely stabilized cosmos, but as history in terms of moving on, leaving things behind and striking out towards new horizons yet unseen."[32] Rather than the religious sanctioning of the present, the experience of revelation led the ancient people of God to "a break-away from the present towards the future."[33] Thus, revelation-as-promise gave rise to Israel's unique concept of history as linear and initiated its prophetic tendencies, which constantly called for greater righteousness in light of God's faithfulness and future kingdom.

Moltmann finds the same idea of revelation as promise at work in the New Testament church. It experienced Christ as an event of promise and proclaimed his death and resurrection as promises of God's future kingdom.[34] It also experienced the Holy Spirit as the "earnest" of the promised future of Christ. In the resurrection of the crucified Christ and in the sending of the Spirit God promised his own righteousness in history, life overcoming death in the resurrection of all the dead and a kingdom of God in a new totality of being.[35] Based on these promises the early church lived in hope with a view toward the future and toward mission, experiencing the faithfulness of God while remaining restless for the coming of God's kingdom of righteousness.

---

[30]Ibid., 99–102.
[31]Ibid., 228.
[32]Ibid., 102.
[33]Ibid., 100.
[34]Ibid., 139–40.
[35]Ibid., 203.

According to Moltmann, revelation-as-promise does not impart facts but kindles faith and hope. Nevertheless, he averred, there is a kind of knowledge engendered by promise, the knowledge of things hoped for, a prospective, anticipatory, provisional and fragmentary knowledge that always remains open and strains beyond itself.[36] In his view, this knowledge is not the same as futurology, which seeks to predict the future based on present trends and tendencies. Instead, it is knowledge of the future based on the promise of God in Christ. More specifically, "it knows the future in striving to bring out the tendencies and latencies of the Christ event of the crucifixion and resurrection, and in seeking to estimate the possibilities opened up by this event."[37] For him, the Bible is not itself revelation and is not verbally inspired, but it is a witness to the promissory history of God.[38] The Bible contains the narratives of God's promises and human responses to those promises, but its primary value lies in pointing beyond itself to the coming kingdom of God: "In these accounts of the past we encounter the promissory history of the future of God. We find the future in the past, see the future revealed and anticipated in the past, and find ourselves taken up into this history of liberation."[39] Thus, the authority of Scripture is instrumental: God uses the Bible and the Spirit to bring about his kingdom and is glorified in them. Like everything else, however, the Scriptures themselves are not already perfect but "will be fulfilled in perfection in the kingdom of the coming glory."[40]

Moltmann's driving desire to provide an alternative to transcendence theology and immanence theology is evident already in his doctrine of revelation. Instead of conceiving of revelation as a supernatural incursion into history from above or as a natural capacity of humans in history, he described it as the promise of totally new and unexpected events in the future that can be only anticipated in the present. The futurity of the events signals the transcendence of revelation, which contradicts the present and opens it to a new totality of being not already inherent in it.[41] Revelation is not the

---

[36]Ibid.

[37]Ibid.

[38]Moltmann, *Experiment Hope*, 8.

[39]Ibid., 7.

[40]Jürgen Moltmann, "The Fellowship of the Holy Spirit—Trinitarian Pneumatology," *Scottish Journal of Theology* 37 (1984): 278.

[41]Moltmann, *Theology of Hope*, 85.

unveiling of already existing truth but the "apocalypse of the promised future of the truth."[42] Even their historical fulfillments do not exhaust God's promises: "In every fulfillment the promise, and what is still contained in it, does not yet become wholly congruent with reality and thus there always remains an overspill."[43] Revelation, therefore, is transcendent in the way the future is transcendent. But it is also immanent in the way the future is imminent to the present. The future kingdom of glory does not yet exist, but it is not absent from the present, either. It is "present" in its effects: "As compared with what can now be experienced, it brings something new. Yet it is not for that reason totally separate from the reality which we can now experience and have now to live in, but, as the future that is really outstanding, it works upon the present by awaking hopes and establishing resistance."[44]

Moltmann reconstructs God as the "power of the future." Moltmann's new approach to transcendence and immanence based on futurity is crucial to his doctrine of God. The Tübingen theologian drew the closest possible link between God's own being and the future kingdom of glory in which God will be fully present and manifest in the world. Consequently, "God is not 'beyond us' or 'in us,' but ahead of us in the horizons of the future opened up to us in his promises," so that "the 'future' must be considered as a mode of God's being."[45] Moltmann was fully convinced that if God already existed, whether above us or in us, reality could not be truly historical and God would be responsible for what happens in the world now. History would fall back into meaninglessness or annihilation, as in the epiphany religions. It would have no future open to the truly new. Furthermore, every evil and innocent suffering of history would by necessity be a reflection of God, insofar as either God can but does not want to overcome it, or he cannot and therefore is not really God.

Crucial for Moltmann is the reality of history as what is to be contradicted. Because of the evil and suffering in it, he argued, "God is not the ground of this world and not the ground of existence, but the God of the coming kingdom which transforms this world and our existence radically."[46]

---

[42]Ibid., 84.
[43]Ibid., 105.
[44]Ibid., 227.
[45]Moltmann, *Theology of Hope*, 85.
[46]Ibid.

God's transcendence, then, does not lie in his being the Creator and Sustainer of a world that already exists. Transcendence is God's being the power that transforms the present world from the perspective of its future by negating what is negative in it and by drawing it into the kingdom of glory. Similarly, God's immanence is his imminent futurity impinging on every moment, contradicting its contradictions of the glory of the future kingdom. Moltmann did not conceive of this dualistically, however. For him, the future does penetrate into the present, releasing events that work to propel it forward into its future. These proleptic, anticipatory events are works of God in which he himself is truly present in suffering and power, and hence he is immanent in the world. The greatest among these occurrences are the events of Jesus Christ, especially his crucifixion and resurrection, and the sending of the Holy Spirit.

Consequently, Moltmann conceives of God's presence in the world trinitarianly. If God's transcendence lies in his *coming* ("Adventus") out of the future to the world, contradicting its negativities, his immanence lies in his *becoming* together with the world in the trinitarian history of the kingdom of glory within the world. His vision of God's transcendence and immanence as the presence of the future constitutes Moltmann's doctrine of God as "eschatological, Trinitarian panentheism." As will be seen, he regards the immanence of God as a real history of the triune God within world history. At the same time he sees this history not as development or evolution but as prolepsis and anticipation.

Moltmann's eschatological ontology and doctrine of God as future is difficult for many people to grasp because they are conditioned to think of the present as determined by the past or by a power above the world. An illustration from Jesus' own life, however, may shed some light of understanding on Moltmann's point. Throughout his earthly, human life Jesus' deity was hidden. He was God incarnate but in a very real sense not yet fully who and what he would be in his glorification after his resurrection. Jesus' whole earthly life was lived toward his crucifixion and resurrection and glorification. But only when the latter happened would his life be illumined and, in a sense, become what it was. Jesus' resurrection determined his life's meaning and being. And yet, his deity did not have to await his resurrection; his resurrection preappeared, for example, in his miracles and in his transfiguration. Those were proleptic events—the future happening ahead of time. During his earthly life he existed under the conditions of history, in weakness and suffering. And yet, he was already proleptically the resurrected and glorified Lord *because* that was his future. There is a sense, then, in which during his preresurrection life he was "not yet" the Lord of resurrected glory and also "already" that. His true being as resurrected and glorified God-man stood in his future, but it also determined who he was already. And yet it determined it by canceling out and contradicting the weakness, injustice and suffering of his torture and death.

Now project that onto the screen of world history. The kingdom of glory is the true being of creation, but it is not yet. But, although not yet, it is in a sense already because God enters from there, from the future, into history to cancel out its incompleteness in suffering, death and decay. But only when God is all in all, everything to everyone, in his kingdom of glory, will what has been true in a hidden and incomplete, anticipatory way be fully real. Standing where we stand within history, surrounded by evil and innocent suffering, we must say that *for us* God does not yet exist because his kingdom of glory *is* his deity. When we are there, as God already is, we will look back and say that God always was the true Lord and Creator of the world, but not the providential ruler of all the horrors of history.

Moltmann elucidates the trinitarian history of the kingdom. More than any other twentieth-century theologian, Moltmann explored the interconnections between the Trinity and the kingdom of God. This was his special burden in *The Crucified God* and *The Trinity and the Kingdom*, although it reappears in *The Spirit of Life* and *The Coming of God*. For him, the key to understanding God's identity as historical, and thus as immanent, is the doctrine of the Trinity as understood from the event of the cross of Jesus Christ. Through a penetrating analysis of the cross event, the theologian of hope concluded that it not only has an effect on humanity in the dynamic of reconciliation, but it also has an effect on God. The cross is the occasion in which God constitutes himself as Trinity within history: "What happened on the cross was an event between God and God. It was a deep division in God himself, in so far as God abandoned God and contradicted himself, and at the same time a unity in God, in so far as God was at one with God and corresponded to himself."[47] This is dialectical thinking at its best or worst.

For Moltmann, the "Trinity" is a shorter version of the passion narrative of Christ. The basis and ground of the Trinity is the separation-in-unity God experienced within himself in this event. The Trinity cannot be understood apart from the cross, and the cross cannot be understood apart from the Trinity. From his interpretation of the cross, Moltmann drew several radical conclusions. Because it is linked intrinsically to the event of the cross, the Trinity is historical; it is constituted in and through suffering and conflict, and it takes different forms throughout the history of God's kingdom on the way to its future fulfillment in glory. Moltmann radically rejected the idea of an immutable, impassable God removed from the sufferings and conflicts of history. What happens in history happens "in God," because the cross opens God to the world:

> If one conceives of the Trinity as an event of love in the suffering and the death of Jesus—and that is something which faith must do—then the Trinity is no self-contained group in heaven, but an eschatological process open for men on earth, which stems from the cross of Christ.[48]

Moltmann's account of the "historical being of God" in *The Crucified God* began a project of reinterpreting the nature of God, which differs radically from both traditional Christian theism and process theology while preserving elements of both. Although the project remained incomplete in that book, he took it up again in later books. Moltmann's reinterpretation broke boldly from classical theism by asserting God's real historicity on the basis of God's suffering the death of the Son in the event of the cross. Consequently, the cross is not extrinsic to God's own being, as if God would be exactly who and what he is without it. Rather, it constitutes God's being as Trinity through the dialectic of the separation and unity between Father and Son. In Moltmann's words, "This means that God's being is historical and that he exists in history. The 'story of God' then is the story of the history of man."[49]

And yet Moltmann's program differed from process theology in signif-

---

[47]Jürgen Moltmann, *The Crucified God*, trans. R. A. Wilson and John Bowden (New York: Harper & Row, 1974), 244.

[48]Ibid., 249.

[49]Jürgen Moltmann, "The 'Crucified God': God and the Trinity Today," in *New Questions on God*, ed. Johannes Metz (New York: Herder and Herder, 1972), 35.

icant ways. He rejected any idea of development in God and asserted that the historicity of God is a free act of God's love. God's experiences of conflict, pain and suffering in history are not due to some inherent dependence of God on the world. They are due to God's voluntary self-limitation out of love. Moltmann's passionate, trinitarian God is not Whitehead's fellow sufferer who understands, but is rather the Father of Jesus Christ who "has decided from eternity for seeking love, and in his decision to go outside of himself lies the conditions for the possibility of this experience."[50] Moltmann's suffering God not only understands, as in process thought; he also helps. His trinitarian suffering in the cross releases into the world the Spirit of the unity of the Father and Son that works toward the world's transformation. But above all, unlike process theology, Moltmann kept in view always the transcendent future of God's kingdom of glory which is the final consummation of history—God's and the world's. Against process theology he asserted, "If there is no new creation of all things, there is nothing that can withstand the Nothingness that annihilates the world."[51]

God's loving and gracious choice to allow his own life to be constituted by the world's history entails self-limitation. Moltmann explained, "In order to create a world 'outside' himself, the infinite God must have made room beforehand for a finitude in himself."[52] Similarly, in order to redeem the godforsaken world God enters the godless space created by his self-limitation and suffers it, thus bringing it within his divine life in order to conquer it. This, then, is the point of the trinitarian history of the cross: "By entering into the Godforsakenness of sin and death (which is Nothingness), God overcomes it and makes it part of his eternal life: 'If I make my bed in hell, thou art there.'"[53] So God's self-limitation preserves both his transcendence and his immanence. Because he is limited, he is vulnerable and historical and includes the pain and suffering of the world while conquering it. Nevertheless, because this limitation is self-chosen and not imposed by

---

[50]Jürgen Moltmann, "The Trinitarian History of God," *Theology* 78 (December 1975): 644.

[51]Moltmann, *God in Creation*, 79. For an excellent comparison and contrast of Moltmann's doctrine of God with process theology, see John J. O'Donnell, *Trinity and Temporality: The Christian Doctrine of God in the Light of Process Theology and the Theology of Hope* (Oxford: Oxford University Press, 1983), 159–200.

[52]Moltmann, *God in Creation*, 86.

[53]Ibid., 91.

his nature or anything outside himself he remains transcendent. God's self-limitation is not a matter of fate or destiny but of freedom and love.

According to Moltmann, then, God's relationship with the world cannot be expressed either in terms of classical theism, which he believed pictures God as invulnerable, or in the categories of process panentheism, which pictures God as a pathetic, finite being trapped in endless codependence with the world. However, Moltmann did appropriate the term "panentheism" for his doctrine of the Trinity. He called it trinitarian panentheism and claimed it preserves and deepens the truths in both classical theism and process theology while avoiding their weaknesses.[54] Whether that is the case is debatable. The entire structure of his concept of God depends on the coherence of its foundations, which lies in the idea that God's love unites freedom and necessity while transcending them. Moltmann argued that God did not have to create and enter into the world and its history, but at the same time he asserted that there could be no "otherwise." Although he found such talk merely an example of "creative antitheses," to some of his readers it appears to flirt with sheer contradiction.

Moltmann develops an eschatological, trinitarian, panentheistic doctrine of God. After *The Crucified God*, which resounded with radical sayings about God and suffering and "conflict in God," Moltmann wrote a series of theological monographs reflecting further on his concept of God's relationship with the world. It is important to know and absorb the fact that, for Moltmann, none of the traditional concepts will work. In light of God's revelation in the cross and the sending of the Spirit, classical theism, deism, pantheism, process panentheism and atheism are impossible. All are too deeply flawed to serve Christian theology well. Classical theism separates God too far from suffering to make sense of God in view of the horrors of the twentieth century such as the Holocaust. Deism also separates God too far from the world and leaves God in a transcendent sphere where he does not do anything except judge. Pantheism depersonalizes God and identifies God with the world, which intensifies the problem of evil. Process panentheism leaves God weak and unable to help. Atheism divests reality of meaning. Moltmann's whole theological career was spent attempting to

---

[54]Ibid., 98–103.

create a new concept of God that would do greater justice to God's essence as love in light of the horrors of history.

Moltmann began this reconstruction of the God-world relation in *The Crucified God* by saying that God identifies with the suffering world on the cross. He continued in *The Church in the Power of the Spirit* by arguing that God helps the suffering by sending the Spirit, God himself in immanent power, into the world to relieve suffering by working out the coming kingdom proleptically through the church. In *The Trinity and the Kingdom* he traced out the historical patterns of God's own trinitarian life in relation to the world and the history of the coming kingdom. There he set forth this thesis:

> The history in which Jesus is manifested as "the Son" is not consummated and fulfilled by a single subject. The history of Christ is already related in trinitarian terms in the New Testament itself. So we start from the following presupposition. *The New Testament talks about God by proclaiming in narrative the relationships of the Father, the Son and the Spirit, which are relationships of fellowship and are open to the world.*[55]

This is panentheistic in a new and different way than any panentheism before. For Moltmann, God allows the history of the world to determine the relationships among the persons of the Trinity. For example, the Father sends the Son and the Spirit and yet is dependent on them for his own glory in the kingdom. The main point is that the world makes a difference to God. The coming of the kingdom of glory, which is the work of all three persons of the Trinity in varying ways, is an event of God's own self-realization. God benefits also. The history of God as the changing relationships among Father, Son and Spirit is the history of the kingdom and thus inseparable from the history of the world. God is no monarch ruling from heaven; God is the loving community of three persons open for the world. While there may be an inner-trinitarian life of God that is not wholly constituted within history, it is stamped by the cross and other events of salvation history.[56] The cross of the Son and the joy of love in glorification through the Spirit put their impress on the inner life of the triune God from eternity to eternity.[57]

---

[55]Jürgen Moltmann, *The Trinity and the Kingdom*, trans. Margaret Kohl (San Francisco: Harper & Row, 1981), 64.
[56]Ibid., 160.
[57]Ibid., 161.

Moltmann's panentheistic idea of God and the world, shaped around the concept of God as ever-changing community that includes the world and its history, has a political impact. For him, hierarchy is bad. Even God chooses not to remain in a hierarchical relationship over the world but enters into it to the point of becoming victim of history's horrors while retaining power to draw the world to its final goal. Moltmann uses this doctrine of the Trinity to provide a criticism of "political and clerical monotheism." "The notion of a divine monarchy in heaven and on earth, for its part, generally provides the justification for earthly domination—religious, moral, patriarchal or political domination—and makes it a hierarchy, a 'holy rule.'"[58] His own reconstructed doctrine of God as triune, historical being points toward nonhierarchical community as the right ordering of society. Vulnerable love is God's own being and so it is what God intends for people as well.

Moltmann's panentheistic view of God reaches its point closest to traditional panentheism (e.g., Hegel and process theology) in *God in Creation*. There he emphasizes the "perichoretic relationship" between God and the world—a relationship of fellowship, mutual need and mutual interpenetration[59]—and strongly suggests a model of the world as God's body.[60] Here he is seeking to promote Christian environmentalism and so emphasizes the earth as God's habitat and the scene of God's coming kingdom of glory. It is not humanity's to do with as it will *because* it is where God dwells. Harming the earth is harming God. Toward the end of *God in Creation* he discusses the future kingdom of glory as the "Sabbath" in which God rests from his creative work and enjoys their fruits:

> On the Sabbath the resting God begins to "experience" the beings he has created. The God who rests in the face of his creation does not dominate the world on this day; he "feels" the world; he allows himself to be affected, to be touched by each of his creatures. He adopts the community of creation as his own milieu.[61]

Reigning, lordship, judgment and praise of God are all muted if not absent from Moltmann's later works. God's goal for persons is not that they

---

[58]Ibid., 190–92.
[59]Moltmann, *God in Creation*, 258.
[60]Ibid., 150.
[61]Ibid., 279.

be his servants or children but his friends, and "in friendship the distance enjoyed by sovereignty ceases to exist."[62]

Moltmann took his panentheistic vision of God and the world further in *The Spirit of Life*. In reaction against the modern notion of human consciousness of the self as absolute (Descartes), he argued, "If the immediate self-consciousness is constitutive for the space of all possible experience, then *narcissism* is the logical and practical consequence of this anthropocentric view of the world."[63] This modern idea of self-consciousness "has domination as its lodestone"[64] and therefore must be abandoned by Christians. But what will take its place? For Moltmann, experience of God in all things replaces the absoluteness of self-consciousness: "I would suggest abandoning the narrow reference to the modern concept of 'self-consciousness,' so that we can discover transcendence in every experience, not merely in experience of the self. For this, the term *immanent transcendence* offers itself."[65] From this he moves to the suggestion that, on the basis of the traditional idea of the Holy Spirit as the source of all life (Augustine, Calvin), we realize that it is possible to experience God in all things and to experience all things in God.[66] This leads him to "a panentheistic vision of the world in God, and God in the world."[67] Moltmann's purpose is to emphasize the importance of all life. The kingdom of God is life abundant. It is already in the immanence of God in the world and the world in God, but it will be fulfilled only in the eschatological sabbath of God when God is all in all. On the way to that future, however, we should conceive of all life, including the whole world, as precious and seek to promote its livingness out of a culture of death.

The Coming of God is Moltmann's last great systematic treatise. There he reaffirms his key theme of God's futurity and steps beyond anything he wrote previously about God's relationship with the world of time and space. Near its beginning he repeats his basic motif from *Theology of Hope*: "The

---

[62]Moltmann, *Trinity and the Kingdom*, 221.
[63]Jürgen Moltmann, *The Spirit of Life: A Universal Affirmation*, trans. Margaret Kohl (Minneapolis: Fortress, 1992), 31.
[64]Ibid.
[65]Ibid., 34.
[66]Ibid., 35, 36.
[67]Ibid., 211.

472 THE JOURNEY OF MODERN THEOLOGY

eschaton is neither the future of time nor timeless eternity. It is God's coming and his arrival."[68] However, later in the book he seems to take a step back from his strong emphasis on God's futurity to embrace what has come to be called open theism. On the basis of God's self-limitation, Moltmann asserts that in relation to creation God "restricts his eternity so that in this primordial time he can give his creation time, and leave it time. God restricts his omniscience in order to give what he has created freedom."[69] God restricts himself in order to "fit into" creation as well as to give creation freedom.

In this vision, God goes along with creation's history toward its future in his kingdom of glory. It is in that ultimate future, even beyond the historical, messianic kingdom of Jesus Christ (premillennialism), that the whole creation will itself become "the *house of God*, the *temple* in which God can dwell, the *home country* in which God can rest."[70] Then the present partial participation of God in creation and creation in God will be complete and God and the world will interpenetrate each other (*perichoresis*). This is a trinitarian process and end point:

> This trinitarian interpretation of the process of God's glorification in the history of Christ's self-surrender, raising and presence in the Spirit, must clearly be understood not exclusively but inclusively. The fellowship between Christ and God in the process of mutual glorification [by the Spirit] is so wide open that the community of Christ's people can find a place in it. . . . In view of the cosmic dimensions of this divine eschatology of the mutual glorification of the Father and the Son and the Spirit, it will even be permissible to say that the mutual relationships of the Trinity are so wide open that in them the whole world can find a wide space, and redemption, and its own glorification.[71]

Then all limitation will cease and God will be the "space" in which everything dwells in fullness of life. Moltmann makes clear that this hope, expectation, of absolute, universal life that embraces God and creation in total unity-in-difference will be a universal reconciliation (*apokatastasis*).[72]

---

[68]Moltmann, *Coming of God*, 22.
[69]Ibid., 282.
[70]Ibid., 307.
[71]Ibid., 335.
[72]Ibid., 254–55.

Moltmann stimulates theological reflection, controversy and some confusion. Without doubt Moltmann introduced several powerful new images and concepts into late-twentieth-century Christianity. No other theologian has done more to explore the implications of eschatology and the cross for God's being. Taking his cue from Bonhoeffer's statement that "only the suffering God can help," the theologian of hope opened up a new chapter in modern theology in which the suffering of God became a new orthodoxy that few seriously questioned. Furthermore, he helped revitalize the doctrine of the Trinity in late modern theology. And he gave birth to a new eschatological orientation in theology that provided creative new ways of conceiving of God's transcendence and immanence.

At the same time, Moltmann's theology is riddled with tensions if not contradictions. Eschatological ontology has yet to receive satisfactory explanation. For example, left unexplained is how the future, which is still open, can impinge on and influence the present. Is God, who is present and active in history, future to himself? And how real are the agonies, sufferings and victories of the present if the future kingdom of glory is assured by God? Does that assured future reality not imply something like an epiphany theology, something Moltmann so vehemently rejected?

Part of the problem with Moltmann is that each of his books represents a slight, sometimes significant, twist in his theological pilgrimage. He was not a systematician in the usual sense. There are unifying threads that tie his many volumes together, but there are also apparent contradictions that he does not acknowledge. How can God be the power of the future who has no future but guarantees the arrival of his kingdom of glory *and* have self-limited omniscience? Does Moltmann sometimes want to have his cake and eat it too? Also, does his doctrine of the Trinity imply tritheism—three gods? Apparently, for him, the immanent Trinity in which Father, Son and Holy Spirit are perfectly united is eschatological. But he can always claim that the future is the locus of being so perfect triune unity is already true for God even if throughout history there are different patterns of the three persons' relationships that sometimes include tension and conflict. It seems that Moltmann has wanted the best of several theological worlds: process theology, classical trinitarian theism, Hegel's dynamic panentheism, Luther's theology of the cross. Whether he unifies the best of them coherently or throws elements of them together eclectically is debatable.

What about modernity? In what sense is Moltmann a modern theologian other than that he worked during the modern era? And what of postmodernity that was challenging classical modernism during the later part of the twentieth century? The theologian of hope was critical of both modernism and postmodernism, although he never spelled out in great detail his responses to either one. One book where he did interact explicitly with modernity is *God for a Secular Society* (1999). There he explained that modernity grew out of Christianity but turned against true Christianity creating an idolatrous religion of domination and subjugation in its place. Humanity, especially Western humanity, displaced God. For him, the main challenge of modernity to Christianity is not epistemological ("What can I know?") but political in the broadest sense. He says, "The founders of the modern age thought of a new, glorious era for the whole human race; but we are surviving on islands of prosperity planted in a sea of mass misery."[73] Why? Because, he declares, "we have lost God, and God has left us, so we are bothered neither by the suffering of others which we have caused, nor by the debts which we are leaving behind us for coming generations."[74] The theologian of hope, who is also a political theologian, affirms the basic humanitarian ideals of the Enlightenment but argues that they depend on belief in and relationship with God:

> There is only one alternative to the humanitarian ideas of human dignity and the universality of human rights [fruits of modernity], and that alternative is barbarism. There is only one alternative to the ideal of eternal peace, and that is a permanent state of war. There is only one alternative to faith in the One God and hope for his kingdom, and that is polytheism and chaos.[75]

By "polytheism" Moltmann means powerful individuals seeing themselves as gods with the right to dominate and control and subjugate the earth and people. What does modernity need? Not apologetics in any traditional sense. Not rational proofs of God's existence but "Hope for God

---

[73]Jürgen Moltmann, *God for a Secular Society: The Public Relevance of Theology*, trans. Margaret Kohl (Minneapolis: Fortress, 1999), 16.
[74]Ibid.
[75]Ibid., 17.

without triumphalism."[76] In this context, a chapter on "Theology in the Project of Modernity," he delivered one of his most concise statements of his eschatological theology as it relates to politics. (And for him, "politics is the widest context of every Christian theology."[77]) What modern people need, he argued, is a new sense of God who is to come:

> That is to say, he will appear in his full God-ness only in his kingdom. But where does God already come now? Where are we so certain of his presence that we can live and act with the assurance of God and ourselves? The messianism of modern times said: with God we will enter into lordship over the earth, and with Christ we will judge the nations [colonialism]. This messianic dream became a nightmare for the nations, and made an excessive demand on the people concerned, a demand which ended in cold despair: a "God-complex." But it is not in our domination that the coming God is present; it is in our suffering [with others who suffer], in which he is present through his life-giving Spirit. It is not in our strength that the grace that raises us up is made perfect; it is in our weakness.[78]

All that is to say that Moltmann's main concern with modernity is not the usual acids of modernity. For him, the challenge of modernity is a political challenge, a social challenge. And Christianity's right response is not accommodation, correlation or rejection; it is suffering sacrifice, the theology of the cross.

The same is true of Moltmann's response to the challenges of modern science. He is not bothered by the scientific revolution, although he clearly does not accept naturalism. He believes in the bodily resurrection of Jesus including the empty tomb and in the return of Christ. For him, the challenge of modern science is not to belief but to life. The attitude that science should do whatever it can do is destructive and, unhindered by an ethical and ultimately theological vision of the dignity of the earth and humanity, leads to injustice and devastation. Nature, he argues, is not our "property" to do with as we wish. We human beings are *"one part* of the wider family of nature, which we have to respect."[79] Similarly, we have to respect the

---

[76]Ibid., 18.
[77]Ibid., 44.
[78]Ibid., 18.
[79]Ibid., 99.

dignity of every person, regardless of his or her ability to produce or contribute to society. Science, cut loose from respect for life rooted in belief in God as creator, leads to life-threatening moral irresponsibility.[80] Without a vision of God, and persons as created in God's image, science will be used to cut short life. Only a theological vision can control science's drive toward total control even to the point of death for those who are perceived as weak and powerless to contribute. Modernity needs religion, but the right kind of religion, to realize that

> God has a relationship with every embryo, every severely handicapped person, and every person suffering from one of the diseases of old age, and he is honoured and glorified in them when their dignity is respected. Without the fear of God, God's image will not be respected in every human being, and the reverence for life will be lost, pushed out by utilitarian criteria. But in the fear of God there is no life that is worthless and unfit to love.[81]

8.b. WOLFHART PANNENBERG REVITALIZES RATIONAL FAITH IN HISTORY'S GOD

Pannenberg is known for seeking to explain the rationality of Christian faith and hope, and yet his faith journey began with a mystical experience. According to his own testimony, his "single most important experience" occurred at age sixteen while walking home from school through woods during sundown on a winter afternoon.[82] Suddenly he was attracted by a light in the distance. When he approached the spot he found himself flooded, even elevated, by a sea of light. Years later he regarded this experience as Jesus Christ claiming his life even though he was not at the time yet a Christian. Over the ensuing years this experience has become the basis for Pannenberg's sense of calling.

Pannenberg's turn toward a rational faith began during high school (German *Gymnasium*). He had been reading Nietzsche and thought that Christianity was responsible for the horrors of history. However, his literature teacher, a Christian, impressed him with the idea that perhaps true Christianity is not the cause of Europe's and the world's woes. Because he

---

[80]Ibid., 84.
[81]Ibid.
[82]For his account of these experiences see Wolfhart Pannenberg, "God's Presence in History," *The Christian Century* (March 11, 1981), 260–63.

was wrestling with the deeper meaning of reality, he decided to look more closely at the Christian faith by studying philosophy and theology. From this project he concluded that Christianity is the best philosophy, a conclusion that launched his life as a Christian and career as a theologian.

Eventually Pannenberg worked with Moltmann in the formation of what has come, rightly or wrongly, to be called eschatological theology or the theology of hope. In profound agreement with Moltmann, Pannenberg embraced the idea of God's futurity, eschatological ontology, and belief that Jesus' resurrection is the proleptic event of God's coming kingdom. However, he soon moved in a direction quite different from Moltmann's dialectical approach to theology. Pannenberg wanted theology to be scientific in the German sense of *wissenschaftlich*—a disciplined and orderly path to knowledge that does not engage in special pleading based on appeals to authority or faith. Responding to modern skepticism and demands for the reasonableness of belief, he stated, "In the face of this modern attack upon the meaningfulness of the Christian faith, theology cannot retreat to the standpoint of authority."[83] His appeal to rationality is clearly set forth in this axiom: "Every theological statement must prove itself on the field of reason, and can no longer be argued on the basis of unquestioned presuppositions of faith."[84] Clearly he was breaking away from Barth, with whom he studied in Basel, and all forms of what he considered subjectivist theology including existentialism, pietism and dialectical theology.

Over the last third of the twentieth century Pannenberg emerged as one of the few remaining world-class theologians—theologians whose thought had to be wrestled with and could not be ignored. His prolific program of writing made it difficult for anyone to keep up with him, but he became a mentor to many young theologians of especially the 1970s and 1980s. Even those who strongly disagreed with him, and they were legion, had to interact with him and give him credit for his profound knowledge of and engagement with philosophy, science and theology. His reputation came to depend on two main ideas: God as future ("God does not yet exist"[85]) and Christianity

---

[83]Wolfhart Pannenberg, *Basic Questions in Theology*, trans. George Kelm (Minneapolis: Augsburg Fortress, 1971), 2:51.

[84]Ibid., 2:54.

[85]Wolfhart Pannenberg, *Theology and the Kingdom of God*, ed. Richard John Neuhaus (Philadelphia: Westminster Press, 1969), 56.

as rational. In both cases, however, the ordinary meanings of words like "future" and "rational" cannot be assumed. He meant what *he* meant by them and not necessarily what others mean by them. Closely related to both of these ideas is Pannenberg's well-known defense of the bodily resurrection, including the empty tomb, as a historical event knowable by critical historical reason and not just by faith or encounter. He radically rejected Bultmann's entire program of demythologization without falling back on fundamentalism. He regarded existentialism not as the "good luck" of modern Christianity but as the bane of modern theology. And he viewed the resurrection as the guarantee of the final end of history in God's kingdom, when not only will God be "all in all" but also finally himself.

Pannenberg helps create a new circle of theologians. Pannenberg was born in Stettin, Germany, now part of Poland, in 1928. After his intellectual conversion to Christianity during high school, he enrolled in the University of Berlin to study philosophy and theology. While there he became impressed with Barth, whose theology he at first interpreted as an attempt to establish the sovereignty of God to claim all of reality for the God of the Bible. But study with Barth in Basel resulted in a certain uneasiness with Barth's perceived dualism between natural knowledge of God and divine revelation in Jesus Christ. He came to break radically with Barth's dialectical theology and rejection of any appeal to rational foundations for faith. Eventually he expressed strong exception to Barth's theology of the Word of God based on faith, that is, theology from above. He believed that approach "ghettoizes" Christianity, thereby reducing its public influence. He wrote, "When the foundation of theology is left to a venture [of faith] in this way, not only is its scientific status endangered, but also the priority of God and his revelation over human beings, on which, for Barth, everything rests."[86] Also, "Barth's apparently so lofty objectivity about God and God's word turns out to rest on no more than the irrational subjectivity of a venture of faith with no justification outside itself."[87]

After studying with Barth, Pannenberg moved to Heidelberg, where he studied under such scholars as von Rad, Hans von Campenhausen (1903–1989), Old and New Testament scholars respectively, and his main theological

---

[86]Wolfhart Pannenberg, *Theology and the Philosophy of Science*, trans. Francis McDonagh (Philadelphia: Westminster Press, 1976), 272.
[87]Ibid., 273.

mentor, ecumenical thinker Edmund Schlink (1903–1984). During his years at Heidelberg his thinking concerning revelation, history, faith and reason took shape partly through a discussion group in theology that came to be known as the Pannenberg circle. The conclusions of this group, aimed against all forms of subjectivism in theology, including especially Bultmann's existentialism, were published in *Revelation as History* (1961). While that book may not have fallen like a bombshell on the playground of the theologians, as did Barth's *Epistle to the Romans*, it did announce a new path for modern theology away from reliance on authority and faith and away from any dualism between salvation history and ordinary world history. It constituted a public rejection of Barth and Bultmann and the whole subjectivist (as the Pannenberg circle saw it) stream of theology of post–World War I neo-orthodox theology.

After graduating from Heidelberg with a doctorate in theology, Pannenberg taught at the Wuppertal church academy with Moltmann. During those few years the two theologians together forged the theology of the future or eschatological theology. Both were profoundly influenced by Bloch and his eschatological ontology (see 8.a.). Both gained attention by saying things like "God does not yet exist." Later the two colleagues had a falling out over politics and over who first thought of making use of Bloch's eschatological ontology for an eschatological theology.[88] After Wuppertal, Pannenberg taught theology at the University of Mainz (1961–1968) and then the University of Munich, where he retired in 1993. At Munich he headed the Institute for Fundamental Theology and Ecumenism, which was involved in the Protestant-Catholic dialogues of the 1980s and 1990s that led to a concordat about justification by faith.

Pannenberg not only taught in Germany. He served two stints as guest professor at American universities—Chicago and Claremont. At Chicago his

---

[88]Some of what I know about Pannenberg comes from lengthy personal conversations with him. In August 1981, he told me in his office that Moltmann stole his ideas from him. I have heard from some of Moltmann's students that he said the same about Pannenberg. I also talked with Pannenberg in Munich about the reasons for his break with Moltmann, and he told me it was mainly over politics. Moltmann is a socialist whereas Pannenberg is a conservative. I discerned another reason for their lack of friendship: Pannenberg is very friendly to the Catholic Church, and Josef Cardinal Ratzinger, later Pope Benedict XVI, is one of Pannenberg's best friends. They became acquainted when the cardinal was archbishop of Munich. Moltmann leans more toward the free church tradition and even toward aspects of the radical Reformation (Anabaptism). However, their friendship was healed. Some of these matters are discussed in Moltmann, *A Broad Place.*

office was next to Tillich's, and he became friends with the existentialist theologian even though they were moving in opposite directions theologically. At
Claremont he became friendly with Cobb, who thought Pannenberg's theology was consistent with process thought. That turned out not to be the case,
and their friendship suffered over it. Again, however, as with Moltmann, they
were reconciled.[89] Pannenberg also traveled widely lecturing on theology. His
literary output is almost unrivaled in modern theology. Among his major
works are *Jesus—God and Man* (1964 and 1966, two volumes in German; 1968,
one volume in English), *Theology and the Philosophy of Science* (1973), *Anthropology in Theological Perspective* (1985) and the three-volume *Systematic
Theology* (1988–1993). Perhaps his most important early programmatic
statement was *Theology and the Kingdom of God* (1969). While he wrote hundreds of articles, chapters in edited volumes and books, the last mentioned
one remains the key statement of his theological project's main themes.

Pannenberg attempts to make Christian theology truly scientific. One of
his driving motives is to return Christian theology to the status of a science.
By "science" he means *Wissenschaft*—truth discovered or at least supported
by reason. Since arriving at Munich he was concerned about continuing attempts to marginalize theology and even expel it from the state universities.
He believed that dialectical and existentialist theologies contributed to these
efforts by placing theology in a walled-off space protected from criticism by
special pleading. He wanted theology once again to be truly public by
making rationally supported universal truth claims. Against what he saw as
the increasing subjectivizing of theology at least since Kierkegaard, Pannenberg declared, "*My* truth cannot be mine alone. If I cannot in principle
declare it to be truth for all—though perhaps hardly anyone else sees this—
then it pitilessly ceases to be truth for me also."[90] Also, "without a sound
claim to universal validity Christians cannot maintain a conviction of the
truth of their faith and message."[91] This is especially true in the modern age,

---

[89]Again, much of what I know about Pannenberg's relationships with Tillich and Cobb come
from his own mouth. I was present at Pannenberg's sixtieth birthday celebration in Chicago
when he and Cobb toasted each other warmly.

[90]Wolfhart Pannenberg, *Systematic Theology*, trans. G. W. Bromiley, 3 vols. (Grand Rapids: Eerdmans, 1991), 1:51.

[91]Wolfhart Pannneberg, *Anthropology in Theological Perspective* (Philadelphia: Westminster
Press, 1985), 15.

Pannenberg says.[92] The Enlightenment made it impossible for Christians or anyone else to base public, universal truth claims on authority or subjective experience alone. In order to be taken seriously as a matter of truth and not mere opinion (or superstition), theology must become scientific.

Why was Pannenberg so adamant about the public nature of theology and the universality of its truth claims? That is, why is it so important to him that theology be scientific? He was very concerned about secularism and atheism and the effect they would have on society unless they are countered by religion. Pannenberg believes that only God provides the proper ground for human freedom and dignity and that without religion these realities cannot be sustained. In contrast to atheism, which often claims that the existence of God would undermine human freedom, he argued that "the basis of freedom as something held in common can be provided only by a personal reality of a supra-personal kind, which by contrast to a human reality would be a pure act of freedom."[93] But in order to guard and even promote freedom and dignity, radical secularism must be countered with rational arguments and not leaps of faith or appeals to authority. For Pannenberg, much of modern theology, especially under the spell of existentialism, has helped secularism take over the public intellectual realms where policies are developed. Theology must, therefore, remain in the state universities and retake its public role as foundation for human dignity and freedom. This became his whole theological burden, to answer the question

> How can theology make the primacy of God and his revelation in Jesus Christ intelligible, and validate its truth claims, in an age when all talk about God is reduced to subjectivity, as may be seen from the social history of the time and the modern fate of the proofs of God and philosophical theology?[94]

Pannenberg knows well there are no easy answers to such a question. Modern Christian theology has wrestled with the question and answered it in multiple ways, but he is convinced that the general drift has been toward subjectivizing the faith with the result that it is thought to be a private matter. The privatization of religion is a major symptom of modern secularity and,

---

[92]Pannenberg, *Basic Questions*, 2:50–52.
[93]Wolfhart Pannenberg, *The Idea of God and Human Freedom*, trans. R. A. Wilson (Philadelphia: Westminster Press, 1973), 114.
[94]Pannenberg, *Systematic Theology*, 1:128.

Pannenberg believes, has been aided and abetted by theologies that appeal primarily to authority or personal experience.[95] So how should theology proceed in this modern context? How can theology recover its scientific status so that its claims will at least be heard and seriously considered?

First, Pannenberg argues, Christian theology must want to be a public discipline and not the private language of the church. That cannot be taken for granted. But he is certain that both proclamation and public ethics depend on it, insofar as Christians want their worldview, their belief system, to influence society for the good. Christians should care enough about the world to want to fill the vacuum of "universal obligatoriness" in modern society. In other words, Pannenberg warns, without religion, relativism if not nihilism rules. Contemporary secular culture is ruled by "anomie"—lawlessness—because there is no transcendent, universally binding power.[96] And the problem is that "the appeal to the authority of Scripture and to a proclamation grounded in this is no longer sufficient to establish the legitimacy of faith."[97] What is needed, then, is a rational theology grounded in public reasons, one that appeals to the same criteria of truth to which the best secular thinkers appeal. An obvious objection at this point is noted by the German theologian: "Is not modern reason so fashioned that it leaves absolutely no room for Christian faith other than a subjectivity which lacks any intersubjective binding force? Is not any attempt at a rational accounting of the Christian faith foredoomed to vain compromise?"[98] He does not agree that the answer must be yes; reason itself is intersubjective and a gift of God not to be eschewed. However, he warns that, contrary to much modern, secular thought, "there really is [no] such a thing as 'the' reason, which is so monolithic in form that theology can only be dashed to pieces against it."[99] In other words, Pannenberg wishes to base the truth of Christianity on reason without accepting any particular definition of reason offered especially by persons hostile to religion. Reason that rules out God from the beginning is not rational. Reason must be open to all reality for which there is evidence, including rational arguments, and must not close off investigation from the beginning.

---

[95]Pannenberg, *Theology and the Philosophy of Science*, 265.
[96]Pannenberg, *Basic Questions*, 2:53.
[97]Ibid.
[98]Ibid., 2:54.
[99]Ibid.

So, what will make Christian theology scientific again? Pannenberg's most basic rule is that in order for something to count as science it must be intersubjective.[100] That is, it must offer reasons that can make sense to all reasonable people. Put negatively, it must not be esoteric. Basing Christian truth on personal experience alone privatizes it and makes it esoteric and thus not scientific. (Think of the difference between astronomy and astrology. The former is a science, not because it knows everything or can prove every hypothesis, but because it uses only intersubjective reasoning. The latter is esoteric, not scientific, because it uses private knowledge not open to public verification or falsification.) Pannenberg believes that, against his own will, Barth and his dialectical theology followers reduced Christianity to an esoteric discipline and thus removed its public influence.

Second, in order to be scientific, theology must be open to radical criticism including self-criticism.[101] What makes a discipline scientific is its openness to correction. Christian theology, then, must be open to criticism and correction from any reasonable (i.e., not esoteric) source. But that means, in order to be truly scientific, theology must put forth all its truth claims as hypotheses to be tested. This is perhaps his most controversial claim: "It is part of the finite nature of theological knowledge that even in theology the idea of God remains hypothetical and gives way to man's knowledge of the world and himself, by which it must be substantiated."[102] In correlation with this, theology cannot separate itself from other sciences but must remain open to their testing and criticism.

> Its real task is to examine the validity of the thesis of faith as a hypothesis. In doing this it cannot . . . have a field of investigation which can be separated or isolated from others. Though it considers everything it studies in particular relation to the reality of God, it is not a specialized positive science. The investigation of God as the all-determining reality involves all reality.[103]

In other words, in order to be properly scientific, theology must listen to and be open to correction by the settled facts of other sciences. The risk involved is that it may find its object turning into another one. That is, the-

---

[100]Pannenberg, *Theology and the Philosophy of Science*, 301.
[101]Ibid., 261.
[102]Ibid., 300.
[103]Ibid., 296.

ology must remain open to the possibility that it will be absorbed into some other science if its truth claims are falsified.[104]

It is important to stop at this point and correct a common misconception about Pannenberg's idea that theology's truth claims must be hypotheses. Critics have said that he undermines the passion of faith and the authority of revelation. *It must be understood, however, that in all this he is talking about theology and not about personal faith.* Pannenberg does not say that an individual Christian or church cannot have strong beliefs and hold them passionately. What he is saying is that insofar as theology intends to be a discipline, a science, with a public hearing, it must play by the same rules every science plays by. To alleviate some worries Pannenberg says, "This does not mean that present knowledge of the content [of revelation] is impossible, given the premise that God makes it possible for us to know him through his work in history. Even so, all such knowledge will always be preliminary."[105] By "preliminary" he means open to correction and ultimately proven only eschatologically.

Third, what are the intersubjective criteria for truth in theology? A science has to operate according to intersubjective criteria. It does not have to have indubitable foundations; Pannenberg is no foundationalist. However, there must be criteria for testing truth claims. First, Pannenberg admits, not reluctantly, that Christian knowledge of God is based on divine revelation: "no knowledge of God and no theology are conceivable that do not proceed from God and are not due to the working of his Spirit."[106] The question is not, then, whether God has given a revelation of himself; Christianity presupposes it. All sciences begin with certain presuppositions. The question is "whether theology is right in what it says about God, and by what right it says it."[107] That is where reason comes into play. Theology uses two criteria to test its own hypotheses. First, there is a negative criterion, which is logic: "no argumentation is possible, even in theology, unless there is recognition of the basic principles of identity and contradiction. These principles have always been especially presupposed in efforts to present the systematic unity

---

[104]Ibid., 300.
[105]Pannenberg, *Systematic Theology*, 1:16.
[106]Ibid., 1:2.
[107]Ibid., 1:7.

of Christian doctrine."[108] In brief, theology that contradicts itself is false. Pannenberg does not rule out paradox, but for him it is always a task for further thought.[109] Second is theology's (really any science's) positive criterion, which is coherence: "Systematic theology ascertains the truth of Christian doctrine by investigation and presentation of its coherence as regards both the interrelation of the parts and the relation to other knowledge."[110]

How does theology use these criteria to establish the truth of its claims? First, a basic principle for Pannenberg is the historicity of truth itself. "Time belongs to the essence of truth and of reality itself."[111] Ultimately, truth is that which will appear in the future, at the end of history.[112] This is part of his eschatological ontology; the future determines the present and past (see 8.a.). The reason is that the meaning of anything depends on its context, and the ultimate context of anything is universal history, which will be complete only at the end of history. Thus, only the end of history will reveal with certainty the truth of anything. Until history is finished and reality is whole and unified, everything remains provisional, even truth itself. Every science hypothesizes about the ultimate truth while remaining open to correction. Correction comes through logic and experience. The truth of a statement about reality depends on its coherence with other things considered true. That worldview, philosophy of reality, is most true that is most coherent. Thus,

> dogmatics as systematic theology proceeds by way of both assertion and hypothesis as it offers a model of the world, humanity, and history as they are grounded in God, a model which if it is tenable, will "prove" the reality of God and the truth of Christian doctrine, showing them to be consistently conceivable, and also confirming them, by the form of presentation.[113]

Pannenberg appeals to human existence and experience to support Christian faith with reason. Pannenberg approaches the task of supporting the truth of Christian faith rationally in two ways. First is what

---

[108]Ibid., 1:21.

[109]This comes from a personal conversation with Pannenberg in Munich on January 29, 1982. See Wolfhart Pannenberg, *Jesus—God and Man*, trans. Lewis Wilkin and Duane Priebe (Philadelphia: Westminster Press, 1968), 157.

[110]Pannenberg, *Systematic Theology*, 1:22.

[111]Pannenberg, "God's Presence in History," 260.

[112]Wolfhart Pannenberg, *Grundfragen systematischer Theologie* (Göttingen: Vandenhoeck & Ruprecht, 1980), 2:117. Translations are by this writer.

[113]Pannenberg, *Systematic Theology*, 1:60.

he calls fundamental theology, which has nothing to do with fundamentalism. It seeks to support the truth of Christianity by rooting belief in God in anthropology—human existence and experience generally considered. Second is the resurrection of Jesus Christ as the key to the meaning of history. First we will consider the first of these two prongs of his rational theology. Fundamental theology is Pannenberg's alternative to natural theology. Natural theology appealed to the existence or structures of the physical universe, nature, to ground belief in God's existence. Fundamental theology appeals to human existence and experience to justify belief in God. Here is one area where Pannenberg's modern tendencies appear. Christian theology in the modern age, he argues in *Anthropology in Theological Perspective*, must provide its foundation in general anthropological studies.[114] By "anthropology" here he means philosophical anthropology, not biological or archeological anthropology. Philosophical anthropology is the study of what it means to be human. Pannenberg asserts:

> Christians cannot but try to defend the claim of their faith to be true . . . in
> the modern age they must conduct this defense on the terrain of the interpre-
> tation of human existence and in the debate over whether religion is an indis-
> pensable component of humanness or, on the contrary, contributes to
> alienate human beings from themselves.[115]

The reason this is the approach that must be taken in the modern age is that modern science has closed all the gaps that constituted traditional natural theology. The physical universe, nonhuman nature, can now be exhaustively explained by science. What cannot be explained without reference to God is humanity itself.

Pannenberg argues that the best of modern philosophical anthropology focuses on the human person's "exocentricity" or openness to the world. (Here "world" means the whole of reality including the future.) Another term for it is "basic trust." "Human openness to the world, the capacity for objectivity in relation to the objects of our world, thus has an implicitly religious dimension of depth."[116] This depth dimension of human existence

---

[114]Pannenberg, *Anthropology in Theological Perspective*, 15.
[115]Ibid.
[116]Ibid., 2.

points to the fact that the question of human beings about themselves, their self-consciousness, and the question about divine reality belong inseparably together.[117] Thus, "only in relation to God can human beings become fully themselves."[118] Pannenberg admits this is not a "proof of the existence of God" in any traditional sense, but it shows that *the question of God* belongs to the very humanity of man. "For in one way or another, as long as human beings live, they live on the basis of a fundamental trust which sustains their life—whether it is God or an idol in which they put their trust."[119] Pannenberg takes more than five hundred pages to spell it all out and defend it using numerous philosophers and social scientists, but his ultimate conclusion is that "thus the idea of a divine reality that transcends everything finite is part of the religious thematic of human life, as is the idea of some kind of immortal destiny for one's own being beyond transiency and death."[120]

If this is not a proof of God's existence, what is it, and what is its use? Pannenberg believes philosophical anthropology can establish that humans are not mere, highly evolved animals. Human experience cannot be explained without reference to something transcendent. Ultimately, only the God of the Judeo-Christian tradition, the all-determining, personal (or suprapersonal) reality can explain humanity in its depth dimensions beyond physical drives. He goes on in *Anthropology in Theological Perspective* to talk about the Christian doctrine of sin and how it, too, explains human experience better than any alternative. His argument is not that someone who denies God is stupid; it is that someone who denies God cannot explain his or her own self-transcendence in creativity, rational reflection, basic trust or drive toward evil. There are many aspects of human experience that cannot be explained without reference to something or someone beyond nature. This is, he says, an indirect proof of God and of Christian faith. God is "co-given" in human experience.

The point is that in modernity "the existence of God has not only become doubtful but the content of the concept of God has also become unclear."[121]

---

[117]Ibid.
[118]Ibid., 73.
[119]Ibid.
[120]Ibid., 74.
[121]Pannenberg, *Systematic Theology*, 1:64.

In other words, it cannot be taken for granted. Nor will preaching convince many people:

> Nevertheless, the possibility of proving an anthropological need for rising above the finite to the thought of the infinite and absolute still has significance for the truth claim of all religious talk about God, even for Christian proclamation of the divine act of revelation in Jesus Christ. All talk about God must validate itself by being able to make the world of experience a proof of its power, showing what it is in everyday experience.[122]

Pannenberg also supports Christian faith with history. Contrary to what some critics have thought, Pannenberg does not believe that God can be known apart from his self-revelation. Over the years he has repeated this axiom (in different ways): "God can be known only if he gives himself to be known. The loftiness of the divine reality makes it inaccessible to us unless it makes itself known."[123] The question is where or how God reveals himself. The appeal to human experience described above is not about revelation; Pannenberg does not believe, as Schleiermacher did, that God is revealed in universal human experience. Rather, universal human experience supports belief in God with reason. For Pannenberg, God's self-revelation appears both directly and indirectly in history.

For him, universal history, history as a whole, is a medium of revelation. This is similar to what Hegel believed, and Pannenberg acknowledges that. But there are also significant differences.[124] As will be seen, for Pannenberg, revelation is primarily at the end of history. Also, he wants to protect the freedom of God in history in a way Hegel did not. Pannenberg is aware that critics, especially those in the neo-orthodox camp, will argue that God is revealed only in his Word (e.g., Barth's three forms of the Word of God). In contradiction he argues, "We simply have to rid ourselves of the notion that only the communication of a primary knowledge of deity can be revelation."[125] In other words, God can be truly revealed indirectly through events and not only directly through "Word."

---

[122]Ibid., 1:106.
[123]Ibid., 1:189.
[124]See Wolfhart Pannenberg, "The Significance of Christianity in the Philosophy of Hegel," in *The Idea of God and Human Freedom*, trans. R. A. Wilson (Philadelphia: Westminster Press, 1973), 161–95.
[125]Pannenberg, *Systematic Theology*, 1:195.

For Pannenberg, then, history is the medium of God's revelation:

The development of biblical ideas of revelation leads to a point at which human historical experience becomes an express theme in demonstration of the power and deity of the gods, and the related claim is made that the God of the Bible will prove himself to be the one God of all people, or has already shown himself to be this one God in Jesus Christ.[126]

God's revelation, then, is God's self-proof through history. History is a contest of the gods. Which god or God will turn out to be the "all-determining reality"? (By this Pannenberg does not mean meticulous determinism as in some forms of Calvinism; he means the being who decides the meaning of the whole of history and therefore of its parts.) Pannenberg believes that the God of Abraham, Isaac and Jacob, the God of the philosophers, the God of Jesus Christ are one and the same God. Philosophical theology has not always had it right, but at its best it has always pointed toward God as the all-determining reality. The point is that, for him, it is not true that (as Pascal declared) the God of the philosophers is not at all the God of the Bible. Pannenberg declares, against all forms of Christian subjectivism, that God's revelation in history is "open to anyone who has eyes to see."[127] And a person does not need special "lenses" provided by the Holy Spirit to "see" God revealed in history. However, before the ultimate end of history, even God's revelation is provisional because it is anticipatory of that final revelation when all possibility of doubt will be removed.[128] On the way to that future revelation, revelation is always indirect and provisional leaving room for doubt. The kingdom of God, God's rule, will be the final and complete revelation of God as Lord beyond doubt. Right now, at every point in history before the consummation, every event of revelation is open to debate, and that is where faith enters. Christians have faith that what they see in history, God's revelation of himself as Lord, is true even when it cannot be proven beyond doubt or debate.

This is where Pannenberg's other radical claim enters the picture. Pannenberg's principle is, "The deity of God is his rule."[129] From this he concludes that

---

[126]Ibid., 1:196.
[127]Ibid., 1:249.
[128]Ibid., 1:238, 247.
[129]Pannenberg, *Theology and the Kingdom of God*, 55.

it is necessary to say that, in a restricted but important sense, God does not yet exist. Since his rule and being are inseparable, God's being is still in the process of coming to be. Considering this, God should not be mistaken for an objectified being presently existing in its fullness.[130]

This is why process theologians like Cobb once thought Pannenberg was some kind of process thinker. Later, however, it became clear he was not. People with a tendency to run away with that often-quoted statement "God does not yet exist" need to stop and realize what the German theologian means by "in a restricted . . . sense." For Pannenberg, God himself has no future; God is the future of the world determining the future of all that is present.[131] The future, he adamantly asserts, is not an "empty category."[132] Rather, "God in his very being is the future of the world,"[133] and this is not just a matter of appearance or finite perspective.[134] From the future God rules over the world, determining its being and meaning. Creation is from the future.[135] By "creation" in this sense Pannenberg means "unifying power." From the future God draws the world into unity. The kingdom of God, God's lordship, is the unity of humanity under God's manifest (not debatable) rule. But that is future for us even if not for God. God has no future conditioning him.[136]

These are, by all accounts, enigmatic statements. They refer to the eschatological ontology already discussed in the section on Moltmann's theology. However, they need some clarification here in order to shed light on Pannenberg's idea of revelation, reason and God. The only way to understand them is to realize that for him, as for many German thinkers, the order of knowing and the order of being are inseparable. If the meaning of something is truly debatable, even the best use of reason cannot establish it, then it does not yet fully exist. God's being as God is *strittig*, open to debate, throughout history. There is room for doubt. For one thing, evil and innocent suffering demonstrate this. God's rule is not yet; therefore God is

---

[130]Ibid., 56.
[131]Ibid.
[132]Ibid.
[133]Ibid., 61.
[134]Ibid., 63.
[135]Ibid., 59.
[136]Ibid., 63.

not yet. When God rules there will be no doubt; his existence will be beyond debate. Only then will he fully exist. All that is true—from the finite perspective. But Pannenberg does not mean *only* from the finite perspective because that has ontological reality. From the finite point of view, before God's rule is established, God does not yet exist. However, God does not have that perspective. For himself, as the power of the future that has no future conditioning him, his being is complete. There is no becoming in God. *We creatures, however, cannot take God's perspective.* For us it is true that God does not yet exist. The full reality of God, God's rule, is doxological—an expression of faith made in an attitude of worship.[137]

So, for Pannenberg, all of history, including certain special, anticipatory events, reveals God. But this will be proven beyond doubt only in the future. On the way to that future

> as the revelation of God in his historical action moves towards the still out-standing future of the consummation of history, its claim to reveal the one God who is the world's Creator, Reconciler, and Redeemer is open to future verification in history, which is as yet incomplete, and which is still exposed, therefore, to the question of its truth. This question is given an ongoing answer in the life of believers by the power of revelation to shed light on their life experiences.[138]

Crucial to Pannenberg's whole theological project has been to claim that the future lordship of God has preappeared within history. History, conditional and provisional as it is, has within it events that can only be called proleptic—the future happening ahead of time. The most important such event is the resurrection of Jesus: "the event of the resurrection of Jesus is itself . . . an anticipation of the end, [though] not the end itself. Its difference from the eschatological future of the general resurrection is nevertheless only a quantitative, not a qualitative one."[139] In other words, Jesus' resurrection was the future event of the resurrection of all the dead preappearing in one person.

---

[137]This explanation of "God does not yet exist" comes directly from Pannenberg. It was expressed in a lengthy and detailed theological conversation over lunch in Munich on Friday, January 29, 1982. See also Roger E. Olson, "Wolfhart Pannenberg's Doctrine of the Trinity," *Scottish Journal of Theology* 43:2 (1990): 175–206.

[138]Pannenberg, *Systematic Theology*, 1:257.

[139]Wolfhart Pannenberg, *Basic Questions in Theology*, trans. G. W. Bromiley (Minneapolis: Fortress, 2008), 1:179.

Pannenberg's argument is that if Jesus was raised from the dead, it had to be by God, and it proves, as much as it is possible to prove anything before the end, that Jesus is one with God and the God of Jesus is Lord of all.

On the resurrection of Jesus Pannenberg breaks with modernity and liberal and neo-liberal theologies. He believes it is irrational to decide ahead of time, before considering the evidence, that an event cannot have happened. But his modern commitments reappear in the way he goes about establishing the historicity of the resurrection. He makes no appeal to faith; his appeal is solely to historical verification.[140] Pannenberg believes that Jesus' unique unity with God (his divinity) was not established by his words or deeds but only by his resurrection from the dead.[141] "Only because the end of the world is already present in Jesus' resurrection is God himself revealed in him."[142] One of Jesus' claims that even most critical-historical scholars of the Gospels admit is genuine is his claim to be the "Son of God."[143] This claim was not verified even by his miracles, as there were many miracle workers in the ancient world. However, "if Jesus has been raised, this for a Jew can only mean that God himself has confirmed the pre-Easter activity of Jesus."[144] Also, "if Jesus, having been raised from the dead, is ascended to God and if thereby the end of the world has begun, then God is ultimately revealed in Jesus."[145] How does this relate to verifying the resurrection of Jesus as historically true? Pannenberg argues there is no other rational explanation for the rise of the early church and its Gentile mission: "The transition to the Gentile mission is motivated by the eschatological resurrection of Jesus as resurrection of the crucified One."[146] He spells it out in more detail:

> The resurrection of Jesus would be designated as a historical event in this sense: If the emergence of primitive Christianity . . . can be understood . . . only if one examines it in the light of the eschatological hope for a resurrection from the dead, then that which is so designated is a historical event,

---

[140]Pannenberg, *Jesus—God and Man*, 99.
[141]Ibid., 53.
[142]Ibid., 69.
[143]Ibid., 53.
[144]Ibid., 67.
[145]Ibid., 69.
[146]Ibid., 70.

even if we do not know anything more particular about it. Then an event that is expressible only in the language of the eschatological expectation is to be asserted as a historical occurrence.[147]

It is not possible here, given space limitations, to trace out in detail all the steps of Pannenberg's argument for the historicity of the resurrection. Suffice it to say that he believes it is a real event (including the empty tomb) and not just the "rise of faith" in the hearts of the disciples (Bultmann's and Tillich's restitution theory). And he believes historical research can confirm it as much as any historical event can be confirmed. To rule it out in advance because it is supernatural is arbitrary. Historical research has to examine and decide these things, not philosophical commitments. On the basis of rational belief in the resurrection of Jesus, Christians reasonably make the claim that the end of history, history's fullness and completeness, is the kingdom of the God of Jesus who does not yet exist and yet appears in Jesus Christ before the end. Until the end comes, however, even this will remain open to possible falsification; it remains a hypothesis to be tested by the ongoing events of history.

Pannenberg works out a Christology from below. He contrasts two theological approaches to the deity of Jesus Christ (his humanity not being in debate). First is "Christology from above," which begins with his deity and then asks how he could be also man. Second is his preferred approach, "Christology from below," which begins with the "human *Gestalt* of Jesus," the pattern of his life including his resurrection, and works toward his deity based on his unique humanity. Pannenberg's rather shocking formula for his new, reconstructed Christology, which is not incarnational but revelational, is "as this man, Jesus is God."[148] Jesus' deity is based on his unity with God established by his resurrection; in him God revealed his lordship, his rule, which is inseparable from his deity, and thus determined him as one with himself: "as *this* man, as man in this particular, unique situation, with this particular historical mission and this particular fate—as this man Jesus is not just man, but from the perspective of his resurrection from the dead . . . he is one with God and thus is himself God."[149]

---

[147]Ibid., 98.
[148]Ibid., 323.
[149]Ibid.

But if the resurrection "made" him one with God and thus God, was he God before the resurrection? Or is this just a fancy form of adoptionism, as some critics have charged? To answer this and to ground the real, onto-logical deity of Jesus Christ without talk of preexistence or descent from heaven, Pannenberg turns to his eschatological ontology. Once the resur-rection happened, it *retroactively* determined that Jesus' whole life was God's perfect self-revelation and "self-realization" within history so that he was ontologically united with God all along even though that was *strittig*, debatable, until the resurrection. Similarly, the resurrection, being the pro-leptic appearing of the future kingdom of God, God's lordship and deity beforehand, in history, unites Jesus with God in eternity:

> The confirmation of Jesus' unity with God in the retroactive power of his res-urrection makes the hiddenness of this unity during Jesus' earthly life com-prehensible and thus makes room for the genuine humanity of this life. . . . [Thus] out of his eternity, God has through the resurrection of Jesus, which was always present to his eternity, entered into a unity with this one man which was at first hidden. This unity illuminated Jesus' life in advance, but its basis and reality were revealed only by his resurrection.[150]

This is Pannenberg's alternative to the orthodox doctrine of Jesus Christ (the hypostatic union), which he thinks inevitably leads to a dualism of the person of Christ. His alternative Christology could be called a "two states" doctrine of Jesus Christ—his human state and his divine state. From one perspective, they are successive, but from God's perspective they are per-fectly united. Everything here depends on the cogency of the concept of "retroactive causation" intrinsic to eschatological ontology.

Long after he wrote *Jesus—God and Man*, Pannenberg revised his Chris-tology without denying anything in the earlier version. He added an el-ement—Jesus' unity with God based on Jesus' self-differentiation from the Father and God's self-realization in the history of Jesus Christ. What divides humanity from God is "lack of differentiation of himself from God."[151] Human self-estrangement results from that because it amounts to idolatry of self. However, "the deeper and clearer the self-differentiation from God . . .

---

[150]Ibid., 322.
[151]Pannenberg, *Grundfragen systematischer Theologie*, 2:144.

the deeper and closer the unity with God."[152] Jesus actively differentiated himself from God saying, for example, that only God is good. By "self-differentiation from God" Pannenberg means humility before God. Full communion with God results from highest involvement for the cause of God combined with the spiritual poverty of self-differentiation from God.[153]

> In the self-differentiation of Jesus from the Father this relationship [trinitarian Father-Son relationship] is so realized that at the same time the self-realization of God comes to its goal in him; Jesus in his self-differentiation from the Father belongs himself to the divinity of God as the eternal Son from whom the redemption of the world proceeds.[154]

Pannenberg constructs an eschatological doctrine of the Trinity. How does Pannenberg view God in relation to the world? The answer is very complex and cannot be explained here in the detail it deserves. A few general comments will have to suffice. First, as strongly hinted above, God realizes or actualizes himself through the world's discovery of him and in becoming its unifying Lord. Jesus Christ is the pinnacle of this self-realization of God.[155] Does this mean a dependence of God on the world? Pannenberg's answer is similar to Moltmann's, a kind of voluntary panentheism: "Because God is love, having once created a world in his freedom, he finally does not have his own existence without this world, but over against it and in it in the process of its ongoing consummation."[156] Pannenberg joins (borrows from?) Dorner to express God's relationship with the world as "the self-realization [*Selbstverwirklichung*] of God in the working out of his lordship over his creation."[157] And this is where the Trinity enters the picture of Pannenberg's idea of the God-world relation. If God were a single monad, an undifferentiated unity without any multiplicity, he could not come to self-realization in and through the world without divinizing the world as part of himself. This was Hegel's problem. The Trinity is the solution:

---

[152]Ibid.

[153]Ibid., 2:144–45.

[154]Ibid., 2:145.

[155]See Roger E. Olson, "The Human Self-Realization of God: Hegelian Elements in Pannenberg's Christology," *Perspectives in Religious Studies* 13:3 (1986): 207–23.

[156]Pannenberg, *Systematic Theology*, 1:447.

[157]Pannenberg, *Grundfragen systematischer Theologie*, 2:141.

> Divine working and human seeking interlace in this process of the self-real-
> ization of God. But in the moment in which the self of God is definitively
> found—as is possibly the truth of the history of Jesus—this interlacing is
> absorbed [*wird aufgenommen*] in the identity of the divine essence itself as
> trinitarian self-relation of God in the distinction of the Father and the Son
> through the Spirit who binds both together, who is as much a Spirit of self-
> differentiation as of community.[158]

The doctrine of the Trinity is central to Pannenberg's mature doctrine of
God. If God realizes himself, comes to himself, in and through the self-
differentiation of the Son Jesus from the Father so that Jesus belongs eternally to the very essence of God, then there are at least two persons in God.
The revelation of God in this way cannot be understood without community of two in one God. Their oneness lies in their unity of interdependence. Without the Son, Jesus, the Father would not be God in the way he
is and without the Father the Son, Jesus, would not be God as he is. The
Spirit is the personal love that binds the Father and Son and glorifies them.
The following quotation is possibly the clearest expression of Pannenberg's
idea of the Trinity. It is not easy to understand and can hardly be para-
phrased, so here it is:

> As the Father is present to the world for its salvation through the sending and
> death of the Son, and as his fatherly love is thus revealed, the Son has actu-
> alized [realized] the deity of God in the world and glorified in it God's name
> and kingly rule. Certainly this glorifying in the world presupposes constant
> glorifying in God's eternity. Yet in the world the kingly rule of the Father is
> first glorified by the Son and Spirit as the incarnate Son, by obedience to his
> mission, glorifies the name of the Father among us, and as the Spirit teaches
> us to see herein the mission of the obedient Son. Since we cannot separate
> the deity of God from his royal lordship, it follows that the irruption of the
> future of this lordship in the work of the Son has as its content the absolute
> reality of God in and for the world. Because, however, the sending of the Son
> and Spirit is from the Father, in relation to the fulfillment of the mission by
> the obedience of the Son and the work of the Spirit, we thus may speak of a
> self-actualization of the trinitarian God in the world.[159]

---

[158]Ibid., 2:143.
[159]Wolfhart Pannenberg, *Systematic Theology*, trans. G. W. Bromiley, 3 vols. (Grand Rapids: Eerdmans, 1994), 2:392–93.

One thing is clear from this: Pannenberg regards history as the basis for God's triunity. Then the question arises, would God be triune, would there be a Trinity, without the world and its history (in which Jesus Christ appears)? Pannenberg affirms an immanent Trinity, that God is Father, Son and Holy Spirit in himself, eternally. Ultimately, Pannenberg, who values reason so highly, falls into paradox in trying to state the relationship between the immanent or ontological Trinity and the economic or historical Trinity: "It is certainly true of all the persons specifically that they are there before the process of God's self-actualizing in the world of his creation by historical revelation. It is also true that their deity is the result of this process."[160]

Pannenberg answers deep theological questions and raises more. Clearly one of Pannenberg's main motives is to insert Christian theology into the modern intellectual conversation. In almost everything he writes about, one eye is kept on Christian tradition and one eye is kept on modernity. He is not primarily an accommodationist theologian; it is none of his intention to reconstruct doctrines to correlate with secular thought. However, in a way probably not true of any premodern Christian theology, he wants to make Christian doctrines intelligible to rational modernists. And he wants theology to be respected by them as a science among the sciences. However, he is not a foundationalist or a naturalist. That is, he does not believe in indubitable foundations of fact (whether self-evident truths or empirical perceptions) that justify all knowledge such that knowledge includes only what reason can prove. His unique eschatological approach to truth and knowledge, their provisional rationality based on history, has caused some commentators to label him postfoundationalist as if he belongs to the postmodern intellectual milieu.[161] That is certainly debatable. What is beyond debate (if anything is) is that Pannenberg seeks to make Christian theology reasonable without accepting some presupposed definition of rationality that, for example, rules out the supernatural.

One of the questions Pannenberg answered helpfully, at least according to most critics, is how there might be a rational basis for belief in God that

---

[160]Ibid., 2:393–94.
[161]See LeRon Shults, *The Postfoundationalist Task of Theology: Wolfhart Pannenberg and the New Theological Rationality* (Grand Rapids: Eerdmans, 1999).

is not subject to the criticisms of natural theology. Pannenberg's work in philosophical anthropology, correlating it with Christian anthropology, goes far toward demonstrating that belief in God is intrinsic to human nature even when God is not named. At least the question of God is presupposed in human existence and experience. His idea of human exocentricity, openness to the world, is very carefully crafted in conversation with a multitude of modern philosophers, social psychologists and anthropologists. This helps to show that belief in God, and perhaps even belief in the Christian God, does not require a leap of faith. Also, especially conservative Christian theologians have found his work on the historicity of the resurrection helpful in countering not only secular skepticism but also liberal and neo-liberal denials of its very possibility.

However, Pannenberg's theology raises some questions it does not satisfactorily answer. His doctrine of revelation is completely nonpropositional, which raises questions about how doctrine is constructed. Nowhere does he explain exactly his sources or norms for theology. They seem to be Scripture, tradition, reason and experience, but his doctrine of Scripture is weak. Ultimately, he appeals not to Scripture per se, which is not inspired in any traditional sense, but to "the gospel."[162] Scripture is "inspired" insofar as it communicates the gospel. "Certainly the scriptures are to be understood as divinely inspired, . . . but only insofar as they witness to the Gospel of Jesus Christ." This is not far from the neo-orthodox idea of biblical inspiration. The same problem bedevils it: How does one derive or justify doctrine from the gospel when it is embedded in Scripture and Scripture as a whole is not considered inspired? That becomes especially problematic when Pannenberg rejects the Holy Spirit as the source of Scripture's authority. He bases Scripture's authority on the gospel in it and the fact that the apostles wrote it. But one could ask, so what?

Here we arrive at a fundamental dilemma in Pannenberg's theology—its source and norm for doctrine. What justifies considering Scripture special? What justifies deriving doctrines from it and using it to justify them? Even Pannenberg does this to a certain extent. Traditionally, Protestant theology,

---

[162]This comes from Wolfhart Pannenberg, "On the Inspiration of Scripture," unpublished essay given to this writer by Pannenberg after this writer requested something written to explain his view of Scripture's authority.

from Luther to Calvin to Barth, has talked about the inner testimony of the Holy Spirit, not just in the individual but in the church. Pannenberg radically rejects what we might call the Holy Spirit principle which underlies the Scripture principle. "One cannot run away from the dilemma of the question of the truth in relation to the Christian message by appealing to the Holy Spirit."[163] The question he does not answer satisfactorily, however, is exactly how the truth of the Christian message is to be held with any degree of passionate commitment. He seems too comfortable with holding Christian claims as hypotheses. But that would seem necessary unless the Holy Spirit is the guarantor of the truth of the Christian message. One contemporary of Pannenberg's who especially criticized him for this is Helmut Thielicke (1908–1986), who wrote against Pannenberg that his theology does not take seriously enough the fallenness of humanity:

> A basic conviction of biblical anthropology is that man is a prisoner of his defection from God, that he is a sinner, and that the bondage of his will brings him under extreme constraint. The sayings of Jesus . . . about blocked ears and blinded eyes and hardened hearts make this very clear. Their point is simply that there is no accessibility of the event of revelation unless it makes itself accessible. "The natural man does not perceive the things of the Spirit of God" (1 Corinthians 2:14), nor, therefore, the things of the Word and event that this Spirit alone discloses.[164]

Without doubt Pannenberg's doctrine of the Holy Spirit is his weakest. He refers to the Holy Spirit as a divine "field of force" and warns against any use of the Spirit to subjectivize faith: "If the Spirit is understood as the new life that appeared in Christ, and which operates in our present in a provisional and only initiatory way as our common future, then there is a safeguard against the subjectivistic emptying of the confession of the Holy Spirit."[165] It seems to many critics that he depersonalizes the Holy Spirit. Certainly he is afraid of using the Holy Spirit in any epistemological way. His fear of subjectivism may carry him too far away from the effect of God on the human heart and mind.

---

[163]Pannenberg, *Basic Questions in Theology*, 1:34.
[164]Helmut Thielicke, *The Evangelical Faith: Theology of the Holy Spirit*, trans. G. W. Bromiley, 3 vols. (Grand Rapids: Eerdmans, 1974), 3:xxvii.
[165]Pannenberg, *Basic Questions in Theology*, 2:43.

Finally, what about Pannenberg and modern science? One thesis of this book is that much modern theology is consciously or unconsciously constructed or reconstructed to avoid conflicts with science. That is certainly truer of some theologians than others. Some have separated faith so entirely from science, as having to do with entirely unrelated realities, that there is in principle no possibility that they might conflict. Some have accommodated radically to whatever scientists say, even if their theories are unproven and conflict with basic Christian beliefs. Some have fought modern science and declared it secular and therefore unchristian. Christians should ignore or even condemn it. Pannenberg's relationship with modern science is more nuanced than any of those approaches. He does not want to fall into a dualism where science and theology cannot touch or even conflict. Because he is determined that theology be a science among the sciences, even if primarily a human and not a physical science, he is loath to separate them into watertight compartments.

Pannenberg has engaged in many dialogues with scientists and published quite a lot about the relation between theology and the natural sciences. He has been a frequent contributor to the journal *Zygon*, which is devoted to dialogue between theology and science. He comes at this dialogue in different ways, but one overriding theme is the contingency of nature in part and in whole. He redefines laws of nature so that they are not iron-clad mechanisms that rule out the new and unpredictable. He says that the deterministic view of nature that ruled classical science before the advent of quantum physics in the twentieth century was a kind of religious faith.[166] He means, of course, that it was not truly scientific. He finds many openings in contemporary physics for acts of God. He examines major twentieth-century scientific models of the universe and how nature works, such as that of Carl Friedrich von Weizsäcker (1912–2007), and concludes that "all [these] models allow one to speak of a continuing creative activity of God in world events."[167]

The point here is not to examine in detail Pannenberg's view of modern science but only to say that he believes nothing about its best established

---

[166]A. M. Klaus Müller and Wolfhart Pannenberg, *Erwägungen zu einer Theologie der Natur* (Gütersloh: Gütersloher Verlagshaus Gerd Mohn, 1970), 38.

[167]Ibid., 63. Translation is this writer's.

theories conflicts with Christian belief even though it is possible that such could be the case. In other words, theology and science are not about entirely different phenomena. He looks for "parallels" between them and believes he finds them in physics and biology especially.[168] He does not seem afraid of science; it appears that he would gladly adjust Christian belief if necessary to accord with facts or well-established theories. Christianity, for him, is primarily about endings, not beginnings. That changes much in the science versus religion debate.

---

[168]Wolfhart Pannenberg, "Theological Questions to Scientists," *Zygon* 16:1 (1981): 65–76.

9

Liberation Theologies
Protest Injustice
and Oppression

 &

While 1960s radical theologians were celebrating secularity and accommodating to modernity and while theologians of hope were pointing to the future, new voices of protest were demanding a hearing in theology. Previously, almost all major, academic theologians were white, middle class and male. The 1960s and 1970s, however, was a time of social unrest. Race riots broke out in many American cities. European universities underwent student protests and reorganizations based on them. Young men burned draft cards in public, and young women burned bras to protest sexism in society. Ché Guevara (1928–1967) became a guerilla hero in Latin America and around the world. Martin Luther King Jr. (1929–1968) and Malcom X (1925–1965) marshaled African Americans and sympathetic whites to overturn segregation and racism. Betty Friedan (1921–2006) founded the National Organization for Women (NOW) to liberate women from second-class status and gain equality with men in every area of society. Anyone who lived through the years between 1960 and 1975 remembers the social turmoil and revolutionary temper of the times. It was exhilarating for some, frightening for others and both for many.

A Paradigm Shift Begins to Affect Theology

Until the 1960s, modernity was generally considered a benefit to humanity except by some conservative religious people. Theologians wrestled with the epistemological issues raised by modernity: whether belief in God is rational, whether faith is a legitimate basis for belief. Theologians also wrestled with issues of reality such as whether miracles are possible. At the least it is safe to say modernity was assumed to be mainly about liberating humans from authoritative tradition to, as Kant said, think for themselves. (Not everyone agreed this was a good thing.) Suddenly, some philosophers and theologians began to question whether that was what modernity was about and whether it was even beneficial for all people. The term "postmodern" had been used for a century before 1970 for various purposes, but beginning sometime in the 1960s and 1970s it took on a new connotation summarized in pithy style by philosopher Jean-François Lyotard (1924–1998) in a groundbreaking book titled *The Postmodern Condition: A Report on Knowledge* (1979). According to Lyotard, postmodernism is "incredulity towards meta-narratives."[1] Many people began to regard modernity itself as a "grand narrative"—a totalizing scheme of thought that pretends to encompass all knowledge and explain all experience. Especially oppressed minorities and women began to point out the tendency of modernity to promote domination by educated and economically privileged people. So far, anyway, they pointed out, it had not done much for African Americans, women and people of the Global South (what was then called the Third World).

Many postmodern thinkers began to argue that epistemology should not be the main focus of philosophy and theology; their main concerns should be liberation from oppression. Modernity generally assumed a paradigm of knowing that favored educated, Euro-American, white males. The Enlightenment itself was constructed by them. Postmoderns, including liberationists of all kinds, argued that there is no one paradigm of knowing that covers all people. Perhaps no book did more to undermine confidence in the hegemony of the Enlightenment and its accompanying faith in science than *The Structure of Scientific Revolutions* (1962) by philosopher of science

---

[1]Jean-François Lyotard, *The Postmodern Condition: A Report on Knowledge*, trans. Geoff Bennington and Brian Massumi (Minneapolis: University of Minnesota Press, 1984), xxiv.

Thomas Kuhn (1922–1996). Kuhn argued, persuasively for many people, that even the natural sciences do not operate by pure evidence and reason alone. He introduced the idea of "paradigm shift" to describe how science functions. A paradigm is like a metanarrative, a grand perspective on reality and how it works. Even scientists work under the influence of paradigms that themselves cannot be proven true or false. For example, Newton's paradigm of physics viewed the universe as a machine. During the twentieth century it was being gradually replaced by a new perspective, a new paradigm of science, called quantum physics, that pictures the universe more organically and open to novelty and contingency. Scientists under the sway of the Newtonian paradigm were reluctant to give it up even when the preponderance of evidence demonstrated its fundamental flaws. Paradigm change is almost always gradual and painful, and even the most rational, purportedly objective thinkers resist it.

Around the same time two sociologists, Peter Berger and Thomas Luckmann, published a groundbreaking and some would say revolutionary book titled *The Social Construction of Reality* (1966) that launched a new paradigm of epistemology called the sociology of knowledge. The basic idea was that no knowledge is, as Enlightenment thinkers claimed, purely objective. Instead, knowledge is always influenced, if not determined, by social location and perspective based on vested interests. That is, reality is constructed or at least construed according to an individual's and social group's inherited or developed economic, political and tribal perceived needs or desires. A major desire is to protect power. Thus, for example, one group of people may view another as inferior, when they are not, because it is to their advantage to keep them in an inferior socioeconomic status.

These were among the revolutionary ideas of the 1960s that began to undermine the modern project and promote interest in postmodernism. (As of the second decade of the twenty-first century, there is still no consensus about what that means beyond Lyotard's minimal definition.) They also gave impetus to a new paradigm of theology called liberation theology, which has many forms. Every group that perceives itself as oppressed develops its own form of liberation theology, but all of them have certain basic things in common. Underlying them all is a sense that Christian theology, by and large, bought into modernity to the detriment of oppressed minorities whose unique experiences and perspectives were submerged in the overwhelmingly white, male and economically privileged Enlightenment-based modern project.

Liberation Theology Arises and Becomes Controversial

Liberation theology, in all its forms, is difficult for many privileged people to understand. Sociologists of knowledge would suggest that difficulty arises in part from a deep aversion to understanding it because it challenges social privilege. Beyond finding it difficult to understand, many privileged people have misrepresented it as prone to violence and as rooted in Marxism more than Christianity. Such caricatures would not survive and flourish if there were not some truth in them, but the popular images of liberation theology that arose in reaction to it, especially during the 1970s through the 1990s, were often distorted. One Baptist seminary in the South ordered its professors not to discuss liberation theology with students. The seminary's leaders did not want students to even know about it. Others, especially conservative Christians, both Protestant and Catholic, promoted harsh images of it. They latched onto certain examples that they knew would undermine attempts to understand it or take it seriously. For example, Columbian priest and university professor Camilo Torres (1929–1966) abandoned his life of privilege to join a guerilla group attempting to overthrow the government. He was killed in his first militant revolutionary attack against the government. After his death, his admirers collected his writings and published them as *Revolutionary Priest: The Complete Writings and Messages of Camilo Torres* (1971). Critics of liberation theology often implied that all Latin American liberation priests and theologians were violent revolutionaries. They were not. A better example was Dom Helder Camara (1909–1999), a Brazilian archbishop and icon of liberation theology in South America. When he became archbishop he refused to move into the traditional episcopal palace near the cathedral and turned it into a homeless shelter. His *Spiral of Violence* (1971) called for an end to all violence.

The issue of violence has haunted liberation theology at least since the Torres case. And, around the same time, in the late 1960s and early 1970s, some black power militants called for race riots to oppose what they saw as systemic oppression of African Americans. The leading black theologian, James Cone (b. 1938), refused to condemn calls for a race war and even hinted that such might be the only way for African Americans to achieve justice. Whites, and some blacks, were shocked when Cone, a professor at Union Theological Seminary in New York City, wrote, "It is important to point out that no one can be nonviolent in an unjust society."[2] What he meant was that injustice itself is a form of violence. But Cone went further and wrote, "We [blacks] have reached our limit of tolerance, and if it means death with dignity or life with humiliation, we will choose the former. And if that is the choice, we will take some honkies with us."[3] At the same time, however, Martin Luther King Jr. was advocating pacifism even in the face of lynchings and police violence against peaceful protesters. Later, Cone softened his rhetoric and stopped hinting at racial violence as a means of liberation for oppressed African Americans. But critics of liberation theology will remember and hold against him his early flirtations with violent revolution.

Much discussion has surrounded the question of liberation theology's beginning. Can it be dated? According to liberation theology scholar David Tombs, "The actual birth of liberation theology and the church's option for the poor can be dated to mid-1968."[4] In May and August Catholic leaders in Latin America met and called for the church to realign itself with the poor majority. Previously, and to some extent long afterwards, the Catholic hierarchy in Latin America was aligned with oppressive, dictatorial regimes. The bishops called for change and opened the door to liberation theology. One of the first theologians to walk through that door and who became acknowledged as the father of Latin American liberation theology was Gustavo Gutiérrez (b. 1928), a Peruvian priest who wrote the bible of the movement, *A Theology of Liberation* (1971). Afterwards numerous Catholic priests and theologians throughout Latin America embraced liberation theology, which began to decline during the 1990s with the fall of world communism and the rise of democratically elected socialist regimes in many Latin American countries.[5]

---

[2]James Cone, *God of the Oppressed* (New York: Harper & Row, 1975), 219.
[3]James Cone, *A Black Theology of Liberation*, 2nd ed. (Maryknoll, NY: Orbis, 1987), 15.
[4]David Tombs, *Latin American Liberation Theology* (Boston: Brill, 2002), 115.
[5]Credit should be given here to Rubem Alves (b. 1933), whose *A Theology of Human Hope* (1969) may have been the first true book of liberation theology. However, Gutiérrez has come to be credited with bringing liberation theology to the world with *A Theology of Liberation*.

The women's liberation movement also began in the 1960s with Betty Friedan and NOW and other women intellectuals in Europe and North America calling for an end to patriarchy—the sexist social paradigm in which men are considered or at least treated as superior to women. Feminist theology is not always recognized as a form of liberation theology, but it should be. Catholic sociologist-theologian Mary Daly (1928–2010) wrote *The Church and the Second Sex* (1968) and then *Beyond God the Father: Toward a Philosophy of Women's Liberation* (1973). In both books she criticized the male-dominated hierarchy of the Catholic Church and argued for a new, nonhierarchical paradigm for church governance. In *Beyond God the Father* she pointed toward a new language for God based on women's experience. Eventually Daly left the Catholic Church and Christianity and turned to mother goddess religion (Wicca) as a form of protest against what she considered the hopelessly patriarchal Christian religion. A theologian influenced by Daly was fellow Catholic Rosemary Radford Ruether (b. 1936), author of several volumes on liberation theology who wrote *Sexism and God-Talk: Toward a Feminist Theology* (1983), which became the manifesto of Christian feminist theology for at least the next two decades. Unlike Daly, Ruether did not express hostility toward men or abandon Christianity for mother goddess worship. Her proposals for revising Christianity, however, were far-reaching and closely paralleled black theology and Latin American liberation theology (except for the issue of violence, which feminist theology has never advocated). She borrowed heavily from Tillich in reconstructing the doctrine of God, whom she called "God/ess" or "the Matrix of Being." Her main goal was to abolish hierarchical social systems which she identified with patriarchy.

Cone taught at Union Theological Seminary, a fact that helped him launch his black theology project. It is hard to ignore the Charles Augustus Briggs Distinguished Professor of Systematic Theology at such a prestigious Protestant seminary when he writes as he did in books like *God of the Oppressed* (1975) and *A Black Theology of Liberation* (1970). Gutiérrez taught theology at Peru's leading Catholic university and then at the University of Notre Dame. Daly taught at Boston College, a prestigious Jesuit university. Ruether taught at Garrett-Evangelical Theological Seminary of Northwestern University and the Pacific School of Religion, two highly regarded

Protestant seminaries. These theologians intended to ruffle feathers and even create controversy, and they accomplished both. But none of them intended to create controversy for its own sake or to make names for themselves. Their common concern was with structural oppression in churches and in societies and liberation of people suffering that oppression. All of them built on the works of earlier thinkers, and each had his or her followers who went in various directions. But especially Cone, Gutiérrez and Ruether stand out as the fathers and mother of liberation theology, and so they will be the case studies in this chapter.

Liberation Theology Creates a Paradigm Shift in Theology

Liberation theology is difficult for some people to grasp because they come to it with expectations based on traditional theological methods. Liberation theology is different. The different types of liberation theology do not intend to follow well-trod paths of either orthodox or liberal theologies. Liberation theology represents a new approach to doing theology. However, all the liberation theologians were influenced by previous theologians. Cone borrowed heavily from Barth. Gutiérrez was influenced by European political theologies and especially Johannes Metz (b. 1928). Ruether was influenced by Tillich and process theology. However, liberation theology begins differently, with alternative aims and intentions, and proceeds differently, with nontraditional sources and norms. All three forms of liberation theology share much in common, especially in terms of this new paradigm for doing theology. First, then, we will look at their family resemblances as liberation theologies. Afterwards, in the following sections each one will be examined for its uniqueness even from other liberation theologies.

The place to begin in understanding liberation theology is at the deepest level—liberation theology's driving motives. Karl Marx famously said that philosophy before him had attempted to understand the world while his goal was to change it. That approach is common to all liberation theologies—to change society more than understand God. They all think understanding God and changing society go together, but their priority is not intellectual discovery of new thoughts about traditional Christian doctrines. Their priority is promoting fundamental changes in the way society is ordered and that at its deepest levels. Deconstructing and reconstructing

Christian doctrine happens, to various degrees, as they examine social structures, but their first concern is to expose and protest against oppression that dehumanizes people and forge pathways toward human liberation from oppression within a Christian frame of reference.[6] That is why liberation theology can properly be called protest theology. Its goal is not objective knowledge; it is denunciation of the existing orders of society that oppress people and annunciation of new forms of life, of community, that liberate the oppressed and oppressors alike.[7] In other words, this theology intends to be prophetic, not scientific in the usual sense. There is no interest in cool, rational objectivity. In fact, liberation theologians, borrowing from the sociology of knowledge, do not believe that exists.

A second common feature is liberation theology's starting point, which is praxis. Gutiérrez famously defined liberation theology as "critical reflection on praxis."[8] "Praxis" means active involvement in a project, usually a social project. In the case of all liberation theologies, the praxis from which theology begins and on which it reflects is solidarity with the oppressed in their struggle for liberation, in other words, denunciation and annunciation. This is crucial to liberation theology's paradigm shift. Traditional theology begins with an attitude of faith in God's revelation or with a scientific examination of evidences for Christian belief (natural theology or foundational theology). Liberation theology is closest to the first approach—"faith seeking understanding." However, the faith it seeks to understand is liberating praxis. That is not to say that all liberation theologians are indifferent to orthodoxy, but all are more committed to orthopraxy—right practice defined as involvement with *God* in liberating the oppressed. What are oppression and liberation? For all liberation theologians, oppression is any social structure, whether formal or merely custom or social habit (e.g., racism), that dehumanizes people, that keeps

---

[6]This sketch of liberation theology's common features is drawn from deep and broad reading in these theologians and their commentators and critics. One book that does something like this is *Liberation Theologies: The Global Pursuit of Justice* by Alfred T. Hennelly, S.J. (Mystic, CT: Twenty-third Publications, 1997). This writer has been lecturing and writing on liberation theology for thirty years, has met and had conversations with most of the leading liberation theologians and has participated in liberation theology conferences.

[7]Gustavo Gutiérrez, *A Theology of Liberation: History, Politics and Salvation*, rev. ed., trans. Caridad Inda and John Eagleson (Maryknoll, NY: Orbis, 1973), 136.

[8]Ibid., 5.

them from being able to achieve their full humanity by denying them equality or basic human needs. Liberation is active freedom from such social structures and customs such that the oppressed become able to live fully equal human lives.

A third family resemblance of liberation theology is its context. According to all liberation theologians, theology should not be universal in the sense of the same everywhere. How can theology be the same in an affluent, all-white, North American suburb as in a South American barrio or favela where children go hungry and people live in subhuman conditions? Theology should be local, all liberation theologians agree. "Local" does not necessarily mean geographically limited; it can also mean focused on and for a particular group of people suffering a specific form of oppression. Liberation theologians do not deny that some doctrines are universal, but they would all say that universal doctrines must be made relevant to the needs of a particular social situation and understood through the eyes of those who suffer oppression. Put another way, doctrinal orthodoxy is finished. There is nothing to add to Christian orthodoxy except to make it relevant to oppression. An example is Brazilian Catholic theologian Leonardo Boff (b. 1938), who wrote *Trinity and Society* (1986) with an eye on the application of the doctrine of the Trinity to Latin American poverty. According to Boff, "the community of Father, Son and Holy Spirit becomes the prototype of the human community dreamed of by those who wish to improve society and build it in such a way as to make it into the image and likeness of the Trinity."[9] For Boff, only those involved in the struggle for a true community of equals can understand the Trinity correctly. But Boff would not argue that his formulation of the Trinity is universal; it is grounded in the Latin American liberation movement. If others find inspiration and guidance in it, fine. But he does not pretend to write in an ivory tower divorced from his social location and its struggles.

A fourth common feature is twofold: God has a "preferential option" for the poor and oppressed, and the poor and oppressed have a "privileged insight into God." This double-sided principle has been called the "epistemological break" that sets liberation theology apart from every other form of

---

[9]Leonardo Boff, *Trinity and Society*, trans. Paul Burns (Maryknoll, NY: Orbis, 1988), 7.

theology.[10] That God is on the side of the oppressed in their struggle for liberation from oppression is taken as a first principle, a basic fact, by all liberation theologians. Perhaps no liberation theologian has expressed it more clearly than Cone, who wrote, "Because God has made the goal of blacks God's own goal, black theology believes that it is not only appropriate but necessary to begin the doctrine of God with an insistence on God's blackness. The blackness of God means that God has made the oppressed condition God's own condition."[11] The other side of the coin (the fifth common feature) is that "those who want to know who God is and what God is doing must know who black persons are and what they are doing. . . . Knowing God means being on the side of the oppressed, becoming *one* with them, and participating in the goal of liberation."[12] Liberation theologians often point to the exodus in Israel's history to justify the idea that God favors the oppressed and sides with them in their struggle against oppression. This does not mean, however, that God hates oppressors or that only the oppressed can be saved. It means that knowledge of who God is and what God wills is inseparable from gaining the consciousness of the oppressed.

Sixth, all liberation theologians agree that there is a consciousness of oppression rooted in oppressed experience and that this is both a source and norm for theology. Ruether expresses this axiom of liberation theology from a feminist perspective:

> Human experience is the starting point and the ending point of the hermeneutical circle. . . . The uniqueness of feminist theology lies not in its use of the criterion of experience but rather in its use of *women's* experience, which has been almost entirely shut out of theological reflection in the past. The use of women's experience in feminist theology, therefore, explodes as a critical force. . . . Feminist theology makes the sociology of theological knowledge visible, no longer hidden behind mystifications of objectified divine and universal authority.[13]

Out of women's experience arises what Ruether calls the feminist critical principle: "Whatever denies, diminishes, or distorts the full humanity of

---

[10]Theo Witvliet, *A Place in the Sun: Liberation Theology in the Third World* (Maryknoll, NY: Orbis, 1985), 24ff.

[11]Cone, *Black Theology of Liberation*, 63.

[12]Ibid., 65.

[13]Rosemary Radford Ruether, *Sexism and God-Talk: Toward a Feminist Theology* (Boston: Beacon Press, 1983), 12.

women is . . . appraised as not redemptive. . . . [It] must be presumed not to reflect the divine."[14] Every liberation theology begins with the experience of a particular oppressed group; therefore liberation theology is, like liberal theology, theology from below. However, liberal theology did not identify the human experience that serves as theology's source and norm as that of an oppressed group. Liberation theology does. This rootedness in experience does not mean that liberation theology rejects the authority of Scripture or tradition; it means both are interpreted through the lens of an oppressed group's experience. But they all insist this is not unique to them; Scripture and tradition and even reason itself have always been interpreted through the lens of a privileged group's experience.

Seventh, all liberation theologies agree that liberation of the oppressed is a work of the oppressed themselves. They cannot and should not wait for the privileged group in society to extend equality; they should take it. Black theologians quote King, who wrote in his famous 1963 letter from Birmingham jail, "We know through painful experience that freedom is never voluntarily given by the oppressor; it must be demanded by the oppressed."[15] Whether it be black theology, Latin American liberation theology or feminist theology (or any other specific type), it seeks to be theology done by and for the oppressed themselves in support of oppressed people's struggle for liberation. Cone supported the black power movement of the 1960s partly because it was African Americans seeking to free themselves and not waiting for reform granted by the white majority.[16] Ruether was not appealing to the Catholic hierarchy or men in general to grant women equality; she was calling on women to rise up and take equality. (After all, women represent at least 51 percent of the population in most countries including the United States.) Gutiérrez wrote *The Power of the Poor in History* (1979), in which he stated, "The theology of liberation is rooted in a revolutionary militancy. . . . It is not the perspective of an elite, or of little groups, but is one of organizations—which the popular movement, and the Christian people within that popular movement, build for themselves."[17]

---

[14]Ibid., 18–19.

[15]Quoted in Diana L. Hayes, *And Still We Rise: An Introduction to Black Liberation Theology* (Mahwah, NJ: Paulist Press, 1996), 64.

[16]Ibid., 62–66.

[17]Gustavo Gutiérrez, *The Power of the Poor in History*, trans. Robert R. Barr (Maryknoll, NY:

Eighth, liberation theologians believe that social reform, such as religious political progressives advocate, is too slow and timid. Liberation theology is not the old social gospel; it is revolutionary. Of course, the moment someone mentions "revolution" people get nervous about violence. However, the late twentieth century saw several nonviolent revolutions such as in the Philippines, where the Catholic hierarchy gave permission to the people to oust Ferdinand Marcos in 1986. That they did by massive demonstrations and noncooperation. Marcos had to leave because powerful people sided with the poor and oppressed. No guns were fired. Revolution does not have to be violent. However, liberation theologians point out the irony of Americans celebrating their own violent revolution every July 4 while condemning other people's revolutions. The point here is that liberation theologians, including feminist theologians, are not calling for gradual reform of social orders; they are calling for radical change in social structures and customs. Gutiérrez called for a "cultural revolution" to bring about, insofar as possible, a society free of all injustice and exploitation. For him, nothing less will do than "the creation of a fraternal society of equals, in which there are no oppressors and no oppressed."[18] Black theologians and feminists also envision revolutionized social conditions free of racism and sexism, and they were willing to acknowledge that this will probably not happen without conflict of some kind. This revolutionary change in social conditions, liberation theologians argue, is part of salvation. "Holistic salvation" includes abolition of injustice.

The ways in which liberation theology represents a paradigm shift in theology should be obvious. Objectivity is not valued; involvement is the door to good theology. Correct doctrine or right understanding is not the goal; right praxis and social revolution are the goals. Knowledge is tied inextricably with oppressed consciousness and the struggle for liberation. Progress and development are not the keys to social change; revolution is. Another way in which liberation theology represents a paradigm shift is its response to modernity. For liberation theologians, the challenge of modernity is not so much unbelief as oppression, and the Enlightenment is viewed as mostly beneficial to the privileged classes. Gutiérrez acknowl-

---

Orbis, 1983), 205.
[18]Gutiérrez, *Theology of Liberation*, 159.

edges some benefits of the Enlightenment for all people but argues that "the grand claim of the Enlightenment" (like one of Lyotard's grand narratives) has been an ideology of the "bourgeois class."[19] (Here "bourgeois" means property-owning class as distinct from the poor.) It fostered individualism, private ownership and an overemphasis on reason. It raised questions and concerns that modern theology attempted to address intellectually. However, according to Gutiérrez,

> our question is not how to speak of God in an adult world. That was the old question asked by progressivist theology. No, the interlocutor of the theology of the liberation is the "*nonperson*," the human being who is not considered human by the present social order—the exploited classes, marginalized ethnic groups, and despised cultures. Our question is how to tell the non-person, the nonhuman, that God is love, and that this love makes us all brothers and sisters.[20]

Feminist theologians would add women to the list of human beings not considered fully human by the present social order. This is another aspect of liberation theology's paradigm shift—its response to modernity. To them, modernity has been a mixed blessing. It cracked open the door to equality for all (as in the French Revolution), but it did not push it open or even allow the oppressed to move through it. They all say that theology needs to stop obsessing about modern skepticism and unbelief (after all, all the intellectual answers have been given) and focus attention on the poor, the oppressed, left behind by modernity's failed project of progress.

James Cone Promotes a Black Theology of Liberation

Cone was not the first or only black theologian, but he became the most famous and influential spokesman for academic African American theology. Before Cone gained that status, several African American voices were raised in protest against racism and what Patrick Bascio calls *The Failure of White Theology* (1994). In 1969, just before Cone's *A Black Theology of Liberation* brought this form of liberation theology to public attention, a group of African American church leaders set forth a concise description of black theology:

---

[19]Gutiérrez, *Power of the Poor in History*, 176.
[20]Ibid., 193.

Black Theology is a theology of black liberation. It seeks to plumb the black
condition in the light of God's revelation in Jesus Christ, so that the black
community can see that the gospel is commensurate with the achievement of
black humanity. Black Theology is a theology of "blackness." It is the affirmation of black humanity that emancipates black people from white racism,
thus providing authentic freedom for both white and black people. It affirms
the humanity of white people in that it says No to the encroachment of white
oppression.[21]

The cultural context of black theology is the condition of continuing
racism against African Americans in the United States. It has its counterparts in other parts of the world and especially South Africa, where a distinctive form of black theology helped bring down apartheid. Generally
speaking, however, black theology arose in the context of the American
black power movement of the 1960s. The above statement expresses the
view of all black theologians, but Cone was not satisfied with it. He did not
think it went far enough in protesting white racism and oppression of
blacks in the United States. He was not interested in affirming the humanity
of white people or even in reconciliation between whites and blacks. His
distinctive declaration was that "God is black." In order for whites to
become pleasing to God they must identify with blackness by becoming
black with God.

Cone was born in Arkansas and grew up with the experiences of poverty
and racism. He graduated from traditionally black Philander Smith College
in Little Rock and then attended Garrett-Evangelical Divinity School of
Northwestern University in Evanston, Illinois. He earned his PhD from that
university and wrote his dissertation on the theology of Barth. After
teaching at a couple mostly African American colleges, he joined the faculty
of prestigious Union Theological Seminary in 1970 and became its Augustus H. Briggs Professor of Systematic Theology in 1977. His first book
was *Black Theology and Black Power*, followed closely by *A Black Theology
of Liberation*. Other major publications include *God of the Oppressed*,
Martin and Malcolm and America: A Dream or a Nightmare? (1992) and *The*

---

[21]"Statement by the National Committee of Black Churchmen, June 13, 1969," reprinted in
Black Theology: A Documentary History, 1966–1979, ed. Gayraud S. Wilmore and James H.
Cone (Maryknoll, NY: Orbis, 1979), 101.

Cross and the Lynching Tree (2011). Cone is an ordained minister of the denomination he grew up in, the African Methodist Episcopal Church. Over the years his voice has become less militant without diminishing his clarion call for justice especially for African Americans. He remains the father of black theology even as his voice is sometimes not completely in harmony with other black theologians such as the more moderate J. Deotis Roberts, Duke Divinity School professor of theology and author of *Liberation and Reconciliation: A Black Theology* (1971).

Other American black theologians of note, many of who were influenced by Cone, include Gayraud Wilmore, Joseph R. Washington, Albert B. Cleage, James H. Evans, Major Jones, Henry Mitchell and Willie Jennings. There is great variety among them, and some might not even consider themselves liberation theologians, but all have contributed to the phenomenon called black theology. Cone, however, towers over them all as the most influential voice of black theology.

It is impossible to understand Cone's black theology apart from the black power movement of the 1960s. While most progressive whites and many African Americans were watching King and his civil rights movement, a different African American movement was growing out of black rage against continuing injustices in American society. Those associated with the black power movement were not patient with reform; they wanted revolution as described above—not necessarily violent but radical change. Roberts describes the black power movement and its reception by black theology well:

> Black power, in affirming the empowerment of blacks, also speaks to the need for revolutionary social transformation. For black people to accept injustice and inhuman treatment passively is to partake in the system that enslaves them. The Christian faith is revolutionary in its very nature. It is the responsibility of Christians, aware of their stake in blackness in a white racist society, to keep the pressure on.[22]

Among the leaders associated with the black power movement were Malcolm X, Stokely Carmichael (1941–1998) and Eldridge Cleaver (1935–

---

[22]J. Deotis Roberts, *Black Theology Today: Liberation and Contextualization* (New York: Edwin Mellen, 1983), 158–59.

1998). All were high-profile protesters against racism in America in the 1960s and all sounded different from King, who talked about racial reconciliation and peace. It was into this volatile context of black rage that Cone stepped with *Black Theology and Black Power*, in which he declared that black power is "Christ's central message to twentieth-century America."[23] He defined black power as the "complete emancipation of black people from white oppression by whatever means black people deem necessary."[24]

For Cone, black theology builds on black power with the addition of God's revelation in Jesus Christ. Black theology is analyzing the black condition in light of that revelation and faith in it. In Jesus, Cone argued, black people find the "soul" necessary to destroy white racism.[25] The distinctive note, however, of black theology is the elevation of black experience to the status of a theological norm. Cone's critical principle even for theology was that "black theology is not prepared to accept any doctrine . . . which contradicts the black demand for freedom now."[26] In true liberation fashion, Cone defined theology as the "study of the being of God in the world in light of the existential situation of an oppressed community, relating the forces of liberation to the essence of the gospel, which is Jesus Christ."[27] In other words, for Cone, theology is not the attempt to devise a universal, coherent system of doctrines in line with tradition or accommodated to modernity. Theology is practical; it begins with the consciousness of a particular group of oppressed people and their struggle for liberation. It is for them and not for everyone. That is, it is not meant to address every conceivable question or fit the experience of every group. Cone defined black theology as "survival theology" "because it seeks to provide the theological dimensions of the struggle for black identity"[28] without which blacks in the United States cannot survive. It is survival theology and therefore speaks with passion.[29] And because it is survival theology it is for blacks only. He warned, "It will be difficult for white theologians to participate in

---

[23]James H. Cone, *Black Theology and Black Power* (New York: Seabury, 1969), 1.
[24]Ibid., 6.
[25]Ibid., 117.
[26]Ibid., 120.
[27]Cone, *Black Theology of Liberation*, 1.
[28]Ibid., 13–14.
[29]Ibid., 17–20.

this reality—because of their identification with unreality."[30] By "unreality" he meant the "camouflaged" racism of white privilege that he believed was endemic to American society. For all these reasons, black theology is different. Cone admitted it is "necessary to break with traditional theological concerns"[31] in order for African Americans to achieve liberation.

The difference of black theology appears also in Cone's description of theology's sources and norms. The first is "black experience," by which he meant "a life of humiliation and suffering."[32] But it is also "catching the spirit of blackness and loving it."[33] It is "a way of living in an insane environment."[34] "It comes from . . . carving out an existence in a society that says you do not belong."[35] Summing up, Cone says of black experience that it is

> a source of black theology because this theology seeks to relate biblical revelation to the situation of blacks in America. This means that black theology cannot speak of God and God's involvement in contemporary America without identifying God's presence with the events of liberation in the black community.[36]

Many white people protested that theology should be for all people, but Cone and other black theologians responded that "normal theology" has always been done by and for white people; white people just do not see that. Black people do.

Black history and black culture are two more sources and norms for black theology.[37] Cone acknowledges Barth's warning against identifying God's Word, revelation, with any culture. That is what led to the phenomenon of German (Nazi) Christians in the 1930s. But Cone dismisses that as not applying to oppressed culture. Instead he turned to Tillich's method of correlation so that "God's revelation comes to us in and through the cultural situation of the oppressed."[38] Theology properly done by and for African Americans, then, must relate God's Word positively to black

---

[30]Ibid., 20.
[31]Ibid.
[32]Ibid., 23.
[33]Ibid., 25.
[34]Ibid.
[35]Ibid.
[36]Ibid.
[37]Ibid., 25–29.
[38]Ibid., 28.

history and culture. But Cone did not mean it should use only black history and culture for the task of being relevant; it must look to them as sources of divine revelation. "God's word is our word; God's existence is our existence. This is the meaning of black culture and its relationship to divine revelation."[39]

What about Jesus Christ? Cone acknowledged Jesus as "God's revelatory event . . . in person."[40] "He is the event of God, telling us who God is by what God does for the oppressed. In Christian thinking the man Jesus must be the decisive interpretive factor in everything we say about God because he is the plenary revelation of God."[41] However, for Cone, Jesus Christ is not just a past event or person; he is "present today in the midst of all societies effecting his liberation of the oppressed."[42] What about Scripture? In what sense is it a source and norm for black theology? Cone affirmed that it is, but he also cautioned against identifying it with revelation itself or viewing it as supernaturally inspired or infallible. Its main value lies in its witness to Jesus Christ the liberator of the oppressed. "The meaning of scripture is not to be found in the words of scripture as such but only in its power to point beyond itself to the reality of God's revelation—and in America, that means black liberation."[43] Finally, what about tradition? Cone dismissed it as any source or norm for black theology except insofar as it provides examples and impetus for liberation. "Black theology is concerned only with the tradition of Christianity that is usable in the black liberation struggle. As it looks over the past, it asks: 'How is the Christian tradition related to the oppression of blacks in America?'"[44]

Cone summed up everything about his black theology's attitude toward sources and norms by referring to Jesus Christ: "The norm of all God-talk which seeks to be black-talk is the manifestation of Jesus as the black Christ who provides the necessary soul for black liberation."[45] This means that Christian God talk, at least for African Americans, must undergo radical revision. It must talk about God as liberator of the oppressed[46] and not just

---

[39]Ibid.
[40]Ibid., 30.
[41]Ibid.
[42]Ibid.
[43]Ibid., 32.
[44]Ibid., 35.
[45]Ibid., 38.
[46]Ibid., 60.

"the oppressed" as an abstract concept or any other oppressed than blacks. Cone did not deny that there are other oppressed groups, but he believed that the oppression of blacks in the United States is unique and must be the focus of all talk of God as liberator. Perhaps Cone's most famous claim is that "God is black."[47] This was a statement designed to make people pay attention, and many took it entirely too literally. What does it mean if not that God literally has black skin (which Cone did not mean)? Cone believed that traditional theology, especially in the United States, had identified God with whiteness; from his perspective "God is white" is what most people believe. That means most people tend to think of God as the justifier of white culture. By "God is black" Cone meant that God identifies with African Americans in their struggle for liberation from white racism.

It is important to allow Cone to explain for himself:

> The blackness of God, and everything implied by it in a racist society, is the heart of the black theology doctrine of God. There is no place in black theology for a colorless God in a society where human beings suffer precisely because of their color. The black theologian must reject any conception of God which stifles black self-determination by picturing God as a God of all peoples. Either God is identified with the oppressed to the point that their experience becomes God's experience, or God is a God of racism. . . . Because God has made the goal of blacks God's own goal, black theology believes that it is not only appropriate but necessary to begin the doctrine of God with an insistence on God's blackness. The blackness of God means that God has made the oppressed condition God's own condition.[48]

What ramifications does that have for the doctrine of God? Cone focuses attention on the doctrine of God's sovereignty. A black God cannot be imaged as the providential ruler of history. Cone rejected traditional Christian doctrines of God's sovereignty as controlling providence. If that is what providence means, Cone said, "it is difficult, if not impossible, to avoid the conclusion that all human suffering is in accordance with the divine plan. This would mean that the death of six million Jews, the genocide of Amerindians, the enslavement and lynching of blacks, and every other inhumanity, happened 'within the knowledge and will of God.' Only op-

---

[47]Ibid., 63.
[48]Ibid.

pressors can make such a claim."[49] For Cone, God's blackness means that God is not the ruler of history but the liberator of the oppressed. And God's omnipotence does not mean that God can do literally anything; it means "the power to let blacks stand out from whiteness and to be."[50]

Another shocking claim by Cone was that in order to know God savingly, "we must become black with God!"[51] Again, he did not mean becoming literally black as in skin color. Rather, "to receive God's revelation is to become black with God by joining God in the work of liberation."[52] When Cone talked about salvation and knowing God he was not talking about avoiding hell and going to heaven in the afterlife. Without in any way denying life after death, his focus was entirely on this life and changing this world.[53] It seems that Cone was suggesting that white people can become black. That would be their only hope for salvation, by which he meant being with God and doing God's will. In *God of the Oppressed* he held out a bare hope that some whites could become black:

> I am not ruling out the *rare* possibility of conversion among white oppressors . . . of white people becoming black. But conversion in the biblical sense is a *radical* experience, and it ought not to be identified with white sympathy for blacks or with a pious feeling in white folks' hearts. In the Bible, conversion is closely identified with repentance, and both mean a radical "reorientation of one's whole life and personality, which includes the adoption of a new ethical line of conduct."[54]

In other words, in order to be saved and know God truly, a white person must give up white privilege and enter into solidarity with oppressed African Americans in their struggle against racism.

Cone's Theology Creates Controversy and Raises Consciousness

Some of Cone's harshest critics have been other African American theologians and even some who identify with black theology. In *Liberation and Reconciliation* Roberts criticized Cone for rejecting reconciliation between

---

[49]Ibid., 80.
[50]Ibid., 81.
[51]Ibid., 65.
[52]Ibid., 66.
[53]See Cone's discussion of life after death in *Black Theology of Liberation*, 135–42.
[54]Cone, *God of the Oppressed*, 241.

whites and blacks as a goal of black theology. According to him, "authentic existence for blacks and whites can only be realized finally in reconciliation between equals in the body of Christ."[55] In another book, Roberts launched a full-scale critique of Cone for a variety of weaknesses he perceived in the latter's theology. Perhaps his harshest criticism is that "a moral paralysis remains inherent in Cone's theological method"[56] because he seemed to give permission to radical African American activists to use violence. "Young angry black militants were seeking moral guidance. They asked for bread; he cast them a stone."[57] By way of response to Roberts, Cone wrote, "A word about reconciliation too soon or at the wrong time to the oppressors only grants them more power to oppress black people."[58] In a new foreword to the 1986 edition of *A Black Theology of Liberation* Cone expressed regret for some omissions and oversights in the book but by and large stood by its strident language, claiming it was necessary given the depth of depravity of the "heresy" of white racism in the United States.[59]

Another African American criticism of Cone's theology came from women who accused him of overlooking the oppression of women even by black men. They pointed out that sexism is different from racism and just as harmful. Womanist theologian Delores Williams criticized Cone and other male black theologians for ignoring the unique experience of African American women in their constructions of black theology.[60] Throughout the 1990s and the first decade of the twenty-first century, womanist theology has combined insights of feminist theology with black theology to formulate a unique liberation theology based on black women's experience of oppression at the hands of white and black males and white women. Womanist theology places "black women's experience and ideas at the center of analysis."[61] Womanist theologians often look to the writings of Alice Walker, such as *The Color Purple* (1982), for inspiration. If experience

---

[55]J. Deotis Roberts, *Liberation and Reconciliation: A Black Theology* (Philadelphia: Westminster Press, 1971), 25.
[56]Roberts, *Black Theology Today*, 39.
[57]Ibid.
[58]Cone, *God of the Oppressed*, 243.
[59]Cone, *Black Theology of Liberation*, xv.
[60]Delores Williams, *Sisters in the Wilderness: The Challenge of Womanist God-Talk* (Maryknoll, NY: Orbis, 1993), 269.
[61]Quoted from Patricia Hill Collins in Hayes, *And Still We Rise*, 139.

of oppression and struggle for liberation are the appropriate contexts for theology, womanist theologians argue, then no group of people in the United States has more claim for privileged insight into God than African American women.

Naturally, Cone received harsh criticism from many white theologians and nontheologians. Perhaps the most symbolic example of that was widespread reaction to Jeremiah Wright's sermons quoted in a March 2008 national news report during Barack Obama's presidential campaign. Excerpts were taken from Wright's sermons that revealed influence by Cone. Some commentators claimed that Cone was a radical, anti-American, even Marxist theologian and that Wright was his disciple. For the most part, however, white theologians have been relatively silent about Cone. Stanley J. Grenz (1950–2005) expressed the views of many theologians by saying that

> Black theology elevated experience to the status of norm for theology. In this way, it merely reflected the methodology characteristic of the earlier liberalism, of course. But Black theology took this approach one step farther. Its norm was not universal human experience, but the specific experience of the Black community described in terms of oppression. As a result, Black theology became a massive reinterpretation program. The traditional Christian narrative of salvation and the theological categories traditionally used in its articulation . . . were cast in political-economic-social and specifically ethnic . . . terms, in contrast to the spiritual-cosmic and universally human die that beautified classical theology.[62]

Gustavo Gutiérrez Develops a Liberation Theology for Latin America

With good reason Gutiérrez has been called the father of Latin American liberation theology. He was building on the earlier works of people like Bartolomé de Las Casas (1484–1566), a Spanish priest who defended the Native Americans of South America against the conquistadors, who often considered them subhuman. Las Casas argued to the emperor of Spain that the native inhabitants were human, created in God's image, and therefore deserving of respect and justice. He linked salvation with social justice and pointed out that the Spaniards were placing their own salvation in jeopardy

---

[62]Stanley J. Grenz and Roger E. Olson, *20th Century Theology: God and the World in a Transitional Age* (Downers Grove, IL: InterVarsity Press, 1992), 209–10.

by treating the Indians cruelly.[63] Gutiérrez also built on the works of European political theologians Metz and Moltmann (see 8.a.). He was familiar with European theology, as he studied in Europe in the 1950s. In 1960 the Peruvian priest began teaching theology at the Catholic University in Lima. Throughout the coming decade he read deeply in radical social theory and participated in discussions with fellow Catholic priests and theologians from around South America. One person with whom he formed a friendship was Camilo Torres whom he urged not to join a guerilla group. Nevertheless, Gutiérrez was impressed with Torres's commitment to the poor and dream of a just society.[64]

During the 1960s events in both church and society propelled Gutiérrez to develop his theology of liberation, which he published in *A Theology of Liberation, The Power of the Poor in History, We Drink from Our Own Wells* (1984) and other writings. First was the Second Vatican Council held in Rome (1962–1965). Although it did not change Catholic doctrine, it did open the doors of the church to new insights into application and practice. No longer was all Catholic theology bound to Rome; it was possible for Catholic theologians to create indigenous theologies, unique to their own contexts, so long as they did not contradict Catholic dogma. A second development was the rise of national security states in many Latin American countries in reaction to events in Cuba under Fidel Castro. Many countries were led by new, militant, right-wing governments supported by the United States. These often persecuted and even killed dissidents, especially those who advocated socialism. Third was the series of meetings of Latin American bishops culminating in Consejo Episcopal Latinamericano (Latin American Episcopal Conference; CELAM II) in 1968. There the Catholic leaders shocked the world by criticizing the church's traditional alliance with ruling powers and condemning "institutionalized violence" against the poor and dissenters. The fourth development was the rise of base communities in many Latin American countries. These are small groups of mostly poor people who meet outside the confines of the institutional church, often led by a radical priest, to discuss the implications of the biblical message for

---

[63]Gutiérrez, *Power of the Poor in History*, 205.
[64]Robert McAfee Brown, *Gustavo Gutiérrez: An Introduction to Liberation Theology* (Maryknoll, NY: Orbis, 1990), 34.

their social situation and to support each other in community development. Occasionally these base communities generated revolutionary action committees, so they were considered subversive by many ruling military juntas.

By 1971 Latin America was in what Argentinian liberation theologian José Miguez Bonino (1924–2012) called a "revolutionary situation."[65] Gutiérrez's burning question was about the church's and theology's role in that situation. Unlike anywhere else in the world, the Catholic Church was the established church in most of the South American continent and throughout Central America. His concern was with the church and its response to structural poverty, institutionalized violence and the revolutionary situations many Latin American countries found themselves in. Thus, Gutiérrez sought to forge a distinctly Latin American theology, one relevant to the social context of Latin America in the 1970s. The first and most basic principle of his theology, then, is that good theology is always contextual; there is no universal theology. What is developed in Rome or Tübingen or New York may not be relevant or even true for Latin American Christians. A theology imposed from afar may even be oppressive. For Gutiérrez and other Latin American liberation theologians, such theologies are unsuitable for Latin Americans because

> here faith is lived by the poor of this world. Here the theological reflection seeking self-expression has no intention of being a palliative for these sufferings and refuses integration into the dominant theology. Here theology is ever more conscious of what separates it from the dominant theologies, conservative or progressive.[66]

Like Cone, Gutiérrez believes that the radical nature of an evil, in this case poverty and institutionalized violence, requires a theological response. For him it is similar to the situation in Germany in the 1930s. During that time of Nazi domination, Christian theology should have responded more specifically than it did. With a few exceptions, however, the dominant theology in Germany either ignored the situation or accommodated to it. It is impossible to understand Gutiérrez and other Latin American liberation theologians apart from this perception of their cultural context.

---

[65]José Miguez Bonino, *Doing Theology in a Revolutionary Situation* (Philadelphia: Fortress, 1975).
[66]Gutiérrez, *Power of the Poor*, 186.

The questions theology must address in Latin America, Gutiérrez believes, are different from the ones the dominant theologies of Europe and
North American have addressed. There, theology has been obsessed with
intellectual questions raised by modernity. The main one in the 1960s and
1970s was how to speak of God in a secular world. The task of Latin
American theology, in contrast, is not conditioned by the unbeliever's questions but by the question of the "nonperson": "the human being who is not
considered human by the present social order—the exploited classes, mar-
ginalized ethnic groups, and despised cultures."[67] That is not to say that
Gutiérrez or other Latin American liberation theologians reject everything
about theologies developed in other social contexts. In fact, as a Roman
Catholic, he borrows heavily from them and especially the *nouvelle théologie*
("new theology") of French Catholic theologians that helped bring about
the new openness to the world evidenced by the Second Vatican Council.
The influence of Karl Rahner (see 10.a.) is especially evident in his thought.[68]
The point here is not that Gutiérrez discarded or ignored everything of the
dominant theology or theologies developed outside of Latin American; the
point is that he argued for a culturally relevant theology, one developed by
Latin Americans themselves, even if partially borrowed from elsewhere.

One cannot understand Gutiérrez and other Latin American liberationists without understanding the nature of poverty in that part of the
world. At the time Gutiérrez wrote *A Theology of Liberation*, more than half
of children in Peru died before the age of five.[69] In Brazil, the top 2 percent
of landowners controlled 60 percent of the arable land whereas 70 percent
of the rural householders were landless. In Peru, workers who previously
supported six persons had to provide for eight with less than half their
former incomes. In El Salvador, a family of six needed $333 per year to
survive, but more than half the population earned less than that. Throughout
Latin America poverty had reached catastrophic levels. One priest turned
liberation theologian said he was in constant contact with persons "who
simply live by competing with the swine and the vultures for what they can

---

[67]Ibid., 193.
[68]Brown, *Gustavo Gutiérrez*, 25.
[69]Ibid., 52.

find in the garbage dumps."[70] As the poor grew poorer, the tiny rich minority prospered. Many who protested these conditions mysteriously disappeared or were assassinated; Archbishop Oscar Romero of El Salvador in 1980 was gunned down by a government-sponsored death squad while saying Mass in a church. The reason was his public call for young Salvadoran soldiers to refuse orders to shoot their fellow countrymen.[71] Gutiérrez concluded:

> What we are faced with is a situation that takes no account of the dignity of human beings, or their most elemental needs, that does not provide for their biological survival, or their basic right to be free and autonomous. Poverty, injustice, alienation, and the exploitation of human beings by other human beings combine to form a situation that the Medellín conference [CELAM II] did not hesitate to condemn as "institutionalized violence."[72]

In the face of this inhuman situation, the Peruvian theologian argued, a radical break with the socio-political-economic status quo is necessary.[73] Such a break was already in the works. Latin America was experiencing revolutionary ferment, so that, in Gutiérrez's words, "a broad and deep aspiration for liberation inflames the history of humankind in our day, liberation from all that limits or keeps humans from self-fulfillment, liberation from all impediments to the exercise of freedom."[74] The question, then, was not whether the church should get involved or take sides. The question, according to the liberation theologians, was whose side the church would take—that of the oppressors, as usual, or that of the poor and oppressed.

A basic principle of all liberation theology, according to Gutiérrez, is God's preferential option for the poor: "the poor deserve preference not because they are morally or religiously better than others, but because God is God, in whose eyes 'the last are first.' This statement clashes with our narrow understanding of justice; this very preference reminds us, therefore, that

---

[70] Quoted from Leonardo Boff in Dean William Ferm, *Profiles in Liberation* (Mystic, CT: Twenty-third Publications, 1988), 125.

[71] Brown, *Gutiérrez*, 39.

[72] Gutiérrez, *Power of the Poor*, 28.

[73] It is not possible here to give a detailed account of the liberation theologians' criticism of capitalism. For the best brief statement of it see Bonino, *Doing Theology in a Revolutionary Situation*, 21–37.

[74] Gutiérrez, *Theology of Liberation*, 18.

God's ways are not ours."[75] Preference for the poor means that even though God loves all people, he identifies with the poor, reveals himself to the poor and sides with the poor in a special way. Above all, it means that in the class struggle God sides with the poor against every oppressor who would exploit or dehumanize them. This basic principle determines the shape of the next: theology as critical reflection on praxis. For Gutiérrez and other liberation theologians theology begins and arises out of commitment to the liberation of the poor. That is what praxis means to them. Theological reflection, then, is bringing God's Word to bear on such Christian involvement on behalf of the poor in order to support and purify it. In many ways this understanding forms a reversal of classical theological method and of modernity's way of discovering knowledge. For liberation theologians, theological reflection is never detached, merely theoretical or objective. Gutiérrez and others, then, were staging another Copernican revolution in theological method involving an epistemological break from tradition and theology accommodated to modernity. Knowledge of God, they claimed, always involves active obedience in liberating the oppressed. Parallels with Cone's black theology are obvious here. According to Gutiérrez, "to know God is to work for justice. There is no other path to reach God."[76]

What is revelation for Gutiérrez and liberation theologians generally? And what role does Scripture play in theology? If praxis is the first act of theology, reflection is its second act. And, for Christian theology, reflection on praxis requires revelation. But revelation is more than the Bible. It encompasses the entire historical project of God's liberating activity in history. Liberation theology links God closely with history, avoiding speculation about God in himself. According to Gutiérrez, God's liberation of his people from bondage and oppression in the Old Testament forms the "theophany of God." God appears and enters history in the great events such as the exodus. In the New Testament a new dimension of God's relationship with history appears: "In Jesus Christ God not only reveals himself in history, he becomes history."[77] Of course, the Peruvian theologian did not mean that God and history merge; he was speaking of the incarnation as

---

[75]Ibid., xxxviii.
[76]Ibid., 10.
[77]Gutiérrez, *Power of the Poor*, 13.

the ultimate point of God's historical revelation and the point where God himself enters into history. Scripture is the primary source and normative record of the revelatory activity of God on behalf of the poor and oppressed. However, God's activity is not confined to the past; it is ongoing. Revelation continues. Gutiérrez was not talking there about new doctrines being revealed; he was speaking of the ongoing work of God in liberating people. Scripture forms one set of revealed truths, but "the deposit of faith" is not limited to it. On the contrary, revelation "lives in the Church where it rouses Christians to commitments in accordance with God's will and also provides criteria for judging them in the light of God's word."[78] Theology, then, is a hermeneutical circle that moves between praxis and reflection on praxis using Scripture, tradition and God's continuing liberating activity as norms.

Gutiérrez argued that too often Christianity has viewed salvation and Christian mission in purely spiritual terms—as paths to heaven that have nothing to do with changing this world. Against such spiritualizing, he talked about salvation as "integral liberation" and mission as "liberating praxis." Again, nothing he wrote or said denied the reality of heaven or salvation as reconciliation between God and the human person. He wanted to build on what theology had already determined about those matters by making salvation more holistic, applying it to all of life including the social world. However, Gutiérrez went beyond the gospel of "soup, soap and salvation" by saying that there can be no otherworldly encounter with God; God is either encountered in and through "conversion to the neighbor" or not at all.[79] True salvation is integral because it involves all dimensions of human existence. He was not interested in discovering the minimal requirements for entrance into heaven. Salvation, for him, is the activity of God and human beings working together to bring about the full humanization of all relationships. The concern of liberation theologians is that we all become "sisters and brothers"[80] by abolishing unjust social systems that oppress, exploit and alienate people. Gutiérrez made clear throughout his writings that, for him, as for most liberation theologians, this means abolishing capitalism and the system of private property that has resulted in

---

[78]Gutiérrez, *Theology of Liberation*, xxxiv.
[79]Ibid., 118.
[80]Gutiérrez, *Power of the Poor*, 64.

Latin America's extreme duality of wealth and poverty. Without baptizing socialism as a Christian ideology, *the* path to social salvation, he did recommend it as one necessary way to redeem the oppressive social systems of Latin America.

For Gutiérrez, Christian mission included more than saving souls. Rather, the mission of the church in Latin America is to transform society toward the kingdom of God. Solidarity with the poor in their struggle, teaching them to understand the true causes of their poverty ("conscientization") and supporting and encouraging popular efforts to throw off oppression are all means of salvation. According to Gutiérrez, "any effort to build a just society is liberating. And it has an indirect but effective impact on the fundamental alienation. It is a salvific work, although it is not all of salvation."[81] For many critics of liberation theology such a statement raised the question of violence. Does "any effort" include violence? Most liberation theologians, including Gutiérrez, believe that violence is never ideal, but as a last resort it may be a necessary means of bringing about justice—even for Christians. He preferred that any revolution be nonviolent, but he refused to criticize those who, like Guevara and Torres, found it necessary to participate in armed struggle against the violence of the established orders: "We cannot say that violence is all right when the oppressor uses it to maintain or preserve 'order,' but wrong when the oppressed use it to overthrow this same order."[82] The main means of Christian mission, however, he argued, are nonviolent prophetic denunciation of the oppressive structures of society and annunciation of God's will for total liberation from all that dehumanizes people—especially poverty.

Gutiérrez Sheds Light and Draws Criticism

Critics of Latin American liberation theology have been legion. For whatever reason, more criticism has been aimed at it than at black theology even though they are quite similar in terms of basic impulses. Some observers have questioned whether theology ought to be so totally contextualized. Would not a fully contextualized theology eliminate the basis for condemning torture or terrorism?[83] Does liberation theology close itself off

---

[81]Gutiérrez, *Theology of Liberation*, 104.
[82]Gutiérrez, *Power of the Poor*, 28.
[83]See Max L. Stackhouse, "Torture, Terrorism and Theology: The Need for a Universal Ethic,"

from outside criticism by claiming that theology is fully contextual? Others
have questioned whether the blame for Latin American poverty can be so
entirely laid at the feet of outsiders such as international corporations and
insiders such as military dictators and their oligarchies. Is it not possible
that some, if not much, of it results from conditions specific to the cultures
of Latin America?[84] Yet other critics question whether it is biblically or
theologically sound to say that God favors the poor, solely because they are
poor. One wrote that "when we accept the idea of a divine bias, we are being
unfaithful to our ministry to the whole people of God."[85] Some critics have
objected to liberation theologians' use of Marxism. Marxist categories such
as class warfare, they say, cannot be used as a tool of social analysis without
liberation theology being drawn into its atheistic view of history and humanity. Marxism's understanding of the economic causes of human alienation, for example, cannot be separated from Marx's own view of the human
person as the product of one's self-creation through work rather than as a
creature of God.[86]

Evangelical theologian J. Andrew Kirk offered an objection to liberation theology's method that applies to every form of it and not just its
Latin American manifestation. Kirk asked whether theory and reflection
can be made secondary to praxis. Does not right praxis presuppose some
view (theory and reflection) of what is right and what is wrong? And
does that not mean for Christians that Scripture, not praxis, must be the
ultimate source and norm? Kirk insightfully argued that in order to
avoid a new ideologizing of the Christian message (such as happened
with the German Christians in the 1930s), Gutiérrez's theological method
must be turned around. Some preunderstanding of right praxis versus
wrong praxis must set the stage for theological reflection, he noted. And
if our preunderstanding is not drawn from Scripture, it will come from
some ideology:

The Christian Century (October 8, 1986), 861–63.

[84]Michael Novak, *The Spirit of Democratic Capitalism* (New York: Simon and Schuster, 1982).
Criticism of liberation theology is scattered throughout this book.

[85]Sam A. Portaro Jr., "Is God Prejudiced in Favor of the Poor?" *The Christian Century* (April 24,
1985), 404–5.

[86]Wolfhart Pannenberg, "Christianity, Marxism and Liberation Theology," *Christian Scholar's
Review* 18:3 (March 1989): 861–63.

For this reason, we insist that the task of modern theology should be a consciously critical reflection on God's Word in the light of contemporary praxis of liberation. If this is not the order of our methodology then the phrase (in Gutiérrez's definition), "in the light of God's Word," ultimately becomes emptied of content.[87]

Kirk's point is that "right praxis ultimately depends on right theory."[88]

Many other questions have been raised about liberation theology such as whether it tends to reduce salvation to social transformation and whether it identifies God too much with history. Liberation theologians have not been eager to engage critics in dialogue; they assert that outsiders, especially people of privilege, cannot understand what is going on in their contexts and theologies. They also claim that theology should be judged by its fruits and not by the strength of its intellectual arguments.[89] Their defenders sometimes impute evil motives to those who question their orthodoxy. Robert McAfee Brown, for example, charged, "The church can suffer fools gladly, but it has a harder time with prophets, particularly when they threaten to interfere with profits."[90] Archbishop Camara famously declared that when he gave bread to the poor, people called him a saint, but when he asked why the poor have no bread, they called him a communist.[91] A major reason for liberation theologians' impatience with criticism is their commitment to the sociology of knowledge. To them, such criticism usually arises from those who do not suffer oppression and therefore have no consciousness of it or the urgency of liberating people from it.

As of this writing, Gutiérrez and other Latin American liberation theologians such as Boff and Jon Sobrino (b. 1938) are still writing and teaching, but by most accounts a crisis has occurred for their movement that shone so brightly in the 1970s and 1980s. Boff and Sobrino have been silenced by the Vatican for periods of time. Other major Latin American liberation theologians have passed from the scene, as have their main North American

---

[87]J. Andrew Kirk, *Liberation Theology: An Evangelical View from the Third World* (Atlanta: John Knox, 1979), 193.

[88]Ibid., 198.

[89]Gutiérrez, *Power of the Poor*, 198.

[90]Brown, *Gutiérrez*, 155.

[91]Quoted in John Dear, *Peace Behind Bars: A Peacemaking Priest's Journal from Jail* (Lanham, MD: Sheed and Ward, 1995), 65.

and European defenders such as Brown (1920–2001) and German theologian Dorothee Sölle (1929–2003). Without any doubt the Vatican has sought to reduce the influence of liberation theology, although Gutiérrez has escaped sanctions. At the same time Latin America itself has undergone profound changes both religious and secular. Pentecostalism has attracted a greater following among the poor than has liberation theology and its base communities. Some Latin American countries have experienced democracy and socialism. Also, the fate of the Sandinista regime in Nicaragua, led by revolutionaries steeped in liberation theology, diminished liberation theology's credibility in some people's eyes. Finally, the fall of world communism and the apparent triumph of Western-style democracy and capitalism have at least temporarily drawn attention away from liberation theology. Tombs concludes:

> During the 1990s, liberation theology lost its momentum as an organized theological movement and faced a crisis of relevance in the terminology of liberation. However, its commitment to the poor and oppressed and its methodological approach to theology remained highly relevant, and this is very likely to continue.[92]

Rosemary Radford Ruether Develops a Theology for the Women's Movement/Feminism

Ruether's Christian feminism goes far beyond seeking equality of women with men. This becomes apparent throughout her feminist writings but nowhere more clearly than in *Gaia and God*. There she identifies that from which both women and men need to be liberated as patriarchy. As she and other Christian feminists define it, patriarchy is a mentality and social system in which men's ways of living, including especially the needs for "invulnerable and dominating power over others," oppress not only women but also other men and nature. She writes:

> The "liberation of women" cannot be seen simply as the incorporation of women into alienated male styles of life, although with far fewer benefits, for this simply adds women to the patterns of alienated life created by and for men. . . . What is necessary is a double transformation of both women and

---

[92]Tombs, *Latin American Liberation Theology*, 292.

men in their relation to each other and to "nature." . . . It is the male rather than the female life-style that needs, however, the deeper transformation. Males need to overcome the illusion of autonomous individualism, with its extension into egocentric power over others.[93]

The liberation of women and nature from the typical male pattern of life means empowering women and more. It means achieving true interdependency of women and men and nature.[94] As concrete steps in such liberation from patriarchy, or as signs that it is happening, Ruether points to demilitarization and deep ecology. Her recommended path to those ends is the building of "strong base communities of celebration and resistance" in which people learn what it means to live completely equal, interdependent lives in harmony with the earth.[95] For Ruether, that is the path of revolutionary change.

Ruether was born in Georgetown, Texas, in 1936. Georgetown is a university town not far from Austin. She was raised in a humanistic home environment by a Catholic mother and an Episcopalian father. Her father died when she was twelve; then she and her mother moved to California, where the future feminist theologian grew up and gained her education. She graduated from Methodist-related Claremont Graduate School of Theology with a PhD in classics and patristics. Her first teaching position was at the historically African American Howard University's School of Religion. Then she taught at Methodist-related Garrett-Evangelical Divinity School of Northwestern University, Episcopal-related Pacific School of Religion (part of the Graduate Theological Union) and finally as visiting professor at Claremont. Throughout her teaching career she became known as one of the earliest advocates of liberation theology. Then she published her magnum opus, *Sexism and God-Talk*, which remains for many the bible of Christian feminist theology. Her other books include the aforementioned *Gaia and God*, *Women Church* (1987) and *Women and Redemption* (1998). One of her major accomplishment was the formation, together with other Christian feminists, of the Women Church movement beginning in 1983.

---

[93]Rosemary Radford Ruether, *Gaia and God: An Ecofeminist Theology of Earth Healing* (San Francisco: HarperSanFrancisco, 1992), 265–66.
[94]Ibid., 266.
[95]Ibid., 268–69.

Women Church is a network of women-led Christian liturgical communities patterned after the Latin American base communities. Men are welcome but normally are not allowed to lead. The purpose of the churches is to give women space to develop their own religious leadership.

Ruether's feminist theology, like feminist theology in general, developed in three distinct but not necessarily chronological steps. These remain permanent moments or aspects of Christian feminism in general. Ruether begins with a critique of the past—a "recovery of the dangerous memory of women's oppression" by the male patriarchal church and culture. The second step or moment seeks alternative biblical and extrabiblical traditions that support, in Ruether's characterization, "women's personhood, her equality in the image of God, her equal redeemability, her participation in prophecy, teaching and leadership."[96] Finally, Ruether sets forth her own method of theology, which includes revisioning Christian categories. "Every theological doctrine and concept had to be examined anew in light of the growing awareness that women had been oppressed in the church at least as systematically as in other parts of society."[97] Ruether outlined the task of feminist theology as clarifying the vision of the feminist community of faith and clarifying the criteria for testing what is authentic. Such reconstruction is necessary, she explained, because the primary source of feminist faith cannot be the church, tradition or Scripture. Rather,

> the patriarchal distortion of all tradition throws feminist theology back upon the primary intuitions of religious experience itself: namely, the belief in a divine foundation of reality which is ultimately good, which does not wish evil or create evil, but affirms and upholds our autonomous personhood as women, in whose image we are made.[98]

As Ruether and other feminist theologians look back over two thousand years of Christian history and even today they see a dark history of patriarchal oppression of women. For her and them, the entire history of Judeo-Christian tradition is marked by the invisibility and subjugation of women and their domination by men. Church fathers called women "defective males"

---

[96]Rosemary Ruether, "Feminist Theology in the Academy," *Christianity and Crisis* 45:3 (March 4, 1985): 59.

[97]Pamela Dickey Young, *Feminist Theology/Christian Theology: In Search of Method* (Minneapolis: Fortress, 1990), 13.

[98]Ruether, "Feminist Theology in the Academy," 61.

and blamed them for men's sins. Medieval theologians regarded women as "misbegotten males," and the Protestant Reformers did nothing to change the status of women in church or society. Even Barth considered woman second to man in the covenants of nature and grace.[99] Feminists like Ruether conclude that their analysis of Christian tradition illustrates its need to be purged of sexism before it can be useful. It reflects the pervasive sin of androcentrism, the worldview "in which men possess all dignity, virtue and power in contrast to women who are seen as inferior, defective, less than fully human, the alien, or 'other' in relation to the male human norm."[100] This androcentric world view infected even the Christian doctrine of God: "Insofar as Christianity has given to the symbolism of father and son a central, determinative role in shaping its theology and practice, it is androcentric."[101] According to Ruether, this androcentrism permeates the whole of Christian theology:

> Starting with the basic assumption that the male is the normative human person and, therefore, also the normative image of God, all symbols, from God-language and Christology to church and ministry, are shaped by the pervasive pattern of the male as center, the female as subordinate and auxiliary.[102]

When women with a feminist consciousness look at that tradition "an entire social and symbolic universe crumbles within and outside them. They recognize in the familiar the deeply alien."[103] They cannot be Christians without making fundamental alterations in it.

We should not assume that Ruether's and other feminist theologians' critique of tradition involves only rejection and condemnation. A major part of her and their task is the recovery of the lost stories of women. Ruether's *Women and Redemption* constitutes a sustained archeology of women's contributions to Christianity beginning with Jesus, who was, in Ruether's reconstruction, an iconoclast against all forms of hierarchy and domination including patriarchy.[104] From there she recounts the stories of women

---

[99]Ruether, *Sexism and God-Talk*, 94–99.

[100]Ibid., 173.

[101]Anne E. Carr, *Transforming Grace: Christian Tradition and Women's Experience* (San Francisco: Harper & Row, 1988), 136.

[102]Ruether, "Feminist Theology and the Academy," 59.

[103]Ibid.

[104]Rosemary Radford Ruether, *Women and Redemption: A Theological History* (Minneapolis: Fortress, 1998), 19.

mystics, reformers, Christian humanists, abolitionists and early modern feminists. For her, these examples of liberated women throughout church history function as a kind of "canon outside the canon" of Scripture. But Ruether's aim in developing her Christian feminism goes beyond critiquing tradition and rediscovering the forgotten history of Christian women. Rather, as Ruether points out, her aim is a total revolution against hierarchically structured culture: "Culturally, sexism defines the whole system of reality, from 'matter' to 'God.' One cannot challenge sexism without the dethronement of the cultural universe as an authentic and good model of life."[105] Her *God and Gaia* is a manifesto of such a cultural revolution. She calls for "a fundamental restructuring of all . . . relations from systems of domination/exploitation to ones of biophilic mutuality."[106] "What is necessary," she wrote, "is a double transformation of both women and men in their relation to each other and to 'nature.'"[107] "This change of consciousness is one that recognizes that real 'security' lies, not in dominating power and the impossible quest for total invulnerability, but rather in the acceptance of vulnerability, limits, and interdependency with others, with other humans and with the earth."[108]

How does Ruether reach her theological conclusions? How does feminist theology work? Ruether, like all feminist theologians, regards women's experience, as defined by feminists, as the center and norm of all theological reflection:

> The uniqueness of feminist theology lies not in its use of the criterion of experience but rather in its use of *women's* experience, which has been almost entirely shut out of theological reflection in the past. The use of women's experience in feminist theology, therefore, explodes as a critical force, exposing classical theology, including its codified traditions, as based on *male* experience rather than on universal human experience. Feminist theology makes the sociology of theological knowledge visible, no longer hidden behind mystifications of objectified divine and universal authority.[109]

---

[105]Ruether, *Sexism and God-Talk*, 178.
[106]Ruether, *God and Gaia*, 258.
[107]Ibid., 265.
[108]Ibid., 269.
[109]Ruether, *Sexism and God-Talk*, 13.

What does Ruether mean by "women's experience"? Here it is helpful to turn to another feminist theologian who explicates it more concisely and clearly. According to Pamela Dickey Young, women's experience differs from men's in five ways: Women experience their bodies differently; women have different socialized experiences; women now have feminized consciousness; women have different historical experience; and women have different individual experiences that can serve as catalysts for change.[110] Other feminist theologians have expressed that women's natures are more "transformative and person-centered" than men's.[111] Others have identified the unique aspects of women's experience as relationality, nondualism, intuitiveness and communality. Despite the differing descriptions, all feminist theologians agree that the primary experience of women is oppression at the hands of patriarchal society.

But why should either gender's experience be determinative for theology? Shouldn't theology's sources and norms be neutral and universal? Ruether vehemently rejected this suggestion with the retort that all theology so far considered standard and orthodox has been male-oriented. Men's experience has not only colored theology; it has determined the content and form. Feminist theology is drawing on women's experience, which has not been taken into account up until now. In true postmodern fashion, she denies that there is any gender-neutral, objective theological standpoint, and "one cannot wield the lever of criticism without a place to stand."[112] Drawing, then, on women's experience, Ruether expresses "the critical principle of feminist theology," which also implies a positive one: "What does promote the full humanity of women is of the Holy, it does reflect true relation to the divine, it is the true nature of things, the authentic message of redemption and the mission of redemptive community."[113] It is difficult not to see the parallels here with Cone's black theology and Gutiérrez's Latin American liberation theology.

Ruether does not rely solely on women's experience to defend her feminist critical principles. She also finds their source in the "prophetic-

---

[110]Young, *Feminist Theology/Christian Theology*, 53–56.
[111]Carr, *Transforming Grace*, 127.
[112]Ruether, *Sexism and God-Talk*, 18.
[113]Ibid., 19.

liberating tradition" of Scripture. In her estimation, theology makes use of numerous sources and norms—first and foremost women's experience but also Scripture, non-Christian pagan religions, marginal and "heretical" movements within Christianity, philosophies such as liberalism, romanticism and Marxism, and contemporary stories of women's oppression and liberation. However, the ultimate norm for interpreting what is divine revelation lies in the prophetic-liberating tradition of which Jesus is the historical paradigm. Thus, "feminist readings of the Bible can discern a norm within Biblical faith by which the Biblical texts themselves can be criticized. . . . On this basis many aspects of the Bible are to be frankly set aside and rejected."[114] The prophetic-liberating tradition is the vision of a completely egalitarian, nonhierarchical society unmarked by patterns of domination and submission. The employment of this norm for theology will result in an explicit critique of patriarchy, as well as the deepening and transformation of all "the liberating and prophetic visions" so that they include what they did not include—women.[115]

For Ruether, the central tenet of Christian theology needing transformation in the light of women's experience and the feminist critical principles is the doctrine of God. She believes it has been dominated by male-oriented dualism arising out of patriarchal images of society. "Dualism" divides what essentially belongs together and sets them over against each other in hierarchically arranged orders of good and evil, domination and subordination.[116] While claiming that males are not intrinsically evil, Ruether argued that men display a marked tendency toward psychic and social dualisms that women do not.[117] Insofar as theology has been dominated by male-oriented thinking, it has been characterized by a set of dualisms that have served to subjugate and dehumanize women, including nature/spirit, transcendence/immanence, soul/body, creation/redemption, male/female, good/evil. Dualism tends to assign a positive value to one side and a neg-

---

[114]Ibid., 23.

[115]Ibid., 32.

[116]This is a cursory summary of a key element of Ruether's critique of traditional theology in *Sexism and God-Talk* and other writings. One important passage where this critique of patriarchy as dualism is found is in chapter 3 of *Sexism and God-Talk*, "Woman, Body and Nature: Sexism and the Theology of Creation," 72–92.

[117]Ibid., 112.

ative value to the other. Dualist thinking has led to assigning negative value to women along with nature, body and even creation. Patriarchy specializes in dualism; it tends to see all of reality that way including God and world.

Like all feminist theologians, Ruether is critical of male imagery and language for God. It is obviously oppressive to women. But she wishes to go further and critique not only the father image for God but also any parent image of God as patriarchal, because it implies dualism and hierarchy: "Patriarchal theology uses the parent image for God to prolong spiritual infantilism as virtue and to make autonomy and assertion of free will a sin."[118] Searching for a nondualistic, nonpatriarchal reference for God, Ruether turned to Tillich's concept of God as the ground of being, which she prefers to call the "primal Matrix" or "God/ess." For her, God/ess is not a transcendent, personal being but "the transcendent matrix of Being that underlies and supports both our own existence and our continual potential for new being."[119] God/ess is no more to be identified with spirit, transcendence or maleness than with matter, immanence and femaleness. In fact, God/ess embraces all such dualities in a dynamic unity, so that there is no "great chain of being" with the divine at the top and inanimate nature at the bottom. Because of its unity with God/ess, all reality is radically equal.[120] Ruether's reconstructed doctrine of God is clearly a form of panentheism if not pantheism. In *God and Gaia* she comments:

> Ecofeminist theology and spirituality has tended to assume that the "Goddess" we need for ecological well-being is the reverse of the God we have in the Semitic monotheistic traditions; immanent rather than transcendent, female rather than male identified, relational and interactive rather than dominating, pluriform and multicentered rather than uniform and mono-centered. But perhaps we need a more imaginative solution to these traditional oppositions than simply their reversal, something more like Nicholas of Cusa's paradoxical "coincidence of opposites," in which the "absolute maximum" and the "absolute minimum" are the same.[121]

---

[118]Ibid., 69.
[119]Quoted in Mary Hembrow Snyder, *The Christology of Rosemary Radford Ruether: A Critical Introduction* (Mystic, CT: Twenty-third Publications, 1988), 107.
[120]Ruether, *Sexism and God-Talk*, 86–87.
[121]Ruether, *God and Gaia*, 247.

One hesitates to say "in other words," because Ruether's concept of God is vague at best. However, it seems safe to say her God/ess is not very much like the God of traditional Christian tradition, and that is her point.

One of Christian feminist theology's main challenges is to explain how a male Savior can be the Savior of women. Most of them regard Jesus Christ as a paradigm of true humanity—humanity freed of the evil of patriarchal attitudes and behavior patterns. Ruether rises to the challenge again using Tillich's concept of Christ as the "new being." Like him, she rejects the classical Christology of Chalcedon (hypostatic union), which, she wrote, is neither a consistent evolution of Jewish messianic hope nor "a faithful rendering of the messianic announcement of Jesus of Nazareth and his views of the coming Reign of God."[122] In its stead, in a manner reminiscent of classical liberal theology, she elevated her rendition of the historical Jesus as a first-century feminist: "Once the mythology about Jesus as Messiah or divine *Logos*, with its traditional masculine imagery is stripped off, the Jesus of the synoptic Gospels can be recognized as a figure remarkably compatible with feminism."[123] In her account, Jesus was the liberator who denounced the power and status relationships that defined privilege and deprivation.[124] He did not proclaim himself but pointed beyond himself to the new humanity to come, the redemptive humanity enjoying perfect community free of dualisms and hierarchies. Ruether identified the new humanity with "Christ." Thus, Jesus was the Christ only in the sense that he represented the new humanity and served as its forerunner. Consequently, "Christ, as redemptive person and Word of God, is not to be encapsulated 'once-for-all' in the historical Jesus. The Christian community continues Christ's identity."[125] One has to wonder if Women Church is, then, "Christ."

The radical nature of Ruether's theology is illustrated in a "Feminist Midrash" (interpretive story) at the beginning of *Sexism and God-Talk*. The story is a highly imaginative and symbolic account of the history of salvation involving a female deity, "the Queen of Heaven," who is above Yahweh, and a figure who appeared to Mary Magdalene after Jesus rose from the dead

---

[122]Ruether, *Sexism and God-Talk*, 116.
[123]Ibid., 135.
[124]Ibid., 137.
[125]Ibid., 138.

and disappeared—a figure "taller and more majestic [than Jesus] . . . regal and yet somehow familiar, a woman like [Mary] herself."[126] The figure tells Mary that she is now the "continuing presence of Christ" who will "continue the redemption of the world."[127] The midrash closes with what cannot be brushed off as mere story, because it clearly intends to provide its interpretation in theological idiom: "With Jesus' death, God, the heavenly Ruler, has left the heavens and has been poured out upon the earth with his blood. A new God is being born in our hearts to teach us to level the heavens and exalt the earth and create a new world without masters and slaves, rulers and subjects."[128] Clearly, Ruether's feminist theology is much more than a development within orthodox Christianity committed to the goal of women's equality. On the contrary, to her it necessarily includes radical, sweeping revisions in every area of Christian thought and life.

Ruether Sparks Interest and Becomes a Lightning Rod

Even most critics have agreed that feminist theology has done a great service to the Christian community by pointing out the evils of androcentrism, patriarchy and sexism. Its theologians, including especially Ruether, have often helped the churches to become more inclusive and therefore truer to the image of God as both male and female and to the universality of the gospel. In spite of these gains, however, critics often point out that this theology goes too far in its radical revision of the Christian symbols and threatens a new schism within the body of Christ between women and men. Should there be a theology based entirely on the experience of one group of people? Is it true that no theology can be relevant to both men's and women's experiences? Has Ruether created a new dualism between male and female with her theology based on women's experience and controlled by a presupposed feminist critical principle? These are obvious questions, and they echo ones raised to black theology and Latin American liberation theology. Are these special-interest theologies that can guide the whole church? Are they perhaps overly contextualized? Or, should they perhaps be viewed as protest theologies, not meant to replace all traditional theology but to supplement and provide correction to them? What be-

---

[126]Ibid., 8.
[127]Ibid.
[128]Ibid., 11.

comes of them if the evils they identify are overcome? What is theology
after racism or institutionalized violence that keeps the poor in poverty and
patriarchy? Presumably these three theologians do not look that far ahead;
the situations they are protesting are so severe and prolonged that there is
no need, they might say, for such long-range thinking.

One especially incisive critic of feminist theology is herself a feminist
theologian. Young, referred to earlier, argued that in spite of its great service
in recovering women's experience as a source of theology, feminist theology
has by and large gone too far in cutting itself loose from the Christian tradition. It has allowed principles from outside that heritage to become controlling norms for its account of what is truly Christian. The problem, she
believes, should be obvious:

> Basically the person employing the term [Christian] can use it however he or
> she wishes. This means, then, that whereas feminist theologians may claim
> the use of "Christian" for whatever liberates women, if there is nothing that
> can be derived from the tradition itself that can be used normatively to argue
> that this is what Christianity is all about, then others can use the tradition in
> less liberating ways.[129]

In other words, even though Ruether and other feminist theologians
appeal to the person of Jesus as warrant for their doctrinal reformulations,
they sacrifice the right to call their theologies Christian when they hold
women's experience—as defined by feminists—as a norm that controls
what in his life and teachings is normative and what is not. Young believes
this methodology leads toward relativism: "If one appeals only to a member's self-identification as a criterion for deciding what is and what is not
part of a given religious tradition, one is left with a relativism that must
accept all without judgment or discernment."[130] In short, women's experience cannot serve as the ultimate norm for something that claims to be a
form of Christian theology. Without the objective norms of the transcul-
tural and gender-transcending Word of God and at least general outlines of
the Christian tradition of orthodoxy, Christianity can become whatever any
individual or group says it is.

---

[129]Young, *Feminist Theology/Christian Theology*, 74.
[130]Ibid., 77.

Ruether's doctrines of God and Christ illustrate the inherent weakness in its methodology. Her and other feminist theologians' reformulations of these doctrines seem to hold little in common with classical Christianity. Because hierarchy is assumed to be patriarchal and therefore evil, God (or God/ess) cannot be Father or even Parent. Because dualism is a male-oriented, oppressive way of regarding reality, God (God/ess) and the world cannot be absolutely different. Elizabeth Achtemeier, a noted biblical scholar and theologian, argued that this identification of God or God/ess with the world will ultimately lead feminist theology into a religion different from Christianity, if it has not done so already:

> No religion in the world is so old as is this immanentist identification of God with creation. It forms the basis of every nonbiblical religion, except Islam; and if the church uses language that obscures God's holy otherness from creation, it opens the door to corruption of the biblical faith in that transcendent God who works in creation only by his Word and Spirit. Worshippers of a Mother Goddess ultimately worship the creation and themselves, rather than the Creator.[131]

These are harsh words, but they come from another woman theologian. Feminist theologians may say both she and Young lack feminized consciousnesses. They do not think all women are automatically in touch with women's experience.

Liberation Theologies Become the First Postmodern Theologies

All forms of liberation theology, black, Latin American, feminist, share certain characteristics. One of them most pertinent to this book's theme is their reactions to modernity. Whether they should be categorized as postmodern or not, there is definitely in them a postmodern impulse.[132] Their epistemology is nonfoundationalist. Their focus is local and contextual. They make use of the sociology of knowledge. They do not believe in the myth of progress. Revolution, not reform, is their goal. Most importantly, perhaps, they are more interested in deconstruction than reconstruction.

---

[131]Elizabeth Achtemeier, "The Impossible Possibility: Evaluating the Feminist Approach to Bible and Theology," *Interpretation* 42 (January 1988): 57.

[132]Some scholars of modern theology do categorize liberation theology as postmodern. See Terrence W. Tilley, ed., *Postmodern Theologies: The Challenge of Religious Diversity* (Maryknoll, NY: Orbis, 1995), 119–29.

To be sure, they all engage in some limited reconstruction of Christian doctrines, but their guiding impulse is unmasking the oppressive tendencies of traditional Christianity and showing how it has served as an ideology to support the vested interests of privileged and powerful people. The idea that postmodernism is necessarily relativistic is a myth. None of the liberation theologians are sheer relativists. They all envision an absolute that can be called justice, and they all are concerned to show how far short of it all past and present social arrangements, including Christian ones, fall. Above all, modernity is not their context except insofar as it has contributed to oppression. They all tend to see it as at best a mixed blessing.

Finally, liberation theologians are not interested in the question of how to reconcile the natural sciences with Christianity. They prefer to leave that to others, and they tend to see it as a distraction from what should be the main concern of contemporary Christianity, which is using social science to move Christianity toward comprehensive liberation. It is difficult even to find any discussion of science (except the social sciences) in their writings. This reveals that, like some modern theologians before them, liberation theologians believe the essence of Christianity is not doctrine but ethics. It is not about explaining the way things are in the universe and nature; it is about explaining how things ought to be. In this way, the spirit of Ritschl and classical liberal theology, including the social gospel, lives on in them.

10

CATHOLIC THEOLOGIANS
ENGAGE WITH MODERNITY

Pope John XXIII was supposed to be a mere caretaker of the Catholic Church until the cardinals could agree on someone younger. He was unexpectedly elected in 1958 and died in the middle of the event for which he is most remembered—the Second Vatican Council (1962–1965). Vatican II was the first ecumenical council since Vatican I in the 1870s. During that time, the Catholic hierarchy had restrained Catholic modernism and all attempts by Catholic scholars to come to terms with modernity (see 2.d.). However, slowly, throughout the twentieth century, a new type of Catholic theology developed that fit neither the category "modernism" nor "integralism" (traditional). It has been called the *nouvelle théologie*, or new theology, because it was created primarily in France and its main formulator was a French Catholic theologian named Henri de Lubac (1896–1991). De Lubac was influenced by Blondel (see 2.d.). Like Blondel, de Lubac wanted to emphasize the intrinsic work and presence of grace in human beings in contrast to the emphasis on its extrinsic nature in much scholastic Catholic theology. (These concepts are discussed in chapter 2, so they will not be explained here.)

Nouvelle théologie is a broad category that encompasses many progressive Catholic theologians. It spawned new research into the theology of

Thomas Aquinas, the medieval Angelic Doctor whose theology has been considered official for Roman Catholics for centuries. It also sought to discover ways in which the best of modern scholarship and Catholic biblical studies and theology could interact. It was not, however, modernist in the same sense as the theologies of Loisy or Tyrrell that were, even to advocates of the *nouvelle théologie*, too accommodated to modernity. Throughout the post–World War II era, Catholic theologians and biblical scholars and some members of the magisterium (hierarchy) pressed gently for reforms in the church's approach to the modern world. No one expected Pope John XXIII to bring about such reforms; everyone expected him to hold down the fort, so to speak, until the cardinals and a future pope could decide which direction to take. However, the new pope called a new council, meaning that all bishops were invited to Rome to deliberate about the future direction of the church. Like almost everything else of the 1960s the council was revolutionary, not in the sense of changing dogmas or overthrowing tradition but in the sense of remodeling or updating the church (*aggiornamento*). Included was a new openness to modernity and Catholic use of modern methods of scholarship. In many people's eyes, the council threw open the windows of the church and let the fresh breezes of the modern world blow in. By all accounts Vatican II was the beginning of a new era for Roman Catholics around the world.

Two of the leading Catholic theologians at the council were Karl Rahner (1904–1984) of Austria and Hans Küng (b. 1928) of Switzerland. Rahner taught theology at the University of Innsbruck; Küng taught theology at Tübingen. The former was an elder statesman of Catholic theology and, after the close of the council, produced a progressive, modern interpretation of the faith. The latter was just beginning to show his abilities and true colors. In the wake of Vatican II he styled himself as a modern Luther continuously challenging the church to continue further and faster with openness to modernity. Although both can be considered progressives in contemporary Catholic theology, Rahner was the more conservative (or at least cautious) of the two.

Both Rahner and Küng sought to bring heaven and earth together without losing the distinction between them. That is, much of their theological energies were consumed with developing the immanence of transcendence. They believed that traditional Catholic theology had been too dualistic in its approach to the basic problems of nature and grace, transcendence and immanence. In their own ways each sought to overcome that perceived dualism and do justice to the presence of God's Spirit in the world and in humanity. The influences of Rahner and Küng and other offspring of the *nouvelle théologie* fostered tremendous changes in European and American Catholic theology after Vatican II. However, under John XXIII's successor, Paul VI (1963–1978), a reaction began to set in. The conservative reaction has become increasingly powerful and intense during the tenures of John Paul II (1978–2005) and Benedict XVI (2005–2013). In the midst of all this turmoil and confusion within the church, Rahner and Küng have stood out. They have been regarded as visionaries and trailblazers courageously pointing the direction for the future. Moderates look more to Rahner while more liberal and radical progressives look to Küng. Conservatives are wary of both.

A third modern Catholic theologian, one who reacted more against modernity than accommodated to it, was Hans Urs von Balthasar (1905–1988), who was not invited to Vatican II but whose theology influenced the council nevertheless. Balthasar was, like Küng, Swiss. But there the similarity ends. Like Rahner, he was influenced by and is considered part of the *nouvelle théologie* movement in Catholic theology. His reputation and influence began to wax after his death. During the first decades of the twenty-first century his name is being mentioned as frequently as, if not more often than, Rahner's and Küng's when scholars discuss influential twentieth-century Catholic thinkers.

10.A. KARL RAHNER FINDS GOD IN HUMAN EXPERIENCE

Rahner was criticized many times for the high level of abstraction in his theological writings. He once received an anonymous cartoon that depicted him as a "theological nuclear physicist" lecturing to a group of fascinated "multipliers"—people who take his message in the next frame of the cartoon to a group of "popularizers." After the lecture, one of the popularizers stands in a pulpit and expounds Rahner's message to a congregation. Jesus stands to one side listening and says, "I don't understand." The intended point was that Rahner's theology is too difficult to explain—even to the person it is supposed to be about! Something inevitably gets lost in the translation. Rahner's response when reminded of this humorous criticism was, "That's just the way it is when you're a theology teacher."[1]

In spite of the abstruse nature of much of his theology, Rahner has become the most influential Catholic theologian of the twentieth century and is still widely read and discussed, even by Protestants, in the twenty-first century. According to one of his interpreters, he functions as "a kind of universal god-father to contemporary Roman Catholic theology."[2] He has been compared with Thomas Aquinas, Schleiermacher, Barth and Tillich. By the time of his death his influence had reached into nearly every Catholic seminary and university theology faculty in the world, as well as into the Vatican itself. It is impossible to understand the changes that took place in Catholic theology in the latter half of the twentieth century without paying attention to Rahner's role in making them possible. One example is his leadership role in the Second Vatican Council. His activities there gained him a worldwide reputation as an advocate of cautious change. Certain of his unique concepts worked their way into several of the sixteen declarations passed by the council. Rahner became recognized as "the most powerful man at the Council."[3]

Rahner's is a mediating theology. That is, his theology seeks a middle ground between two extremes that have been at war with each other in the Catholic Church for more than a century. Many people are attracted to his thought precisely because of this mediating tendency. One extreme Rahner sought to avoid is integralism—the approach that seeks to preserve the integrity of traditional Catholicism at all costs. While integralism provides a safe harbor for theology in the storms of modernity, Rahner found it a haven of false security and irrelevance. At the other extreme is modernism—the approach that seeks relevance to the point of accommodation to modern, secular culture. Rahner strived valiantly to steer his theology between these two extremes. In an interview he expressed the essence of his

---

[1]Karl Rahner, *I Remember: An Autobiographical Interview with Meinhold Krauss*, trans. Harvey D. Egan, S.J. (New York: Crossroad, 1985), 19.
[2]George Vass, *The Mystery of Man and the Foundations of a Theological System*, vol. 2 of *Understanding Karl Rahner* (Westminster, MD: Christian Classics. 1985), 118.
[3]Herbert Vorgrimler, *Understanding Karl Rahner: An Introduction to His Life and Thought*, trans. John Bowden (New York: Crossroad, 1986), 99.

approach: "Theology must be so presented that it encourages a genuine dialogue between the best of traditional thought and exigencies of today."[4]

Rahner rises to fame and influence. The future theologian was born in
the Black Forest city of Freiburg in Germany. His family was devoutly
Catholic, and he followed his brother Hugo into the Jesuit order. The order
assigned him to become a professor of philosophy and sent him to several
schools, eventually to the University of Freiburg, where he studied under
Heidegger. His dissertation on Thomas Aquinas's theory of knowledge was
rejected by the Catholic faculty because they found it too heavily influenced
by Heidegger. Eventually it was published as *Spirit in the World* (1939), his
first philosophical book, and received high acclaim as a work of genius. The
young German scholar began his teaching career at the University of Innsbruck, which was closed by the Nazis during World War II. Eventually he
returned and lectured at the reopened Catholic school until 1964, when he
moved to the University of Munich. After a falling-out with other faculty
members he relocated to the University of Münster, where he taught dogmatic theology. He retired from teaching and returned to Munich, where he
remained at the Jesuit house near the university until just before his death.

Even in retirement Rahner was extremely busy. He traveled extensively,
speaking at ecumenical dialogue events and giving advice to theological
councils, conferences, cardinals and popes. The size of his written output
rivals that of Barth and Tillich. By the time he died more than sixteen
hundred books and articles had been published under his name. His most
important articles were collected and published in a twenty-three-volume
set titled *Theological Investigation* (1982–1992), which contains more than
nine thousand pages. He also wrote a one-volume systematic theology near
the end of his life, *Foundations of Christian Faith* (1978), which provides an
excellent introduction to his life's work by concisely summarizing its major
methods and themes. When asked to formulate briefly its purpose Rahner
provided an exquisitely succinct summary of his entire theology:

> I really only want to tell the reader something very simple. Human persons
> in every age, always and everywhere, whether they realize it and reflect upon

---

[4]*Karl Rahner in Dialogue: Conversations and Interviews, 1965–1982*, ed. Paul Imhof and Hubert
Biallowons, trans. Harvey D. Egan (New York: Crossroad, 1986), 22.

it or not, are in relationship with the unutterable mystery of human life that we call God. Looking at Jesus Christ the crucified and risen one, we can have the hope that now in our present lives, and finally after death, we will meet God as our own fulfillment.[5]

Rahner explains the transcendental method of theology. Rahner's theology was a response to the secular loss of the transcendence of God stemming from modernity. The forces of extreme immanence that led to such phenomena as secular theology and death of God theology (see chap. 7) were recognized by Rahner long before their full manifestation in the 1960s radical theologies. His entire career was a struggle against the common idea that one had to choose between the majesty and sovereignty of God on the one hand and the autonomy and freedom of humans on the other hand. He expressed his lifelong conviction by declaring that "the dilemma of the 'immanence' or 'transcendence' of God must be overcome without sacrificing the one or the other concern."[6] His theological method reflects this conviction. He sought to show that ordinary human experience is unintelligible without the transcendent, holy mystery called God and that the holy mystery of God must be encountered and known in and through the historical environment people experience in daily life. The key to understanding Rahner's approach to theology is his "transcendental method." Because this method is so philosophical, it is best to look first at his attitude toward philosophy.

Like Tillich and unlike Barth, Rahner considered philosophy an essential moment or aspect of theology's work. The place for the involvement of philosophy in theology lay in what Rahner called "fundamental theology," which "comprises the scientific substantiation of the fact of the revelation of God in Jesus Christ."[7] In other words, fundamental theology constructs the foundations for dogmatic or systematic theology by rationally justifying belief in God's revelation in Jesus. It attempts to show through philosophical reflection on human experience that belief in this revelation is not arbitrary or a sheer leap of faith but rests on sound intellectual grounds. Ultimately,

---

[5]Ibid., 147.

[6]Karl Rahner, *Foundations of Christian Faith: An Introduction to the Idea of Christianity*, trans. William V. Dych (New York: Seabury, 1978), 87.

[7]Karl Rahner, *Hearers of the Word*, trans. Michael Richards (New York: Herder and Herder, 1969), 17.

then, fundamental theology's purpose is to make Christian belief possible with intellectual honesty.[8] The basic tool of Rahner's fundamental theology is "transcendental reflection" on human experience as "open to receive revelation." Humans are not only parts and products of the natural world; they are also oriented toward an infinite, mysterious horizon of being that Christians know as God. In other words, human beings are transcendent.[9] They transcend nature and themselves in every act of questioning and thinking. They are not closed in on themselves but open toward, oriented to and receptive of divine revelation. To demonstrate this philosophically was Rahner's great task, one that consumed most of his theological energy.

Rahner borrowed his tool of transcendental reflection from modern philosophers such as Kant, Heidegger and Joseph Maréchal (1878–1944). Transcendental reflection seeks to discover the necessary conditions for known facts. It asks, given the undeniable reality of a particular phenomenon, what must be real in the mind or the universe for it to exist. What are its necessary a priori conditions? A crude illustration of this mode of reflection is science's discovery of the planet Neptune. Scientists deduced its existence from observing certain irregularities in the movements of Uranus that could be explained only by the existence of an unseen planet. Through a kind of transcendental process they knew about Neptune before seeing in through a telescope in 1846.[10] The point of transcendental reflection in philosophy is similar: to discover the preconditions for human knowledge and experience, or, in Rahner's words, to ask, "What is the a priori transcendental condition for the possibility of [human] subjectivity?"[11]

Rahner focused attention on what he called "transcendental experiences" to show that humans are naturally oriented toward God. These are ordinary, universal human experiences such as questioning the meaning of life. These experiences show that God is not alien to human nature but an intrinsic part of it as the necessary condition for them. In Hearers of the Word the Jesuit theologian focused on the phenomenon of human cognition—the

[8]Rahner, Foundations, 12.

[9]Rahner, Hearers, 53.

[10]Michael J. Buckley, "Within the Holy Mystery," in A World of Grace: An Introduction to the Themes and Foundations of Karl Rahner's Theology, ed. Leo J. O'Donovan (New York: Seabury, 1980), 34.

[11]Rahner, Hearers, 56.

experience of knowing a thing as a thing—in order to establish metaphysically that some relationship to the infinite necessarily precedes any knowledge of finite things. Forming any intellectual judgments about things—drawing conclusions about them—necessarily involves setting things apart from oneself and yet seeing them in relation to oneself. It also involves separating them from, yet seeing them in relation to, the whole of reality. To know a thing, which is different from simply seeing or feeling it, is to transcend both oneself and the thing in an act of abstraction that cannot be explained by nature alone.[12] Abstraction, then, is the uniquely human intellectual act of forming concepts about things. It is not merely sensing them or remembering them (animals are capable of both) but also recognizing them as particular cases of classes of things. One sees a number of beings and interprets them as human or questions their humanity. For Rahner, that phenomenon is a mysterious human capacity that signals something transcendent—a relationship to Being itself, to the whole of reality. The necessary background for such an act is the whole of reality. But the whole of reality is not a thing. It cannot be comprehended but exists only as an infinite horizon toward which humans move in their subjectivity.

What Rahner was attempting to establish in *Hearers of the Word* was a unique and mysterious human capacity that cannot be explained by thinking of humans as highly evolved animals, just products of nature. He spoke of it as

> a *capacity* of dynamic self-movement of the spirit, given *a priori* with human nature, directed towards all possible objects. It is a movement in which the particular object is, as it were, grasped as an individual factor of this movement towards a goal, and so consciously grasped in a pre-view of this absolute breadth of the knowable.[13]

Because the "absolute breadth of the knowable" cannot be known by ordinary human cognition except as a mysterious absolute horizon, it must reveal itself. Otherwise it remains a sheer mystery, and the meaning of particular things remains ultimately unintelligible. At this point Rahner introduces God into his fundamental theology. Metaphysical-transcendental reflection

---

[12]Ibid., 57.
[13]Ibid., 59–60.

on human subjectivity was not meant to be any sort of proof of God's existence. It was designed to be a proof of a human capacity for divine revelation. Without the self-revelation of the infinite horizon of knowing and being toward which the human person is inwardly oriented, all things would be ultimately meaningless. Rahner considered his phenomenology of human transcendence proof that human nature is spirit, as well as matter, and that a certain openness to God forms the inner core of that spiritual nature.[14] From this, Rahner drew the conclusion that "man is at least the one who must listen for a revelation from a free God speaking in *human words.*"[15]

Rahner called this natural transcendence of humanity its *potentia oboedientialis*—potential for obedience—to a possible revelation.[16] He believed that a purely philosophical, transcendental inquiry into the structure of human experience could show that it is naturally inclined toward receiving God's Word. The *potentia oboedientialis* means that "man is that existent thing who stands before the free God who may possibly reveal himself."[17] So strong is this potency that Rahner considered it a kind of knowledge of God imbedded within human nature itself. In every act of cognition, in every transcendental experience in which humans reach out beyond themselves and their finite world toward an infinite horizon of meaning, hope and love, they show that they always already know God implicitly.[18] However, this implicit knowledge of God is unthematic and nonreflexive; it is preconscious, latent and often dormant or even rejected. Nevertheless, it remains a knowledge of and relation to God that is intrinsic to human nature.[19]

The purpose of Rahner's highly sophisticated philosophical anthropology was to provide rational support for Augustine's claim that humans are created restless until they find their rest in God. In more popular jargon, all humans have a God-shaped empty place in their beings that can be filled only by God. Rahner believed that the proof of this could be found through transcendental inquiry into the a priori conditions for human

---

[14]Ibid., 53.

[15]Ibid., 155.

[16]Ibid., 161.

[17]Ibid., 101.

[18]Ibid., 65–66.

[19]Louis Roberts declares that for Rahner, "man exists only by virtue of the fact that he is always on his way to God, whether he knows it explicitly or not and whether he wills it or not." Louis Roberts, *The Achievement of Karl Rahner* (New York: Herder and Herder, 1967), 37.

knowing. But what is the value of this inquiry? Why did Rahner go to such heights and lengths of subtle abstraction to discover this implicit knowledge of God? The answer lies in the secular impulse of the modern world and its overwhelming tendency to place God and humanity either in tension or identity. Rahner was trying to show that, contrary to the accusations of such modern thinkers as Nietzsche and Sartre, God is not a threat to human self-fulfillment. Rather, God is the necessary horizon of human subjectivity and therefore belongs essentially to human nature itself. And contrary to pantheists who would identify God with humanity, he attempted to show that there is a radical difference between the finite and the infinite, signaled by the ultimate mysteriousness of the absolute horizon of human subjectivity. The human person is intrinsically, inwardly related to a holy mystery in and through human subjectivity. Yet the holy mystery remains transcendent—even to the transcendence of the human subject that reaches out toward it. If that holy mystery is to be known (beyond the bare knowledge of it in the *potentia oboedientialis*), it must make itself known.

Rahner posits a supernatural presence of God to every human person. One of Rahner's most distinctive ideas is what he called the "supernatural existential." According to Rahner, not only are humans always by nature open to God (*potentia oboedientialis*), they are also always supernaturally elevated by God in that transcendental openness so that they actually have an experience of God. God, Rahner claimed, communicates himself to every human person in a gracious offer of free grace, so that God's presence becomes an "existential," a constitutive element, in every person's humanity.[20] Without the supernatural existential, humans would remain a question struggling for an answer, open to something beyond themselves, a holy mystery, an infinite horizon, unknown and completely transcendent. But because of it, humans find the terminal point of their transcendence within themselves as gracious, personal, loving presence.[21]

This universal presence of God to every human person is "the light that lights everyone coming into the world," but it is not part of their natural equipment. Although it is an existential, and thus a permanent, constituent

---

[20]Rahner, *Foundations*, 116.
[21]Ibid., 129.

part of them, it is not "natural." It is completely gracious and therefore supernatural. Rahner took great pains to make this clear and thereby avoid any hint of the heresy of immanentism—making God part of the creature's own being. He clarified the matter this way: "This communication [of God] is not to be understood in a pantheistic or gnostic way as a natural process of emanation from God. It is to be understood rather as the freest possible love because he could not have refrained from this and been happy in himself."[22] Although it is supernatural, this divine presence is not extrinisic. The whole point of the supernatural existential is to overcome extrinsicism and intrinsicism. It does not contradict human nature because it comes as an elevation of transcendental openness of that nature to God. Thus, in true Catholic fashion, grace (the supernatural existential) fulfills and does not contradict nature (*potentia oboedientialis*).

According to Rahner, then, humans are not only beings open to God and divine revelation; they are also recipients of God's gracious self-communication. "Man," he wrote, "is the event of a free, unmerited and forgiving, and absolute self-communication of God."[23] This is the first kind of divine revelation—original experience of God in and through the prevenient grace of the supernatural existential. Like the *potentia oboedientialis*, however, it is transcendental, not "categorical" (specific, concrete, historical). It does not communicate special revelation of God but exists within the human person as an offer of personal knowledge of and relationship with God. By itself it remains unthematic and nonreflexive, but it does provide a "point of contact" for thematic, reflexive knowledge of God in historical, special revelation.[24]

At this point many students of Rahner wonder what the difference is between the *potentia oboedientialis* and the supernatural existential, and they ask why both are necessary to Rahner's theological method. First, for Rahner, the *potentia oboedientalis* is part of human persons' natural equipment. It is a philosophical-anthropological fact discovered through transcendental inquiry. It is part of the image of God in humanity. Every human person has it by virtue of being created human by God rather than something other than

---

[22]Ibid., 123–24.
[23]Ibid., 116.
[24]Ibid., 131.

human. The supernatural existential, however, is not part of any person's natural equipment but comes as a self-communication of God to it. It is added, as it were, to every human person's natural humanity. Therefore, it cannot be discovered by a purely philosophical-anthropological inquiry. It cannot be found through transcendental reflection alone. However, neither does it contradict nature or philosophy. According to Rahner, "it is the most self-evident thing of all, and at the same time it cannot be logically deduced from anything else."[25] Second, the *potentia oboedientialis* contains no real presence or knowledge of God *except as question*. It is the human striving toward God in all experience. The supernatural existential, however, conveys real knowledge and experience of God as an offer of redeeming grace. It is more than just a question; it conveys an offer, even though it still does not bestow the gift of redeeming grace itself. Only together, therefore, do the *potentia oboedientialis* and the supernatural existential do any good for the human person or the theologian.

Rahner recognizes the reality of "anonymous Christians." One of Rahner's most controversial ideas was what he called the "anonymous Christian."[26] Traditional Catholic theology says there is no salvation outside the church. Rahner asserted that whoever freely cooperates with the gracious presence of God in the supernatural existential can and will be saved—apart from any special, historical revelation of God or explicit knowledge of Jesus Christ. This is possible only because of the supernatural existential; the *potentia oboedientialis* cannot save. God, Rahner says, has a universal will for salvation: "There is a serious, effective and universal salvific will of God in the sense of that salvation which the Christian means by his own Christian salvation."[27] That, too, is traditional Catholic doctrine. But Rahner broke with common Catholic belief by saying that "anyone who does not close himself to God in an ultimate act of his life and his freedom through free and personal sin for which he is really and subjectively guilty and for which he cannot shirk responsibility, this person finds his salvation."[28] Also,

---

[25]Ibid., 123.
[26]Karl Rahner, "Anonymous Christians," in *Theological Investigations*, 23 vols. (London: Darton, Longman and Todd, 1969; New York: Seabury, 1974), 6:390–91, 393–95.
[27]Rahner, *Foundations*, 147.
[28]Ibid., 143.

> if someone lives life in a final and fundamental attitude of fidelity, of love, of
> surrender, of unconditional obedience to conscience, whether it is "useful" or
> not, I would call that person someone saved, someone who lives in the grace
> of God, whether or not that fundamental orientation comes to explicit con-
> ceptualization in the individual.[29]

An anonymous Christian, then, is someone not explicitly Christian who is
nevertheless implicitly Christian and saved. It is possible, however, only because of the supernatural existential which is a universal offer of salvation
to every person. There is a sense in which, for Rahner, God is an equal opportunity savior. A person can be saved by the grace of God even if he or
she is an atheist because salvation is not by beliefs or works but by grace
through obedience to conscience.

Rahner identifies a revelation above transcendental. Rahner distinguishes between two types of revelation. The first has just been described.
Our natural and supernatural orientations toward God constitute "transcendental revelation." This revelation, mediated through transcendental
experiences, provides an implicit knowledge of God as question and offer.
But it remains unthematic and prereflective. It communicates God, but not
specific information about God that could be formulated conceptually and
reflected on. Transcendental revelation reaches out toward a holy mystery
that remains for it infinite, indefinable and ineffable.[30] Transcendental
revelation forms the a priori basis for a second type of revelation which
Rahner calls "categorical" or "real" revelation, specific revelation in history
through events, words and symbols. These two aspects of revelation—transcendental and categorical—are distinct yet interdependent. Both are necessary to revelation. Rahner defined categorical revelation as that self-
revelation of God which

> is not simply given with the spiritual being of man as transcendence, but
> rather has the character of an event. It is dialogical, and in it God speaks to
> man, and makes known to him something which cannot be known always
> and everywhere in the world simply through the necessary relation of all re-
> ality in the world to God in man's transcendence.[31]

---

[29]*Karl Rahner in Dialogue*, 115.
[30]Rahner, *Foundations*, 60–61.
[31]Ibid., 171.

Categorical revelation, then, discloses the inner reality of God that cannot be discovered through transcendental revelation alone. That inner reality includes the personal character of God and his free relationship to spiritual creatures.[32]

Categorical revelation occurs throughout history and across cultures whenever and wherever people by God's grace actualize their natural and supernatural transcendentality and "break through," as it were, to a reflective knowledge of God. Every religion is an attempt at such a break through. Consequently, "in all religions there are individual moments of such a successful mediation . . . when the supernatural, transcendental relationship of man to God through God's self-communication becomes self-reflexive."[33] In such moments, people of any religion or no religion can become anonymous Christians. However, because of human depravity every such event of revelation remains partial and intermixed with error. Because universal categorical revelation (natural, general revelation) remains always partial and fallible, Rahner posits the existence of a second, higher type of categorical revelation which he described as "public, official, particular and ecclesially constituted revelation."[34] By this he meant the prophetic revelation found primarily in the Bible on which the church is based. This revelation is different in degree rather than in kind from universal categorical revelation: "Something comes to expression in the prophets which fundamentally is present everywhere and in everyone, including ourselves who are not called prophets."[35] Hence, the particular, historical revelation contained in the Bible is not a "bolt out of the blue" but a fulfillment and completion of the universal self-communication of God, both transcendental and categorical.[36]

Finally, Rahner arrived at the highest revelation, revelation in an absolute sense. Because in him we find the incarnation of God, the unsurpassable climax of all revelation is Jesus Christ. As absolute revelation, Jesus Christ provides the touchstone for interpreting the entire universal history of revelation. But even here Rahner denies an absolute break with the rest of revelation. The incarnation of God in Jesus is the highest point of God's

---

[32]Ibid.
[33]Ibid., 173.
[34]Ibid., 174.
[35]Ibid., 158.
[36]Ibid., 161.

self-communication, the most intense mediated immediacy of God's presence in human history and experience. For Rahner, the entire history of the cosmos, including evolution, contains the seed of God's absolute self-communication, which comes to fruition in the incarnation. Even the divine-human reality of Jesus Christ is not for him a "bolt out of the blue"; rather it too is the fulfillment of the self-transcendence of creation itself, the "omega point" toward which all things in creation gravitate.[37] Nevertheless, it provides a touchstone for distinguishing the particular and official revelation from the universal and incomplete revelation in history.

Rahner contributes to the renaissance of trinitarian theology. One of the things Rahner is most famous for is his construction of the doctrine of the Trinity. He wrote several treatises on it including *The Trinity* (1974). Perhaps his most lasting contribution to contemporary trinitarian thought is his development of what has come to be known as Rahner's Rule: "The 'economic' Trinity is the 'immanent' Trinity and the 'immanent' Trinity is the 'economic' Trinity."[38] It is customary in trinitarian theology to distinguish between God's threefold activity toward what is outside of himself in history (the economic Trinity) and the threefoldness of God in himself in eternity without a world (the immanent Trinity). Rahner believed that throughout Christian history these two aspects of the Trinity became separated so that theologians speculated on the intratrinitarian relations completely apart from any salvation-historical activity of the three persons. For example, some theologians suggested that any one of the three persons of the Trinity could have become incarnate, not only the Son, and that all activities of the Trinity in the world are activities of the entire Trinity (*opera trinitatis ad extra indivisa sunt*). Rahner rejected this thesis. It falsely separates God-in-himself from history, and it seems to make the incarnation superfluous to God's own being, as if God would be the same without it. In such a case, there could be no real self-communication of God to creatures in history.[39]

---

[37]Rahner's connection of Christ, and especially the incarnation, with human evolution parallels the theology of Teilhard de Chardin in many ways. Teilhardian motifs are especially evident in the section of *Foundations* titled "Christology Within an Evolutionary View of the World" (178–206).

[38]Karl Rahner, *The Trinity*, trans. Joseph Donceel (New York: Seabury, 1974), 22. The term "Rahner's Rule" was coined by Ted Peters, "Trinity Talk, Part 1," *Dialog* 26 (winter 1987): 46.

[39]Rahner, *The Trinity*, 99–101.

Against this speculative focus on God-in-himself and the immanent Trinity Rahner argued there is no warrant for making any statements about the intratrinitarian relations apart from what God actually is and does among us in history and that the economic activity of the three persons in human history for our salvation must be recognized as the real presence of the immanent Trinity. This thesis raises questions about God's immutability. If the economic Trinity *is* the immanent Trinity and vice versa, does God change in and through history? The doctrine of the immanent Trinity, whatever its defects, was meant to guard against a dissolution of God in history. God would remain God in the same way without the world and his activities in it as with them. Rahner's answer was typically ambiguous: "God can become something. He who is not subject to change in himself can *himself* be subject to change *in something else.*"[40] The creature—especially the human creature—was created by God in such a way (*potentia oboedientialis*) that it is a proper vehicle for God's own self-expression and therefore of God's own becoming in it. The creature is "the grammar of God's possible self-expression."[41] By emptying himself in assuming human nature to himself, God "becomes" without changing.

According to Rahner, this is a proper, "dialectical" interpretation of God's immutability. In his relationship with creatures God remains true to himself without being static. God himself actualizes potentialities in both creation and himself in such a way that he does not lose himself and the world does not become God. Yet both become something in and through their relation with the other; they enter into a real history with each other without merging together. For Rahner, then, the immanent Trinity and the economic Trinity are joined in history in the event of the incarnation, which is the primary event of God's becoming. In Jesus Christ the Logos, the second person of the Trinity, became a human person. This becoming could not have left the intratrinitarian being of God untouched. The incarnation signals a true history in God. Yet even in this event God remained the same. He became in and through another to which he emptied himself and which he added to himself. Also, Rahner's Rule means *only* the Son of God, the Logos, could have become incarnate. There is that about the second person

---

[40]Rahner, *Foundations*, 220.
[41]Ibid., 223.

of the Trinity, in relation to the Father, that made him and not the Father or the Holy Spirit the suitable person to become human.

The effect of Rahner's Rule and his overall doctrine of the Trinity as involving a becoming in God has been profound in Christian theology in the latter part of the twentieth century and early twenty-first century. One runs into the rule everywhere in trinitarian thought. It is almost taken for granted even as scholars debate its exact meaning.[42] Why? One reason for the near demise of the doctrine of the Trinity in modern theology is its apparent speculative nature. Especially classical liberal theologians throughout the nineteenth century found little use for it in ethics, which they considered the essence of Christianity. Rahner believed one reason for that was that most people came to think of the Trinity as the immanent Trinity which, torn away from the economic Trinity, is speculative. However, kept together with the economic Trinity the immanent Trinity is about the relationality and becoming of God, God's historicity. Then it is no longer merely speculative. However, Rahner did not want to dissolve the Trinity into history, which would result in modalism—the idea that the three persons are only manifestations of God in history. His rule is intended to avoid both dangers—a merely speculative trinitarian doctrine about a self-enclosed, immutable circle in heaven and a modalistic dissolving of the community of God as mere temporal manifestations like masks God wears.

Rahner propounds Jesus as the "absolute Savior." Not surprisingly, Rahner's account of the person of Jesus Christ is "transcendental Christology." It inquires about the transcendental preconditions for the appearance of such a God-man or "absolute Savior," as Christians claim the man Jesus of Nazareth was and is. Rahner cited as the central question, "Is something like an absolute savior or God-man . . . an idea which is intelligible to some extent, prescinding from the question whether and where this idea has been realized?"[43] His answer was yes. Through an inquiry into human transcendental experience he concluded that searching for a God-man within history is a basic human activity.[44] Again, the point is to show

---

[42]See various interpretations explicated in Chung-Hyun Baik, *The Holy Trinity—God for God and God for Us: Seven Positions on the Immanent-Economic Trinity Relation in Contemporary Trinitarian Theology* (Eugene, OR: Pickwick, 2011).

[43]Ibid., 228–29.

[44]Ibid., 296.

that belief in Jesus as God is not a concept entirely foreign to the deepest needs and hopes of humanity; it is not a bolt out of the blue or, as Kierkegaard argued, "absolute paradox." It is not irrational. In fact, universal human experience is open to it and remains unfulfilled without it.

Whether Jesus is indeed such an absolute Savior is another question. Although transcendental Christology cannot prove Jesus' absolute saviorhood, it can provide a point of contact between anthropology and Christian faith in Jesus as the Savior of the world. Rahner found the ultimate basis for the Christian claim that Jesus is the absolute Savior in the historical combination of Jesus' self-consciousness and his resurrection. Jesus claimed to bear in himself a "new and unsurpassable closeness of God which on its part will prevail victoriously and is inseparable from him."[45] This closeness Jesus called the "coming and arrival of God's kingdom," and he challenged people to accept or reject this God who had come close in himself. From this Rahner offered this conclusion:

> Jesus, then, is the historical presence of this final and unsurpassable word of God's self-disclosure: this is his claim and he is vindicated in this claim by the resurrection. He is of eternal validity and he is experienced in this eternal validity. In this sense in any case he is the "absolute savior."[46]

What of the church's claim that Jesus was and is not only the absolute Savior of the world—the fulfillment of the deepest human hopes and aspirations—but also God incarnate? Rahner believed that the ontological divinity of Jesus Christ could be established from his function as absolute Savior. An absolute Savior, he argued, must be more than merely a human prophet. Only God himself in self-communicating grace can save absolutely. Any merely human mediation of a message from God would fall short of a real presence of God transforming and "divinizing" the world. Furthermore, Rahner argued, an absolute event of salvation must be an event in the very life of God himself.[47]

We can understand these assertions properly only against the background of Rahner's view of final and ultimate—"absolute"—salvation. Such

---

[45]Ibid., 279.
[46]Ibid., 280.
[47]Ibid., 300–301.

salvation, which human transcendentality strives toward, involves much more than a "message" from God. It necessarily includes the real presence of God in the very depths of creaturely existence, transforming it in grace toward higher union with God. In a word, it is "divinization." Absolute salvation brings a grand result: "Now God and the grace of Christ are present as the secret essence of every reality we can choose."[48] Such a union of God and humanity, which preserves their distinctness, cannot be produced by a mere prophet. If Jesus was and is the event of absolute salvation, as Rahner believed his resurrection established, then he could not have been less than God present in man—Immanuel, "God with us." Rahner affirmed and defended the classical christological doctrine of the hypostatic union which states that Jesus Christ is one person with two natures—human and divine. His defense rested on transcendental and historical grounds. If Jesus' entire consciousness was indeed permeated by radical and complete surrender to God, and if what he accomplished by his life, death and resurrection constituted the final and absolute event of salvation, then he could be no other than God incarnate.[49]

But wouldn't that contradict Jesus' true humanity? Rahner adamantly rejected any hint of Docetism—the view that Jesus' humanity was unreal or a mere "livery" of God. Jesus was as much human as anyone else, even to the extent of being fallible in his own consciousness about many things.[50] His divine consciousness was apparently transcendental and therefore unthematic and nonreflexive (not available to his conscious mind) during his formative years. And it never overwhelmed or displaced his finite human consciousness. How can the finite creature, in this case Jesus' humanity, and the infinite being of God unite in a single entity such as the person of Jesus? That is the mystery of the hypostatic union, a mystery that has never been satisfactorily solved. Rahner believed he had an insight that would open up that mystery at least to some extent. The clue lay in his concept of humanity as the "cipher of God."

Rahner elevates humanity's status to "cipher of God." According to Rahner's theological anthropology, humans are never merely creaturely, immanent, closed in on themselves and nature. Rather, as we have seen, we

---

[48]Ibid., 228.
[49]Ibid., 303.
[50]Ibid., 249.

are transcendent while remaining finite. That human nature is transcendentally open to God is a fundamental philosophical fact. Theologically, in view of the incarnation, one must say that our human God-openness is intended by God as the potential for divine self-expression. In other words, the human person is the creature that is incomplete without incarnation. God is the mystery of humanity, and humanity is the cipher of God. Humanity is the question; God is the answer. Just as the question participates in the answer and the answer participates in the question while transcending it, so God and humanity belong essentially together. God has decided it will be so.[51] "When God wants to be what is not God, man comes to be."[52] This is one of the most telling statements in Rahner's entire theology. It indicates that for him, the purpose for the creation of humanity, if not the cosmos as a whole, is the incarnation. Humanity is created to be the "cipher of God," the symbol and vehicle of God's self-expressive presence.

Consequently, the incarnation does not contradict true humanity but brings it to its greatest possible fulfillment. According to Rahner, the assumption that in order to be truly human Jesus had to have some independent existence over against God is fundamentally mistaken, because "closeness and distance, or being at God's disposal and being autonomous, do not vary for creatures in inverse, but rather in direct proportion."[53] Therefore, Jesus Christ could be the most radically human, autonomous and free precisely because his humanity was made closest to God by its assumption into eternal union with the Logos in the incarnation. For Rahner, the incarnation, then, was the ultimate accomplishment and fulfillment of both God and humanity. In it God's desire to express himself outwardly through what is not God came to fulfillment. At the same time, the incarnation comprises fulfillment of the human search for an absolute Savior and human radical openness to God. All things, therefore, in heaven and on earth were fulfilled in Jesus Christ.

Rahner leaves a thought-provoking and ambiguous legacy. Without any doubt Rahner was one of the most creative theologians of the twentieth century, and he remains a source of much theological creativity into the

---

[51]Ibid., 224–27.
[52]Ibid., 225.
[53]Ibid., 226.

twenty-first century. Theologians still refer to Rahner's Rule when writing about the doctrine of the Trinity. He opened up ways of thinking about the God-world relationship that avoided both extrinsicism and intrinsicism, both too much transcendence of God over against the world and too much immanence of God in the world. That also applies to the old discussion about nature and grace that is so important in Catholic thought. For Rahner, nature and grace are not at all set over against one another, which is what Catholic thought at its best has always said. But Rahner showed ways for Catholic theology to think about them that avoided pitfalls in developing further that tricky relationship. For him, especially human nature is always already graced by God, but that universal being graced by God is supernatural and not natural. Many Catholic and some Protestant theologians have found much inspiration in his idea of the supernatural existential.

Another area of Rahner's constructive contribution to modern theology is his positive and yet cautious interaction with modernity. He drew on the best of modern philosophy while doggedly remaining faithful to the rich heritage of Catholic theology. Some have compared his use of Heidegger and existentialism, for example, with Thomas Aquinas's use of Aristotle. Both demonstrated points of congeniality with non-Christian philosophies in order to contextualize the Christian message and make it relevant to culture. Rahner refused to be intimidated by modern prejudices against metaphysical thinking and theological speculation and, for many people, recovered a sense of the beauty and grandeur of the mind's ability to grasp something of the mystery of God. Rahner may have provided the greatest impulse and path for faithful renewal of Catholic thought since Thomas Aquinas in the thirteenth century.

And yet, even sympathetic critics have questions about Rahner's contribution and concepts. The main issue is his ambiguity. According to his student George Vass, many of his central concepts are "eel-like."[54] For example, the supernatural existential is a highly unstable concept. If the theologian emphasizes the universal aspect denoted by the term "existential," the concept may easily fall into intrinsicism and become little more than another religious a priori like Schleiermacher's God-consciousness. But if

---

[54]Vass, *Mystery of Man*, 99.

one puts the emphasis on the supernatural aspect, the supernatural existential may easily fall into extrinsicism and become little more than another theological assertion of the transcendence of God's self-revelation and its alien nature to humanity. The question is whether an "existential" (something universal to human existence) can be "supernatural" (not part of humanity's natural equipment).

The supernatural existential is not the only ambiguous Rahner concept. His rule that the economic Trinity is the immanent Trinity and vice versa has spawned much discussion and given rise to much debate. On one side are arrayed theologians who interpret it as virtually denying any God-in-himself (or God-in-themselves) apart from history. Catholic theologian Catherine Mowry LaCugna comes close to that in her work on the Trinity entitled *God for Us* (1973). On the other side, German Catholic theologian and cardinal Walter Kaspar takes an opposite approach in *The God of Jesus Christ* (1984). The issue is whether Rahner's Rule means unity or identity of the immanent and economic aspects of the Trinity. Obviously Rahner himself left it unclear.

Finally, as to examples of Rahner's ambiguity, his account of humanity as the cipher of God raises questions about possible panentheism. His overall theory implies that God needs the world for his self-actualization in self-expression and that creation is not fully good until the incarnation unites it with God. There is a sense in which it appears that God and the world need each other for fulfillment. The specter that haunts Rahner's theology begins to look more and more like the ghost of Hegel, whose panentheistic philosophy of the "true infinite" that includes the finite in itself blurred the distinction between God and creation. The house of modern theology has been haunted by Hegel's ghost ever since he lectured on philosophy of religion in Berlin, and Rahner's theology has not been completely exorcised of it.

What about Rahner and modernity? There can be no doubt that the Jesuit theologian took it as his task to respond to what he saw as the major challenges of modernity. But he did not think those were what most people thought. He was not particularly concerned with evolution or biblical criticism, which is not to say he did not see some problems with the ways in which they were explained or used. Rather, for him, modernity's main challenge to Christianity lay in its tendency to secularize humanity such that

God is unnecessary for human fulfillment. Modernity tended to portray the human as finding self-realization in production whether it be art or machines. And the "transcendental self" was gradually seen as godlike so that humanity replaced God. Or God was viewed as a depth dimension of human existence. Overall, modernity pitted humanity against God and vice versa such that God, at least as Christian theism has understood God as a transcendent-immanent person, is a hindrance to human freedom. Rahner worked tirelessly to demonstrate that this is not so. For him, humanity can be shown to be open to God as the mystery of its own existence, the horizon toward which it always faces and without which it loses meaning and dignity. In all that he did not accommodate to modernity, at least not consciously or completely, but strived to open modernity and Christianity to each other in mutually transforming integration.

10.B. HANS KÜNG ADVOCATES A NEW PARADIGM OF CATHOLIC THEOLOGY

On December 18, 1979, Küng was skiing in the Austrian Alps when the message arrived: The Vatican had declared him not a Catholic theologian. This was the culmination of a decade-long struggle between the world-famous theologian and Rome's Sacred Congregation for the Doctrine of the Faith (sometimes called the Holy Office). Rarely does such a theological controversy make headlines around the world, but in this case the secular media had portrayed Küng as a modern-day Luther challenging the monolithic and immobile Catholic establishment. The professor rushed back to Tübingen to save his teaching position at the university and contact his publishers to be sure his current book would not be delayed by the news. He need not have worried. The news only enhanced his prestige and position both at the university and among his publishers and the reading public. Overnight he became a progressive martyr and the leading Catholic spokesman for reform in the Catholic Church.

Küng becomes a thorn in the Vatican's side. Küng was born in a Catholic village in Switzerland in 1928. After a traditional Catholic upbringing and early education he traveled to Rome to begin his studies toward the priesthood, a vocation he settled on rather quietly during his last years of *Gymnasium* (high school). In Rome he received a traditional theological

education at the prestigious Gregorian University. Throughout the 1950s
Küng became increasingly uncomfortable with the Vatican's heavy-handed
approach to well-intentioned adaptations of Catholic thought to modernity.
He also read Sartre and Barth. He later confessed that both served as liber-
ators of his own philosophical and theological thought. He was ordained
and celebrated his first mass in St. Peter's Cathedral in Rome in October
1954 and shortly afterwards moved to Paris to work toward his doctorate in
theology. There he came under the influence of theologians of the *nouvelle
théologie*. His studies in Paris set him on a theological trajectory that would
be marked by ecumenical openness, progressive, critical orthodoxy and
positive dialogue with secular science, philosophy and world religions.[55]

Küng's first book was a revision of his doctoral dissertation on Barth's
doctrine of justification. *Justification: The Doctrine of Karl Barth and a
Catholic Reflection* was published with a brief "letter to the author" by
Barth in 1957. It created a small stir because of its main thesis that "on the
whole there is fundamental agreement between the theology of Barth and
that of the Catholic Church."[56] Although Barth did not necessarily agree,
he embraced the book's author as a younger colleague and friend and invited him to have dialogue in his seminars in Basel. The Catholic hierarchy
was less enthusiastic. Only later did Küng discover that the Sacred Congregation for the Doctrine of the Faith opened a file on him shortly after the
book's publication. This would set the stage for lifelong conflict between
Küng and the Catholic hierarchy. Throughout the 1960s he was primarily
concerned with challenging and reinterpreting Catholic teachings about
the nature of the church. In *Structures of the Church* (1962), *The Church*
(1967) and *Infallible?* (1970) he presented strong biblical, historical and
theological criticisms of the hierarchical authority of the Catholic Church,
its resistance to change and especially the dogma of the infallibility of the
pope. His writings on the church gained him the undying enmity of powerful leaders in Rome and caused even some of his friends to distance
themselves from him.

---

[55]These biographical details are taken from two main sources: Küng's autobiography *Hans Küng:
My Struggle for Freedom*, trans. John Bowden (Grand Rapids: Eerdmans, 2003) and Robert
Nowell, *A Passion for Truth: Hans Küng and His Theology* (New York: Crossroad, 1981).

[56]Hans Kung, *Justification: The Doctrine of Karl Barth and a Catholic Reflection*, trans. Thomas
Collins et al. (New York: Thomas Nelson and Sons, 1964), 282.

In 1960 Küng accepted a position teaching fundamental theology at the University of Tübingen. This was a most unusual invitation for a thirty-two-year-old scholar. He remained there in spite of controversy and conflict with the Vatican and the German bishops of the Catholic Church and routinely drew huge crowds of students to his lectures. Even before the Second Vatican Council opened in 1962 Küng was already explaining what it should accomplish in *The Council, Reform and Reunion* (1960). He articulated high hopes for visible unity between Catholics and Protestants and urged change in the Catholic Church toward greater openness toward modernity. Much of his later career as a theologian can be interpreted in light of his disappointment over the outcome of the council.

Küng is one of the most prolific theologians with massive new books appearing every year or two. Among his most widely read and discussed ones are *On Being a Christian* (1974) and *Does God Exist?* (1978). Both are lengthy, detailed discussions of Christian theology in the light of modernity. The first is his one-volume systematic theology written mainly for laypeople but with great erudition. It was a best seller in Germany and sold widely in the United States as well. The second is Küng's book of apologetics defending belief in God as a "rational choice." It, too, sold well in Germany and represented a major challenge to atheism. What eventually brought about the withdrawal of his *missio canonica* (formal license to teach Catholic theology) was his Christology in *On Being a Christian*. There he presented Jesus as a religious reformer and as God's representative among people, but his doctrinal statement of Jesus' deity fell short of dogmatic standards. One especially harsh critic charged that he represented Jesus as a maverick reformer courageously standing up against the religious establishment of his time and thus as "the man who would be Küng!"

The Swiss theologian's reputation and career were greatly enhanced by the Vatican's treatment of him. More than a thousand students demonstrated on his behalf in Tübingen's public square. Newspapers and scholarly societies around the world published editorials and declarations condemning the Vatican's act as a "new Inquisition." His book sales skyrocketed, and invitations to speak and teach poured in from around the world. The University of Tübingen set up a special institute for Küng to lead and kept him as a professor in spite of the fact that Catholic students could no longer take his courses for credit toward their ministerial licenses. Küng, now freed from most restraints, embarked on a crusade against what he considered the backwardness of the Vatican. When asked in 1989 what he thought of the popular Pope John Paul II, he replied, "We'll just have to wait for him to die," and expressed hope that the next pope would carry out the reforms begun by Vatican II.[57] In 1990 he published an especially biting critique of Rome titled "Longing for John XXIV: In Memory of Pope John XXIII."[58]

Two of Küng's books that are not as well-known but nevertheless important for understanding his theology are his massive study of Hegel's Christology titled *The Incarnation of God* (1970) and *Theology for the Third Millennium* (1987). When asked, he expressed his opinion that the first one was his finest and most fundamental theological contribution.[59] The second was a more programmatic treatise on theological method in which he advocated paradigm change in theology as culture moved from being modern to being postmodern. Beginning in 1985 with the publication of *Christianity and the World Religions*, he increasingly turned his attention toward interreligious dialogue and the development of an ecumenical world ethic that he hoped would reduce violence in the world.

Küng argues for a "critical rationality" in theology. Rahner referred to Küng as a liberal Protestant in Catholic disguise. There is no question that he, like Erasmus during the Reformation, wishes to remain within the Catholic Church and change it from within. His theological method, however, is much more akin to that of modern Protestant theology than to classical Catholic thought. He stands in the tradition of Schleiermacher and Tillich while also drawing heavily on Barth. In fact, it could be said that his entire project is an attempt to mediate between Catholic and Protestant streams of contemporary theology.

To analyze Küng's theological method we have to look first at his epistemological starting point, which he calls "critical rationality," then inspect his view of the rationality of belief in God before moving to his proposal for a postmodern paradigm including his view of theology's sources and norms.

---

[57]Küng communicated this to the author in personal conversation in Houston, Texas, in March 1989.
[58]Hans Küng, *Reforming the Church Today: Keeping Hope Alive*, trans. Peter Heinegg et al. (New York: Crossroads, 1990), 64–71.
[59]From conversation with the author in March 1989.

Finally, we will examine his reconstructions of the doctrines of God and the person of Jesus Christ.

In *Does God Exist?* the Swiss theologian defended the rational credentials of basic Christian theism against the onslaughts of such modern atheists as Feuerbach, Marx, Nietzsche and Freud. Through careful analysis of the grounds for their objections to belief in God he discovered that, although atheism cannot be conclusively refuted, neither can it be conclusively substantiated. His assessment of Nietzsche is typical: "If we look dispassionately behind the mask of the prophet, visionary, emotional thinker, preacher, his atheism also was not really justified, but assumed as a datum."[60] Laboriously, Küng built his case throughout the book: Atheism is not more rational than belief in God. Neither belief nor unbelief is provable; both are "basic decisions" on which everything else in a person's life rests. His appeal to basic decisions forms a part of the epistemological approach he calls critical rationality. He believes this approach to knowledge is more appropriate both to the modern scientific mind and to Christian belief than either critical rationalism or fideism.

Critical rationalism is the concept of reason stemming from Descartes and espoused in the twentieth century by philosophers Karl Popper (1902–1994) and Hans Albert (b. 1921), among others, which insists on mathematical-like proofs and disproofs as the basis of all true knowledge. In other words, it is a form of foundationalism. It is also similar to what is called positivism in its view of empirical verification and falsification as criteria of truth. Küng argues that such an epistemology is inappropriate because it assumes the existence of some Archimedean point of reference for objective knowledge.[61] Belief in reason, then, would require some suprarational belief in the rationality of the universe. Consequently, he added, "all knowledge . . . contains a 'presupposition' that can be described as a 'matter of faith.'"[62] Furthermore, Popper's critical rationalism ignores the "multiple dimensionality" and "complex stratification" of reality by reducing everything to empirical data.[63]

---

[60]Hans Küng, *Does God Exist? An Answer for Today*, trans. Edward Quinn (Garden City, NY: Doubleday, 1980), 403.
[61]Ibid., 449.
[62]Ibid., 464.
[63]Ibid., 124.

But, for Küng, fideism, or irrationality, is just as inappropriate as dogmatic rationalism. Therefore, he outlined a middle way between the two
extremes which he called "the way of critical rationality." This approach
recognizes the fundamentally uncertain condition of reality and of our
human grasp of it, as well as the multiple varieties of reality, and builds
from suprarational fundamental decisions that can at best be rationally
justified beliefs about the nature of reality. Such basic attitudes or commitments cannot be proved or disproved, conclusively verified or falsified.
Nevertheless, they are rationally justified insofar as they fit human experience as a whole. He applied this method of critical rationality to belief
in God in *Does God Exist?* Building from Kant, he asserted that neither
God's existence nor God's nonexistence can be proved, for it lies beyond
the grasp of human reason.[64] Nevertheless, belief in God is not an irrational leap of faith or a sacrifice of the intellect. Rather, it is a rationally
justified fundamental trust that can be verified indirectly through the "experienced reality of man and the world."[65] In other words, if God exists,
certain universal human questions are answered and certain universal
human experiences are explained. Ultimately, uncertain reality itself receives coherence, meaning and a ground of being, if God exists. If God
does not exist, reality remains uncertain and there can be no ground,
basis or support for fundamental trust.

Does God Exist? represents a sustained indirect proof of the rationality of
belief in God. That is far from a proof of God's existence, but Küng believes
that all that is necessary today is to show that belief in God is not irrational, as
many secularists claim, but rationally justified. Much of the force of his argument stems from his critique of atheism. While it is rationally irrefutable,
he averred, "denial of God implies an ultimately unjustified fundamental
trust in reality."[66] Küng's argument for theism's rationality begins with the
necessity of taking an attitude toward uncertain reality: Reality is either ultimately trustworthy or untrustworthy. Either the universe is a home for
humans full of meaning and value or it is a sheer accident devoid of any transcendent meaning or purpose. If we choose to believe the latter, we are by

---

[64]Ibid., 544.
[65]Ibid., 550.
[66]Ibid., 571.

definition nihilists, an option that cannot be maintained consistently in practice. Nihilism provides no ground for aesthetics or ethics; rather, everything is meaningless. Most people, including atheists, however, do not believe that; they find fundamental or basic trust a compelling attitude.

If we opt for fundamental trust, Küng argues, we must choose once more: Uncertain reality either has a ground and source that overcomes its absolute uncertainty or it does not. It is ruled either by a divine providence or by chance. The choice to believe that reality is ruled by a personal transcendent-immanent God is rationally justified because it provides ground and support to fundamental trust, whereas atheism does not. Compared with traditional natural theology and its opposite, Kierkegaardian (or Barthian) defiance of reason, the Swiss theologian's approach is modest. He placed his method of verifying the truth of God's existence "between Karl Barth and Vatican 1."[67] He claimed, however, that this approach is the best one today, because it preserves both rationality and faith, something even natural science must do.[68]

Küng constructs a postmodern paradigm for theology. Küng's reliance on critical rationality flowed into his method of reinterpreting Christian belief for today. Not only apologetics but also systematic theology must be thoroughly critical if it is to be taken seriously by modern or postmodern culture. He argued, "In theological science, the rules are no different in principle from the rules of other sciences. Here, too, irrationality, unjustified reactions, subjectivist decisions, cannot be permitted."[69] At the same time, rationality must not be so absolutized that it becomes an ideology binding the transcendent Word of God at the outset. In systematic theology as in apologetics, he desired to inhabit a space between extremes. He called for a new, postmodern paradigm for theology.[70] In this he was influenced by Thomas Kuhn and *The Structure of Scientific Revolutions* (discussed in

---

[67]Ibid., 536.

[68]Ibid., 111.

[69]Ibid., 337.

[70]Küng is not the only contemporary theologian to use the term "postmodern" to describe a new approach to theology in the light of a culture-wide critique of certain aspects of modernity. There is, however, no consensus about what postmodern theology is. Küng is one theologian who is seeking to fill the concept with content. For other attempts, see David Ray Griffin, William A. Beardslee and Joe Holland, *Varieties of Postmodern Theology* (Albany: State University of New York Press, 1989).

chap. 9). According to Kuhn, scientific revolutions, paradigm shifts, are not purely rational processes. Scientists are reluctant to give up old ways of viewing nature and methods for studying it and do so only gradually or by sheer conversion when forced to by overwhelming evidence. In fact, it is usually young Turks in the scientific community, such as Einstein, who force such paradigm changes.[71]

Küng believes that Kuhn's analysis of paradigm change holds true in every science—including theology. The history of Christian theology can be analyzed in terms of shifts, not just from one type of theology to another, but from one "entire constellation of beliefs, values and techniques" to another. An example of such a paradigm shift in Christian theology is the Protestant Reformation, which represented more than merely a shift in emphasis or interpretation. It was a radical shift in the foundations of theology away from medieval scholasticism and authoritarian traditionalism toward a concentration on Scripture and faith. Changing along with the Reformation involved more than turning a new leaf or altering an opinion. It required a kind of conversion—albeit not an irrational leap. In Küng's view, the Catholic Church and Christianity as a whole are ripe for a paradigm shift as radical as that of the Reformation. Any new paradigm, he argued in *Theology for the Third Millennium*, must be "postmodern," comprising "an immanent critique of modernity" and "sober, upright movement forward to the future."[72] One should not read too much into this use of "postmodern"; Küng did not mean what many think it means (e.g., truth claims as power plays). We must allow him to tell us what he means by this essentially contested concept.

One of Küng's favorite concepts is the Hegelian idea of *Aufhebung* (see 1.d.). There is no good English word to translate it, but Küng's idea of postmodernity provides a good opportunity to explain it. A postmodern paradigm would be the *Aufhebung* of modernity (that is, culture based on the Enlightenment), in that it would transcend modernity without canceling it out entirely. The enduring, positive values of modernity would be

---

[71]For an excellent discussion of paradigm change in both natural science and in theology, see Hans Küng, *Theology for the Third Millennium: An Ecumenical View*, trans. Peter Heinegg (New York: Doubleday, 1988), 123–69.

[72]Ibid., 6.

preserved, while its outmoded aspects would be transcended by something new. Modernity, Küng averred, must be "preserved, critiqued, and transcended" in a new postmodern paradigm of culture that includes philosophy and theology.[73] Hence, he is not opposed to the Enlightenment; he even believes that it is impossible to go back behind it. The rise of critical reason, science and the historical-critical method of inquiry and the Enlightenment emphasis on human freedom and autonomy can never be reversed. Theology must be among the first to acknowledge this. But such negative, even unscientific, elements of modern culture as dogmatic rationalism and the myth of inevitable progress must be transcended by a higher vision of reason and a more realistic assessment of experience. We have seen this basic response to the Enlightenment and modernity illustrated in Küng's idea of critical rationality.

Küng called for a new, post-Enlightenment paradigm for theology, a "contemporary-ecumenical paradigm" resulting in a "critical ecumenical theology."[74] In *Theology for the Third Millennium* he did not provide a complete picture of the new paradigm that he saw struggling to be born in contemporary theology, but he did provide some principles, norms and guidelines for its birth and development. Above all, like new scientific paradigms, the new theological one must stand in both continuity and discontinuity with previous theological paradigms.[75] Küng brought to the fore a number of competing paradigms, attempting to expose their weaknesses while preserving their strengths. For example, "Catholic Traditionalism," represented especially by the nineteenth-century textbook theology of Denziger,[76] was correct to preserve the unity and continuity of Christian teaching but wrong to make "sound Catholic teaching" the be-all and end-all of the Christian message.[77] Another alternative is that of Barth. The

---

[73]Ibid., 8–9.
[74]Ibid., 127.
[75]Ibid., 154.
[76]"Denziger" is common shorthand for the *Enchiridion Symbolorum et Definitionum* (*Handbook of Creeds and Definitions*) of which Heinrich Denziger was the editor. The first edition was published in 1854; the last, based on materials he left, was published after Denziger's death in 1908. The volume was for many years considered a semi-official, authoritative compendium of Catholic doctrine and served as a kind of conservative, written magisterium for testing the orthodoxy of Catholic theologians and their writings.
[77]Ibid., 185.

Swiss Protestant initiated a change from the modern to the postmodern paradigm. But he would need to go further in embracing critical methodology and openness to the truth in world religions in order to establish his theology as the basic model for the third millennium.[78]

Küng develops a new theological method for the new paradigm. Küng laid down two basic poles between which a new theological paradigm must be equally balanced: "a theology from the perspective of Christian origins and the Christian center, against the horizon of today's world."[79] In other words, theology must work with two sources or norms: "God's revelatory speaking in the history of Israel and the history of Jesus,"[80] on the one hand, and "our own human world of experience"[81] on the other hand. He affirmed Tillich's method of correlation between these two sources/norms of theology, while suggesting a significant alteration. He advocated a "critical correlation" in which there is sometimes genuine "critical confrontation" between them.[82] Hence, the new paradigm theologian must not expect from the outset that there will always be smooth continuity and harmony within the gospel message, even as understood through the best historical-critical exegesis, and modern human experience. Sometimes conflict and confrontation will arise. This is why Küng calls his paradigm postmodern rather than modern. When conflict happens the primacy must be given to the Christian message itself and not to the horizon of modern experience.

The strong emphasis on the primacy of the Christian gospel over the "horizon of human experience" marks a significant point of difference between Küng's method and both classical liberalism and neoliberalism. One can only wish that he would provide more concrete examples of such primacy. Generally, he is more interested in discussing the importance of correlating the Christian message with contemporary human experience. Nevertheless, he insisted on this point of continuity with traditional paradigms of theology both Catholic and Protestant:

---

[78]Ibid., 190–91.
[79]Ibid., 106.
[80]Ibid., 108.
[81]Ibid., 116.
[82]Ibid., 122.

All this means that a drastic, paradigmatic upheaval can take place in Christian theology—if it is to be and remain Christian—always and only on the *basis* of the Gospel, and ultimately *on account* of the Gospel, but never *against* the Gospel. The Gospel of Jesus Christ himself—much as the testimonies to him must be deeply probed by means of historic-criticism—is no more at the theologian's disposal, to rule on its truth, than history is for the historian or the Constitution is for the constitutional lawyer.[83]

Concretely, this means, for example, that Küng rejects the trend among certain Christian theologians to remove Jesus Christ from the center of Christianity and for the sake of interreligious understanding replace him with simply God. The Catholic thinker considers this point a genuine watershed, "Caesar's Rubicon," which he cannot cross if he is to remain a Christian theologian.[84]

Küng's emphasis on the primacy of the gospel in any new Christian theological paradigm does not mean, however, that he sides with conservatives or evangelicals who wish to base the gospel on the verbal inspiration of the Bible. He wishes to preserve as the primary source/norm of theology Jesus Christ as unique Lord and Savior of humanity, not the entire Bible. For Küng, believing the Bible infallible is as much a mistake as regarding the pope as infallible. Infallibility belongs only to God; the writers of the Bible were merely fallible human witnesses to God's revelation to Israel and in Jesus Christ. One must not elevate the Bible to the position of paper pope, as he believed happened in Protestant fundamentalism and evangelicalism. Rather, we must make a clear distinction between even the New Testament and the gospel.[85] The gospel is imbedded in the New Testament in the person of Jesus Christ. Only sound "critico-historical method" can rediscover this *norma normans* (norming norm) of theology which must then be applied to the rest of the Bible. In other words, at times the Bible must be used against itself.

Küng called for "a historico-critically responsible dogmatic theology" based on "historic-critically grounded exegesis."[86] As we will see, this raises the question, even for some of Küng's most sympathetic critics, of what the

---

[83]Ibid., 159.
[84]From personal conversation in Houston, Texas, March 1989.
[85]Küng, *Theology for the Third Millennium*, 193.
[86]Ibid., 194.

true *norma normans* of his critical ecumenical paradigm will be: the New Testament, as he has occasionally indicated in past writings,[87] the person of Jesus Christ, the "Gospel of Jesus Christ" or historic-critical methodology?[88] As a Catholic, Küng must find a place for Christian tradition in his theological method. He relegates it to a secondary status within the overall source/norm of the Christian message. The gospel of Jesus Christ holds first place as the *norma normans*, the touchstone of truth, even over the Bible. The tradition of church teaching, including apparently even the Bible itself, as well as the church fathers, councils, popes and so forth, constitutes the *norma normata* (normed norm), the secondary norm for determining validity within the Christian message.[89] Critics charge that Küng has neglected church tradition as constituting any essential ingredient in determining the structure and course of the new theological paradigm.

All of the immediately preceding material deals with Küng's view of the first pole or source/norm of the new critical-ecumenical paradigm of theology—the Christian message. His account resembles that of dialectical theology, with a strong dose of historical-critical method thrown in. The core and touchstone of the Christian message is Jesus Christ plus the gospel message about him, which Küng has formulated in this way: "In the light and in the power of Jesus we can in the world of today live, act, suffer and die in a truly human way; utterly committed to our fellow-man because utterly sustained by God."[90] The Bible, and especially the New Testament, participates in this *norma normans* of theology as its historical vehicle, but it is not itself above criticism. Like the church as a whole, the Bible is "indefectible" in the whole, while not at all infallible. God makes his truth shine forth through the Bible's human mistakes. Church tradition helps in identifying the truth of the Christian message and should be respected as a secondary source/norm of theology, but it is even more open to correction and revision than the Bible.

The second pole and source/norm of the new critical-ecumenical theological paradigm is "the horizon of human experience," that is, "our present-

---

[87]Ibid., 59.
[88]Catherine Mowry LaCugna, *The Theological Methodology of Hans Küng* (Chico, CA: Scholars Press, 1982), 182–83.
[89]For an excellent, detailed discussion of Küng's view of tradition see ibid., 95–103.
[90]Quoted in Nowell, *Passion for Truth*, 246.

day world of experience with all its ambivalence, contingency, and changeableness."[91] Among other things, the pole of experience establishes the necessity of critical reason in understanding and evaluating truth claims, confirms the assumption of a scientific view of the natural world and its processes (that is, a modern worldview) and demands a generous, tolerant inclusivism of all faiths toward each other. Küng worked out the correlation between the Christian message and critical rationality in *Does God Exist?* In *On Being a Christian* he explored the correlation between Christian belief and the modern, scientific worldview. In *Christianity and the World Religions* he discussed with representatives of the major faith traditions the relationship of Christian truth to other religions. In each case he managed to hold firmly to Jesus Christ as the source/norm of Christianity in the face of overwhelming objections and problems arising out of the secular culture and non-Christian religions. At the same time, at least in the eyes of critics, he also relativized, ignored or denied much of traditional Christian belief in favor of non-Christian truth claims.

Küng revises classical Christian theism with the "historicity of God." Like many twentieth-century theologians, Küng is concerned with overcoming the God/world dualism he sees implicit in much traditional theology, while avoiding any hint of pantheism. In other words, he seeks to discover God's transcendence *in* immanence. He worked out his doctrine of God primarily through critical dialogue with Hegel, as evidenced in *The Incarnation of God*. In spite of large areas of disagreement with Hegel, who had also taught at Tübingen, Küng is clearly dazzled by the German philosopher's overall vision of the dialectical unity of God and the world. Consequently he sought to delineate a "post-Hegelian" concept of God that would transcend while preserving (*aufheben*) both traditional Christian theism and Hegelian panentheism. Such a view of God would rule out any "naïve anthropomorphic or even enlightened deistic picture of God on the basis of a supra- or even extra-terrestrial God deemed to exist alongside or over against this world and man."[92] At the same time, it

---

[91]Küng, *Theology for the Third Millennium*, 166. It is interesting that Küng reversed the order of these two poles in the two places in this book where they are explicitly mentioned in relation to each other.

[92]Ibid., 237.

would go beyond Hegel. It would lead to a new conception of the living God based on a dialectic of love, instead of Hegel's dialectic of knowledge, and would discover "*God* in the world, *transcendence* in immanence, the *beyond* in the here-and-now."[93]

Through a meticulous examination of Hegel's philosophical theology, Küng revealed his areas of agreement and disagreement with the great German philosopher. He quickly discounted the charges of pantheism against Hegel, while acknowledging the truth of the charge of panentheism. In Hegel, God and the world—or God and humanity—are not "rolled into one." Nevertheless, they are united in intrinsic, reciprocal unity-in-differentiation, so that Hegel's God "is rarely described as a living, active person in an I-Thou relationship, but rather as a creatively present universal life and Spirit."[94] The Swiss theologian disagreed with this Hegelian diminution of God's personhood, as well as with the inevitable cancellation of grace that follows any intrinsic, essential unity of God and humanity. Against Hegel he declared, "What is entailed by a God of grace is a God who lives *in* the world itself, present but not caged within it, immanent within it yet also transcending it . . . close to and yet at the same time also other than the world."[95] Küng is likewise uncomfortable with Hegel's tendency to make God a prisoner of his own philosophical system and of the God-world totality ("monism of Spirit"). Apparently, God's freedom, which is presupposed by God's grace, is for Küng one of those nonnegotiable items of the central core of the Christian message.

At the same time, Küng found much to embrace in Hegel's concept of God and God's relationship with the world. In contrast to the all too static and otherworldly God of traditional theism, Hegel's God is living, dynamic and capable of suffering, and it includes its antithesis in itself, rather than standing aloof from the world's history. This picture of God, Küng argued, is more compatible with and conducive to a full understanding of the incarnation than is the Greek-inspired theism of much traditional Christian theology. In the light of the incarnation, Küng asked, "Should not God's transcendence, immutability and unchangeability be subjected to a

---

[93]Ibid.
[94]Ibid., 133.
[95]Ibid., 288.

thoroughgoing reinterpretation?"[96] He answered his query in the affirmative and declared that such a reinterpretation might be aided by "walking in Hegel's footsteps" (up to a point), because the German thinker's concept of God "is manifestly better suited to express what must be stated by a classical Christology which has been thought through to the end."[97]

Küng identified three key points where Hegel's concept of God could make a contribution to a renewed Christian doctrine of God: the suffering of God, the dialectic within God and God's involvement in becoming.[98] We will treat the three in reverse order, beginning with God's involvement in becoming. In Küng's estimation, a major task for contemporary Christian thinking is to develop an understanding of God's historicity. In fact, the divine historicity is the main theme of *The Incarnation of God*. God's incarnation, the author affirmed, means that the divine attributes must be interpreted in light of God's unity with Jesus' birth, life, suffering, death and resurrection. He explained, "Man's salvation is entirely dependent on the fact that God himself does not hold aloof from this history and that it is God himself and not just a man who takes the stage in this man."[99] Consequently, the traditional affirmations of God's immutability and impassability, which Küng saw as based primarily on Greek metaphysics rather than on the Bible, must be reconsidered and revised in light of God's presence in Jesus. This God is one who is capable of entering history and making it his own. He is a living, dynamic, historical God who becomes, not by necessity, but because he chooses to do so out of grace and overflowing love.

God's involvement in history does not signal a deficiency or even self-development, as if God *has* to become something to realize himself. In asserting this, Küng strenuously rejected both Hegel and Whitehead. A God who would need to become something would be "a pallid imitation of human wretchedness."[100] Nevertheless, God does become, he added, and thus God possesses a "basic historicality" that flows out of his own inner dynamic life. In his discussion of God's basic historicity Küng avoided the question whether God changes in his becoming. Yet by reading between

---

[96]Ibid., 455.
[97]Ibid., 457.
[98]Ibid., 458.
[99]Ibid., 449.
[100]Ibid., 455.

the lines, we can deduce something about Küng's attitude toward this crucial question. On the one hand, he rejected any notion of God's changeableness in the sense of being subject to change by necessity. He also has no use for any concept of irrational or capricious changeableness in God. On the other hand, he also rejected strict unchangeableness in the sense of being untouched by the history of pain and suffering in the world, especially in Jesus' life and death. Once again, Küng's thinking is dialectical, moving between two false extremes. God can and does change, he affirmed, in full consistency with his own character by identification with finitude, temporality and suffering in Christ. Yet such change is not a denial or diminution of his deity, but constitutes its highest manifestation.[101]

Küng became more speculative when he delved into the hidden aspect of God's being which makes such historicity possible. Hegel's second contribution, he argued, is the dialectic within God himself. God can become because he always already includes finitude and imperfection in his own infinite being. This is a version of Hegel's idea of God, or Absolute Spirit, as the *wahrhaft Unendliche*—the true infinite—that does not stand alongside the finite but includes it. In Küng's words, "the living Christian God is therefore a God who does not exclude but includes his antithesis."[102] Greek metaphysics, he noted, on which traditional Christian theism is largely based, could not conceive of such a God. For him, this dialectical unity of infinity and finitude within God's eternal being is the basis for God's self-humiliation in Christ. His entire thesis in *The Incarnation of God* is summed up in one passage dealing with this speculative vision of God's dynamic, dialectical being:

> God is not *forced*, but he is able to do what he does in history; and he has a power and ability to perform these acts which are rooted in his nature. The nature of the living God is a nature which is capable of self-humiliation, even though not compelled to take this path, a nature which contains within itself the power for gracious self-externalisation.[103]

These two theses concerning God, based on perceived "contributions of Hegel," form the foundation for Küng's revision of God's transcendence and

---

[101]Ibid., 450–51.
[102]Ibid., 452.
[103]Ibid.

immanence. Throughout his writings he repeatedly emphasized that a viable modern or postmodern concept of God must not separate God from the world: No worldless God and no godless world! God is to be conceived as present and revealed in the world and its history without being dissolved in them. God embraces the world in a loving gesture of self-abnegation, so that he becomes deeply embedded in its history and its history becomes part of him. This is possible because God already contains the finite within himself. But does that not lead back to Hegel's panentheism in which God is not God without a world? Can Küng avoid it in any way other than by sheer assertion that it cannot be? Why does he not avail himself of the doctrine of the Trinity, like other contemporary theologians such as Moltmann and Eberhard Jüngel have done, to explain how God can become in time and history without losing himself? In the final analysis Küng's doctrine of God leans dangerously close to panentheism; he avoids the fallacy by asserting that to preserve God's freedom and grace that position cannot be true.

The emphasis on God's suffering is the third Hegelian contribution Küng embraced. Because God contains his antithesis in himself, he is able to suffer without being pathetic. Once again, the Swiss theologian wended his way dialectically between two false opposites: God as apathetic and God as pathetic. The former extreme is the fault early Christianity inherited from Greek metaphysics. The latter is the error of process theology and other modern metaphysical conceptions of God that are based on the modern concept of the ultimacy of change. The God of the incarnation, Küng asserted, is one who suffers freely and out of grace, not out of necessity or need.[104] That God suffers is almost a truism in post–World War II theology. In a single generation the traditional doctrine of God's impassibility has been overturned, so that it is now almost heresy (in some circles) to affirm it. Nevertheless, one must question whether Küng's account of the basis for God's suffering is better than that provided by process theology. God's suffering, for him, is based on his free choice to identify with Christ's sufferings. Yet, it is also based on the divine inner dialectic in which God always already includes the tension of antithesis within himself. He is the infinite that includes the finite, perfection that includes imperfection, life that includes

---

[104]Ibid., 445–46.

death. Such a God would seem to be bound up with historicity and suffering. For such a God, involvement with the world and identification with its pain and misery would seem to be a given rather than a free, gracious choice.

Küng accused Hegel of "sublating" the graciousness of God's relationship with the world in his philosophical system. Yet he also affirmed that the Christian God "is here *and* hereafter, distant *and* near, above the world *and* within the world, future *and* present. God is oriented to the world: There is no God without a world. And the world is wholly ordered to God: there is no world without God."[105] Küng's intention to balance God's transcendence and immanence is reflected in the first part of this affirmation. The second part, however, raises the question as to whether he has fallen into Hegel's error of tying God too closely to the world to the detriment of both. It would be wrong, however, to accuse Küng of emphasizing exclusively the immanence of God. He never tires of reasserting the transcendent freedom of God over the world. He is aware that the tendency toward immanentism in contemporary theology has led to a serious crisis in every area of theology. However, his ready acceptance of certain aspects of Hegel's ontology, such as the dialectical unity of the infinite and finite, pushes him unwittingly toward the pitfall of chaining God to the world and thus reducing the graciousness of God's relationship with us.

Küng expounds a functional Christology. No aspect of Küng's theology has been as controversial as his Christology. Even the German bishops of the Catholic Church were more upset over it than over his ecclesiology. His Christology was the straw that broke the proverbial camel's back. Although action was already underway to discipline him in some way, when *On Being a Christian* appeared in 1974 and church leaders had the opportunity to evaluate the author's statements about Jesus Christ, it seemed inevitable to many that he would receive a harsh sentence. Yet Küng considers his theology radically Christocentric. His intention in his Christology is to return to the earliest biblical teachings about Jesus Christ and place that testimony at the heart of the Christian message. As he explained, "Christianity is based not on myths, legends, or fairy tales, and not merely on a teaching . . . but primarily on a historical personality: Jesus of Nazareth, who is believed as God's Christ."[106] Why then all the controversy?

---

[105]Küng, *On Being a Christian*, 306.
[106]Küng, *Theology for the New Millennium*, 111.

Küng made clear in *On Being a Christian* that his approach to expounding the faith for today would be consistently from below. He wanted to communicate Christian belief to modern men and women not by presupposing any dogmas of the church but by beginning with their questions and experiences, in order to provide a rational justification for faith today.[107] The Catholic thinker carried this approach into his Christology, investigating who Jesus is by following the path from the history of Jesus to the church's confession of him as the Christ—the same path traversed by the first disciples.[108] Nothing was particularly new in this approach. Pannenberg, for example, had followed it in his Christology. The controversy was not over the method so much as over the results of the process.

Küng spent hundreds of pages of *On Being a Christian* exploring the historical personality of Jesus. Jesus was not a "pious legalist" or a "revolutionary." Rather, in Küng's portrayal, he was a man totally consumed with God's cause—the well-being of others—a man who had a unique experience of God as his Abba and devoted himself without reservation to the kingdom of God. In the end, he was raised up by God and "exalted" to glory. (Küng made clear, however, that these are metaphors that can only give hints of what became of Jesus Christ after his death.) Clearly, the Catholic theologian (as he still was then) considered Jesus a unique human being. Because of who he was, what he did and the fate he suffered, "the true *man* Jesus of Nazareth, is for faith the real *revelation* of the one true *God*."[109] He is God's "representative, delegate, deputy" and "the living pointer to God the Father."[110]

What Küng's critics were looking for, however, was some positive statement of Jesus' divinity, some affirmation of the ontological incarnation of God in Jesus, some acknowledgment that Jesus could be said to *be* God. This they could not find in *On Being a Christian*. In discussing Jesus' preexistence—an appropriate point for an affirmation of his divinity—Küng interpreted the doctrine as meaning only that Jesus' ultimate origin was from God.[111] This affirmation could be made about anyone, especially any prophet. It seemed that he was subscribing to the "ideal preexistence"

---

[107]Küng, *On Being a Christian*, 83.
[108]Küng, *Incarnation of God*, 493.
[109]Ibid., 444.
[110]Ibid., 391–92.
[111]Ibid., 447.

theory, that Jesus preexisted in the mind and will of God but not as the second person of the Trinity.[112] In one brief passage he provided his "up-to-date positive paraphrase of the ancient Chalcedonian formula 'truly God and truly man.'" Once again, he stated that Jesus was "God's advocate and deputy, representative and delegate" and the "permanently reliable ultimate standard of human existence."[113] This, he wrote, was to stand "against all tendencies to deify Jesus."[114] Naturally, Küng was accused by his critics of adoptionism and christological reductionism akin to liberal and neo-liberal Protestant theology's functional Christology. This is one reason Rahner labeled him a liberal Protestant.

Küng leaves a questionable legacy of traditionalism and accommodation. Küng was one of the twentieth century's most prolific and popular theologians, and he continues to be both a beacon and lightning rod well into the twenty-first century. For many people he is a symbol of progressive Christian thought. For others he is the epitome of the arrogant academic rebel against tradition. Among those who know him and his theology indifference is rare. Some of the controversial points of his theology have already been indicated. Here the main question will be about his status as a modern or postmodern theologian.

One of the problems of modern theology since the Enlightenment and certainly since Schleiermacher is accommodation to modernity. How much is too much? The Roman Catholic hierarchy believes Küng's is too much. And yet he calls his own theological method postmodern, not modern. Here we need to dispense with the notion that it is truly postmodern. When *Theology for the Third Millennium*, where he claimed the label "postmodern" for his theology, was published in 1987 the term "postmodern" was still very unclear especially in theological circles. Some theologians were calling their very traditional theologies postmodern orthodoxy, and yet in philosophy the label increasingly meant deconstructionism—the technique of

---

[112]Küng's doctrine of the Trinity is underdeveloped and extremely vague. It seems that for him the "Spirit" is the presence of God the Father and the "Son" is Jesus. Thus, there is no immanent, eternal, ontological Trinity, but only a historical and functional Trinity. However, this can only be surmised because he provides very little to go on in interpreting his concept of God's triunity. See *On Being a Christian*, 477.

[113]Ibid., 449–50.

[114]Ibid., 449.

exposing the ideological tendencies of literature and philosophical and theological truth claims. In theology "postmodern" was an essentially contested concept and a popular one that many different thinkers wanted to own. It was something of a buzzword that drew attention. It waited to be filled with content. It could mean any approach to practicing theology that was not modernist. Even process theology, as modern as it is, was being labeled postmodern by some people who wanted to reinvigorate it with panache. It is very doubtful that the theological method spelled out by Küng should be categorized as postmodern in the second decade of the twenty-first century, when that label is coming in intellectual circles to mean something more specific and definitely other than rejection of rationalism. Critical rationality may not be exactly modern, but neither does it fit the antifoundationalism and emphasis on suspicion usually associated with postmodernism.

One sympathetic critic of Küng's theological method was Catherine Mowry LaCugna (1952–1997), who clearly viewed it as more modern than traditionally Christian or postmodern. The question she focused her criticism on was the Swiss theologian's real final criterion for truth in theological reconstruction. Is it Scripture, the "gospel" within Scripture or the historical-critical method? She correctly observed that a distinction must be made between Küng's theoretical methodology (his stated intentions) and his applied methodology (what he does).[115] (This is the distinction made in this book about Tillich's method of correlation.) After rigorous investigation she concluded that "formally speaking . . . in Küng's theoretical methodology there appears to be a lively, if not difficult, tension between faith and history, in which the historical strand conditions but does not determine the strand of faith."[116] In other words, Küng cannot make up his mind which he will choose as the ultimate norm for theological truth, should a conflict arise between critical historical reason and clear biblical teaching and the church's traditional teaching about Jesus Christ. At least he never clearly opted for historical criticism over faith in the teachings of the Bible about the gospel. In fact, as seen earlier here, he stated that in such a conflict situation the gospel wins out over critical reason.

---

[115]LaCugna, *Theological Methodology*, 174.
[116]Ibid., 178.

LaCugna concluded, however, that in his applied methodology Küng gives undue weight to the historical-critical method of discovering truth. While Jesus Christ is supposed to be the criterion of all truth and truth itself, the "real Christ" seems to be accessible only through historical-critical analysis.[117] In practice, then, he elevates critical reason above, or at least alongside of, Jesus Christ himself, and certainly above both Scripture and tradition. But does not this approach serve to raise the individual critical exegete or some group of critical scholars above the absolute claim of the gospel, which is available only through Scripture and the Christian tradition? If so, then the charge that Küng is a liberal Protestant, accommodated to modernity, is largely sustained. That charge arises more sharply than ever in relation to his specific reconstructions of Christian doctrines. His account of the God-world relation leaves the prior actuality of God unclear. In several instances he indicated a marked preference for Hegel's very modern "dialectical unity of God and the world." He likewise expressed strong distaste for the entire concept of the supernatural and blatantly denied that the concept of miracles makes any sense: "Physically, a supernatural intervention by God in the world would be nonsense."[118] What should a Christian believe about such important dimensions of biblical piety as prayer? It comes as no surprise that Küng hardly discusses prayer in his major doctrinal or apologetic writings. Finally, he portrayed Jesus as a special, even unique, human person, but not as God incarnate (in spite of the title of one of his most important books). Nothing he said about Jesus in his quasi-systematic theology that includes a massive section on Christology comes close to ascribing deity to him.

It seems that after all the magnificent apologetics, when it comes to doctrine we are left with a fairly weak, liberal or neo-liberal Protestant theology in which historical criticism and the modern, scientific worldview play the leading roles. In spite of his claim to discover and adhere to a postmodern paradigm, Küng's real, functional methodology is deeply imbued with the spirit of modernity. True, Popper's critical rationalism is criticized as is positivism, two closely related radical extensions of the modern spirit into

---

[117]Ibid., 194–95.
[118]Küng, *Does God Exist?* 653.

epistemology. A close reading of *On Being a Christian*, however, cannot miss the frequent accommodations to modernity and especially the underlying, implicit rejection of the supernatural. Küng's Christianity is demythologized and redesigned to fit, not atheism or secularism, but the modern scientific worldview.

10.C. HANS URS VON BALTHASAR BASES CHRISTIAN TRUTH ON BEAUTY

According to Balthasar, the gospel is like a magnificent painting or a gripping drama; it radiates beauty that fulfills and transforms. Modernity's basic problem is forgetfulness of beauty; secularity empties the world of glory. Only the sacred can answer humanity's longing for the beautiful, the harmonious, the glorious. Modernity relegated these to the subjective realm leaving humans disconnected from anything truly satisfying. The drama of God in Jesus Christ is intrinsically beautiful and glorious and therein lies its superiority to dry-as-dust secularism and rationalism.

Balthasar examined "man's search for God," hidden within the search for meaning, beauty and purpose, in the whole history of philosophy and concluded, "Searching is the basic characteristic of the human being."[119] He concluded that all philosophical attempts to discover truth, beauty and goodness, the universal "transcendentals" of philosophy and religion, resulted in dead ends. At best, "the God of the philosophers is a mild, timeless, diffuse light,"[120] a pale reflection of something or Someone that satisfies the human longing for satisfaction. Of all the philosophical and religious systems, he inquired,

> Is there nowhere a unity of these fragments of theory and practice? Is there not anywhere beside all these false trails a road which will take us through the forest of being? If so, then there is only one. Something would have to happen which the blind person's fumbling cannot take into account in the search: namely, that suddenly another hand would seize his and take over the lead. This other hand would not be the hand of a fellow human being.[121]

---

[119]Hans Urs von Balthasar, *The von Balthasar Reader*, ed. Medard Kehl and Werner Löser, trans. Robert J. Daly and Fred Lawrence (New York: Crossroad, 1982), 188.
[120]Ibid., 191.
[121]Ibid., 190.

According to Balthasar, "the human being in its search for truth can never arrive by philosophizing—of however simple or academic a kind—at the statement 'God is love.'"[122] And yet *only* that satisfies. Only the revelation of God in Jesus Christ can take the hand of lost people "searching for God" and lead them to their goal.

How does he know this? Where does he place his confidence that this is true? Not on a rational, philosophical foundation such as traditional natural theology or apologetic proofs or on a leap of faith. Instead, Balthasar appeals to the "Aha!" experience of beauty a person has who sits in silence and contemplates a great work of art and is suddenly transformed by it. In Munich, Germany, where he studied and taught, people sit in enormous rooms in the *Alte Pinakothek* (Old Gallery of Art) such as the Rubens-Saal (Rubens Room) and for hours stare at twenty-foot-high paintings by the Old Masters. Contemplation of their form and symbolism as well as their style and color delivers an experience of beauty unparalleled elsewhere. According to Balthasar,

> if one reflects for a while on this [the love of God in Jesus Christ], keeping in mind the whole fate of Jesus up to his cross, then perhaps the realization might begin to dawn that here occurred God's final, never-to-be-exceeded self-revelation. That in this existence and in this dying abandonment by God, God has proclaimed his final "word" which from that point rings undiminished down the centuries. What more then could be said than this?[123]

In contrast to the majority of modern theologians, Balthasar believed that contemplation is a necessary component in apprehension of truth. Christian theology studies the great drama of God's eventful revelation and activity for the salvation of humanity in an attitude of openness to truth, beauty and goodness. In this posture, the person receives the hand of God to lead him or her on the journey toward ultimate satisfaction.

Balthasar follows an unusual path to theological fame. On June 30, 1988, Pope John Paul II sent a telegram to Joseph Cardinal Ratzinger (b. 1927; the future Pope Benedict XVI). The pope asked the cardinal to honor the just deceased priest-theologian Hans Urs von Balthasar with a homily at his fu-

---

[122]Ibid., 193.
[123]Ibid.

neral. John Paul II had decided to name Balthasar a cardinal of the Catholic Church, but the Swiss theologian died before he could receive the honor. Ratzinger, then Prefect of the Congregation for the Doctrine of the Faith, delivered a glowing eulogy for a theologian who long labored in relative obscurity, shunned by the leaders of his church and sometimes vilified as a fanatic and heretic. Among other things he said of the deceased theologian:

> Henri de Lubac [an influential Catholic theologian] has called Balthasar possibly the most cultured person of our time. Actually, the arc of his works spans from the predecessors of Socrates to Freud, Nietzsche, and Berthold Brecht; it embraces the entire Western heritage of philosophy, literature, art and theology. But in this vast adventure of the spirit, his interest was not the curiosity to know a great deal, nor the power that comes from having many skills. If he wished to gather the treasures of Egypt into the storehouse of our Faith (to speak the language of the Church Fathers), he also knew that such treasures can bear fruit only in a converted heart, while on the shoulders of the unconverted they become a destructive burden. He knew that fullness of knowledge turns to unhappiness in the face of the extent of the still unknown and to despair over our impotence to achieve the essential: being a person, life itself. What Balthasar wanted may well be encapsulated in a single phrase of St. Augustine: "Our entire task in this life, dear brothers, consists in healing the eyes of the heart so they may be able to see God."[124]

After his death, Balthasar's theology gradually began to be read and celebrated by both Catholics and Protestants. Before that, he was best known, especially among Protestants, for his magisterial study of the theology of Karl Barth titled *The Theology of Karl Barth* (1951/1961). His person and work were the subject of controversy in the Catholic Church, although after the Second Vatican Council they grew into greater appreciation. Three factors account for this ambiguity of his reputation among Catholics. First, he was noted for criticizing the standard neo-scholastic theology of Catholic thought that reigned throughout much of the late nineteenth and early to mid-twentieth centuries. He frequently referred to it as dry and lifeless. While he had no sympathy for Catholic modernism (see 2.d.), he did believe Catholic theology needed to a new approach to make it vital and relevant.

---

[124]Josef Ratzinger, "Homily at the Funeral Liturgy for Hans Urs von Balthasar," *Communio: International Catholic Review* 15 (winter 1988): 512.

Second, Balthasar was considered at the least eccentric because of his attachment to a mystic named Adrienne von Speyr (1902–1967), a Swiss physician who converted to Catholicism under Balthasar's guidance. She then became his spiritual director, and he spent numerous hours over many years writing down her spiritual insights. He clearly believed her to be a prophet. Because he and she founded a secular institution for the propagation of her revelations and other matters, Balthasar was relieved of his Jesuit orders, or he gave them up. He remained a priest, however, and a devoted son of the Catholic Church.

Finally, third, before the Second Vatican Council, Balthasar was widely considered an adherent of the *nouvelle théologie*. For Catholic integralists (conservatives, usually neo-scholastics), the *nouvelle théologie* was regarded with suspicion as bordering on the immanentalist error of Catholic modernism. That is, traditionalists thought these *nouvelle* theologians were advocating an overly immanent view of God as part of nature so that the line between the human and the divine was blurred. *Nouvelle théologie* was largely vindicated by Vatican II, and Balthasar's reputation grew. However, only after his death has he been widely considered one of the few truly great Catholic theologians of the modern age.

Unlike some other theologians described in this book, Balthasar did not begin life in humble circumstances. The "von" in his name indicates nobility; his family stood in a long line of Swiss families of noble heritage and wealth. He was born in the Alpine town of Lucerne and early felt called to the priesthood. He studied at several German, Austrian and Swiss universities eventually receiving his doctoral degree in Germanic studies from the University of Zurich. He joined the Society of Jesus and was ordained in 1936. In 1939, on the eve of World War II, he was teaching theology in Munich. As a Swiss citizen he was allowed to leave Germany and spent the rest of his life in Basel, where he came into close contact with Barth. Balthasar served as a chaplain to students in Basel and gave lectures, some of which Barth attended. In 1950 he left the Jesuits and, together with von Speyr, founded an institute called the *Johannesgemeinschaft* (Community of John) and a publishing house known as the *Johannesverlag* (John Publisher). The Jesuits did not consider this work compatible with being a Jesuit. There is more than a suspicion that their distancing from Balthasar had something to do with his attachment to and reverence for von Speyr.

Although Balthasar had worked hard to prepare the way for the Second Vatican Council, unlike Rahner he was not invited to participate. That was a slap in his face by the hierarchy. However, as alluded to already, the outcome of the council was influenced by his theology, and his standing in Catholic circles was enhanced by it. Later he bemoaned what he saw as the liberalizing direction of some post–Vatican II Catholic theology. He stoutly defended clerical celibacy, restriction of ordination to males and rules against contraception. To some he was a conservative, a traditionalist. To others he was a progressive. To most he has been something of an enigma, even if a brilliant one.[125]

Throughout the 1990s and into the twenty-first century, Balthasar's star has risen steadily and rapidly, even among Protestant theologians. Most of his books are still in print, and book-length studies of his thought are being published every year. Many doctoral dissertations are being written about his theology, and scholarly symposia are being held at professional society meetings. Most Catholic universities in Europe and the United States, as well as some Protestant ones, hold graduate seminars devoted to his theology. The papacy of Benedict XVI was increasingly promoting Balthasar as a model theologian for Catholics.

Balthasar's writings fill many volumes that weigh down shelves and boggle minds. Many theologians, among them Barth and Rahner, were prolific writers. Few rival Balthasar, however, whose prodigious output is almost beyond recounting. His magnum opus is the three sets of books on systematic theology published under the general titles *The Glory of the Lord* (seven volumes), *Theo-Drama* (five volumes) and *Theo-Logic* (three volumes). Volume 1 of *The Glory of the Lord*, titled *Seeing the Form* (1961), encompasses 691 pages in English translation (1984). His collected essays, published under the general title *Explorations in Theology*, fill four large volumes. His monographs (books on individual subjects) in English trans-

---

[125]David Moss and Edward T. Oakes, "Introduction," in *The Cambridge Companion to Hans Urs von Balthasar*, ed. Edward T. Oakes and David Moss (Cambridge: Cambridge University Press, 2004), 1–7. The facts about Balthasar's life and career here come from this source and Medard Kehl, "Hans Urs von Balthasar: A Portrait," in *The von Balthasar Reader*, ed. Medard Kehl and Werner Löser, trans. Robert J. Daly and Fred Lawrence (New York: Crossroad, 1982), 3–54.

lation number forty-five; more are yet to be translated. Some estimate his actual number of books at more than one hundred.

Few can claim to have read all of Balthasar's published works; even fewer can claim to have absorbed and understood them. Even Balthasar scholars have usually read only some. A greater problem than reading everything he wrote, however, is summarizing his thought in any systematic way. By all accounts he was not a strictly linear or systematic thinker. In spite of his broad and deep grasp of philosophy from Plato to Heidegger and of theology and culture in general, he was primarily a contemplative, and his writings reveal it. Although they are sprinkled with biblical references and quotations and references to and quotations from numerous great thinkers of history, they tend to be somewhat impressionistic—almost like stream of consciousness. He was writing as he thought. That is not to say he was not using research; he most certainly was. It is only to say that his style confounds the reader looking for the usual procedure from point A to point Z with each unit of thought building directly on something more basic and general before it.

Two of Balthasar's most astute English interpreters, the editors of *The Cambridge Companion to Hans Urs von Balthasar*, Edward T. Oakes and David Moss, say that the common response to the Swiss theologian is "perplexity"[126] because "in Hans Urs von Balthasar we encounter a man teeming with paradoxes."[127] One perplexing paradox is that his theology is traditional and idiosyncratic.[128] That is, on the one hand, Balthasar afforded great authority to Scripture and tradition, especially the church fathers, and, on the other hand, was not afraid to introduce new and even sometimes radical twists to traditional beliefs. Also, he was distinctly antimodern while displaying profound knowledge and understanding of modern philosophy, science and culture. He was opposed to too much accommodation to modernity (which he saw in much modern theology) without being fundamentalist or obscurantist. In many of these aspects he provided a Catholic parallel to Barth, his Protestant dialogue partner in Basel.

---

[126]Moss and Oakes, "Introduction," in *The Cambridge Companion to Hans Urs von Balthasar*, ed. Edward T. Oakes and David Moss (Cambridge: Cambridge University Press, 2004), 1.
[127]Ibid., 6.
[128]Ibid., 7.

Balthasar propounds his big idea. Every theologian has a big idea—a key insight that forms the center of his or her theological project. Schleiermacher's was *Gefühl*—humanity's feeling of utter dependence, or God-consciousness. Barth's was revelation of God as self-revelation, especially in Jesus Christ. Tillich's was God as being itself as answer to the human predicament. Rahner's was the supernatural existential. All were discovered and propounded to some degree in relation to modernity even if primarily against it. What was Balthasar's big idea? As of yet there is no consensus about that among Balthasar scholars. And yet, it seems fairly obvious: Being is love. It is not obvious to everyone because he used so many terms besides love to describe the nature of being—especially the so-called philosophical transcendentals (attributes of being) truth, beauty, goodness and oneness. But for him, they all resolve into love as love is properly understood as self-giving. For Balthasar, the highest and best truth available to humanity is that God's self-giving in Jesus Christ alone satisfies human longing for the true, the good and the beautiful.

Balthasar expressed this basic idea in numerous ways. "It is exclusively in God's reaching to us that our stretching to God reaches its goal."[129] If that sounds prosaic, especially after studying other theologians who said something similar (e.g., Augustine's idea of the "restless heart"[130]), it is not so once one sees what the Swiss theologian meant by "God's reaching to us." Another way he expressed it is "only the eternal God can fulfill the longing gaze of human freedom."[131] According to Balthasar, what humanity has always been longing for, stretching toward, is infinite love, a love beyond the finite loves of this world. By "love" he definitely did not mean a feeling. He meant a giving of self that is absolutely selfless and all-including. The closest analogy is the mother's loving gaze at her infant child. But even that is not infinite love. Ultimately, for Balthasar, infinite love can be expressed and experienced only in absolute being's going out of itself (himself) into death and hell for the sake of the loved. We will return to that.

So, according to Balthasar, the entire story of human thought, philosophy, religion and culture is wrapped up in the unending, world-transcending

---

[129]*The von Balthasar Reader*, 22.
[130]Augustine wrote in his *Confessions* that our hearts are restless until they find their rest in God.
[131]*The von Balthasar Reader*, 103.

search for being as love, for infinite love. Philosophy does not deliver even though it reaches toward it: "The God of the philosophers is a mild, timeless, diffuse light."[132] In other words, natural reason, at its best, can deliver something of value, but it cannot reach the goal. Ultimately, humanity's longing, stretching, searching for love can be fulfilled and finalized only in God's self-revelation in Jesus Christ, which is distinctly not an idea but an event:

> No religion or world view has dared to think and proclaim something of this kind about God, human beings, and the world; therefore Christianity remains without analogy, and it rests not on an "idea" but on a fact—Jesus Christ—which, in the unity of claim, cross and resurrection, remains an unsplittable atom. It depends on him whether we can dare to address being as love, and thus all beings as worthy of love, an idea to which the face of the world would otherwise have hardly brought us.[133]

What Balthasar meant by "something of this kind" is yet to be explored; it has to do with self-giving on the part of absolute being—even unto death.

Crucial to Balthasar's big idea (about an event) is beauty. All philosophy and religion deal with what he calls the transcendentals mentioned above. Beauty stands out for him as the bridge connecting humanity's universal searching and Christianity's message about the event. One of his main complaints is that modern Western philosophy and religion have largely forgotten beauty. Beauty has been reduced to something subjective—what pleases the senses—in the eye of the beholder. Not so for much of traditional philosophy and religion, however. According to him, real beauty is not "a mere perception of a delightful vision" but "the 'aesthetic' experience of the awesome glory of divine being."[134] Beauty is harmony, glorious goodness, peace, form. Beauty overcomes the dualisms that break and fragment existence. Modern Western people have largely lost "aesthetic knowledge," the ability to apprehend real beauty. That needs to be restored because "without aesthetic knowledge, neither theoretical nor practical reason can attain to their total completion."[135]

---

[132]Ibid., 191.
[133]Ibid., 113.
[134]Hans Urs von Balthasar, *The Glory of the Lord: A Theological Aesthetics 1: Seeing the Form*, trans. Erasmo Leiva-Merikakis, ed. Joseph Fessio and John Riches (San Francisco: Ignatius Press, 1982), 158.
[135]Ibid., 147.

How can aesthetic knowledge be restored to modern Western people? That is a major part of Balthasar's project. He wanted to draw a picture, as it were, that would bring out people's latent sense of beauty and appeal to them as that which alone can satisfy their deepest longings and desires. But he realized the obstacles were formidable. Much modern Western culture and religion stands in the way. Catholic neo-scholasticism and Protestantism took their share of criticism from Balthasar as responsible for the demise of aesthetic knowledge. A basic presupposition of his, however, is that "the beautiful brings with it a self-evidence that enlightens without mediation."[136] The person who is open to beauty in a contemplative way will be grasped when confronted by it. In fact, a Christian, Balthasar said, is someone who has been "snatched up by the beauty of Christ" and thus "inflamed by the most sublime of beauties."[137]

Balthasar did not think, however, that a person with the most heightened aesthetic knowledge or sensibility could reach saving knowledge of God without a special impartation of God's grace. Such a special impartation of grace, however, he believed, is always already at work in the world of philosophy and religion, leading people who seek toward the fullness of glory. The self-revelation of God in Jesus Christ, he averred, is not the canceling but the fulfilling of "man's entire philosophical-mythological questioning."[138] About non-Christian philosophies, world views, mythologies and religions he wrote, in language reminiscent of C. S. Lewis, that "it could be the case . . . that God's true light also falls upon figures of human imagination (myths) and speculation (philosophies), and that this light can lead them and their partial truths to the God of revelation."[139]

So, what for Balthasar is ultimately beautiful, that toward which all humanity's striving and seeking reaches and that which alone can fulfill and perfect them? In a phrase, the "condescension of divine love."[140] Of the mission of Christian theology he wrote that "we have a real and inescapable obligation to probe the possibility of . . . a genuine relationship between theological beauty and the beauty of the world."[141] In other words, the

---

[136]Ibid., 36.
[137]Ibid., 33.
[138]Ibid., 141.
[139]Ibid., 152.
[140]Ibid., 121.
[141]Ibid., 78.

theologian's task is to discover the natural and supernatural bridges between beauty in the world, including humanity's searching and striving for
it, and the condescension of divine love in Jesus Christ. The act of faith, he
posited, is always "both 'supernatural' (because sustained by the light of
grace) and 'natural' (as the perfect fulfillment of spiritual aspirations)."[142]
In other words, persons brought to faith in Christ discover there the answer
to their natural strivings, but the answer is from above, so to speak, and not
from below. However, and this is a major "however," for Balthasar, even the
striving and yearning and questioning of the natural person is a result of
grace. This point brings us to one of his main propositions: that there is no
such thing as "pure nature" from a Christian point of view.

Balthasar calls belief in "pure nature" theologically dangerous. Every
theologian writes out of a context of concern. Balthasar's overriding concern
was with religious and secular belief in "pure nature." To him, religious belief
in pure nature leads to secularism. And secular thought has to reduce nature
to pure nature—nature stripped of grace, divorced from the supernatural,
shorn of mystery and depth. And he saw the culprits all around him.

For Balthasar, the ultimate villain is "the catastrophe of nominalism."[143]
Nominalism is the denial of the reality of universals such as truth, beauty
and goodness. It reduces these to concepts if not mere words. The result of
nominalism, which lies at the root of modernity, is "a dessicated and dreary
secularized Christianity"[144] bereft of everything that makes Christianity
beautiful. If beauty is just in the eye of the beholder, as nominalism has it,
then even Jesus Christ is not truly beautiful. The root problem of modernity
and the religions of modernity, including most modern theology, according
to Balthasar, is lack of aesthetics:

> Once the perception of God's innate beauty and of the inherent and self-estab-
> lishing attractiveness of revelation disappears, it becomes impossible for the
> ordinary citizen of the world to see any value in being religious at all or to see
> in Christianity the very embodiment of God's [beautiful] condescension.[145]

---

[142]Ibid., 145.
[143]Edward T. Oakes, *Pattern of Redemption: The Theology of Hans Urs von Balthasar* (New York:
    Continuum, 1994), 180.
[144]Ibid., 177.
[145]Ibid., 171.

When beauty goes, with it eventually go truth and goodness because these are all inseparable in being. And God goes with them, even where God is still spoken about.

Nominalism led to modernity; modernity led to secularity; secularity led to a void of meaning, an emptiness, a striving without finding. Ultimately, Balthasar said, "modern man has had the frightful misfortune that God in nature has died for him."[146] Because of its overwhelming anthropocentrism, modernity has led to a situation where "in whatever mirror of nature he [the human] may look, he will always ultimately see himself."[147] Modern culture that "approaches things from a merely rationalistic and technical point of view . . . completely misunderstands its own being."[148] That is because in all their striving and searching and seeking after meaning human persons are ultimately spiritual and not merely natural. This is because, as Balthasar says in somewhat philosophical language, "the unity of the consciousness of mankind cannot be expressed otherwise than as a question that is open towards what is above, that is to God."[149]

It will be helpful, even necessary, to stop momentarily and note that in his polemics against modernity and pure nature Balthasar was not attacking science. He explicitly rejected Christian apologetics that turns against modern science: "Today we see clearly that we cannot fight science with Scripture, because the aim of God's revelation in the Bible is not to teach men science. But how dearly had this understanding to be paid for!"[150] (He was referring to the Galileo affair.) For him, science is not the enemy of God or Christianity. The enemy is belief in pure nature. Science cannot say whether nature is devoid of everything sacred or spiritual; it studies only the mechanics of nature. It is not equipped to discover the mysterious depths of nature in grace. That is a matter for philosophy and religion. And in modernity both have largely failed.

To sum up Balthasar's attitude toward modernity, then, he called it "a tragic epoch" in the history of humanity.[151] That is because "men can no longer

---

[146]Hans Urs von Balthasar, *The God Question and Modern Man*, trans. Hilda Graef (New York: Seabury, 1967), 100.
[147]Ibid., 26.
[148]Ibid., 33.
[149]Ibid., 77.
[150]Ibid., 93.
[151]Ibid., 143.

love each other without God."[152] But even bare belief in "a god" will not suffice to fix humanity's desperate situation. Life on earth is becoming unbearable, he warned, without the incarnation.[153] Only the incarnation provides the eventful answer to humanity's longing search for self-giving love.

What exactly did Balthasar mean by "pure nature"? And why is it so pernicious? Pure nature would be nature devoid of grace, nature on its own, independent of anything sacred. Pure nature would be nature that is sufficient in itself to which grace would be at best an attachment rather than something intrinsic and fulfilling. Pure nature is set over against the spiritual; spirit is its counterpart and not necessary to it. A belief system that includes pure nature is necessarily dualistic and tends toward secularity. A basic premise of Balthasar's and, he would say, a basic presupposition of Christianity, is that "nature was never without spirit [especially] in humanity."[154] This is an expression of what we learned as intrinsicism in Catholic theology, especially in the *nouvelle théologie* going back to its precursor Blondel (see 2.d.). Balthasar was not only opposed to nominalism, modernity and secularism; he also vehemently opposed a type of Catholic thought called neo-scholasticism that reigned supreme in Catholic theology after the defeat of modernism in the first decade of the twentieth century.

According to Balthasar, and other theologians associated with *nouvelle théologie*, neo-scholasticism was guilty of the same sin as modern secularism. Neo-scholasticism was guilty, he charged, of extrinsicism—making grace extrinsic, external to nature. It portrayed nature as devoid of grace so that grace, the supernatural gifts, including love, is "added on," as it were, to nature. In stark contrast, Balthasar asserted that "love is built into the foundations of living beings."[155] Again, he did not mean love as in romantic love; he meant love as in self-giving love or at least the longing for it. As he saw it, neo-scholastic Catholic theology separated the natural and the supernatural, nature and grace, into two separate compartments, one above the other.[156] Their relationship was portrayed as extrinsic rather than organic.

---

[152]Ibid.
[153]Ibid., 144.
[154]*The von Balthasar Reader*, 78.
[155]Ibid., 87.
[156]Hans Boersma, *Nouvelle Théologie and Sacramental Ontology* (Oxford: Oxford University Press, 2009), 119.

Without going into all the details, it should be obvious why and how Balthasar saw this as playing into the hands of secularism. It robs the world of mystery, true beauty, goodness and value. Grace, the supernatural realm, God's own love, is then viewed as dispensable for nature to be what it is. Nature becomes ordinary, empty and unspiritual.

Balthasar rebuilds the world from its foundations. Balthasar was not interested in tinkering with neo-scholasticism or accommodating to modern secularity; nor was he particularly concerned with responding to the acids of modernity except those that reduced humanity to bare, pure nature. What he was interested in was, as one interpreter put it, "rebuilding the world from its foundations."[157] Expressed differently, he "never abandoned his insistence that modernity [and neo-scholasticism] has been consistently looking at reality through the wrong end of the telescope."[158] He wanted to turn the telescope around and see reality wholly differently—through the lens of the gospel and the church fathers. Two key, interrelated ideas stand out as crucial to Balthasar's ambitious project: nature as always already graced, and the *analogia entis*—the analogy of being.

Against both secular and religious forms of extrinsicism, belief in pure nature, Balthasar insisted on the presence of grace in nature. His main concern was the human person as already graced in his or her nature as evidenced by openness to God. With Rahner and many other *nouvelle théologie* Catholic thinkers, "man as spirit is open to God."[159] No person is devoid of any relation to God. On this hangs human dignity and value: "Every . . . person receives his highest dignity and freedom from his relation to God: for a person cannot be viewed and recognized in any other way."[160]

Something Balthasar is especially known for is his defense of the concept of the analogy of being. It is a concept rooted in classical Catholic thought going back to Thomas Aquinas, even though the Angelic Doctor did not mention it by that name. One of the Swiss theologian's mentors was a Polish Catholic philosopher-theologian named Erich Przywara (1889–1972; pro-

---

[157]Edward T. Oakes, "Envoi: The Future of Balthasarian Theology," in *The Cambridge Companion to Hans Urs von Balthasar*, ed. Edward T. Oakes and David Moss (Cambridge: Cambridge University Press, 2004), 269.

[158]Ibid.

[159]Balthasar, *The God Question and Modern Man*, 48.

[160]Ibid., 37.

nounced "shevara") who made this idea the centerpiece of his thought. At its most basic level, the analogy of being, *analogia entis*, claims that there exists a real ontological (having to do with being) relation between created beings and God who is absolute being.[161] The connection between this and Balthasar's idea of nature always already graced by God's supernatural gift of his presence should be obvious. Balthasar's intrinsicism demands that there be an analogy between God and created being that is not only notional; it must also be ontological.

The danger in this idea is immediately apparent—especially to neoscholastic Catholics and Protestants. (Modern secular thinkers have not gotten this far with Balthasar. They still struggle with the ideas of grace and the supernatural.) If there exists an analogy of being between God and the creature, even the human person created in God's image and likeness, then what of God's transcendent otherness? What of God's holiness? Christian tradition has always emphasized God's transcendence and otherness from creatures. God is said to be not like anything in creation. Luther talked about God's hiddenness; Barth wrote about God's "wholly otherness." Wouldn't analogy of being bring God down to creaturely size—even if bigger?

Balthasar wanted to stress first that God is with us, that the created order of nature, including human nature, is not devoid of God's real presence and activity. What does it mean that nature is always already graced?[162] One example is that for him, "the logic of the creature is not alien to the logic of God."[163] Second, Balthasar wished to stress just as emphatically that, in spite of the analogy, God is other than us. He insisted, against Barth, who claimed the analogy of being was the "invention of the anti-Christ,"[164] that it does not scale God down to creation's being; it does not make God and humanity, for example, of the same species. Analogy allows for more than proportional difference. In other words, God's being is a different quality of being and not

---

[161]Fergus Kerr, "Balthasar and Metaphysics," in *The Cambridge Companion to Hans Urs von Balthasar*, ed. Edward T. Oakes and David Moss (Cambridge: Cambridge University Press, 2004), 226. For an in-depth study of the Barth-Przywara-von Balthasar debate over the *analogia entis* see Keith L. Johnson, *Karl Barth and the* Analogia Entis (London: T & T Clark, 2011).
[162]John Webster, "Balthasar and Karl Barth," in *The Cambridge Companion to Hans Urs von Balthasar*, ed. Edward T. Oakes and David Moss (Cambridge: Cambridge University Press, 2004), 250.
[163]Ibid.
[164]Oakes, *Pattern of Redemption*, 41.

just a different quantity of it. It is not that God just has more being; it is that God wholly transcends the created order while at the same time giving it a participation in his reality by grace. Because of that gracious elevation, nature, creation, bears a resemblance to God. Again, an example is in order. Truth, beauty and goodness are present in nature *because* of God, not because these have some autonomous existence apart from God. These transcendental attributes of being are genuinely present in creation and can be known by creatures even though they are archetypally God's alone.

A terrible controversy broke out between Barth and Przywara and then between Barth and Balthasar over the analogy of being. Barth warned that it opened the door to pantheism—a blurring of the line between God and creation. And it threatened to rob grace of its gratuity—its freedom, its gift-nature. In other words, Barth worried, if God is somehow ontologically present in creation, then his redemption of creation is not totally free. By redeeming fallen creation God would be saving himself. It would be necessary and not absolutely free. In *The Theology of Karl Barth* Balthasar accused Barth of constructing and tearing down a straw man. For him, "once the straw man is seen for what it is, much of the force . . . falls away."[165] Basically, Balthasar explained that the analogy of being is the only way to avoid the pure nature fallacy, which opens the door to secularism, and it preserves God's transcendence, and thus the gratuity of grace, by saying the relationship between God and creation always remains analogy and not identity. And, the *Catholic* Swiss theologian repeatedly affirmed the declaration of a medieval church council that the dissimilarity between God and creation is always greater than the similarity.

The debate between Balthasar and Barth over the analogy of being reminds one of Barth's debate with Brunner (see 5.a.). It seems that Barth misunderstood at least Balthasar's concept of it. Still, there does seem to remain one perhaps subtle difference, even after theologians have worked on the matter and declared that Barth's concept of the "analogy of faith" and Balthasar's concept of the analogy of being are "two ways of understanding the one revelation of God."[166] The difference is that, for Barth, the relationship between God and the world is always one of confrontation, or at

---

[165]Webster, "Balthasar and Karl Barth," 249.
[166]Ibid., 250.

least contains that element. For Balthasar, the relationship between God, while not one of continuity (as in pantheism and panentheism), is always one of fulfillment. This is at least a difference of emphasis.

So, what does it mean that Balthasar sought to "rebuild the world from its foundations"? He answered that in *The God Question and Modern Man*:

> We are not concerned with re-interpreting or newly formulating either the act or the contents of faith. But its actual essence should become simple and transparent, it should be reborn and resurrected from the primeval sources of revelation; we would integrate into [it] those elements which it needs in order to attain its fullness, that is to say especially hope and love.[167]

In other words, Balthasar was not interested in reconstructing Christianity; he was interested in resurrecting it by means of an "archeology of alienated beauty."[168] That is, by stirring up the innate capacity in people to recognize the beautiful and to display Christian truth, the event of God's self-giving in Jesus Christ, as the truly beautiful. By exposing all forms of extrinsicism as false and by expressing a theology of grace in nature that does justice to God's transcendence as well as God's immanence.

Balthasar was not interested in producing a rational system of Christian theology. He was interested in demonstrating how beauty leads to God and how the supernatural beauty of grace connects to the beauty of the natural. He was interested in being God's servant in showing to modern people the beauty of God's infinity and self-giving. He wanted his theology to overcome the habit in which Christians "settle down in the visible . . . with the modern mind that is turned toward the world."[169] He was fully aware that, to rebuild the universe, to turn the world around from this forgetfulness of beauty, it would take more than a new theology. Rather, he wrote, "Christians must be more intensely on fire with the love of God."[170] Nevertheless, he hoped that he could be an instrument "to bring back mankind, and especially Christendom, to a more adequate idea of God. . . . The Christian answer must know how . . . to change it into something that brings light and

---

[167]Balthasar, *The God Question and Modern Man*, 141.
[168]Oakes, *Pattern of Redemption*, 159.
[169]Balthasar, *The God Question and Modern Man*, 100.
[170]Ibid., 101.

unity."[171] As one commentator noted, his books are not meant to "systematize revelation" ("for to arrange something in a system is to imply we have gained a kind of control over it").[172] They are meant rather "to set things into motion in the heart of the reader."[173] They are exercises in contemplative theology intended to point the way out of modern blindness and deafness to beauty and toward a more adequate idea of God.

Balthasar offers a "more adequate idea of God." Balthasar's doctrine of God begins with God's self-revelation in Jesus Christ as self-giving love. For him, that is the beauty of being itself, that it freely gives itself away for the other. No world religion or philosophy has offered such a beautiful vision of ultimate reality. But it did not come like a bolt out of the blue, delivered from heaven against everything people ever thought, experienced or anticipated. For him, the graced, natural experience that yearns for such an infinite love begins with the mother's gaze on her child and the child's first experience in the world which is that gaze. That is only an analogy of God's love, but it is an analogy. And from that moment on, or from whatever first experience a person has of love, even if only yearning for it, he or she knows deep inside that there must be love at the heart of being or else life is absurd.

For Balthasar, absoluteness of love demonstrates absoluteness of being.[174] And absoluteness of love and being is exactly what is revealed in Jesus Christ. "It is utterly incomprehensible that the absolute love (which in the triune life is completely satisfied in itself) should, for the sake of the sinner (which I am), empty itself of its divine form and go into the outermost darkness to die."[175] Yet this drama contains an "inner harmony" that is incomparable in its beauty. The drama begins with "the risk God has taken in entrusting his creatures with genuine freedom."[176] "Ultimately God could only take such a risk if he threw himself into the balance, assumed the risk himself, and of himself opened a way where there was no way."[177] Right away, then, at the beginning of his doctrine of God, Balthasar steps aside from tradition,

---

[171]Ibid., 97.
[172]Oakes, *Pattern of Redemption*, 135.
[173]Ibid., 139.
[174]*The von Balthasar Reader*, 102.
[175]Ibid., 126.
[176]Ibid., 199.
[177]Ibid.

taking the biblical narrative of God's love ultimately seriously. God risks; God puts himself at risk. God radically enters into history with his creatures, giving over to them his own destiny which meant the cross.

This Balthasar identifies as Christianity's "outrageous claim"[178]—that the God who is absolute being and absolute freedom is also absolute love and that he demonstrated it by "coming over to our side"[179] in Jesus Christ. But the Swiss theologian did not stop there. He dared to talk about God dying and even being dead. Of the incarnation he wrote that "he [God] does not thereby cease to be himself; indeed he shows precisely through this what he is in himself, what he is and what he can do. God can be dead without ceasing to be eternal life."[180] Balthasar did not mean, like Altizer, that God annihilated himself in the incarnation and death of Jesus Christ. He heartily affirmed the resurrection of Jesus from death. However, Balthasar was not timid about talking of God's death—especially in relation to "Holy Saturday"—a major theme of his theology. In stark, paradoxical fashion he wrote of the triune God, revealed in Jesus and especially his death, "He is so full of life (so very much love) that he can afford to be dead."[181]

Balthasar was willing to jettison some traditional Catholic notions of God's transcendence, especially impassability (that God is incapable of suffering), in order to take fully seriously the impact of the incarnation and death of Christ on God himself. He warned that this drama, God-with-us in Jesus, "must be enveloped in the radiance of mystery. It cannot be neatly resolved and rationally surveyed, but rather is full of blessed paradoxes."[182] But he meant it when he declared about the event of the cross, "Here the love between Father and Son has adopted the mode of estrangement . . . in order to include in itself all men's estrangement through sin."[183] The ultimate mystery in all this is Holy Saturday—Christ's, God's, descent into hell. This is the ultimate "condescension of divine love"—that God went to hell with the dead. On Holy Saturday, Balthasar

---

[178]Ibid., 195.
[179]Ibid., 199.
[180]Ibid., 200.
[181]Ibid., 113.
[182]Balthasar, *The God Question and Modern Man*, 141.
[183]Ibid., 117.

averred, God was "(out of an ultimate love . . .) dead together with them."[184]

What Christ, God incarnate, did in hell on Holy Saturday is a mystery, but Balthasar was not shy about expressing it anyway. ("Expressing" is not the same as "explaining.") There, in hell, he wrote, God took over the "hellish desolation of the creature" and "transmuted [it] into an expression of love."[185] Clearly, he was going against the belief common among Christians that on Holy Saturday Christ went into Hades, the abode of the dead, to preach the good news of his atoning death for sins to Old Covenant believers who were waiting there. Then, so some tradition says, he took them to paradise. (This doctrine of the "harrowing of hell" is based on Matthew 12:40; Acts 2:27, 31; 1 Peter 3:19-20; 4:6; and Ephesians 4:8-10. It is also based on expressions about Christ descending into hell in the ancient ecumenical creeds.) Balthasar believed, based largely on von Speyr's revelations, that Christ did not merely preach in hell or Hades but identified with the dead in their estrangement from God. His descent into hell, then, is part of his atoning work for humanity and an event in the life history of God—part of the "theo-drama" that is revelation.

Balthasar's is a radical reworking, a reconstruction, of traditional Christian theism. His interpreter Edward Oakes says of the Swiss theologian's concept of Holy Saturday that it "constitutes his single greatest innovation to the tradition."[186] What is so radical about it is that Jesus' descent into hell, for Balthasar, "involves nothing less than a change in the relationship between God and the world that affects the relations within the Godhead."[187] It is the "incorporation of godforsakenness into the trinitarian relations."[188] And it implies a radical kenosis (self-emptying) in God himself and not only in the humanity of Jesus. There is within the trinitarian life of God, Balthasar dared to speculate, an "emptying of each Person for the other."[189] The essence of love is self-giving, so within the eternal life of God, which forms the background of the incarnation and cross event, the persons of the Trinity give themselves to each other in selfless love. Balthasar summed

---

[184]*The von Balthasar Reader*, 153.
[185]Ibid., 172.
[186]Oakes, *Pattern of Redemption*, 237.
[187]Ibid., 243.
[188]Ibid., 247.
[189]Ibid., 290.

up his entire doctrine of God: "No truth of revelation, from the Trinity to the Cross and Judgment, can speak of anything else than the glory of God's poor love—which of course is something much different than what we here below imagine by the name love. No, it is Spirit and Fire."[190]

The upshot is that, for Balthasar, hell is a real place, but we are to hope that, because of Holy Saturday, it is empty. According to him, "the dogma [of the church] is that hell exists, not that people are in it."[191] He was not a universalist, in which case he would have definitely affirmed the universal reconciliation of all with God. He explained his position clearly in *Dare We Hope "That All Men Be Saved"?* His own view is expressed in a quote from another theologian:

> Will it really be *all men* who allow themselves to be reconciled? No theology or prophecy can answer this question. But love *hopes all things* (I Cor. 13:7). It cannot do otherwise than to hope for the reconciliation of all men in Christ. Such unlimited hope is, from the Christian standpoint, not only permitted but *commanded.*[192]

Balthasar's view may rightly be labeled a "qualified universalism of hope" because it does not affirm universal salvation; it hopes for it. Responding to critics he wrote, "I never spoke of certainty but rather of hope."[193]

Balthasar stimulates enthusiasm and criticism among theologians. After his death a cult has arisen around Balthasar and his theology. He is called the Catholic Barth and a modern-day equivalent of Thomas Aquinas. Numerous, mostly laudatory, books and articles are pouring forth from publishing houses. A Catholic publisher in San Francisco is dedicated mostly to his writings. Why this seeming sudden surge of interest in a theologian most of whose works were composed in the 1950s and 1960s? A possible answer lies in what some see as his affinities with postmodernism.[194] Balthasar was a perspectivalist; he did not believe in the modern myth of detached impartiality, of "bare facts," of purely objective knowledge.[195] In-

---

[190]Quoted in ibid., 298.
[191]Quoted in ibid., 306.
[192]Quoted from Hermann-Josef Lauter in *Dare We Hope "That All Men Be Saved"?* trans. David Kipp and Lothar Krauth (San Francisco: Ignatius Press, 1988), 213.
[193]Ibid., 18.
[194]Oakes, "Envoi," 272–73.
[195]Balthasar, *The Glory of the Lord*, 122.

stead, like many postmodern thinkers, he argued that all reasoning takes place from within a horizon of faith[196] whether it is called faith or not. That is, knowledge is not limited to what can be proven rationally, by the method of foundationalism; it includes whatever is discovered by means of the rationality appropriate to a particular sphere of experience and research. There is no universal rationality or view from nowhere. And apprehension of beauty is a kind of sixth sense that modernity has too often ignored to its detriment, leading to a dreary landscape of contemporary culture.

In spite of his popularity and enthusiastic embrace by people as different as Pope Benedict XVI and Reformed theologian Hans Boersma, Balthasar had and has his critics. He referred to his critics in *Dare We Hope?* After a litany of harsh attacks on his position from conservatives and liberals, he concluded, "So be it; if I have been cast aside as a hopeless conservative by the tribe of the left, then I now know what sort of dung-heap I have been dumped upon by the right."[197] He was ambiguous enough in some of his theological constructions and conclusions to be relegated to near heresy by opposite camps. His criticisms of neo-scholasticism throughout the 1950s, before Vatican II, brought him much grief. His virtual expulsion from the Society of Jesus was the cause of tremendous sorrow to him. He rarely responded to cruel comments about his relationship with von Speyr, whom he treated as a living saint and prophet. Here, however, our focus will be on substantial criticisms of specific theological positions.

First, Balthasar has been accused of not truly understanding modernity.[198] His criticisms of modernity focused primarily on its forgetfulness of mystery and beauty. Some defenders of modernity argue that romanticism was also part of modernity and indirectly influenced him. One sympathetic commentator admits, "The symbolic-holistic understanding of the fathers of the church and not the critical-analytic reflection of the moderns is what forms the real horizon of his thought."[199] The criticism becomes stronger, however, when some critics accuse Balthasar of being premodern, a throwback to medievalism if not to the ancient era of the church fathers.

---

[196]Larry Chopp, "Revelation," in *The Cambridge Companion to Hans Urs von Balthasar*, ed. Edward T. Oakes and David Moss (Cambridge: Cambridge University Press, 2004), 13.

[197]Balthasar, *Dare We Hope?* 19–20.

[198]Kehl, "Hans Urs von Balthasar: A Portrait," 5.

[199]Ibid.

Without doubt he had affinities with and sympathy for the Christianity of those earlier times, but nobody can fault him with being ignorant of modern thought or for condemning all of it outright.

Balthasar directly addressed this concern (viz., his alleged premodernism) in *The God Question and Modern Man*. There he admitted that many of the "old views and customs [of Christendom] hallowed by habit have become empty and meaningless."[200] He averred that Christians should not just oppose modernity and its culture but strive to give a Christian shape to whatever the times offer.[201] "Thus the contemporary concept of God . . . has a style [like modern art] which the Christian ought to recognize and in which he ought to express himself. . . . By interpreting them rightly he will help both himself and his times."[202] That hardly sounds like a premodern conservative. He was harshly critical of much of modern culture and thought but no more so than many secular postmodernists. And he did not recommend Christian withdrawal from the world, for "this demonic situation cannot be mastered by desertion."[203] Instead, he recommended acceptance of "religious responsibility for the world."[204]

Another area of criticism of Balthasar's theology lies in his doctrine of God. Does his account of the inner-trinitarian life of God amount to tritheism—belief in three gods? This issue is raised by the Archbishop of Canterbury, Rowan Williams (b. 1950), in his essay on Balthasar in *The Cambridge Companion to Hans Urs von Balthasar*. The fact that Williams, then one of the highest prelates in the world, would write a chapter in a book about Balthasar says much about the Swiss theologian's ascendency and influence. Williams gently raises the issue of possible tritheism in Balthasar's doctrine of the Trinity especially in relation to his teaching about "difference" between the three persons and unity through action especially in self-giving. The real problem, Williams notes, is when Balthasar says that the persons of the Godhead worship each other.[205] However, the archbishop calls Balthasar's

---

[200]Balthasar, *The God Question and Modern Man*, 91.
[201]Ibid.
[202]Ibid., 92.
[203]Ibid., 57.
[204]Ibid., 59.
[205]Rowan Williams, "Balthasar and the Trinity," in *The Cambridge Companion to Hans Urs von Balthasar*, ed. Edward T. Oakes and David Moss (Cambridge: Cambridge University Press, 2004), 50.

account of the Trinity "a bit like tritheism" and compares it with Barth's doctrine which, he says, is "a bit like Sabellianism" (modalism).[206]

Perhaps Balthasar's harshest critic to date is a Catholic theologian, Alyssa Lyra Pitstick, who argued that the Swiss theologian's teaching about Holy Saturday fell into absolute conflict with authoritative Catholic doctrine. She accused it of contradicting Catholic tradition's authoritative dogma of God's immutability and of implying tritheism. She wrote:

> The conclusions that Balthasar's theology of Christ's descent into hell neither represents the traditional doctrine nor is compatible with it hardly need be drawn. The contrast is not a matter of subtlety of interpretation, but essential differences on the most central features of the doctrine . . . one finds that Balthasar's theology of Holy Saturday is observed in a straightforward manner to be new, different from the traditional Catholic doctrine, or incompatible with it.[207]

Her book gave rise to a flurry of articles in journals such as *First Things* defending Balthasar; she responded, and the debate continues.[208] With Benedict XVI on his side, however, the ultimate outcome of the debate (whether Balthasar should be considered orthodox) does not seem to be seriously in doubt.

---

[206]Ibid.

[207]Alyssa Lyra Pitstick, *Light in Darkness: Hans Urs von Balthasar and the Catholic Doctrine of Christ's Descent into Hell* (Grand Rapids: Eerdmans, 2007), 344.

[208]A simple Internet search using her name and Balthasar's together with "*First Things*" will bring up numerous links to articles by leading Balthasar scholars defending him against Pitstick's charges and to her responses.

11

EVANGELICAL THEOLOGY
COMES OF AGE AND WRESTLES
WITH MODERNITY

The place was St. Louis, Missouri, and the time was April 1942. The people meeting for the first time were representatives of many Protestant denominations that considered themselves evangelical but not fundamentalist. They were opposed to the general drift of Protestantism toward liberal and neo-liberal theology, but they were also dissatisfied with the way fundamentalism had evolved since its beginnings in the late nineteenth and early twentieth centuries. For the most part, these conservative Christian men and women would have called themselves fundamentalists fifty years before because they affirmed what they considered the traditional essentials of Protestant orthodoxy: the inspiration and authority of the Bible, the deity and humanity of Jesus Christ, his virgin birth, miracles and bodily resurrection, the Trinity, salvation by grace through faith alone, a supernatural world view, the visible return of Jesus Christ. However, between 1925 and 1942, in their estimation, fundamentalism had become narrow, overly dogmatic (e.g., requiring belief in premillennialism for authentic Christianity), anti-intellectual, negative toward culture and separatistic. These fundamentalists wanted a new identity and a new movement. They

founded the National Association of Evangelicals (NAE) as a diverse umbrella group of nonfundamentalist, conservative Protestant Christians to
rival the fundamentalist American Council of Christian Churches (ACCC)
and the more liberal (modernist) Federal Council of Churches, later renamed the National Council of Churches (NCC).

Thus was the new evangelical movement launched.[1] As fundamentalists also called themselves evangelicals (as do many others including
many Lutherans) scholars have sometimes labeled this new movement neoevangelicalism or postfundamentalist evangelicalism. The National Association of Evangelicals grew to include more than fifty American denominations and hundreds of Christian organizations. Many Protestants who
sympathized with its aims did not formally join but loosely associated with
the movement. (For example, the Southern Baptist Convention, America's
largest Protestant denomination, never joined the NAE but frequently sent
nonvoting representatives to its board meetings. Southern Baptist individuals played leading roles in the new evangelical movement.) The NAE
drew up a minimal statement of basic beliefs that could be affirmed by all
its members including conservative Presbyterians and Pentecostals. The
purpose of the organization was to give Protestants who could not join
either the ACCC or the NCC a means of cooperation and fellowship. One
of the group's first acts was to found a World Relief Commission to give
physical aid to victims of disasters and poverty around the world.

What the NAE lacked at first was a figurehead, a charismatic leader who
could speak for this diverse group of conservative Protestants in the public
square. Soon, however, such a person emerged and was embraced by all
new evangelicals—Billy Graham (b. 1918). Throughout the 1950s and 1960s
and into the 1970s and 1980s he became the informal pope of the evangelical movement worldwide. He had no magisterial authority, but his ethos
of irenic conservative evangelical piety was by consensus considered the
touchstone of the evangelical movement. In a very real sense, evangelicals

---

[1]The information about evangelicalism here is drawn from a variety of sources including Joel
Carpenter, *Revive Us Again: The Reawakening of American Fundamentalism* (New York: Oxford
University Press, 1997); George Marsden, *Understanding Fundamentalism and Evangelicalism*
(Grand Rapids: Eerdmans, 1991); Mark Noll, *American Evangelical Christianity: An Introduction* (Malden, MA: Blackwell, 2001); and Jon R. Stone, *On the Boundaries of American Evangelicalism: The Postwar Evangelical Coalition* (New York: St. Martin's Press, 1999).

in this sense were people who loved Graham and looked to him for spiritual and theological leadership. Because he was not a theologian but an evangelist, Graham looked for and found a nonfundamentalist, conservative evangelical theologian to speak for him and for the new evangelical movement. That person was Carl F. H. Henry (1913–2003). Together with other evangelical intellectuals Henry helped found the flagship seminary of the new movement, Fuller Theological Seminary, and the movement's mouthpiece publication, *Christianity Today*. Henry was recognized by *Time* magazine as "the leading theologian of the nation's growing Evangelical flank" (February 14, 1977, 82).

Evangelicalism was and is not a theological movement per se, but it has spawned numerous theologians and schools of theology who share in common the basic tenets of the NAE (basic Protestant orthodoxy) and a supernatural worldview but from there go in many different directions. Some are strict Calvinists while others are passionate Wesleyans. Some are dispensationalists who look for a rapture of Christians before Christ's return, and others are amillennialists who do not believe in an earthly rule of Christ after his return. Some hold high the inerrancy of the Bible (with qualifications fundamentalists normally do not allow) while others prefer to talk about the Bible's dynamic inspiration and infallibility. (These are subtle differences to outsiders but topics of debate among evangelical scholars—just as they were for hundreds of years among orthodox Protestants.) Most important for this story of modern theology, all theologians associated with this new evangelical movement, now well over half a century old, reject the more extreme claims of modernity without rejecting everything of modernity, as is the fundamentalists' tendency. Specifically, evangelicals reject naturalism, positivism (an extreme form of rationalism that rules out revelation and faith), historicism, skepticism and secularism. However, most of their leaders value higher education, critical biblical scholarship (minus naturalistic presuppositions), the value of the arts and sciences, dialogue and cooperation with nonevangelicals (which fundamentalists do not) and science (devoid of naturalism). Evangelicals oppose liberal theology, including neo-liberalism, and are wary of neo-orthodoxy and dialectical theology. To liberal and neo-orthodox Protestants, evangelicals seem little different from fundamentalists; to fundamentalists they seem little different from liberals. Evangelicals pride themselves on a *via media* between those extremes of absolute rejection of modernity and maximal accommodation to it.

During the second half of the twentieth century and first decades of the twenty-first century evangelicalism has spawned numerous theologians. An evangelical theologian is one who works from a confessional basis of at least the NAE's statement of faith (many affirm their own denomination's statement of faith, which may be more detailed), believes in and has experienced the new birth, conversion to Jesus Christ by faith, and is associated by affiliation or affinity with the broad evangelical movement. The movement as a whole beyond the NAE has no definite boundaries, so exactly who is and who is not an evangelical theologian is often disputed. There is no authoritative office that decides such things. Generally considered evangelical are theologians such as E. J. Carnell (1919–1967), one-time president of Fuller Seminary and author of numerous books of apologetics, philosophy and theology; Donald G. Bloesch (1928–2010), professor of theology at the University of Dubuque Theological Seminary and author of numerous books of evangelical theology; David Wells (b. 1939), long-time professor of theology at evangelical Gordon-Conwell Theological Seminary and author of many books of conservative Protestant theology; Clark Pinnock (1937–2010), professor of theology at several evangelical institutions and author of numerous books of evangelical theology; Millard Erickson (b. 1932), professor of theology, evangelical seminary dean and author of many books including the most widely used evangelical systematic theology (*Christian Theology* 1983–1985); Bernard Ramm (1916–1992), professor of theology at numerous evangelical colleges, universities and seminaries and author of dozens of books of evangelical apologetics and theology; Thomas Oden (b. 1931), liberal Methodist convert to evangelicalism, long-time professor at Drew University Divinity School and author of a massive evangelical systematic theology; and, finally, Stanley J. Grenz (1950–2005), professor of theology at several evangelical seminaries and author of many books associated with postconservative evangelical theology.

This is only a representative selection of leading evangelical theologians; many others could be named. This list runs the gamut of the diverse types of evangelical theologians from traditional Reformed (Wells) to progressive, postconservative Arminian (Pinnock). Evangelicals are not all readers of academic theology; some leading popularizers of theology include Francis Schaeffer (1912–1984), C. S. Lewis (1898–1963; not a member of the new evangelical movement but a writer popular among evangelicals), John Stott (1921–2011), Charles Colson (1931–2012) and John Piper (b. 1946; a theologian in his own right but author of mainly popular evangelical books). What do all these thinkers and writers have in common in spite of vast differences about secondary matters such as the sacraments, the end times and the gifts of the Spirit? They all claim to be born again, adhere to biblical authority as the supreme norm for faith and practice, believe in the reality of the supernatural including miracles (with varying degrees of interest), are Protestants and stand apart from fundamentalism and theological liberalism and neo-liberalism. Some are critically favorable to Barth's theology (e.g., Bloesch) while others reject Barth (e.g., Schaeffer). They all inhabit a middle ground between religious reactions to modernity.

Here three evangelical theologians will be described and analyzed especially in terms of their attitudes toward modernity. With the exception of Henry, the selection is somewhat arbitrary; only Henry stands out as the obvious choice to represent evangelical theology, which is not to say all evangelical theologians agree with him methodologically. Which will be remembered fifty to a hundred years hence as the outstanding evangelical thinkers of the late twentieth and early twenty-first centuries is anyone's guess. The reason for selection here is representation of types of evangelical theology especially in terms of responses to modernity: conservative (generally suspicious of and rejecting modernity), moderate (critical appropriation of modernity) and postconservative (more postmodern than modern).

Carl Henry Liberates Evangelical Theology from Fundamentalism (but Not Entirely)

Henry was a restless fundamentalist. He had an inquiring mind and thirst for knowledge through higher education; he chafed at fundamentalism's angularity and anti-intellectualism. He agreed passionately with all the fundamentals of the faith as defined by fundamentalism, and he was extremely suspicious of modernity, liberal theology and neo-orthodoxy. Yet, he saw the fundamentalist movement as failing adequately to engage with the world outside its closed subculture. A major turning point for him and for evangelicalism generally was *The Uneasy Conscience of Modern Fundamentalism*, in which Henry chastised his fellow fundamentalists for several sins of omission. The basic problem he saw was their lack of social concern. Their humanitarianism, benevolent regard for the welfare of humanity, had slowly evaporated.[2] As a result, Henry argued, their movement divorced the Christian faith from the great social reform movements; it shied away from preaching the kingdom of God as a present reality and withdrew from the task of shaping the mindset of society. In 1947 Henry still considered himself a fundamentalist, even though his pursuit of two doctorates in philosophy and theology, one at a liberal university, was already moving him to the movement's margins. But he feared that unless someone spoke out, fundamentalism would soon be reduced to an insignificant sect with no impact on the wider culture. Therefore, he boldly challenged his colleagues to action, claiming that "the hour is ripe now, if we seize it rightly, for a rediscovery of the Scriptures and of the meaning of the incarnation for the human race."[3] He envisioned nothing less than the reemergence of "historic Christianity" as a vital "world ideology," and this because of his conviction that "the redemptive message has implications for all of life."[4] His book was a major parting of the ways between fundamentalism and the new evangelicalism of which Henry would become the leading theological spokesman.

Henry was born into a family of German immigrants in New York City. Christian conversion came to him as a result of influences from outside his home. While working as a promising young journalist he came in contact with a godly elderly woman he affectionately called Mother Christy and several members of an evangelically oriented Oxford Group (Moral Re-Armanent). Through their prodding and as a result of his own fascination with the biblical accounts of Jesus' resurrection the young journalist experienced conversion on June 10, 1933.[5] Following that experience Henry moved away from journalism and toward theological studies. In the fall of 1935 he enrolled in Wheaton College, a flagship school of the fundamen-

---

[2]Carl F. H. Henry, *The Uneasy Conscience of Modern Fundamentalism* (Grand Rapids: Eerdmans, 1947), 16.

[3]Ibid.. 9.

[4]Ibid., 68.

[5]Carl F. H. Henry, *Confessions of a Theologian* (Waco, TX: Word, 1986), 44.

talist movement that would become a center of evangelical academic activity. One factor contributing to his choice of Wheaton was a lecture delivered by the college's president, J. Oliver Buswell, that emphasized the
importance of reason for faith. Henry's years at Wheaton set the direction
for his subsequent life. It established his relationship with evangelicalism
(at that time beginning to emerge out of fundamentalism) and brought him
into friendship with several people, including Graham, who would become
respected leaders of the evangelical movement. But most significantly for
his theology, Henry was influenced by his Wheaton philosophy professor
Gordon Clark (1902–1985). Clark was an advocate of a rationalistic approach to evangelical Christianity.

After Wheaton, Henry enrolled in Northern Baptist Theological Seminary, which had been founded by fundamentalists within the Northern
Baptist Convention (NBC, now the American Baptist Churches) as an alternative to the more liberal University of Chicago Divinity School, also af-
fliated with the NBC. He earned a ThD from Northern in 1942, the birth year
of the NAE. Armed with these credentials and a determination to make his
mark on the emerging new evangelical movement, Henry launched his academic career, which began at Northern. He became a founding faculty
member of Fuller Seminary in Pasadena, California, and earned a PhD from
Boston University. From there he went on to become the founding editor of
Christianity Today, intended to be the conservative alternative to the more
liberal and mainline *Christian Century*. He served there until 1967, when he
left the magazine in a dispute with board members over its future direction.[6]
Then he taught theology at a number of evangelical institutions and served
as lecturer at large for the world's largest poverty-relief organization, World
Vision, an evangelical organization. Henry authored many books and numerous articles and traveled around the world speaking about topics of conservative theology dear to his heart. His magnum opus, *God, Revelation and
Authority* (six volumes), was published between 1976 and 1983. When he
died in 2003 *Christianity Today* honored him with an article. Beeson Seminary dean and evangelical theologian Timothy George wrote, "Henry cut a
wide and deep swath across the landscape of American Christianity and the

---

[6]For Henry's perspective on the developments at *Christianity Today*, see ibid., 264–301.

world evangelical movement. Indeed . . . Henry practically invented what . . . became known as evangelicalism." [7]

Henry Attacks Subjectivism and Irrationalism

Throughout his career as a theologian Henry had one main theme—that Protestant accommodations to modernity had led to Christianity's demise as salt and light in the world and that only a return to biblical authority could rescue it from oblivion. His secondary theme was that evangelical theology would follow the same path to oblivion if it budged one inch from its historic commitment to the verbal inspiration and inerrancy of the Bible. To many that sounds fundamentalist, but Henry was not a fundamentalist in the sectarian, anti-intellectual sense of someone who separates from every doctrinally impure person. Henry was a man possessed of towering intellect who began with firm belief in the Bible as God's Word and an un-wavering commitment to traditional, orthodox doctrines. And yet, he was willing to go almost anywhere to meet and engage in dialogue with people of other persuasions. In such dialogues, however, he argued boldly for the superiority of basic evangelical orthodoxy to all alternative theological methods and systems.

According to Henry, all the failings and frustrations of modern the-ology can be traced back to a single but two-sided problem: Christian subjectivism and defection from biblical authority. But, clearly, for Henry, surrounding these is a single larger problem, and that is accom-modation to modernity. If it were not for modernism and modern theo-logians' fear of its corrosive effects subjectivism and defection from bib-lical authority would not be a problem. Instead, what Henry saw was that, beginning at least with Schleiermacher and continuing with Barth, modern theology had escaped from the acids of modernity by running away from rationality into subjectivisms of experience and faith alone. Henry was all about standing up to modernity and challenging its he-gemony—especially in religion. For example, in the face of naturalism, to which he thought many forms of modern theology had succumbed, he wrote, "Naturalism can provide no conclusive reason why radical

---

[7]Timothy George, "Inventing Evangelicalism: No One Was More Pivotal to the Emerging Move-ment Than Carl F. H. Henry," *Christianity Today* (March 2004), 48–51.

self-interest should not be the high altar on which all principles can be advantageously sacrificed. Indeed, naturalism can give no reason for taking reason or even itself seriously."[8] In the face of modern doubt and skepticism, naturalism and rationalism and against Christian flight with its claims into a safe, subjective realm that cannot be touched by these, Henry stood up against all that and reaffirmed what he thought was the conservative Protestant theological consensus.

The above quote about naturalism illustrates Henry's basic approach to truth. For him, the ultimate criterion of truth is reason, but not Enlightenment rationalism. Henry insisted on a distinction. Enlightenment rationalism, beginning with Descartes, focused on self-evident truths and made the thinking subject the center of truth and reality. And it reduced knowledge to what can be proven rationally. Contrary to what many people expect of evangelicals, based on stereotypes drawn from movies such as *Leap of Faith*, Henry did not appeal to emotion or inward faith or anything else subjective. Nor did he agree with strict rationalism. Instead, for him, the ultimate standards of truth, and therefore of what counts as knowledge, are logical consistency and explanatory power.[9] His basic thesis is that "Christianity does not disdain the canons of rationality. It offers a comprehensive logical network of beliefs."[10] And, "there can be but one comprehensive system of truth. If the true system is comprehensive, every false system must contain contradictions."[11] What he meant is that there can be only one absolutely comprehensive and logically consistent system of truth because anything different from it would contradict it, and two contradictory systems of truth cannot both be true.

The ultimate support for Christianity's belief system is its comprehensiveness, consistency and explanatory power. What invalidates all competing systems of truth, including naturalism, is their lack of comprehensiveness, consistency and explanatory power. (Henry added comprehensiveness to the other two criteria of truth when looking at competing worldviews. A worldview always claims to be comprehensive, so one that is not fails to be a

---

[8]Carl F. H. Henry, *Towards a Recovery of Christian Belief* (Wheaton, IL: Crossway, 1990), 113–14. This book well summarizes Henry's entire theological method.
[9]Ibid., 53.
[10]Ibid., 80.
[11]Ibid., 88.

worldview. Among those that are comprehensive, offering answers to all of life's urgent questions, logical consistency and explanatory power kick in to determine their truthfulness.) According to Henry, "what invalidates secular views is their inability to account for existence and meaning."[12] He would apply the same criteria to all worldviews, including orthodox Christianity, and he was confident it would prevail in terms of comprehensiveness, consistency and explanatory power. If someone asked Henry why logic is so important, as opposed to, say subjective experience, he would argue that subjective experience is a poor basis for universal beliefs. As Luther once said, "Experience is a wax nose any knave can twist to suit his own countenance." In other words, Henry believed that Christian truth is public truth and that it should shape all aspects of life including public life. What people have in common, he believed, is reason. Not reason as a particular philosophy and certainly not reason as it was distorted by the Enlightenment into positivist rationalism, but reason as logic—that contradictions are always sure signs of error.

To Christians who appealed to experience as the basis of their beliefs Henry said, "If we profess to be Christian, neither our own experience nor anyone else's can be the basis of our religious affirmation."[13] To Christians who question how we can trust reason, even to judge the truth of the Bible and Christian doctrines, Henry responded, "In a universe where the *Logos* is the source and support of created existence, logic is the *form* of reality."[14] This is called logos theology, and Henry learned it from Clark, who harked back to Origen and early Christian Platonism to argue that rationality, rooted in God himself and his creation, is built into the fabric of the universe *and* into human minds so that minds are capable of using reason to understand the universe and even God. According to Henry, if we assume anything else, we are lost in a sea of subjectivism which leads to relativism so that knowledge itself becomes impossible. It then becomes impossible to adjudicate between competing truth claims.

Henry Criticizes Modernity, Liberal Theology and Fideism
Unlike fundamentalists, Henry did not just preach against modernism

---

[12]Ibid., 91.
[13]Ibid., 100.
[14]Ibid., 95.

outside or inside the churches and call for repentance and separation. He saw it as his duty and that of every intellectually gifted evangelical Christian to demonstrate the superiority of the orthodox Christian life and worldview. One way of doing that was to point out the cultural condition of late modern societies and the incoherence of every secular philosophy of life. According to him, because of the Enlightenment's anthropocentric shift away from God and to the centrality and authority of the individual thinking subject, "the West has lost its moral and epistemic compass bearings. It has no shared criterion for judging whether human beings are moving up or down, standing still, or merely on the move only God knows where."[15] He believed any reasonable person could see that Western culture flourished and made tremendous progress so long as its compass was Scripture: "Thanks to its Scriptural commitments, the West towered head and shoulders over its pagan past."[16] As a result of modernity's defection from the authority of the Bible, however, "secular scholars seem unable to tell us where we are."[17] In other words, nothing is objectively better or worse, just different. The result is a culture adrift and a society mired in relativism.

Henry specifically blamed this cultural anomie on the Enlightenment that "relied on philosophical arguments from the not-God, that is, from nature, or from the pattern of history, or from mankind—especially from human mind and conscience."[18] This was accompanied by and resulted in modern philosophy's abandonment of "revelatory Biblical theism" in favor of "speculative theism," by which Henry probably meant deism.[19] The result, Henry argued, was eventual complete departure from Western culture's Christian theistic roots so that finally post-Christian culture believes that "Nature alone is the ultimate reality; Man is essentially a complex animal; Truth and the good are relative and changing."[20]

Henry then turned his criticism toward the Christian churches and their theologies. In his view, liberal Christianity (a very broad category) accommodated to modernity with devastating results:

---

[15]Ibid., 15.
[16]Ibid., 16.
[17]Ibid.
[18]Ibid., 20.
[19]Ibid.
[20]Ibid., 21.

Ongoing dilution of the essentials of Biblical theism, through concessions to one and then another neoteric [sic] speculative theory, seriously impaired Judeo-Christian core beliefs. University scholars eagerly truncated the living God of the Bible, sundering Him from nature and history and paying only grudging, temporary tribute to this or that surviving morsel of the West's Christian inheritance. Repeated deference to novelties, to which Scriptural concepts were routinely adjusted, finally forfeited cognitive initiative to contemporary conjectural alternatives to the Biblical view.[21]

In other words, according to Henry, liberal theology became a series of attempts to fit into modernity at any cost resulting in a near total loss of classical Christianity.

However, Henry traditionally reserved his harshest criticisms for nonliberal theologies that embrace subjectivism in the name of faith. The enemies within the camp (often even of evangelicalism) are "fideists [like] Søren Kierkegaard and certain Neo-orthodox theologians who dismiss public reason and rational tests as irrelevant to religious truth claims."[22] Such theologies, he declared, are not to be confused with evangelical orthodoxy: "Evangelical theists consider unacceptable any irrationalist claim that intellectual absurdity renders religious beliefs worthy or that spiritual obedience demands a 'leap of faith' indifferent to rational considerations."[23] The *Time* article about Henry was headlined "Theology for the Tent Meeting," which missed the mark of Henry's concern. (The headline writer clearly did not read the article.) The dean of evangelical theologians complained often and bitterly, "All too many Americans . . . believe . . . that a satisfying religious experience can be had without worrying about propositional truths."[24] And by propositional truths he meant rationally defensible truth claims about reality outside the individual's emotional states. Henry viewed the fundamental disease of nearly all modern theology and religion as subjectivism, abandonment of objective, rational truth claims and the Christian worldview as a rationally defensible system of such claims about reality.

---

[21]Ibid., 31.
[22]Ibid., 39.
[23]Ibid.
[24]Ibid., 28–29.

Henry Explains Evangelical Presuppositionalism as the Right Theological Method

So, how can the mess modern theology, including much evangelical theology, finds itself in be fixed? According to Henry, there is only one way—a return to biblical authority as the foundation for the Christian life and worldview that then also informs all of culture. He was not advocating Enlightenment foundationalism, however, but rather what he called presuppositionalism. He argued that "Christians should feel no compulsion to taper their transcendent theistic epistemology to the preferences of hostile philosophers."[25] Also,

> to engage in authentic truth Christianity need not subscribe to secular statements of how we must ideally conduct theological inquiry. The Christian religion is not obliged antecedently to accept extraneous theories of truth or to accommodate its own alternative to them as the price of earnest metaphysical elaboration and discussion.[26]

He specifically mentioned "neo-Kantians, logical positivists, existentialists" among others. "To establish the 'credibility' of Christian inquiry by first exhibiting its compatibility with alien theories is merely to negotiate away Christianity's uniqueness."[27] According to Henry, every worldview, philosophy and even science begins with unprovable assumptions or presuppositions that are faith-based (which does not make them irrational unless they can produce no other credentials). "Without faith neither science nor philosophy nor theology can make progress."[28] So Christianity should not be embarrassed that it begins with certain basic presuppositions. These govern its worldview, which turns out to be the most comprehensive, consistent and powerfully explanatory worldview. That is what justifies them as proper starting points.

Christianity's proper presuppositions are, according to Henry, two governing axioms: the basic ontological axiom which is "the living God," and the basic epistemological axiom which is "divine revelation." Because every science begins with unprovable axioms, "it is wholly legitimate for the

---

[25]Ibid., 45.
[26]Ibid., 44.
[27]Ibid.
[28]Ibid.

Christian philosopher to begin with what he knows as a Christian."[29] But if Christianity is to have explanatory power as a worldview, it must be a coherent system of propositions, truth claims about reality. That is also the case if it is to be tested for its truth status and demonstrated superior to competing worldviews. "Propositional expressibility is . . . a precondition for evaluating any system. A system [i.e., worldview] that is not propositionally expressible involves no shareable truth claims and can in no way be tested."[30] But that means, then, that the revelation Christianity begins with must be propositional. One of Henry's most basic and often criticized (even by other evangelicals) claims is that "divine revelation is a mental activity."[31] In other words, the living God speaks in understandable ways to the intellect. That is revelation. True, revelation may include more than just propositions, but for revelation to be useful to theology it must have a propositional component that is also rational and univocal. That is, it must have a literal component and not be merely symbolic or expressive.

Here is the briefest and clearest statement of his theological method by Henry:

> The Christian's primary ontological axiom is the one living God, and his primary epistemological axiom is divine revelation. On these basic axioms depend all the core beliefs of Biblical theism, including divine creation, sin and the Fall, the promise and provision of redemption, the Incarnation of God in Jesus of Nazareth, the regenerate Church as a new society, and a comprehensive eschatology. And yet a metaphysical view that professes to make sense of all reality and life and involves a universal truth claim must adduce some epistemological justification if it is to escape dismissal as fideism or sheer faith that derogates reason.[32]

So, the Christian worldview, "Biblical theism," is based on two axioms, presuppositions, and is true because it is, as a whole, rationally superior to all competing worldviews. In a way better than they, it passes the criteria of comprehensiveness, consistency and explanatory power.

What, then, does theology do? "The task of Christian theology is to exhibit

---

[29]Ibid., 67.
[30]Ibid., 71.
[31]Ibid., 55.
[32]Ibid., 49.

the content of biblical revelation as an orderly whole."[33] But this presupposes that the Bible is "Christian theology's authoritative verifying principle."[34] Here a critic might ask whether, in Henry's view, that is really Scripture or logic. He would probably say both, but when one is attempting to construct the Christian worldview and a system of Christian beliefs, Scripture is the supreme source even if logic is the supreme norm.[35] The point here is that theology's task is not to draw on extrabiblical sources or norms (remember that logic is for Henry built into creation by the God of the Bible) or to correlate revelation with extrabiblical culture or philosophy. Theology's task is only to construct a system of doctrines faithful to the Bible as God's inspired, inerrant, authoritative revelation. At this point Henry's method looks very much like Hodge's.

Because Scripture is presupposed to be God's propositional revelation and because it is theology's sole supreme source and norm, it must be inspired and inerrant. This is a major point of Henry's theology. He believed that all the problems of modern theology, and possibly of culture as well, stem from a loss of faith in the Bible's inspiration and inerrancy which are necessary to its authority.[36] The Bible is authoritative because it is inspired by God; it is inerrant for the same reason. And its inerrancy comes back around to be necessary to its authority. Any denial of the verbal inspiration of the Bible, Henry argued, leads inexorably to a loss of its authority. The same is true of its inerrancy. He defined inspiration as "the Holy Spirit superintended the scriptural writers in communicating the biblical message . . . safeguarding them from error."[37] Furthermore, it is "a supernatural influence upon divinely chosen prophets and apostles whereby the Spirit of God assures the truth and trustworthiness of their oral and written proclamations."[38] The Bible is essential for theology because "it inscripturates divinely revealed truth in verbal form."[39] Its inerrancy means that Scripture is true in all that it reveals, not that everything in it (e.g., poetry and parables) must be taken literally.

---

[33] Carl F. H. Henry, *God, Revelation and Authority*, 6 vols. (Waco, TX: Word, 1976–1983), 1:215.
[34] Henry, *Toward a Recovery of Christian Belief*, 55.
[35] To the best of this writer's knowledge Henry never says this, but it seems to be what he would have to say given his strong emphasis on logic as the universal test of all truth.
[36] Henry set forth his understanding of inspiration, inerrancy and infallibility in *God, Revelation and Authority*, 4:103–219.
[37] Ibid., 166–67.
[38] Ibid., 129.
[39] Ibid.

Henry's account of revelation and the Bible is nearly identical with Hodge's and is consistent with the conservative evangelical tradition going back to Calvin in the Reformation. However, he avoided some of the more extreme positions found in certain fundamentalist circles. He was quick to reject any suggestion that the Bible was the product of divine dictation.[40] Nor did inerrancy imply technical precision of accuracy or exactness of New Testament quotations of the Old. In other words, unlike many fundamentalists, Henry qualified "inspiration" and "inerrancy" so that they fit the phenomena of Scripture.[41] Some critics have wondered if he killed especially inerrancy with the death of a thousand qualifications. Might not "infallible" be a more fitting term for the Bible's truthfulness? Henry did not think so, but many other conservative evangelical scholars did and do.[42]

If there is one doctrine that has caused the most consternation, confusion and controversy among postfundamentalist evangelicals since 1942 it is biblical inerrancy. Henry staunchly defended it as necessary for inspiration and authority; if the Bible contains real errors, it cannot be of divine origin or trustworthy. Other evangelical theologians have vigorously denied that claim preferring a view of Scripture as "perfect with respect to purpose" but not inerrant in matters of science and history.[43] Although he vigorously defended the concept of inerrancy, with many qualifications, Henry did not go so far as to make it a doctrinal test for evangelical faith as did some of his colleagues. The somewhat reactionary elevation of inerrancy as the "superbadge of evangelical orthodoxy," he lamented, "deploys energies to this controversy that evangelicals might better apply to producing comprehensive theological and philosophical works so desperately needed in a time of national and civilizational crisis."[44] This is one thing that marked Henry as postfundamentalist—his denial that belief in biblical inerrancy is a fundamental of Christianity. He did, however, think it inconsistent to affirm biblical inspiration and authority while denying biblical inerrancy.

---

[40]Ibid., 138.
[41]For Henry's discussion of what inerrancy does and does not imply, see ibid., 201–10.
[42]For example, Reformed evangelical theologian Harry Boer in *Above the Battle? The Bible and Its Critics* (Grand Rapids: Eerdmans, 1977).
[43]See Jack B. Rogers and Donald K. McKim, *The Authority and Interpretation of the Bible: An Historical Approach* (San Francisco: Harper & Row, 1979).
[44]Carl F. H. Henry, "Reaction and Realignment," *Christianity Today* (July 2, 1976), 30 [1038].

The only remarkable thing about Henry's theology is its method (rational presuppositionalism). Otherwise, his account of biblical theism is virtually identical with Protestant orthodoxy: supernatural worldview, biblical authority, deity and humanity of Christ, Trinity and salvation by grace through the atoning death of Jesus Christ.

What about science? How did Henry respond to modern science? His approach was identical with Hodge's more than a century earlier: Christianity has nothing to fear from science so long as science sticks to its proper realm and role, which is physical nature and servanthood. Science becomes a threat to Christianity only when it oversteps its limits and makes metaphysical claims about the whole of reality. Scientism is the modern tendency to put the physical sciences on a pedestal and pretend they can explain everything and whatever they cannot explain lies outside the real. Henry wrote very little about science except to object to scientism. At the end of an essay on "Theology and Science," he attempted to put science firmly in its place:

> The fact is that empirical science has no firm basis whatever on which to raise objections to Christianity, not because scientific and historical concerns are irrelevant to revelation and faith, but because scientists must allow for possible exceptions to every rule they affirm, and for the empirical vulnerability of the rules themselves.[45]

In other words, science must always remain humble especially about its limitations. It cannot rule on the truth of worldviews or claims to exceptions to natural laws. All of science's conclusions are opinions open to possible future revision. Christians should never allow these to unhinge confidence in basic Christian truth.

Henry Continues to Serve as the Evangelical Gold Standard

That does not mean Henry does not have his critics, even among evangelicals. However, among both evangelicals and nonevangelical theologians, Henry remains years after his death the most widely recognized spokesman for evangelical theology. All evangelical theologians admire and respect him even as some of them criticize what they see as his overemphasis on the rationality of revelation and Christianity. Some also criticize his

---

[45]Henry, *God, Revelation and Authority*, 1:175.

stringent insistence on verbal inspiration and inerrancy of the Bible or his presuppositional approach to apologetics.

British evangelical theologian Alister McGrath (b. 1953) represents one type of evangelical criticism of Henry's theological method. Speaking of his emphasis on logic McGrath says that "Henry risks making an implicit appeal to a more fundamental epistemological foundation . . . leading to the conclusion that the authority of Scripture itself is derived from this more fundamental authority."[46] Also, McGrath accuses Henry of reducing the Bible to "a code book of theological ordinances."[47] In other words, as with Hodge a century earlier, Henry risks portraying the Bible as nothing more than a not-yet-systematized systematic theology or philosophy (biblical theism), thus reducing it to facts waiting to be organized. According to McGrath and other critics, this ignores the narrative nature of revelation. On both counts, McGrath concludes that Henry's theology rests on "the Old Princeton School, especially the writings of Charles Hodge and Benjamin B. Warfield, in which the influence of Enlightenment presuppositions is particularly noticeable."[48] This is ironic, given that Henry so vehemently opposed theological accommodation to the Enlightenment and the culture of modernity it spawned.

A nonevangelical theologian expresses many evangelicals' concerns about Henry's approach to theology. Gary Dorrien, Reinhold Niebuhr Professor of Social Ethics at Union Theological Seminary, comments (clearly referring to Henry among others):

> Evangelicals are prone to fret that everything will be lost if they have no ground of absolute certainty or no proof that Christianity is superior to Islam or Buddhism. This fear drives them to impose impossible tests on Christian belief. Inerrancy or the abyss! It also drives them to invest religious authority in a posited epistemological capacity that exists outside the circle of Christian faith. The truth of Christianity is then judged by rational tests that are not only external to Christian revelation but given authority over revelation.[49]

---

[46]Alister McGrath, *A Passion for Truth: The Intellectual Coherence of Evangelicalism* (Downers Grove, IL: InterVarsity Press, 1996), 170.

[47]Quote from Bernard Ramm, ibid.

[48]Ibid., 174.

[49]Gary Dorrien, *The Remaking of Evangelical Theology* (Louisville, KY: Westminster John Knox, 1998), 201.

He labels Henry and other conservative evangelicals like him "antimodernist modernizers"[50] because, he believes, while decrying modernity they succumb to its demands for rational certainty and treat Scripture as a textbook of rational propositions.

Another group of critics of Henry's theology are evangelical evidentialists. These are conservative Protestants who believe the truth status of what Henry calls biblical theism, the Christian worldview, depends on evidence, not logic. They are not opposed to logic, but to them it is not the main criterion of the truth of a worldview that makes historical claims. For evangelical evidentialists like John Gerstner (1914–1996), who once called Henry a fideist because of his presuppositionalism, the truth of Christianity rests on the historical verifiability of the resurrection of Jesus. They think it is invalid to begin Christian theology with presupposed axioms and then make its truth rest on its comprehensiveness, consistency and explanatory power. They do not deny those characteristics of biblical theism, but they think several competing worldviews might have them, and it is difficult to determine their quality. What is not so difficult, the evangelical evidentialists argue, is to prove beyond a reasonable doubt that Jesus was raised from death by the power of God thus verifying his lordship. From there everything essential to historic Christianity follows.[51] This approach would also meet the objections of McGrath and Dorrien because it, too, seeks to base the truth of Christianity on reasons external to Christianity itself (viz., historical research). Henry rejected it because it could at best provide probability.[52]

Bernard Ramm Encourages Evangelicals to Come to Terms with Modernity

Our second case study in evangelical theology is Bernard Ramm. Ramm's fame among evangelicals may be waning, but his influence is still very much alive even where he is not explicitly named. Because he taught at many evangelical institutions, a large number of evangelical theologians studied under him and carried his basic outlook throughout their careers. Because he

---

[50]Ibid., 13.
[51]See John Gerstner, *Reasons for Faith* (Grand Rapids: Soli Deo Gloria, 1997). It was originally published in 1960 by Harper and Brothers.
[52]Henry, *Towards a Recovery of Christian Belief*, 77.

wrote numerous books of apologetics, ethics and theology, his influence even on those who never met him was broad and often deep. Ramm is included here because, especially in his later writings, he presented an alternative to Henry's rationalistic approach to evangelical theology. Also, he was not nearly as opposed to modernity as was Henry, even though he could hardly be called an advocate of modernity. He believed it was important for evangelicals to come of age by taking modernity seriously rather than shunning it and denigrating it. Some conservative evangelicals saw his leanings toward the theology of Barth as dangerous and perhaps even a defection from evangelicalism. However, they should pay attention to two of his last books, both of which were strong affirmations of orthodox Protestant doctrines (*Offense to Reason* about original sin [1985] and *An Evangelical Christology* [1993] about the person of Jesus Christ). The point is that Ramm represents a different flavor of evangelical theology from Henry's even though they agreed on basic Christian doctrines. Ramm had a long career as a theologian and went through many changes, so here attention will be given to one of his last contributions: *After Fundamentalism* (1983).[53]

In *After Fundamentalism* Ramm returned to a theme he had visited in *The Christian View of Science and Scripture* (1954). It had become a classic of the break of evangelicals from fundamentalism. There Ramm, who majored in science in his undergraduate studies, criticized fundamentalist "obscurantism"—the habit of ignoring facts because one's mind is already made up. There Ramm called on conservative Christians to face up to modern science's discoveries and stop condemning science as essentially godless. And he insisted that they adjust their views of the natural world to science's "material facts."[54] An example was the age of the earth. Ramm noted that many conservative Christians still believed and defended a scientifically indefensible estimate of the age of creation. According to him, the Bible says nothing about the age of creation; that is science's territory, and Christians should look to science for that answer. At the same time he

---

[53]Ramm told this writer (summer 1985) that this was not his preferred title for the book and that he believed the publisher's title choice hurt the book's sales. His preferred title was the subtitle: *The Future of Evangelical Theology*. Perhaps the publisher thought there were already too many books with similar titles.

[54]Bernard L. Ramm, *The Christian View of Science and Scripture* (Grand Rapids: Eerdmans, 1954), 29–30. See also 43, 169, 238, 244.

warned that Christians need not adapt to every theory of science and certainly not to those that conflicted with the basic truths of Scripture. *The Christian View of Science and Scripture* represented a major parting of the ways between fundamentalists, most of whom continued to reject science as inimical to faith, and evangelicals who at least wanted to correlate biblical theism with the best of modern science.

In *After Fundamentalism* Ramm once again picked up the issue of religious obscurantism, which he defined as "the denial of the validity of modern learning."[55] The entire book is a sustained argument that evangelicals must come to terms with modern learning without inappropriately accommodating to modern theories that fundamentally conflict with basic, orthodox Christianity. After exposing secular and religious reactions to the Enlightenment, Ramm concluded, "If the Enlightenment collapsed orthodoxy as an option for Europe's intelligentsia, and if liberal Christianity was born as a reaction to the Enlightenment, it seems obvious to me that evangelical theology must come to its terms with the Enlightenment."[56] The context of that thesis statement makes clear that Ramm was not advocating liberal accommodation but taking the Enlightenment seriously and not running from it, which he saw as a common evangelical habit.

Ramm then suggested that evangelicals develop a "new paradigm in theology" that takes the Enlightenment and modernity more seriously than obscurantism but avoids needless accommodations to them. For him, "the critical issue is whether evangelical theology needs a new paradigm in theology or not."[57] The turning point for answering that question, he argued, is a theologian's sense of the Enlightenment's permanence as a cultural revolution:

> If an evangelical feels that the Enlightenment and modern learning have ushered in a new cultural epoch, which in turn has precipitated into existence a new and radical set of issues for evangelical theology, then such a person will feel the need for a new paradigm. If an evangelical feels that the Enlightenment is but one more chapter in the history of unbelief, then he or she will not feel that a new paradigm is necessary.[58]

---

[55]Bernard Ramm, *After Fundamentalism: The Future of Evangelical Theology* (San Francisco: Harper & Row, 1983), 19.
[56]Ibid., 8.
[57]Ibid., 25.
[58]Ibid., 25–26.

Clearly, Ramm felt that a new evangelical paradigm of theology is necessary because to deny that the Enlightenment ushered in a new cultural epoch and to ignore or condemn it as sheer unbelief so that one does not need to come to terms with it dooms evangelical theology to obscurantism and ultimate irrelevance.

So, what did Ramm see as the "old paradigm" that had to change? For him, and for many moderate to progressive evangelicals who followed him, it was the theological method of Hodge and the Old Princeton School of theology. Ramm believed most evangelicals were stuck in Hodge's view of Scripture, which ultimately made it impossible for them to come to terms with modern learning. And it resulted in their embrace of obscurantism. The problem with that paradigm, Ramm, argued, is its view of Scripture. According to Ramm, Hodge held that "whenever the authors of Scripture . . . speak of factual or scientific matters or matters of the natural order, they are supernaturally protected from error, so even in these matters they make true statements."[59] Ramm pointed out that for Hodge and his contemporary conservative evangelical disciples, "there are no errors of any conceivable kind and from any conceivable source in Holy Scripture."[60] For Ramm, this "is not a working solution."[61] All evangelicals, in distinction from the most conservative fundamentalists, claim that Scripture was not dictated by God; Scripture's authors were fully human and creatures of their ancient cultures. And yet, somehow, their worldviews did not infect what they wrote. Against this Ramm stated, "If the writers of Holy Scripture are truly children of their cultures, then they express themselves in the terms, concepts and vocabulary of their culture. . . . They wrote as anybody would write in their times and in their cultures."[62] To say otherwise is to fall back into belief in inspiration as dictation, implicitly denying the humanness of the authors, and to ignore the manifest examples of cultural conditioning in the Bible.

What Ramm was arguing is that evangelical insistence on verbal inspiration and comprehensive inerrancy of the Bible is impossible without sacrificing the intellect; it is sheer obscurantism. His proposed solution is to

---

[59]Ibid., 44.
[60]Ibid., 45.
[61]Ibid.
[62]Ibid., 47.

learn from Barth to distinguish between "the human, fallible media of revelation and the divine, infallible truth Scripture contains."[63] Shortly before
After Fundamentalism was published, a group of conservative evangelical
scholars had met in Chicago to write *The Chicago Statement on Biblical Inerrancy* (1978). Their purpose was to explain and defend biblical inerrancy.
Henry was their theological guide. Ramm commented that "it is very difficult to see how the positive affirmations [of inerrancy] can stand in the
light of the subsequent qualifications . . . as with Hodge, it is more an affirmation of its version of Holy Scripture than a working solution."[64] By "affirmation" here Ramm meant "assertion" without reason.

Much to the dismay and chagrin of his more conservative evangelical
counterparts, Ramm urged evangelicals to make a paradigm shift away
from Protestant scholasticism (the Old School Princeton theology of
Hodge) and toward the Barthian version of neo-orthodoxy. Barth, he said,
viewed Scripture and the Word of God as distinct realities. "The Word of
God exists 'in, with, and under' the culturally conditioned text."[65] This, he
proposed, has some distinct advantages:

> It does not make the wholesale concessions to the Enlightenment that charac-
> terized the solution of liberal Christianity. It does not suffer from the internal
> contradiction of Hodge's solution nor from the imponderables of working with
> that solution. It does not need to resort to obscurantism in matters of science
> and biblical criticism. At the same time, it stoutly defends the theological in-
> tegrity of Holy Scripture as vigorously as any orthodox person would.[66]

Ramm offered to his fellow evangelicals (some of whom by this time no
longer considered him truly evangelical) the thesis that Barth's theology is
the best paradigm for "our times." "As a paradigm, it means that we do not
need to defend Barth at every point. It may be that the best service of Barth
to evangelical theology is not to give us a theology but to open windows to
the fact that there are other alternatives [open] to evangelical theology than
the options that emerged in the nineteenth century [e.g., liberal theology]."[67]

---

[63]Ibid., 45.
[64]Ibid., 45–46.
[65]Ibid., 47.
[66]Ibid.
[67]Ibid, 48–49.

Ramm Divides Evangelicals

Generally speaking, the conservatives Ramm appealed to rejected his proposal and criticized him for capitulating to neo-orthodox subjectivism. Many rejected him as no longer truly evangelical. He found evangelical institutions increasingly closed to him and ended up teaching at a moderate to liberal Baptist seminary in California. However, many younger evangelicals were inspired by Ramm to investigate Barth, and many came to agree with him that Barth's paradigm of theology is better for evangelicals taking seriously modern learning. It meant that one did not have to defend every statement in Scripture. At the same time, Scripture is the unique witness to God's revelation in the history of Israel and especially Jesus Christ. Theology, then, is no longer organizing the propositions of the Bible. It is wisely discerning the implications of God's revelation embedded in the Bible. Science is no longer a threat, nor is fair biblical criticism. It does not mean that the Barth-inspired theologian must agree with everything Barth said or that modernity claims. It means that one does not have to run from the material facts which include contradictions and cultural conditioning in Scripture.

Ramm was not the only evangelical theologian making the same argument. Throughout the 1970s and 1980s another one, Donald Bloesch, was trying to turn evangelicals toward Barth. While he disagreed with many aspects of Barth's theology, Bloesch saw his sacramental view of Scripture and the Word of God as compelling. He used the analogy of a light bulb to illustrate it: "One might say that the Bible is the Word of God in a formal sense—as a light bulb is related to light. The light bulb is not itself the light but its medium."[68] Throughout his seven-volume *Christian Foundations* Bloesch recommended Barth's general approach to theology to both evangelicals and so-called mainstream Protestants. Like Ramm, he came to reject strict biblical inerrancy as impossible not only in light of the actual phenomena of Scripture but also in light of modern science and historical knowledge: "We must never say that the Bible teaches theological or historical error, but we need to recognize that not everything reported in the Bible may be in exact correspondence with historical and scientific fact as

---

[68]Donald G. Bloesch, *Holy Scripture: Revelation, Inspiration and Interpretation* (Downers Grove, IL: InterVarsity Press, 1994), 59.

we know it today."[69] Together, the Ramm-Bloesch approach to "progressive evangelical theology"[70] (Bloesch's term that fits the later Ramm as well) caught on among younger evangelical thinkers tired of what they saw as the lingering effects of fundamentalism in evangelical thought.

One such younger evangelical theologian was Clark Pinnock, who, like Ramm, taught at many evangelical colleges and seminaries, wrote dozens of books of apologetics and theology and underwent a paradigm shift of his own in mid-career. Without espousing Barthian theology, Pinnock advocated being "honest and observant in regard to the human side of Scripture." He wrote, "I see a kind of theological synthesis possible in which the Bible remains normative, but in which it is read afresh under the illumination of the Spirit who makes it live for us."[71] His article concluded with a quote from Ramm. Later, in *The Scripture Principle* (1984) and *Tracking the Maze* (1990), Pinnock moved further in a Barthian direction stating that "I would want to admit that there are things in the Bible that are history like but not likely to be historical."[72] He also affirmed cultural conditioning in the Bible and declared, "The Bible is not a book full of timeless truths"[73] and "The Bible exists to tell the Christian story and to testify to the decisive events in the narrative."[74] Pinnock became more of a lightning rod of controversy for conservative evangelicals when he embraced open theism, the view that God's omniscience does not include foreknowledge of future free decisions yet to be made by creatures. Neither Ramm nor Bloesch went there. However, critics of their common view of Scripture and theological method saw a connection, a slippery slope, between denial of the Hodge-

---

[69]Ibid., 36–37.
[70]Bloesch's self-designation as a "progressive evangelical" was communicated to me in personal conversation with him. Toward the end of his career we became friends and had many correspondences and face-to-face conversations. In his writings he tended to label himself a "centrist" who intended to model "ecumenical orthodoxy." See his volume in *Foundations* titled *Jesus Christ: Savior and Lord* (Downers Grove, IL: InterVarsity Press, 2005), 11–12. When asked (by me) what he meant by "progressive evangelical" he responded that he values and makes use of biblical criticism. I would add that his distinction between the Word of God and the words of Scripture is progressive among evangelicals.
[71]Clark Pinnock, "An Evangelical Theology: Conservative and Contemporary," *Christianity Today* (January 5, 1979), 29.
[72]Clark Pinnock, *Tracking the Maze: Finding Our Way Through Modern Theology from an Evangelical Perspective* (San Francisco: Harper & Row, 1990), 161.
[73]Ibid., 175.
[74]Ibid., 172.

ian view of Scripture and theological method and eventual departure from basic Christian orthodoxy.

Throughout the 1990s and the first decade of the twenty-first century evangelicalism and especially evangelical theologians fell apart over controversies about biblical inerrancy, theological method, God's foreknowledge and the roles of men and women in the church and home. To the heirs of Ramm, Bloesch and Pinnock it seemed a new fundamentalism was emerging that wanted to exclude all fresh consideration of traditional conservative interpretations. To heirs of Henry and others like him, such as Wells, it seemed a new liberalism was evolving among evangelical theologians.[75] One evangelical theologian in particular emerged as the lightning rod for evangelical controversy. He was a follower of Ramm who also admired Bloesch and Pinnock (while disagreeing with the latter about open theism) named Stanley Grenz, our third case study in evangelical theology.

Stanley Grenz Proposes a Postconservative Paradigm for Evangelical Theology

Grenz died tragically at the pinnacle of his theological career just as many, especially young evangelicals, were finding in his theology a way to remain evangelical in an increasingly postmodern culture. Without any doubt he was the leading thinker of what some were calling "postconservative evangelicalism."[76] He passed away suddenly, unexpectedly, in his sleep in 2005 at age fifty-five. He had just finished (or nearly finished, so that his

---

[75]For two opposite accounts of this division see David Wells, *No Place for Truth: Or Whatever Happened to Evangelical Theology?* (Grand Rapids: Eerdmans, 1993) and Kenneth J. Collins, *The Evangelical Moment: The Promise of an American Religion* (Grand Rapids: Baker Academic, 2005).

[76]This is a label Grenz himself never used, but it fit his theological program well. The label was first used by Fuller Seminary theology professor Jack Rogers in *Confessions of a Conservative Evangelical* (1974). His title for the book was *Confessions of a Post-conservative Evangelical*, but the publisher changed it. The published title did not fit the book well, as it is an account of how Rogers, like many other evangelicals in the 1960s and 1970s, became disillusioned with conservative evangelicalism as represented by Henry. Pinnock used the label for post–Vatican II Catholic theologians in *Tracking the Maze*. This writer used it in an article published in *Christian Century* announcing the emergence of a new type of evangelical theology building on the works of Ramm, Bloesch and Pinnock and represented especially by Grenz: "Postconservative Evangelicals Greet the Postmodern Age," *The Christian Century* (May 3, 1995), 480–83. Evangelical theologian Kevin Vanhoozer used it independently in some of his early writings but later dropped it. For a detailed explanation of the postconservative paradigm see Roger E. Olson, *Reformed and Always Reforming: The Postconservative Approach to Evangelical Theology* (Grand Rapids: Baker Academic, 2007).

teaching assistant could finish) the second volume of his projected multi-volume systematic theology under the overarching title *The Matrix of Christian Theology*.[77]

Grenz taught theology at several evangelical seminaries and at Regent College in Vancouver, Canada. When he died he was on the faculty of Carey Theological College in the same city. Grenz was a prolific author with about twenty-five volumes to his credit as well as hundreds of articles. He gained a following especially among young Christians attracted to the emerging church movement. His paradigm change was not toward greater openness to modernity; it was away from fundamentalism and modernism and toward engagement with postmodernity. For Grenz, modernity was dying out in the last decade of the twentieth century and postmodernity was replacing it as the common cultural mood in the early twenty-first century. For him, rushing to correlate evangelicalism with modernity was a project behind the times. What was needed, he believed, was critical engagement of evangelicals with postmodern culture—something not yet fully defined but gradually replacing Enlightenment-based modernity.

Grenz announced his project in *Revisioning Evangelical Theology: A Fresh Agenda for the 21st Century*. First, he called for evangelical theology to rediscover and embrace its pietist roots. He defined evangelicalism as "an experiential piety cradled in a theology."[78] For him, the central, defining character of evangelicalism is not doctrine but "a distinctive spirituality."[79] That distinctive spirituality is what Grenz called "convertive piety."[80] He clearly distinguished this from Schleiermacher's liberal distortion of pietism in which he viewed the essence of religion and Christianity as universal God-consciousness. Instead, for Grenz, the essential, unifying core of evangelical Christianity is conversion to Jesus Christ and the life of devotion to him growing out of that. He affirmed doctrine and theology as important but relegated them to secondary status after evangelicalism's

---

[77]The first volume was *The Social God and the Relational Self: A Trinitarian Theology of the Imago Dei* (Louisville, KY: Westminster John Knox, 2001). The second volume, based on his outlines, notes and manuscripts and completed shortly after his death, was *The Named God and the Question of Being: A Trinitarian Theo-Ontology* (Louisville, KY: Westminster John Knox, 2005).

[78]Stanley J. Grenz, *Revisioning Evangelical Theology: A Fresh Agenda for the 21st Century* (Downers Grove, IL: InterVarsity Press, 1993), 35.

[79]Ibid., 31.

[80]Ibid., 47.

"shared religious experience . . . couched in a shared theological language."[81] Grenz was critical of the propositional approach to revelation (Henry and Hodge), Scripture and theological method. In his estimation, this was an overly rationalistic accommodation to modernity that centered on the cognitive powers of the rational individual. His thesis was that "if our theology is to speak the biblical message in our contemporary situation, we must shed the cloak of modernity and reclaim the more profound community outlook in which the biblical people of God were rooted."[82]

Grenz went on to argue that evangelical theology should be an everongoing conversation between three sources and norms: the biblical message, which has primacy; the theological heritage of the church, which is secondary to the biblical message; and "the thought forms of the historical-cultural context in which the contemporary people of God seek to speak, live and act."[83] By "the biblical message" Grenz meant "the Bible as canonized by the church" but especially "the kerygma as inscripturated in the Bible."[84] This was similar to the Barthian move proposed by Ramm and Bloesch: a distinction between the Bible and the Word of God in it. Theology, Grenz argued, "is not merely the systematic repetition of the content of the Bible."[85] Rather, it is our best attempt to say what all three sources and norms require within the context of a believing community with a shared experience of God through Jesus Christ. "A truly helpful theology must articulate the biblical kerygma, in a way understandable by contemporary culture, while maintaining a fundamental unity with the one people of God throughout history."[86]

To propositionalist evangelicals of the Henry flavor, Grenz's proposal sounded mushy and even relativistic. Harsh condemnation was heaped on him for departing from evangelical orthodoxy or at least setting the stage for such departure.[87] Critics especially disliked Grenz's inclusion of the

---

[81]Ibid., 38.
[82]Ibid., 73.
[83]Ibid., 93.
[84]Ibid.
[85]Ibid., 94.
[86]Ibid., 104.
[87]See, for example, Millard Erickson, *The Evangelical Left: Encountering Postconservative Evangelical Theology* (Grand Rapids: Baker, 1997) and Millard Erickson et al., eds., *Reclaiming the Center: Confronting Evangelical Accommodation in Postmodern Times* (Wheaton, IL: Crossway, 2004).

thought forms of the historical-cultural context as one of theology's sources and norms. They thought it set the stage for theological accommodation to secular culture. Grenz thought they had already accommodated to secular culture by focusing so heavily on revelation's propositional aspect and by making theology a rational effort governed by comprehensiveness, logic and explanatory power (a lá Henry). The response to Grenz's proposal for revisioning evangelical theology deepened the divide between the followers of Hodge and Henry, on the one side, and Ramm and Bloesch on the other.

In 2000 and 2001 Grenz produced two major works on evangelical theology focusing especially on postmodernity and theological method: *Renewing the Center* and *Beyond Foundationalism* coauthored with John Franke. In the first book Grenz called for a "reconstructive evangelical theology" that would turn away from the Enlightenment-based, individualistic and rationalistic approach of an evangelical foundationalism toward a more tradition- and community-based approach. His analysis and critique of the former, more traditional evangelical theological method was that it imitated modernity's obsession with scientific certainty: "Neo-evangelicals routinely assume that the task of the theologian is to apply the scientific method, assisted by the canons of logic, to the deposit of revelation found in Scripture in the quest to compile the one, complete, timeless body of right doctrines."[88] This, he argued, is an approach to knowledge being outmoded by postmodernity with its postfoundationalist epistemology, and not suited to the experiential nature of evangelical faith, which puts the heart first and the head second. It also closes the door prematurely to revision of doctrines and theological systems as if once the perfect one is found it cannot be altered in light of new knowledge.

Grenz proposed that evangelical theology be viewed much as all the sciences are viewed in postmodernity (e.g., under the influence of Thomas Kuhn)—as "construction projects."[89] As there are no indubitable epistemological foundations, the test of truth will be coherence.[90] This is different, however, from Henry's approach in that Grenz did not think rational certainty

---

[88]Stanley J. Grenz, *Renewing the Center: Evangelical Theology in a Post-Theological Era* (Grand Rapids: Baker Academic, 2000), 77.
[89]Ibid., 248.
[90]Ibid., 205.

was possible even in theology. Also, no theology can ever claim to be final and complete. The churches, he averred, will always need "doctrinal retrieval and reformation" in view of new light from God's Word and changes happening in culture.[91] Critics missed that he constantly affirmed the "primacy of the Spirit speaking through the Word over culture."[92] They thought he was giving equal weight to culture and Scripture. He was not and made that abundantly clear. Grenz offered this description of his new evangelical theology:

> Theology is progressive in that it is an ongoing discipline that repeatedly gives rise to new ways of looking at old questions, brings into view previously undeveloped aspects of the Christian belief-mosaic, and occasionally even advances the church's knowledge of theological truth.[93]

In *Beyond Foundationalism* Grenz, together with Franke, demonstrated the meaning of his recognition of culture as a "pillar of theology" together with the biblical witness and tradition. He believed that postmodernity (not postmodernism) offered certain advantages to Christian theology:

> Two aspects of the postmodern ethos are especially important for theological method: the fundamental critique and rejection of modernity, and the attempt to live and think in a realm of chastened rationality characterized by the demise of modern epistemological foundationalism.[94]

By "epistemological foundationalism" Grenz meant any view of knowledge that based everything on indubitable foundations that are self-evidently true. Postmodernity says there are no such foundations. Also by foundationalism Grenz meant the search for rational certainty in a total system of truth. Postmodernity has no time for that. Grenz thought that traditional evangelical theology would become irrelevant in a postmodern culture because of its ties to foundationalism.

Again, as in two books before, Grenz described postmodern theology as a conversation. The ultimate partner in the conversation is the Holy Spirit: "It is not the Bible as a book that is authoritative, but the Bible as the instrumentality of the Spirit: the biblical message spoken by the Spirit through

---

[91]Ibid., 345.
[92]Ibid., 211.
[93]Ibid., 343.
[94]Stanley J. Grenz and John Franke, *Beyond Foundationalism: Shaping Theology in a Postmodern Context* (Louisville, KY: Westminster John Knox, 2001), 19.

the text is theology's norming norm."[95] Furthermore, the whole purpose of theology's conversation, which includes the voices of tradition and culture, is to enter into and work within the overall Christian story, the narrative of God's creative and redemptive work in the world through Israel, Jesus Christ and the church. For Grenz, revelation is primarily narrative, not propositional-cognitive. Therefore, theology should never imitate philosophy; its task is different. Theology is about assisting the Christian community in its performance of the dramatic story of God that is still unfolding. He endorsed British evangelical scholar N. T. Wright's metaphor of theology as the fifth act of a five-act play in which the first four acts are completed and the actors, together with the play's director, must faithfully improvise the not-yet-written fifth act.[96] The theologian is like the director of the faithfully improvising actors—to keep pointing them back to the first four acts (corresponding with Scripture and tradition), helping them improvise in light of new conditions.

Grenz's vision of evangelical theology is postmodern because it rejects any single foundation and is always open to the future as it listens to the Spirit of God speaking through Scripture, guiding the church toward new ways of thinking. "The truly Reformed tradition," he said, "is by its very nature 'open.' And this 'openness,' in turn, preserves the dynamic nature of tradition."[97] Also, it is postmodern because theology must be done in community. It cannot be an individual enterprise.[98] It is not postmodern in the sense of being deconstructive, exercising suspicion toward all metanarratives. But it is postmodern in not seeing the Christian metanarrative as totalizing (excluding the possibility of truth elsewhere and attempting to impose itself on everyone). It is postconservative in the way it handles creeds and confessional statements and systems of theology:

> They are helpful as the provide insight into the faith of the church in the past and as they make us aware of the presuppositions of our own context. In addition, they stand as monuments to the community's reception and proclamation of the voice of the Spirit. Despite their great stature, such resources

---

[95]Ibid., 69.
[96]Ibid., 128.
[97]Ibid., 125.
[98]Ibid., 91.

do not take the place of canonized Scripture as the community's constitutive authority. Moreover, they must always and continually be tested by the norm of canonical scripture.[99]

An example of Grenz's revised evangelical theological method, postmodern and postconservative, is his development of the concept of the Christian as "ecclesial self" in *The Social God and the Relational Self.* There he weaves together several strands of Scripture, tradition and postmodern culture to argue that God's purpose is through the Spirit indwelling believers to gather the church into the divine, trinitarian life. This requires viewing the Trinity as a community (social Trinity) and the Christian person as called to exist in perichoretic relationship with other believers in the corporate personality of the church and all together to be elevated into the trinitarian life of God. "In short, the indwelling Spirit leads and empowers the church to fulfill its divinely mandated calling to be a sacrament of trinitarian communion, a temporal, visible sign of the eternal, dynamic life of the triune God."[100] He meant this ontologically and not merely metaphorically.

Grenz Inspires Young Evangelicals and Alienates Conservatives

For whatever reason, Grenz became for conservative evangelical theologians the symbol of all that was going wrong in evangelical theology around the turn of the twenty-first century. He was accused of cultural relativism, capitulation to postmodernism and subjectivism, and even compared with Schleiermacher. One sustained critique was offered by conservative biblical scholar and theologian D. A. Carson, who portrayed Grenz as evangelicalism's Schleiermacher, leading evangelicals away from objective truth into a swamp of subjective experience and doctrinal drift. About Grenz Carson wrote, "He prefers the direction illumined by Schleiermacher, arguing that the three sources or norms for theology are Scripture, tradition, and culture. This is, to say the least, decidedly unhelpful."[101] He explained why it is unhelpful: "I cannot escape the dreadful feeling that modern evangelicalism in the West more successfully effects the gagging of God . . . than all the

---

[99]Ibid., 124.
[100]Stanley J. Grenz, *The Social God and the Relational Self: A Trinitarian Theology of the Imago Dei* (Louisville, KY: Westminster John Knox, 2001), 336.
[101]D. A. Carson, *The Gagging of God: Christianity Confronts Pluralism* (Grand Rapids: Zondervan, 1996), 481.

post-modernists together."[102] By "the gagging of God" Carson meant silencing God's voice speaking propositional truths in Scripture. One thing Carson failed to acknowledge, however, is Grenz's frequent assertions that in the theological conversation, Scripture has primacy over tradition and culture. He wrote about Grenz as if he argued for an equality of culture with Scripture. He did not.

Evangelical Theology Becomes an Illusion

By the end of the first decade of the twenty-first century it was clear that there is no such thing as *the* evangelical theology. Evangelicals, including the movement's theologians, agree on certain basic worldviews, perspectives and doctrinal affirmations. Those were stated at the beginning of this chapter. However, when it comes to theological method and relationships with modernity and postmodernity, fragmentation appears. But that is not new. The evangelical movement, going back to its founding fathers Jonathan Edwards and John Wesley, both born in 1703 and both revivalists, has always been an unstable compound of two very different religious impulses. On the one hand are those evangelicals who see orthodoxy, right doctrine, as the permanent, enduring essence of evangelical Christianity. They are heirs of the Puritans, Protestant scholastics and the Old Princeton School theologians. For them, Christianity is above all a doctrinal system. And, for most of them, everything of any importance was settled either during the Reformation or shortly afterwards and Hodge summed it up and put it in a nice package in his systematic theology. These are also the heirs of Edwards.

Other evangelicals look back to the pietists and Wesley as the primary saints in their great cloud of witnesses. These pietist evangelicals regard conversion and a personal relationship with Jesus as more important than right doctrine. They also tend to emphasize Christian virtues and practices over doctrines. For them, experiencing God in a transforming way is the essence of Christianity with doctrine trailing a somewhat distant second.

These two groups found each other and joined hands in the face of the overwhelming threats of secularism and theological liberalism. They cooperated and accepted each other as evangelicals so long as Graham was active, serving as the glue that held evangelicalism together as one

---

[102]Ibid., 488.

movement. When Graham began to fade away into retirement and inactivity, the divide between these two types of evangelical Protestantism widened and deepened, or at least became more noticeable. Representatives on both sides began to snipe at the other side. Eventually they stopped talking to each other except to cast aspersions. Now, evangelical theology is not one theology. Two very different mindsets have evolved out of the old division. Grenz represents the pietist-Wesleyan side while Carson represents the puritan-Reformed side.

12

POSTMODERN THEOLOGIANS
REBEL AGAINST MODERNITY

Two events happened in 1951 that cause some scholars to date postmodernity from that year.[1] A philosopher named W. V. O. Quine (1908–2000) published an article titled "Two Dogmas of Empiricism" that resonated with many thinkers dissatisfied with Enlightenment approaches to knowledge. Quine's article was a manifesto for a move away from classical foundationalism and toward an "epistemological holism." That is, knowledge in the postmodern era would no longer have to be based on indubitable facts in order to count as knowledge. Quine suggested that postmodern knowledge would be more like a web than a building. The upshot is a reduction of certainty based on strict rationalism. That same year, 1951, was also the year of philosopher Ludwig Wittgenstein's death (b. 1889). Wittgenstein talked about knowledge as existing within "language games" and that there is no universal language game. The rules that apply in one language game such as physics do not apply in another such as psychology. Wittgenstein's influence on postmodern thought is inestimable.

---

[1]See Nancey Murphy, *Beyond Liberalism and Fundamentalism: How Modern and Postmodern Philosophy Set the Theological Agenda* (Valley Forge, PA: Trinity Press International, 1996), 87.

Postmoderns Step Away from Foundationalism

Both Quine and Wittgenstein were precursors to and pioneers of the cultural mood that has come to be called postmodernity. There were others, such as Nietzsche and philosopher of science Thomas Kuhn (see chap. 9). Appropriately, postmodernity and postmodernism are not clear and distinct ideas ("appropriately" because "clear and distinct ideas" was a major test of knowledge for Descartes, the father of philosophical modernism). A person can read twenty-five books on postmodernism and come away with twenty-five or more definitions. Part of the postmodern condition is not knowing for sure what it means. It is an emerging cultural and philosophical mood more than a definite movement. Jean-François Lyotard (also discussed in chap. 9) tried to provide a unifying definition of postmodernity as "incredulity toward meta-narratives." That definition caught on, but some postmoderns do not accept it and many debate its exact meaning. There does not seem to be, however, any universal definition of postmodernity or postmodernism other than a cultural and philosophical dissatisfaction with modernity.

Theologian Kevin Vanhoozer offers as good a description (not definition) of postmodern thought as any. According to him, "modern thought was characterized by a drive for certitude, universality, and perhaps, above all, *mastery*. All that was to be achieved through objective, universal reason starting from 'a view from nowhere.'"[2] Vanhoozer goes on to describe postmodernity's philosophical and theoretical turn:

> Postmodern philosophers . . . rebelled against the so-called "Enlightenment project" that sought universal human emancipation through the light of universal human reason, deployed through the powers of modern technology, science, and democracy. Postmodern thinkers rejected the idea that "reason" names a neutral and disinterested perspective from which to pursue truth and justice. Specifically, postmodern theory rejects the following modern postulates: (1) that reason is absolute and universal, (2) that individuals are autonomous, able to transcend their place in history, class, and culture (3) that universal principles and procedures are objective whereas preferences are subjective.[3]

---

[2]Kevin J. Vanhoozer, "Theology and the Condition of Postmodernity," in *The Cambridge Companion to Postmodern Theology*, ed. Kevin J. Vanhoozer (Cambridge: Cambridge University Press, 2003), 8.

[3]Ibid.

Another way of stating this succinctly is that postmodern theory rejects foundationalism with all of its baggage.

Foundationalism is the mode of knowledge inextricably tied to the Enlightenment and modernity. John Thiel has helpfully described foundationalism:

> "Foundations" for knowledge can be described as universal and so undebatable principles of argumentation, or as justifying belief itself not in need of justification, or as an immediately available, universal, and noninferential mode of knowing to which other claims must appeal for their validity. However differently foundations be portrayed, their defenders all err [according to postmoderns] in a similar way by according extraordinary privilege to what is no more than an assumption about how beliefs are justified.[4]

In other words, Enlightenment foundationalism can take different forms depending on what are considered the proper foundations for knowledge, but all agree that in order for something to count as knowledge it must be rigorously and rationally based on first principles, facts that are beyond dispute. Quine's epistemological holism, one postmodern alternative to foundationalism, rejects the existence of such foundations and suggest coherence among ideas as the criterion of truth for any system of beliefs. Other postmoderns look to narratives, grand but not totalizing stories, as the alternatives to foundations. In that case, all knowledge exists within, arises from and is judged by adequacy to the given story about reality that sustains a tradition and its form of life.

The purpose of foundationalism was to avoid dogmatism and relativism. The seventeenth-century wars of religion inspired Enlightenment thinkers to look for a way of knowing independent of traditions, stories, subjective perspectives and religious or political authorities. The rise of the scientific revolution also moved them in that direction. Foundationalism was supposed to provide certainty apart from revelation, tradition or faith. And it was supposed to emancipate people from those. According to some scholars, however, it did anything but those things. Philosopher Stephen Toulmin says that "the dream of *foundationalism*—i.e., the search for a permanent and unique set of authoritative principles for human knowledge—proves to be just a dream, which has its appeal in moments of intellectual crisis, but

---

[4]John E. Thiel, *Nonfoundationalism* (Minneapolis: Fortress, 1994), 82–83.

fades away when matters are viewed under a calmer and clearer light."[5] Toulmin goes on to level the popular postmodern accusation that Enlightenment foundationalism and the modern rage for mastery it gave rise to have had the consequence of a new bondage of the masses to the domination of an intellectual elite of society whose aim, whether conscious or not, has been to support the political power of the wealthy.

Postmodernism Seeks a New Way to Know

Postmodern thinkers find fault, in varying degrees, with all the major themes and commitments of modernity spelled out in the earliest chapters of this book. But their main objection is to the totalizing effect of modernity. The modern mind became the single standard for all discourse so that what counts as knowledge is what can be proven by means of modern methods and criteria of truth. Everything else was relegated to the categories of opinion or superstition. Modernity promoted the myths of complete objectivity of the individual knower (the view from nowhere); progress through education, reason, science and technology; and the universe as a great machine ruled by inexorable laws describable in mathematical equations. Perhaps nothing contributed more to the deaths of those myths than the world wars of the twentieth century. World War I was a meaningless war between neighboring European nations most of which were allegedly thoroughly modern in ethos. New weapons, developed by modern science, devastated the combatants and civilians. World War II witnessed what many considered the most enlightened nation, Germany, waging total war against civilian populations in Poland and Russia and genocide against Jews. One effect of the wars was to raise questions about modernity's myths.

It is important to distinguish between postmodernity as a cultural mood and postmodernism as a philosophical set of attitudes about knowledge and reality. The former is an amorphous, pervasive and popular mood marked by skepticism about grand claims to truth if not truth itself. Postmoderns are people who tend to question authority just because it is authority, tradition just because it is tradition and truth claims just because they are claims. Some scholars consider this mood hypermodern rather than truly post-

---

[5]Stephen Toulmin, *Cosmopolis: The Hidden Agenda of Modernity* (Chicago: University of Chicago Press, 1990), 174.

modern. It tends to be destructive rather than constructive and, all too often, a lazy excuse for radical individualism. Postmodernism, however, as a set of philosophical concerns and attitudes, constitutes a serious disenchantment with modernity and determination to find something to replace it without tossing aside all of the Enlightenment's achievements.

Philosopher of religion Diogenes Allen says of postmodernism that "it is not a denial of all its [modernity's] achievements, nor a despair over being able to speak in a reliable, though limited and fallible, way about our world and about ourselves."[6] Nancey Murphy and James McClendon, a philosopher and a theologian respectively, argue that postmodern thought, as opposed to popular postmodernity, is not destructive but constructive. They "single out three important and interrelated tendencies in [postmodern] philosophy: holism in epistemology, a focus on discourse or use in philosophy of language, and a focus on tradition and community in ethics."[7] Other scholars point out other constructive moves made by postmodern philosophy. These three point to a postfoundationalist epistemology that focuses on coherence among beliefs as the test of truth, meaning as function in language (how words are used as opposed to Descartes's "clear and distinct ideas") and morality defined in terms of character developed within communities shaped by traditions.

The postmodern ethos, then, is marked not only by rejection but also and even more by the struggle to find a workable alternative to the Enlightenment's modernist rationalism and naturalism. To be sure, some postmodern thinkers are more interested in deconstructing hidden ideologies of power and domination in literature and politics and even religion. Even they, however, are not interested in stopping there. Overall and in general, postmodern thinkers, as opposed to postmodern popularizers, are serious philosophers who have discovered the crumbling foundations of modernity and wish to replace them with more modest, realistic and useful modes of thinking and living.

Christians Respond to Postmodernism in Different Ways

Christian philosophers and theologians have responded to postmodernism in radically different ways depending on how they view its basic impulses.

---

[6]Diogenes Allen, "The End of the Modern World," *Christian Scholar's Review* 22:4 (June 1993): 340.
[7]Nancey Murphy and James McClendon Jr., "Distinguishing Modern from Postmodern Theologies," *Modern Theology* 53:3 (April 1989): 191.

Christian philosopher Alan Padgett offers a helpful delineation of four Christian responses to postmodernism. He describes them using four images of ways Christian scholars have treated the postmodern challenge: the ostrich, the bogeyman, the best buddy and the critical dialogue partner. Padgett recommends the stance of critical dialogue partner. This means, he says, studying the best postmodern thinkers carefully and paying attention to their insights without embracing them uncritically.[8] One Christian scholar who has attempted to help others see the values in postmodern thought is Allen, who claims, "The end of the modern world means that Christianity is liberated from the narrow, constricting, asphyxiating stranglehold of the modern world."[9] For example, he says, because of postmodernism "the philosophical and scientific bases for excluding the possibility of God have collapsed."[10] In fact, according to Allen, "in a post-modern world Christianity is intellectually relevant."[11]

Another Christian philosopher who has done much to introduce postmodernism to Christian audiences as helpful is Merold Westphal, whose constant message has been that postmodernism, though not itself Christian, can be an ally of Christianity. For example, a major theme of postmodernism is the destabilizing of "modernity's proud pretensions" to God-like status for the rational subject. He asks,

> Doesn't the Christian theologian, whether the preacher in the pulpit or the professor in the seminary, want to say the same thing? Atheistic postmodernism says that we are not God because there is no God. Christian thought says we are not God because only God is God. In spite of deep disagreement about God, there is a deep agreement between Christians and postmodern thinkers that we are not God and should not claim divine status for our knowledge.[12]

Westphal is not saying that all postmodern thinkers are atheists or that Christians ought to accept postmodern thought uncritically. He is, however, advocating Padgett's approach as critical dialogue partner to Christian en-

---

[8]Alan Padgett, "Christianity and Postmodernity," *Christian Scholar's Review* 26:2 (winter 1996): 129.

[9]Allen, "End of the Modern World," 340.

[10]Ibid., 342.

[11]Ibid., 345.

[12]Merold Westphal, "Blind Spots: Christianity and Postmodern Philosophy," *The Christian Century* (June 14, 2003), 33.

counter with postmodern philosophy, a major impulse of which is to dethrone (deconstruct) powerful ideologies that elevate modern men and women of reason and science to God-like status. In other words, Christianity and postmodernism share a concern to tear down idols.

Not all Christians are as sanguine as Padgett, Allen and Westphal about relations between postmodernism and Christianity. Many liberal and conservative theologians, to say nothing of preachers and popular writers, have condemned postmodernism as "cognitive nihilism" and sheer relativism. Much of this is based on misreadings of postmodern thinkers such as Jacques Derrida (1930–2004) and Emmanuel Levinas (1906–1995). The extent to which such criticisms are valid for other postmodern philosophers such as Michel Foucault (1926–1984) and Richard Rorty (1931–2007) is debatable. Most certainly, however, not all postmodernists are guilty of those sins. Murphy thinks she knows why conservative theologians and liberal theologians both tend to reject postmodernism. According to her analysis it is because both approaches to theology are largely based on modern assumptions and methods. Both, in separate ways, have accommodated to modernity even though especially conservatives deny it. According to her, however, "foundationalism has had a powerful influence on the development of modern theology."[13] Liberals and conservatives, whom she calls fundamentalists, are brothers under the skin insofar as both are based on foundationalism:

> Theologians have conceived of theology as a building needing a sturdy foundation. But what is that foundation to be? The short answer is that there are only two options: Scripture and experience. Conservative theologians have chosen to build upon Scripture; liberals are distinguished by their preference for experience. This forced option has been one cause of the split between liberals and conservatives.[14]

The split, however, if Murphy is right, is a surface one. Foundationalism lies at the root of conservative theology just as much as at the root of liberal theology. Her case study of that is Hodge (see chap. 3). Another candidate would be Henry (see chap. 11). Both and many other conservative theolo-

---

[13]Murphy, *Beyond Liberalism and Fundamentalism*, 12.
[14]Ibid.

gians view Scripture as the indubitable foundation for all teachings. What makes these conservative theologians modern is not just that they view Scripture as authoritative; it is that they treat it as the unchallengeable, inerrant source of all doctrines for the sake of establishing rational certainty.

Murphy also relegates most liberal theology to the modern category.[15] This has been a major theme of this book—that liberal and neo-liberal theologians have by and large capitulated to modernity by elevating universal human experience to the primary source and norm of Christian theology. Whether that be Schleiermacher's God-consciousness or Tillich's ultimate concern, liberal theologians have sought to use an account of universal human religiousness (a religious a priori) to justify Christian truth claims to the detriment of revelation and faith. Both conservatives and liberals object most strenuously to postmodernism because they are committed to modernity whether they know it or not. (It is usually conservative theologians who are but do not know it and often vehemently reject it.)

Two broad categories of Christian theologians have rigorously engaged in the task of critical dialogue with postmodern philosophy to the extent of shaping their theological methods and projects around it. They are postliberals and deconstructionists. (There is also deconstructionism in other disciplines, but here the term will be used to describe a particular approach to postmodern theology.) Postliberalism is just as essentially contested as postmodernism itself. It is anything but a clear and distinct idea, and it is not a movement. It is an ethos or general approach to doing theology. It is a conversation among somewhat like-minded Christian theologians who seek to transcend the liberalism of their teachers and the left-middle-right spectrum of modern theology using narrative, tradition and community and a focus on Christian practices to revision Christianity away from captivity to modernism.

Deconstructionism is a mode of Christian theology that focuses on commitment to the "other" and critical exposure of the violent tendencies in all thought systems to move theology away from ideological idolatry toward openness to the new, the different and the unexpected. Their similarity lies in their common refusal of modernism as the necessary context

---

[15]Ibid., 22-28.

for theological creativity. Their difference lies in their attitudes and approaches to Christian community, to the church. Postliberals highly value
the church while deconstructionists are characteristically suspicious of all
community life and especially institutions.

12.A. Postliberal Theologians and Stanley Hauerwas Develop a Third Way in Theology

One evening in 1985 two theologians associated with Duke University sat in
a backyard in Durham, North Carolina, discussing the condition of modern
theology and especially its liberal/conservative divide. A book by George
Lindbeck (b. 1923), *The Nature of Doctrine*, had just been published.[16]
Stanley Hauerwas (b. 1940) and William Willimon (b. 1946) came up with
an idea for an article that would describe an alternative to the liberal/con-
servative divide in Protestant theology. Referring to Lindbeck's book, Hauerwas says in his autobiography:

> In light of this book, we saw an opportunity to describe an emerging theo-
> logical development associated with people as diverse as Hans Frei, David
> Kelsey, Will Campbell, John Yoder, Walker Percy, and Flannery O'Connor.
> We wanted to argue for a theological transformation that would involve the
> recovery of the centrality of the church and the liturgy for Christian for-
> mation. As we talked about it in my backyard, we concluded that the problem
> with most pastors and theologians was that the way they went about their
> business did not require the existence of God.[17]

Most likely that article was "Embarrassed by God's Presence,"[18] a manifesto of what many call postliberal theology—not a movement, Hauerwas
and Willimon wrote, but a mood. That mood, they explained, is best expressed this way:

> We are no longer content . . . to stand on the periphery, hat in hand, apolo-
> getically trying to translate our religious convictions into terms palatable to
> the world. Rather, we are now ready to say that our convictions lay down a

---

[16]George A. Lindbeck, *The Nature of Doctrine: Religion and Theology in a Postliberal Age* (Philadelphia: Westminster Press, 1984).
[17]Stanley Hauerwas, *Hannah's Child: A Theologian's Memoir* (Grand Rapids: Eerdmans, 2010),
193–94.
[18]Stanley Hauerwas and William Willimon, "Embarrassed by God's Presence," *The Christian
Century* (January 30, 1985), 98–100.

program, a vision, a paradigm for accommodating the world to the gospel . . . there is an aggressive, anti-establishment spirit among [postliberals] that we think is right. That is, they challenge both the academy and the church to realize that business as usual cannot continue if Christians are to be intellectually and socially of service in our time.[19]

Postliberals share a mood in theology. Hauerwas and Willimon went on to coauthor a book further explaining the postliberal mood, as they felt and interpreted it. Its main thesis was that "the church is a colony, an island of one culture in the middle of another. In baptism our citizenship is transferred from one dominion to another, and we become, in whatever culture we find ourselves, resident aliens."[20] According to Hauerwas and Willimon, modern theology and churches have allowed themselves to be determined by the agenda of modernity; they have succumbed to cultural accommodation to European and American modes of thought and life stemming largely from Enlightenment principles. Their main concern has been "How do we make the gospel credible to the modern world?"[21] They have unconsciously distorted the gospel in the process of attempting to translate it for moderns.[22] The main question theologians and all Christians should ask, they argued, is not how to make the gospel intelligible to moderns but "Can we so order our lives in the [Christian] colony that the world might look at us and know that God is busy?"[23]

Postliberalism is another essentially contested concept in contemporary theology. Hauerwas and Willimon do not speak for all who consider themselves postliberal. Like "postmodern," "postliberal" is difficult to pin down and describe in a way its own theologians would appreciate. It is not a cohesive movement. There are a few things that can be said about it with some degree of assurance, however.

First, postliberalism has two fathers who were both professors at Yale Divinity School, which is one reason it is sometimes called the new Yale theology. They are Hans Frei (1922–1988) and Lindbeck. Frei's groundbreaking

---

[19]Ibid., 98.
[20]Stanley Hauerwas and William H. Willimon, *Resident Aliens: Life in the Christian Colony* (Nashville: Abingdon, 1989), 12.
[21]Ibid., 19.
[22]Ibid., 21.
[23]Ibid., 92.

book that helped launch narrative theology, a major ingredient in post-liberalism, is *The Eclipse of Biblical Narrative* (1974). His *The Identity of Jesus Christ* (1975) was an experiment in narrative Christology and became a major catalyst for postliberal theology. Lindbeck's *The Nature of Doctrine*, although a small book, became a bible of postliberal theology. Most who associate themselves with postliberalism or who are generally thought of that way were either students of Frei and Lindbeck or heavily influenced by them.

Second, postliberals consciously seek to develop a third way in contemporary theology that avoids what they see as the accommodationist tendencies of both conservative theology and liberal theology. Gary Dorrien highlights this attempt to develop a third way in theology by postliberals:

> No theological perspective has a commanding place or an especially impressive following these days [2001]. Various theologies compete for attention in the highly pluralized field, and no theology has made much of a public impact. One significant and inescapable development, however, has been the emergence of a "postliberal" theology, a major attempt to revive the neo-orthodox ideal of a "third way" in theology.[24]

Dorrien and other observers have noted the heavy reliance of postliberals on Barth, even though none of them follow Barth completely or uncritically.

Third, postliberals make certain postmodern moves in developing their third way in theology. This is probably a controversial claim about postliberalism. Some of its advocates and defenders will no doubt object to its inclusion with deconstructionist theology in a section on postmodern theologies. However, such a protest would probably be based on an assumption that "postmodern" equates with cognitive nihilism and relativism. As has already been explained, that is not necessarily the case. Murphy and McClendon rightly argue that postliberalism is "through and through postmodern."[25] One example of postliberalism's postmodern tendencies is postliberal theologian William Placher's contention that "there are no reasons

---

[24]Gary Dorrien, "A Third Way in Theology? The Origins of Postliberalism," *The Christian Century* (July 4–11, 2001), 16.

[25]Murphy and McClendon, "Distinguishing Modern from Postmodern Theologies," 206–7. See also Murphy, *Beyond Liberalism and Fundamentalism*, 127–31.

not internal to some tradition."[26] Most, if not all, postliberals would agree
with Placher, a student of Lindbeck, that "all argument operates within some
particular tradition, that there is no universal standard of rationality."[27]

Fourth, postliberal theologians believe contemporary Christianity must
recover the stance that "the Bible absorbs the world." This axiom has been
expressed by postliberals in many different ways, but the essential idea is
the same. It was expressed as a basic principle by Frei in *The Eclipse of Biblical Narrative* and reiterated by Lindbeck in *The Nature of Doctrine*. This is
the briefest expression of what is called narrative theology, which all postliberals adopt to some degree. Placher explains its meaning most clearly:

> Frei proposes a radical solution. Suppose we do not start with the modern
> world. Suppose we start with the biblical world, and let those narratives
> define what is real, so that *our* lives have meaning to the extent that we fit
> them into *that* framework. . . . If we do that, then the truth of the biblical nar-
> ratives does not depend on connecting them to some other *real* world. *They*
> describe the real world.[28]

It is extremely important not to misunderstand this principle that lies at
the heart of postliberalism. Postliberals are not saying that Christians must
take everything in the Bible literally or even that the Bible is inerrant. Rather,
Frei's narrative theology and postliberalism in general view the Bible as a
realistic narrative that, in spite of flaws, conveys a picture of reality that
serves as the lens through which Christians view reality. Underlying this
idea of narrative-shaped knowing is the assumption, absolutely contrary to
modernity, that "narration . . . is a more basic category than either explanation or understanding."[29] Added to that is that "creation and redemption
constitute the story necessary for us [Christians] to know who we are. Such
knowledge comes only through the telling of this story."[30] Postliberals love
to point out that this is not unique to Christians. All systems of belief, all
worldviews, know from within some story about reality.

---

[26]William Placher, *Unapologetic Theology: A Christian Voice in a Pluralistic Conversation* (Louisville, KY: Westminster John Knox, 1989), 117.
[27]Ibid., 123.
[28]Ibid., 161.
[29]Stanley Hauerwas, *With the Grain of the Universe: The Church's Witness and Natural Theology*
(Grand Rapids: Brazos Press, 2001), 206.
[30]Ibid., 207.

Placher explains narrative theology, as expressed by Frei, very clearly and succinctly:

> On this view, the biblical narratives (1) lay out the shape of the world in which, they claim, we live and (2) depict the character of a God to whom they call us to respond. On both counts, they make some general claims about the truth of the story they tell, and those claims are important to the meaning of the narrative. But in neither case is accurately detailed history the point of the text.[31]

This is one area where narrative theology/postliberalism diverges from fundamentalism. Both emphasize the necessity of the Bible for authentic Christianity. Both say that the Bible absorbs the world in the sense explained above. But for narrative theology/postliberalism "letting these stories [the biblical narratives] convey to us who God is in a way that only a story could does not commit us to the truth of each episode."[32] Conservative critics of postliberalism have often charged it with reducing Christian truth to nice fiction. Nothing could be further from the truth even though it admits that much in the Bible may be history-like without being historical. Placher falsifies the critics' claims:

> I have repeatedly emphasized that all argument operates within some particular tradition, that there is no universal standard of rationality. But . . . as a Christian I believe that the central claims of Christian faith are true—not merely "true for Christians" or "true within the context of the Christian tradition" but in a strong sense just plain true. . . . The way we can go about justifying a belief is always context dependent, but the truth claimed for that belief is not.[33]

Fifth, postliberal theologians believe, contrary to most conservative evangelicals like Hodge and Henry, that doctrinal claims are secondary to the church's primary language. Another way of putting it is that doctrinal claims are the church's second-order language. Christianity's first-order language is the language of worship and witness. Doctrine is regulative, not constitutive of Christian discourse. Lindbeck spells this out in *The Nature of Doctrine*. Religion, he argues, is like a culture and its language; it takes

---

[31]Placher, *Unapologetic Theology*, 131.
[32]Ibid., 132.
[33]Ibid., 123.

training to learn it unless one grows up in it. It is not just a belief system: "a religion can be viewed as a kind of cultural and/or linguistic framework or medium that shapes the entirety of life and thought."[34] This is similar to what Wittgenstein meant by a "language game." It is a communal phenomenon that shapes subjectivity, a form of life that gives rise to experience and identity. It is a symbol system like a language:

> To become religious involves becoming skilled in the language, the symbol system of a given religion. To become a Christian involves learning the story of Israel and of Jesus well enough to interpret and experience oneself and one's world in its terms. A religion is above all an external word . . . that molds and shapes the self and its world, rather than an expression or thematization of a preexisting self or of preconceptual experience.[35]

Lindbeck calls this his "cultural-linguistic" theory of religion and doctrine and contrasts it with the liberal "experiential-expressive" theory and the conservative "cognitive-propositional" theory.[36]

According to Lindbeck's theory of religion, doctrines are communally constituted rules for speech and conduct, much like the grammar of a language. The language of faith is what Christians do by worshiping, promising, obeying, exhorting, preaching and witnessing. All that is shaped by the biblical narrative and takes place within the context of a community traditioned by that narrative. Doctrines are the rules of the grammar of that language of faith:

> Just as grammar by itself affirms nothing either true or false regarding the world in which language is used, but only about language, so theology and doctrine, to the extent that they are second-order activities, assert nothing either true or false about God and his relation to creatures, but only speak about such assertions. These assertions, in turn, cannot be made except when speaking religiously, i.e., when seeking to align oneself and others performatively with what one takes to be most important in the universe by worshiping, promising.[37]

This view of doctrine as regulative, like grammar, has shocked many conservatives and liberals alike. That is because they have gotten used to thinking of their doctrinal affirmations as metaphysical claims about reality.

---

[34]Lindbeck, *Nature of Doctrine*, 33.
[35]Ibid., 34.
[36]Ibid., 16.
[37]Ibid., 69.

Critics of postliberalism have charged that Lindbeck's theory constitutes a denial of the truth of Christianity. That is because they equate Christianity with doctrines. But Lindbeck is not denying the truth of doctrines. He is saying their truth is of a different kind from metaphysical claims about external, ultimate reality in and of itself. Doctrines govern religious language and, in turn, are constituted by the biblical narrative. The point is that doctrines are not the essence of religion; narrative and worship are.

Not all postliberals are entirely pleased with Lindbeck's account of doctrines. All agree that doctrines are second order to the first-order language of the biblical narrative and the community's worship and witness. That is, doctrines function in a servant role. They are ministerial rather than magisterial. At the same time, they regulate and govern, but not apart from the biblical narrative, which is revelation itself (after Jesus Christ, who is the subject of the canonical story). Theologian George Hunsinger (b. 1945) disagrees mildly with Lindbeck about the nature of doctrines. While he agrees that "becoming religious is something like learning a language,"[38] he is afraid that Lindbeck's rule theory of doctrine cannot do justice to "the truth claims of Christian discourse."[39] Still, Hunsinger, like all postliberals, considers doctrine regulative rather than constitutive of religion, including Christianity.

Sixth, and finally, postliberal theologians believe the true mode of Christian discourse toward those outside the Christian community is witness and not apologetics. They do not mean "witness" as in evangelical street witnessing or mass evangelism. They mean being the church in the midst of the world. Public discipleship is the best way to convince unbelievers that "God is busy," as Hauerwas put it. The problem with all apologetics, postliberals aver, is that it requires the Christian to step outside his or her Christian commitments to adopt, however briefly, universally acceptable warrants for believing. The problem with that is twofold: no such universally acceptable warrants for believing exist, and by stepping outside distinctively Christian grounds for believing the apologist has to treat as authoritative some alternative story, worldview, rationality. No postliberal theologian expresses the postliberal case against apologetics (including

---

[38]George Hunsinger, "Postliberal Theology," in *The Cambridge Companion to Postmodern Theology*, ed. Kevin J. Vanhoozer (Cambridge: Cambridge University Press, 2003), 54.
[39]Ibid., 45.

natural theology) more strongly than Hauerwas: "If what Christians believe about God and the world could be known without witness, then we would have evidence that what Christians believe about God and the world is not true."[40] Also, "the only truthful way to make Christianity attractive is through witness."[41] For Hauerwas, all Christian attempts at apologetics involve accommodation to modernity, which means having to assume that the Christian God does not exist in order to work their way back to believing in God on the basis of entirely secular premises. "I am suggesting that Christians in modernity have lost the ability to answer questions about the truthfulness of what we believe because we have accepted beliefs about the world that presuppose that God does not matter."[42]

Postliberals answer their critics. Placher sums up this sixth point of postliberalism well when he says, "Confronted by our culture's standards of what makes sense and what doesn't, postliberal theology invites Christians to say 'We don't look at things that way,' and to nurture communities that offer an alternative vision."[43] As one might expect, this aspect of postliberalism, which is inseparable from the others, has drawn much criticism from conservative and liberal theologians. While expressing real appreciation for some aspects of narrative theology and postliberalism, conservative evangelical theologian Alister McGrath raises the question of the truth of the biblical story for them:

> For evangelicals, postliberalism reduces the concept of "truth" to "internal consistency." There can be no doubt that intrasystematic consistency is a quality which is to be admired. However, it is perfectly possible to have an entirely coherent system which has no meaningful relation to the real world. Christianity is not simply about interpreting the narrated identity of Jesus, or giving a coherent account of the grammar of faith. It is about recognizing the truth of Jesus Christ as Saviour and Lord.[44]

Postliberals would probably respond that McGrath and other conservative critics are confusing the actuality of what is believed with the how of

---

[40]Hauerwas, *With the Grain of the Universe*, 207.
[41]Ibid., 215.
[42]Ibid., 231.
[43]Placher, *Unapologetic Theology*, 19.
[44]Alister McGrath, *A Passion for Truth: The Intellectual Coherence of Evangelicalism* (Downers Grove, IL: InterVarsity Press, 1995), 153–54.

believing. Just because there are no external, non-Christian warrants for believing what Christians believe and confess does not mean what they believe in and confess does not exist. And just because doctrines are regulative and not constitutive, second-order and not first-order language, does not mean they are fictions.

Liberal or neo-liberal theologians have also criticized postliberalism for allegedly relegating Christianity to a ghetto of faith cut off from the public discourse of the world outside the church. One especially harsh liberal critic is James Gustafson (b. 1925), who accused postliberalism of a "pernicious . . . sectarian temptation" which "legitimates a withdrawal of Christianity from its larger cultural environs."[45] Especially Placher has felt the force of such criticism and responded from a postliberal perspective in articles and books. He borrows Frei's language of "ad hoc apologetics" to describe how postliberalism approaches public theology. It means that "we should let the common ground we share with a given conversation partner set the starting point for that particular conversation, not looking for *universal* rules or assumptions for human conversation generally."[46] There are no such universal rules or assumptions. Postliberalism is not opposed to public conversations about what Christians believe, but it opposes shifting over to non-Christian assumptions in order to support and defend Christian belief. There are no neutral, disinterested, unstoried assumptions for the Christian and the non-Christian to use in attempting to persuade each other. But that does not mean Christians cannot speak up in the marketplace of ideas and witness to their beliefs or enter into conversations based on shared common ground with non-Christians.

Hauerwas rises to fame, influence and cult status. Hauerwas is known for many things. Among them is salty speech. Unlike most theologians, he has few qualms about sprinkling his public lectures with profanities. He attributes that to his early years as a bricklayer in Texas, where he was born and raised. Some religious groups, however, will not invite him to speak fearing what he might say. That does not bother him; he has more than enough invitations to speak. In fact, it would be safe to say he is the most sought-after theologian in the United States if not the world. He receives

---

[45]Quoted in Placher, *Unapologetic Theology*, 19.
[46]Ibid., 167.

numerous invitations to speak and appear on panels every month. In his autobiography he bares his soul about many things, including the ups and downs of his marriages and friendships. And he admits to not knowing what he believes. He confesses that he tries to be a "church theologian" but is "not interested in what I believe. I am not even sure what I believe. I am much more interested in what the church believes."[47] Anyone who reads Hauerwas, however, discovers quickly that there are some things he believes passionately, and they are not always what the church believes. He is noted, for example, for his commitment to nonviolence including noncoercion. And he is well-known for his aversion to any Christian accommodation to modern culture and especially to American values. Hauerwas does not consider himself a card-carrying member of any theological club or tribe whether it be liberal or conservative, neo-orthodox or postliberal. Postliberals, however, often include him among themselves and value his work, and scholars of postliberalism often list him among its proponents.

There can be no doubt that Hauerwas is a cult figure, a force of nature, a leader and spokesman for a cause. And he has accumulated a large following of devotees who devour everything he writes. Many of them are much younger than he. He denies that he ever wanted this, but if not, he has done much to bring it about anyway. Even his friends often note that he has a tendency to express his views in extreme ways and then qualify them to soften the rough edges. But, at least to his followers, he sounds like a prophet more than a calm scholar speculating about the metaphysical properties of God. That is at least partly because of his extroverted personality and partly because he regards ethics as theology's main task. He is actively disinterested in the questions that consume so much theological energy. For him, theology is practical and pastoral, and ethics is its primary mode.[48] However, ethics is not about commands or rules so much as about virtue and character. He is a pioneer in what has come to be called virtue ethics, whose focus is on the kind of people Christians ought to be rather than on duties or rational decisions about right and wrong in specific situations. He

---

[47]Hauerwas, *Hannah's Child*, 254.
[48]Stanley Hauerwas, *The Peaceable Kingdom: A Primer in Christian Ethics* (Notre Dame, IN: University of Notre Dame Press, 1983), xvii. This is not to say that Hauerwas does not care about doctrines. Rather, he regards dogma and ethics as inseparable. His choice is to focus on ethics.

never tires of saying that "to be a Christian is not principally to obey certain commandments or rules, but to learn to grow into the story of Jesus as the form of God's kingdom,"[49] and "Christian ethics is concerned more with who we are than what we do."[50] For him, who we are, or should be, as Christians, is nonviolent Jesus people: "Nonviolence is not one among other behavioral implications that can be drawn from the gospel but is integral to the shape of Christian convictions."[51] And this peaceful (not passive) character is shaped by community; it is no individualistic decision or self-creation.[52] These and other themes of Hauerwas's theology have found strong resonance with many especially younger Christians while they have been harshly criticized by others. If Hauerwas is anything he is controversial.

Life began for Stanley Hauerwas in small-town Texas in 1940. Raised in an evangelical Methodist home and church, he attended Methodist-related Southwestern College in Georgetown, now a suburb of Austin. His decision to become a theologian was a long process that came to conclusion only while he was studying for the ministry at Yale Divinity School. There he came into contact with influential theologians such as Paul Holmer (1916–2004), Gustafson, Julian Hartt (1911–2010) and Frei. Hauerwas received his PhD in Christian ethics from Yale in 1968. His first teaching position was at Lutheran Augustana College in Rock Island, Illinois, after which he taught theology and ethics at the University of Notre Dame. There he almost became Catholic but finally decided to remain Methodist. While at Notre Dame he met Mennonite theologian John Howard Yoder (1927–1997), who was then teaching at Associated Mennonite Biblical Seminary, also in Indiana. Hauerwas was so impressed with Yoder, who had studied with Barth in Switzerland, that he brought him to Notre Dame, where he became the first Anabaptist to teach at a Catholic university. Yoder became, much to many observers' surprise, a major influence on Hauerwas's developing theology and Christian ethics. It was surprising because, then as still to some extent, Mennonites were considered sectarians unworthy of serious attention except perhaps in courses of study about the radical Reformation.

---

[49]Ibid., 30.
[50]Ibid., 33.
[51]Ibid., xvi.
[52]Ibid., 33.

After fourteen years at Notre Dame, Hauerwas accepted an invitation from Methodist-related Duke Divinity School at Duke University to join its faculty. There he became its star theologian and remains well into the age when most people retire. By all accounts he is a person of boundless energy, an avid runner, prolific writer, frequent preacher and guest speaker, gadfly by means of editorials and essays commenting on world affairs. In 2001, he was named America's "best theologian" by *Time*.[53] The day after he delivered the prestigious Gifford Lectures in Scotland, terrorists flew airplanes into the World Trade Center's Twin Towers in New York City. Hauerwas, a known pacifist, was asked to respond to that and to America's war against Iraq. In typical Hauerwas fashion, against the grain of cultural drift, he argued against the war, reminding especially Christians that violence is never the way of Jesus or the gospel. He lost several close friends because of his stance.[54]

Hauerwas's publications are numerous. Among his most important books not already mentioned are *A Community of Character* (1981), *The Peaceable Kingdom* (1983), *After Christendom?* (1991) and *With the Grain of the Universe* (2001). *The Hauerwas Reader* (2003) comprises seven hundred pages including excerpts from many of his books and articles. When contemplating his published corpus one is tempted to say with the medieval Spanish bishop about the collected works of Augustine, "Anyone who says he has read all of this is a liar."

Hauerwas criticizes Christian accommodation to modernity. The most important, overriding theme of Hauerwas's theology is the distinctiveness of the gospel over against culture and especially the culture created by modernity. He is not so concerned with the natural sciences, except insofar as they claim too much authority over too much territory, as with politics broadly defined. (Here, as in the writings of Yoder, "politics" does not mean partisan politics or even just government; it refers to the ways in which people organize their common life together.) According to Hauerwas, the great temptation facing Christianity has always been what he calls Christendom—the amalgamation of the gospel with pagan or secular culture. Christendom is when Christians pretend that the culture they create is

---

[53]Jean Bethke Elshtain, "Theologian: Christian Contrarian," *Time* (September 17, 2001), 76–77.
[54]The biographical information about Hauerwas is taken from *Hannah's Child*, 269–71. His article appeared in *Time* (February 23, 2003).

Christian. The last gasp of Christendom in the West has been Christian the-ology's attempt to make the gospel credible to the modern world by trans-lating it into terms modern people can understand and accept.[55] Examples of this are Schleiermacher and Tillich. Schleiermacher adjusted the gospel to appeal to Christianity's "cultured despisers." Tillich practiced correlation be-tween the gospel and non-Christian culture, especially modernity. In both cases, and in liberal and neo-liberal theologies generally, Hauerwas asserts, these modern interpretations of the gospel have distorted it.[56]

The Duke theologian argues that theologians like Schleiermacher and Tillich have, since the Enlightenment, sought to demonstrate that the gospel can be translated into terms that are meaningful and compelling for those who do not share Christianity's particularistic beliefs about Jesus.[57] "Such theologians try to locate the 'essence' of religion in a manner that frees religion from its most embarrassing particularistic aspects."[58] Hauerwas's main illustrations of this bad habit are drawn from Christian social ethics. Two of his primary examples are Rauschenbusch, a father of the social gospel in the United States, and Reinhold Niebuhr, the twentieth century's leading public theologian and Christian ethicist. Like most liberals and neo-liberals, he charges, these theologians and their followers succumbed to Christendom by attempting to downplay the distinctive, particularistic claims of the gospel of Jesus Christ in order to speak into the public, secular conversations about American political life. These theologians, in their own ways, thought the primary task of Christian ethics was to support and sustain the moral resources of American society.[59] "For Niebuhr and the social gospelers the subject of Christian ethics was America."[60]

This complaint of Hauerwas's needs some explanation. He would say that is because most American Christians have gotten so used to thinking of Christianity and America together that they have trouble separating the two. That is a modern form of the sin of Christendom peculiar to the United

---

[55]Hauerwas and Willimon, *Resident Aliens*, 19.
[56]Ibid., 21.
[57]Stanley Hauerwas, "On Keeping Theological Ethics Theological," in *The Hauerwas Reader*, ed. John Berkman and Michael Cartwright (Durham, NC: Duke University Press, 2001), 52.
[58]Ibid., 53.
[59]Ibid., 65.
[60]Ibid., 60.

States, even though it has parallels in other societies. What exactly is it Hauerwas objects to in this liberal project of public social ethics and the theology that underwrites it? He believes and argues that whenever Christians
attempt to do "public theology and ethics" on the same ideological territory
as non-Christians they sacrifice something essential to the gospel. They
have to water it down in order to make Christian ethics universal for society at large. "In the hope of securing societal good, the task of Christian
ethics became the attempt to develop social strategies that people of
goodwill could adopt even though they differed religiously and morally."[61]
An example Hauerwas returns to repeatedly is the theology and ethics of
Reinhold Niebuhr. In order to inject Christianity into the public discussion
of public policy, Niebuhr, he argues, had to define justice in a way that required compromise of the gospel of Jesus Christ. (Here Hauerwas is informed by and agrees with Yoder in *The Politics of Jesus* [1972].) In other
words, in order to be players in the public political arena, Christian theologians and ethicists such as Niebuhr had to take less than fully seriously the
way of Jesus Christ and the gospel. "As American society becomes increasingly secular, Christian ethicists come to think that, if they wish to remain
political actors, they must translate their convictions into a nontheological
idiom. But once such a translation is accomplished, why is the theological
idiom needed at all?"[62]

Nowhere does Hauerwas make this case against Christian cultural accommodation in theology and ethics clearer than in his Gifford Lectures.
In *With the Grain of the Universe* he strenuously argues that secular modernity has seduced Christian thinkers away from the gospel. But he puts
the blame not on secular modernity or American culture but squarely on
Christians themselves for adopting natural theology as their basis for
knowing God. In this he follows Barth closely. He brings the two points
together. Natural theology and Christendom, apologetics and "neo-
Constantinianism," are intertwined in the modern cultural subversion of the
gospel. "When Christianity is tempted to become a civilizational religion in
a manner that makes witness secondary to knowing the truth about God,
Christians lose the skills necessary to make known to themselves and others

---

[61]Ibid., 61.
[62]Ibid., 68.

how what we believe is true to the way things are."[63] The natural theology of post-Enlightenment Christendom is foundational or fundamental theology that seeks to correlate human experience, as defined by modernity, with Christianity. In other words, it is anthropology. Niebuhr is guilty of this, according to Hauerwas. "Niebuhr assumed that the truth of Christianity consisted in the confirmation of universal and timeless myths about the human condition that made Christianity available to anyone without witness."[64] By "witness" here Hauerwas means the particular confession of Jesus Christ as God and Savior. He means Christian convictions based on the gospel. Modern natural theology, often disguised, as in the case of Niebuhr, sets witness aside in order to make Christianity palatable to modern, secular people. "The truth-fulfilling conditions of Christian speech have been compromised in the interest of developing an ethic for Christians in liberal social orders."[65] (By "liberal" here Hauerwas means the classical liberalism of individualism, freedom and inherent rights.)

All this criticism of modern Christian theological ethics can be made concrete with the case of violence. Hauerwas believes that nonviolence is part and parcel of the gospel of Jesus Christ. "Nonviolence is not one among other behavioral implications that can be drawn from the gospel but is integral to the shape of Christian convictions."[66] "Nonviolence . . . is at the very heart of our understanding of God."[67] Underlying this emphasis on nonviolence is Hauerwas's (and Yoder's) conviction that "the nature and reality of the kingdom is manifest throughout Jesus' life and ministry."[68] The life and ministry of Jesus displayed a radical alternative to the world's valuing of power, coercion and control. The cross event demonstrates this. The Sermon on the Mount proves it. Hauerwas, following Yoder, thinks it is the height of folly and compromise to interpret the Sermon on the Mount as a counsel of perfection not applicable to life here and now. Even though the Sermon on the Mount is meant to be followed, Jesus did not try to control history, and neither should Christians. "The task of the Christian

---

[63]Hauerwas, *With the Grain of the Universe*, 32.
[64]Ibid., 38–39.
[65]Ibid., 38.
[66]Hauerwas, *Peaceable Kingdom*, xvi.
[67]Ibid., xvii.
[68]Ibid., 85.

people is not to seek to control history, but to be faithful to the mode of life of the peaceable kingdom."[69] Thus, for Hauerwas, for Christians, justice can never be learned apart from the kingdom of God lived and proclaimed by Jesus. Justice, the central issue for any Christian social ethic, "never comes through violence, nor can it be based on violence."[70] Since modern nation-states are built and kept on violence, Christians cannot give them ultimate loyalty or even treat their social ethic as support for them.

For Hauerwas, then, Christian accommodation to modernity displays itself nowhere more clearly than in liberal theologians' attempts to develop justifications for Christian beliefs and ethics based on universal principles available without witness. "The more theologians seek to find the means to translate theological convictions into terms acceptable to the non-believer, the more they substantiate the view that theology has little of importance to say in the area of ethics."[71] This is because "Christian ethicists [like Niebuhr] accepted an account of the social good that failed to manifest the struggle and the transformation of the self necessary for any adequate account of the moral life."[72] That account of the social good includes, but is not limited to, a distinctively modern concept of freedom. In modernity, and especially in the United States, Hauerwas avers, "freedom itself is at once the necessary and sufficient condition for being moral."[73] This freedom, which is not real freedom from a Christian perspective, is inextricably tied to individualism. Modernity elevated individual freedom to godlike status; it has become an idol. Too many modern theologians and Christian ethicists have assumed its value and adjusted Christianity to accommodate it. Hauerwas argues that true freedom is not modern freedom, the individual's freedom from constraint to create himself or herself, but character shaped by virtues. "Freedom is a quality that derives from having a well-formed character. Put in traditional terms, only the truly good person can be the truly free person . . . freedom follows from courage and the ability to respond to a truthful story."[74] Also, "we are most free when

---

[69] Ibid., 106.
[70] Ibid., 114.
[71] Hauerwas, "On Keeping Theological Ethics Theological," 69.
[72] Ibid., 70.
[73] Hauerwas, *Peaceable Kingdom*, 8.
[74] Ibid., 37.

we are formed by a story that helps us live appropriate [sic] to the reality that our life is a gift."[75]

Individualism, freedom as personal rights to self-determination, co-ercion and violence, nation-states—these are the products of modernity, not the gospel, says Hauerwas. Modern natural theology is the attempt to correlate Christianity with them in order to make the gospel fit modern society. That is our Christendom. It is a betrayal of the gospel.

Hauerwas emphasizes story, tradition, community and witness. According to Hauerwas, modern culture and society are so imbued with values contrary to the gospel that the only Christian response is to live as witnesses to the truth of the gospel in the Christian colony. For too long the church has allowed the world to set its agenda; now it is time for the church to set its own agenda based on the way of Jesus Christ and the gospel of the kingdom. The church must be the alternative community to the violent one of the nation-state. Hauerwas and Willimon say, "We would like a church that again asserts that God, not nations, rules the world, that the boundaries of God's kingdom transcend those of Caesar, and that the main political task of the church is the formation of people who see clearly the cost of discipleship and are willing to pay the price."[76] Undergirding this task must be a recognition of the essential nature of story, tradition, community and witness.

Hauerwas rejects modern foundationalism in favor of narrative. The-ology, he says, must be done without indubitable foundations.[77] None exist. Following philosopher Alasdair MacIntyre (b. 1929) Hauerwas argues that all existence is narratively formed.[78] There is no mid-air view from nowhere that does not already see reality as something in particular because of a story. All ethics is done from within a story about reality. Even modernity is a narrative or set of narratives about reality and values. So, "all accounts of the moral life are narrative dependent."[79] Christians must learn to see the world through the lens of the gospel narrative, the story of Jesus Christ.

---

[75]Ibid., 46.
[76]Hauerwas and Willimon, *Resident Aliens*, 48.
[77]Hauerwas, *Peaceable Kingdom*, xxiv.
[78]Ibid., 35.
[79]Ibid., 61.

That is their only foundation.[80] (But it is not a foundation as in Enlightenment foundationalism because it is not self-evident or indubitable for everyone. Nothing is.) "As Christians we claim we learn most clearly who God is in the life and death of Jesus Christ," and "We become holy by becoming citizens of God's kingdom, thereby manifesting the unrelenting love of God's nature."[81] Hauerwas leaves no doubt that he believes in the truth of the biblical story, even though he does not believe every single element of it must be literal or historical. "Christians claim or attribute authority to Scripture because it is the irreplaceable source of the stories that train us to be a faithful people."[82] The task of Christian ethics is imaginatively to help Christians understand the implications of that story of Jesus and God's kingdom for life. Christian life is a continuous journey of locating our lives in relation to his. "By learning to be followers of Jesus we learn to locate our lives within God's life, within the journey that comprises his kingdom."[83] The biblical story of Israel and Jesus Christ absorbs the world. For the Christian, all of reality is seen through that framework.

This task of Christian ethics, this Christian journey of character formation, is never individualistic, Hauerwas asserts. "Christian ethics are church-dependent."[84] Again, this is not unique to Christian ethics.

> It is important to recognize that all ethics, even non-Christian ethics, arise out of a tradition that depicts the way the world works, what is real, what is worth having, worth believing. Tradition is a function and a product of community. So all ethics, even non-Christian ethics, make sense only when embodied in sets of social practices that constitute a community.[85]

This is one belief that makes Hauerwas postmodern and postliberal. He radically rejects any "heroic, individualist ethic" such as posited by Kant.[86] For him, the moral life requires a "tradition of moral wisdom."[87] That is because real morality is rooted in character and not in abstract principles

---

[80]Ibid., 67.
[81]Ibid.
[82]Ibid., 70.
[83]Ibid., 75.
[84]Hauerwas and Willimon, *Resident Aliens*, 71.
[85]Ibid., 79.
[86]Ibid.
[87]Hauerwas, "On Keeping Theological Ethics Theological," 71.

memorized and applied in ethical crisis situations. For Christians, that tradition of moral wisdom begins with the story of Jesus and continues through the lives of the saints—the church. "Such a tradition is not a 'deposit' of unchanging moral 'truth,' but is made up of the lives of men and women who are constantly testing and developing that tradition through their own struggle to live it."[88] Learning such a tradition and how to be shaped by it requires community. "Christians believe that to live well, we need not only a community, but a community of a particular kind. We need a community of people who are capable of being faithful to a way of life, even when that way of life may be in conflict with what passes as 'morality' in the larger society."[89]

Hauerwas strongly believes that what passes for morality in the larger society will always be different from that of the Christian colony. That is because, even though he does not say it quite this way, Christian ethics is rooted in something supernatural and particular. It is not even on the same plane as natural ethics or ethics arising out of other narratives such as paganism. There may be common ground now and then, here and there, but Christian ethics assumes the cross and resurrection of Jesus Christ; it is not a philosophy or based on one. Christendom is the desire and attempt to correlate Christian ethics with some mythical universal, rational ethical system independent of the Christian story, tradition and church in order to make Christianity publicly acceptable and therefore powerful. That always results in the cultural subversion of Christianity as Christians find it necessary to, for example, give up the supernatural. (Hauerwas does not use that term; he might even object to it. However, it is clear that he believes Christianity, including Christian ethics, is not rooted in nature or reason but in revelation.) What then is the task of Christian ethics if not to discover universal ethical principles that are in harmony with Christian values? "Our task as theologians," he says, "remains what it has always been: namely to exploit the considerable resources embodied in particular Christian convictions which sustain our ability to be a community faithful to our belief that we are creatures of a graceful God."[90]

---

[88]Ibid.
[89]Ibid., 73.
[90]Ibid., 73–74.

Doesn't the Christian church have a social strategy? According to Hauerwas, and this is possibly his most controversial claim, the church *is* the Christian social strategy.[91] "The overriding political task of the church is to be the community of the cross."[92] Another way of putting this is that the church's social strategy is witness—witness by being the church. The foremost way it does this is by being peaceful. But "peaceful" does not mean "passive." Hauerwas rejects Christian withdrawal from the world.[93] However, he admits that being the church, as the church should be, will bring tension between it and the violent "culture of death" (abortion, capital punishment, war). "God's peaceable people cannot but appear to the world as 'violent people' just to the extent that they challenge the normality of violence."[94] The church does not seek to control or manipulate the world. It seeks only to witness to the world by being the peaceable people of God. The job of transforming the world toward God's peaceable kingdom is God's, not Christians'.

Hauerwas argues for an ethics of virtue. Hauerwas is dissatisfied with traditional approaches to ethics, especially modern ones. Most modern ethics, including Christian theological ones, is what he calls "quandary ethics." Quandry ethics focuses on moral dilemmas and seeks rules or principles to solve them. Quandry ethics is either deontological or consequentialist. Deontological emphasizes duty and believes there are absolute rules of right and wrong that always determine what a person should do. Consequentialist emphasizes outcomes and believes that while rules and principles may be helpful, right and wrong are determined by the results of decisions. Hauerwas's approach is to reject both as bases for Christian ethics because it should be about virtue and character. About quandary ethics of both kinds he avers, "Such a concentration on 'quandries' obscures the fact that they make sense only in the light of convictions that tell us who we are. Our most important moral convictions are like the air we breathe: we never notice them because our life depends on them."[95]

In place of quandary ethics Hauerwas more than recommends virtue ethics. The focus of Christian ethics should not be on rules or consequences

---

[91]Hauerwas and Willimon, *Resident Aliens*, 43.
[92]Ibid., 47.
[93]Hauerwas, *With the Grain of the Universe*, 220.
[94]Ibid., 227.
[95]Hauerwas, *Peaceable Kingdom*, 4.

or even on predetermining the right decisions in moral dilemmas. The focus should instead be on transformation of character. "We can only know God by having our lives transformed through initiation into the kingdom."[96] Christian ethics' first task, then, is not to inculcate obedience to rules or attention to consequences but a transforming vision of the world. This normally happens through the community of God's people and the individual's training in the Christian story that takes place there. It is a process of being shaped by Christian communal wisdom. To be sure, there will be actions Christians believe are prohibited or enjoined, but Christian ethics does not start with them or focus on them. Rather, "Christian ethics . . . is dependent on a community's wisdom about how certain actions are prohibited or enjoined for the development of a particular kind of people."[97] The church's ethical witness to the world is not its prohibitions or moral demands but being "nothing less than a people whose ethic shines as a beacon to others illuminating how life should be lived well."[98]

Hauerwas anticipates the question how his approach to ethics helps Christians make right moral decisions. He is confident that sound Christian character formation within sound Christian community in which the Jesus story absorbs the world will lead to right decision making. When a mature, spiritually formed Christian faces a moral decision it "makes itself if we know who we are and what is required of us."[99] "Those committed to living faithfully do not have to decide constantly whether to be faithful or not."[100] According to Hauerwas, Christianity regards the moral life very differently than moderns do. In modernity the moral life is rational; to know the good is to do the good. Education becomes the means to ethical formation and decision making. When absolutes leave the scene, as happened in late modernity, values clarification takes the place of moral education. In either case, however, the solution to ethics is knowing facts and how to use them. Christian ethics is very different. It views the moral life as a journey guided by the Christian tradition of moral wisdom internalized: "for Christians the moral life is to be seen as a journey through life sustained by fidelity to the

---

[96]Ibid., 29.
[97]Ibid., 54.
[98]Ibid., 34.
[99]Ibid., 129.
[100]Ibid.

cross of Christ, which brings a fulfillment no law can ever embody."[101]

Hauerwas stands apart from modern theology. Hauerwas's theology has been and is being worked out within the context of modernity, but it is clearly antimodern. Not antimodern in every possible sense, but antimodern in the sense of pitting authentic Christianity against the ethos of modernity. But what is the ethos of modernity for him? Jeffrey Stout has it right about Hauerwas: "No theologian has done more to inflame Christian resentment of secular political culture."[102] In other words, the modernity Hauerwas is against is not modern science per se or modern achievements for human rights such as abolition of slavery. For him, modernity is a political phenomenon in the broadest sense of the word *political*. Its epistemology, foundationalism, is not politically neutral. (In this he would agree with Toulmin in *Cosmopolis*.) And Hauerwas's antimodernism shows especially in his firm opposition to Christian accommodation to American values, which are largely based on modernity. William Meyer rightly notes that Hauerwas's entire theological project is opposed to the "Constantinian legacy" and the modern American churches' "age-old attempt to integrate Christ and Culture into a synergistic whole."[103] Hauerwas resists above all "the assumption that the gospel can be 'adapted and domesticated' in such a way as to 'fit American values into a loosely Christian framework,' thereby making theology and the church 'culturally significant.'"[104]

What specific modern beliefs and values so integral to modern American culture and so seductive to American Christians does Hauerwas oppose? Most of those have already been stated. Once again, they are not modern medicine or modern rights for all *except insofar as* these become idols that people worship and *except insofar as* these seduce people into thinking they are immortal or individual selves free to create their own realities in godlike fashion. The problem with modern American culture, however, is precisely that these seductions are so rampant. The aspect of modern American (but not only American) culture Hauerwas sees as especially radically contrary to the gospel is its violence.

---

[101]Hauerwas, "On Keeping Theological Ethics Theological," 70.
[102]Jeffrey Stout, *Democracy and Tradition* (Princeton, NJ: Princeton University Press, 2004), 140.
[103]William J. Meyer, *Metaphysics and the Future of Theology: The Voice of Theology in Public Life* (Eugene, OR: Pickwick, 2010), 295.
[104]Ibid.

To far too great an extent, Hauerwas argues, modern American Christianity, including much theology, has served only to underwrite Americanism. Underlying all the pretensions of modern culture, Hauerwas claims, is its assumption of Enlightenment-based rationalism, foundationalism, which assumes that knowledge is what autonomous reason can discover and prove with everything else counting as opinion rather than fact. The Kantian divorce between facts and values is so ingrained in modern culture, including American, that even most Christians assume it. For Hauerwas, all these aspects of modernity are so foreign to and even hostile to the gospel that the Christian church must stand apart (not withdrawn) and become an alternative witness living communally by an entirely different story and set of values. It must resist the temptations of cultural respectability and societal power.

The problem with most modern theology, Hauerwas boldly declares, is that it has succumbed to those temptations. One way it did that is by its various methods of apologetic theology and correlations with modernity. His message is that "by pursuing the modern goals of intelligibility and credibility as part of a strategy of cultural apologetics, the theology of translation gravely distorted the gospel and domesticated it in relation to modern culture."[105] This is nowhere more evident than in modern theology's acquiescences to naturalism (e.g., denial of the resurrection) and justifications of violence. The only cure for this disease, according to Hauerwas, is for the church to become a witness of an alternative polis, not as a strategy of immunization by withdrawal, as in some Anabaptist and fundamentalist churches, but in order to transform the culture, as God chooses, by example. "The church . . . is not to *make* the world the kingdom, but to be faithful to the kingdom by showing to the world what it means to be a community of peace."[106]

Hauerwas draws harsh criticism and responds. Probably the most common criticism of Hauerwas's theology is the charge of sectarianism. In his autobiography he mentions one particularly painful "broadside" against him by a friend—Gustafson. It came in a paper Gustafson read at a meeting of the Catholic Theological Society in which he called Hauerwas's theology

---

[105]Ibid., 296.
[106]Hauerwas, *Peaceable Kingdom*, 103.

"sectarian, fideistic, tribalist."[107] Hauerwas comments that his position can "seem quite threatening to anyone committed to the status quo."[108] Gustafson's charge has been repeated many times by others, including Stout, another of Hauerwas's friends. According to Stout, Hauerwas is guilty of "dualism" between church and world. That is, Hauerwas draws a "rigid and static line between Christian virtue and liberal vice."[109] One example of this, Stout says, is Hauerwas's abandonment of any concept of justice except one based on the ethics of Jesus and the gospel. He challenges Hauerwas to stop bashing the "liberal straw man" and rediscover the language of justice.[110]

A possible example of this accusation against Hauerwas is the popularity among many liberal Christian ethicists of the secular ethic of John Rawls (1921–2002), author of the extremely influential *A Theory of Justice* (1971). Rawls attempted to develop a secular theory of justice based on reason alone that he called "justice as fairness." Many liberal and even some conservative Christian ethicists have found it attractive, not as a complete theory of justice but as a secular analogue to Christian ideas of justice. For those Christians doing exactly what Hauerwas condemns, attempting to discover points of contact between the gospel and the best of modern, secular thought, Rawls has often seemed helpful. Hauerwas never tires of criticizing Rawls for laboring under the delusion of a narrative-independent, purely rational, universal concept of justice. But even more, he never tires of criticizing Christians who latch onto Rawls or other secular thinkers to tie their Christianity to his modern, secular philosophy. Gustafson and Stout find Hauerwas's criticisms a retreat from Christian public engagement in shaping society's policies. To them, he wants to retreat into a Christian ghetto and witness to the world without taking responsibility for it.

Hauerwas offers a sustained response to Gustafson's and others' charge of sectarianism in the introduction to *Christian Existence Today*. Without calling it wrong, that is, a misunderstanding, he says it is an oversimplification of his position.[111] First, he says, underlying the charge of sectarianism is the suspicion that he is a theological fideist. In fact, he reports, he knows

---

[107]Hauerwas, *Hannah's Child*, 208.
[108]Ibid., 209.
[109]Stout, *Democracy and Tradition*, 154.
[110]Ibid., 160.
[111]Stanley Hauerwas, *Christian Existence Today* (Grand Rapids: Brazos Press, 2001), 3.

that Gustafson and other critics have identified him that way, claiming that
he makes Christian claims impervious to criticism. This he adamantly
denies: "Nothing I have said is meant to protect theology or Christians from
such [viz., scientific] challenges."[112] But, he continues, "I do not assume that
such confrontations will necessarily result in victory for the challenger."[113] In
other words, according to Hauerwas, theological truth claims are not
immune, impervious, to outside criticism. Theology is not such an isolated
language game as to be in principle unfalsifiable. Then he turns the tables on
his critics: "Rather than asserting that material theological convictions *must*
be revised in the light of science, should not Gustafson [and others] indicate
which scientific conclusions should be considered and why?"[114] Then he
offers up his own implicit criticism of theologians who have adopted naturalism because they think science requires it:

> Certainly I see no reason why the central affirmations of the Christian faith
> need to be surrendered or denaturalized [perhaps he means naturalized] in
> terms of the mere activity of science, and I am unaware of any scientific con-
> clusion that would require such revision—particularly those about the ul-
> timate end of the human life or even the world that so impress Gustafson.
> The history of modern theology is littered with the wrecks of such revision
> done on the basis of a science that no longer has any credence; which is but a
> way of saying that while I have eminent respect for scientific work, I am less
> confident . . . that it is meaningful to assign to science qua science an over-
> riding veridical status.[115]

Hauerwas's second response to the accusation of fideism is an admission. He admits that he and his critics probably disagree about one
aspect of Christianity crucial to him. It may, he says, be the aspect most
troubling to Gustafson and others. "For I have argued that the very content
of Christian convictions requires that the self be transformed if we are
adequately to see the truth of the convictions—e.g., that I am a creature of
a good creator yet in rebellion against my status as such."[116] He admits that
knowing the truth of basic Christian convictions requires transformation,

---

[112]Ibid., 9.
[113]Ibid.
[114]Ibid.
[115]Ibid.
[116]Ibid., 10.

but he denies that he has ever said there are no reality checks to which Christians must pay attention.[117]

It seems that, in response to the charge of fideism, Hauerwas ought to admit that he embraces a soft form of it, one that allows there to be external challenges and bridges between Christianity and other forms of life that make similar truth claims about existence. Hard-core fideism, such as one finds among certain so-called Wittgensteinian fideists such as D. Z. Phillips (1934–2006), is not Hauerwas's position, however, and he is right to defend it against accusations that it is. (Gustafson had lumped Hauerwas into that category.) Postliberals in general chafe at the charge of fideism, but it is hard to know why except that the term carries with it a certain stigma of implied obscurantism. That is what distinguishes soft from hard fideism, however. The fideism espoused by Barth and the postliberals is one that is open to dialogue and criticism but refuses to acknowledge some narrative independent view from nowhere that floats above all metaphysical commitments and is purely, objectively rational. For them, contrary to Kant's ideal of religion within the limits of reason, reason always functions within the limits of *some* religious or quasi-religious belief system.

Hauerwas then takes up the charge of sectarian irresponsibility for the world. He responds:

> My call for Christians to recover the integrity of the church as integral to our political witness does not entail that Christians must withdraw from the economic, cultural, legal, and political life of our societies. It does mean, however, that the form of our participation will vary given the nature of the societies in which we find ourselves.[118]

He goes on to give examples. He agrees with the Mennonite (and other Anabaptist) practice of Christians not using law courts to sue each other, "but that does not entail that Christians are to avoid all contact with the law."[119] Also, he says, Christians must withdraw their support from the secular order whenever it resorts to violence. "At that point and that point alone Christians must withhold their involvement with the state."[120] That

---

[117]Ibid., 11.
[118]Ibid., 14.
[119]Ibid.
[120]Ibid., 15.

hardly commits him to a sectarian stance, that is, Christian withdrawal from social involvement in public affairs. "Indeed," he says, "I believe it to be the responsibility of Christians to work to make their societies less prone to resort to violence."[121]

Again, in a statement that implies strong criticism, Hauerwas declares:

> If my work appears sectarian in our time I suspect it is because in the name of being responsible too many Christians are under the illusion we live in societies in which we can be at home because the societies are our creations. To reclaim alien status in contexts which were once thought home requires transformation of social and intellectual habits that cannot help but be a wrenching process.[122]

But why doesn't Hauerwas admit to the charge of sectarianism? Again, as with fideism, postliberals in general are loath to accept such a label, probably because of the stigma it carries. However, as with fideism, there are two varieties of sectarianism, and Hauerwas clearly falls into one of them. Sectarianism can be hard core, in which case it advocates total withdrawal of the church from society—sometimes to the point of geographical separation. Some Anabaptist communities practice that. Soft sectarianism, however, is the refusal of Christendom, the denial of the church's responsibility to shape the public polis. It does not have to reject all attempts to influence it. Many sectarian groups throughout the ages have taken that approach. Traditionally, all Anabaptists and most Baptists, with their strong emphasis on separation of church and state, have been soft sectarians.

How has Hauerwas demonstrated his soft sectarianism? His commitment to pacifism is one way. He does not advocate Christians resisting the draft, for example, or serving as conscientious objectors when called to military service. The softness of his sectarianism appears in his public "An Appeal to Abolish War" addressed "To Christian Leaders and Theologians"[123] and co-authored with his friend Enda McDonagh. It is a ringing call for Christians to work toward the abolition of war, which requires involvement with governments. Hauerwas defends his involvement in this effort by saying,

---

[121]Ibid.
[122]Ibid.
[123]Stanley Hauerwas, *War and the American Difference: Theological Reflections on Violence and National Identity* (Grand Rapids: Baker Academic, 2011), 40–42.

The eschatological convictions that shape Christian nonviolence assume this is God's world. Accordingly, we do not believe that the boundary between church and world is a barrier that cannot be breached. Indeed we believe that the division between church and world is permeable.[124]

So much for the charge of hard-core sectarianism. Still, Hauerwas is not likely to run for president and not only because he is not qualified to be president. Being president means being commander in chief of the armed forces. And while Hauerwas disavows Christian withdrawal from government and politics, his definition of violence as including involvement in coercive force would seem to forbid any Christian holding public office in the United States. It seems that he sometimes wants to have his cake and eat it too.

One last criticism that must be dealt with is the oft-repeated one that Hauerwas makes the church the "binding medium" of the gospel such that the church becomes the message as much or more than the gospel itself. Meyer charges, "By making the church constitutive of the gospel, Hauerwas runs the danger of fostering hubris and idolatry, on the one hand, and the danger of conceptual confusion and irrelevance on the other."[125] The point is that, according to critics like Meyer, Hauerwas overlooks the demonic potential of any collective group. Hauerwas already responded to that in his response to Gustafson, however, by calling for reality checks on the church from both inside and outside it. But the more serious charge Meyer and other critics level is that Hauerwas falls into the danger of an "ecclesiastically-constituted gospel."[126] Allegedly he confuses the gospel itself with the church such that there can be no prophetic proclamation of the gospel independent of the church. Witness to the gospel must always be something the church does and, in that witness, it points back to itself.

Meyer and other critics seem to suffer a confusion of their own. For example, everyone agrees that, normally, God uses humans to spread the gospel. But nobody claims that means the gospel *is* the humans who spread it. Hauerwas is saying that, normally, there is no individualistic Christianity and that God has constituted the church as his witness. Nowhere does he say or imply that the church as an organized institution is constitutive of the

---

[124]Ibid., 39.
[125]Meyer, *Metaphysics and the Future of Theology*, 320.
[126]Ibid., 324.

gospel. For him, admittedly, it is a necessary (because God says so) medium of the gospel, but in this case the medium is not the message. It and the message are inextricably related, but the medium is always subject to correction by the message. Meyer's and others' accusation seems almost silly.

12.B. JOHN CAPUTO DECONSTRUCTS RELIGION WITH THE KINGDOM OF GOD

John Caputo is a postmodern philosopher who, by his own confession, loves God without knowing exactly what he is loving. "What do I love when I love my God?" is a question that haunts him and all of his writings. But he did not invent the question; it comes from his favorite philosopher, Derrida, who got it from Augustine. Like Derrida, Caputo loves questions more than definite answers, but often some kind of indefinite answer is uncontained in the question. The use of "uncontained" is purposeful; for Caputo, as for Derrida, answers often only haunt questions just as "impossibles" often haunt possibilities. The prefixes "un-" and "im-" are (un)popular with deconstructionists like Derrida and Caputo. When one wanders/wonders into deconstructionism it is like finding oneself in Alice's Wonderland. Nothing is quite as it seems or as expected. The wanderer/wonderer has to learn a new vocabulary and way of thinking and using words. What does Caputo even mean by "God"? That is intentionally uncertain.

One thing is certain. Caputo's theology is radical and revolutionary, turning things upside down in order to get to the bottom of things. Deconstruction is how it is done. But there are as many definitions of "deconstruction" as of "postmodern." Caputo is one philosopher, obsessed with theology, who defines it and uses it influentially—especially for Christians. Here he serves as the representative of radical, postmodern, deconstructive theology. There have been and are others; Caputo is the choice because he is easier to understand than most and his writing sparkles with wit and wisdom. His description of how modernity mishandled religion is an example:

> So, in modernity, the question of God is profoundly recast. Instead of beginning on our knees, we are all seated solemnly and with stern faces on the hard benches of the court of Reason as it is called into session. God is brought before the court, like a defendant with his hat in his hand, and required to give an account of himself, to show His ontological papers, if He expects to

win the court's approval. In such a world, from [medieval theologian] Anselm's point of view, God is already dead, even if you conclude that the proof is valid, because whatever you think you have proven or disproven is not the God he experiences in prayer and liturgy but a philosophical idol. Is there or is there not a sufficient reason for this being to be?, the court wants to know. If there are reasons, are they empirical or a priori? Are they good or bad? That is what the court has assembled to decide. What does the defendant have to say for himself? What's that you say? Nothing but a few hymns, some pious prayers, and a bit of incense? Whom can he call in his defense? Shakers and Quakers and Spirit-seers all in heat? Next case![127]

In true postmodern fashion, Caputo reveals the faults and flaws of modernity without throwing the baby out with the bathwater; the Enlightenment and the culture it spawned brought about many good things. But, for Caputo, especially its treatment of religion was and is abominable. Not that he wants to return to premodern religion. Not at all. What Caputo attempts to show throughout his writings on religion and Christianity is that postmodern disillusionment with the totalizing rationalism of the Enlightenment opens up doors for religion it closed. For him, postmodernity means, among other things, postsecularity: the "death of the death of God."[128] And it all began with Kierkegaard, the "prime progenitor" of postmodernism and Caputo's muse, along with Derrida. For him, Kierkegaard was the original deconstructor of Enlightenment rationalism. Caputo intends to carry on that project, applying the "weak force" (Caputo loves oxymorons) of deconstruction to everything that pretends to be final, ultimate and absolute.

Caputo becomes a philosopher who does theology. Caputo (Jack to his friends) was born in Philadelphia in 1940. He grew up Catholic and has always remained a son of the church if not a particularly faithful one. He earned his first degree from La Salle University and his master of arts from Villanova University. His PhD in philosophy is from Bryn Mawr College. He taught philosophy at Villanova University from 1968 until 2004, when he became Thomas R. Watson Professor of Religion at Syracuse University in New York. There he taught both philosophy and theology, gradually moving into the role of philosophical theologian with special emphasis on

---

[127]John D. Caputo, *On Religion* (London: Routledge, 2001), 46.
[128]Ibid., 56.

Christian theology. He retired in 2011 while continuing to lecture in both the United States and Europe and write books and articles on his favorite subjects: continental philosophy (especially postmodernism) and theology (with special emphasis on deconstructionism). He is professor emeritus at both Villanova and Syracuse. Much to his own surprise he has become a favorite thinker among postmodern Christians including many in the so-called emergent church movement. Popular emergent Christian thinker and writer Peter Rollins (b. 1973), author of *How (Not) to Speak of God* (2006) has incorporated ideas from Caputo into his books and lectures.

What is notable about Caputo's philosophical journey is his shift from pure philosophy (whatever that is) to Christian theology. In his major treatise on God, *The Weakness of God*, he almost apologetically confesses to having "a weakness for theology."[129] (As often, his use of the term "weakness" there is intended as a play on words, in this case on the title and theme of the book.) In the professional scholarly academy, one is supposed to be either a philosopher or a theologian and never both. Especially philosophers are not supposed to cross over and do Christian theology. In typical fashion Caputo thumbs his nose at such (to him) silly, modern rules and transgresses a boundary. His *Philosophy and Theology* constitutes his defense. In postmodernity, he argues, the old boundaries and high walls that modernity built around reason and science and philosophy have come down.[130] Now, after the deconstruction of modernity, we must "think of philosophers and theologians . . . as fellow sailors on that ocean, venturers and adventurers out over seventy thousand fathoms, old salts telling the rest of us stories while we, like youngsters with bulging eyes, take in every word."[131] (Caputo loves metaphors.) In other words, to put the point more philosophically, "philosophy and theology are different but companion ways to nurture what I call the *passion for life.*"[132]

Caputo is the author of many books, most of them about continental philosophy and postmodern theology. His first book was *The Mystical Element in Heidegger's Thought* (1978). Already he was beginning to dabble in

---

[129]John D. Caputo, *The Weakness of God: A Theology of the Event* (Bloomington: Indiana University Press, 2006), 1.
[130]John D. Caputo, *Philosophy and Theology* (Nashville: Abingdon, 2006), 68.
[131]Ibid., 69.
[132]Ibid.

the religious hidden within the philosophical. His second book was *Heidegger and Aquinas* (1982)—an attempt to show points of congeniality between an atheist, existentialist philosopher and the Angelic Doctor of Catholic thought. Other notable books by Caputo include *The Prayers and Tears of Jacques Derrida* (1997)—another project in demonstrating the religious side of an allegedly atheist philosopher—and *Deconstruction in a Nutshell* (1997), perhaps the clearest explanation of deconstructionism in print. In 2007 Caputo did something truly surprising, as did Baker Academic: he published *What Would Jesus Deconstruct?* with a publisher historically known for publishing evangelical books. Not that Caputo was becoming evangelical (except perhaps for his idea of the kingdom of God), but he made use of *In His Steps* (1897), a popular book among evangelical Christians, and a popular question among evangelicals: "W.W.J.D.?" (What Would Jesus Do?) to demonstrate deconstruction on American religion.

Caputo has become an icon among postmodern Christians, including some evangelicals who think he has much to contribute even if he is not an evangelical Christian. (Exactly what kind of Christian, other than radical, that he is, is debatable. He leaves it intentionally undecidable—another one of his favorite words.) Among them is evangelical Christian philosopher Keith Putt (b. 1955), who has concentrated much of his writing on Caputo's prophetic value to purifying Christianity of its bondage to modernity. Another is James Olthuis (b. 1938), author of several articles on Caputo's philosophy and theology and editor of *Religion Without Religion: The Prayers and Tears of John Caputo* (2002). The postmodern philosopher has expressed surprise and some degree of bemusement at his popularity among progressive evangelical thinkers.

Caputo has become one of the foremost American interpreters of the philosophy of Derrida and especially of connections between Derrida's philosophy of deconstruction and the ideas of Kierkegaard and Levinas, a leading French postmodern philosopher. Rightly or wrongly, Caputo has striven to correct what he sees as misconceptions of deconstructionism among its critics. If he is right, few critics have gotten it right. By all accounts, it is not easy to get deconstructionism right. There is something elusive if not esoteric about it. As Caputo never tires of pointing out, it has wrongly been mistaken for "a kind of anarchistic relativism in which 'anything goes.'"[133] Derrida and deconstructionism, he says, have been blamed for almost everything: "For ruining American departments of philosophy, ... for ruining the university itself, ... for dimming the lights of the Enlightenment, for undermining the laws of gravity, for destroying all standards ... and also for Mormon polygamy."[134] According to Caputo this is all wrong, but it is evidence that deconstructionism is not simple to understand. If he is right, however, it is not all *that* difficult, and he makes it his business to break through the confusion and make it as clear as possible because he thinks it has great prophetic value. According to him and his mostly positive interpreters Rollins, Putt and Olthuis, deconstruction is not destructive but "deeply and profoundly affirmative."[135] But he admits it is "too complicated to summarize."[136] However, he does his best, and here we will, too.

Deconstruction gives ordinary words new meanings. One thing that complicates deconstructionism is its sometimes esoteric use of ordinary words. In order to understand deconstructionism, one has to learn some new terminology. The words may be familiar, but their meanings in this philosophy and the theology that has grown out of it are not—to most people. Caputo is a master at explaining them. (One almost gets the feeling from other deconstructionist philosophers and theologians that they do not want people to understand them.) If you are wondering what deconstructionism is, you must be patient for a bit. It will become clearer with the explanations of its key terms.

First is "deconstruction" itself. The word has entered into popular culture; it is heard in television situation comedies and read in entertainment magazines. Those uses of it have little or nothing to do with its meaning in postmodern philosophy and theology. In popular parlance "deconstruction" is usually a fancy way of saying "destruction." When something is torn down or exposed as fraudulent it is said to be deconstructed. That is not its meaning in philosophy or theology. However, there is no simple definition of deconstruction. Like "postmodern," everyone who uses it seems to give it a slightly different (sometimes radically different) meaning. So, here, its

---

[133]John D. Caputo, ed., *Deconstruction in a Nutshell: A Conversation with Jacques Derrida* (New York: Fordham University Press, 1997), 37.

[134]Ibid., 41.

[135]Ibid.

[136]Ibid., 32.

meaning is drawn from Caputo, who draws his from Derrida. But Caputo refuses to give a single, definite definition of deconstruction because that would be against the spirit of deconstruction. Deconstruction is not a thing or even a technique; it is an event—what happens when something hidden within a present idea or reality is uncovered and explodes, not to destroy but to open up new possibilities: "the business of deconstruction is to open and loosen things up."[137] "Deconstruction is a way of giving things a new twist; it is bent on giving things a new bent."[138] But these are not what one does to something; it is already being done in them. Deconstruction is the discovery of that hidden, disturbing element within a text or institution that is striving to move it beyond itself.

The closest Caputo comes to defining deconstruction is his description of its "meaning and mission," which is to show that

> things—texts, institutions, traditions, societies, beliefs, and practices of whatever size and sort you need—do not have definable meanings and determinable missions, that they are always more than any mission would impose, that they exceed the boundaries they currently occupy. What is really going on in things, what is really happening, is always to come. Every time you try to stabilize the meaning of a thing, to fix it in its missionary position, the thing itself, if there is anything at all, slips away.... A "meaning" or a "mission" is a way to contain and compact things, like a nutshell, gathering them into a unity, whereas deconstruction bends all its efforts to stretch beyond these boundaries, to transgress these confines, to interrupt and disjoin all such gatherings. Whenever it runs up against a limit, deconstruction presses against it.[139]

It is impossible to understand this, or to understand deconstruction, as Caputo means it, without moving on to "the impossible," another term with an unusual meaning.

According to Caputo, deconstruction is all about "the relentless pursuit of *the* impossible."[140] Lest anyone yawn and go to sleep, having given up trying to crack this code, it will be helpful to jump ahead a little and name some

---

[137]Ibid., 42.
[138]Ibid.
[139]Ibid., 32.
[140]Ibid.

"impossibles." Caputo lists some of them: justice, gift, hospitality, love. One all Americans are familiar with is democracy. Caputo says that deconstruction is all about "the experience of the impossible."[141] But what is impossible about democracy or justice or any of the other alleged impossibles? And if they are impossible, why are they important? This is exactly where Americans, especially, stumble when attempting to understand deconstruction. Americans are instrumentalists; they tend to be interested in what is—and what is possible. They want to solve problems, and anything considered impossible is uninteresting. Caputo, however, says, "The impossible is more interesting than the possible and provokes more interesting results, provided that anything at all results."[142] Democracy is impossible *if* what is meant, and this is what Caputo means, *the democracy to come*—his term for perfect, pure democracy. Actual democracy is not bad; it just is not perfect. Deconstruction wants to make it better—more like the democracy to come—perfect, pure democracy. But exactly what that is is not precisely known. It is something both hidden within present democracy and always not yet present.

Caputo's and Derrida's favorite example is the difference between law and justice. Justice is impossible but inescapable; it is a "quasi-transcendental"—an ideal without which we cannot live but that cannot ever be fully instantiated. We have only an inkling of what it is really like; it lurks hidden within things like the laws of a country and is always coming, never fully arriving. Laws, the legal system, may pretend to be just (in fact, most do, and that is the problem), but they never are completely just. "Justice is never found in the present order, is never present to itself, is never gathered unto itself. . . . Justice calls, justice is to come, but justice does not exist."[143] The answer to "What good is something impossible?" is in that statement; it is the purifying standard, the perfect circle nobody can draw, the absolute equality no group achieves, the desire never quite satisfied. Concrete laws, legal systems, need the impossible of justice to hold them accountable, to open them up to the new and unexpected, to the singular that was not thought of yet when the laws were written. Justice is the hundredth percentile on a standardized test no test-taker can achieve.

---

[141]Ibid.
[142]Ibid., 33.
[143]Ibid., 154.

Another word for the "impossible," as Caputo means it, is the "undeconstructible." A basic working principle of deconstruction is that whatever is constructed can be deconstructed—in the sense of subjected to criticism and opened up to the unforeseen and unexpected. But some things, the impossibles, cannot be deconstructed because they were never constructed in the first place and are absolutes. They are not absolutes in some metaphysical sense of existing or having substantial reality behind things that appear, but they are absolutes in the sense of being transcendental, future, unavailable, not able to be manipulated. They "break in" (or "break out") eventfully through deconstruction. They are justice, democracy (to come), love, gift, hospitality. "Deconstruction," Caputo explains, "is the endless, bottomless, affirmation of the absolutely undeconstructible."[144]

Another important concept for Caputo's deconstructionism is "event." Deconstructionism is antimetaphysical, which means it does not believe in what Caputo calls "the Secret." The Secret is the really real thing-in-itself behind appearances, the ultimate reality that lies above everyday experiences that is somehow objectively real, static and knowable by reason or mystical apprehension. It is the "Presence"—whatever is supposed to be true, final, already always there. The secret of deconstructionism is that there is no secret. As Derrida famously said, "There is nothing outside the text." In other words, everything is interpretation and deconstructible— except "the impossible," which is not deconstructible but does not exist. The "event," in deconstruction language, is the breaking in or out of the impossible, its appearance in the flux of time and history. The event is the deconstruction that opens up the closed and that explodes the supposedly settled. It is transformation. For example, justice is always an event. It must be enacted; it is not a condition.[145] "Justice is the welcome *given* to the other in which I do not . . . have anything up my sleeve, it is the hospitality that I extend to the other, the expenditure without return."[146] Justice, then, breaks into our present from the future; its arrival is always a moment, not a thing. "In a deconstruction, our lives, our beliefs, and our practices are

---

[144]Ibid., 42.

[145]Ibid., 138.

[146]Ibid., 149.

not destroyed but forced to reform and reconfigure—which is risky business."[147] That is an event.

Yet another crucial term for Caputo's deconstructionism is "the other." For this Caputo relies heavily on the philosophy of Levinas, who made it the center of his entire thought. The "other" is the strange, the different, the not identical, the singular that cannot be assimilated. Deconstructionism is "the politics of the other."[148] "Deconstruction is a way to prevent the text [or institution or whatever] from becoming an idol, which like a deep well . . . simply sends back to us our own image."[149] Our natural tendency is to gravitate toward identity, familiarity, sameness, so we tend to shut out the different, the strange and the other. But the other is transcendence; it calls to us and we have an obligation to it. Transformation, the event, justice, happens only in encounter with and adjustment to the other.

> A deconstruction of a text or an institution, of a discourse or a practice, amounts to the claim that all these formulations are subject to the sway of *différence*, which is Derrida's way of saying that they are subject to the need for constant revisiting and revising, rereading and reworking.[150]

This seems to be the underlying or overarching motive and motif of deconstruction: the claim of the other, our obligation to it, its breaking into and disrupting closed identity that is a form of idolatry. For Caputo, deconstruction "delivers the shock of the other to the forces of the same."[151] "In a deconstruction, the 'other' is the one who tells the truth on the 'same.'"[152] Who is the other? For Caputo, Jesus answered that in his parable of the Good Samaritan. For him, the other is the outsider, the enemy, the weak and hurting, the person in need, the powerless and homeless. These are they for

---

[147]John D. Caputo, *What Would Jesus Deconstruct? The Good News of Postmodernism for the Church* (Grand Rapids: Baker Academic, 2007), 27. Astute readers may have caught what seems, on the surface, to be agreement between Caputo and Moltmann and Pannenberg with regard to the power of the future. However, Caputo is not interested in ontotheology—attempts to describe God's being. At least to some extent both Moltmann and Pannenberg are so interested, even if they redefine God's being as futurity. Caputo would no doubt reject their eschatological ontology as an impermissible attempt to identify God as being rather than as event.
[148]Caputo, *Weakness of God*, 268, 276.
[149]John D. Caputo, *More Radical Hermeneutics* (Bloomington: Indiana University Press, 2000), 211.
[150]Ibid., 200.
[151]Caputo, *What Would Jesus Deconstruct?* 26.
[152]Ibid., 29.

whom deconstruction is intended. Bringing together several of deconstructionism's terms, Caputo says that "justice is the relation to the other"[153] and
"deconstruction is the affirmation of the coming [event] of the other."[154]

Finally, another key concept for Caputo's deconstructionism is the
"messianic." He borrows and adapts it from Derrida. In brief, the messianic is the coming, the eventful arrival, of justice in breaking open
sameness to otherness. According to Caputo, "deconstruction takes the
specific form of a democratic messianism."[155] It is the claim and coming
of "absolute hospitality."[156] It is postmodernism's and especially deconstructionism's alternative to modernity's myth of progress. Modernity
believed in continual reform of, for example, institutions, through
reason. Deconstruction believes in a "pure form of hope"[157] called "the
messianic" or "messianicity." It is hope because it does not depend on our
powers of reason or calculation; it depends on the new, the unexpected,
the arrival of the impossible. It is the "incoming of the other."[158] It destabi-
lizes identity and breaks open self-protective enclosures.[159] It "breaks the
spell of present constructions."[160] Caputo notes and capitalizes on what
he calls this "messianic tone" of Derrida's deconstructionism. "The messianic future of which deconstruction dreams, its desire and its passion,
is the unforeseeable future to come, absolutely to come, the justice, the
democracy, the gift, the hospitality to come."[161] For Caputo this contains
a religious impulse and calls for a "New Enlightenment"[162] that is open
to faith which is presupposed by deconstructive gestures.[163] Deconstruction, having a "messianic structure of promise,"[164] depends on
something spiritual that transcends Enlightenment rationalism. It is
postsecular in that it "moves beyond all Enlightenment debunking of

---

[153]Caputo, *Deconstruction in a Nutshell*, 17.
[154]Ibid., 53.
[155]Ibid., 173.
[156]Ibid.
[157]Caputo, *Philosophy and Theology*, 65.
[158]Caputo, *Deconstruction in a Nutshell*, 108.
[159]Ibid., 107.
[160]Ibid., 162.
[161]Ibid., 156.
[162]Ibid., 54.
[163]Ibid., 22.
[164]Ibid.

religion and chastises the Enlightenment for having chased away one ghost too many."[165] By this account, deconstruction depends on a "prophetic fervor" of "faith in the unforeseeable and incalculable figure" of justice, democracy to come, absolute hospitality.[166]

Caputo portrays Jesus as the ultimate deconstructor. Philosophers usually do not talk about Jesus. Caputo does not hesitate. For him, Jesus is the prophet of deconstruction, the proclaimer of the madness of the kingdom of God who challenges all closed systems and institutions and subjects them to deconstruction. For Caputo, deconstruction never happens except "in the name" of some undeconstructible, some impossible, quasi-transcendental absolute such as justice, the gift, hospitality. And for him, going beyond Derrida, the kingdom of God is the ultimate symbol of the undeconstructible that deconstructs everything that has been humanly constructed—including the church. Borrowing terminology from liberation theology (Caputo is not a liberationist), the kingdom of God serves as deconstructionism's critical principle. It is the reservoir, as it were, the cipher, to use a different metaphor, for all that is undeconstructible and impossible in the name of which all that is and is possible should be deconstructed.

But from where does Caputo get this idea of the kingdom of God? What is his method? In true continental (which usually means French) philosophical style, Caputo does not worry much about epistemology. Modernity is all about epistemology; Caputo, following Derrida, is not obsessed with it. In true postmodern fashion, he rejects foundationalism in all its forms. There are no indubitable foundations for knowledge. Knowing is always a matter of perspective—"seeing as." Caputo firmly rejects the Enlightenment "principle of sufficient reason" as an idol and therefore needing deconstruction. He opposes modernity's "fetishizing of reason"[167] on the grounds that it amounts to a play of power (and power always corrupts) and ignores the fact that, as certain premoderns such as Augustine and Anselm knew, even reason rests on certain unprovable assumptions so that "seeing as," perspective, is inescapable.[168] In postmodernity, he asserts,

---

[165]Ibid., 159.
[166]Ibid., 175.
[167]Caputo, *Philosophy and Theology*, 29.
[168]Ibid., 56.

"the distinction between philosophy and theology is drawn between two kinds of faith, by which I mean two kinds of 'seeing as.'"[169] Furthermore, following Wittgenstein, Caputo argues, "Religion constitutes an irreducible paradigm of its own, a language game of its own, a perspective of its own."[170] In sum, Caputo, together with most postmodern thinkers, sees "the world [as] a lot more complicated than the moderns [foundationalists] think, a lot messier, less well-programmed, less rule-governed, more open-ended and open-textured."[171]

The upshot of Caputo's critique, deconstruction, of modernity is to reject its idea that only what can be proven can be called "knowledge."[172] According to him, the "postmodern turn" in philosophy is the wheels coming off the Enlightenment.[173] It is not that he wants to go back to premodernity, but he thinks postmodernity and premodernity have certain things in common and one of them is openness to the sacred, to transcendence, to religion. For him, "postmodernity is the condition under which we today conduct the business of philosophy and theology, of science and art, of politics and religion, of just about everything."[174] That condition includes suspicion of the "affection for systems" displayed by, among others, Hegel, and that haunted Kierkegaard. By "systems" he means ideologies—closed and totalizing explanations of reality that exercise power over and exclude every perspective but their own. All this means that, for Caputo, religion is back in the game, so to speak; it can count as knowledge. That does not mean every religious claim or belief is true; it means that they cannot be ruled out of court from the beginning.

In concert with other postmoderns, and especially with postliberals, Caputo regards all knowledge as arising within story. All we have are stories, and all are "permanently susceptible to the crisis of interpretation."[175] That is what "seeing as" means—interpreting reality through the lens of some story. Then, he asks the modernist question and answers it:

---

169 Ibid., 57.
170 Ibid., 53.
171 Ibid., 48.
172 Ibid., 29–31.
173 Ibid., 35.
174 Ibid., 37.
175 Caputo, *More Radical Hermeneutics*, 200.

Has everything gone to the devil? I would say there is nothing to do but tell and retell old stories and work with our texts. It is unceasingly a question of telling stories, good stories, the best ones possible, and it is possible to pit story against story, to see which one wins out, not because of some macho storytelling power of the narratival subject, but because we are struck by the trauma of alterity [otherness] in a story, by the shock of transcendence, by the blow which is invariably delivered by something divine.[176]

What is the "shock of transcendence" that marks a story as likely to be true? For Caputo it is the breaking in of the other, the revelation of the call of obligation to the other. It is the "contradiction of our freedom"[177] to do whatever we want to with ourselves within our enclosed identity and with our vested interests. And this is exactly what the Christian story of Jesus and the kingdom of God does.

For Caputo, "Christianity is a story that at a crucial point depends upon knowing what to make of an empty tomb."[178] What he means by "an empty tomb" is the continuing relevance of the prophet Jesus, the messianic revealer of the kingdom of God. For him, revelation is not something ready-made, unambiguous and authoritative—as if there would be no decisions to make. "We ought not to imagine revelation as if it were a matter of taking dictation from a divine speaker."[179] Rather, revelation is the *what* revealed in the "poetics of the kingdom" in Jesus' life, death and teaching. He dwells especially on Jesus' parables and his "prophetic impatience."[180] The poetics of the kingdom "provides a *politica negativa* [negative politics], a critical voice rather like the voice of a prophet against the king, like Amos."[181] This "politics of the kingdom" revealed by Jesus would be "marked by madness of forgiveness, generosity, mercy, and hospitality."[182] This is a sign of its truth; it calls us to break out of the same, the predictable, identity, the programmable, and to adjust ourselves to the breaking in of the other, the impossible, the undeconstructible—especially justice.

---

[176]Ibid., 216.
[177]Ibid., 218.
[178]Ibid., 196.
[179]Ibid., 209.
[180]Caputo, *What Would Jesus Deconstruct?* 83.
[181]Ibid., 87.
[182]Ibid., 88.

Does this mean that Christianity is simply doing what Jesus did? Not at all. That would be a complete misunderstanding of the kingdom. Rather,

> nothing is settled by identifying what Jesus did in the New Testament and then trying to literally reproduce it today. . . . It is *our responsibility* to breathe with the spirit of Jesus, to implement, to invent, to convert this poetics into praxis, which means to make the political order resonate with the radicality of someone whose vision was not precisely political.[183]

Caputo sounds like Reinhold Niebuhr when he says, "The model that Jesus sets is impossible . . . a theo-poetics of the impossible."[184] For Niebuhr, the Sermon on the Mount and Jesus' life and teaching revealed the impossible possibility of perfect love that can only be incarnated as justice. Caputo means something similar, only for him justice is also impossible. What is possible is law, and Jesus came to deconstruct law and every possibility by opening it up to justice.

Before moving on, it will be helpful to recapitulate Caputo's theological method, which may sound like anything but a method to modernist ears. In a manner very similar to postliberalism, Caputo regards the Jesus story of the kingdom of God, the poetics of the kingdom, as the story that, for the Christian, absorbs the world. That is what he means by Derrida's "there is nothing outside the text." The Christian life is an adventurous, eventful journey toward the kingdom of God in which the world is constantly being deconstructed. For the Christian disciple of Jesus, "the kingdom comes to contradict the world and contest the world's ways, and it always looks like foolishness to the world's good sense."[185] The world's "good sense" is law, violence, sameness, control, manipulation, predictability, settling for the lesser of two evils. The world's good sense includes "just war." Deconstruction is the kingdom's way of opening up the world to the rule of God— justice, peace, otherness, the new and different, love for enemies, forgiveness. Scripture is the Christian's guide on this journey, a map, as it were, but not territory. (No map is the territory it displays.) Scripture is not "supernatural assertions" but "invitations to transform our lives" and the

---

[183]Ibid., 95.
[184]Ibid., 100.
[185]Caputo, *Weakness of God*, 108.

world.[186] "Scripture is the site of an event"[187]—the event of transformation toward the kingdom of God. "They [Scripture's stories] are to be read for their imaginative power to portray the life-transforming character of the kingdom, not literalized as if they were giving eyewitness reports of super-natural occurrences."[188] None of this needs proof; it is not a matter of evidence or logic. It is a matter of grace.[189] It is being grasped by a vision, a "weak force," a call that comes through a poetics, not through reason, although there is nothing irrational about it.[190]

Caputo fleshes out "the kingdom of God." Clearly, for Caputo, the kingdom of God is the key to deconstruction and therefore to the prophetic way of life that marks authentic Christianity. But what is it, exactly? "It" is not the right word; "event" is the right word. The kingdom of God, true Christianity, is not a state of affairs or a system or an institution. It is neither "real" (present) nor "unreal" (absence) but "hyper-real,"[191] which is the same as "impossible" in the technical sense explained above. According to Caputo, Jesus' vision of the kingdom of God is that of an "anarchic field of reversals and displacements" or "sacred anarchy," for short.[192] It exists as promise and call, not presence or construct. Its content, if it has any, is "whenever pow-erlessness exerts its force, whenever the high and mighty are displaced by the least among us."[193] Unlike any other kingdom, it is "organized around the power of the powerless, by forces that are weak."[194] For Caputo, the ul-timate symbol of this is the cross of Christ in which "the power of God is embodied in the helpless body whose flesh is nailed to the cross."[195] (He has been reading Bonhoeffer and Moltmann.)

According to Caputo, the kingdom of God is the event of hospitality in which the powerful and mighty welcome the powerless and strangers in such a way that they become equals. The kingdom "calls" to radical hospi-

---

[186]Ibid., 117–19.
[187]Ibid., 119.
[188]Ibid., 239.
[189]Caputo, *What Would Jesus Deconstruct?* 51.
[190]Caputo, *Weakness of God*, 103.
[191]Ibid., 9.
[192]Ibid., 14.
[193]Ibid.
[194]Ibid., 29.
[195]Ibid., 54.

tality so that *"doing* hospitality is what *constitutes* membership in the kingdom."[196] By hospitality Caputo does not mean inviting friends over for dinner or giving a room to the missionary visiting your church. Radical hospitality is turning one's home over to the homeless person. It is welcoming the enemy with open arms of forgiveness. It is setting aside all the rules to do justice to the singular individual whose situation does not fit the rules. It is allowing one's own identity (or the identity of a culture or institution) to be destabilized and transformed by encounter with the other. All that is beyond the possible; it lies in the realm of the impossible, which is why it is so important. Settling for the possible is the surest way to be left out of the kingdom.

Caputo realizes how crazy all this sounds, but he insists that Jesus was crazy—by the world's standards. Here is where Caputo and Hauerwas could shake hands. The latter could just as well have written what the former wrote about the kingdom, Christianity and the world:

> Kierkegaard could not have been more biblical and more prophetic when he insisted that Christianity stands in permanent structural opposition to this world, to the kingdom of this world, and that it is a sign of decadence in Christianity . . . to have sat down to table with the world, to have made peace with that *cosmos* upon which it is called to make war.[197]

Both Hauerwas and Caputo, to say nothing of Kierkegaard, would mean war in a figurative sense—as opposition, prophetic critique, deconstruction.

One way in which Christianity has succumbed to the world is ethics. Caputo famously wrote *Against Ethics* (1993), by which he did not mean Christians or anyone should be unethical or immoral. Rather, he meant that the messianic, the kingdom of God, transcends ethics. "If ethics is concerned with duties then I am against ethics," he declared. "I think that we should put an end to ethics."[198] Ethics, in his meaning of it, is calculating what is right before the singular situation occurs. And it functions by rules. All ethical rules, however, are at best provisional, and "the singular situations of daily life fly too close to the ground to be de-

---

[196]Ibid., 269.
[197]Ibid., 48.
[198]Caputo, *More Radical Hermeneutics*, 185.

tected by the radar of ethical theory."[199] Deconstruction, the poetics of the kingdom, crazily goes beyond ethics, not by "leveling the laws but [by] loosening them up."[200] It also does not demolish authority and the "force of law" but, like Jesus, "divests the authority of the law of the trappings of absoluteness."[201]

A word of caution is in order here. Caputo is not saying what some others have said—that the kingdom of God is a transcendent ideal above or ahead of us—out there somewhere waiting to be discovered or coming at us as something totally foreign. His view is much more subtle. It is deconstructive. For him, the kingdom of God, justice and love, forgiveness and hospitality, are not "somewhere else," but "stirring within" the things they disturb. For example, "the event of justice stirs within the rule of law."[202] It exists (but not like a thing exists), like every impossible, undeconstructible, as a "simmering potency" within a name. For example, "democracy." On the one hand, it is our form of government. On the other hand, it is the simmering potency within the concept; it is the "call" hidden within the practice. According to Caputo, "it would be 'idolatrous' to identify the event of something like democracy with its present state of affairs."[203] True democracy is that democracy to come that exceeds any actual state of affairs; it is impossible because it exceeds even the foreseeable and expectations.[204] But it is already there, in present democracies, not as what they are but as what they should be. The kingdom of God, then, is not the church. Here is where Caputo and Hauerwas might part company. For the former, the church is always provisional and deconstructible. "The church is a provisional construction, and whatever is constructed is deconstructible, while the kingdom of God is that in virtue of which the church is deconstructible."[205] A church under deconstruction would be constantly reinventing itself in an ongoing process of renewal in light of the kingdom of God. But the kingdom of God is already stirring within it.

---

[199]Ibid., 173.
[200]Ibid., 189.
[201]Ibid., 199.
[202]Caputo, *What Would Jesus Deconstruct?* 66.
[203]Ibid., 60.
[204]Ibid.
[205]Ibid., 35.

Caputo admits that this means "trouble." However, "the good news deconstruction bears to the church is to provide the hermeneutics of the kingdom
of God. The deconstruction of Christianity is not an attack on the church
but a critique of the idols to which it is vulnerable."[206]

Caputo reconceives God as "event." Without doubt one of Caputo's
most subtle and controversial ideas is that God is not an entity but an
event. Also, hand in hand with that, is the idea that God is not omnipotent but "weak." God, he declares, is not sovereign but "pitches his tent
among beings by identifying with everything the world casts out and
leaves behind."[207] "God" is the call for us to do the same. "The voice of
God, the Word of God, the Spirit of God, is the call that calls us without
causality, power or prestige, calling upon what is best in us."[208] Caputo
defines God's transcendence as "not . . . an eminent omnipotent onto-
power capable of leveling tall buildings and reducing his enemies . . . to
ashes, but as the weak force of a call."[209] Two factors cause him to arrive at
this concept of God. First, power corrupts, and coercive power is always
evil. So, "strong theologies," theologies that conceive of God as omnipotent being, are always in league with human power. Second, Jesus is our
best clue to the nature and character of God, and Jesus did not exercise
worldly power or strong force but allowed himself to be crucified. "God"
is the event of the call to transformation that claims us through Jesus
Christ for the weak force of the kingdom of God. "The name of God is the
name of an event, of an event that comes calling at our door, which can
and must be translated into the event of hospitality."[210]

Caputo's description of God as event gives rise to many questions, and he
does not seem particularly interested in answering them the way most people
want them answered. He is more than disinterested in speculation into the
structure of God—God's being or existence or attributes. To him, such questions and investigations always lead away from what is most important—the
kingdom of God as God's call on our lives and our response. He says,

---

[206]Ibid., 137.
[207]Caputo, *Weakness of God*, 45.
[208]Ibid., 41.
[209]Ibid., 38.
[210]Ibid., 269.

It is in or under the name of God that the event calls upon us. It is not what we call God that is at issue, but what God calls. Then again, it is not what God calls that is at issue, but the response, which is first and only testimony to the call, which is from a worldly point of view a weak force, like a kiss.[211]

However, he says enough to suggest how he thinks about God. "God is not a supreme being, but a certain holy 'ought' without being."[212] Also, "God can be God only if my relationship to God is oblique, while my relationship to the neighbor is frontal."[213] That would seem to make our relationship with God a purely horizontal one without any verticality. "God," then, is encountered only in obligation to the other and loving response. Perhaps the clearest expression of Caputo's concept of God is that God is not an entity in the order of existence or being but "the excess of the promise, of the call."[214] And "the name of God is the name of an event rather than an entity, of a call rather than a cause, of a provocation or a promise rather than of a presence. . . . We will do better to think of God in terms of weakness rather than of outright strength."[215]

What, then, of Jesus' miracles? Caputo relegates the miracles to the realm of "magic" while seeking to retain the "religion" in the stories.[216] He chooses as a case study the story of Jesus' raising Lazarus from the dead. The resuscitation of a corpse would be magic, something Caputo has no use for. What is important in the story is not that but the image of Jesus it portrays which is an image of God: "The figure upon which I seize in the story of Lazarus is that of Jesus weeping, which is the figure of the weakness of God. . . . The divinity is in the weakness, not the power."[217] Caputo makes clear that he values historical-critical study of the Bible and that he accepts modern science's conclusion that there are no supernatural interventions in nature.[218] We should abide by these achievements of the Enlightenment and not fall into premodern superstition and belief in magic. However, he says, "neither should we be

---

[211]Ibid., 97.
[212]Ibid., 271.
[213]Ibid.
[214]Ibid., 11.
[215]Ibid., 12.
[216]Ibid., 238–39.
[217]Ibid., 257–58.
[218]Ibid., 112.

stampeded by our debt to historical-critical studies, which lays literalism and creationism and fundamentalisms to rest . . . into an Enlightenment blindness to these narratives or a rationalist insensitivity to the claim they make upon us."[219]

Is not easy to tell exactly what Caputo thinks about God, and he admits as much when he wrestles with Augustine's and Derrida's question, "What do I love when I love my God?" One thing is clear: Caputo embraces "the death of the ontotheological God of classical theism."[220] Caputo's God is not a "metaphysical mechanic" or "cosmic force" that controls the universe or even intervenes to fix it.[221] God, for him, is not an object like a planet or even a law of nature; he or it cannot be discovered and described in a mathematical formula or theological system. One possible way of thinking about Caputo's God is as the impossible stirring within the life and death of Jesus Christ, calling humans into the kingdom through transformation. In other words, not as real or unreal but as hyper-real. In a strange, counterintuitive way, deconstruction (at least as taught by Derrida and Caputo) views the hyperreal as more real than the ordinarily real and, of course, the unreal. And yet, the hyperreal is never here. It is not, as the Germans put it, *vorhanden*—available at hand. God, then, if this interpretation is correct, is not envisioned by Caputo as dead and gone, a lá Nietzsche or Altizer, or present and complete, but potential, providing we understand potential as more "real" than the actual. But all that, Caputo would probably say, is metaphysical mumbo-jumbo that avoids the real point which is that we are called to transformation.

Caputo is cautiously embraced and interrogated. As mentioned earlier, Caputo has his admirers and critics. One person who is both is Putt, who has written several book chapters and scholarly articles analyzing and critiquing Caputo's theology. Another who is both admirer and critic is Olthuis. Both are evangelical Christians who approach Caputo confessionally. While he is formally a Catholic, his work does not display any interest in being confessionally orthodox. Both Putt and Olthuis are Christians committed to gen-

---

[219]Ibid., 120.

[220]B. Keith Putt, "The Existence of Evil and the Insistence of God: Caputo's Poetics of the Event as a Discourse on Divine Intervention," unpublished paper, 12.

[221]Ibid., 14–15.

erous orthodoxy, orthodox Christianity broadly understood. Their areas of appreciation and criticism of Caputo's theology are similar, so emphasis here will be given to Putt, whose work on Caputo is ongoing.

As a confessional Christian, Putt finds Caputo's postmodern turns helpful and hopeful. Much to his credit and Christianity's benefit, he says, Caputo demonstrates that "the Enlightenment dismissal of religion and faith is itself an illusion."[222] At the same time, he suggests, there is "one flaw" in Caputo's theology. It has to do with an inconsistency in his attitude toward modernity. According to Putt, Caputo

> rejects . . . any possibility that an event of God's grace might break into the genuine structures of existence and intervene relationally into the personal lives of individuals who respond to its messianic call. The one thing that Caputo seems always to have up his sleeve is a somewhat inconsistent and reductive adherence to modernist criteria of history and science.[223]

In other words, Putt suggests, Caputo has not followed through with his postmodern project consistently. Nor is his own theology of the event internally consistent. He debunks the idol of science and claims that it is not the god modernity has made it out to be. Putt is on to something with his criticism. Here is what Caputo wrote about science in *Deconstruction in a Nutshell* (a fairly recent publication):

> A "deconstruction" of natural science, were it undertaken seriously and with a sufficient sense of gravity, would be good news. Its effect would be to keep the laws of science in a self-revising, self-questioning mode of openness to the "other," which here would mean the scientific "anomaly," the thing that defies or transgresses the law. . . . A deconstructive approach to science would keep the scientific community open to the upstarts, the new ideas. . . . A deconstructive approach to natural science would maintain that the "laws" of science are always deconstructible (revisable) just in virtue of an [sic] science to come, one that is presently unforeseeable. A deconstructive approach to science would be good news and hard science. The sneaking suspicion that something may be wrong with what we currently believe, while keeping a watchful eye that current paradigms not be taken dogmatically, that some-

---

[222]B. Keith Putt, "Poetically Negotiating the Love of God: An Examination of John D. Caputo's Recent Postsecular Theology—A Review Essay," *Christian Scholar's Review* 37 (2008): 487.
[223]Ibid., 496.

thing else, something other, still to come, is being missed—that deeply deconstructive frame of mind goes to the heart of hardball science, if it has a heart![224]

Putt's question is how this fits with Caputo's rigid rejection of miracles as
"magic" and belief in them as superstition.

Putt rightly wants to soften Caputo's stance: "I suggest that he follow
his wise apothegm and loosen up a bit. . . . At times, Caputo tends toward
a rigidity in his theology of weakness, a rigidity driven by his com-
mendable passion to redeem the kingdom of God from the corruption of
traditional ontotheology."[225] Putt accuses Caputo of "fraternizing" too
closely with the "false dilemma fallacy"—too many either-ors haunt his
theology.[226] "One need not reduce divine intervention to magic or
nothing."[227] God, Putt warns, does not have to be impotent to not be
omnipotent.[228] He points out that Caputo himself sometimes uses the
language of divine intervention—especially when he writes about the
Spirit working through deconstruction to transform people and institutions. "There it is," Putt says, "that is precisely how Caputo's poetics of
the event can remain a discourse on divine intervention. God intervenes
in the world as the Spirit of motivation and encouragement. The still,
small voice of God lures us and cajoles us with the promise of the 'impossible to come.'"[229] Putt insightfully concludes that Caputo's denial of
God's intervening power "actually runs contrary to his own deconstructive hermeneutical tradition."[230]

Similarly, Putt points out an inconsistency in Caputo's doctrine of God.
Carrying further his critique of Caputo's either-or tendency, Putt argues
that the deconstructionist philosopher "writes as if one must either interpret God as an entity within the massive structures of metaphysical
speculation *or* one must not interpret God as an entity at all."[231] Putt calls
for a third way, a middle ground, in which God is envisioned as an entity

[224]Caputo, *Deconstruction in a Nutshell*, 73–74.
[225]Putt, "Existence of Evil," 29.
[226]Ibid., 33.
[227]Ibid., 34.
[228]Ibid., 39–40.
[229]Ibid., 35.
[230]Ibid., 37.
[231]Ibid., 33.

but not as a totalizing one.[232] In other words, Caputo seems to fear that describing God as an entity makes him (or it) the all-determining reality, the supreme being, the cosmic dictator that exercises coercive force. Putt concludes that "one need not reduce existing to exhausting."[233] Putt is suggesting that there is much middle ground between that and not being an entity at all.

Another possible weakness in Caputo's theology is his treatment of the church. This is probably the weakness Hauerwas would point out if he commented on Caputo's theology. Following Derrida, Caputo expresses strong reservation about community. Community has the inbuilt tendency to become totalizing and exclusive whereas "dissociation, separation, is the condition of my relation to the other."[234] Caputo believes that community always includes an element of inhospitality that must be deconstructed in the name of the other. Deconstruction "troubles community" by challenging its self-protective enclosure.[235] This carries over into his thoughts about "church." The problem is not only that he calls the church "provisional" and "deconstructible"; it is also and even more that he refers to the church as "Plan B."[236] What he means is clear: the church is not necessary to the kingdom of God or to Jesus' prophetic mission and ours. Caputo leaves no positive place for the church in his theology. It is just another human institution needing deconstruction and transformation. Hauerwas would agree that the church is not the kingdom of God and that every church needs improvement, but he would shudder at Caputo's cavalier treatment of the church as if it were a mere afterthought of the apostles when Jesus did not return as expected.

One thing critics of Caputo (as well as admirers) need to remember is that he is a philosopher. That is not to say he should not be taken seriously, but he makes no pretense of being personally committed to any orthodoxy or confessional posture. He does claim to be a Christian, however, and that opens him up to interrogation by Christian theologians—something he does not

---

[232]Ibid.
[233]Ibid.
[234]Caputo, *Deconstruction in a Nutshell*, 14. This is a quote from Derrida with which Caputo later expresses agreement.
[235]Ibid., 107–8.
[236]Caputo, *What Would Jesus Deconstruct?* 35.

exactly enjoy. Those interrogating him, however, also need to remember that he has come a long way on his personal journey from pure philosophy to theology. Along the way he has discovered the poetics of the kingdom and stumbled into demythologizing and process theology and neo-orthodoxy and, much to his bemusement, evangelicalism. Perhaps he has far to go to count as a "real theologian" (whatever that is). He will probably best be remembered by both philosophers and theologians as a gadfly, a troublemaker, a prophet. And with that reputation he would almost certainly be content.

CONCLUSION

This book has been like one of the diaries my mother kept of our family vacations when I was kid—the story of a journey, only this one was filled with more tension than most of our family trips. And unlike most of them, anyway, it has not had a clear destination. The Christian family has been fragmented and often at odds throughout its modern odyssey. And its destination has been much disputed. Its starting point was the Enlightenment and its guides were Christian tradition and modern foundationalism. Attempts to follow both often ended up in dead ends. Some family members chose to follow only one of the guides, ignoring the other one. Others sought to reconcile the two guides with limited success. Finally, a rebel child named Jack left both guides and launched off on his own without a guide except an impossible dream.

The journey of modern theology began with efforts to reconstruct the vehicle and ended (so far) with projects to deconstruct it. Along the way numerous Christian thinkers tinkered with it, tried to tune it up or refurbish it as it supposedly was before the journey began.

Whatever metaphor one prefers for describing it, there can be little doubt that the story of modern theology's journey is one filled with tension, confusion, occasional triumphs, some tragedies and many surprises. Some observers of the journey may think all roads lead eventually to the same destination, but that would be difficult to defend as many of the paths go in absolutely opposite directions.

The study of modern theology can lead a person obsessed with poet Wallace Stevens's "blessed rage for order" to Eastern Orthodoxy—a form of Christianity largely untouched by the Enlightenment and modernity. Most of us in the West, however, and many in the so-called younger churches of the Global South, too, cannot escape modernity. Even postmoderns are still swimming in the modern cultural water as they critique it as polluted and foul. Christians throughout the past two to three hundred years have found themselves in the same situation as Christians in the Roman Empire during the church's first two to three centuries. "What has Athens to do with Jerusalem?" was their question. Ours has been "What has Wittenberg or Rome to do with Königsberg [Kant]?" Almost every Christian thinker says at least "something." Working out that relationship between the gospel, Christian tradition and modernity has not been easy.

During the first decade of the twenty-first century, three and a half centuries after the beginning of the Enlightenment, many young Christians are choosing to opt out of the journey of modern theology insofar as it still follows maps created by Descartes, Locke, Hume, Kant and Hegel. The most vital Christian youth movements seem to be the young, restless, Reformed new Calvinism rediscovering premodern Christianity with Calvin and Jonathan Edwards, and the postmodern emerging church movement reveling in irony toward all ideologies, including modernity, and searching for a new map or enjoying the journey without one. To a large extent studies of Schleiermacher, Barth and Tillich are greeted with yawns by both groups.

The problem is that the paths of these and other modern theological trailblazers are often still being followed even where their names are unknown. It is better for contemporary Christians to know about those who journeyed before them; otherwise, chances are, they will fall into the same ruts and waste time going around in the same circles. While learning about them, they may find surprising signs that point forward, out of impasses in which they have found themselves caught.

The big, lingering theological question hovering over the story of this journey of modern theology is where God has been. Has God abandoned his people? Where was God when the radical theologians of the 1960s declared him dead? Or has God perhaps abandoned theology as it took leave of him? Is God alive and well in popular religion? I do not think there are easy answers to those questions, but I am confident God does not abandon his people even as he allows them to wander around in the wilderness for a number of years.

To lay my cards on the table for all finally to see—I think the comparison between modernity, as the cultural context of modern Western Christianity, and Hellenism, as the cultural context of ancient Christianity in the Roman world, is misleading. Secularism, a major product of the Enlightenment, and especially naturalism and rationalistic foundationalism, represent something new in human history. Balthasar describes this powerfully in *The God Question and Modern Man.*

Balthasar (see 10.c.) argued that before the modern era humanity always had some form of natural religion in addition to whatever revealed religion was believed in and followed. Nature, in other words, was always viewed as open to the supernatural and creation itself was seen as "charged with the grandeur of God" (or gods or the divine). Secularism, stemming from the Enlightenment, took this away from humanity and attempted to put man in place of the sacred, the divine. Nature, the created order, the world, was reduced to a machine. The result has been a severe loss of mystery, beauty and hope.

Many conservative Christians think the main problem with modernity is loss of authority, especially of the authority of the Bible and church tradition. There is that, no doubt. However, written authority can be "the letter" that kills (2 Cor 3:6); only the Spirit gives life. The worst result of modernity has been loss of the spiritual dimension of life. Secularism has reduced reality to the ordinary, the predictable, the banal. It has relegated everything spiritual to the realm of private opinion if not superstition. The reaction has been proliferation of all kinds of cults, mystery religions, New Age spiritual technologies and fundamentalisms. One scholar of cults and new religions explained their abundance in late modernity by saying that when the secular policemen of modern culture get too heavy with their naturalistic nightsticks the people start smuggling the gods in brown paper bags.[1]

---

[1] I heard church historian Martin Marty say this on several occasions.

The entirely new challenge of modernity, then, has been antisupernatu-ralism. By "supernaturalism" I do not mean gullible belief in every reported miracle story; I mean that reality and agency which transcends the natural even as it imbues nature with a dimension above the merely material. Those theologies that jumped on the antisupernatural bandwagon of modern sci-entism and rationalist philosophy sold out not only Christianity, the gospel, but humanity as well. In my opinion, the heroes of this story of modern theology are neither the deep accommodationists nor the reactionaries but the theologians who held firmly to the gospel of Jesus Christ, within a su-pernatural frame of reference, seeking to communicate it in as relevant a way possible to contemporary culture, namely, Barth (Protestant) and Balthasar (Catholic). That is not to endorse everything either one said; it is to say they are to be applauded for swimming against the stream of modern secular culture without abdicating Christian responsibility for the world.[2]

Also, both Barth and Balthasar rose above the tendency of much modern theology to reduce theology to Kant's realm of practical reason—ethics. Al-though they could not rightly be called metaphysical theologians, with all the baggage that carries, both affirmed that Christian theology makes truth claims about reality; it is not merely about human experience or values. A major thesis of this study of modern theology is that it has been over-shadowed and, too often, intimidated by modern science. Many modern Christian theologians were so intimidated that they redefined Christianity so that, in principle, it cannot conflict with science. That sounds good, but the cost is too high. Knowledge was handed over to the so-called hard sci-ences so that what was left to theology was opinion and value judgments only. It is not far from there to superstition.

In the twenty-first century, much Christian theology is overcoming its fear of science and reclaiming ground it surrendered in its subjectivizing of belief either Kantian style or by means of existentialism. Theologian and

---

[2]As always, there will be people who debate whether Barth should be called a supernaturalist. Everything depends on what "supernatural" means. I regard anyone who believes in the bodily resurrection of Jesus Christ, including the empty tomb, a supernaturalist on some level. In my use of it, "supernatural" does not necessarily imply that God must or even ever does intervene in or violate nature and its regularities. I take it that Reid (as discussed in 1.e.) and Bushnell (discussed in 4.b.) provided accounts of the supernatural and miracles that do not imply that God or God's special activity must violate nature.

physicist John Polkinghorne (mentioned in 6.b.) is leading the way toward a new integrationism in which theology and science inhabit overlapping but not competing spheres of knowledge.

In spite of my criticisms of much modern theology, I can truly say that I have learned from every theologian and movement described in this book, and many not mentioned here as well. As the saying goes, God can strike a heavy blow (to one's comfort zone and settled opinions) even with a crooked stick. I hope my readers can truly say the same.

People often ask me to predict the future of theology. I refuse. It is a fool's errand. Everyone who tried to predict the future around 1901 (the first year of the twentieth century) turned out to be mostly wrong. On the heels of the nineteenth century especially Europeans and Americans were full of optimism and hope. The twentieth century was to be "the Christian century"—the century during which the kingdom of God would dawn or education and technology would banish ignorance and misery. If the twentieth century taught us anything, it should be not to predict the future. All I can say is, whatever the future brings, it is likely to be interesting. I look toward the Global South and its young churches to breathe new breath into Christianity and possibly into theology as well. It seems we in the modern West have followed every path to the journey's end. Now we are going around in circles. Perhaps an African or Asian voice will speak into our postmodern milieu and point the way forward.